FOLKLORE IN THE OLD TESTAMENT

FOLKLORE
IN THE OLD
TESTAMENT

Sir James G. Frazer

Studies in Comparative Religion,
Legend, and Law

Abridged Edition

AVENEL BOOKS
NEW YORK

This 1988 edition is published by Avenel Books, distributed
by Crown Publishers, Inc., 225 Park Avenue South, New
York, New York 10003, by arrangement with The Council
of Trinity College, Cambridge.
Printed and Bound in the United States of America.
Library of Congress Cataloging-in-Publication Data
Frazer, James George, Sir, 1854-1941.
Folk-lore in the Old testament : studies in comparative
religion, legend, and law /
by Sir James George Frazer. — Abridged ed.
p. cm.
Reprint. Originally published: New York : Macmillan, 1923.
Includes index.
ISBN 0-517-67251-0
1. Folklore in the Bible. 2. Bible. O.T.—Criticism,
interpretation, etc.   I. Title.   II. Title: Folklore in the Old
Testament.
BS625.F7 1988   88-8123
398.2—dc19   CIP

h g f e d c b a

SANTAE TRINITATIS APUD CANTABRIGIENSES

COLLEGIO VENERABILI

MAGNIS MAGNORUM INGENIORUM INCUNABULIS

SPLENDIDO LITTERARUM DOCTRINARUMQUE LUMINI

TUTO VIRORUM DOCTORUM ADVERSUS FORTUNAE TEMPESTATES

PORTUI AC PERFUGIO

PARVULUM PRO TANTIS IN ME COLLATIS BENEFICIIS MUNUSCULUM

PIO GRATOQUE ANIMO

MORTALIS IMMORTALI OFFERO

FOREWORD

If Herodotus is called the "Father of History," Sir James George Frazer should rightly hold the title of "Father of Anthropology." A lifelong scholar whose works and theories were mined at his desk from the wealth of information provided by more physically adventurous colleagues and explorers, Frazer pioneered the comparative method of analysis in studying the folklore and religions of the civilized and uncivilized worlds.

Frazer's omnivorous scholarship and extraordinary commitment gave rise to a vast number of books; many of his works were multi-volume sets that underwent several further revisions and expansions. The most famous of these is *The Golden Bough*, his seminal work on the uses and development of magic, customs, social practices, and religion among primitive peoples; it withstood three separate and differing editions and filled thirteen volumes in its final unabridged form.

Though extraordinary in its own right and unique to his time, Frazer's scholarship has become fatally flawed in the eyes of modern anthropologists; his works are now faulted by the academic world for their lack of historical and scientific perspective. But how many men and women can lay claim to such a life's work? The breadth, depth, richness of idea, and ornamentation of language that characterize Frazer's writing makes reading him a singular experience in any era.

Folklore in the Old Testament shows a typical Frazerian development. The seed of the book was planted when Frazer was asked to contribute an essay to the Tylor Festschrift, a volume of essays published in 1907 in honor of anthropologist E.B. Tylor's seventy-fifth birthday. Some eleven years later, in 1918, his 73-page essay, "Folk-Lore in the Old Testament," was published in a thick three-volume set with the same title. Finally, in 1923, Frazer made his work available to the general public in an abridged edition; this is the edition reprinted here. His abridgement, as he wrote in his 1923 Preface, shortened and omitted certain chapters, and almost virtually eliminated the footnotes referring to his authorities and sources.

v

Reading Frazer is like seeing the Tower of Babel magically reconstructed, brick by brick, before one's very eyes. He is a master craftsman charged not only with finding the diverse fragments of myth and culture, but also with laying out the multi-colored pieces in their logical order, and mortaring them by the sweat of his intellect into a whole tower, a rational discipline. Few people have the strength or the mind to imagine the structure; still fewer dare to undertake the actual building. Traversing the eternal narrative of the Old Testament, exploring the roots of Western civilization and the fascinating parallels present in other cultures both ancient and modern, Frazer attempts to weld the bricks of our world into a single, finite tower. Whether he has succeeded or failed with *Folklore in the Old Testament*, you must judge for yourself.

B.L.H. MASTERSON

New York
1988

PREFACE
TO THE ABRIDGED EDITION

IT has been suggested to me that an abridged edition of *Folk-lore in the Old Testament* might be welcome to a number of readers who have neither the means to buy nor the leisure to read the original edition in three portly volumes. In deference to this opinion I have accordingly prepared the present abridgement by omitting some chapters altogether and shortening most of the rest. In particular, to gain space for the text, I have struck out almost all the footnotes, containing the references to authorities, except in a very few cases where a word of explanation seemed desirable, or where, in quoting from the Old Testament, I deemed it necessary to give my reasons for adopting a reading different from that of the Authorized or the Revised English version. Readers who desire to learn the source of any particular statement must therefore consult the volumes of the larger edition, which is fully documented.

It was observed by Renan that to a philosophical mind, occupied with the investigation of origins, the human past offers but three histories of primary interest—the history of Greece, the history of Israel, and the history of Rome. To these three histories, which all rest on the evidence of written documents, we may now add at least a fourth, to wit, the history of mankind in ages and in countries to which the art of writing was unknown. For since the time when Renan gave to the world his great history of Israel and of early Christianity, our knowledge of the human past has been vastly enlarged and enriched, on the one hand, by the discoveries of prehistoric archaeology, and, on the other hand, by a more exact study of savage races, who represent for us more or less accurately the various stages of social evolution through which the ancestors of the civilized races passed long ago. Taken together, these comparatively new sciences lift to some extent the veil which has hitherto hung over the infancy of mankind; they allow us to pierce, if I may say so, the dead wall which till lately appeared to block the path of the inquirer beyond the limits of classical antiquity; they open up a seemingly endless vista of man's thought and activity as they existed in those dim and incalculable ages which elapsed between the emergence of our species on earth and its full maturity in civilized humanity. Hence the ardour with which the studies of folk-lore and prehistoric archaeology are pursued at the present day by ever-widening circles of inquirers. We may almost say that among the forces which are moulding and transforming the enlightened opinion of our time these humanistic disciplines are beginning to exert an influence only second to that impulse which the amazing advances of the physical sciences within living memory have impressed on the general movement of thought; for the question of the validity of beliefs and the worth of institutions can hardly be divorced from the question of their origin, on which archaeology and folk-lore are continually throwing new light.

In the present work I have attempted, on the lines of folk-lore, to trace some of the beliefs and institutions of ancient Israel backward to earlier and cruder stages of thought and practice which have their analogies in the faiths and customs of existing savages. If I have in any measure succeeded in the attempt, it should henceforth be possible to view the history of Israel in a truer, if less romantic, light as that of a people not miraculously differentiated from all other races by divine revelation, but evolved like them by a slow process of natural selection from an embryonic condition of ignorance and savagery.

J. G. FRAZER.

5th June 1923.

PREFACE

MODERN researches into the early history of man, conducted on different lines, have converged with almost irresistible force on the conclusion, that all civilized races have at some period or other emerged from a state of savagery resembling more or less closely the state in which many backward races have continued to the present time; and that, long after the majority of men in a community have ceased to think and act like savages, not a few traces of the old ruder modes of life and thought survive in the habits and institutions of the people. Such survivals are included under the head of folk-lore, which, in the broadest sense of the word, may be said to embrace the whole body of a people's traditionary beliefs and customs, so far as these appear to be due to the collective action of the multitude and cannot be traced to the individual influence of great men. Despite the high moral and religious development of the ancient Hebrews, there is no reason to suppose that they formed an exception to this general law. They, too, had probably passed through a stage of barbarism and even of savagery; and this probability, based on the analogy of other races, is confirmed by an examination of their literature, which contains many references to beliefs and practices that can hardly be explained except on the supposition that they are rudimentary survivals from a far lower level of culture. It is to the illustration and explanation of a few such relics of ruder times, as they are preserved like fossils in the Old Testament, that I have addressed myself in the present work. Elsewhere I have had occasion to notice other similar survivals of savagery in the Old Testament, such as the sacrifice of the first-born, the law of the uncleanness of women, and the custom of the scapegoat; but as I am unwilling to repeat what I have said on these topics, I content myself with referring readers, who may be interested in them, to my other writings.

The instrument for the detection of savagery under civilization is the comparative method, which, applied to the human mind, enables us to trace man's intellectual and moral evolution, just as, applied to the human body, it enables us to trace his physical evolution from lower forms of animal life. There is, in short, a Comparative Anatomy of the mind as well as of the body, and it promises to be no less fruitful of far-reaching consequences, not merely speculative but practical, for the future of humanity. The application of the comparative method to the study of Hebrew antiquities is not novel. In the seventeenth century the method was successfully employed for this purpose in France by the learned French pastor Samuel Bochart, and in England by the learned divine John Spencer, Master of Corpus Christi College, Cambridge, whose book on the ritual laws of the ancient Hebrews is said to have laid the foundations of the science of Comparative Religion. In our own age, after a lapse of two centuries, the work initiated by these eminent scholars and divines was resumed in Cambridge by my revered master and friend William Robertson Smith, and the progress which the study made during his lifetime and since his too early death is due in a large measure to the powerful impulse it received from his extraordinary genius and learning. It has been my ambition to tread in the footsteps of these my illustrious predecessors in this department of learning, and to carry on what I may be allowed to call the Cambridge tradition of Comparative Religion.

It is a familiar truth that the full solution of any one problem involves the solution of many more; nay, that nothing short of omniscience could suffice to answer all the questions implicitly raised by the seemingly simplest inquiry. Hence the investigation of a point of folk-lore, especially in the present inchoate condition of the study, naturally opens up lines of inquiry which branch out in many directions; and in following them we are insensibly drawn on into wider and wider fields of inquiry, until the point from which we started has almost disappeared in the distance, or, to speak more correctly, is seen in its proper perspective as only one in a multitude of similar phenomena. So it befell me when, many years ago, I undertook to investigate a point in the folk-lore of ancient Italy; so it has befallen me now, when I have set myself to discuss certain points in the folk-lore of the ancient Hebrews. The examination of a particular legend, custom, or law has in some cases gradually broadened out into a disquisition and almost into a treatise. But I hope that, apart from their immediate bearing on the traditions and usages of Israel, these disquisitions may be accepted as contribu-

tions to the study of folk-lore in general. That study is still in its
infancy, and our theories on the subjects with which it deals must
probably for a long time to come be tentative and provisional,
mere pigeon-holes in which temporarily to sort the multitude of
facts, not iron moulds in which to cast them for ever. Under these
circumstances a candid inquirer in the realm of folk-lore at the
present time will state his inferences wtih a degree of diffidence
and reserve corresponding to the difficulty and uncertainty of the
matter in hand. This I have always endeavoured to do. If anywhere I have forgotten the caution which I recommend to others,
and have expressed myself with an appearance of dogmatism which
the evidence does not warrant, I would request the reader to correct
all such particular statements by this general and sincere profession
of scepticism.

Throughout the present inquiry I have sought to take account
of the conclusions reached by the best modern critics with regard to
the composition and dates of the various books of the Old Testament; for I believe that only in the light of these conclusions do
many apparent discrepancies in the sacred volume admit of a logical
and historical explanation. Quotations are generally made in the
words of the Revised English Version, and as I have occasionally
ventured to dissent from it and to prefer a different rendering or
even, in a very few places, a different reading, I wish to say that,
having read the whole of the Old Testament in Hebrew attentively,
with the English Version constantly beside me, I am deeply impressed by the wonderful felicity with which Translators and
Revisers alike have done their work, combining in an extraordinary
degree fidelity to the letter with justice to the spirit of the original.
In its union of scrupulous accuracy with dignity and beauty of
language the English Revised Version of the Old Testament is,
as a translation, doubtless unsurpassed and probably unequalled in
literature.

The scope of my work has obliged me to dwell chiefly on the
lower side of ancient Hebrew life revealed in the Old Testament, on
the thaces of savagery and superstition which are to found in its
pages. But to do so is not to ignore, far less to disparage, that
higher side of the Hebrew genius which has manifested itself in a
spiritual religion and a pure morality, and of which the Old Testament is the imperishable monument. On the contrary, the revelation of the baser elements which underlay the civilization of ancient
Israel, as they underlie the civilization of modern Europe, serves

rather as a foil to enhance by contrast the glory of a people which, from such dark depths of ignorance and cruelty, could rise to such bright heights of wisdom and virtue, as sunbeams appear to shine with a greater effulgence of beauty when they break through the murky clouds of a winter evening than when they flood the earth from the serene splendour of a summer noon. The annals of savagery and superstition unhappily compose a large part of human literature; but in what other volume shall we find, side by side with that melancholy record, psalmists who poured forth their sweet and solemn strains of meditative piety in the solitude of the hills or in green pastures and beside still waters; prophets who lit up their beatific visions of a blissful future with the glow of an impassioned imagination; historians who bequeathed to distant ages the scenes of a remote past embalmed for ever in the amber of a pellucid style? These are the true glories of the Old Testament and of Israel; these, we trust and believe, will live to delight and inspire mankind, when the crudities recorded alike in sacred and profane literature shall have been purged away in a nobler humanity of the future.

J. G. FRAZER.

1 BRICK COURT TEMPLE,
LONDON, 26 May 1918.

CONTENTS

		PAGE
Foreword .	. . . .	v
Preface (1923)	. . . .	vii
Preface (1918)	. . . .	ix

PART I

THE EARLY AGES OF THE WORLD

CHAPTER I

THE CREATION OF MAN

Two different accounts of the creation of man in Genesis	1
The Priestly and the Jehovistic narratives	2
The Jehovistic the more primitive	3
Babylonian and Egyptian parallels	3
Greek legend of the creation of man out of clay	3
Australian and Maori stories of the creation of man out of clay . . .	4-5
Tahitian tradition: creation of woman out of man's rib	5
Similar stories of the creation of woman in Polynesia	5
Similar Karen and Tartar stories	6
Other stories of the creation of man in the Pacific	6
Melanesian legends of the creation of men out of clay	6
Story of the creation of man in Celebes	6-7
Stories told by the Dyaks of Borneo	7
Legend told by the natives of Nias	7-8
Stories told by the natives of the Philippines	8-9
Indian legends of the creation of man	9-10
Cheremiss story of the creation of man	10
African stories of the creation of man	10-11
American stories of the creation of man	11-14
Our first parents moulded out of red clay	14-15

CHAPTER II

THE FALL OF MAN

§ 1. *The Narrative in Genesis*

The temptation and the fall, the woman and the serpent . . .	15-16
The two trees	16
The Tree of Life and the Tree of Death	16-17
The Creator's good intention frustrated by the serpent . . .	17
The serpent's selfish motive for deceiving the woman	18
Widespread belief in the immortality of serpents	18
Story of the Fall, a story of the origin of death	19

xiii

§ 2. *The Story of the Perverted Message*

	PAGE
Hottentot story of the Moon and the hare	20
Bushman story of the Moon and the hare	20-21
Nandi story of the Moon and the dog	21
Hottentot story of the Moon, the insect, and the hare	22
Bushman story of the Moon, the toroise, and the hare	22-23
Gold Coast story of God, the sheep, and the goat	23
Ashantee story of God, the sheep, and the goat	23-24
Togoland story of God, the dog, and the frog	24-25
Bantu story of God, the chameleon, and the lizard	25
The miscarriage of the message of immortality	26

§ 3. *The Story of the Cast Skin*

Supposeed immortality of animals that cast their skins	26
How men missed immortality and serpents, etc., obtained it	26-27
Belief that men formerly cast their skins and lived for ever	27-29
Belief that men used to rise from the dead after three days	29-30
How men missed immortality and the Moon obtained it	30
Bahnar story how men used to rise from the dead	30-31
Rivalry between men and serpents, etc., for immortality	31

§ 4. *The Composite Story of the Perverted Message and the Cast Skin*

Galla story of God, the blue bird, and the serpent	31-32
Stories of the Good Spirit, men, and serpents	32

§ 5. *Conclusion*

Original form of the story of the Fall of Man	32-33

CHAPTER III

THE MARK OF CAIN

The theory that the mark was a tribal badge	33-34
Homicides shunned as infected	34
Attic law concerning homicides	34
Seclusion of murderers in Dobu	34-35
Belief in the infectiousness of homicides in Africa	35
Earth supposed to spurn the homicide	36
Wanderings of the matricide Alcmaeon	36
Earth offended by bloodshed and appeased by sacrificed	36-37
The homicide's mark perhaps a danger-signal to others	37-38
The mark perhaps a protection against the victim's ghost	38
Ceremonies to appease the ghosts of the slain	38-39
Seclusion of murderer through fear of his victim's ghost	39-40
Bodily marks to protect people against ghosts of the slain	40
Need of guarding warriors against the ghosts of the slain	41
Various modes of guarding warriors against the ghosts of the slain	41-42
Faces or bodies of manslayers painted in diverse colours	42-44
The mark of Cain perhaps a disguise against the ghost of Abel	44-45
Advantage of thus interpreting the mark	45

CONTENTS

CHAPTER IV

THE GREAT FLOOD

§ 1. *Introduction*

PAGE

Huxley on the Great Flood 46
The present essay a study in folk-lore 46
Bearing of flood stories on problems of origin and diffusion . . 47-48

§ 2. *The Babylonian Story of a Great Flood*

Babylonian tradition recorded by Berosus 48-49
Nicolaus of Damascus on the flood 49
Modern discovery of the original Babylonian story . . 49-50
The Gilgamesh epic 50
Journey of Gilgamesh to Ut-napishtim 50
Ut-napishtim's story of the Great Flood 51
The building of the ship—the embarkation—the storm . . 51-52
The sending forth of the dove and the raven—the landing . 52-53
Other fragmentary versions of the Babylonian story . . 53-54
Sumerian version of the flood story 54-56
The flood story borrowed by the Semites from the Sumerians . 56

§ 3. *The Hebrew Story of a Great Flood*

The story compounded of two different narratives . . 56-57
The Priestly Document and the Jehovistic Document . . 57-60
Late date and ecclesiastical character of the Priestly Document . 57-59
Its contrast with the Jehovistic Document . . . 59
Verbal differences between the Priestly and the Jehovistic Documents 60-61
Material differences between the documents in the flood story . 61
The Jehovistic document the older of the two . . . 62
Dependence of the Hebrew on the Babylonian story of the flood 62-64
Fanciful additions made to the flood story in later times . . 64-66

§ 4. *Ancient Greek Stories of a Great Flood*

Deucalion and Pyrrha 66-67
Aristotle and Plato on Deucalion's flood 67-68
Athenian legend of Deucalion's flood 68
The grave of Deucalion and the Water-bearing Festival at Athens 68
Story of Deucalion's flood at Hierapolis on the Euphrates . 68-69
Water festival and prayers at Hierapolis 69-70
Deucalion, the ark, and the dove 70
Noah's flood on coins of Apamea Cibotos in Phrygia . . 70
Greek traditions of three great floods. The flood of Ogyges . 70-71
Dates assigned by ancient authorities to the flood of Ogyges . 71
The flood of Ogyges and the vicissitudes of the Copaic Lake . 71
The flood of Dardanus. Home of Dardanus at Pheneus . 72
Alternations of the valley of Pheneus between wet and dry . 72-73
Samothracian story of great flood consequent on opening of Darda-
    nelles 73-74
The Samothracian story partially confirmed by geology . 74-75
The Samothracian story probably a speculation of an early phi-
    losopher 75
Story of Deucalion's flood perhaps an inference from the configura-
    tion of Thessaly 75-76
The Vale of Tempe 76-77
The Greek flood stories probably myths of observation . . 77-78

§ 5. *Ancient Indian Stories of a Great Flood*

PAGE

The story in the *Satapatha Brahmana*. Manu and the fish . . 78-79

§ 6. *Modern Indian Stories of a Great Flood*

Stories told by the Bhils and Kamars of Central India . . . 79-80
Story told by the Anals of Assam 80-81

§ 7. *Stories of a Great Flood in Eastern Asia*

Stories told by the Karens and Singphos of Burma . . 81-82
Story told by the Bahnars of Cochin China . . . 82
Stories told by the aborigines of the Malay Peninsula . 82-83
Story told by the Lolos of Southern China . . 83-84
Kamchadale story of a great flood 84
Mongolian story of a great flood 84

§ 8. *Stories of a Great Flood in the Indian Archipelago*

Story told by the Bataks of Sumatra 84
Story told by the natives of Engano . . . 84-85
Stories told by the Dyaks of Borneo . . . 85-86
Story told by the natives of Celebes . . . 86
Story told by the natives of Rotti 86-87
Story told by the Andaman Islanders . . . 87-88

§ 9. *Stories of a Great Flood in Australia*

Story told by the Kurnai of Victoria . . . 88-89
Stories told by other tribes of Victoria . . . 89

§ 10. *Stories of a Great Flood in New Guinea and Melanesia*

Stories told by the natives of New Guinea . . . 89-90
Fijian story of a great flood 90-91
Melanesian story of a greeat flood 91

§ 11. *Stories of a Great Flood in Polynesia and Micronesia*

Wide diffusion of such stories in the Pacific . . 91-92
Tahitian legends of a great flood . . . 92-94
Hawaiian legend of a great flood . . . 94
Maori legend of a great flood 94-96
Story of a great flood told by the Pelew Islanders . . 96-97

§ 12. *Stories of a Great Flood in South America*

Stories told by the Indians near Rio de Janeiro . . 97-98
Story told by the Caingangs of Southern Brazil . . 98-99
Story told by the Carayas of Brazil . . . 99-100
Story told by other Indians of the Purus River . . 100
Story told by the Muratos of Ecuador . . . 100-101
Story told by the Araucanians of Chili . . . 101
Story told by the Ackawois of British Guiana . . 101-103
Story told by the Arawaks of British Guiana . . 103
Story told by the Macusis of British Guiana . . 103-104
Stories told by the Indians of the Orinoco . . . 104

PAGE

Story told by the Cañaris of Ecuador 104-105
Stories told by the Peruvian Indians 105-106
Story told by the Chiriguanos of Bolivia 106-107
Story told by the Fuegians 107

§ 13. *Stories of a Great Flood in Central America and Mexico*

Stories told by the Indians of Panama and Nicaragua . . 107
Mexican tradition of a great flood 107
Michoacan legend of a great flood 107-108
Story told by the Huichol Indians of Mexico . . . 108-109
Stories told by the Cora Indians of Mexico . . . 109-110

§ 14. *Stories of a Great Flood in North America*

Story told by the Papagos of Arizona 110
Story told by the Pimas 111
Stories told by the California Indians 111-112
Story told by the Natchez of the Lower Mississippi . . 112
Story told by the Mandan Indians 112
Annual Mandan ceremonies commemorative of the flood . 112-114
Story told by the Cherokee Indians 114-115
Story of a Great Flood widely spread among the Algonquins . 115
Story told by the Montagnais Indians of Canada . . 115-116
Story told by the Crees 116
The Algonquin story told in full by the Chippeways . . 116-119
An Ojibway version of the same story 119-120
Another version of the same story told by the Blackfoot Indians 120
Another version of the same story told by the Crees . . 121
Another version of the same story told by the Dogrib and Slave Indians 121
Another version of the same story told by the Hareskin Indians 121-122
Stories of a Great Flood told by the Tinneh Indians . . 122-123
Stories told by the Tlingit Indians of Alaska . . . 123-125
Story told by the Haida Indians of Queen Charlotte Islands . 125
Story told by the Thompson Indians of British Columbia . 125-126
Stories told by the Indians of Washington State . . 126
Story told by the Indians of the Lower Columbia River . 126-127
Stories told by the Eskimo and Greenlanders . . . 126-127

§ 15. *Stories of a Great Flood in Africa*

General absence of flood stories in Africa 129
Reported traces of such stories 129-130
Stories of a Great Flood reported in East Africa . . 130-131

§ 16. *The Geographical Diffusion of Flood Stories*

Absence of flood stories in a great part of Asia . . . 131
Rarity of flood stories in Europe 132
Absence of flood stories in Africa 132
Presence of flood stories in the Indian Archipelago, New Guinea,
    Australia, Melanesia, Polynesia, and America . . 132
The Hebrew flood story derived from the Babylonian . . 133
Most other flood stories apparently independent of the Babylonian 133
Greek flood stories not borrowed from the Babylonian . 133-134
Ancient Indian story probably independent of the Babylonian . 134
Wide diffusion of the Alonquin story in North America . 135
Evidence of diffusion in South America and Polynesia . 135

CONTENTS

§ 17. *The Origin of Stories of a Great Flood*

PAGE

Old theory of a universal deluge supported by evidence of fossils   135-136

Survivals of the theory of a universal deluge in the nineteenth century 136-137

Stories of a Great Flood interpreted as solar, lunar, or stellar myths   137

Evidence of geology against a universal deluge . . . 137

Philosophical theories of a universal primeval ocean . . 137-138

Many flood stories probably reminiscences of real events . . 138

Memorable floods in Holland 138

Floods caused by earthquake waves in the Pacific . . . 139

Some flood stories in the Pacific probably reminiscences of earthquake waves 139-140

Inundations caused by heavy rains 140

Babylonian story explained by annual inundation of the Euphrates valley 140-142

Diluvial traditions partly legendary, partly mythical . . 142

Myths of observation based on geological configuration and fossils   142

All flood stories probably comparatively recent . . . 142-143

CHAPTER V

THE TOWER OF BABEL

The Tower of Babel and the confusion of tongues . . 143-144

Later Jewish legends as to the Tower of Babel . . . 144

The Tower of Babel probably a reminiscence of a temple-tower   144-145

Two such ruined temple-towers at Babylon 145

Ruined temple-tower at Ur of the Chaldees . . . 145-146

Theories as to the primitive language of mankind . . 146-147

African stories like that of the Tower of Babel . . . 147-148

Story told of the pyramid of Cholulu in Mexico . . 148-149

Karen and Mikir versions of the Tower of Babel . . 150

Admiralty Islands version of the Tower of Babel . . . 150

Stories as to the origin of the diversity of tongues in Greece, Africa, Assam, Australia, and America 150-152

PART II

THE PATRIARCHAL AGE

CHAPTER I

THE COVENANT OF ABRAHAM

The Patriarchal Age described in Genesis 153

God's covenant with Abraham 153-154

Hebrew covenant by cutting a sacrificial victim in two . . 154

Similar Greek models of ratifying oaths . . . 154-155

Similar modes of swearing among the Scythians . . . 155

Similar ceremonies at peacemaking in East Africa . . 155-157

Ceremonies at peacemaking in South Africa . . . 157

Similar ceremonies among tribes of Assam . . . 157-158

Two theories of the ceremonies, the retributive and the sacramental or purificatory 158

The retributive theory implied in some cases . . . 158

Ceremony at peacemaking among the Awome of Calabar . 158-159

CONTENTS

PAGE

Retributive theory confirmed by Greek and Roman practice . . 159
Retributive theory illustrated by an Assyrian inscription . 159-160
Similar sacrifices and imprecations in the ritual of barbarous tribes 160-161
The slaughter of the victim symbolizes the fate of the perjurer . 161
The sacramental or purificatory theory 161-162
Bisection of victims in purificatory ceremonies . . . 162
The purificatory theory confirmed by a modern Arab rite . 162-163
Similar rites observed by Chins, Koryaks, and gipsies . . 163
Significance of the passage between the pieces of the victim . 163
Robertson Smith's sacramental interpretatoin of the Hebrew rite 163-164
The interpretation confirmed by savage rituals . . . 164-166
Half-skeleton of bisected human body found at Gezer . . 166
The half-skeleton probably a relic of human sacrifice . . . 167
Alternative explanations, the purificatory and the covenantal, of the
    bisection of human victims 167
The purificatory or protective explanation of the rite . . 167-169
Discovery of another half-skeleton of a human victim at Gezer . 169
The half-skeleton not explicable as a foundation sacrifice . . 170
Conventional explanation of half-skeleton confirmed by Wachaga pratice 170
Retribution theory of Hebrew rite confirmed by Wachaga parallel 171
Retributive and sacramental theories complementary . . 171-172

CHAPTER II

THE HEIRSHIP OF JACOB OR ULTIMOGENITURE

§ 1. *Traces of Ultimogeniture in Israel*

The character of Jacob 172
His alleged frauds on his brother and father . . . 172
Theory that Jacob, as the younger son, was the heir . . . 173
Traces of junior right or ultimogeniture in patriarchal history . 174
Traces of ultimogeniture in the history of David . . . 175

§ 2. *Ultimogeniture in Europe*

Borough English in England 175-176
Ultimogeniture in France 176-177
Ultimogeniture in Friesland and Germany 177-178
Ultimogeniture in Russia 178
Ultimogeniture in Hungary 178

§ 3. *The Question of the Origin of Ultimogeniture*

Blackstone on the origin of Borough English . . . 179
Ultimogeniture among the Turks and Mongols . . . 180

§ 4. *Ultimogeniture in Southern Asia*

The Lushais of Assam, their migratory cultivation . . 180-182
Youngest son a chief's heir among the Lushais . . . 182
Ultimogeniture in private families among the Lushais . 182-183
Ultimogeniture among the Angamis of Assam . . . 183
Ultimogeniture among the Meitheis of Assam . . . 183-184
Ultimogeniture among the Kachins or Singphos of Burma . 184-185
Systems of ownership dependent on systems of agriculture . 185
Economic advance from migratory agriculture and communal won-
    ership to permanent agriculture and individual ownership . 186

PAGE

The Kachins practise both migratory and permanent agriculture 186-187
Ultimogeniture among the Kachins of China . . . 187
Ultimogeniture among the Shans of China 188
Ultimogeniture among the Chins 189
Compromise between ultimogeniture and primogeniture among the
    Hkamies 189
Ultimogeniture among the Lolos of China 189
Heirship of youngest daughter among the Khasis and Garos of Assam 190
Mother-kin among the Khasis 190
Youngest daughter the heir among the Khasis . . . 190-191
Why daughters rather than sons are heirs among the Khasis 191-192
The Garos 192-193
Mother-kin among the Garos 193-194
Heirship of the youngest daughter among the Garos . . 194
Original home of Mongolian tribes practising ultimogeniture 194-195
Ultimogeniture among the Mrus 195
The Hos or Larka Coles of Bengal 195-196
Ultimogeniture and primogeniture among the Hos . . 196-197
The Bhils of Central India 197-198
Ultimogeniture among the Bhils 198
Ultimogeniture among the Badagas of Southern India . 198
Traces of ultimogeniture in the Malay region and Georgia . 198-199

§ 5. *Ultimogeniture in North-eastern Asia*

Ultimogeniture among the Yukaghirs 199-200
Ultimogeniture among the Chukchee 200-201
Ultimogeniture among the Koryaks 201

§ 6. *Ultimogeniture in Africa*

Rarity of ultimogeniture in Africa 201
Rights of youngest sons among the Bogos, Suks, and Turkans 201-202
Ultimogeniture among the Ibos of Southern Nigeria . . 202

§ 7. *The Origin of Ultimogeniture*

Why youngest sons are preferred as heirs 202
Why youngest daughters are preferred as heirs . . 202-203
Preference for youngest sons natural among pastoral tribes . 203-204
Ultimogeniture tends to pass into primogeniture . . . 204

CHAPTER III

JACOB AND THE KIDSKINS: OR THE NEW BIRTH

§ 1. *The Diverted Blessing*

Story of Jacob's trick perhaps a reminiscence of a legal ceremony 204-205
How Jacob, disguised as his elder brother, obtained the blessing 205-206
Displacement of an elder by a young son in the succession . 206

§ 2. *Sacrificial Skins in Ritual*

East African tribes in relation to the Semites . . . 206-207
Fat and skin of animals in Galla rite of adoption . . 207
Rings made from skins of sacrificial victims in East Africa . 207
Kikuyu ceremony of the new birth 207-209

PAGE

Assimilation of mother and child to sheep and lamb . . . 209
Sacrificial skins at Kikuyu ceremony of adoption . . 209-210
Sacrificial skins at circumcision in East Africa 210
Sacrificial skins at marriage in East Africa 211
Sacrificial skins at covenants in East Africa 211
Sacrificial skins in another Kikuyu rite 211-212
Sacrificial skins at sacrifices in East Africa 212-213
Sacrificial skins in sickness, etc., in East Africa . . 213-214
Sacrificial skins at expiations among the Wachaga . . . 214
Sacrificial skins at expiations among the Wawanga . . 214-215
Sacrificial skins at transference of government in East Africa . 215
Victim's skin intended to identify the wearer with the animal . 215-216

§ 3. *The New Birth*

Legal fiction of a new birth to effect a change of status . . 216
Fiction of new birth at adoption in antiquity and the Middle Ages 216-217
Fiction of new birth at adoption among Slavs and Turks . . 217
Fiction of new birth at adoption among the Klemantans . . 217
Fiction of new birth at adoption among the Bahima . . 217-218
Fiction of new birth enacted in Greece and India by persons erro-
    neously thought to be dead 218
Fiction of new birth to raise a Brahman to the rank of a god . 219
Fiction of new birth in India as Expiation for breach of custom 219-220
Fiction of new birth from a metal cow as expiation in India . 220
Fiction of new birth from a golden cow to raise Maharajahs of Tra-
    vancore to Brahman rank 220-222
Fiction of new birth from a live cow in India . . . 222-223
Rite of new birth tends to dwindle into an abridged form . . 223

§ 4. *Conclusion*

Jacob and the kidskins in relation to the rite of the new birth . 223

CHAPTER IV

JACOB AT BETHEL

§ 1. *Jacob's Dream*

Jacob sent away to Laban in Haran 223-224
His dream of the heavenly ladder at Bethel 224
The stone at Bethel set up and anointed 225

§ 2. *Dreams of the Gods*

Belief that gods reveal themselves to men in dreams . . . 225
Dreams in the sanctuary of Amphiaraus at Oropus . . 225-226
Dreams in the sanctuary of Aesculapius at Epidaurus . . 226-228
Dream oracle of Ino or Pasiphae in Laconia 228
Dream oracles in ancient Italy 228

§ 3. *The Heavenly Ladder*

African tales of heavenly ladders 228-229
Toradja tales of creepers connecting earth and heaven . . . 229
Stories of heavenly ladder, etc., in Sumatra and Madagscar . 229-230
Ladders to facilitate the descent of gods or spirits . . . 230

§ 4. *The Sacred Stone*

	PAGE
Popularity of the sanctuary at Bethel	231
Sacred stones at Canaanite and Hebrew sanctuaries	231
Stones worshipped by the ancient Arabs and Greeks	231-232
Worship of stones in the Banks Islands and New Hebrides	232-233
Worship of stones in Samoa	233
Worship of stones in the Indian Archipelago	233-234
Worship of stones in Africa	234
Worship of stones among the North American Indians	234
The Gruagach stones in the highlands of Scotland	235
Sacred stones anointed in Norway	235
Sacred stones anointed in classical antiquity	235
Sacred stones anointed in India	235-236
Sacred stones anointed in the Kei Islands, Madagascar, and Africa	236
The anointed stone at Bethel	237
Many Bethels (*baitylia*) in Canaan	237
The standing stones (*masseboth*) of Canaanite sanctuaries	237

CHAPTER V

JACOB AT THE WELL

Jacob's meeting with Rachel at the well	237-238
The weeping of Jacob at meeting Rachel	238
Weeping at the meeeting of friends in the Old Testament	238-239
Weeping at meeting among the Maoris	239-241
Weeping as a salutation in the Adaman Islands and India	241
Weeping as a salutation among the American Indians	241-243

CHAPTER VI

THE COVENANT ON THE CAIRN

Jacobs' return to the land of his fathers	243-244
His dispute with Laban	244-245
The reconciliation and covenant at the cairn	245
The cairn personified as a witness	246
Rude stone monuments beyond Jordan	246-247
Stones employed to give stability to covenants	247
The stone at marriage in India	247-248
Oaths on stones in Scotland	248
Oaths on stones in Africa and India	248-249
Religious and magical uses of stones in oaths	249
Twofold aspect of the cairn in Jacob's covenant	249-250
Procopius on a detection of perjury	250
Cairns as witnesses in modern Syria	250

CHAPTER VII

JACOB AT THE FORD OF THE JABBOK

Jacob's descent into the glen of the Jabbok	251
Jacob's wrestle with a mysterious adversary at the ford	251-252
His adversary perhaps the jinnee of the river	252
The wrestling of Greek heroes with water-sprites	252-253
Shape-shifting in such encounters	253

PAGE

Propitiation of water-spirits at fords 253-254
Rivers worshipped by Bantu tribes of South Africa . . . 254
Offerings to rivers at crossing them in Africa . . . 254
Ceremonies at crossing rivers in South India . . . 255
Ceremonies of the Agoni at crossing river . : . . 255-256
Punishments inflicted on river-spirits . . : . . 256
Punishing or fighting the spirits of the sea . . . 256-257
The sinew that shrank; American Indian parallels . . . 257
Ancient Mexican parallel to Jacob's nocturnal wrestle . 257-258

CHAPTER VIII

JOSEPH'S CUP

Joseph's divining cup 258
Divination by appearances in water in antiquity . . . 258-259
Divination by appearances in water or ink in modern Egypt . 259-260
Divination by appearances in water in Scandinavia and Tahiti . 260
Divination by appearances in water in New Guinea, and among the
    Eskimo 260-261
Other ways of divining by a vessel of water 261
Divination by things dropped into water 261
Divination by tea-leaves in a cup 261
Divination by molten lead or wax in water 262

PART III

THE TIMES OF THE JUDGES AND THE KINGS

CHAPTER I

MOSES IN THE ARK OF BULRUSHES

National history of Israel begins with Moses 263
Exposure and preservation of the infant Moses . . . 264
Exposure and preservation of Romulus 265
Exposure and preservation of Sargon 266
Exposure and preservation of Prince Karna in the *Mahabharata* 266-267
Exposure and preservation of Trakhan, king of Gilgit . . 267-268
Water ordeal to test the legitimacy of children . . . 268-269

CHAPTER II

SAMSON AND DELILAH

Incongruity of Samson among the judges . . . 269-270
Samson's strength in his hair: the secret betrayed . . 270-272
Belief in East Indies that a man's strength is in his hair . . 272
Belief in Europe that the power of a witch is in her hair . 272
Similar belief as to witches in India and Mexico . 272-273
Niasian story of king whose strength was in his hair . 273-274
Ancient Greek stories like that of Samson and Delilah . 274
Russian story of Koshchei the Deathless . . . 274-276
Serbian story of the warlock True Steel 276
Serbian story of the dragon of the mill . . . 276-277
Islay story of the giant and the egg 277-278

PAGE

Argyleshire story of the giant and the thorn . . . 278-279
Indian story of the ogre king of Gilgit 279-281
Resemblance of all these stories to the Samson legend . . . 281
Transposition of the hero and the villain 281-282
The harlequins of history 282

CHAPTER III

THE BUNDLE OF LIFE

The wilderness of Judea 283-284
David and Abigail 284
"The bundle of life" 285
Belief that souls can be abstracted from their bodies . . . 285
Souls extracted to keep them out of harm's way . . . 285-286
Bundles of sticks and stones as receptacles of souls in Central Aus-
tralia 286-287
Analogy of these bundles to "the bundle of life" . . . 287-288
Ezekiel on women who hunt and catch souls . . . 288
The art of hunting and catching souls 288-289
Trapping souls in Celebes 289
"Houses of the soul" denounced by Isaiah 290
"Houses of the soul" perhaps scent-bottles 290-291
Folk-lore and poetry 291

CHAPTER IV

THE WITCH OF ENDOR

Saul and Samuel 291
The character of Saul 291-292
The eve of battle 292
Saul resolves to consult the ghost of Samuel . . . 293
Saul and the witch of Endor 293-295
Necromancy among the ancient Hebrews 295-296
Necromancy in the Gilgamesh epic 296
Necromancy among the ancient Greeks 296-297
The oracles of the dead 297
The oracle of Aornum in Thesprotis 297-298
Oracles imparted by the dead in dreams 298-299
Dream oracle of the dead in Italy 299
Dream oracles on graves in North Africa 299-300
Dream oracles on graves in Celebes 300
Evocation of the ghosts of Darius, Achilles, and Homer . . 300
Lucan on the evocation of the dead 300-301
Horace and Tibullus on the evocation of the dead . . . 301
Evocation of the dead by Nero and Caracalla . . . 301
Necromancy in Africa 301
Oracles of dead kings among the Baganda . . . 301-302
Oracles of dead chiefs among the Bantu tribes of Rhodesia . 302
Evocation of the dead among the negroes of West Africa . 302-303
Consultation of the dead by means of their images . . 303
Evocation of the dead among the Maoris 303
Evocation of the dead in Nukahiva 303-304
Evocation of the dead in New Guinea and Celebes . . 304
Evocation of the dead in Borneo 304
Evocation of the dead among the Bataks of Sumatra . . 304-305
Evocation of the dead among the Eskimo . . . 305
Necromancy and evocation of the dead in China . . 305-307
Wide diffusion of necromancy 307

CHAPTER V

THE SIN OF A CENSUS

	PAGE
Aversion of Jehovah to the numbering of Israel . . .	307-308
Aversion of Congo peoples to count themselves or their children	308
Aversion of East African tribes to count themselves or their cattle	308-309
Aversion to the Hottentots to be counted . . .	309
Aversion to numbering people and things in North Africa .	309-310
Mode of counting measures of grain in Palestine . . .	310
Aversion to counting leaves in the Shortlands . . .	310
Aversion to counting fruit or people among American Indians .	310
Superstitious objection to counting in Europe . . .	310-312
Jewish objection to a census probably superstitious . .	312
Later relaxation of the rule	313

CHAPTER VI

THE KEEPERS OF THE THRESHOLD

The Keepers of the Threshold in the temple at Jerusalem . .	313
Modern Syrian superstition about treading on a threshold .	313-314
Keepers of the Threshold at Peking in the Middle Ages . .	314
Not to tread on the threshold of a Tartar prince's hut . .	314
Respect for thresholds of caliphs of Baghdad and kings of Persia	314-315
Respect for thresholds of Fijian chiefs	315
Respect for thresholds in Africa	315-316
Respect for thresholds among aborigines of India and the Kalmuks	316
Conditional prohibitions to touch the threshold . . .	316
Practice of carrying a bride over the threshold . .	316-317
Practice of carrying a bride over the threshold among Aryan peoples	317-318
The practice not a relic of marriage by capture . . .	318
Sanctity of the threshold	319
Belief that the threshold is haunted by spirits . . .	319
Custom of burying the dead at the doorway	320
Stillborn children buried under the threshold to ensure rebirth .	320
Abortive calves buried under the threshold in Eng'and .	320-321
Sanctity of the threshold and the theory of rebirth . .	321
Sacrifice of animals at thresholds	321
Brides stepping over blood at the threshold . . .	322
Sacrifices to the dead at the threshold among the Bambaras .	322
Sanctity of the threshold in relation to spirits . . .	322

CHAPTER VII

SACRED OAKS AND TEREBINTHS

The oak and the terebinth in Palestine	322
Three species of oaks in Palestine	322-323
Veneration for oaks in Palestine	323-324
Sacred oak groves in Northern Syria	324
Sacred oaks beside the tombs of Mohammedan saints . .	324
The *Wely* or reputed tomb of a saint under a sacred tree .	324-325
These shrines (*Mukâms*) the real objects of worship in Palestine .	325
Description of these shrines	326
Mode of worship at the shrines	326-327
Sanctity of the trees at the shrines	327

PAGE

Antiquity of the worship at these "high places" . . . 327
Modern examples of these local sanctuaries . . . 327-328
Sacred oak trees hung with votive rags 328
Daughters of Jacob associated with oaks 328
Hebrew words for oak and terebinth 329
Terebinths in Palestine 329
Sacred terebinths hung with votive rags 329
The spirit or saint (Wely) in the tree 330-331
The oak predominantly the sacred tree of Palestine . . 331
Worship of oaks denounced by Hebrew prophets . . . 331-332
Bloody sacrifices to sacred oaks 332
Bloody sacrifices to sacred trees in Africa . . . 332-333
Jehovah associated with sacred oaks or terebinths . . 333
The oracular oak or terebinth at Shechem . . . 333-334
The oak associated with the king 334
The oak or terebinth of Mamre 334-335
The three angels worshipped at the tree 335
The three gods in the holy oak at Romove . . . 335
Church built by Constantine "at the oak of Mamre" . . 335
Annual festival at the terebinth or oak of Mamre . . 336
The end of the Jewish nation at the terebinth or oak of Mamre . 337

CHAPTER VIII

THE HIGH PLACES OF ISRAEL

The high places formerly legitimate seats of worship . . . 337
Abolition of worship at the high places 338
Green trees a prominent feature of the high places . . 338-339
Wooded heights still seats of religious worship in Palestine . . 339
Sacred groves, relics of ancient forests, on high places among the
    Akikuyu 339-340
Sacred groves, relics of ancient forests, among the Mundas . 340-341
Analogy of the grove deities to the Baalim 341
Sacred groves, relics of ancient forests, on high places among the
    Afghans 341-342
Sacred groves, relics of ancient forests, on high places among the
    Cheremiss 342
The Baalim of Canaan probably old woodland deities . . 342
The sacred pole (asherah) and its analogue in Borneo . . 342-343

CHAPTER IX

THE SILENT WIDOW

Restrictions laid on mourners for fear of the ghost . . . 343
Silence perhaps imposed on Hebrew widows 343
Silence of widows in Africa and Madagascar . . . 343-344
Silence of widows among North American Indians . . . 344
Silence of widows in some tribes of North Australia . . 344-345
Silence of widows among the Arunta of Central Australia . 345-346
Silence of widows among the Unmatjera and Kaitish . . 346
Silence of widows and other female mourners among the War-
    ramunga 346-347
Silence of widows among the Dieri 347
The motive for silence a fear of the ghost 347-348
Confirmation from position in which widow stands to her deceased
    husband's younger brother 348-349
Similar customs and beliefs perhaps in ancient Israel . . 349

PART IV

THE LAW

CHAPTER I

THE PLACE OF THE LAW IN JEWISH HISTORY

PAGE

Late date of Pentateuchal legislation in its present form   .   350
Law a gradual growth   350-351
Legislation and codification   351
Many Hebrew laws older than the date of their codification   .   352
Historical reality of Moses, the founder of Israel .   .   .   352-353
Three bodies of law in the Pentateuch   353
The Book of the Covenant   353-354
The Deuteronomic Code   354
Josiah's reformation: written code substituted for oral tradition   354-355
The religious effect of the substitution   355
Date of the composition of the Deuteronomic Code uncertain   .   355-356
Ethical and religious character of Deuteronomy   .   .   .   356-357
Theoretical inadequacy and practical inconvenience of the one sanctuary 357
Destruction of local sanctuaries perhaps regretted by the peasants   357-358
The reformation powerless to avert the national ruin   .   .   358-359
The second reformation after the Exile, resulting in the Priestly
    Code   359-360

CHAPTER II

NOT TO SEETHE A KID IN ITS MOTHER'S MILK

"Not to seethe a kid in its mother's milk" one of the original Ten
    Commandments   360-361
The original version of the Ten Commandments   .   .   .   361-362
Contrast between the ritual and the moral versions of the Decalogue   363
The ritual version the older of the two   363
Suggested explanations of the command not to seethe a kid in its
    mother's milk   364-365
Aversion of pastoral tribes in Africa to boil milk for fear of injuring
    the cows   364
The aversion based on sympathetic magic   364-365
Parallel superstitions as to oranges and lees of wine   .   .   365
Objection to boil milk among pastoral tribes of Central and East
    Africa   365-367
Traces of similar beliefs in Europe   367
The Hebrew command perhaps similarly explicable   .   .   368
The boiling of flesh in milk thought to injure the cows   .   .   368
Other rules of sympathetic magic observed by pastoral peoples   .   369
Milk-vessels not to be washed with water   369
Pastoral Bahima will not wash themselves with water   .   .   369
Cows thought to be affected by the material of milk-vessels   .   369
Objection of pastoral tribes to let milk touch flesh   .   .   369-370
Flesh and milk not to be eaten together in pastoral tribes   .   370-371
Jewish rule not to eat flesh and milk together   .   .   .   371-372
Vegetables and milk not to be eaten together in pastoral tribes   .   372-373
Pastoral tribes discourage agriculture for fear of hurting their cattle   373-374
Some pastoral tribes eschew the flesh of certain wild animals for fear
    of hurting their cattle   374-375
Aversion of pastoral tribes to game perhaps due to fear of hurting
    their cattle   375-376

PAGE
Pastoral tribes eat such wild animals as they think resemble cattle . 375
Hebrew law of clean and unclean animals perhaps based on their sup-
posed likeness or unlikeness to cattle 376
Hebrew customs as to milk and flesh diet probably derived from pas-
toral stage of society 377

CHAPTER III

CUTTINGS FOR THE DEAD

Hebrew customs of cutting the body and shearing the hair in
mourning 377-378
Similar Philistine and Moabite customs 378
The customs forbidden in the Deuteronomic code . . . 378
The customs forbidden in the Levitical code 379
Both customs common in mourning throughout the world . . 379
Arab custom of scratching the face and shearing the hair in mourning 379
Similar mourning customs in ancient Greece 379-380
Assyrian, Armenian, and Roman custom of scratching faces in mourning 380
Faces gashed and hair shorn by mourners among Scythians, Huns,
Slavs, and Caucasian peoples 380-381
Bodies scratched and hair shorn by mourners in Africa . . 381
Bodies lacedated and hair shorn by mourners in Indian tribes of
North America 381-384
Bodies lacerated and hair shorn by mourners in Indian tribes of
South America 384
Bodies lacerated by mourners among the Turks and tribes in Suma-
tra, New Guinea, and the New Hebrides 385
Hair shorn and offered to the dead by mourners in Halmahera . 385
Bodies lacerated and hair shorn by mourners in Tahiti . . 386-387
Bodies lacerated by mourners in Hawaii 387-388
Bodies lacerated by mourners in Tonga 388-389
Bodies lacerated in mourning in Samoa, Mangaia, and the Marquesas
Islands 389
Bodies lacerated and hair shorn by mourners among the Maoris 389-390
Bodies lacerated and hair shorn by mourneres among the Australian
aborigines 390-392
Blood of mourners applied to the corpse or the grave . . 392-393
Severed hair of mourners applied to the corpse . . . 393
Bodies lacerated and hair shorn by mourners among the Tasmanians 393
Body lacerated and hair shorn perhaps as disguise against ghost . 393
Fear of ghost shown in Australia mourning customs . . 393-394
Desire to propitiate ghost shown in Australian mourning customs 394
Offerings of blood and hair to the dead 394
How the blood may be thought to benefit the dead . . 395-396
How the hair may be thought to benefit the dead . . . 396-397
Customs of cutting the body and shearing the hair in mourning evi-
dence of a worship of the dead . . . . . ° 397

CHAPTER IV

THE OX THAT GORED

Homicidal ox to be stoned to death 397-398
Blood revenge extended by Kukis to animals and trees . . 398
Trees that have caused a death felled by Ainos . . . 398
Homicidal weapons destroyed or rendered useless . . . 399
Homicidal buffaloes put to death in Malacca and Celebes . . 399

PAGE

Arab treatment of homicidal animals 400
Punishment of worrying dog in the *Zend-Avesta* 400
Trial of animals and things in ancient Athens . . . 400-401
Trial of animals and things recommended by Plato . . 401-402
Trial and punishment of things in Thasos 402
Statues punished at Olympia and Rome 402-403
Animals punished in ancient Rome 403
Trial and punishment of animals in modern Europe . . . 403
Ecclesiastical jurisdiction over wild animals and vermin . 403-404
Mode of proceedings against animals in ecclesiastical courts . . 404
Examples of the prosecution of animals in Europe . . . 405
Lawsuit brought by St. Julien against coleopterous insects . . 405
Lawsuit against rats at Autun 405-406
Proceedings taken by the Stelvio against field-mice . . 406-407
Proceedings taken by Berne against vermin called *inger* . 407-408
Proceedings against Spanish flies at Coire and leeches at Lausanne 408
Proceedings against caterpillars at Villenose and Strambino . 408-409
Proceedings against caterpillars in Savoy 409-410
Proceedings against ants in Brazil 410-411
Proceedings against rats and mice in Bouranton . . . 411-412
Trial and punishment of domestic animals by the civil power . 412
Trial and execution of a homicidal sow at Savigny . . 412-413
Execution of sows at various places 413
Execution of other animals in France 413-414
Execution of a cock at Bâle for laying an egg . . . 414
Execution of dogs in New England 414
Animals cited as witnesses in Savoy 415
The bell of La Rochelle punished for heresy 415
The English law of deodand 415-416
Adam Smith on the punishment of lifeless objects . . . 416
The primitive personification of things reflected in primitive law 416-417

CHAPTER V

THE GOLDEN BELLS

Jewish priest's robe hung with golden bells 417
Sound of the bells perhaps intended to drive off demons . 417-418
Clash of bronze to drive away spirits in antiquity . . . 418
Use of church bells to drive away evil spirits . . . 418-419
Longfellow on church bells in *The Golden Legend* . . 419-420
The Passing Bell 420
The Passing Bell rung to banish demons 420-421
Dante on the Vesper Bell 421
Bret Harte on the Angelus 421-422
Renan on the bells of Rome and Venice 422
Importance of the emotional side of folk-lore . . . 422
Church bells rung to drive away witches 422-423
The bellman and his benediction 423
Milton, Herrick, and Addison on the bellman . . . 423-424
Church bells rung to drive away thunderstorms . . . 424-425
Consecration of bells: inscriptions on bells . . . 425-426
Delrio on the consecration and ringing of church bells . 426
Bacon on the ringing of bells in thunderstorms . . . 426
Famous bells 426
The bells of Caloto in South America 426-427
Bells used by the Bateso to exorcize thunder and lightning . 427-428

PAGE

Gongs beaten by the Chinese in thunderstorms 428
Church bells thought by New Guinea people to ban ghosts . 428-429
Bells used by the Pueblo Indians in exorcism 429
Gongs beaten by the Chinese to exorcize demons . . . 430
Bells used by the Annamese in exorcism 430
Religious use of bells in Burma 430
Bells and metal instruments sounded at funerals and in mourning
    among primitive folk 431
Gongs and bells used in Borneo to drive off demons . . 431-432
Bells attached to an honoured visitor among the Dyaks . . 432-433
Bells worn by priests in India and children in China . . 433
Bells worn by children in Africa to keep off demons . . 433-434
Bells rung to keep demons from women after childbirth . . 434
The infant Zeus and the Curetes 34
Evil spirits kept off at childbirth by armed men among the Tagalogs
    of the Philippines 435
Evil spirits kept off at childbirth by armed men among the Kachins of
    Burma 435-436
Evil spirits kept off at childbirth by clash of metal, etc., among
    various peoples 436
Precautions against Silvanus at childbirth among the Romans . 436-437
Tinkling anklets worn by girls among the Sunars . . . 437
Bells used by girls at circumcision among the Nandi . . . 437
Bells used to ward off demons on the Congo and the Victoria Nyanza 437-438
Use of bells by priests, prophets, and medicine-men in Africa 438-439
Function of the Jewish priest's golden bells 439

INDEX 441

FOLKLORE IN THE OLD TESTAMENT

PART I

THE EARLY AGES OF THE WORLD

CHAPTER I

THE CREATION OF MAN

ATTENTIVE readers of the Bible can hardly fail to remark a striking discrepancy between the two accounts of the creation of man recorded in the first and second chapters of Genesis. In the first chapter, we read how, on the fifth day of creation, God created the fishes and the birds, all the creatures that live in the water or in the air; and how on the sixth day he created all terrestrial animals, and last of all man, whom he fashioned in his own image, both male and female. From this narrative we infer that man was the last to be created of all living beings on earth, and incidently we gather that the distinction of the sexes, which is characteristic of humanity, is shared also by the divinity; though how the distinction can be reconciled with the unity of the Godhead is a point on which the writer vouchsafes us no information. Passing by this theological problem, as perhaps too deep for human comprehension, we turn to the simpler question of chronology and take note of the statements that God created the lower animals first and human beings afterwards, and that the human beings consisted of a man and a woman, produced to all appearance simultaneously, and each of them reflecting in equal measure the glory of their divine original. So far we read in the first chapter. But when we proceed to peruse the second chapter, it is somewhat disconcerting to come bolt on a totally different and, indeed, contradictory account of the same momentous transaction. For here we learn with surprise that God created man first, the lower animals next, and woman last of all, fashioning her as a mere afterthought out of a rib which he abstracted from man in his sleep. The order of merit in the two narratives is clearly reversed. In the first narrative the deity begins with fishes and works steadily up through birds and beasts to man and woman. In the second narrative he begins with man and works downwards through the lower animals to woman, who apparently marks the nadir of the divine workmanship. And in this second version nothing at all is said about man and woman being made in the image of God. We are simply told that "the Lord God formed man of the dust of the ground, and breathed into his nostrils the breath of life; and man became a living soul." Afterwards, to relieve the loneliness of man, who wandered without a living companion in the beautiful garden which had been created for him, God fashioned all the birds and beasts and brought them to man, apparently to amuse him and keep him company. Man looked at them and gave to them all their names; but still he was not content with these playmates, so at last, as if in despair, God created woman out of an insignificant portion of the masculine frame, and introduced her to man to be his wife.

The flagrant contradiction between the two accounts is explained very simply by the circumstance that they are derived from two different and originally independent documents, which were afterwards combined into a single book by an editor, who pieced the two narratives together without always taking pains to soften or harmonize their discrepancies. The account of the creation in the first chapter is derived from what is called the Priestly Document, which was composed by priestly writers during or after the Babylonian captivity. The account of the creation of man and the animals in the second chapter is derived from what is called the Jehovistic Document, which was written several hundred years before the other, probably in the ninth or eighth century before our era. The difference between the religious standpoints of the two writers is manifest. The later or priestly writer conceives God in an abstract form as withdrawn from human sight, and creating all things by a simple fiat. The earlier or Jehovistic writer conceives God in a very concrete form as acting and speaking like a man, modelling a human being out of clay, planting a garden, walking in it at the cool of the day, calling to the man and woman to come out from among the trees behind which they had hidden themselves, and making coats of skin to replace the too scanty garments of fig-leaves with which our abashed first parents sought to conceal their nakedness. The charming naïvety, almost the gaiety, of the earlier narrative contrasts with the high seriousness of the later; though we cannot but be struck by a vein of sadness and pessimism running under the brightly coloured picture of life in the age of innocence, which the great Jehovistic artist has painted for us. Above all, he hardly attempts to hide his deep contempt for woman. The lateness of her creation, and the irregular and undignified manner of it—made out of a piece of her lord and master, after all the lower animals had been created in a regular and decent manner—sufficiently mark the low opinion he held of her nature; and in the sequel his misogynism, as we may fairly call it, takes a still darker tinge, when he ascribes all the misfortunes and sorrows of the human race to the credulous folly and unbridled appetite of its first mother.

Of the two narratives, the earlier or Jehovistic is not only the more picturesque but also the richer in folk-lore, retaining many features redolent of primitive simplicity which have been carefully effaced by the later writer. Accordingly, it offers more points of comparison with the childlike stories by which men in many ages and countries have sought to explain the great mystery of the beginning of life on earth. Some of these simple tales I will adduce in the following pages.

The Jehovistic writer seems to have imagined that God moulded the first man out of clay, just as a potter might do, or as a child moulds a doll out of mud; and that having kneaded and patted the clay into the proper shape, the deity animated it by breathing into the mouth and nostrils of the figure, exactly as the prophet Elisha is said to have restored to life the dead child of the Shunammite by lying on him, and putting his eyes to the child's eyes and his mouth to the child's mouth, no doubt to impart his breath to the corpse; after which the child sneezed seven times and opened its eyes. To the Hebrews this derivation of our species from the dust of the ground suggested itself all the more naturally because, in their language, the word for "ground" (adamah) is in form the feminine of the word of "man" (adam). From various allusions in Babylonian literature it would seem that the Babylonians also conceived man to have been moulded out of clay. According to Berosus, the Babylonian priest, whose account of creation has been preserved in a Greek version, the god Bel cut off his own head, and the other gods caught the flowing blood, mixed it with earth, and fashioned men out of the bloody paste; and that, they said, is why men are so wise, because their mortal clay is tempered with blood divine. In Egyptian mythology Khnoumou, the Father of the Gods, is said to have moulded men out of clay on his potter's wheel.

So in Greek legend the sage Prometheus is said to have moulded the first men out of clay at Panopeus in Phocis. When he had done his work, some of the clay was left over, and might be seen on the spot long afterwards in the shape of two large boulders lying at the edge of a ravine. A Greek traveller, who visited the place in the second century of our era, thought that the boulders had the colour of clay, and that they smelt strongly of human flesh. I too, visited the spot some seventeen hundred and fifty years later. It is a forlorn little glen, or rather hollow, on the southern side of the hill of Panopeus, below the long line of ruined but still stately walls and towers which crowns the grey rocks of the summit. It was a hot day in late autumn—the first of November—and after the long rainless summer of Greece the little glen was quite dry; no water trickled down its bushy sides, but in the bottom I found a reddish crumbling earth, perhaps a relic of the clay out of which Prometheus modelled our first parents. The place was solitary and deserted: not a human being, not a sign of human habitation was to be seen; only the line of mouldering towers and battlements on the hill above spoke of the busy life that had long passed away. The whole scene, like so many else in Greece, was fitted to impress the mind with a sense of the transitoriness of man's little bustling existence on earth compared with the permanence and, at least, the outward peace and tranquillity of nature. The impression was deepened when I rested, in the heat of the day, on the summit of the hill under the shade of some fine holly-oaks, and surveyed the distant prospect, rich in memories of the past, while the sweet perfume of the wild thyme scented all the air. To the south the finely cut peak of Helicon peered over the low intervening ridges. In the west loomed the mighty mass of Parnassus, its middle slopes darkened by pine-woods like shadows of clouds brooding on the mountain side; while at its skirts nestled the ivy-mantled walls of Daulis overhanging the deep glen, whose romantic beauty accords so well with the loves and sorrows of Procne and Philomela, which Greek legend associated with the spot. Northwards, across the broad plain to which the steep bare hill of Panopeus descends, the eye rested on the gap in the hills through which the Cephissus winds his tortuous way to flow under grey willows, at the foot of barren stony hills, till his turbid waters lose themselves, no longer in the vast reedy swamps of the now vanished Copaic Lake, but in a dark cavern of the limestone rock. Eastward, clinging to the slopes of the bleak range of which the hill of Panopeus forms part, were the ruins of Chaeronea, the birthplace of Plutarch; and out there in the plain was fought the fatal battle which laid Greece at the feet of Macedonia. There, too, in a later age, East and West met in deadly conflict, when the Roman armies under Sulla defeated the Asiatic hosts of Mithridates. Such was the landscape spread out before me on one of those farewell autumn days of almost pathetic splendour, when the departing summer seems to linger fondly, as if loth to resign to winter the enchanted mountains of Greece. Next day the scene had changed: summer was gone. A grey November mist hung low on the hills which only yesterday had shone resplendent in the sun, and under its melancholy curtain the dead flat of the Chaeronean plain, a wide, treeless expanse shut in by desolate slopes, wore an aspect of chilly sadness befitting the battlefield where a nation's freedom was lost.

We cannot doubt that such rude conceptions of the origin of mankind, common to Greeks, Hebrews, Babylonians, and Egyptians, were handed down to the civilized peoples of antiquity by their savage or barbarous forefathers. Certainly stories of the same sort have been recorded among the savages and barbarians of to-day or yesterday. Thus the Australian blacks in the neighbourhood of Melbourne said that Pund-jel, the Creator, cut three large sheets of bark with his big knife. On one of these he placed some clay and worked it up with his knife into a proper consistence. He then laid a portion of the clay on one of the other pieces of bark and shaped it into a human form; first he made the feet, then the legs then the trunk, the arms, and the head. Thus he made a clay man on each of the two pieces of bark; and being well pleased with his handiwork, he danced round them for joy. Next he took stringy bark from the eucalyptus tree, made hair of it, and stuck it on the heads of his clay men. Then he looked at them again, was pleased with his work, and again danced around them for joy. He then lay down on them, blew his breath hard into their mouths, their noses, and their navels; and presently they stirred, spoke, and rose up as full-grown men. The Maoris of New Zealand say that a certain god, variously named Tu, Tiki, and Tane, took red riverside clay, kneaded it with his own blood into a likeness or image of himself, with eyes, legs, arms, and all complete, in fact, an exact copy of the deity; and having perfected the model, he animated it by breathing into its mouth and nostrils, whereupon the clay effigy at once came to life and sneezed. So like himself was the man whom the Maori Creator Tiki fashioned that he called him *Tiki-ahua,* that is, Tiki's likeness.

A very generally received tradition in Tahiti was that the first human pair was made by Taaroa, the chief god. They say that after he had formed the world he created man out of red earth, which was also the food of mankind until bread-fruit was produced. Further, some say that one day Taaroa called for the man by name, and when he came he made him fall asleep. As he slept, the Creator took out one of his bones (*ivi*) and made of it a woman, whom he gave to the man to be his wife, and the pair became the progenitors of mankind. This narrative was taken down from the lips of the natives in the early years of the mission to Tahiti. The missionary, William Ellis, who records it observes: "This always appeared to me a mere recital of the Mosaic account of creation, which they had heard from some European, and I never placed any reliance on it, although they have repeatedly told me it was a tradition among them before any foreigner arrived. Some have also stated that the woman's name was Ivi, 'which would be by them pronounced as if written *Eve*. Ivi is an aboriginal word, and not only signifies a bone, but also a widow, and a victim slain in war. Notwithstanding the assertion of the natives, I am disposed to think that *Ivi,* or Eve, is the only aboriginal part of the story, as far as it respects the mother of the human race." However, the same tradition has been recorded in other parts of Polynesia besides Tahiti. Thus the natives of Fakaofo or Bowditch Island say that the first man was produced out of a stone. After a time he bethought him of making a woman. So he gathered earth and moulded the figure of a woman out of it, and having done so he took a rib out of his left side and thrust it into the earthen figure, which thereupon started up a live woman. He called her Ivi (Eevee) or "rib" and took her to wife, and the whole human race sprang from this pair. The Maoris also are reported to believe that the first woman was made out of the first man's ribs. This wide diffusion of the story in Polynesia raises a doubt whether it is merely as Ellis thought, a repetition of the Biblical narrative learned from Europeans.

However, the story of the creation of the first woman out of a rib of the first man meets us elsewhere in forms so closely resembling the Biblical account that they can hardly be independent of it. Thus the Karens of Burma say that God "created man, and of what did he form him? He created man at first from the earth, and finished the work of creation. He created woman, and of what did he form her? He took a rib from the man and created the woman." Again, the Bedel Tartars of Siberia have a tradition that God at first made a man, who lived quite alone on the earth. But once, while this solitary slept, the devil touched his breast; then a bone grew out from his ribs, and falling to the ground it grew long and became the first woman. Thus these Tartars have deepened the cynicism of the writer in Genesis by giving the devil a hand in the creation of our common mother. But to return to the Pacific.

The Pelew Islanders relate that a brother and sister made men out of clay kneaded with the blood of various animals, and that the characters of these first men and of their descendents were determined by the characters of the animals whose blood had been mingled with the primordial clay; for instance, men who have rat's blood in them are thieves, men who have serpent's blood in them are sneaks, and men who have cock's blood in them are brave. According to a Melanesian legend, told in Mota, one of the Banks Islands, the hero Qat moulded men of clay, the red clay from the marshy riverside at Vanua Lava. At first he made men and pigs just alike, but his brothers remonstrated with him, so he beat down the pigs to go on all fours and made man walk upright. Qat fashioned the first woman out of supple twigs, and when she smiled he knew she was a living woman. The natives of Malekula, one of the New Hebrides, give the name of Bokor to the great being who kneaded the first man and woman out of clay.

The inhabitants of Noo-hoo-roa, in the Kei Islands, say that their ancestors were fashioned out of clay by the supreme god, Dooadlera, who breathed life into the clay figures. According to the bare'e-speaking Toradjas of Central Celebes there were at first no human beings on the earth. Then i Lai, the god of the upper world, and i Ndara, the goddess of the under world, resolved to make men. They committed the task to i Kombengi, who made two models, one of a man and the other of a woman, out of stone or, according to others, out of wood. When he had done his work, he set up his models by the side of the road which leads from the upper to the under world, so that all spirits passing by might see and criticize his workmanship. In the evening the gods talked it over, and agreed that the calves of the legs of the two figures were not round enough. So Kombengi went to work again, and constructed another pair of models which he again submitted to the divine criticism. This time the gods observed that the figures were too pot-bellied, so Kombengi produced a third pair of models, which the gods approved of, after the maker had made a slight change in the anatomy of the figures, transferring a portion of the male to the female figure. It now only remained to make the figures live. So the god Lai returned to his celestial mansion to fetch eternal breath for the man and woman; but in the meantime the Creator himself, whether from thoughtlessness or haste, had allowed the common wind to blow on the figures, and they drew their breath and life from it. That is why the breath returns to the wind when a man dies.

The Dyaks of Sakarran in British Borneo say that the first man was made by two large birds. At first they tried to make men out of trees, but in vain. Then they hewed them out of rocks, but the figures could not speak. Then they moulded a man out of damp earth and infused into his veins the red gum of the kumpang-tree. After that they called to him and he answered; they cut him and blood flowed from his wounds, so they gave him the name of Tannah Kumpok or "moulded earth." Some of the Sea Dyaks, however, are of a different opinion. They think that a certain god named Salampandai is the maker of men. He hammers them into shape out of clay, thus forming the bodies of children who are to be born into the world. There is an insect which makes a curious clinking noise at night, and when the Dyaks hear it, they say that it is the clink of Salampandais hammer at his work. The story goes that he was commanded by the gods to make a man, and he made one of stone; but the figure could not speak and was therefore rejected. So he set to work again, and made a man of iron; but neither could he speak, so the gods would have none of him. The third time Salampandai made a man of clay, and he had the power of speech. Therefore the gods were pleased and said, "The man you have made will do well. Let him be the ancestor of the human race, and you must make others like him." So Salampandai set about fashioning human beings, and he is still fashioning them at his anvil, working away with his tools in unseen regions. There he hammers out the clay babies, and when one of them is finished he brings it to the gods, who ask the infant, "What would you like to handle and use?" If the child answers, "A sword," the gods pronounce it a male; but if the child replies, "Cotton and a spinning-wheel," they pronounce it a female. Thus they are born boys or girls, according to their own wishes.

The natives of Nias, an island to the south-west of Sumatra, have a long poem descriptive of the creation, which they recite at the dances performed at the funeral of a chief. In this poem, which is arranged in couplets after the style of Hebrew poetry, the second verse repeating the idea of the first in somewhat different language, we read how the supreme god, Luo Zaho, bathed at a celestial spring which reflected his figure in its clear water as in a mirror, and how, on seeing his image in the water, he took a handful of earth as large as an egg, and fashioned out of it a figure like one of those figures of ancestors which the people of Nias construct. Having made it, he put it in the scales 'and weighed it; he weighed also the wind, and having weighed it, he put it on the lips of the figure which he had made; so the figure spoke like a man or like a child, and God gave him the name of Sihai. But though Sihai was like God in form, he had no offspring; and the world was dark, for as yet there was neither sun nor moon. So God meditated, and sent Sihai down to earth to live there in a house made of tree-fern. But while as yet he had neither wife nor child, he one day died at noon. However, out of his mouth grew two trees, and the trees budded and blossomed, and the wind shook the blossoms from the trees, and blossoms fell to the ground and from them arose diseases. And from Sihai's throat grew a tree, from which gold is derived; and from his heart grew another tree, from which men are descended. Moreover, out of his right eye came the sun, and out of his left eye came the moon. In this legend the idea of creating man in his own image appears to have been suggested to the Creator by the accident of seeing his own likeness reflected in a crystal spring.

The Bila-an, a wild tribe of Mindanao, one of the Philippine Islands, relate the creation of man as follows. They say that in the beginning there was a certain being named Melu, of a size so huge that no known thing can give any idea of it; he was white in colour, and had golden teeth, and he sat upon the clouds, occupying all the space above. Being of a very cleanly habit, he was constantly rubbing himself in order to preserve the whiteness of his skin unsullied. The scurf which he thus removed from his person he laid on one side, till it gathered in such a heap as to fidget him. To be rid of it he constructed the earth out of it, and being pleased with his work he resolved to make two beings like himself, only much smaller in size. He fashioned them accordingly in his own likeness out of the leavings of the scurf whereof he had moulded the earth, and these two were the first human beings. But while the Creator was still at work on them, and had finished one of them all but the nose, and the other all but the nose and one other part. Tau Dalom Tana came up to him and demanded to be allowed to make the noses. After a heated argument with the Creator, he got his way and made the noses, but in applying them to the faces of our first parents he unfortunately placed them upside down. So warm had been the discussion between the Creator and his assistant in regard to the noses, that the Creator quite forgot to finish the other part of the second figure, and went away to his place above the clouds, leaving the first man or the first woman (for we are not told which) imperfect; and Tau Dalom Tana also went away to his place below the earth. After that a heavy rain fell, and the two first of humankind nearly perished, for the rain ran off the tops of their heads into their up-turned nostrils. Happily the Creator perceived their plight and coming down from the clouds to the rescue he took off their noses and replaced them right end up.

The Bagobas, a pagan tribe of South-eastern Mindanao, say that in the beginning a certain Diwata made the sea and the land, and planted trees of many sorts. Then he took two lumps of earth, shaped them like human figures, and spat on them; so they became man and woman. The old man was called Tuglay, and the old woman, Tuglibung. They married and lived together, and the old man made a great house and planted seeds of different kinds, which the old woman gave him.

The Kumis, who inhabit portions of Arakan and the Chittagong hill tracts in Eastern India, told Captain Lewin the following story of the creation of man. God made the world and the trees and the creeping things first, and after that he made one man and one woman, forming their bodies of clay; but every night, when he had done his work, there came a great snake, which, while God was sleeping, devoured the two images. This happened twice or thrice, and God was at his wits' end, for he had to work all day and could not finish the pair in less than twelve hours; besides, if he did not sleep, "he would be no good," as the native narrator observed with some show of probability. So, as I have said, God was at his wits' end. But at last he got up early one morning and first made a dog and put life into it; and that night, when he had finished the images, he set the dog to watch them, and when the snake came, the dog barked and frightened it away. That is why to this day, when a man is dying, the dogs begin to howl; but the Kumis think that God sleeps heavily nowadays, or that the snake is bolder, for men die in spite of the howling of the dogs. If God did not sleep, there would be neither sickness nor death; it is during the hours of his slumber that the snake comes and carries us off. A similar tale is told by the Khasis of Assam. In the beginning, they say, God created man and placed him on earth, but on returning to look at the work of his hands he found that the man had been destroyed by the evil spirit. This happened a second time, whereupon the deity created first a dog and then a man; and the dog kept watch and prevented the devil from destroying the man. Thus the work of the deity was preserved. The same story also crops up, with a slight varnish of Hindoo mythology, among the Korkus, an aboriginal tribe of the Central Provinces of India. According to them, Rawan, the demon king of Ceylon, observed that the Vindhyan and Satpura ranges were uninhabited, and he besought the great god Mahadeo to people them. So Mahadeo, by whom they mean Siva, sent a crow to find for him an ant-hill of red earth, and the bird discovered such an ant-hill among the mountains of Betul. Thereupon the god repaired to the spot, and taking a handful of the red earth he fashioned out of it two images, in the likeness of a man and a woman. But no sooner had he done so than two fiery horses, sent by Indra, rose from the earth and trampled the images to dust. For two days the Creator persisted in his attempts, but as often as the images were made they were dashed in pieces by the horses. At last the god made an image of a dog, and breathed into it the breath of life, and the animal kept off the fiery steeds of Indra. Thus the god was able to make the two images of man and woman undisturbed, and bestowing life upon them, he called them Mula and Mulai. These two became the ancestors of the Korku tribe.

A like tale is told, with a curious variation, by the Mundas, a primitive aboriginal tribe of Chota Nagpur. They say that the Sun-god, by name Singbonga, first fashioned two clay figures, one meant to represent a man and the other a woman. But before he could endow the figures with life, the rose, apprehensive of what in future he might endure at their hands, trampled them under its hoofs. In those days the horse had wings and could move about much faster than now. When the Sun-god found that the horse had destroyed his earthen figures of men, he first created a spider and then fashioned two more figures like those which the horse had demolished. Next he ordered the spider to guard the effigies against the horse. Accordingly the spider wove its web round the figures in such a way that the horse could not break them again. After that, the Sun-god imparted life to the two figures, which thus became the first human beings.

The Cheremiss of Russia, a Finnish people, tell a story of the creation of man which recalls episodes in the Toradjan and Indian legends of the same event. They say that God moulded man's body of clay and then went up to heaven to fetch the soul, with which to animate it. In his absence he set the dog to guard the body. But while he was away the Devil drew near, and blowing a cold wind on the dog he seduced the animal by the bribe of a fur-coat to relax his guard. Thereupon the fiend spat on the clay body and beslavered it so fully, that when God came back he despaired of ever cleaning up the mess and saw himself reduced to the painful necessity of turning the body outside in. That is why a man's inside is now so dirty. And God cursed the dog the same day for his culpable neglect of duty.

Turning now to Africa, we find the legend of the creation of mankind out of clay among the Shilluks of the White Nile, who ingeniously explain the different complexions of the various races by the differently coloured clays out of which they were fashioned. They say that the creator Juok moulded all men out of earth, and that while he was engaged in the work of creation he wandered about the world. In the land of the whites he found a pure white earth or sand, and out of it he shaped white men. Then he came to the land of Egypt and out of the mud of the Nile he made red or brown men. Lastly, he came to the land of the Shilluks, and finding there black earth he created black men out of it. The way in which he modelled men was this. He took a lump of earth and said to himself, "I will make man, but he must be able to walk and run and go out into the fields, so I will give him two long legs, like the flamingo." Having done so, he thought again, "The man

must be able to cultivate his millet, so I will give him two arms, one
to hold the hoe, and the other to tear up the weeds." So he gave
him two arms. Then he thought again, "The man must be able
to see his millet, so I will give him two eyes." He did so accordingly. Next he thought to himself, "The man must be able to eat
his millet, so I will give him a mouth." And a mouth he gave him
accordingly. After that he thought within himself, "The man
must be able to dance and speak and sing and shout, and for these
purposes he must have a tongue." And a tongue he gave him
accordingly. Lastly, the deity said to himself, "The man must be
able to hear the noise of the dance and the speech of great men, and
for that·he needs two ears." So two ears he gave him, and sent
him out into the world a perfect man. The Fans of West Africa say
that God created man out of clay, at first in the shape of a lizard,
which he put in a pool of water and left there for seven days. At
the end of the seven days God cried, "Come forth," and a man
came out of the pool instead of a lizard. The Ewe-speaking tribes
of Togo-land, in West Africa, think that God still makes men out
of clay. When a little of the water with which he moistens the
clay remains over, he pours it on the ground, and out of that he
makes the bad and disobedient people. When he wishes to make a
good man he makes him out of good clay; but when he wishes to
make a bad man, he employs only bad clay for the purpose. In
the beginning God fashioned a man and set him on the earth; after
that he fashioned a woman. The two looked at each other and
began to laugh, whereupon God sent them into the world.

The story of the creation of mankind out of clay occurs also in
America, among both the Eskimo and the Indians, from Alaska to
Paraguay. Thus the Eskimo of Point Barrow, in Alaska, tell of a
time when there was no man in the land, till a certain spirit named
á sĕ lu, who resided at Point Barrow, made a clay man, set him up
on the shore to dry, breathed into him, and gave him life. Other
Eskimo of Alaska relate how the Raven made the first woman out
of clay, to be a companion to the first man; he fastened water-grass
to the back of the head to be hair, flapped his wings over the clay
figure, and it arose, a beautiful young woman. The Acagchemem
Indians of California said that a powerful being called Chinigchinich
created man out of clay which he found on the banks of a lake;
male and female created he them, and the Indians of the present
day are the descendants of the clay man and woman.

According to the Maidu Indians of California the first man and
woman were created by a mysterious personage named Earth-
Initiate, who descended from the sky by a rope made of feathers.
His body shone like the sun, but his face was hidden and never seen.
One afternoon he took dark red earth, mixed it with water, and
fashioned two figures, one of them a man and the other a woman.
He laid the man on his right side and the woman on his left side,
in his house. He lay thus and sweated all that afternoon and all

that night. Early in the morning the woman began to tickle him
in the side. He kept very still and did not laugh. By and by he
arose, thrust a piece of pitch-wood into the ground, and fire burst
out. The two people were very white. No one to-day is so white
as they were. Their eyes were pink, their hair was black, their
teeth shone brightly, and they were very handsome. It is said
that Earth-Initiate did not finish the bands of the people, because
he did not know how best to do it. The coyote, or prairie-wolf,
who plays a great part in the myths of the Western Indians, saw
the people and suggested that they ought to have hands like his.
But Earth-Initiate said, "No, their hands shall be like mine."
Then he finished them. When the coyote asked why their hands
were to be like that, Earth-Initiate answered, "So that, if they are
chased by bears, they can climb trees." The first man was called
Kuksu, and the first woman was called Morning-Star Woman.

The Dieugño Indians, or, as they call themselves, the Kawakipais,
who occupy the extreme south-western corner of the State of California, have a myth to explain how the world in its present form
and the human race were created. They say that in the beginning there was no earth or solid land, nothing but salt water,
one vast primeval ocean. But under the sea lived two brothers,
of whom the elder was named Tcaipakomat. Both of them kept
their eyes shut, for if they had not done so, the salt water would
have blinded them. After a while the elder brother came up to
the surface and looked about him, but he could see nothing but
water. The young brother also came up but on the way to the
surface he incautiously opened his eyes, and the salt water blinded
him; so when he emerged he could see nothing at all, and therefore
he sank back into the depths. Left alone on the face of the deep,
the elder brother now undertook the task of creating a habitable
earth out of the waste of waters. First of all he made little red
ants, which produced land by filling up the water solid with their
tiny bodies. But still the world was dark, for as yet neither sun
nor moon had been created. Tcaipakomat now caused certain black
birds with flat bills to come into being; but in the darkness the
birds lost their way and could not find where to roost. Next
Tcaipakomat took three kinds of clay, red, yellow, and black, and
thereof he made a round flat thing, which he took in his hand and
threw up against the sky. It stuck there, and beginning to shed
a dim light became the moon. Dissatisfied with the faint illumina-
tion of this pallid orb, Tcaipakomat took more clay, moulded it
into another round flat disc, and tossed it up against the other side
of the sky. It stuck there and became the sun, lighting up everything with his beams. After that Tcaipakomat took a lump of
light-coloured clay, split it partly up, and made a man of it. Then
he took a rib from the man and made a woman of it. The woman
thus created out of the man's rib was called Sinyaxau or First
Woman (from *siny*, "woman," and *axau*, "first'"). From this first

man and woman, modelled by the Creator out of clay, mankind is descended.

The Hopi or Moqui Indians of Arizona similarly believe that in the beginning there was nothing but water everywhere, and that two deities, apparently goddesses, both named Huruing Wuhti, lived in houses in the ocean, one of them in the east, and the other in the west; and these two by their efforts caused dry land to appear in the midst of the water. Nevertheless the sun, on his daily passage across the newly created earth, noticed that there was no living being of any kind on the face of the ground, and he brought this radical defect to the notice of the two deities. Accordingly the divinities met in consultation, the eastern goddess passing over the sea on the rainbow as a bridge to visit her western colleague. Having laid their heads together they resolved to make a little bird; so the goddess of the east made a wren of clay, and together they chanted an incantation over it, so that the clay bird soon came to life. Then they sent out the wren to fly over the world and see whether he could discover any living being on the face of the earth; but on his return he reported that no such being existed anywhere. Afterwards the two deities created many sorts of birds and beasts in like manner and sent them forth to inhabit the world. Last of all the two goddesses made up their mind to create man. Thereupon the eastern goddess took clay and moulded out of it first a woman and afterwards a man; and the clay man and woman were brought to life just as the birds and beasts had been so before them.

The Pima Indians, another tribe of Arizona, allege that the Creator took clay into his hands, and mixing it with the sweat of his own body, kneaded the whole into a lump. Then he blew upon the lump till it began to live and move and became a man and a woman. A priest of the Natchez Indians in Louisiana told Du Pratz "that God had kneaded some clay, such as that which potters use, and had made it into a little man; and that after examining it, and finding it well formed, he blew upon his work, and forthwith that little man had life, grew, acted, walked, and found himself a man perfectly well shaped." As to the mode in which the first woman was created, the priest frankly confessed that he had no information, the ancient traditions of his tribe being silent as to any difference in the creation of the sexes; he thought it likely, however, that man and woman were made in the same way.

The Michoacans of Mexico said that the great god Tucapacha first made man and woman out of clay, but that when the couple went to bathe in a river they absorbed so much water that the clay of which they were composed all fell to pieces. To remedy this inconvenience the Creator applied himself again to his task and moulded them afresh out of ashes, but the result was again disappointing. At last, not to be baffled, he made them of metal. His perseverance was rewarded. The man and woman were now perfectly watertight; they bathed in the river without falling in pieces, and by their union they became the progenitors of mankind. According to a legend of the Peruvian Indians, which was told to a Spanish priest in Cuzco about half a century after the conquest, it was in Tiahuanaco that the human race was restored after the great flood which had destroyed them all, except one man and woman. There in Tiahuanaco, which is about seventy leagues from Cuzco, "the Creator began to raise up the people and nations, that are in that region, making one of each nation of clay, and painting the dresses that each one was to wear. Those that were to wear their hair, with hair; and those that were to be shorn, with hair cut; and to each nation was given the language that was to be spoken, and the songs to be sung, and the seeds and food that they were to ᵴow. When the Creator had finished painting and making the said nations and figures of clay, he gave life and soul to each one, as well men as women, and ordered that they should pass under the earth. Thence each nation came up in the places to which he ordered them to go." The Lengua Indians of Paraguay believe that the Creator, in the shape of a beetle, inhabited a hole in the earth, and that he formed man and woman out of the clay which he threw up from his subterranean abode. At first the two were joined together, "like the Siamese twins," and in this very inconvenient posture they were sent out into the world, where they contended, at great disadvantage, with a race of powerful beings whom the beetle had previously created. So the man and woman besought the beetle to separate them. He complied with their request and gave them the power to propagate their species. So they became the parents of mankind. But the beetle, having created the world, ceased to take any active part or interest in it. We are reminded of the fanciful account which Aristophanes, in the *Symposium* of Plato, gives of the original condition of mankind; how man and woman at first were knit together in one composite being, with two heads, four arms, and four legs, till Zeus cleft them down the middle and so separated the sexes.

It is to be observed that in a number of these stories the clay out of which our first parents were moulded is said to have been red. The colour was probably intended to explain the redness of blood. Though the Jehovistic writer in Genesis omits to mention the colour of the clay which God used in the construction of Adam, we may perhaps, without being very rash, conjecture that it was red. For the Hebrew word for man in general is *adam,* the word for ground is *adamah,* and the word for red is *adom;* so that by a natural and almost necessary concatenation of causes we arrive at the conclusion that our first parent was modelled out of red earth. If any lingering doubt could remain in our mind on the subject, it would be dissipated by the observation that down to this day the soil of Palestine is of a dark reddish brown, "suggesting," as the writer who notices it justly remarks, "the connection between Adam and the ground from which he was taken; especially is this colour noticeable when the soil is newly turned, either by the plough or in digging." So remarkably does nature itself bear witness to the literal accuracy of Holy Writ.

CHAPTER II

THE FALL OF MAN

§ 1. *The Narrative in Genesis.*—With a few light but masterly strokes the Jehovistic writer depicts for us the blissful life of our first parents in the happy garden which God had created for their abode. There every tree that was pleasant to the sight and good for food grew abundantly; there the animals lived at peace with man and with each other; there man and woman knew no shame, because they knew no ill; it was the age of innocence. But this glad time was short, the sunshine was soon clouded. From his description of the creation of Eve and her introduction to Adam, the writer passes at once to tell the sad story of their fall, their loss of innocence, their expulsion from Eden, and the doom of labour, of sorrow, and of death pronounced on them and their posterity. In the midst of the garden grew the tree of the knowledge of good and evil, and God had forbidden man to eat of its fruit, saying, "In the day that thou eatest thereof thou shalt surely die." But the serpent was cunning, and the woman weak and credulous: he persuaded her to eat of the fatal fruit, and she gave of it to her husband, and he ate also. No sooner had they tasted it than the eyes of both of them were opened, they knew that they were naked, and filled with shame and confusion they hid their nakedness under aprons of fig-leaves: the age of innocence was gone for ever. That woeful day, when the heat of noon was over and the shadows were growing long in the garden, God walked there, as was his wont, in the cool of the evening. The man and woman heard his footsteps, perhaps the rustling of the fallen leaves (if leaves could fall in Eden) under his tread, and they hid behind the trees, ashamed to be seen by him naked. But he called them forth from the thicket, and learning from the abashed couple how they had disobeyed his command by eating of the fruit of the tree of knowledge, he flew into a towering passion. He cursed the serpent, condemning him to go on his belly, to eat dust, and to be the enemy of mankind all the days of his life: he cursed the ground, condemning it to bring forth thorns and thistles: he cursed the woman, condemning her to bear children in sorrow and to be in subjection to her husband: he cursed the man, condemning him to wring his daily bread from the ground in the sweat of his brow, and finally to return to the dust out of which he had been taken. Having relieved his feelings by these copious maledictions, the irascible but really kind-hearted deity relented so far as to make coats of skins for the culprits to replace their scanty aprons of fig-leaves; and clad in these new garments the shamefaced pair retreated among the trees, while in the west the sunset died away and the shadows deepened on Paradise Lost.

In this account everything hinges on the tree of the knowledge of good and evil: it occupies, so to say, the centre of the stage in the great tragedy, with the man and woman and the talking serpent grouped round it. But when we look closer we perceive a second tree standing side by side with the other in the midst of the garden. It is a very remarkable tree, for it is no less than the tree of life, whose fruit confers immortality on all who eat of it. Yet in the actual story of the fall this wonderful tree plays no part. Its fruit hangs there on the boughs ready to be plucked; unlike the tree of knowledge, it is hedged about by no divine prohibition, yet no one thinks it worth while to taste of the luscious fruit and live for ever. The eyes of the actors are all turned on the tree of knowledge; they appear not to see the tree of life. Only, when all is over, does God bethink himself of the wondrous tree standing there neglected, with all its infinite possibilities, in the midst of the garden; and fearing lest man, who has become like him in knowledge by eating of the one tree, should become like him in immortality by eating of the other, he drives him from the garden and sets an angelic squadron, with flaming swords, to guard the approach to the tree of life, that none henceforth may eat of its magic fruit and live for ever. Thus, while throughout the moving tragedy in Eden our attention is fixed exclusively on the tree of knowledge, in the great transformation scene at the end, where the splendours of Eden fade for ever into the light of common day, the last glimpse we catch of the happy garden shows the tree of life alone lit up by the lurid gleam of brandished angelic falchions.

It appears to be generally recognized that some confusion has crept into the account of the two trees, and that in the original story the tree of life did not play the purely passive and spectacular part assigned to it in the existing narrative. Accordingly, some have thought that there were originally two different stories of the fall, in one of which the tree of knowledge figured alone, and in the other the tree of life alone, and that the two stories have been unskilfully fused into a single narrative by an editor, who has preserved the one nearly intact, while he has clipped and pared the other almost past recognition. It may be so, but perhaps the solution of the problem is to be sought in another direction. The gist of the whole story of the fall appears to be an attempt to explain man's mortality, to set forth how death came into the world. It is true that man is not said to have been created immortal and to have lost his immortality through disobedience; but neither is he said to have been created mortal. Rather we are given to understand that the possibility alike of immortality and of mortality was open to him, and that it rested with him which he would choose; for the tree of life stood within his reach, its fruit was not forbidden to him, he had only to stretch out his hand, take of the fruit, and eating of it live for ever. Indeed, far from being prohibited to eat of the tree of life, man was implicitly permitted, if not encouraged, to partake of it by his Creator, who had told him expressly, that he might eat freely of every tree in the garden, with the single exception of the tree of the knowledge of good and evil. Thus by planting the tree of life in the garden and not prohibiting its use, God apparently intended to give man the option, or at least the chance, of immortality, but man missed his chance by electing to eat of the other tree, which God had warned him not to touch under pain of immediate death. This suggests that the forbidden tree was really a tree of death, not of knowledge, and that the mere taste of its deadly fruit, quite apart from any question of obedience or disobedience to a divine command, sufficed to entail death on the eater. The inference is entirely in keeping with God's warning to man, "Thou shalt not eat of it; for in the day that thou eatest thereof thou shalt surely die." Accordingly we may suppose that in the original story there were two trees, a tree of life and a tree of death; that it was open to man to eat of the one and live for ever, or to eat of the other and die; that God, out of good will to his creature, advised man to eat of the tree of life and warned him not to eat of the tree of death; and that man, misled by the serpent, ate of the wrong tree and so forfeited the immortality which his benevolent Creator had designed for him.

At least this hypothesis has the advantage of restoring the balance between the two trees and of rendering the whole narrative clear, simple, and consistent. It dispenses with the necessity of assuming two original and distinct stories which have been clumsily stitched together by a botching editor. But the hypothesis is further recommended by another and deeper consideration. It sets the character of the Creator in a far more amiable light; it clears him entirely of that suspicion of envy and jealousy, not to say malignanty and cowardice, which, on the strength of the narrative in Genesis, has so long rested like a dark blot on his reputation. For, according to that narrative, God grudged man the possession both of knowledge and of immortality; he desired to keep these good things to himself, and feared that if man got one or both of them, he would be the equal of his maker, a thing not to be suffered at any price. Accordingly he forbade man to eat of the tree of knowledge, and when man disregarded the command, the deity hustled him out of the garden and closed the premises, to prevent him from eating of the other tree and so becoming immortal. The motive was mean, and the conduct despicable. More than that, both the one and the other are utterly inconsistent with the previous behaviour of the deity, who, far from grudging man anything, had done all in his power to make him happy and comfortable, by creating a beautiful garden for his delectation, beasts and birds to play with, and a woman to be his wife. Surely it is far more in harmony both with the tenor of the narrative and with the goodness of the Creator to suppose, that he intended to crown his kindness to man by conferring on him the boon of immortality, and that his benevolent intention was only frustrated by the wiles of the serpent.

But we have still to ask, why should the serpent practice this deceit on man? what motive had he for depriving the human race of the great privilege which the Creator had planned for them? Was his interference purely officious? or had he some deep design behind it? To these questions the narrative in Genesis furnishes no answer. The serpent gains nothing by his fraud; on the contrary he loses, for he is cursed by God and condemned thenceforth to crawl on his belly and lick the dust. But perhaps his conduct was not so wholly malignant and purposeless as appears on the surface. We are told that he was more subtle than any beast of the field; did he really show his sagacity by blasting man's prospects without improving his own? We may suspect that in the original story he justified his reputation by appropriating to himself the blessing of which he deprived our species; in fact, that while he persuaded our first parents to eat of the tree of death, he himself ate of the tree of life and so lived for ever. The supposition is not so extravagant as it may seem. In not a few savage stories of the origin of death, which I will relate immediately, we read that serpents contrived to outwit or intimidate man and so to secure for themselves the immortality which was meant for him, for many savages believe that by annually casting their skins serpents and other animals renew their youth and live for ever. The belief appears to have been shared by the Semites; for, according to the ancient Phoenician writer Sanchuniathon, the serpent was the longest-lived of all animals, because it casts its skin and so renewed its youth. But if the Phoenicians held this view of the serpent's longevity and the cause of it, their neighbours and kinsfolk the Hebrews may well have done the same. Certainly the Hebrews seem to have thought that eagles renew their youth by moulting their feathers; and if so, why not serpents by casting their skins? Indeed, the notion that the serpent cheated man of immortality by getting possession of a life-giving plant which the higher powers had destined for our species, occurs in the famous Gilgamesh epic, one of the oldest literary monuments of the Semitic race and far more ancient than Genesis. In it we read how the deified Utnaphistim revealed to the hero Gilgamesh the existence of a plant which had the miraculous power of renewing youth and bore the name "the old man becomes young": how Gilgamesh procured the plant and boasted that he would eat of it and so renew his lost youth; how, before he could do so, a serpent stole the magic plant from him, while he was bathing in the cool water of a well or brook; and how, bereft of the hope of immortality, Gilgamesh sat down and wept. It is true that nothing is here said about the serpent eating the plant and so obtaining immortality for himself; but the omission may be due merely to the state of the text, which is obscure and defective, and even if the poet were silent on this point, the parallel versions of the story, which I shall cite, enable us to supply the lacuna with a fair degree of probability. These parallels further suggest, though they cannot prove, that in the original of the story, which the Jehovistic writer has mangled and distorted, the serpent was the messenger sent by God to bear the glad tidings of immortality to man, but that the cunning creature perverted the message to the advantage of his species and to the ruin of ours. The gift of speech, which he used to such ill purpose, was lent him in his capacity of ambassador from God to man.

To sum up, if we may judge from a comparison of the versions dispersed among many people, the true original story of the Fall of Man ran somewhat as follows. The benevolent Creator, after modelling the first man and woman out of mud and animating them by the simple process of blowing into their mouths and noses, placed the happy pair in an earthly paradise, where, free from care and toil, they could live on the sweet fruits of a delightful garden, and where birds and beasts frisked about them in fearless security. As a crowning mercy he planned for our first parents the great gift of immortality, but resolved to make them the arbiters of their own fate by leaving them free to accept or reject the proffered boon. For that purpose he planted in the midst of the garden two wondrous trees that bore fruits of very different sorts, the fruit of one being fraught with death to the eater, and the other with life eternal. Having done so, he sent the serpent to the man and woman and charged him to deliver this message: "Eat not of the Tree of Death, for in the day ye eat thereof ye shall surely die; but eat of the Tree of Life and live for ever." Now the serpent was more subtle than any beast of the field, and on his way he bethought him of changing the message; so when he came to the happy garden and found the woman alone in it, he said to her, "Thus saith God: Eat not of the Tree of Life, for in the day ye eat thereof he shall surely die; but eat of the Tree of Death, and live for ever." The foolish woman believed him, and ate of the fatal fruit, and gave of it to her husband, and he ate also. But the sly serpent himself ate of the Tree of Life. That is why men have been mortal and serpents immortal ever since, for serpents cast their skins every year and so renew their youth. If only the serpent had not perverted God's good message and deceived our first mother, we should have been immortal instead of the serpents; for like the serpents we should have cast our skins every year and so renewed our youth perpetually.

That this, or something like this, was the original form of the story is made probable by a comparison of the following tales, which may conveniently be arranged under two heads, "The Story of the Perverted Message" and "The Story of the Cast Skin."

§ 2. *The Story of the Perverted Message.*—Like many other savages, the Namaquas or Hottentots associate the phases of the moon with the idea of immortality, the apparent waning and waxing of the luminary being understood by them as a real process of alternate disintegration and reintegration, of decay and growth repeated perpetually. Even the rising and setting of the moon is interpreted by them as its birth and death. They say that once on a time the Moon wished to send to mankind a message of immortality and the hare undertook to act as messenger. So the Moon charged him to go to men and say, "As I die and rise to life again, so shall you die and rise to life again." Accordingly the hare went to men, but either out of forgetfulness or malice he reversed the message and said, "As I die and do not rise to life again, so you shall also die and not rise to life again." Then he went back to the Moon, and she asked him what he had said. He told her, and when she heard how he had given the wrong message, she was so angry that she threw a stick at him which split his lip. That is why the hare's lip is still cloven. So the hare ran away and is still running to this day. Some people, however, say that before he fled he clawed the Moon's face, which still bears the marks of the scratching, as anybody may see for himself on a clear moonlight night. But the Namaquas are still angry with the hare for robbing them of immortality. The old men of the tribe used to say, "We are still enraged with the hare, because he brought such a bad message, and we will not eat him." Hence from the day when a youth comes of age and takes his place among men, he is forbidden to eat hare's flesh, or even to come into contact with a fire on which a hare has been cooked. If a man breaks the rule, he is not infrequently banished the village. However, on the payment of a fine he may be readmitted to the community.

A similar tale, with some minor differences, is told by the Bushmen. According to them, the Moon formerly said to men, "As I die and come to life again, so shall ye do ; when ye die, ye shall not die altogether but shall rise again." But one man would not believe the glad tidings of immortality, and he would not consent to hold his tongue. For his mother had died, he loudly lamented her, and nothing could persuade him that she would come to life again. A heated altercation ensued between him and the Moon on this painful subject. "Your mother's asleep," says the Moon. "She's dead," says the man, and at it they went again, hammer and tongs, till at last the Moon lost patience and struck the man on the face with her fist, cleaving his mouth with the blow. And as she did so, she cursed him, saying, "His mouth shall be always like this, even when he is a hare. For a hare he shall be. He shall spring away, he shall come doubling back. The dogs shall chase him, and when they have caught him they shall tear him to pieces. He shall altogether die. And all men, when they die, shall die outright. For he would not agree with me, when I bid him not to weep for his mother, for she would live again. 'No,' says he to me, 'my mother will not live again.' Therefore he shall altogether become a hare. And the people, they shall altogether die, because he contradicted me flat when I told him that the people would do as I do, returning to life after they were dead." So a righteous retribution overtook the sceptic for his scepticism, for he was turned into a hare, and a hare he has been ever since. But still he has human flesh in his thigh, and that is why, when the Bushmen kill a hare, they will not eat that portion of the thigh, but cut it out, because it is human flesh. And still the Bushmen say, "It was on account of the hare that the Moon cursed us, so that we die altogether. If it had not been for him, we should have come to life again when we died. But he would not believe what the Moon told him, he contradicted her flat." In this Bushmen version of the story the hare is not the animal messenger of God to men, but a human sceptic who, for doubting the gospel of eternal life, is turned into a hare and involves the whole human race in the doom of immortality. This may be an older form of the story than the Hottentot version, in which the hare is a hare and nothing more.

The Nandi of British East Africa tell a story in which the origin of death is referred to the ill-humour of a dog, who brought the tidings of immortality to men, but, not being received with the deference due to so august an embassy, he changed his tune in a huff and doomed mankind to the sad fate to which they have ever since been subject. The story runs thus. When the first men lived upon the earth, a dog came to them one day and said, "All people will die like the Moon, but unlike the Moon you will not return to life again unless you give me some milk to drink out of your gourd and beer to drink through your straw. If you do this, I will arrange for you to go to the river when you die and to come to life again on the third day." But the people laughed at the dog, and gave him some milk and beer to drink off a stool. The dog was angry at not being served in the same vessels as a human being, and though he put his pride in his pocket and drank the milk and beer from the stool, he went away in high dudgeon, saying, "All people will die, and the Moon alone will return to life." That is why, when people die, they stay away, whereas when the Moon goes away she comes back again after three days' absence. If only people had given that dog a gourd to drink milk out of, and a straw to suck beer through, we should all have risen from the dead, like the Moon, after three days. In this story nothing is said as to the personage who sent the dog with the message of immortality to men; but from the messenger's reference to the Moon, and from a comparison with the parallel Hottentot story, we may reasonably infer that it was the Moon who employed the dog to run the errand, and that the unscrupulous animal misused his opportunity to extort privileges for himself to which he was not strictly entitled.

In these stories a single messenger is engaged to carry the momentous message, and the fatal issue of the mission is set down to the carelessness or malice of the missionary. However, in some narratives of the origin of death, two messengers are despatched, and the cause of death is said to have been the dilatoriness or misconduct of the messenger who bore the glad tidings of immortality. There is a Hottentot story of the origin of death which is cast in this form. They say that once the Moon sent an insect to men with this message, "Go thou to men and tell them, 'As I die, and dying live, so ye shall also die, and dying live.'" The insect set off with this message, but as he crawled along, the hare came leaping after him, and stopping beside him asked, "On what errand art thou bound?" The insect answered, "I am sent by the Moon to men, to tell them that as she dies, and dying lives, they also shall die, and dying live." The hare said, "As thou art an awkward runner, let me go." And away he tore with the message, while the insect came creeping slowly behind. When he came to men, the hare perverted the message which he had officiously taken upon himself to deliver, for he said, "I am sent by the Moon to tell you, 'As I die, and dying perish, in the same manner ye shall also die and come wholly to an end.'" Then the hare returned to the Moon, and told her what he had said to men. The Moon was very angry and reproached the hare, saying, "Darest thou tell the people a thing which I have not said? With that she took a stick and hit him over the nose. That is why the hare's nose is slit down to this day.

The same tale is told, with some slight variations, by the Tati Bushmen or Masarwas, who inhabit the Bechuanaland Protectorate, the Kalahari desert, and portions of Southern Rhodesia. The men of old time, they say, told this story. The Moon wished to send a message to the men of the early race, to tell them that as she died and came to life again, so they would die, and dying come to life again. So the Moon called the tortoise and said to him, "Go over to those men there, and give them this message from me. Tell them that as I dying live, so they dying will live again." Now the tortoise was very slow, and he kept repeating the message to himself, so as not to forget it. The Moon was very vexed with his slowness and with his forgetfulness: so she called the hare and said to her, "You are a swift runner. Take this message to the men over yonder: 'As I dying live again, so you will dying live again.'" So off the hare started, but in her great haste she forgot the message, and as she did not wish to show the Moon that she had forgotten, she delivered the message to men in this way, "As I dying live again, so you dying will die for ever." Such was the message delivered by the hare. In the meantime the tortoise had remembered the message, and he started off a second time. "This time," said he to himself, "I won't forget." He came to the place where the men were, and he delivered his message. When the men heard

it they were very angry with the hare, who was sitting at some distance. She was nibbling the grass after her race. One of the men
ran and lifted a stone and threw it at the hare. It struck her right
in the mouth and cleft her upper lip; hence the lip has been cleft
ever since. That is why every hare has a cleft upper lip to this day,
and that is the end of the story.

The story of the two messengers is related also by the negroes of
the Gold Coast, and in their version the two messengers are a sheep
and a goat. The following is the form in which the tale was told
by a native to a Swiss missionary at Akropong. In the beginning,
when sky and earth existed, but there were as yet no men on earth,
there fell a great rain, and soon after it had ceased a great chain
was let down from heaven to earth with seven men hanging on it.
These men had been created by God, and they reached the earth
by means of the chain. They brought fire with them and cooked
their food at it. Not long afterwards God sent a goat from heaven
to deliver the following message to the seven men, "There is something that is called Death; it will one day kill some of you; but
though you die, you will not perish utterly, but you will come to
me here in heaven." The goat went his way, but when he came
near the town he lit on a bush which seemed to him good to eat;
so he lingered there and began to browse. When God saw that
the goat lingered by the way, he sent a sheep to deliver the same
message. The sheep went, but did not say what God had commanded her to say; for she perverted the message and said, "When
you once die, you perish, and have no place to go to." Afterwards
the goat came and said, "God says, you will die, it is true, but that
will not be the end of you, for you will come to me." But the men
answered, "No, goat, God did not say that to you. What the sheep
first reported, by that we shall abide."

In an Ashantee version of the story the two messengers are also
a sheep and a goat, and the perversion of the message of immortality
is ascribed sometimes to the one animal and sometimes to the other.
The Ashantees say that long ago men were happy, for God dwelt
among them and talked with them face to face. However, these
blissful days did not last forever. One unlucky day it chanced that
some women were pounding a mash with pestles in a mortar, while
God stood by looking on. For some reason they were annoyed by
the presence of the deity and told him to be off; and as he did not
take himself off fast enough to please them, they beat him with
their pestles. In a great huff God retired altogether from the world
and left it to the direction of the fetishes; and still to this day
people say, "Ah, if it had not been for that old woman, how happy
we should be!" However, God was very good-natured, and even
after he had gone up aloft, he sent a kind message by a goat to men
on earth, saying, "There is something which they call Death. He
will kill some of you. But even if you die, you will not perish
completely. You will come to me in heaven." So off the goat set

with this cheering intelligence. But before he came to the town he saw a tempting bush by the wayside, and stopped to browse on it. When God looked down from heaven and saw the goat loitering by the way, he sent off a sheep with the same message to carry the joyful news to men without delay. But the sheep did not give the message right. Far from it; she said, "God sends you word that you will die, and that will be an end of you." When the goat had finished his meal, he also trotted into the town and delivered his message, saying, "God sends you word that you will die, certainly, but that will not be the end of you, for you will go to him." But men said to the goat, "No, goat, that is not what God said. We believe that the message which the sheep brought us is the one which God sent to us." That unfortunate misunderstanding was the beginning of death among men. However, in another Ashantee version of the tale the parts played by the sheep and goat are reversed. It is the sheep who brings the tidings of immortality from God to men, but the goat overruns him, and offers them death instead. In their innocence men accepted death with enthusiasm, not knowing what it was, and naturally they have died ever since.

In all these versions of the story the message is sent from God to men, but in another version, reported from Togoland in West Africa, the message is despatched from men to God. They say that once upon a time men sent a dog to God to say that when they died they would like to come to life again. So off the dog trotted to deliver the message. But on the way he felt hungry and turned into a house, where a man was boiling magic herbs. So the dog sat down and thought to himself, "He is cooking food." Meantime the frog had set off to tell God that when men died they would prefer not to come to life again. Nobody had asked him to give that message; it was a piece of pure officiousness and impertinence on his part. However, away he tore. The dog. who still sat hopefully watching the hell-broth brewing, saw him hurrying past the door, but he thought to himself, "When I have had something to eat, I will soon catch froggy up." However, froggy came in first, and said to the deity, "When men die, they would prefer not to come to life again." After that, up comes the dog, and says he, "When men die, they would like to come to life again." God was naturally puzzled, and said to the dog, "I really do not understand these two messages. As I heard the frog's request first, I will comply with it. I will not do what you said." That is the reason why men die and do not come to life again. If the frog had only minded his own business instead of meddling with other people's, the dead would all have come to life again to this day. But frogs come to life again when it thunders at the beginning of the rainy season, after they have been dead all the dry season while the Harmattan wind was blowing. Then, while the rain falls and the thunder peals, you may hear them quacking in the marshes. Thus we see that the frog had his own private ends to serve in distorting the message. He gained for himself the immortality of which he robbed mankind.

In these stories the origin of death is ascribed to the blunder or wilful deceit of one of the two messengers. However, according to another version of the story, which is widely current among the Bantu tribes of Africa, death was caused, not by the fault of the messenger, but by the vacillation of God himself, who, after deciding to make men immortal, changed his mind and resolved to make or leave them mortal; and unluckily for mankind the second messenger, who bore the message of death, overran the first messenger, who bore the message of immortality. In this form of the tale the chameleon figures as the messenger of life, and the lizard as the messenger of death. Thus the Zulus say that in the beginning Unkulunkulu, that is, the Old Old One, sent the chameleon to men with a message, saying "Go, chameleon, go and say, Let not men die." The chameleon set out, but it crawled very slowly and loitered by the way to eat the purple berries of the *ubukwebezane* shrub or of a mulberry tree; however, some people say that it climbed up a tree to bask in the sun, filled its belly with flies, and fell fast asleep. Meantime the Old Old One had thought better of it and sent a lizard post-haste after the chameleon with a very different message to men, for he said to the animal, "Lizard, when you have arrived, say, Let men die." So the lizard ran, passed the dawdling chameleons, and arriving first among men delivered his message of death, saying, "Let men die." Then he turned and went back to the Old Old One who had sent him. But after he was gone, the chameleon at last arrived among men with his joyful news of immortality, and he shouted, saying, "It is said, Let not men die!" But men answered, "Oh! we have heard the word of the lizard; it has told us the word. 'It is said, Let men die.' We cannot hear your word. Through the word of the lizard, men will die." And died they have ever since from that day to this. So the Zulus hate the lizard and kill it whenever they can, for they say, "This is the very piece of deformity which ran in the beginning to say that men should die." But others hate and hustle or kill the chameleon, saying, "That is the little thing which delayed to tell the people that they should not die. If he had only told us in time, we too should not have died; our ancestors also would have been still living; there would have been no disease here on earth. It all comes from the delay of the chameleon."

The same story is told in nearly the same form by other Bantu tribes such as the Bechuanas, the Basutos, the Baronga, the Ngoni, and apparently by the Wa-Sania of British East Africa. It is found, in a slightly altered form, even among the Hausas, who are not a Bantu people. To this day the Baronga and the Ngoni owe the chameleon a grudge for having brought death into the world by its dilatoriness. Hence, when they find a chameleon slowly climbing on a tree, they tease it till it opens its mouth, whereupon they throw a pinch of tobacco on its tongue, and watch with delight the creature writhing and changing colour from orange to green, from green to black in the agony of death ; for so they avenge the great wrong which the chameleon did to mankind.

Thus the belief is widespread in Africa, that God at one time purposed to make mankind immortal, but that the benevolent scheme miscarried through the fault of the messenger to whom he had entrusted the gospel message.

§ 3. *The Story of the Cast Skin.*—Many savages believe that, in virtue of the power of periodically casting their skins, certain animals and in particular serpents renew their youth and never die. Holding this belief, they tell stories to explain how it came about that these creatures obtained, and men missed, the boon of immortality.

Thus, for example, the Wafipa and Wabende of East Africa say that one day God, whom they name Leza, came down to earth, and addressing all living creatures said, "Who wishes not to die?" Unfortunately man and the other animals were asleep; only the serpent was awake and he promptly answered, "I do." That is why men and all other animals die. The serpent alone does not die of himself. He only dies if he is killed. Every year he changes his skin, and so renews his youth and his strength. In like manner the Dusuns of British North Borneo say that when the Creator had finished making all things, he asked, "Who is able to cast off his skin? If any one can do so, he shall not die." The snake alone heard and answered, "I can." For that reason down to the present day the snake does not die unless he is killed by man. The Dusuns did not hear the Creator's question, or they also would have thrown off their skins, and there would have been no death. Similarly the Todjo-Toradjas of Central Celebes relate that once upon a time God summoned men and animals for the purpose of determining their lot. Among the various lots proposed by the deity was this, "We shall put off our old skin." Unfortunately mankind on this momentous occasion was represented by an old woman in her dotage, who did not hear the tempting proposal. But the animals which slough their skins, such as serpents and shrimps, heard it and closed with the offer. Again, the natives of Vuatom, an island in the Bismarck Archipelago, say that a certain To Konokonomiange bade two lads fetch fire, promising that if they did so they should never die, but that, if they refused, their bodies would perish, though their shades or souls would survive. They would not hearken to him, so he cursed them, saying, "What! you would all have lived! Now you shall die, though your soul shall live. But the iguana (*Goniocephalus*) and the lizard (*Varanus indicus*) and the snake (*Enygrus*), they shall live, they shall cast their skin and they shall live for evermore." When the lads heard that, they wept, for bitterly they rued their folly in not going to fetch the fire for To Konokonomiange.

The Arawaks of British Guiana relate that once upon a time the Creator came down to earth to see how his creature man was getting on. But men were so wicked that they tried to kill him; so he deprived them of eternal life and bestowed it on the animals which renew their skin, such as serpents, lizards, and beetles. A some-what different version of the story is told by the Tamanachiers, an Indian tribe of the Orinoco. They say that after residing among them for some time the Creator took boat across to the other side of the great salt water from which he had come. Just as he was shoving off from the shore, he called out to them in a changed voice, "You will change your skins," by which he meant to say, "You will renew your youth like the serpents and the beetles." But unfortunately an old woman, hearing these words, cried out "Oh!" in a tone of scepticism, if not of sarcasm, which so annoyed the Creator that he changed his tune at once and said testily, "Ye shall die." That is why we are all mortal.

The people of Nias, an island to the west of Sumatra, say that, when the earth was created, a certain being was sent down from above to put the finishing touches to the work. He ought to have fasted, but, unable to withstand the pangs of hunger, he ate some bananas. The choice of food was very unfortunate, for had he only eaten river crabs, men would have cast their skins like crabs, and so, renewing their youth perpetually, would never have died. As it is, death has come upon us all through the eating of those bananas. Another version of the Niasian story adds that "the serpents on the contrary ate the crabs, which in the opinion of the people of Nias cast their skins but do not die; therefore serpents also do not die but merely cast their skin."

In this last version the immortality of serpents is ascribed to their having partaken of crabs, which by casting their skins renew their youth and live for ever. The same belief in the immortality of shellfish occurs in a Samoan story of the origin of death. They say that the gods met in council to determine what should be the end of man. One proposal was that men should cast their skins like shellfish, and so renew their youth. The god Palsy moved, on the contrary, that shellfish should cast their skins, but that men should die. While the motion was still before the meeting a shower of rain unfortunately interrupted the discussion, and as the gods ran to take shelter, the motion of Palsy was carried unanimously. That is why shellfish still cast their skins and men do not.

Thus not a few peoples appear to believe that the happy privilege of immortality, obtainable by the simple process of periodically shedding the skin, was once within reach of our species, but that through an unhappy chance it was transferred to certain of the lower creatures, such as serpents, crabs, lizards, and beetles. According to others, however, men were at one time actually in possession of this priceless boon, but forfeited it through the fool-ishness of an old woman. Thus the Melanesians of the Banks

Islands and the New Hebrides say that at first men never died, but that when they advanced in life they cast their skins like snakes and crabs, and came out with youth renewed. After a time a woman, growing old, went to a stream to change her skin; according to some, she was the mother of the mythical or legendary hero Qat, according to others, she was Ul-ta-marama, Change-skin of the world. She threw off her old skin in the water, and observed that as it floated down it caught against a stick. Then she went home, where she had left her child. But the child refused to recognize her, crying that its mother was an old woman, not like this young stranger. So to pacify the child she went after her cast integument and put it on. From that time mankind ceased to cast their skins and died. A similar story of the origin of death is told in the Shortlands Islands and by the Kai, a Papuan tribe of North-eastern New Guinea. The Kai say that at first men did not die but renewed their youth. When their old brown skin grew wrinkled and ugly, they stepped into water, and stripping it off got a new, youthful white skin instead. In those days there lived an old grandmother with her grandchild. One day the old woman, weary of her advanced years, bathed in the river, cast off her withered old hide, and returned to the village, spick and span, in a fine new skin. Thus transformed, she climbed up the ladder and entered her house. But when her grandchild saw her, he went and squalled, and refused to believe that she was his granny. All her efforts to reassure and pacify him proving vain, she at last went back in a rage to the river, fished her wizened old skin out of the water, put it on, and returned to the house a hideous old hag again. The child was glad to see his granny come back, but she said to him, "The locusts cast their skins, but ye men shall die from this day forward." And sure enough, they have done so ever since. The same story, with some trivial variations, is told by natives of the Admiralty Islands. They say that once on a time there was an old woman, and she was frail. She had two sons, and they went a-fishing, while she herself went to bathe. She stripped off her wrinkled old skin and came forth as young as she had been long ago. When her sons came from the fishing they were astonished to see her. The one said, "It is our mother"; but the other said, "She may be your mother, but she shall be my wife." Their mother overheard them and said, "What were you two saying?" The two said, "Nothing! We only said that you are our mother." "You are liars," she retorted, "I heard you both. If I had had my way, we should have grown to be old men and women, and then we should have cast our skin and been young men and young women. But you have had your way. We shall grow old men and old women, and then we shall die." With that she fetched her old skin, and put it on, and became an old woman again. As for us, her descendants, we grow up and we grow old. But if it had not been for those two young scapegraces, there would have been no end of our days, we should have lived for ever and ever.

Still farther away from the Banks Islands the very same story is repeated by the To Koolawi, a mountain tribe of Central Celebes. As reported by the Dutch missionaries who discovered it, the Celebes version of this widely diffused tale runs thus. In the olden time men had, like serpents and shrimps, the power of casting their skin, whereby they became young again. Now there was an old woman who had a grandchild. Once upon a time she went to the water to bathe, and thereupon laid aside her old skin and hung it up on a tree. With her youth quite restored she returned to the house. But her grandchild did not know her again, and would have nothing to do with his grandmother; he kept on saying, "You are not my grandmother; my grandmother was old, and you are young." Then the woman went back to the water and drew on her old skin again. But ever since that day men have lost the power of renewing their youth and must die.

While some peoples have supposed that in the early ages of the world men were immortal in virtue of periodically casting their skins, others have ascribed the same high privilege to a certain lunar sympathy, in consequence of which mankind passed through alternate states of growth and decay, of life and death, corresponding to the phases of the moon, without ever coming to an end. On this view, though death in a sense actually occurred, it was speedily repaired by resurrection, generally, it would seem, by resurrection after three days, since three days is the period between the disappearance of the old moon and the reappearance of the new. Thus the Mentras or Mantras, a shy tribe of savages in the jungles of the Malay Peninsula, allege that in the early ages of the world men did not die, but only grew thin at the waning of the moon and then waxed fat again as she waxed to the full. Thus there was no check whatever on the population, which increased to an alarming extent. So a son of the first man brought this state of things to his father's notice, and asked him what was to be done. The first man, a good easy soul, "Leave things as they are"; but his younger brother, who took a more Malthusian view of the matter, said, "No, let men die like the banana, leaving their offspring behind." The question was submitted to the Lord of the Underworld, and he decided in favour of death. Ever since then men have ceased to renew their youth like the moon and have died like the banana. In the Caroline Islands it is said that in the olden time death was unknown, or rather it was only a short sleep. Men died on the last day of the waning moon and came to life again on the appearance of the new moon, just as if they had wakened from a refreshing slumber. But an evil spirit somehow contrived that when men slept the sleep of death they should wake no more. The Wotjobaluk, a tribe of South-eastern Australia, related that when all animals were men and women, some of them died and the moon used to say, "You up again," whereupon they came to life again. But once on a time an old man said, "Let them remain dead"; and since then anybody has ever come to life again, except the moon, which still continues to do so down to this very day. The Unmatjera and Kaitish, two tribes of Central Australia, say that their dead used to be buried either in trees or underground, and that after three days they regularly rose from the dead. The Kaitish tell how this happy state of things came to an end. It was all the fault of a man of the Curlew totem, who found some men of the Little Wallaby totem in the act of burying a man of that ilk. For some reason the Curlew man flew into a passion and kicked the corpse into the sea. Of course after that the dead man could not come to life again, and that is why nowadays nobody rises from the dead after three days, as everybody used to do long ago. Though nothing is said about the moon in this narrative of the origin of death, the analogy of the preceding stories makes it probable that the three days during which the dead used to lie in the grave, were the three days during which the moon lay "hid in her vacant interlunar cave." The Fijians also associated the possibility, though not the actual enjoyment, of human immortality with the phases of the moon. They say that of old two gods, the Moon and the Rat, discussed the proper end of man. The Moon said, "Let him be like me, who disappear awhile and then live again." But the Rat said, "Let man die as a rat dies." And he prevailed.

The Upotos of the Congo tell how men missed and the Moon obtained the boon of immortality. One day God, whom they call Libanza, sent for the people of the moon and the people of the earth. The people of the moon hastened to the deity, and were rewarded by him for their alacrity. "Because," said he, addressing the moon, "thou camest to me at once when I called thee, thou shalt never die. Thou shalt be dead for but two days each month, and that only to rest thee; and thou shall return with greater splendour." But when the people of the earth at last appeared before Libanza, he was angry and said to them, "Because you came not at once to me when I called you, therefore you will die, one day and not revive, except to come to me."

The Bahnars of Eastern Cochin China explain the immortality of primitive man neither by the phase of the moon nor by the custom of casting the skin, but apparently by the recuperative virtue of a certain tree. They say that in the beginning, when people died, they used to be buried at the foot of a tree called Long Blo, and that after a time they always rose from the dead, not as infants, but as full-grown men and women. So the earth was peopled very fast, and all the inhabitants formed but one great town under the presidency of our first parents. In time men multiplied to such an extent that a certain lizard could not take his walks abroad without somebody treading on his tail. This vexed him, and the wily creature gave an insidious hint to the gravediggers. "Why bury the dead at the foot of the Long Blo tree?" said he; "bury them at the foot of Long Khung, and they will not come to life again. Let them die outright and be done with it." The hint was taken, and from that day men have not come to life again.

In this last story, as in many African tales, the instrument of bringing death among men is a lizard. We may conjecture that the reason for assigning the invidious office to a lizard was that this animal, like the serpent, casts its skin periodically, from which primitive man might infer, as he infers with regard to serpents, that the creature renews its youth and lives for ever. Thus all the myths which relate how a lizard or a serpent became the maleficent agent of human mortality may perhaps be referred to an old idea of a certain jealousy and rivalry between men and creatures which cast their skins, notably serpents and lizards; we may suppose that in all such cases a story was told of a contest between man and his animal rivals for the possession of immortality, a contest in which, whether by mistake or guile, the victory always remained with the animals, who thus became immortal, while mankind was doomed to mortality.

§ 4. *The Composite Story of the Perverted Message and the Cast Skin.*—In some stories of the origin of death the incidents of the perverted message and the cast skin are combined. Thus the Gallas of East Africa attribute the mortality of man and the immortality of serpents to the mistake or malice of a certain bird which falsified the message of eternal life entrusted to him by God. The creature which did this great wrong to our species is a black or dark blue bird, with a white patch on each wing and a crest on its head. It perches on the tops of trees and utters a wailing note like the bleating of a sheep; hence the Gallas call it *halawaka* or "the sheep of God," and explain its apparent anguish by the following tale. Once upon a time God sent that bird to tell men that they should not die, but that when they grew old and weak they should slip off their skins and so renew their youth. In order to authenticate the message God gave the bird a crest to serve as the badge of his office. Well, off the bird set to deliver the glad tidings of immortality to man, but he had not gone far before he fell in with a snake devouring carrion in the path. The bird looked longingly at the carrion and said to the snake, "Give me some of the meat and blood, and I will tell you God's message." "I don't want to hear it," said the snake tartly, and continued his meal. But the bird pressed him so to hear the message that the snake rather reluctantly consented. "The message," then said the bird, "is this. When men grow old they will die, but when you grow old you will cast your skin and renew your youth." That is why people grow old and die, but snakes crawl out of their old skins and renew their youth. But for this gross perversion of the message

God punished the heedless or wicked bird with a painful internal
malady, from which he suffers to this day; that is why he sits
wailing on the tops of trees. Again, the Melanesians, who inhabit
the coast of the Gazelle Peninsula in New Britain, say that To
Kambinana, the Good Spirit, loved men and wished to make them
immortal. So he called his brother To Korvuvu and said to him,
"Go to men and take them the secret of immortality. Tell them
to cast their skin every year. So will they be protected from death,
for their life will be constantly renewed. But tell the serpents
that they must thenceforth die?" However, To Korvuvu acquitted
himself badly of his task; for he commanded men to die, and
betrayed to the serpents the secret of immortality. Since then all
men have been mortal, but the serpents cast their skins every year
and never die. A similar story of the origin of death is told in
Annam. They say that Ngoc hoang sent a messenger from heaven
to men to say that when they reached old age they should change
their skins and live for ever, but that when serpents grew old they
must die. The messenger came down to earth and said, rightly
enough, "When man is old he shall cast his skin; but when serpents
are old they shall die and be laid in coffins." So far so good. But
unluckily there happened to be a brood of serpents within hearing,
and when they learned the doom pronounced on their kind, they
fell into a fury and said to the messenger, "You must say it over
again and just the contrary, or we will bite you." That frightened
the messenger, and he repeated his message, changing the words
thus, "When the serpent is old he shall cast his skin; but when
man is old he shall die and be laid in the coffin." That is why all
creatures are now subject to death, except the serpent, who, when
he is old, casts his skin and lives for ever.

§ 5. *Conclusion.*—Thus, arguing from the analogy of the moon
or of animals which cast their skins, the primitive philosopher has
inferred that in the beginning a perpetual renewal of youth was
either appointed by a benevolent being for the human species or
was actually enjoyed by them, and that but for a crime, an accident,
or a blunder it would have been enjoyed by them for ever. People
who pin their faith in immortality to the cast skins of serpents,
lizards, beetles, and the like, naturally look on these animals as
the hated rivals who have robbed us of the heritage which God or
nature intended that we should possess; consequently they tell
stories to explain how it came about that such low creatures contrived to oust us from the priceless possession. Tales of this sort
are widely diffused throughout the world, and it would be no matter
for surprise to find them among the Semites. The story of the
Fall of Man in the third chapter of Genesis appears to be an abridged
version of this savage myth. Little is wanted to complete its
resemblance to the similar myths still told by savages in many
parts of the world. The principal, almost the only, omission is the
silence of the narrator as to the eating of the fruit of the tree of life

by the serpent, and the consequent attainment of immortality by the reptile. Nor is it difficult to account for the lacuna. The vein of rationalism, which runs through the Hebrew account of creation and has stripped it of many grotesque features that adorn or disfigure the corresponding Babylonian tradition, could hardly fail to find a stumbling-block in the alleged immortality of serpents; and the redactor of the story in its final form has removed this stone of offence from the path of the faithful by the simple process of blotting out the incident entirely from the legend. Yet the yawning gap left by his sponge has not escaped the commentators, who look in vain for the part which should have been played in the narrative by the tree of life. If my interpretation of the story is right, it has been left for the comparative method, after thousands of years, to supply the blank in the ancient canvas, and to restore, in all their primitive crudity, the gay barbaric colours which the skilful hand of the Hebrew artist had softened or effaced.

CHAPTER III

THE MARK OF CAIN

WE read in Genesis that when Cain had murdered his brother Abel he was driven out from society to be a fugitive and a vagabond on earth. Fearing to be slain by any one who might meet him, he remonstrated with God on the hardness of his lot, and God had so far compassion on him that he "set a mark upon Cain, lest any finding him should kill him." What was the mark that God put on the first murderer? or the sign that he appointed for him?

That we have a mere reminiscence of some old custom observed by manslayers is highly probable; and, though we cannot hope to ascertain what the actual mark or sign was, a comparison of the customs observed by manslayers in other parts of the world may help us to understand at least its general significance. Robertson Smith thought that the mark in question was the tribal mark, a badge which every member of the tribe wore on his person, and which served to protect him by indicating that he belonged to a community that would avenge his murder. Certainly such marks are common among peoples who have preserved the tribal system. For example, among the Bedouins of to-day one of the chief tribal badges is a particular mode of wearing the hair. In many parts of the world, notably in Africa, the tribal mark consists of a pattern tattooed or incised on some part of the person. That such marks might serve as a protection to the tribesman in the way supposed by Robertson Smith seems probable; though on the other hand it is to be remembered that in a hostile country they might, on the contrary, increase his danger by advertising him as an enemy. But even if we concede the protective value of a tribal mark, still the explanation thus offered of the mark of Cain seems hardly to fit the case. It is too general. Every member of a tribe was equally protected by such a mark, whether he was a manslayer or not. The whole drift of the narrative tends to show that the mark in question was not worn by every member of the community, but was peculiar to a murderer. Accordingly we seem driven to seek for an explanation in another direction.

From the narrative itself we gather that Cain was thought to be obnoxious to other dangers than that of being slain as an outlaw by any one who met him. God is represented saying to him, "What hast thou done? the voice of thy brother's blood crieth unto me from the ground. And now cursed art thou from the ground, which hath opened her mouth to receive thy brother's blood from thy hand; when thou tillest the ground, it shall not henceforth yield unto thee her strength; a fugitive and a wanderer shalt thou be in the earth." Here it is obvious that the blood of his murdered brother is regarded as constituting a physical danger to the murderer; it taints the ground and prevents it from yielding its increase. Thus the murderer is thought to have poisoned the sources of life and thereby jeopardized the supply of food for himself, and perhaps for others. On this view it is intelligible that a homicide should be shunned and banished the country, to which his presence is a continual menace. He is plague-stricken, surrounded by a poisonous atmosphere, infected by a contagion of death; his very touch may blight the earth. Hence we can understand a certain rule of Attic law. A homicide who had been banished, and against whom in his absence a second charge had been brought, was allowed to return to Attica to plead in his defence; but he might not set foot on the land, he had to speak from a ship, and even the ship might not cast anchor or put out a gangway. The judges avoided all contact with the culprit, for they judged the case sitting or standing on the shore. Clearly the intention of this rule of law was to put the manslayer in quarantine, lest by touching Attic earth even indirectly through the anchor or the gangway he should blast it. For the same reason, if such a man, sailing the sea, had the misfortune to be cast away on the country where his crime had been perpetrated, he was allowed indeed to camp on the shore till a ship came to take him off, but he was expected to keep his feet in sea-water all the time, evidently in order to counteract, or at least dilute, the poison which he was supposed to instill into the soil.

The quarantine which Attic law thus imposed on the manslayer has its counterpart in the seclusion still enforced on murderers by the savages of Dobu, an island off the south-eastern extremity of New Guinea. On this subject a missionary, who resided for seventeen years in the island, writes as follows: "War may be waged against the relatives of the wife, but the slain must not be eaten. The person who kills a relation by marriage must never after partake of the general food or fruit from his wife's village. His wife alone must cook his food. If his wife's fire goes out she is not allowed to take a fire-stick from a house in her village. The penalty for breaking this tabu is that the husband dies of blood-poisoning! The slaying of a blood relation places an even stricter tabu on the slayer. When the chief Gaganumore slew his brother (mother's sister's son) he was not allowed to return to his own village, but had to build a village of his own. He had to have a separate lime-gourd and spatula; a water-bottle and cup of his own; a special set of cooking pots; he had to get his drinking cocoanuts and fruit elsewhere; his fire had to be kept burning as long as possible, and if it went out it could not be relit from another fire, but by friction. If the chief were to break this tabu, his brother's blood would poison his blood so that his body would swell, and he would die a terrible death."

In these Dobuan cases the blood of the slain man is supposed to act as a physical poison on the slayer, should he venture to set foot in, or even to hold indirect communication with, the village of his victim. His seclusion is therefore a precaution adopted in his own interest rather than in that of the community which he avoids; and it is possible that the rules of Attic law in the matter of homicide ought to be similarly interpreted. However, it is more probable that the danger was believed to be mutual; in other words, that both the homicide and the persons with whom he came into contact were thought liable to suffer from blood-poisoning caused by contagion. Certainly the notion that a manslayer can infect other people with a malignant virus is held by the Akikuyu of British East Africa. They think that if a man who has killed another comes and sleeps at a village and eats with a family in their hut, the persons with whom he has eaten contract a dangerous pollution (*thahu*), which might prove fatal to them, were it not removed in time by a medicine-man. The very skin on which the homicide slept has absorbed the taint and might infect any one else who slept on it. So a medicine-man is called in to purify the hut and its inmates.

Similarly among the Moors of Morocco a manslayer "is considered in some degree unclean for the rest of his life. Poison oozes out from underneath his nails; hence anybody who drinks the water in which he has washed his hands will fall dangerously ill. The meat of an animal which he has killed is bad to eat, and so is any food which is partaken of in his company. If he comes to a place where people are digging a well, the water will at once run away. In the Hiáina, I was told, he is not allowed to go into a vegetable garden or an orchard, nor to tread on a threshing-floor or enter a granary, nor to go among the sheep. It is a common, although not universal, rule that he must not perform the sacrifice at the Great Feast with his own hands; and in some tribes, mostly Berber-speaking ones, there is a similar prohibition with reference to a person who has killed a dog, which is an unclean animal. All blood which has left the veins is unclean and haunted by *jnun"* (jinn).

But in the Biblical narrative of the murder of Abel the blood of the murdered man is not the only inanimate object that is personified. If the blood is represented as crying aloud, the earth is represented as opening her mouth to receive the blood of the victim. To this personification of the earth Aeschylus offers a parallel, for he speaks of the ground drinking the blood of the murdered Agamemnon. But in Genesis the attribution of personal qualities to the earth seems to be carried a step further, for we are told that the murderer was "cursed from the ground"; and that when he tilled it, the land would not yield him her strength, but that a fugitive and a wanderer should he be in the world. The implication apparently is that the earth, polluted by blood and offended by his crime, would refuse to allow the seed sown by the murderer to germinate and bear fruit; nay, that it would expel him from the cultivated soil on which he had hitherto prospered, and drive him out into the barren wilderness, there to roam a houseless and hungry vagabond. The conception of earth as a personal being, who revolts against the sin of the dwellers upon it and spurns them from her bosom, is not foreign to the Old Testament. In Leviticus we read that, defiled by human iniquity, "the land vomiteth out her inhabitants"; and the Israelites are solemnly warned to keep God's statutes and judgments, "that the land vomit not you out also, when ye defile it, as it vomited out the nation that was before you."

The ancient Greeks apparently entertained similar notions as to the effect of polluting earth by the shedding of human blood, or, at all events, the blood of kinsfolk; for tradition told how the matricide Alcmaeon, haunted by the ghost of his murdered mother Eriphyle, long wandered restlessly over the world, till at last he repaired to the oracle at Delphi, and the priestess told him that "the only land whither the avenging spirit of Eriphyle would not dog him was the newest land, which the sea had uncovered since the pollution of his mother's blood had been incurred"; or, as Thucydides put it, "that he would never be rid of his terrors till he had found and settled in a country which, when he slew his mother, the sun had not yet shone on, and which at that time was not yet dry land; for all the rest of the earth had been polluted by him." Following the directions of the oracle, he discovered at the mouth of the Achelous the small and barren Echinadian Islands which, by washing down the soil from its banks, the river was supposed to have created since the perpetration of his crime; and there he took up his abode. According to one version of the legend, the murderer had found rest for a time in the bleak upland valley of Psophis, among the solemn Arcadian mountains, but even there the ground refused to yield its increase to the matricide, and he was forced, like Cain, to resume his weary wanderings.

The belief that the earth is a powerful divinity, who is defiled and offended by the shedding of human blood and must be appeased by sacrifice, prevails, or prevailed till lately, among some tribes of Upper Senegal, who exact expiation even for wounds which have merely caused blood to flow without loss of life. Thus at Laro, in the country of the Bobos, "the murderer paid two goats, a dog, and a cock to the chief of the village, who offered them in sacrifice to the Earth on a piece of wood stuck in the ground. Nothing was given to the family of the victim. All the villagers, including the chief, afterwards partook of the flesh of the sacrificed victims, the families of the murderer and his victim alone being excluded from the banquet. If it was an affair of assault and wounds, but blood had not been shed, no account was taken of it. But when blood had been spilt, the Earth was displeased at the sight, and therefore it was necessary to appease her by a sacrifice. The culprit gave a goat and a thousand cowries to the chief of the village, who sacrificed the goat to the Earth and divided the cowries among the elders of the village. The goat, after being offered to the Earth, was also divided among the village elders. But the injured party throughout the affair was totally forgotten and received nothing at all, and that, too, logically enough. For the intention was not to compensate the injured party for his wrong at the cost of the wrongdoer, but to appease the Earth, a great and redoubtable divinity, who was displeased at the sight of bloodshed. In these circumstances there was nothing for the injured party to get. It sufficed that the Earth was pacified by eating the soul of the goat that had been sacrificed to her; for "among the Bobos, as among the other blacks, the Earth is esteemed a great goddess of justice."

Among the Nounoumas, another tribe of Upper Senegal, the customs and beliefs in regard to bloodshed were similar. A murderer was banished for three years and had to pay a heavy fine in cowries and cattle, not as a blood-wit to the family of his victim, but to appease the Earth and the other local divinities, who had been offended by the sight of spilt blood. The ox or oxen were sacrificed to the angry Earth by a priest who bore the title of the Chief of the Earth, and the flesh, together with the cowries, was divided among the elders of the village, the family of the murdered man receiving nothing, or at most only a proportionate share of the meat and money. In the case of brawls where no life had been taken, but blood had flowed, the aggressor had to pay an ox, a sheep, a goat, and four fowls, all of which were sacrificed to pacify the anger of the local deities at the sight of bloodshed. The ox was sacrificed to the Earth by the Chief of the Earth in presence of all the elders of the village; the sheep was sacrificed to the River; and the fowls to the Rocks and the Forest. As for the goat, it was sacrificed by the chief of the village to his private fetish. If these expiatory sacrifices were not offered, it was believed that the gods in their wrath would slay the culprit and all his family.

The foregoing facts suggest that a mark put on a homicide might be intended primarily, not for his protection, but for the protection of the persons who met him, lest by contact with his pollution they should defile themselves and incur the wrath of the god whom he had offended, or of the ghost by whom he was haunted; in short, the mark might be a danger-signal to warn people off, like the special garb prescribed in Israel for lepers.

However, there are other facts which tend to show that the murderer's mark was designed, as the story of Cain implies, for the benefit of the murderer alone, and further that the real danger against which it protected him was further anger of his victim's kinsfolk, but the wrath of his victim's ghost. Here again, as in the Athenian customs already mentioned, we seem to touch the bed-rock of superstition in Attica. Plato tells us that according to a very ancient Greek belief the ghost of a man who had just been killed was angry with his slayer and troubled him, being enraged at the sight of the homicide stalking freely about in his, the ghost's, old familiar haunts; hence it was needful for the homicide to depart from his country for a year until the wrath of the ghost had cooled down, nor might he return before sacrifices had been offered and ceremonies of purification performed. If the victim chanced to be a foreigner, the slayer had to shun the native land of the dead man as well as his own, and in going into banishment he had to follow a prescribed road; for clearly it would never do to let him rove about the country with the angry ghost at his heels.

Again, we have seen that among the Akikuyu a murderer is believed to be tainted by a dangerous pollution (*thahu*) which he can communicate to other people by contact. That this pollution is connected with his victim's ghost appears from one of the ceremonies which are performed to expiate the deed. The elders of the village sacrifice a pig beside one of those sacred fig-trees which play a great part in the religious rites of the tribe. There they feast on the more succulent parts of the animal, but leave the fat, intestines, and some of the bones for the ghost, who is supposed to come that very night and devour them in the likeness of a wild cat; his hunger being thus stayed, he considerately refrains from returning to the village to trouble the inhabitants. It deserves to be noticed that a Kikuku homicide incurs ceremonial pollution (*thahu*) only through the slaughter of a man of his own clan; there is no ceremonial pollution incurred by the slaughter of a man of another clan or of another tribe.

Among the Bagesu of Mount Elgon, in British East Africa, when a man has been guilty of manslaughter and his victim was a member of the same clan and village, he must leave the village and find a new home elsewhere, even though he may settle the matter amicably with the relations of the deceased. Further, he must kill a goat, smear the contents of its stomach on his chest, and throw the remainder upon the roof of the house of the murdered man "to appease the ghost." In this tribe very similar ceremonies of expiation are performed by a warrior who has slain a man in battle ; and we may safely assume that the intention of the ceremonies is to appease the ghost of his victim. The warrior returns to his village, but he may not spend the first night in his own house, he must lodge in the house of a friend. In the evening he kills a goat or sheep, deposits the contents of the stomach in a pot, and smears them on his head, chest, and arms. If he has any children, they must be smeared in like manner. Having thus fortified himself and his progeny, the warrior proceeds boldly to his own house, daubs each door-post with the stuff, and throws the rest on the roof, probably for the benefit of the ghost who may be supposed to perch, if not to roost, there. For a whole day the slayer may not touch food with the hands which shed blood ; he conveys the morsels to his mouth with two sticks cut for the purpose. On the second day he is free to return home and resume his ordinary life. These restrictions are not binding on his wife ; she may even go and mourn over the slain man and take part in his obsequies. Such a pretence of sorrow may well mollify the feelings of the ghost and induce him to spare her husband.

Again, among the Nilotic Kavirondo, another tribe of British East Africa, a murderer is separated from the members of his village and lives in a hut with an old woman, who attends to his wants, cooks for him, and also feeds him, because he may not touch his food with his hands. This separation lasts for three days, and on the fourth day a man, who is himself a murderer, or who has at some time killed a man in battle, takes the murderer to a stream, where he washes him all over. He then kills a goat, cooks the meat, and puts a piece of it on each of four sticks ; after which he gives the four pieces to the murderer to eat in turn. Next he puts four balls of porridge on the sticks, and these also the murderer must swallow. Finally, the goat-skin is cut into strips, and one strip is put on the neck, and one strip around each of the wrists of the homicide. This ceremony is performed by the two men alone at the river. After the performance the murderer is free to return home. It is said that, until this ceremony is performed, the ghost cannot take its departure for the place of the dead, but hovers about the murderer.

Among the Boloki of the Upper Congo a homicide is not afraid of the ghost of the man whom he has killed, when his victim belongs to any of the neighboring towns, because the area within which Boloki ghosts can travel is extremely limited ; but murder, which in that case he might commit with an easy mind, assumes a much more serious complexion when it is perpetrated on a man of the same town, for then he knows himself to be within striking distance of the ghost. The fear of ghostly vengeance now sits heavy on him. There are unfortunately no rites by the observance of which he could allay these terrors, but in default of them he mourns for his victim as though he were a brother, neglecting his toilet, shaving

his head, fasting, and lamenting with torrents of crocodile tears,
Thus the symptoms of sorrow, which the ingenuous European might
take for signs of genuine repentance and remorse of conscience, are
nothing but shams intended to deceive the ghost.

Once more among the Omaha Indians of North America a
murderer, whose life was spared by the kinsmen of his victim, had
to observe certain stringent regulations for a period which varied
from two to four years. He must walk barefoot, and he might eat
no warm food, nor raise his voice, nor look around. He had to
pull his robe about him and to keep it tied at the neck, even in
warm weather; he might not let it hang loose or fly open. He might
not move his hands about, but had to keep them close to his body.
He might not comb his hair, nor allow it to be blown about by the
wind. No one would eat with him, and only one of his kindred
was allowed to remain with him in his tent. When the tribe went
hunting, he was obliged to pitch his tent about a quarter of a mile
from the rest of the people, "lest the ghost of his victim should
raise a high wind which might cause damage." The reason here
alleged for banishing the murderer from the camp probably gives
the key to all the similar restrictions laid on murderers and manslayers among primitive peoples; the seclusion of such persons from
society is dictated by no moral aversion to their crime; it springs
purely from prudential motives, which resolve themselves into a
simple dread of the dangerous ghost by which the homicide is supposed to be pursued and haunted.

Among the Yabim, on the north-eastern coast of New Guinea,
when the kinsmen of a murdered man have accepted a blood-wit
instead of avenging his death, they take care to be marked with
chalk on the forehead by the relatives of the murderer, "lest the
ghost should trouble them for failing to avenge his death, and should
carry off their pigs or loosen their teeth.' In this custom it is not
the murderer but the kinsmen of his victim who are marked, but
the principle is the same. The ghost of the murdered man naturally
turns in fury on his heartless relatives who have not exacted blood
for his blood. But just as he is about to swoop down on them to
loosen their teeth, or steal their pigs, or make himself unpleasant in
other ways, he is brought up short by the sight of the white mark
on their black or coffee-coloured brows. It is the receipt for the
payment in full of the blood-wit; it is the proof that his kinsfolk
have exacted a pecuniary, though not a sanguinary, compensation
for his murder; with this crumb of consolation he is bound to be
satisfied, and to spare his family any molestation in future. The
same mark might obviously be put for the same purpose on the
murderer's brow to prove that he had paid in cash, or whatever
may be the local equivalent for cash, for the deed he had done, and
that the ghost therefore had no further claim upon him. Was the
mark of Cain a mark of this sort? Was it a proof that he had paid
the blood-wit? Was it a receipt for cash down?

It may have been so, but there is still another possibility to be considered. On the theory which I have just indicated it is obvious that the mark of Cain could only be put on a homicide when his victim was a man of the same tribe or community as himself, since it is only to men of the same tribe or community that compensation for homicide is paid. But the ghosts of slain enemies are certainly not less dreaded than the ghosts of slain friends; and if you cannot pacify them with a sum of money paid to their kinsfolk, what are you to do with them? Many plans have been adopted for the protection of warriors against the spirits of the men whom they have sent out of the world before their due time. Apparently one of these precautions is to disguise the slayer so that the ghost may not recognize him; another is to render his person in some way so formidable or so offensive that the spirit will not meddle with him. One or other of these motives may explain the following customs, which I select from a large number of similar cases.

Among the Ba-Yaka, a Bantu people of the Congo Free State, "a man who has been killed in battle is supposed to send his soul to avenge his death on the person of the man who killed him; the latter, however, can escape the vengeance of the dead by wearing the red tail-feathers of the parrot in his hair, and painting his forehead red." The Thonga of South-eastern Africa believe that a man who has killed an enemy in battle is exposed to great danger from his victim's ghost, who haunts him and may drive him mad. To protect himself from the wrath of the ghost, the slayer must remain in a state of taboo at the capital for several days, during which he may not go home to his wife, and must wear old clothes and eat with special spoons off special plates. In former times it was customary to tattoo such a man between the eyebrows, and to rub in medicine into the incisions, so as to raise pimples and to give him the appearance of a buffalo when it frowns. Among the Basutos "warriors who have killed an enemy are purified. The chief has to wash them, sacrificing an ox in the presence of the whole army. They are also anointed with the gall of the animal, which prevents the ghost of the enemy from pursuing them any farther."

Among the Bantu tribes of Kavirondo, in British East Africa, when a man has killed a foe in battle he shaves his head on his return home, and his friends rub a medicine, which generally consists of cow's dung, over his body to prevent the spirit of the slain man from troubling him. Among the Nilotic tribes of Kavirondo, "when a warrior kills another in battle, he is isolated from his village, lives in a separate hut some four days, and an old woman cooks his food and feeds him like a child because he is forbidden to touch any food. On the fifth day he is escorted to the river by another man, who washes him; a white goat is killed and cooked by the attendant, who feeds the man wtih the meat; the goat-skin is cut into strips and put upon the man's wrists and round his head, and he returns to his temporary home for the night. The next day he is again taken to the river and washed, and a white fowl is presented to him. He kills it and it is cooked for him, and he is again fed with the meat. He is then pronounced to be clean and may return to his home. It sometimes happens that a warrior spears another man in battle, and the latter dies from the wound some time after. When death takes place, the relatives go to the warrior and tell him of the death, and he is separated at once from the community until the ceremonies above described have been performed. The people say that the ceremonies are necessary in order to release the ghost of the dead man, which is bound to the warrior who slew him, and is only released on the fulfilment of the ceremonies. Should a warrior refuse to fulfil the ceremonies, the ghost will ask, 'Why don't you fulfil the ceremonies and let me go?' Should a man still refuse to comply, the ghost will take him by the throat and strangle him."

We have seen that among the Nilotic tribes of Kavirondo a very similar ceremony is observed by a murderer for the avowed purpose of freeing himself from the ghost of his victim, which otherwise haunts him. The close resemblance of the ritual in both cases, together with the motives expressly assigned for it, set in the clearest light the essential purpose of the purificatory ceremonies observed by a homicide, whether he is a warrior or a murderer: that purpose is simply to rid the man of his victim's ghost, which will otherwise be his undoing. The intention of putting strips of goat-skin round his head and wrists may be to disguise him from the ghost. Even when no mention is made of the ghosts of the slain by our authorities, we may still safely assume that the purificatory rites performed by or for warriors after bloodshed are intended to appease or repel or deceive these angry spirits. Thus among the Ngoni of British Central Africa, when a victorious army approaches the royal village, it halts by the bank of a stream, and all the warriors who have killed enemies smear their bodies and arms with white clay, but those who were not the first to dip their spears in the blood of the victims, but merely helped to despatch them, whiten their right arms only. That night the manslayers sleep in the open pen with the cattle, and do not venture near their own homes. In the early morning they wash off the white clay from their bodies in the river. The witch-doctor attends to give them a magic potion, and to smear their persons with a fresh coating of clay. This process is repeated on six successive days, till their purification is complete. Their heads are then shaved, and being pronounced clean they are free to return to their own homes. Among the Borâna Gallas, when a war-party has returned to the village, the victors who have slain a foe are washed by the women with a mixture of fat and butter, and their faces are painted red and white. Masai warriors, who have killed barbarians in a fight, paint the right half of their bodies red and the left half white. Similarly a Nandi, who has slain a man of another tribe, paints one side of his body red, and the other side white; for four days after the slaughter he is deemed unclean and may not go home. He must build a small shelter by the river and live there; he may not associate with his wife or sweetheart, and he may only eat porridge, beef, and goat's flesh. At the end of the fourth day he must purify himself by drinking a strong purge made from the *segetet* tree, and by drinking goat's milk mixed with bullock's blood. Among the Wagogo, of East Africa, a man who has killed an enemy in battle paints a red circle round his right eye and a black circle round his left eye.

Among the Thompson Indians of British Columbia it used to be customary for men who had slain enemies to blacken their faces. If this precaution were neglected, it was believed that the spirits of their victims would blind them. A pima Indian who slew one of his hereditary foes, the Apaches, had regularly to undergo a rigid seclusion and purification, which lasted sixteen days. During the whole of that time he might not touch meat or salt, nor look at a blazing fire, nor speak to a human being. He lived alone in the woods attended by an old woman, who brought him his scanty dole of food. He kept his head covered almost the whole time with a plaster of mud, and he might not touch it with his fingers. A band of Tinneh Indians, who had massacred a helpless party of Eskimo at the Copper River, considered themselves to be thereby rendered unclean, and they observed accordingly a number of curious restrictions for a considerable time afterwards. Those who had actually shed blood were strictly prohibited from cooking either for themselves or for others; they might not drink out of any dish nor smoke out of any pipe but their own; they might eat no boiled flesh, but only flesh that was raw or had been broiled at a fire or dried in the sun; and at every meal, before they would taste a morsel, they had to paint their faces with red ochre from the nose to the chin and across the cheeks almost to the ears.

Among the Chinook Indians of Oregon and Washington a man who had killed another had his face painted black with grease and charcoal, and wore rings of cedar bark round his head, his ankles, knees, and wrists. After five days the black paint was washed off his face and replaced by red. During these five days he might not sleep nor even lie down; he might not look at a child nor see people eating. At the end of his purification he hung his head-ring of cedar bark on a tree, and the tree was then supposed to dry up. Among the Eskimo of Langton Bay the killing of an Indian and the killing of a whale were considered to be equally glorious achievements. The man who had killed an Indian was tattooed from the nose to the ears; the man who had killed a whale was tattooed from the mouth to the ears. Both heroes had to refrain from all work for five days, and from certain foods for a whole year; in particular, they might not eat the heads nor the intestines of animals. When a party of Arunta, in Central Australia, are returning from a mission of vengeance, on which they have taken the life of an enemy, they stand in fear of the ghost of their victim, who is believed to pursue them in the likeness of a small bird, uttering a plaintive cry. For some days after their return they will not speak of their deed, and continue to paint themselves all over with powdered charcoal, and to decorate their foreheads and noses with green twigs. Finally, they paint their bodies and faces with bright colours, and become free to talk of the affair; but still of nights they must lie awake listening for the plaintive cry of the bird in which they fancy they hear the voice of their victim.

In Fiji any one who had clubbed a human being to death in war was consecrated or tabooed. He was smeared red by the king with turmeric from the roots of his hair to his heels. A hut was built, and in it he had to pass the next three nights, during which he might not lie down, but must sleep as he sat. Till the three nights had elapsed he might not change his garment, nor remove the turmeric, nor enter a house in which there was a woman. That these rules were intended to protect the Fijian warrior from his victim's ghost is strongly suggested, if not proved, by another Fijian custom. When these savages had buried a man alive, as they often did, they used at nightfall to make a great uproar by means of bamboos, trumpet-shells, and so forth, for the purpose of frightening away his ghost, lest he should attempt to return to his old home. And to render his house unattractive to him they dismantled it and clothed it with everything that to their thinking seemed most repulsive. So the North American Indians used to run through the village with hideous yells, beating on the furniture, walls, and roofs of the huts to drive away the angry ghost of an enemy whom they had just tortured to death. A similar custom is still observed in various parts of New Guinea and the Bismarck Archipelago.

Thus the mark of Cain may have been a mode of disguising a homicide, or of rendering him so repulsive or formidable in appearance that his victim's ghost would either not know him or at least give him a wide berth. Elsewhere I have conjectured that mourning costume in general was originally a disguise adopted to protect the surviving relatives from the dreaded ghost of the recently departed. Whether that be so or not, it is certain that the living do sometimes disguise themselves to escape the notice of the dead. Thus in the western districts of Timor, a large island of the Indian Archipelago, before the body of a man is coffined, his wives stand weeping over him, and their village gossips must also be present, "all with loosened hair in order to make themselves unrecognizable by the *nitu* (spirit) of the dead." Again, among the Herero of South-west Africa, when a man is dying he will sometimes say to a person whom he does not like, "Whence do you come? I do not wish to see you here," and so saying he presses the fingers of his left hand together in such a way that the tip of the thumb protrudes between the fingers. "The person spoken to, now knows that the other has decided upon taking him away (*okutuaerera*) after his death, which means that he must die. In many cases, however, he can avoid this threatening danger of death. For this purpose he hastily leaves the place of the dying man, and looks for an *onganga* (*i.e.* 'doctor,' 'magician'), in order to have himself undressed, washed, and greased again, and dressed with other clothes. He is now quite at ease about the threatening of death caused by the deceased; for, says he, 'Now, our father does not know me' (Nambano tate ke ndyi i). He has no longer any reason to fear the dead."

In like manner we may suppose that, when Cain had been marked by God, he was quite easy in his mind, believing that the ghost of his murdered brother would no longer recognize and trouble him. What the mark exactly was which the divinity affixed to the first murderer for his protection, we have no means of knowing; at most we can hazard a conjecture on the subject. If it is allowable to judge from the similar practices of savages at the present day, the deity may have decorated Cain with red, black, or white paint, or perhaps with a tasteful combination of these colours. For example, he may have painted him red all over, like a Fijian; or white all over, like a Ngoni; or black all over, like an Arunta; or one half of his body red and the other half white, like the Masai and the Nandi. Or if he confined his artistic efforts to Cain's countenance, he may have painted a red circle round his right eye and a black circle round his left eye, in the Wagogo style; or he may have embellished his face from the nose to the chin, and from the mouth to the ears, with a delicate shade of vermilion, after the manner of the Tinneh Indians. Or he may have plastered his head with mud, like the Pimas, or his whole body with cow's dung, like the Kavirondo. Or again, he may have tattooed him from the nose to the ears, like the Eskimo, or between the eyebrows, like the Thonga, so as to raise pimples and give him the appearance of a frowning buffalo. Thus adorned, the first Mr. Smith—for Cain means Smith—may have paraded the waste places of the earth without the least fear of being recognized and molested by his victim's ghost.

This explanation of the mark of Cain has the advantage of relieving the Biblical narrative from a manifest absurdity. For on the usual interpretation God affixed the mark to Cain in order to save him from human assailants, apparently forgetting that there was nobody to assail him, since the earth was as yet inhabited only by the murderer himself and his parents. Hence by assuming that the foe of whom the first murderer went in fear was a ghost instead of a living man, we avoid the irreverence of imputing to the deity a grave lapse of memory little in keeping with the divine omniscience. Here again, therefore, the comparative method approves itself a powerful *advocatus Dei*.

CHAPTER IV

THE GREAT FLOOD

§ 1. *Introduction.*—When the Council of the Royal Anthropological Institute invited me to deliver the annual Huxley lecture, I gratefully accepted the invitation, esteeming it a high honour to be thus associated with one for whom, both as a thinker and as a man, I entertain a deep respect, and with whose attitude towards the great problems of life I am in cordial sympathy. His own works will long keep his memory green; but it is fitting that our science should lay, year by year, a wreath on the grave of one of the most honoured of its exponents.

Casting about for a suitable subject, I remembered that in his later life Huxley devoted some of his well-earned leisure to examining those traditions as to the early ages of the world which are recorded in the Book of Genesis; and accordingly I thought that I might appropriately take one of them for the theme of my discourse. The one which I have chosen is the familiar story of the Great Flood. Huxley himself discussed it in an instructive essay written with all the charm of his lucid and incisive style. His aim was to show that, treated as a record of a deluge which overwhelmed the whole world, drowning almost all men and animals, the story conflicts with the plain teaching of geology and must be rejected as a fable. I shall not attempt either to reinforce or to criticize his arguments and his conclusions, for the simple reason that I am no geologist, and that for me to express an opinion on such a matter would be a mere impertinence. I have approached the subject from a different side, namely, from that of tradition. It has long been known that legends of a great flood, in which almost all men perished, are widely diffused over the world; and accordingly what I have tried to do is to collect and compare these legends, and to inquire what conclusions are to be deduced from the comparison. In short, my discussion of the stories is a study in comparative folk-lore. My purpose is to discover how the narratives arose, and how they came to be so widespread over the earth; with the question of their truth or falsehood I am not primarily concerned, though of course it cannot be ignored in considering the problem of their origin. The inquiry thus defined is not a novel one. It has often been attempted, especially in recent years, and in pursuing it I have made ample use of the labours of my predecessors, some of whom have discussed the subject with great learning and ability. In particular, I would acknowledge my debt to the eminent German geographer and anthropologist, the late Dr. Richard Andree, whose monograph on diluvial traditions, like all his writings, is a model of sound learning and good sense, set forth with the utmost clearness and conciseness.

Apart from the intrinsic interest of such legends as professed records of a catastrophe which destroyed at a blow almost the whole human race, they deserve to be studied for the sake of their bearing on a general question which is at present warmly debated among anthropologists. That question is, How are we to explain the numerous and striking similarities which obtain between the beliefs and customs of races inhabiting distant parts of the world? Are such resemblances due to the transmission of the customs and beliefs from one race to another, either by immediate contact or through the medium of intervening peoples? Or have they arisen independently in many different races through the similar working of the human mind under similar circumstances? Now, if I may presume to offer an opinion on this much-debated problem, I would say at once that, put in the form of an antithesis between mutually exclusive views, the question seems to me absurd. So far as I can judge, all experience and all probability are in favour of the conclusion, that both causes have operated extensively and powerfully to produce the observed similarities of custom and belief among the various races of mankind: in other words, many of these resemblances are to be explained by simple transmission, with more or less of modification, from people to people, and many are to be explained as having originated independently through the similar action of the human mind in response to similar environment. If that is so—and I confess to thinking that this is the only reasonable and probable view—it will follow that in attempting to account for any particular case of resemblance which may be traced between the customs and beliefs of different races, it would be futile to appeal to the general principle either of transmission or of independent origin; each case must be judged on its own merits after an impartial scrutiny of the facts and referred to the one or the other principle, or possibly to a combination of the two, according as the balance of evidence inclines to the one side or to the other, or hangs evenly between them.

This general conclusion, which accepts the two principles of transmission and independent origin as both of them true and valid within certain limits, is confirmed by the particular investigation of diluvial traditions. For it is certain that legends of a great flood are found dispersed among many diverse peoples in distant regions of the earth, and so far as demonstration in such matters is possible, it can be demonstrated that the similarities which undoubtedly exist between many of these legends are due partly to direct transmission from one people to another, and partly to similar, but quite independent, experiences either of great floods or of phenomena which suggested the occurrence of great floods, in many different parts of the world. Thus the study of these traditions, quite apart from any conclusions to which it may lead us concerning their historical credibility, may serve a useful purpose if it mitigates the heat with which the controversy has sometimes been carried on, by convincing the extreme partisans of both principles that in this as in so many other disputes the truth lies wholly neither on the one side nor on the other, but somewhere between the two.

§ 2. *The Babylonian Story of a Great Flood.*—Of all the legends of a Great Flood recorded in literature, by far the oldest is the Babylonian, or rather the Sumerian; for we now know that, ancient as was the Babylonian version of the story, it was derived by the Babylonians from their still more ancient predecessors, the Sumerians, from whom the Semitic inhabitants of Babylonia appear to have derived the principal elements of their civilization.

The Babylonian tradition of the Great Flood has been known to Western scholars from the time of antiquity, since it was recorded by the native Babylonian historian Berosus, who composed a history of his country in the first half of the third century before our era. Berosus wrote in Greek and his work has not come down to us, but fragments of it have been preserved by later Greek historians, and among these fragments is fortunately his account of the deluge. It runs as follows:—

The great flood took place in the reign of Xisuthrus, the tenth king of Babylon. Now the god Cronus appeared to him in a dream and warned him that all men would be destroyed by a flood on the fifteenth day of the month Daesius, which was the eighth month of the Macedonian calendar. Therefore the god enjoined him to write a history of the world from the beginning and to bury it for safety in Sippar, the city of the Sun. Moreover, he was to build a ship and embark in it with his kinsfolk and friends, and to lay up in it a store of meat and drink, and to bring living things, both fowls and four-footed beasts, into the ship, and when he had made all things ready he was to set sail. And when he asked, "And whither shall I sail?" the god answered him. "To the gods; but first thou shalt pray for all good things to men." So he obeyed and built the ship, and the length of it was five furlongs, and the breadth of it was two furlongs; and when he had gathered all things together he stored them in the ship and embarked his children and friends. And when the flood had come and immediately abated, Xisuthrus let fly some of the birds. But as they could find no food nor yet a place to rest, they came back to the ship. And again after some days Xisuthrus let fly the birds; and they returned again to the ship with their feet daubed with clay. A third time he let them fly, and they returned no more to the vessel. Then Xisuthrus perceived that the land had appeared above the water; so he parted some of the seams of the ship, and looking out he saw the shore, and drove the ship aground on a mountain, and stepped ashore with his wife, and his daughter, and the helmsman. And he worshipped the ground, and built an altar, and when he had sacrificed to the gods, he disappeared with those who had disembarked from the ship. And when those who had remained in the ship saw that he and his company returned not, they disembarked likewise and sought him, calling him by name. But Xisuthrus himself was nowhere to be seen. Yet a voice from the air bade them fear the gods, for that he himself for his piety was gone to dwell with the gods, and that his wife, and his daughter, and the helmsman partook of the same honour. And he commanded them that they should go to Babylon, and take up the scriptures which they had buried, and distribute them among men. Moreover, he told them that the land in which they stood was Armenia. And when they heard these things, they sacrificed to the gods and journeyed on foot to Babylon. But of the ship that grounded on the mountains of Armenia a part remains to this day, and some people scrape the bitumen off it and use it in charms. So when they were come to Babylon they dug up the scriptures in Sippar, and built many cities, and restored the sanctuaries, and repeopled Babylon.

According to the Greek historian Nicolaus of Damascus, a contemporary and friend of Augustus and of Herod the Great, "there is above Minyas in Armenia a great mountain called Baris, to which, as the story goes, many people fled for refuge in the flood and were saved; they say too that a certain man, floating in an ark, grounded on the summit, and that remains of the timbers were preserved for a long time. The man may have been he who was recorded by Moses, the legislator of the Jews." Whether Nicolaus of Damascus drew this information from Babylonian or Hebrew tradition may be doubted; the reference to Moses seems to show that he was acquainted with the narrative in Genesis, which he may easily have learned through his patron Herod.

For many centuries the Babylonian tradition of a great flood was known to Western scholars only through its preservation in the Greek fragments of Berosus; it was reserved for modern times to recover the original Babylonian version from the long-lost archives of Assyria. In the course of those excavations at Nineveh, which were one of the glories of the nineteenth century and which made an epoch in the study of ancient history, the English explorers were fortunate enough to discover extensive remains of the library of the great king Ashurbanipal, who reigned from 668 to 626 B.C. in the splendid sunset of the Assyrian empire, carrying the terror of his arms to the banks of the Nile, embellishing his capital with magnificent structures, and gathering within its walls from far and near a vast literature, historical, scientific, grammatical and religious, for the enlightenment of his people. The literature, of which a great part was borrowed from Babylonian originals, was inscribed in cuneiform characters on tablets of soft clay, which were afterwards baked hard and deposited in the library. Apparently the library was arranged in an upper story of the palace, which, in the last sack of the city, collapsed in the flames, shattering the tablets to pieces in its fall. Many of them are still cracked and scorched by the heat of the burning ruins. In later ages the ruins were ransacked by antiquaries of the class of Dousterswivel, who sought among them for the buried treasures not of learning but of gold, and by their labours contributed still further to the disruption and disintegration of the precious records. To complete their destruction the rain, soaking through the ground every spring, saturates them with water containing chemicals, which form in every crack and fissure crystals that by their growth split the already broken tablets into minuter fragments. Yet by laboriously piecing together a multitude of these fragments George Smith, of the British Museum, was able to recompose the now famous epic of Gilgamesh in twelve cantos, or rather tablets, the eleventh of which contains the Babylonian story of the deluge. The great discovery was announced by Mr. Smith at a meeting of the Society of Biblical Archaeology on December the 3rd, 1872.

It was ingeniously conjected by Sir Henry Rawlinson that the twelve cantos of the Gilgamesh epic correspond to the twelve signs of the zodiac, so that the course of the poem followed, as it were, the course of the sun through the twelve months of the year. The theory is to some extent confirmed by the place assigned to the flood legend in the eleventh canto; for the eleventh Babylonian month fell at the height of the rainy season, it was dedicated to the storm-god Ramman, and its name is said to signify "month of the curse of rain." Be that as it may, the story as it stands is an episode or digression destitute of all organic connexion with the rest of the poem. It is introduced as follows :—

The hero of the poem, Gilgamesh, has lost his dear friend Engidu by death, and he himself has fallen grievously sick. Saddened by the past and anxious for the future, he resolves to seek out his remote ancestors Ut-napishtim, son of Ubara-Tutu, and to inquire of him how mortal man can attain to eternal life. For surely, he thought, Ut-napishtim must know the secret, since he has been made like to the gods and now dwells somewhere far away in blissful immortality. A weary and a perilous journey must Gilgamesh accomplish to come at him. He passes the mountain, guarded by a scorpion man and woman, where the sun goes down : he traverses a dark and dreadful road never trodden before by mortal man : he is ferried across a wide sea : he crosses the Water of Death by a narrow bridge, and at last he enters the presence of Ut-napishtim. But when he puts to his great ancestor the question, how man may attain to eternal life, he receives a discouraging reply : the sage tells him that immortality is not for man. Surprised at this answer from one who had been a man and was now himself immortal, Gilgamesh naturally asks his venerable relative to explain how he had contrived to evade the common doom. It is in answer to this pointed question that Ut-napishtim tells the story of the great flood, which runs as follows:—

Ut-napishtim spoke to him, to Gilgamesh: "I will reveal to thee, O Gilgamesh, a hidden word, and the purpose of the gods will I declare to thee. Shurippak, a city which thou knowest, which lies on the bank of the Euphrates, that city was old; and the gods within it, their heart prompted the great gods to send a flood. There was their father Anu, their counsellor the warrior Enlil, their messenger Ninib, their prince Ennugi. The lord of Wisdom, Ea, sat also with them, he repeated their word to the hut of reeds, saying, 'O reed hut, reed hut, O wall, wall, O reed hut hearken, O wall attend. O man of Shurippak, son of Ubara-Tutu, pull down thy house, build a ship, forsake thy possessions, take heed for thy life! Thy gods abandon, save thy life, bring living seed of every kind into the ship. As for the ship which thou shalt build, well planned must be its dimensions, its breadth and its length shall bear proportions each to each, and thou shalt launch it in the ocean.' I took heed and spake into Ea, my lord, saying, 'The command, O my lord, which thou hast given, I will honour and will fulfil. But how shall I make answer unto the city, the people and the elders thereof?' Ea opened his mouth and spake, and he said unto me his servant, 'Thus shalt thou answer and say unto them: Because Enlil hates me, no longer may I abide in your city nor lay my head on Enlil's earth. Down into the deep sea must I go with Ea, my lord, to dwell.'" So Ut-napishtim obeyed the god Ea and gathered together the wood and all things needful for the building of the ship, and on the fifth day he laid down the hull. In the shape of a barge he built it, and on it he set a house a hundred and twenty cubits high, and he divided the house into six stories, and in each story he made nine rooms. Water-plugs he fastened within it; the outside he daubed with bitumen, and the inside he caulked with pitch. He caused oil to be brought, and he slaughtered oxen and lambs. He filled jars with sesame-wine and oil and grape-wine; he gave the people to drink like a river and he made a feast like to the feast of the New Year. And when the ship was ready he filled it with all that he had of silver, and all that he had of gold, and all that he had of living seed. Also he brought up into the ship all his family and his household, the cattle of the field likewise and the beasts of the field, and the handi-craftsmen: all of them he brought in. A fixed time the sun-god Shamash had appointed, saying, "'At eventide the lord of darkness will send a heavy rain. Then enter thou into the ship and shut thy door.' The time appointed drew near, and at eventide the lord of darkness sent a heavy rain. Of the storm, I saw the beginning, to look upon the storm I was afraid. I entered into the ship and shut the door. To the pilot of the ship, even to Puzur-Amurri, the sailor, I committed the (floating) palace and all that therein was. When the early dawn appeared there came up from the horizon a black cloud. Ramman thundered in the midst thereof, the gods Mujati and Lugal went before. Like messengers they passed over mountain and land; Irragal tore away the ship's post. There went Ninib and he made the storm to burst. The Anunnaki lifted up flaming torches, with the brightness thereof they lit up the earth. The whirlwind of Ramman mounted up into the heavens, and all light was turned into darkness." A whole day the tempest raged, and the waters rose on the mountains. "No man beheld his fellow, no more could men know each other. In heaven the gods were afraid of the deluge, they drew back, they climbed up into the heaven of Anu. The gods crouched like dogs, they cowered by the walls. Ishtar cried out like a woman in travail, loudly lamented the queen of the gods with her beautiful voice: 'Let that day be turned to clay, when I commanded evil in the assembly of the gods! Alas, that I commanded evil in the assembly of the gods, that for the destruction of my people I commanded battle! That which I brought forth, where is it? Like the spawn of fish it filleth the sea.' The gods of the Anunnaki wept with her, the gods were bowed down, they sat down weeping. Their lips were pressed together. For six days and six nights the wind blew, and the deluge and the tempest overwhelmed the land. When the seventh day drew nigh, then ceased the tempest and the deluge and the storm, which had fought like a host. Then the sea grew quiet, it went down; the hurricane and the deluge ceased. I looked upon the sea, there was silence come, and all mankind was turned back into clay. Instead of the fields a swamp lay before me. I opened the window and the light fell upon my cheek; I bowed myself down, I sat down, I wept, over my cheek flowed my tears. I looked upon the world, and behold all was sea. After twelve (days?) an island arose, to the land Nisir the ship made its way. The mount of Nisir held the ship fast and let it not slip. The first day, the second day, the mountain Nisir held the ship fast: the third day, the fourth day, the mountain Nisir held the ship fast: the fifth day, the sixth day, the mountain Nisir held the ship fast. When the seventh day drew nigh, I sent out a dove, and let her go forth. The dove flew hither and thither, but there was no resting-place for her, and she returned. Then I sent out a swallow and let her go forth. The swallow flew hither and thither, but there was no resting-place for her, and she returned. Then I sent out a raven and let her go forth. The raven flew away, she beheld the abatement of the waters, she ate, she waded, she croaked, but she did not return. Then I brought all out unto the four winds, I offered an offering, I made a libation on the peak of the mountain. By sevens I set out the vessels, under them I heaped up reed, and cedar-wood, and myrtle. The gods smelt the savour, the gods smelt the sweet savour. The gods gathered like flies about him that offered up the sacrifice. Then the Lady of the gods drew nigh, she lifted up the great jewels which Anu had made

according to her wish. She said, 'Oh ye gods here, as truly as I
will not forget the jewels of *lapis lazuli* which are on my neck, so
truly will I remember these days, never shall I forget them! Let
the gods come to the offering, but Enlil shall not come to the offering, for he took not counsel and sent the deluge, and my people
he gave to destruction.' Now when Enlil drew nigh, he saw the
ship; then was Enlil wroth. He was filled with anger against
the gods, the Igigi (saying), 'Who then hath escaped with his life?
No man shall live after the destruction.' Then Ninib opened his
mouth and spake, he said to the warrior Enlil, 'Who but Ea could
have done this thing? For Ea knoweth every matter.' Then
Ea opened his mouth and spake, he said to the warrior Enlil, 'Thou
art the governor of the gods, O warrior, but thou wouldst not take
counsel and thou hast sent the deluge! On the sinner visit his
sin, and on the transgressor visit his transgression. But hold thy
hand, that all be not destroyed! and forbear, that all be not confounded! Instead of sending a deluge, let a lion come and minish
mankind! Instead of sending a deluge, let a leopard come and
minish mankind! Instead of sending a deluge, let a famine come
and waste the land! Instead of sending a deluge, let the Plague-
god come and slay mankind! I did not reveal the purpose of the
great gods. I caused Atrakhasis to see a dream, and thus be heard
the purpose of the gods.' Thereupon Enlil arrived at a decision,
and he went up into the ship. He took my hand and brought me
forth, he brought my wife forth, he made her to kneel at my side,
he turned towards us, he stood between us, he blessed us (saying),
'Hitherto hath Ut-napishtim been a man, but now let Ut-napishtim
and his wife be like unto the gods, even us, and let Ut-napishtim
dwell afar off at the mouth of the rivers!' Then they took me,
and afar off, at the mouth of the rivers, they made me to dwell."

Such is the long story of the deluge interwoven into the Gilgamesh epic, with which, to all appearance, it had originally no
connexion. A fragment of another version of the tale is preserved
on a broken tablet, which, like the tablets of the Gilgamesh epic,
was found among the ruins of Ashurbanipal's library at Nineveh.
It contains a part of the conversation which is supposed to have
taken place before the flood between the god Ea and the Babylonian Noah, who is here called Atrakhasis, a name which, as we
saw, is incidentally applied to him in the Gilgamesh epic, though
elsewhere in that version he is named not Atrakhasis but Ut-
napishtim. The name Atrakhasis is said to be the Babylonian
original which is Berosus's Greek version of the deluge legend is
represented by Xisuthrus. In this fragment the god Ea commands
Atrakhasis, saying, "Go in and shut the door of the ship. Bring
within thy corn, thy goods and thy possessions, thy (wife?), thy
family, thy kinsfolk, and thy craftsmen, the cattle of the field,
the beasts of the field, as many as eat grass." In his reply the
hero says that he has never built a ship before, and he begs that a

plan of the ship be drawn for him on the ground, which he may follow in laying down the vessel.

Thus far the Babylonian versions of the flood legend date only from the time of Ashurbanipal in the seventh century before our era, and might therefore conceivably be of later origin than the Hebrew version and copied from it. However, conclusive evidence of the vastly greater antiquity of the Babylonian legend is furnished by a broken tablet, which was discovered at Abu-Habbah, the site of the ancient city of Sippar, in the course of excavations undertaken by the Turkish Government. The tablet contains a very mutilated version of the flood story, and it is exactly dated; for at the end there is a colophon or note recording that the tablet was written on the twenty-eighth day of the month Shabatu (the eleventh Babylonian month) in the eleventh year of King Ammizaduga, or about 1966 B.C. Unfortunately the text is so fragmentary that little information can be extracted from it; but the name of Atrakhasis occurs in it, together with references to the great rain and apparently to the ship and the entrance into it of the people who were to be saved.

Yet another very ancient version of the deluge legend came to light at Nippur in the excavations conducted by the University of Pennsylvania. It is written on a small fragment of unbaked clay, and on the ground of the style of writing and of the place where the tablet was found it is dated by its discoverer, Professor H. V. Hilprecht, not later than 2100 B.C. In this fragment a god appears to announce that he will cause a deluge which will sweep away all mankind at once; and he warns the person whom he addresses to build a great ship, with a strong roof, in which he is to save his life, and also to bring into it the beasts of the field and the birds of heaven.

All these versions of the flood story are written in the Semitic language of the ancient people who appear to have preceded the version, found by the American excavators at Nippur and recently deciphered, is written in Sumerian, that is, in the non-Semitic language of the ancient people who appear to have preceded the Semites in Babylonia and to have founded in the lower valley of the Euphrates that remarkable system of civilization which we commonly called Babylonian. The city of Nippur, where the Sumerian version of the deluge legend has been discovered, was the holiest and perhaps the oldest religious centre in the country, and the city-god Enlil was the head of the Babylonian pantheon. The tablet which records the legend would seem, from the character of the script, to have been written about the time of the famous Hammurabi, king of Babylon, that is, about 2100 B.C. But the story itself must be very much older; for by the close of the third millennium before our era, when the tablet was inscribed, the Sumerians as a separate race had almost ceased to exist, having been absorbed in the Semitic population, and their old tongue was already a dead language, though the ancient literature and sacred texts embalmed in it were still studied and copied by the Semitic priests and scribes. Hence the discovery of a Sumerian version of the deluge legend raises a presumption that the legend itself dates from a time anterior to the occupation of the Euphrates valley by the Semites, who after their immigration into the country appear to have borrowed the story from their predecessors the Sumerians. It is of interest to observe that the Sumerian version of the flood story formed a sequel to an account, unfortunately very fragmentary, of the creation of man, according to which men were created by the gods before the animals. Thus the Sumerian story agrees with the Hebrew account of Genesis, in so far as both of them treat the creation of man and the great flood as events closely connected with each other in the early history of the world; and further the Sumerian narrative agrees with the Jehovistic against the Priestly Document in representing the creation of man as antecedent to the creation of the animals.

Only the lower half of the tablet on which this Sumerian Genesis was inscribed has as yet come to light, but enough remains to furnish us with the main outlines of the flood story. From it we learn that Ziugiddu, or rather Ziudsuddu, was at once a king and a priest of the god Enki, the Sumerian deity who was the equivalent of the Semitic Ea; daily he occupied himself in the god's service, prostrating himself in humility and constant in his observance at the shrine. To reward him for his piety Enki informs him that at the request of Enlil it has been resolved in the council of the gods to destroy the seed of mankind by a rain-storm. Before the holy man receives this timely warning, his divine friend bids him take his stand beside a wall, saying, "Stand by the wall on my left side, and at the wall I will speak a word with thee." These words are evidently connected with the curious passage in the Semitic version, where Ea begins his warning to Ut-napishtim. "O reed hut, reed hut, O wall, wall, O reed hut hearken, O wall attend." Together the parallel passages suggest that the friendly god, who might not directly betray the resolution of the gods to a mortal man, adopted the subterfuge of whispering it to a wall of reeds, on the other side of which he had first stationed Ziudsuddu. Thus by eavesdropping the good man learned the fatal secret, while his divine patron was able afterwards to protest that he had not revealed the counsel of the gods. The subterfuge reminds us of the well-known story, how the servant of King Midas detected the ass's ears of his master, and, unable to contain himself, whispered the secret into a hole in the ground and filled up the hole with earth; but a bed of reeds grew up on the spot, and rustling in the wind, proclaimed to all the world the king's deformity. The part of the tablet which probably described the building of the ship and Ziudsuddu's embarkation is lost, and in the remaining portion we are plunged into the midst of the deluge. The storms of wind and rain are described as raging together. Then the text continues: "When for seven days, for seven nights, the rain-storm had raged in the land, when the great boat had been carried away by the wind-storms on the mighty waters, the Sun-god came forth, shedding light over heaven and earth." When the light shines into the boat, Ziudsuddu prostrates himself before the Sun-god and sacrifices an ox and a sheep. Then follows a gap in the text, after which we read of Ziudsuddu, the King, prostrating himself before the gods Anu and Enlil. The anger of Enlil against men appears now to be abated, for, speaking of Ziudsuddu, he says, "Life like that of a god I give to him," and "an eternal soul like that of a god I create for him," which means that the hero of the deluge legend, the Sumerian Noah, receives the boon of immortality, if not of divinity. Further, he is given the title of "Preserver of the Seed of Mankind," and the gods cause him to dwell on a mountain, perhaps the mountain of Dilmun, though the reading of the name is uncertain. The end of the legend is wanting.

Thus in its principal features the Sumerian version of the deluge legend agrees with the much longer and more circumstantial version preserved in the Gilgamesh epic. In both a great god (Enlil or Bel) resolves to destroy mankind by flooding the earth with rain; in both another god (Enki or Ea) warns a man of the coming catastrophe, and the man, accepting the admonition, is saved in a ship; in both the flood lasts at its height for seven days; in both when the deluge has abated, the man offers a sacrifice and is finally raised to the ranks of the gods. The only essential difference is in the name of the hero, who in the Sumerian version is called Ziudsuddu, and in the Semitic version Ut-napishtim or Atrakhasis. The Sumerian name Ziudsuddu resembles the name Xisuthrus, which Berosus gives as that of the hero who was saved from the flood; if the two names are really connected, we have fresh ground for admiring the fidelity with which the Babylonian historian followed the most ancient documentary sources.

The discovery of this very interesting tablet, with its combined accounts of the creation and the deluge, renders it highly probable that the narratives of the early history of the world which we find in Genesis did not originate with the Semites, but were borrowed by them from the older civilized people whom, some thousands of years before our era, the wild Semitic hordes, swarming out of the Arabian desert, found in possession of the fat lands of the lower Euphrates valley, and from whom the descendants of these primitive Bedouins gradually learned the arts and habits of civilization, just as the northern barbarians acquired a varnish of culture through their settlement in the Roman empire.

§ 3. *The Hebrew Story of a Great Flood.*—In the ancient Hebrew legend of a great flood, as it is recorded in the Book of Genesis, Biblical critics are now agreed in detecting the presence of two originally distinct and partially inconsistent narratives, which have been combined so as to present the superficial appearance of a single homogeneous story.   Yet the editorial task of uniting them has been performed so clumsily that the repetitions and inconsistencies left standing in them can hardly fail to attract the attention even of a careless reader.

Of the two versions of the legend thus artificially combined, the one is derived from what the critics call the Priestly Document or Code (usually designated by the letter P) ; the other is derived from what the critics call the Jehovistic or Jahwistic Document (usually designated by the letter J), which is characterized by the use of the divine name Jehovah (Jahweh, or rather Yahweh).   The two documents differ conspicuously in character and style, and they belong to different ages ; for while the Jehovistic narrative is probably the oldest, the Priestly Code is now generally admitted to be the latest, of the four principal documents which have been united to form the Hexateuch.   The Jehovistic document is believed to have been written in Judea in the early times of the Hebrew monarchy, probably in the ninth or eighth century before our era ; the Priestly Code dates from the period after the year 586 B.C., When Jerusalem was taken by Nebuchadnezzar, king of Babylon, and the Jews were carried away by him into captivity.   Both documents are in their form historical, but while the Jehovistic writer displays a genuine interest in the characters and adventures of the men and women whom he describes, the Priestly writer appears to concern himself with them only so far as he deemed them instruments in the great scheme of Providence for conveying to Israel a knowledge of God and of the religious and social institutions by which it was his gracious will that the Chosen People should regulate their lives. The history which he writes is sacred and ecclesiastical rather than secular and civil ; his preoccupation is with Israel as a church rather than as a nation.   Hence, while he dwells at comparative length on the lives of the patriarchs and prophets to whom the deity deigned to reveal himself, he, hurries over whole generations of ccmmon mortals, whom he barely mentions by name, as if they were mere links to connect one religious epoch with another, mere packthread on which to string at rare intervals the splendid jewels of revelation.   His attitude to the past is sufficiently explained by the circumstances of the times in which he lived.   The great age of Israel was over ; its independence was gone, and with it the hopes of wordly prosperity and glory.   The rosy dreams of empire, which the splendid reigns of David and Solomon had conjured up in the hearts of the people, and which may have lingered for a while, like morning clouds, even after the disruption of the monarchy, had long ago faded in the clouded evening of the nation's day, under the grim reality of foreign domination.   Barred from all the roads of purely mundane ambition, the irrepressible idealism of the national temperament now found a vent for itself in another direction.   Its dreams took a different cast.   If earth was shut upon it, heaven was still open; and like Jacob at Bethel, with enemies behind him and before, the dreamer beheld a ladder stretching up beyond the clouds, by which angelic hosts might descend to guard and comfort the forlorn pilgrim. In short, the leaders of Israel sought to console and compensate their nation for the humiliations she had to endure in the secular sphere by raising her to a position of supremacy in the spiritual. For this purpose they constructed or perfected an elaborate system of religious ritual designed to forestall and engross the divine favour, and so to make Zion the holy city, the joy and centre of God's kingdom on earth. With these aims and ambitions the tone of public life became more and more clerical, its interests ecclesiastical, its predominant influence priestly. The king was replaced by the high priest, who succeeded even to the purple robes and golden crown of his predecessor. The revolution which thus substituted a line of pontiffs for a line of temporal rulers at Jerusalem, was like that which converted the Rome of the Caesars into the Rome of the mediaeval Popes.

It is this movement of thought, this current of religious aspirations setting strongly in the direction of ecclesiasticism, which is reflected, we may almost say arrested and crystallized, in the Priestly Code. The intellectual and moral limitations of the movement are mirrored in the corresponding limitations of the writer. It is the formal side of religion in which alone he is really interested; it is in the details of rites and ceremonies, of ecclesiastical furniture and garments, that he revels with genuine gusto. The deeper side of religion is practically a sealed book for him: its moral and spiritual aspects he barely glances at: into the profound problems of immortality and the origin of evil, which have agitated inquiring spirits in all the ages, he never enters. With his absorption in the minutiae of ritual, his indifference to purely secular affairs, his predilection for chronology and genealogy, for dates and figures, in a word, for the dry bones rather than the flesh and blood of history, the priestly historian is like one of those monkish chroniclers of the Middle Ages who looked out on the great world through the narrow loophole of a cloistered cell or the many-tinted glass of a cathedral window. His intellectual horizon was narrowed, the atmosphere in which he beheld events was coloured, by the medium through which he saw them. Thus the splendours of the Tabernacle in the wilderness, invisible to all eyes but his, are as if they had loomed on his heated imagination through the purple lights of a rose-window or the gorgeous panes of some flamboyant oriel. Even in the slow processes or sudden catastrophes which have fashioned or transformed the material universe he discerned little more than the signs and wonders vouchsafed by the deity to herald new epochs of religious dispensation. For him the work of creation was a grand prelude to the institution of the sabbath. The vault of heaven itself, spangled with glorious luminaries, was a magnificent dialplate on which the finger of God pointed eternally to the correct seasons of the feasts in the ecclesiastical calendar. The deluge, which swept away almost the whole of mankind, was the occasion which the repentant deity took to establish a covenant with the miserable survivors; and the rainbow, glowing in iridescent radiance against the murky storm-cloud, was nothing but the divine seal appended to the covenant as a guarantee of its genuine and irrevocable character.

For the priestly historian was a lawyer as well as an ecclesiastic, and as such he took great pains to prove that the friendly relations of God to his people rested on a strictly legal basis, being authenticated by a series of contracts into which both parties entered with all due formality. He is never so much in his element as when he is expounding these covenants; he never wearies of recalling the long series of Israel's title-deeds. Nowhere does this dryasdust antiquary, this rigid ritualist, so sensibly relax his normal severity, nowhere does he so nearly unbend and thaw, as when he is expatiating on the congenial subject of contracts and conveyances. His masterpiece of historical narrative is acknowledged to be his account of the negotiations into which the widowed Abraham entered with the sons of Heth in order to obtain a family vault in which to bury his wife. The lugubrious nature of the transaction does not damp the professional zest of the narrator; and the picture he has drawn of it combines the touches of no mean artist with the minute exactitude of a practised conveyancer. At this distance of time the whole scene still passes before us, as similar scenes may have passed before the eyes of the writer, and as they may still be witnessed in the East, when two well-bred Arab sheikhs fence dexterously over a point of business, while they observe punctiliously the stately forms of courtesies of Oriental diplomacy. But such pictures are rare indeed in this artist's gallery. Landscapes he hardly attempted, and his portraits are daubs, lacking all individuality, life, and colour. In that of Moses, which he laboured most, the great leader is little more than a lay-figure rigged out to distribute ecclesiastical upholstery and millinery.

Very different are the pictures of the patriarchal age bequeathed to us by the author of the Jehovistic document. In purity of outline, lightness and delicacy of touch, and warmth of colouring, they are unsurpassed, perhaps unequalled, in literature. The finest effects are produced by the fewest strokes, because every stroke is that of a master who knows instinctively just what to put in and what to leave out. Thus, while his whole attention seems to be given to the human figures in the foreground, who stand out from the canvas with lifelike truth and solidity, he contrives simultaneously, with a few deft, almost imperceptible touches, to indicate the landscape behind them, and so to complete a harmonious picture which stamps itself indelibly on the memory. The scene, for example, of Jacob and Rachel at the well, with the flocks of sheep lying round it in the noontide heat, is as vivid in the writer's words as it is in the colours of Raphael.

And to this exquisite picturesqueness in the delineation of human life he adds a charming naïvety, an antique simplicity, in his descriptions of the divine. He carries us back to the days of old, when no such awful gulf was supposed to yawn between man and the deity. In his pages we read how God moulded the first man out of clay, as a child shapes its mud baby; how he walked in the garden in the cool of the evening and called to the shamefaced couple who had been skulking behind trees; how he made coats of skin to replace the too scanty fig-leaves of our first parents; how he shut the door behind Noah, when the patriarch had entered into the ark; how he sniffed the sweet savour of the burning sacrifice; how he came down to look at the tower of Babel, apparently because, viewed from the sky, it was beyond his reach of vision; how he conversed with Abraham at the door of his tent, in the heat of the day, under the shadow of the whispering oaks. In short, the whole work of this delightful writer is instinct with a breath of poetry, with something of the freshness and fragrance of the olden time, which invests it with an ineffable and immortal charm.

In the composite narrative of the Great Flood which we possess in Genesis, the separate ingredients contributed by the Jehovistic and the Priestly documents respectively are distinguishable from each other both by verbal and by material differences. To take the verbal differences first, the most striking is that in the Hebrew original the deity is uniformly designated, in the Jehovistic document by the name of *Jehovah* (*Jahweh*), and in the Priestly document by the name of *Elohim*, which in the English version are rendered respectively by the words "Lord" and "God." In representing the Hebrew *Jehovah* (*Jahweh*) by "Lord," the English translators follow the practice of the Jews, who, in reading the Scriptures aloud, uniformly substitute the title *Adonai* or "Lord" for the sacred name of Jehovah, wherever they find the latter written in the text. Hence the English reader may assume as a general rule that in the passage of the English version, where the title "Lord" is applied to the deity, the name Jehovah stands for it in the written or printed Hebrew text. But in the narrative of the flood and throughout Genesis the Priestly writer avoids the use of the name Jehovah and substitutes for it the term *Elohim*, which is the ordinary Hebrew word for God; and his reason for doing so is that according to him the divine name Jehovah was first revealed by God to Moses, and therefore could not have been applied to him in the earlier ages of the world. On the other hand, the Jehovistic writer has no such theory as to the revelation of the name Jehovah; hence he bestows it on the deity without scruple from the creation onwards.

Apart from this capital distinction between the documents, there are verbal differences which do not appear in the English translation. Thus, one set of words is used for "male and female" in the Jehovistic document, and quite a different set in the Priestly. Again, the words translated "destroy" in the English version are different in the two documents, and similary with the words which the English translators represent by "die" and "dried."

But the material differences between the Jehovistic and the Priestly narratives are still more remarkable, and as they amount in some cases to positive contradictions, the proof that they emanate from separate documents may be regarded as complete. Thus in the Jehovistic narrative the clean animals are distinguished from the unclean, and while seven of every sort of clean animals are admitted to the ark, only a pair of each sort of unclean animals is suffered to enter. On the other hand, the Priestly writer makes no such invidious distinction between the animals, but admits them to the ark on a footing of perfect equality, though at the same time he impartially limits them all alike to a single couple of each sort. The explanation of this discrepancy is that in the view of the Priestly writer the distinction between clean and unclean animals was first revealed by God to Moses, and could not therefore have been known to his predecessor Noah; whereas the Jehovistic writer, untroubled by any such theory, naïvely assumes the distinction between clean and unclean animals to have been familiar to mankind from the earliest times, as if it rested on a natural difference too obvious to be overlooked by anybody.

Another serious discrepancy between the two writers relates to the duration of the flood. In the Jehovistic narrative the rain lasted forty days and forty nights, and afterwards Noah passed three weeks in the ark before the water had subsided enough to let him land. On this reckoning the flood lasted sixty-one days. On the other hand, in the Priestly narrative it was a hundred and fifty days before the water began to sink, and the flood lasted altogether for twelve months and ten days. As the Hebrew months were lunar, twelve of them would amount to three hundred and fifty-four days, and ten days added to them would give a solar year of three hundred and sixty-four days. Since the Priestly writer thus assigns to the duration of the flood the approximate length of a solar year, we may safely assume that he lived at a time when the Jews were able to correct the serious error of the lunar calendar by observation of the sun.

Again, the two writers differ from each other in the causes which they allege for the flood; for whereas the Jehovistic writer puts it down to rain only, the Priestly writer speaks of subterranean waters bursting forth as well as of sheets of water descending from heaven.

Lastly, the Jehovistic writer represents Noah as building an altar and sacrificing to God in gratitude for his escape from the flood. The Priestly writer, on the other hand, makes no mention either of the altar or of the sacrifice; no doubt because from the standpoint of the Levitical law, which he occupied, there could be no legitimate altar anywhere but in the temple at Jerusalem, and because for a mere layman like Noah to offer a sacrifice would have been an unheard-of impropriety, a gross encroachment on the rights of the clergy which he could not for a moment dream of imputing to the respectable patriarch.

Thus a comparison of the Jehovistic and the Priestly narratives strongly confirms the conclusion of the critics that the two were originally independent, and that the Jehovistic is considerably the older. For the Jehovistic writer is clearly ignorant of the law of the one sanctuary, which forbade the offering of sacrifice anywhere but at Jerusalem; and as that law was first clearly enunciated and enforced by King Josiah in 61 B.C., it follows that the Jehovistic document must have been composed some time, probably a long time, before that date. For a like reason the Priestly document must have been composed some time, probably a considerable time, after that date, since the writer implicitly recognizes the law of the one sanctuary by refusing to impute a breach of it to Noah. Thus, whereas the Jehovistic writer betrays a certain archaic simplicity in artlessly attributing to the earliest ages of the world the religious institutions and phraseology of his own time, the Priestly writer reveals the reflection of a later age, which has worked out a definite theory of religious evolution and applies it rigidly to history.

A very cursory comparison of the Hebrew with the Babylonian account of the Deluge may suffice to convince us that the two narratives are not independent, but that one of them must be derived from the other, or both from a common original. The points of resemblance between the two are far too numerous and detailed to be accidental. In both narratives the divine powers resolve to destroy mankind by a great flood; in both the secret is revealed beforehand to a man by a god, who directs him to build a great vessel, in which to save himself and seed of every kind. It is probably no mere accidental coincidence that in the Babylonian story, as reported by Berosus, the hero saved from the flood was the *tenth* King of Babylon, and that in the Hebrew story Noah was the *tenth* man in descent from Adam. In both narratives the favoured man, thus warned of God, builds a huge vessel in several stories, makes it water-tight with pitch or bitumen, and takes into it his family and animals of all sorts: in both, the deluge is brought about in large measure by heavy rain, and lasts for a greater or less number of days: in both, all mankind are drowned except the hero and his family: in both, the man sends forth birds, a raven and a dove, to see whether the water of the flood has abated: in both, the dove after a time returns to the ship because it could find no place in which to rest: in both, the raven does not return: in both, the vessel at last grounds on a mountain: in both, the hero, in gratitude for his rescue, offers sacrifice on the mountain: in both, the gods smell the sweet savour, and their anger is appeased.

So much for the general resemblance between the Babylonian

story as a whole and the Hebrew story as a whole. But if we take into account the separate elements of the Hebrew story, we shall see that the Jehovistic narrative is in closer agreement than the Priestly with the Babylonian. Alike in the Jehovistic and in the Babylonian narrative special prominence is given to the number seven. In the Jehovistic version, Noah has a seven days' warning of the coming deluge: he takes seven of every sort of clean animals with him into the ark: he allows intervals of seven days to elapse between the successive despatches of the dove from the ark. In the Babylonian version the flood lasts at its greatest height for seven days; and the hero sets out the sacrificial vessels by sevens on the mountain. Again, alike in the Jehovistic and the Babylonian version, special mention is made of shutting the door of the ship or ark when the man, his family, and the animals have entered into it: in both alike we have the picturesque episode of sending forth the raven and the dove from the vessel, and in both alike the offering of the sacrifice, the smelling of it by the gods, and their consequent appeasement. On the other hand, in certain particulars the Priestly narrative in Genesis approaches more closely than the Jehovistic to the Babylonian. Thus, in both the Priestly and the Babylonian version exact directions are given for the construction of the vessel: in both alike it is built in several stories, each of which is divided into numerous cabins: in both alike it is made water-tight by being caulked with pitch or bitumen: in both alike it grounds on a mountain; and in both alike on issuing from the vessel the hero receives the divine blessing.

But if the Hebrew and Babylonian narratives are closely related to each other, how is the relation to be explained? The Babylonian cannot be derived from the Hebrew, since it is older than the Hebrew by at least eleven or twelve centuries. Moreover, "as Zimmerman has remarked, the very essence of the Biblical narrative presupposes a country liable, like Babylonia, to inundations; so that it cannot be doubted that the story was 'indigenous in Babylonia, and transplanted to Palestine.'" But if the Hebrews derived the story of the great flood from Babylonia, when and how did they do so? We have no information on the subject, and the question can only be answered conjecturally. Some scholars of repute have supposed that the Jews first learned the legend in Babylon during the captivity, and that the Biblical narrative is consequently not older than the sixth century before our era. This view might be tenable if we only possessed the Hebrew version of the Deluge legend in the Priestly recension; for the Priestly Code, as we saw, was probably composed during or after the captivity, and it is perfectly possible that the writers of it acquire a knowledge of the Babylonian tradition either orally or from Babylonian literature during their exile or perhaps after their return to Palestine; for it is reasonable to suppose that the intimate relations which the conquest established between the two countries may have led to a certain diffusion of

Babylonian literature in Palestine, and of Jewish literature in Babylonia. On this view some of the points in which the Priestly narrative departs from the Jehovistic and approximates to the Babylonian may conceivably have been borrowed directly by the Priestly writers from Babylonian sources. Such points are the details as to the construction of the ark, and in particular the smearing of it with pitch or bitumen, which is a characteristic product of Babylonia. But that the Hebrews were acquainted with the story of the great flood, and that too in a form closely akin to the Babylonian, long before they were carried away into captivity, is abundantly proved by the Jehovistic narrative in Genesis, which may well date from the ninth century before our era and can hardly be later than the eighth.

Assuming, then, that the Hebrews in Palestine were familiar from an early time with the Babylonian legend of the deluge, we have still to ask, how and when did they learn it? Two answers to the question have been given. On the one hand, it has been held that the Hebrews may have brought the legend with them, when they migrated from Babylonia to Palestine about two thousand years before Christ. On the other hand, it has been suggested that, after their settlement in Palestine, the Hebrews may have borrowed the story from the native Canaanites, who in their turn may have learned it through the medium of Babylonian literature sometime in the second millennium before our era. Which, if either, of these views is the true one, we have at present no means of deciding.

In later times Jewish fancy tricked out the story of the flood with many new and often extravagant details designed apparently to satisfy the curiosity or tickle the taste of a degenerate age, which could not rest satisfied with the noble simplicity of the narrative in Genesis. Among these tawdry or grotesque additions to the ancient legend we read how men lived at ease in the days before the flood, for by a single sowing they reaped a harvest sufficient for the needs of forty years, and by their magic arts they could compel the sun and moon to do them service. Instead of nine months children were in their mothers' wombs only a few days, and immediately on their birth could walk and talk and set even the demons at defiance. It was this easy luxurious life that led men astray and lured them into the commission of those sins, especially the sins of wantonness and rapacity, which excited the wrath of God and determined him to destroy the sinners by a great flood. Yet in his mercy he gave them due warning; for Noah, instructed by the deity, preached to them to mend their ways, threatening them with the flood as the punishment of their iniquity; and this he did for no less than one hundred and twenty years. Even at the end of that period God gave mankind another week's grace, during which, strange to say, the sun rose in the west every morning and set in the east every night. But nothing could move these wicked men to repentance; they only mocked and jeered at the pious Noah when they saw him building the ark. He learned how to make it from a holy book, which had been given to Adam by the angel Raziel and which contained within it all knowledge, human and divine. It was made of sapphires, and Noah enclosed it in a golden casket when he took it with him into the ark, where it served him as a time-piece to distinguish night from day; for so long as the flood prevailed neither the sun nor the moon shed any light on the earth. Now the deluge was caused by the male waters from the sky meeting the female waters which issued forth from the ground. The holes in the sky by which the upper waters escaped were made by God when he removed two stars out of the constellation of the Pleiades; and in order to stop this torrent of rain God had afterwards to bung up the two holes with a couple of stars borrowed from the constellation of the Bear. That is why the Bear runs after the Pleiades to this day: she wants her children back, but she will never get them till after the Last Day.

When the ark was ready, Noah proceeded to gather the animals into it. They came trooping in such numbers that the patriarch could not take them all in, but had to sit at the door of the ark and make a choice; the animals which lay down at the door he took in, and the animals which stood up he shut out. Even after this principle of natural selection had been rigidly enforced, the number of species of reptiles which were taken on board was no less than three hundred and sixty-five, and the number of species of birds thirty-two. No note was taken, at least none appears to have been recorded, of the number of mammals, but many of them were among the passengers, as we shall see presently. Before the flood the unclean animals far outnumbered the clean, but after the flood the proportions were reversed, because seven pairs of each of the clean sorts were preserved in the ark, but only two pairs of the unclean. One creature, the *reem*, was so huge that there was no room for it in the ark, so Noah tethered it to the outside of the vessel, and the animal trotted behind. The giant Og, king of Bashan, was also much too big to go into the ark, so he sat on the top of it, and in that way escaped with his life. With Noah himself in the ark were his wife Naamah, daughter of Enosh, and his three sons and their wives. An odd pair who also found refuge in the ark were Falsehood and Misfortune. At first Falsehood presented himself alone at the door of the ark, but was refused a passage on the ground that there was no admission except for married couples. So he went away, and meeting with Misfortune induced her to join him, and the pair were received into the ark. When all were aboard, and the flood began, the sinners gathered some seven hundred thousand strong round about the ark and begged and prayed to be taken in. When Noah sternly refused to admit them, they made a rush at the door as if to break it in, but the wild beasts that were on guard round about the ark fell upon

them and devoured some of them, and all that escaped the beasts
were drowned in the rising flood. A whole year the ark floated
on the face of the waters; it pitched and tossed on the heaving
billows, and all inside of it were shaken up like lentils in a pot.
The lions roared, the oxen lowed, the wolves howled, and the rest
bellowed after their several sorts. But the great difficulty with
which Noah had to struggle in the ark was the question of victuals.
Long afterwards his son Shem confided to Eliezer, the servant of
Abraham, the trouble his father had had in feeding the whole
menagerie. The poor man was up and down, up and down, by
day and by night. For the daylight animals had to be fed by day
and the nocturnal animals by night; and the giant Og had his
rations served out to him through a hole in the roof. Though
the lion suffered the whole time from a fever, which kept him
comparatively quiet, yet he was very surly and ready to fly out
on the least provocation. Once when Noah did not bring him
his dinner fast enough, the noble animal gave him such a blow
with his paw that the patriarch was lame for the rest of his natural
life and therefore incapable of serving as a priest. It was on the
tenth day of the month Tammuz that Noah sent forth the raven
to see and report on the state of the flood. But the raven found
a corpse floating on the water and set to work to devour it, so that
he quite forgot to return and hand in his report. A week later
Noah sent out the dove, which at last, on its third flight, brought
back in its bill an olive leaf plucked on the Mount of Olives at
Jerusalem; for the Holy Land had not been ravaged by the
deluge. When he stepped out of the ark Noah wept to see the
widespread devastation wrought by the flood. A thank-offering
for his delivery was offered by his son Shem, for the patriarch
himself was still suffering from the effects of his encounter with
the lion and could not officiate in person.

From another late account we learn some interesting particulars
as to the internal arrangements of the ark and the distribution of
the passengers. The beasts and cattle were battened down in the
hold, the middle deck was occupied by the birds, and the promenade
deck was reserved for Noah and his family. But the men and the
women were kept strictly apart. The patriarch and his sons lodged
in the east end of the ark, and his wife and his sons' wives lodged
in the west end; and between them as a barrier was interposed the
dead body of Adam, which was thus rescued from a watery grave.
This account, which further favours us with the exact dimensions of the ark in cubits and the exact day of the week and of the
month when the passengers got aboard, is derived from an Arabic
manuscript found in the library of the Convent of St. Catherine
on Mount Sinai. The author would seem to have been an Arab
Christian, who flourished about the time of the Mohammedan
conquest, though the manuscript is of later date.

§ 4. *Ancient Greek Stories of a Great Flood.*—Legends of a

destructive deluge, in which the greater part of mankind perished, meet us in the literature of ancient Greece. As told by the mythographer Apollodorus, the story runs thus: "Deucalion was the son of Prometheus. He reigned as king in the country about Phthia and married Pyrrha, the daughter of Epimetheus and Pandora, the first woman fashioned by the gods. But when Zeus wished to destroy the men of the Bronze Age, Deucalion by the advice of Prometheus constructed a chest or ark, and having stored in it what was needful he entered into it with his wife. But Zeus poured a great rain from the sky upon the earth and washed down the greater part of Greece, so that all men perished except a few, who flocked to the high mountains near. Then the mountains in Thessaly were parted, and all the world beyond the Isthmus and Peloponnese was overwhelmed. But Deucalion in the ark, floating over the sea for nine days and as many nights, grounded on Parnassus, and there, when the rains ceased, he disembarked and sacrificed to Zeus, the God of Escape. And Zeus sent Hermes to him and allowed him to choose what he would, and he chose men. And at the bidding of Zeus he picked up stones and threw them over his head; and the stones which Deucalion threw became men, and the stones which Pyrrh threw became women. That is why in Greek people are called *laoi* from *laas*, 'a stone.'"

In this form the Greek legend is not older than about the middle of the second century before our era, but in substance it is much more ancient, for the story was told by Hellanicus, a Greek historian of the fifth century B.C., who said that Deucalion's ark drifted not to Parnassus but to Mount Othrys in Thessaly. The other version has the authority of Pindar, who wrote earlier than Hellanicus in the fifth century B.C.,; for the poet speaks of Deucalion and Pyrrha descending from Parnassus and creating the human race afresh out of stones. According to some, the first city which they founded after the great flood was Opus, situated in the fertile Locrian plain between the mountains and the Euboic Gulf. But Deucalion is reported to have dwelt at Cynus, the port of Opus, distant a few miles across the plain; and there his wife's tomb was shown to travellers down to the beginning of our era. Her husband's dust is said to have rested at Athens. According to Aristotle, writing in the fourth century B.C., the ravages of the deluge in Deucalion's time were felt most sensibly "in ancient Hellas, which is the country about Dodona and the river Achelous, for that river has changed its bed in many places. In those days the land was inhabited by the Selli and the people who were then called Greeks (*Graikoi*) but are now named Hellenes." Some people thought that the sanctuary of Zeus at Dodona was founded by Deucalion and Pyrrha, who dwelt among the Molossians of that country. In the fourth century B.C. Plato also mentions, without describing, the flood which took place in the time of Deucalion and Pyrrha, and he represents the Egyptian priests as ridiculing the Greeks for believing that there had been only one deluge, whereas there had been many. The Parian chronicler, who drew up his chronological table in the year 265 B.C., dated Deucalion's flood one thousand two hundred and sixty-five years before his own time; according to this calculation the cataclysm occurred in the year 1539 B.C.

Various places in Greece claimed the honour of having been associated in a particular manner with Deucalion and the great flood. Among the claimants, as might have been expected, were the Athenians, who, pluming themselves on the vast antiquity from which they had inhabited the land of Attica, had no mind to be left out in the cold when it came to a question of Deucalion and the deluge. They annexed him accordingly by the simple expedient of alleging that when the clouds gathered dark on Parnassus and the rain came down in torrents on Lycorea, where Deucalion reigned as king, he fled for safety to Athens, and on his arrival founded a sanctuary of Rainy Zeus, and offered thank-offerings for his escape. In this brief form of the legend there is no mention of a ship, and we seem to be left to infer that the hero escaped on foot. Be that as it may, he is said to have founded the old sanctuary of Olympian Zeus and to have been buried in the city. Down to the second century of our era the local Athenian guides pointed with patriotic pride to the grave of the Greek Noah near the later and far statelier temple of Olympian Zeus, whose ruined columns, towering in solitary grandeur above the modern city, still attract the eye from far, and bear silent but eloquent witness to the glories of ancient Greece.

Nor was this all that the guides had to show in memory of the tremendous cataclysm. Within the great precinct overshadowed by the vast temple of Olympian Zeus they led the curious traveller to a smaller precinct of Olympian Earth, where they pointed to a cleft in the ground a cubit wide. Down that cleft, they assured him, the waters of the deluge ran away, and down it every year they threw cakes of wheaten meal kneaded with honey. These cakes would seem to have been soul-cakes destined for the consumption of the poor souls who perished in the great flood; for we know that a commemoration service or requiem mass was celebrated every year at Athens in their honour. It was called the Festival of the Water-bearing, which suggests that charitable people not only threw cakes but poured water down the cleft in the ground to slake the thirst as well as to stay the hunger of the ghosts in the nether world.

Another place where the great flood was commemorated by a similar ceremony was Hierapolis on the Euphrates. There down to the second century of our era the ancient Semitic deities were worshipped in the old way under a transparent disguise imposed on them, like modern drapery on ancient statues, by the nominally Greek civilization which the conquests of Alexander had spread over the East. Chief among these aboriginal divinities was the great Syrian goddess Astarte, who to her Greek worshippers mas-

queraded under the name of Hera. Lucian has bequeathed to us a
very valuable description of the sanctuary and the strange rites
performed in it. He tells us that according to the general opinion
the sanctuary was founded by Deucalion, in whose time the great
flood took place. This gives Lucian occasion to relate the Greek
story of the deluge, which according to him ran as follows. The
present race of men, he says, are not the first of human kind;
there was another race which perished wholly. We are of the
second breed, which multiplied after the time of Deucalion. As
for the folk before the flood, it is said that they were exceedingly
wicked and lawless; for they neither kept their oaths, nor gave
hospitality to strangers, nor respected suppliants, wherefore the
great calamity befell them. So the fountains of the deep were
opened, and the rain descended in torrents, the rivers swelled, and
the sea spread far over the land, till there was nothing but water,
water everywhere, and all men perished. But Deucalion was the
only man who, by reason of his prudence and piety, survived and
formed the link between the first and the second race of men; and
the way in which he was saved was this. He had a great ark, and
into it he entered with his wives and children; and as he was
entering there came to him pigs, and horses, and lions, and serpents,
and all other land animals, all of them in pairs. He received them
all, and they did him no harm; nay, by God's help there was a
great friendship between them, and they all sailed in one ark so long
as the flood prevailed on the earth. Such, says Lucian, is the
Greek story of Deucalion's deluge; but the people of Hierapolis,
he goes on, tell a marvellous thing. They say that a great chasm
opened in their country, and all the water of the flood ran away
down it. And when that happened, Deucalion built altars and
founded a holy temple of Hera beside the chasm. "I have seen
the chasm," he proceeds, "and a very small one it is under the
temple. Whether it was large of old and has been reduced to its
present size in course of time, I know not, but what I saw is
undoubtedly small. In memory of this legend they perform the
following ceremony: twice a year water is brought from the sea
to the temple. It is brought not by the priests only, but by all
Syria and Arabia, ay and from beyond the Euphrates many men go
to the sea, and all of them bring water. The water is poured into
the chasm, and though the chasm is small yet it receives a mighty
deal of water. In doing this they say that they comply with the
custom which Deucalion instituted in the sanctuary for a memorial
at once of calamity and of mercy." Moreover, at the north gate of
the great temple there stood two tall columns, or rather obelisks,
each about three hundred and sixty feet high; and twice a year a
man used to ascend one of them and remain for seven days in that
airy situation on the top of the obelisk. Opinions differed as to
why he went there, and what he did up aloft. Most people thought
that at that great height he was within hail of the gods in heaven,

who were near enough to hear distinctly the prayer which he offered
on behalf of the whole land of Syria. Others, however, opined
that he clambered up the obelisk to signify how men had ascended
to the tops of mountains and of tall trees in order to escape from the
waters of Deucalion's flood.

In this late Greek version of the deluge legend the resemblances
to the Babylonian version are sufficiently close; and a still nearer
trait is supplied by Plutarch, who says that Deucalion let loose a
dove from the ark in order to judge by its return or its flight whether
the storm still continued or had abated. In this form the Greek
legend of the great flood was unquestionably coloured, if not
moulded, by Semitic influence, whether the colours and the forms
were imported from Israel or from Babylon.

Another city of Asia Minor which appears to have boasted of
its connexion with the great flood was Apamea Cibotos in Phrygia.
The surname of Cibotos, which the city assumed, is the Greek word
for chest or ark; and on coins of the city, minted in the reigns of
Severus, Macrinus, and Philip the Elder, we see the ark floating
on water with two passengers in it, whose figures appear from the
waist upwards; beside the ark two other human figures, one male
and the other female, are represented standing; and lastly, on the
top of the chest are perched two birds, one of them said to be a
raven and the other a dove carrying an olive-branch. As if to
remove all doubt as to the identification of the legend, the name
Noe, the Greek equivalent of Noah, is inscribed on the ark. No
doubt, the two human figures represent Noah and his wife twice
over, first in the ark, and afterwards outside of it. These coin
types prove unquestionably that in the third century of our era
the people of Apamea were acquainted with the Hebrew tradition
of the Noachian deluge in the form in which the story is narrated
in the Book of Genesis. They may easily have learned it from their
Jewish fellow-citizens, who in the first century before our era were
so numerous or so wealthy that on one occasion they contributed no
less than a hundred pounds weight of gold to be sent as an offering
to Jerusalem. Whether at Apamea the tradition of the deluge was
purely Jewish in origin, or whether it was grafted upon an old
native legend of a great flood, is a question on which scholars are
not agreed.

Though the deluge associated with the name of Deucalion was
the most familiar and famous, it was not the only one recorded by
Greek tradition. Learned men, indeed, distinguished between three
such great catastrophes, which had befallen the world at different
epochs. The first, we are told, took place in the time of Ogyges,
the second in the time of Deucalion, and the third in the time of
Dardanus. Ogyges or Ogygus, as the name is also spelled, is said
to have founded and reigned over Thebes in Boeotia, which, according to the learned Varro, was the oldest city in Greece, having been
built in antediluvian times before the earliest of all the floods.

The connexion of Ogyges with Boeotia in general and with Thebes in particular is further vouched for by the name Ogygian which was bestowed on the land, on the city, and on one of its gates. Varro tells us that the Boeotian Thebes was built about two thousand one hundred years before the time when he was writing, which was in or about the year 36 B.C.; and as the deluge, according to him, took place in the lifetime of Ogyges but after he had founded Thebes, we infer that in Varro's opinion the great flood occurred in or soon after the year 2136 B.C. According to the Church historian Eusebius, the great flood in the time of Ogyges occurred about two thousand two hundred years after the Noachian deluge and two hundred and fifty years before the similar catastrophe in the days of Deucalion. It would seem indeed to have been a point of honour with the early Christians to claim for the flood recorded in their sacred books an antiquity far more venerable than that of any flood described in mere profane writings. The Christian chronicler Julius Africanus depresses Ogyges from the age of Noah to that of Moses; and Isidore, the learned bishop of Seville at the beginning of the seventh century, heads his list of floods with the Noachian deluge, while the second and third places in order of time are assigned to the floods of Ogyges and Deucalion respectively; according to him, Ogyges was a contemporary of the patriarch Jacob, while Deucalion lived in the days of Moses. The bishop was, so far as I am aware, the first of many writers who have appealed to fossil shells imbedded in remote mountains as witnesses to the truth of the Noachian tradition.

If Ogyges was originally, as seems probable, a Boeotian rather than an Attic hero, the story of the deluge in his time may well have been suggested by the vicissitudes of the Copaic Lake which formerly occupied a large part of Central Boeotia. For, having no outlet above ground, the lake depended for its drainage entirely on subterranean passages or chasms which the water had hollowed out for itself in the course of ages through the limestone rock, and according as these passages were clogged or cleared the level of the lake rose or fell. In no lake, perhaps, have the annual changes been more regular and marked than in the Copaic; for while in winter it was a reedy mere, the haunt of thousands of wild fowl, in summer it was a more or less marshy plain, where cattle browsed and crops were sown and reaped. But at all times the water of the lake has been liable to be raised above or depressed below its customary level by unusually heavy or scanty rainfall in winter or by the accidental clogging or opening of the chasms. As we read in ancient authors of drowned cities on the margin of the lake, so a modern traveller tells of villagers forced to flee before the rising flood, and of vineyards and corn-fields seen under water. One such inundation, more extensive and destructive than any of its predecessors, may have been associated ever after with the name of Ogyges.

The theory which would explain the great flood of Ogyges by an extraordinary inundation of the Copaic Lake, is to some extent supported by an Arcadian parallel. We have seen that in Greek legend the third great deluge was associated with the name of Dardanus. Now according to one account, Dardanus at first reigned as a king in Arcadia, but was driven out of the country by a great flood, which submerged the lowlands and rendered them for a long time unfit for cultivation. The inhabitants retreated to the mountains, and for a while made shift to live as best they might on such food as they could procure; but at last, concluding that the land left by the water was not sufficient to support them all, they resolved to part; some of them remained in the country with Dimas, son of Dardanus, for their king; while the rest emigrated under the leadership of Dardanus himself to the island of Samothrace. According to a Greek tradition, which the Roman Varro accepted, the birthplace of Dardanus was Pheneus in North Arcadia. The place is highly significant, for, if we except the Copaic area, no valley in Greece is known to have been from antiquity subject to inundations on so vast a scale and for such long periods as the valley of Pheneus. The natural conditions in the two regions are substantially alike. Both are basins in a limestone country without any outflow above ground: both receive the rain water which pours into them from the surrounding mountains: both are drained by subterranean channels which the water has worn or which earthquakes have opened through the rock; and whenever these outlets are silted up or otherwise closed, what at other times is a plain becomes converted for the time being into a lake. But with these substantial resemblances are combined some striking differences between the two landscapes. For while the Copaic basin is a vast stretch of level ground little above sea-level and bounded only by low cliffs or gentle slopes, the basin of Pheneus is a narrow upland valley closely shut in on every side by steep frowning mountains, their upper slopes clothed with dark pine woods and their lofty summits capped with snow for many months of the year. The river which drains the basin through an underground channel is the Ladon, the most romantically beautiful of all the rivers of Greece. Milton's fancy dwelt on "sanded Ladon's lilied banks"; even the prosaic Pausanias exclaimed that there was no fairer river either in Greece or in foreign lands; and among the memories which I brought back from Greece I recall none with more delight than those of the days I spent in tracing the river from its birthplace in the lovely lake, first to its springs on the far side of the mountain, and then down the deep wooded gorge through which it hurries, brawling and tumbling over rocks in sheets of greenish-white foam, to join the sacred Alpheus. Now the passage by which the Ladon makes its way underground from the valley of Pheneus has been from time to time blocked by an earthquake, with the result that the river has ceased to flow. When I was at the springs of the Ladon in 1895, I learned from a peasant on the spot that three years before, after a violent shock of earthquake, the water ceased to run for three hours, the chasm at the bottom of the pool was exposed, and fish were seen lying on the dry ground. After three hours the spring began to flow a little, and three days later there was a loud explosion, and the water burst forth in immense volume. Similar stoppages of the river have been reported both in ancient and modern times; and whenever the obstruction has been permanent, the valley of Pheneus has been occupied by a lake varying in extent and depth with the more or less complete stoppage of the subterranean outlet. According to Pliny there had been down to this day five changes in the condition of the valley from wet to dry and from dry to wet, all of them caused by earthquakes. In Plutarch's time the flood rose so high that the whole valley was under water, which pious folk attributed to the somewhat belated wrath of Apollo at Hercules, who had stolen the god's prophetic tripod from Delphi and carried it off to Pheneus about a thousand years before. However, later in the same century the waters had again subsided, for the Greek traveller Pausanias found the bottom of the valley to be dry land, and knew of the former existence of the lake only by tradition.

In a valley which has thus suffered so many alternations between wet and dry, between a broad lake of sea-blue water and broad acres of yellow corn, the traditions of great floods cannot be lightly dismissed; on the contrary, everything combines to confirm their probability. The story, therefore, that Dardanus, a native of Pheneus, was compelled to emigrate by a great inundation which swamped the lowlands, drowned the fields, and drove the inhabitants to the upper slopes of the mountains, may well rest on a solid foundation of fact. And the same may be true of the flood recorded by Pausanias, which rose and submerged the ancient city of Pheneus at the northern end of the lake.

From his home in the highlands of Arcadia, the emigrant Dardanus is said to have made his way to the island of Samothrace. According to one account, he floated thither on a raft; but according to another version of the legend, the great flood overtook him, not in Arcadia, but in Samothrace, and he escaped on an inflated skin, drifting on the face of the waters till he landed on Mount Ida, where he founded Dardania or Troy. Certainly, the natives of Samothrace, who were great sticklers for their antiquity, claimed to have had a deluge of their own before any other nation on earth. They said that the sea rose and covered a great part of the flat land in their island, and that the survivors retreated to the lofty mountains which still render Samothrace one of the most conspicuous features in the northern Aegean and are plainly visible in clear weather from Troy. As the sea still pursued them in their retreat, they prayed to the goods to deliver them, and on being saved they set up landmarks of their salvation all round the island and built altars on which they continued to sacrifice down to later ages. And many centuries after the great flood fishermen still occasionally drew up in their nets the stone capitals of columns, which told of cities drowned in the depths of the sea. The cause which the Samothracians alleged for the inundation were very remarkable. The catastrophe happened, according to them, not through a heavy fall of rain, but through a sudden and extraordinary rising of the sea occasioned by the bursting of the barriers which till then had divided the Black Sea from the Mediterranean. At that time the enormous volume of water dammed up behind these barriers broke bounds, and cleaving for itself a passage through the opposing land created the straits which are now known as the Bosphorus and the Dardanelles, through which the waters of the Black Sea have ever since flowed into the Mediterranean. When the tremendous torrent first rushed through the new opening in the dam, it washed over a great part of the coast of Asia, as well as the flat lands of Samothrace.

Now this Samothracian tradition is to some extent confirmed by modern geology. "At no very distant period," says Huxley, "the land of Asia Minor was continuous with that of Europe, across the present site of the Bosphorus, forming a barrier several hundred feet high, which dammed up the waters of the Black Sea. A vast extent of Eastern Europe and of Western Central Asia thus became a huge reservoir, the lowest part of the lip of which was probably situated somewhat more than 200 feet above the sea-level, along the present southern watershed of the Obi, which flows into the Arctic Ocean. Into this basin, the largest rivers of Europe, such as the Danube and the Volga, and what were then great rivers of Asia, the Oxus and Jaxartes, with all the intermediate affluents, poured their waters. In addition, it received the overflow of Lake Balkash, then much larger; and, probably, that of the inland sea of Mongolia. At that time, the level of the Sea of Aral stood at least 60 feet higher than it does at present. Instead of the separate Black, Caspian, and Aral seas, there was one vast Ponto-Aralian Mediterranean, which must have been prolonged into arms and fiords along the lower valleys of the Danube, and the Volga (in the course of which Caspian shells are now found as far as the Kama), the Ural, and the other affluent rivers—while it seems to have sent its overflow, northward, through the present basin of the Obi." This enormous reservoir or vast inland sea, bounded and held up by a high natural dam joining Asia Minor to the Balkan Peninsula, appears to have existed down to the Pleistocene period; and the erosion of the Dardanelles, by which the pent-up waters at last found their way into the Mediterranean, is believed to have taken place towards the end of the Pleistocene period or later. But man is now known for certain to have inhabited Europe in the Pleistocene period; some hold that he inhabited it in the Pliocene or even the Miocene period. Hence it seems possible that the inhabitants of Eastern Europe should have preserved a traditional memory of the vast inland Ponto-Aralian sea and of its partial desiccation through the piercing of the dam which divided it from the Mediterranean, in other words, through the opening of the Bosphorous and the Dardanelles. If that were so, the Samothracian traditions might be allowed to contain a large element of historical truth in regard to the causes assigned for the catastrophe.

On the other hand, geology seems to lend no support to the tradition of the catastrophe itself. For the evidence tends to prove that the strait of the Dardanelles was not opened suddenly, like the bursting of a dam, either by the pressure of the water or the shock of an earthquake, but that on the contrary it was created gradually by a slow process of erosion which must have lasted for many centuries or even thousands of years; for the strait "is bounded by undisturbed Pleistocene strata forty feet thick, through which, to all appearance, the present passage has been quietly cut." Thus the lowering of the level of the Ponto-Aralian sea to that of the Mediterranean can hardly have been sudden and catastrophic, accompanied by a vast inundation of the Asiatic and European coasts; more probably it was effected so slowly and gradually that the total amount accomplished even in a generation would be imperceptible to ordinary observers or even to close observers unprovided with instruments of precision. Hence, instead of assuming that Samothracian tradition preserved a real memory of a widespread inundation consequent on the opening of the Dardanelles, it seems safer to suppose that this story of a great flood is nothing but the guess of some early philosopher, who rightly divined the origin of the straits without being able to picture to himself the extreme slowness of the process by which nature had excavated them. As a matter of fact, the eminent physical philosopher Strato, who succeeded Theophrastus as head of the Peripatetic school in 287 B.C., actually maintained this view on purely theoretical grounds, not alleging it as a tradition which had been handed down from antiquity, but arguing in its favour from his observations of the natural features of the Black Sea. He pointed to the vast quantities of mud annually washed down by great rivers into the Euxine, and he inferred that but for the outlet of the Bosphorus the basin of that sea would in time be silted up. Further, he conjectured that in former times the same rivers had forced for themselves a passage through the Bosphorus, allowing their collected waters to escape first to the Propontis, and then from it through the Dardanelles to the Mediterranean. Similarly he thought that the Mediterranean had been of old an inland sea, and that its junction with the Atlantic was effected by the dammed-up water cutting for itself an opening through the Straits of Gibraltar. Accordingly we may conclude that the cause which the Samothracians alleged for the great flood was derived from an ingenious speculation rather than from an ancient tradition.

There are some grounds for thinking that the flood story which the Greeks associated with the names of Deucalion and Pyrrha may in like manner have been, not so much a reminiscence of a real event, as an inference founded on the observation of certain physical facts. We have seen that in one account the mountains of Thessaly are said to have been parted by the deluge in Deucalion's time, and that in another account the ark, with Deucalion in it, is reported to have drifted to Mount Othrys in Thessaly. These references seem to indicate Thessaly as the original seat of the legend; and the indication is greatly strengthened by the view which the ancients took of the causes that had moulded the natural features of the country. Thus Herodotus relates a tradition that in ancient times Thessaly was a great lake or inland sea, shut in on all sides by the lofty mountains of Ossa and Pelion, Olympus, Pindus, and Othrys, through which there was as yet no opening to allow the pent-up waters of the rivers to escape. Afterwards, according to the Thessalians, the sea-god Poseidon, who causes earthquakes, made an outlet for the lake through the mountains, by cleaving the narrow gorge of Tempe, through which the river Peneus has ever since drained the Thessalian plain. The pious historian intimates his belief in the truth of this local tradition. "Whoever believes," says he, "that Poseidon shakes the earth, and that chasms caused by earthquakes are his handiwork, would say, on seeing the gorge of the Peneus, that Poseidon had made it. For the separation of the mountains, it seems to me, is certainly the effect of an earthquake." The view of the father of history was substantially accepted by later writers of antiquity, though one of them would attribute the creation of the gorge and the drainage of the lake to the hero Hercules, among whose beneficent labours for the good of mankind the construction of waterworks on a gigantic scale was commonly reckoned. More cautious or more philosophical authors contented themselves with referring the origin of the defile to a simple earthquake, without expressing any opinion as to the god or hero who may have set the tremendous disturbance in motion.

Yet we need not wonder that popular opinion in this matter should incline to the theory of divine or heroic agency, for in truth the natural features of the pass of Tempe are well fitted to impress the mind with a religious awe, with a sense of vast primordial forces which, by the gigantic scale of their operations, present an overwhelming contrast to the puny labours of man. The traveller who descends at morning into the deep gorge from the west, may see, far above him, the snows of Olympus flushed with a golden glow under the beams of the rising sun, but as he pursues the path downwards the summits of the mountains disappear from view, and he is confronted on either hand only by a stupendous wall of mighty precipices shooting up in prodigious grandeur and approaching each other in some places so near that they almost seem to meet, barely leaving room for the road and river at their foot, and for a strip of blue sky overhead. The cliffs on the side of Olympus, which the traveller has constantly before his eyes, since the road runs on the south or right bank of the river, are indeed the most magnificent and striking in Greece, and in rainy weather they are rendered still more impressive by the waterfalls that pour down their sides to swell the smooth and steady current of the stream. The grandeur of the scenery culminates about the middle of the pass, where an enormous crag rears its colossal form high in air, its soaring summit crowned with the ruins of a Roman castle. Yet the sublimity of the landscape is tempered and softened by the richness and verdure of the vegetation. In some parts of the defile the cliffs recede sufficiently to leave little grassy flats at their foot, where thickest of evergreens—the laurel, the myrtle, the wild olive, the arbutus, the agnus castus—are festooned with wild vines and ivy, and variegated with the crimson bloom of the oleander and the yellow gold of the jasmine and laburnum, while the air is perfumed by the luscious odours of masses of aromatic plants and flowers. Even in the narrowest places the river bank is overshadowed by spreading plane-trees, which stretch their roots and dip their pendant boughs into the stream, their dense foliage forming so thick a screen as almost to shut out the sun. The scarred and fissured fronts of the huge cliffs themselves are tufted with dwarf oaks and shrubs, wherever these can find a footing, their verdure contrasting vividly with the bare white face of the limestone rock; while breaks here and there in the mountain wall open up vistas of forests of great oaks and dark firs mantling the steep declivities. The overarching shade and soft luxuriance of the vegetation strike the traveller all the more by contrast if he comes to the glen in hot summer weather after toiling through the dusty, sultry plains of Thessaly, without a tree to protect him from the fierce rays of the southern sun, without a breeze to cool his brow, and with little variety of hill and dale to relieve the dull monotony of the landscape. No wonder that speculation should have early busied itself with the origin of this grand and beautiful ravine, and that primitive religion and science alike should have ascribed it to some great primeval cataslysm, some sudden and tremendous outburst of volcanic energy, rather than to its true cause, the gradual and age-long erosion of water.

Hence we may with some confidence conclude that the cleft in the Thessalian mountains, which is said to have been rent by Deucalion's flood, was no other than the gorge of Tempe. Indeed, without being very rash, we may perhaps go farther and conjecture that the story of the flood itself was suggested by the desire to explain the origin of the deep and narrow defile. For once men had pictured to themselves a great lake dammed in by the circle of the Thessalian mountains, the thought would naturally occur to them, what a vast inundation must have followed the bursting of the dam, when the released water, rushing in a torrent through the newly opened sluice, swept over the subjacent lowlands carrying havoc and devastation in its train! If there is any truth in this conjecture, the Thessalian story of Deucalion's flood and the Samothracian story of the flood of Dardanus stood exactly on the same footing: both were mere inferences drawn from the facts of physical geography: neither of them contained any reminiscences of actual events. In short, both were what Sir Edward Tylor has called myths of observation rather than historical traditions.

§ 5. *Ancient Indian Stories of a Great Flood.*—No legend of a great flood is to be found in the Vedic hymns, the most ancient literary monuments of India, which appear to have been composed at various dates between 1500 and 1000 B.C., while the Aryans were still settled in the Punjab and had not yet spread eastward into the valley of the Ganges. But in the later Sanscrit literature a well-marked story of a deluge repeatedly occurs in forms which combine a general resemblance with some variations of detail. It may suffice to cite the oldest known version of the tale, which meets us in the *Satapatha Brahmana,* an important prose treatise on sacred ritual, which is believed to have been written not long before the rise of Buddhism, and therefore not later than the sixth century before Christ. The Aryans then occupied the upper valley of the Ganges as well as the valley of the Indus; but they were probably as yet little affected by the ancient civilization of Western Asia and Greece. Certainly the great influx of Greek ideas and Greek art came centuries later with Alexander's invasion in 326 B.C. As related in the *Satapatha Brahmana* the story of the great flood runs as follows:—

"In the morning they brought to Manu water for washing, just as now also they are wont to bring water for washing the hands. When he was washing himself, a fish came into his hands. It spake to him the word, 'Rear me, I will save thee!' 'Wherefrom wilt thou save me?' 'A flood will carry away all these creatures: from that I will save thee!' 'How am I to rear thee?' It said, 'As long as we are small, there is great destruction for us: fish devours fish. Thou wilt first keep me in a jar. When I outgrow that, thou wilt dig a pit and keep me in it. When I outgrow that, thou wilt take me down to the sea, for then I shall be beyond destruction.' It soon became a *ghasha* (a large fish); for that grows largest of all fish. Thereupon it said, "In such and such a year that flood will come. Thou shalt then attend to me by preparing a ship; and when the flood has risen thou shalt enter into the ship, and I will save thee from it.' After he had reared it in this way, he took it down to the sea. And in the same year which the fish had indicated to him, he attended to the advice of the fish by preparing a ship; and when the flood had risen, he entered into the ship. The fish then swam up to him, and to its horn he tied the rope of the ship, and by that means he passed swiftly up to yonder northern mountain. It then said, 'I have saved thee. Fasten the ship to a tree; but let not the water cut thee off, whilst thou art on the mountain. As the water subsides, thou mayest gradually descend!' Accordingly he gradually descended, and hence that slope of the northern mountains is called 'Manu's descent.' The flood then swept away all these creatures, and Manu alone remained here.

"Being desirous of offspring, he engaged in worshipping and austerities. During this time he also performed a *paka*-sacrifice: he offered up in the waters clarified butter, sour milk, whey, and curds. Thence a woman was produced in a year: becoming quite solid she rose; clarified butter gathered in her footprint. Mitra and Varuna met her. They said to her, 'Who art thou?' 'Manu's daughter,' she replied. 'Say thou art ours,' they said. 'No,' she said, 'I am the daughter of him who begat me.' They desired to have a share in her. She either agreed or did not agree, but passed by them. She came to Manu. Manu said to her, 'Who art thou?' 'Thy daughter,' she replied. 'How, illustrious one, art thou my daughter?' he asked. She replied, 'Those offerings of clarified butter, sour milk, whey, and curds, which thou madest in the waters, with them thou hast begotten me. I am the blessing: make use of me at the sacrifice! If thou wilt make use of me at the sacrifice, thou wilt become rich in offspring and cattle. Whatever blessing thou shalt invoke through me, all that shall be granted to thee!' He accordingly made use of her as the benediction in the middle of the sacrifice; for what is intermediate between the fore-offerings and after-offerings, is the middle of the sacrifice. With her he went on worshipping and performing austerities, wishing for offspring. Through her he generated this race, which is this race of Manu; and whatever blessing he invoked through her, all that was granted to him."

§ 6. *Modern Indian Stories of a Great Flood.*—The Bhils, a wild jungle tribe of Central India, relate that once upon a time a pious man (*dhobi*), who used to wash his clothes in a river, was warned by a fish of the approach of a great deluge. This fish informed him that, out of gratitude for his humanity in always feeding the fish, he had come to give him this warning, and to urge him to prepare a large box in which he might escape. The pious man accordingly made ready the box and embarked in it with his sister and a cock. After the deluge Rama sent out his messenger to inquire into the state of affairs. The messenger heard the crowing of the cock and so discovered the box. Thereupon Rama had the box brought before him, and asked the man who he was and how he had escaped. The man told his tale. Then Rama made him face in turn north, east, and west, and swear that the woman with him was his sister. The man stuck to it that she was indeed his sister. Rama next turned him to the south, whereupon the man contradicted his former statement and said that the woman was his wife. After that, Rama inquired of him who it was that told him to escape, and on learning that it was the fish, he at once caused the fish's tongue to be cut out for his pains; so that sort of fish has been tongueless ever since. Having executed this judgment on the fish for blabbing, Rama ordered the man to repeople the devastated world. Accordingly the man married his sister and had by her seven sons and seven daughters. The firstborn received from Rama the present of a horse, but, being unable to ride, he left the animal in the plain and went into the forest to cut wood. So he became a woodman, and woodmen his descendants the Bhils have been from that day to this. In this Bhil story the warning of the coming flood given by the fish to its human benefactor resembles the corresponding incident in the Sanscrit story of the flood too closely to be independent. It may be questioned whether the Bhils borrowed the story from the Aryan invaders, or whether on the contrary the Aryans may not have learned it from the aborigines whom they encountered in their progress through the country. In favour of the latter view it may be pointed out that the story of the flood does not occur in the most ancient Sanscrit literature, but only appears in books written long after the settlement of the Aryans in India.

The Kamars, a small Dravidian tribe of the Raipur District and adjoining States, in the Central Provinces of India, tell the following story of a great flood. They say that in the beginning God created a man and woman, to whom in their old age two children were born, a boy and a girl. But God sent a deluge over the world in order to drown a jackal which had angered him. The old couple heard of the coming deluge, so they shut up their children in a hollow piece of wood with provision of food to last them till the flood should subside. Then they closed up the trunk, and the deluge came and lasted for twelve years. The old couple and all other living things on earth were drowned, but the trunk floated on the face of the waters. After twelve years God created two birds and sent them to see whether his enemy the jackal had been drowned. The birds flew over all the corners of the world, and they saw nothing but a log of wood floating on the surface of the water. They perched on it, and soon heard low and feeble voices coming from inside the log. It was the children saying to each other that they had only provisions for three days left. So the birds flew away and told God, who then caused the flood to subside, and taking out the children from the log of wood he heard their story. Thereupon he brought them up, and in due time they were married, and God gave the name of a different caste to every child who was born to them, and from them all the inhabitants of the world are descended. In this story the incident of the two birds suggest a reminiscence of the raven and the dove in the Biblical legend, which may have reached the Kamars through missionary influence.

Again, the Anals of Assam say that once upon a time the whole world was flooded. All the people were drowned except one man and one woman, who ran to the highest peak of the Leng hill, where they climbed up a high tree and hid themselves among the branches. The tree grew near a large pond, which was as clear as the eye of a crow. They spent the night perched on the tree, and in the morning, what was their astonishment to find that they had been changed into a tiger and a tigress! Seeing the sad plight of the world, the Creator, whose name is Pathian, sent a man and a woman from a cave on a hill to repeople the drowned world. But on emerging from the cave, the couple were terrified at the sight of the huge tiger and tigress, and they said to the Creator, "O Father, you have sent us to repeople the world, but we do not think that we shall be able to carry out your intention, as the whole world is under water, and the only spot on which we could make a place of rest is occupied by two ferocious beasts, which are waiting to devour us ; give us strength to slay these animals." After that, they killed the tigers, and lived happily, and begat many sons and daughters, and from them the drowned world was repeopled.

§ 7. *Stories of a Great Flood in Eastern Asia.*—According to the Karens of Burma the earth was of old deluged with water, and two brothers saved themselves from the flood on a raft. The waters rose till they reached to heaven, when the younger brother saw a mango-tree hanging down from the celestial vault. With great presence of mind he clambored up it and ate of the fruit, but the flood, suddenly subsiding, left him suspended in the tree. Here the narrative breaks off abruptly, and we are left to conjecture how he extricated himself from his perilous position. The Chingpaws or Singphos of Upper Burma have a tradition of a great flood. They say that when the deluge came, a man Pawpaw Nan-chaung and his sister Chang-hko saved themselves in a large boat. They had with them nine cocks and nine needles. After some days of rain and storm they threw overboard one cock and one needle to see whether the waters were falling. But the cock did not crow and the needle was not heard to strike bottom. They did the same thing day after day, but with no better result, till at last on the ninth day the last cock crew and the last needle was heard to strike on a rock. Soon after the brother and sister were able to leave their boat, and they wandered about till they came to a cave inhabited by two elves or fairies (*nats*), a male and a female. The elves bade them stay and make themselves useful in clearing the jungle, tilling the ground, hewing wood, and drawing water. The brother and sister did so, and soon after the sister gave birth to a child. While the parents were away at work, the old elfin woman, who was a witch, used to mind the baby ; and whenever the infant squalled, the horrid wretch would threaten, if it did not stop bawling, to make mincement of it at a place where nine roads met. The poor child did not understand the dreadful threat and persisted in giving tongue, till one day the old witch in a fury snatched it up, hurried it to the meeting-place of nine roads, and there hewed it in pieces, and sprinkled the blood and strewed the

bits all over the roads and the country round about. But some of
the titbits she carried back to her cave and made into a savoury
curry. Moreover, she put a block of wood into the baby's empty
cradle. And when the mother came back from her work in the
evening and asked for her child, the witch said, "It is asleep. Eat
your rice." So the mother ate the rice and curry, and then went
to the cradle, but in it she found nothing but a block of wood.
When she asked the witch where the child was, the witch replied
tartly, "You have eaten it." The poor mother fled from the house,
and at the cross-roads she wailed aloud and cried to the Great
Spirit to give her back her child or avenge its death. The Great
Spirit appeared to her and said, "I cannot piece your baby together
again, but instead I will make you the mother of all nations of men."
And then from one road there sprang up the Shans, from another the
Chinese, from others the Burmese, and the Bengales, and all the
races of mankind; and the bereaved mother claimed them all as her
children, because they all sprang from the scattered fragments of her
murdered babe.

The Bahnars, a primitive tribe of Cochin China, tell how once
on a time the kite quarrelled with the crab, and pecked the crab's
skull so hard that he made a hole in it, which may be seen down to
this very day. To avenge this injury to his skull, the crab caused
the sea and the rivers to swell till the waters reached the sky, and
all living beings perished except two, a brother and a sister, who were
saved in a huge chest. They took with them into the chest a pair of
every sort of animal, shut the lid tight, and floated on the waters
for seven days and seven nights. Then the brother heard a cock
crowing outside, for the bird had been sent by the spirits to let our
ancestors know that the flood had abated, and that they could come
forth from the chest. So the brother let all the birds fly away, then
he let loose the animals, and last of all he and his sister walked out
on the dry land. They did not know how they were to live, for
they had eaten up all the rice that was stored in the chest. However,
a black ant brought them two grains of rice: the brother planted
them, and next morning the plain was covered with a rich crop. So
the brother and sister were saved.

The Benua-Jakun, a primitive aboriginal tribe of the Malay
Peninsula, in the State of Johor, say that the ground on which we
stand is not solid, but is merely a skin covering an abyss of water.
In ancient times Pirman, that is the deity, broke up this skin, so
that the world was drowned and destroyed by a great flood. However, Pirman had created a man and a woman and put them in a
ship of *pulai* wood, which was completely covered over and had no
opening. In this ship the pair floated and tossed about for a time,
till at last the vessel came to rest, and the man and woman, nibbling
their way through its side, emerged on dry ground and beheld this
our world stretching away on all sides to the horizon. At first all
was very dark, for there was neither morning nor evening, because

the sun had not yet been created. When it grew light, they saw seven small shrubs of rhododendron and seven clumps of the grass called sambau. They said one to another, "Alas, in what a sad plight are we, without either children or grandchildren!" But some time afterwards the woman conceived in the calves of her legs, and from her right calf came forth a male, and from her left calf came forth a female. That is why the offspring of the same womb may not marry. All mankind are the descendants of the two children of the first pair.

The legend of a great flood plays an important part in the traditionary lore of the Lolos, an aboriginal race who occupy the almost impregnable mountain fastnesses of Yunnan and other provinces of South-western China, where they have succeeded in maintaining their independence against the encroachments of the Chinese. They are so far from being savages that they have even invented a mode of writing, pictographic in origin, in which they have recorded their legends, songs, genealogies, and religious ritual. Their manuscripts, copied and recopied, have been handed down from generation to generation. The Lolos believe in patriarchs who now live in the sky, but who formerly dwelt on earth, where they attained to the great ages of six hundred and sixty and even nine hundred and ninety years, thereby surpassing Methuselah himself in longevity. Each family, embracing the persons united by a common surname, pays its devotions to a particular patriarch. The most famous of these legendary personages is a certain Tse-gu-dzih, who enjoys many of the attributes of divinity. He it was who brought death into the world by opening the fatal box which contained the seeds of mortality; and he too it was who caused the deluge. The catastrophe happened thus. Men were wicked, and Tse-gu-dzih sent down a messenger to them on earth, asking for some flesh and blood from a mortal. No one would give them except only one man, Du-mu by name. So Tse-gu-dzih in wrath locked the rain-gates, and the water mounted to the sky. But Du-mu, who complied with the divine injunction, was saved, together with his four sons, in a log hollowed out of a *Pieris* tree; and with them in the log were likewise saved otters, wild ducks, and lampreys. From his four sons are descended the civilized peoples who can write, such as the Chinese and the Lolos. But the ignorant races of the world are the descendants of the wooden figures whom Du-mu constructed after the deluge in order to repeople the drowned earth. To this day the ancestral tablets, which the Lolos worship on set days of the year and on all the important occasions of life, are made out of the same sort of tree as that in which their great forefather found safety from the waters of the deluge; and nearly all the Lolo legends begin with some reference to him or to the great flood. In considering the origin of this flood legend it should be mentioned that the Lolos generally keep a Sabbath of rest every sixth day, when ploughing is forbidden, and in some places women are not allowed to sew or wash clothes. Taken together with this custom, the Lolo traditions of the patriarchs and of the flood appear to betray Christian influence, and Mr. A. Henry may well be right in referring them all to the teaching of Nestorian missionaries; for Nestorian churches existed in Yunnan in the thirteenth century when Marco Polo travelled in the country, and the Nestorian Alopen is said to have arrived in China as early as A.D. 635.

The Kamchadales have a tradition of a great flood which covered the whole land in the early days of the world. A remnant of the people saved themselves on large rafts made of tree-trunks bound together; on these they loaded their property and provisions, and on these they drifted about, dropping stones tied to straps instead of anchors in order to prevent the flood from sweeping them away out to sea. When at last the water of the deluge sank, it left the people and their rafts stranded high and dry on the tops of the mountains.

In a Chinese Encyclopaedia there occurs the following passage: "*Eastern Tartary.*—In traveling from the shore of the Eastern Sea towards Che-lu, neither brooks nor ponds are met with in the country, although it is intersected by mountains and valleys. Nevertheless there are found in the sand very far away from the sea, oyster-shells and the shields of crabs. The tradition of the Mongols who inhabit the country is, that it has been said from time immemorial that in remote antiquity the waters of the deluge flooded the district, and when they retired, the places where they had been made their appearance covered with sand."

§ 8. *Stories of a Great Flood in the Indian Archipelago.*—The Bataks of Sumatra say that, when the earth grew old and dirty, the Creator, whom they called Debata, sent a great flood to destroy every living thing. The last human pair had taken refuge on the top of the highest mountain, and the waters of the deluge had already reached to their knees, when the Lord of All repented of his resolution to make an end of mankind. So he took a clod of earth, kneaded it into shape, tied it to a thread, and laid it on the rising flood, and the last pair stepped on it and were saved. As the descendants of the couple multiplied, the clod increased in size till it became the earth which we all inhabit at this day.

The natives of Engano, an island to the west of Sumatra, have also their story of a great flood. Once on a time, they say, the tide rose so high that it overflowed the island and every living being was drowned, except one woman. She owed her preservation to the fortunate circumstance that, as she drifted along on the tide, her hair caught in a thorny tree, to which she was thus enabled to cling. When the flood sank, she came down from the tree, and saw with sorrow that she was left all alone in the world. Beginning to feel the pangs of hunger, she wandered inland in the search for food, but finding nothing to eat, she returned disconsolately to the beach, where she hoped to catch fish. A fish, indeed, she saw; but when she tried to catch it, the creature glided into one of the corpses that were floating on the water or weltering on the shore. Not to be balked, the woman picked up a stone and struck the corpse a smart blow therewith. But the fish leaped from its hiding-place and made off in the direction of the interior. The woman followed, but hardly had she taken a few steps when, to her great surprise, she met a living man. When she asked him what he did there, seeing that she herself was the sole survivor of the flood, he answered that somebody had knocked on his dead body, and that in consequence he had returned to life. The woman now related to him her experiences, and together they resolved to try whether they could not restore all the other dead to life in like manner by knocking on their corpses with stones. No sooner said than done. The drowned men and women revived under the knocks, and thus was the island repeopled after the great flood.

The Ibans or Sea Dyaks of Sarawak, in Borneo, are fond of telling a story which relates how the present race of men survived a great deluge, and how their ancestress discovered the art of making fire. The story runs thus. Once upon a time some Dyak women went to gather young bamboo shoots for food. Having got them, they walked through the jungle till they came to what they took to be a great fallen tree. So they sat down on it and began to pare the bamboo shoots, when to their astonishment the trunk of the tree exuded drops of blood at every cut of their knives. Just then up came some men, who saw at once that what the women were sitting on was not a tree but a gigantic boa-constrictor in a state of torpor. They soon killed the serpent, cut it up, and carried the flesh home to eat. While they were busy frying the pieces, strange noises were heard to issue from the frying-pan, and a torrential rain began to fall and never ceased falling till all the hills, except the highest were submerged and the world was drowned, all because these wicked men had killed and fried the serpent. Men and animals all perished in the flood, except one woman, a dog, a rat, and a few small creatures, who fled to the top of a very high mountain. There, seeking shelter from the pouring rain, the woman noticed that the dog had found a warm place under a creeper; for the creeper was swaying to and fro in the wind and was warmed by rubbing against the trunk of the tree. She took the hint, and rubbing the creeper hard against a piece of wood she produced fire for the first time. That is how the art of making fire by means of the fire-drill was discovered after the great flood. Having no husband the woman took the fire-drill for her mate, and by its help she gave birth to a son called Simpang-impang, who, as his name implies, was but half a man, since he had only one arm, one leg, one eye, one ear, one cheek, half a body, and half a nose. These natural defects gave great offence to his playmates the animals, and at last he was able to supply them by striking a bargain with the Spirit of the Wind, who had carried off some rice which Simpang-impang had spread out to dry. At first, when Simpang-impang demanded compensation for this injury, the Spirit of the Wind flatly refused to pay him a farthing; but being vanquished in a series of contests with Simpang-impang, he finally consented, instead of paying him in gongs or other valuables, of which indeed he had none, to make a whole man of him by supplying him with the missing parts and members. Simpang-impang gladly accepted the proposal, and that is why mankind have been provided with the usual number of arms and legs ever since.

Another Dyak version of the story relates how, when the flood began, a certain man called Trow made a boat out of a large wooden mortar, which had hitherto served for pounding rice. In this vessel he embarked with his wife, a dog, a pig, a fowl, a cat, and other live creatures, and so launched out on the deep. The crazy ship outrode the storm, and when the flood had subsided, Trow and his wife and the animals disembarked. How to repeople the earth after the destruction of nearly the entire human race was now the problem which confronted Trow; and in order to grapple with it he had recourse to polygamy, fashioning for himself new wives out of a stone, a log, and anything else that came to hand. So he soon had a large and flourishing family, who learned to till the ground and became the ancestors of various Dyak tribes.

The Bare'e-speaking Toradjas of Central Celebes also tell of a flood which once covered the highest mountains, all but the summit of Mount Wawom Pebato, and in proof of their story they point to the sea-shells which are to be found on the tops of hills two thousand feet and more above the level of the sea. Nobody escaped the flood except a pregnant woman and a pregnant mouse, who saved themselves in a pig's trough and floated about, paddling with a pot-ladle instead of an oar, till the waters sank down and the earth again became habitable. Just then the woman, looking about for rice to sow, spied a sheaf of rice hanging from an uprooted tree, which drifted ashore on the spot where she was standing. With the help of the mouse, who climbed up the tree and brought down the sheaf, she was able to plant rice again. But before she fetched down the sheaf, the mouse stipulated that as a recompense for her services mice should thenceforth have the right to eat up part of the harvest. That is why the mice come every year to fetch the reward of their help from the fields of ripe rice; only they may not strip the fields too bare. As for the woman, she in due time gave birth to a son, whom she took, for want of another, to be her husband. By him she had a son and daughter, who became the ancestors of the present race of mankind.

The inhabitants of Rotti, a small island to the south-west of Timor, say that in former times the sea flooded the earth, so that all men and animals were drowned and all plants and herbs beaten down to the earth. Not a spot of dry ground was left. Even the high mountains were submerged, only the peak of Lakimola, in

Bilba, still rose solitary over the waves. On that mountain a man
and his wife and children had taken refuge. After some months
the tide still came creeping up and up the mountain, and the man
and his family were in great fear, for they thought it would soon
reach them. So they prayed the sea to return to his old bed. The
sea answered, "I will do so, if you give me an animal whose hairs
I cannot count." The man thereupon heaved first a pig, then a
goat, then a dog, and then a hen into the flood, but all in vain; the
sea could number the hairs of every one of them, and it still came
on. At last he threw in a cat: this was too much for the sea, it
could not do the sum, and sank abashed accordingly. After that
the osprey appeared and sprinkled some dry earth on the waters,
and the man and his wife and children descended the mountain to
seek a new home. Thereupon the Lord commanded the osprey to
bring all kinds of seed to the man, such as maize, millet, rice, beans,
pumpkins, and sesame, in order that he might sow them and live
with his family on the produce. That is the reason why in Rotti,
at the end of harvest, people set up a sheaf of rice on the open place
of the village as an offering to Mount Lakimola. Everybody cooks
rice, and brings it with betel-nuts, coco-nuts, tobacco, bananas, and
breadfruit as an oblation to the mountain; they feast and dance all
kinds of dances to testify their gratitude, and beg him to grant a
good harvest next year also, so that the people may have plenty
to eat.

The primitive inhabitants of the Andaman Islands, in the Bay
of Bengal, have a legend of a great flood, which may be related
here, though their islands do not strictly belong to the Indian
Archipelago. They say that some time after they had been created,
men grew disobedient and regardless of the commands which the
Creator had given them at their creation. So in anger he sent a
great flood which covered the whole land, except perhaps Saddle
Peak where the Creator himself resided. All living creatures,
both men and animals, perished in the waters, all save two men and
two women, who, having the good luck to be in a canoe at the time
when the catastrophe occurred, contrived to escape with their lives.
When at last the waters sank, the little company landed, but
they found themselves in a sad plight, for all other living creatures
were drowned. However, the Creator, whose name was Puluga,
kindly helped them by creating animals and birds afresh for their
use. But the difficulty remained of lighting a fire, for the flood
had extinguished the flames on every hearth, and all things were
of course very damp. Hereupon the ghost of one of their friends,
who had been drowned in the deluge, opportunely came to the
rescue. Seeing their distress he flew in the form of a kingfisher
to the sky, where he found the Creator seated beside his fire. The
bird made a dab at a burning brand, intending to carry it off in his
beak to his fireless friends on earth, but in his haste or agitation he
dropped it on the august person of the Creator himself, who,

incensed at the indignity and smarting with pain, hurled the blazing brand at the bird. It missed the mark and whizzing past him dropped plump from the sky at the very spot where the four people were seated moaning and shivering. That is how mankind recovered the use of fire after the great flood. When they had warmed themselves and had leisure to reflect on what had happened, the four survivors began to murmur at the Creator for his destruction of all the rest of mankind; and their passion getting the better of them they even plotted to murder him. From this impious attempt they were, however, dissuaded by the Creator himself, who told them, in very plain language, that they had better not try, for he was as hard as wood, their arrows could make no impression on him, and if they dared so much as to lay a finger on him, he would have the blood of every mother's son and daughter of them. This dreadful threat had its effect: they submitted to their fate, and the mollified Creator condescended to explain to them, in milder terms, that men had brought the great flood on themselves by wilful disobedience to his commands, and that any repetition of the offence in future would be visited by him with condign punishment. That was the last time that the Creator ever appeared to men and conversed with them face to face; since then the Andaman Islanders have never seen him, but to this day they continue to do his will with fear and trembling.

§ 9. *Stories of a Great Flood in Australia.*—The Kurnai, an aboriginal Australian tribe of Gippsland, in Victoria, say that a long time ago there was a very great flood; all the country was under water, and all the black people were drowned except a man and two or three women, who took refuge in a mud island near Port Albert. The water was all round them. Just then the pelican, or Bunjil Borun, as the Kurnai call the bird, came sailing by in his canoe, and seeing the distress of the poor people he went to help them. One of the women was so beautiful that he fell in love with her. When she would have stepped into the canoe, he said, "Not now, next time"; so that after he had ferried all the rest, one by one, across to the mainland, she was left to the last. Afraid of being alone with the ferry-man, she did not wait his return on his last trip, but swam ashore and escaped. However, before quitting the island, she dressed up a log in her opossum rug and laid it beside the fire, so that it looked just like herself. When the pelican arrived to ferry her over, he called, "Come on, now." The log made no reply, so the pelican flew into a passion, and rushing up to what he took to be the woman, he lunged out with his foot at her and gave the log a tremendous kick. Naturally he only hurt his own foot, and what with the pain and the chagrin at the trick that had been played him, he was very angry indeed and began to paint himself white in order that he might fight the husband of the impudent hussy who had so deceived him. He was still engaged in these warlike preparations, and had only painted white one half of his black body, when another

pelican came up, and not knowing what to make of such a strange
creature, half white and half black, he pecked at him with his beak
and killed him. That is why pelicans are now black and white;
before the flood they were black all over.

According to the aborigines about Lake Tyers, in Victoria, the
way in which the great flood came about was this. Once upon a
time all the water in the world was swallowed by a huge frog, and
nobody else could get a drop to drink. It was most inconvenient,
especially for the fish, who flapped about and gasped on the dry
land. So the animals laid their heads together and came to the
conclusion that the only way of making the frog disgorge the
waters was to tickle his fancy so that he should laugh. Accordingly they gathered before him and cut capers and played pranks
that would have caused any ordinary person to die of laughing.
But the frog did not even smile. He sat there in gloomy silence,
with his great goggle eyes and his swollen cheeks, as grave as a
judge. As a last resort the eel stood up on its tail and wriggled
and danced, about, twisting itself into the most ridiculous contor-
tions. This was more than even the frog could bear. His features
relaxed, and he laughed till the tears ran down his cheeks and the
water poured out of his mouth. However, the animals had now
got more than they had bargained for, since the waters disgorged
by the frog swelled into a great flood in which many people perished.
Indeed the whole of mankind would have been drowned, if the pelican
had not gone about in a canoe picking up the survivors and so
saving their lives.

§ 10. *Stories of a Great Flood in New Guinea and Melanesia.*—
In the Kabadi district of British New Guinea the natives have a
tradition that once on a time a certain man Lohero and his younger
brother were angry with the people about them, and they put a
human bone into a small stream. Soon the great waters came forth,
forming a sea, flooding all the low land, and driving the people back
to the mountains, till step by step they had to escape to the tops of
the highest peaks. There they lived till the sea receded, when
some of them descended to the lowlands, while others remained on
the ridges and there built houses and formed plantations. The
Valmans of Berlin Harbour, on the northern coast of New Guinea,
tell how one day the wife of a very good man saw a great fish
swimming to the bank. She called to her husband, but at first he
could not see the fish. So his wife laughed at him and hid him
behind a banana-tree, that he might peep at it through the leaves.
When he did catch sight of it at last, he was horribly afraid, and
sending for his family, a son and two daughters, he forbade them to
catch and eat the fish. But the other people took bow and arrow
and a cord, and they caught the fish and drew it to land. Though
the good man warned them not to eat of the fish, they did it notwithstanding. When the good man saw that, he hastily drove a pair of
animals of every sort up into the trees, and then he and his family

climbed up into a coco-nut tree. Hardly had the wicked men consumed the fish than water burst from the ground with such violence that nobody had time to save himself. Men and animals were all drowned. When the water had mounted to the top of the highest tree, it sank as rapidly as it had risen. Then the good man came down from the tree with his family and laid out new plantations.

The natives of the Mamberano River, in Dutch New Guinea, are reported to tell a story of a great flood, caused by the rising of the river, which overwhelmed Mount Vanessa, and from which only one man and his wife escaped, together with a pig, a cassowary, a kangaroo, and a pigeon. The man and his wife became the ancestors of the present race of men; the beasts and birds became the ancestors of the existing species. The bones of the drowned animals still lie on Mount Vanessa.

The Fijians have a tradition of a great deluge, which they call Walavu-levu: some say that the flood was partial, others that it was universal. The way in which the catastrophe came about was this. The great god Ndengei had a monstrous bird called Turukawa, which used to wake him punctually by its cooing every morning. One day his two grandsons, whether by accident or design, shot the bird dead with their bows and arrows, and buried the carcass in order to conceal the crime. So the deity overslept himself, and being much annoyed at the disappearance of his favourite fowl, he sent out his messenger Uto to look for it everywhere. The search proved fruitless. The messenger reported that not a trace of the bird was to be found. But a second search was more successful, and laid the guilt of the murder at the door of the god's grandsons. To escape the rage of their incensed grandfather the young scapegraces fled to the mountains and there took refuge with a tribe of carpenters, who willingly undertook to build a stockade strong enough to keep Ndengei and all his catchpolls at bay. They were as good as their word, and for three months the god and his minions besieged the fortress in vain. At last, in despair of capturing the stockade by the regular operations of war, the baffled deity disbanded his army and meditated a surer revenge. At his command the dark clouds gathered and burst, pouring torrents of rain on the doomed earth. Towns, hills, and mountains were submerged one after the other; yet for long the rebels, secure in the height of their town, looked down with unconcern on the rising tide of waters. At last when the surges lapped their wooden walls and even washed through their fortress, they called for help to a god, who, according to one account, instructed them to form a float out of the fruit of the shaddock; according to others, he sent two canoes for their use, or taught them how to build a canoe for themselves and thus ensure their own safety. It was Rokoro, the god of carpenters, who with his foreman Rokola came to their rescue. The pair sailed about in two large double canoes, picking up the drowning people and keeping them on board till the flood subsided. Others, however, will have it that the survivors saved themselves in large bowls, in which they floated about. Whatever the minor variations may be in the Fijian legend, all agree that even the highest places were covered by the deluge, and that the remnant of the human race was saved in some kind of vessel, which was at last left high and dry by the receding tide on the island of Mbengha. The number of persons who thus survived the flood was eight. Two tribes were completely destroyed by the waters; one of them consisted entirely of women, the members of the other had tails like those of dogs. Because the survivors of the flood landed on their island, the natives of Mbengha claimed to rank highest of all the Fijians, and their chiefs always acted a conspicuous part in Fijian history: they styled themselves "Subject to heaven alone." It is said that formerly the Fijians always kept great canoes ready for use against another flood, and that the custom was only discontinued in modern times.

The Melanesians of the New Hebrides say that their great legendary hero Qat disappeared from the world in a deluge. They show the very place from which he sailed away on his last voyage. It is a broad lake in the centre of the island of Gaua. In the days of Puat the ground now occupied by the lake was a spacious plain clothed with forest. Qat felled one of the tallest trees in the wood and proceeded to build himself a canoe out of the fallen trunk. While he was at work on it, his brothers would come and jeer at him, as he sat or stood there sweating away at his unfinished canoe in the shadow of the dense tropical forest. "How will you ever get that huge canoe through the thick woods to the sea?" they ask him mockingly. "Wait and see," was all he deigned to answer. When the canoe was finished, he gathered into it his wife and his brothers and all the living creatures of the island, down to the smallest ants, and shut himself and them into the vessel, which he provided with a covering. Then came a deluge of rain; the great hollow of the island was filled with water, which burst through the circle of the hills at the spot where the great waterfall of Gaua still descends seaward, with a thunderous roar, in a veil of spray. There the canoe swept on the rushing water through the barrier of the hills, and driving away out to sea was lost to view. The natives say that the hero Qat took away the best of everything with him when he thus vanished from sight, and still they look forward to his joyful return.

§ 11. *Stories of a Great Flood in Polynesia and Micronesia.—* Legends of a great flood in which a multitude of people perished are told by the natives of those groups of islands which under the general names of Polynesia and Micronesia are scattered widely over the Pacific. "The principal facts," we are told, "are the same in the traditions prevailing among the inhabitants of the different groups, although they differ in several minor particulars.

In one group the accounts state, that in ancient times Taaroa, the principal god (according to their mythology, the creator of the world), being angry with men on account of their disobedience to his will, overturned the world into the sea, when the earth sank in the waters, excepting a few *aurus,* or projecting points, which, remaining above its surface, constituted the principal cluster of islands. The memorial preserved by the inhabitants of Eimeo states, that after the inundation of the land, when the water subsided, a man landed from a canoe near Tiataepua, in their island, and erected an altar, or *marae,* in honour of his god."

In Tahiti the legend ran as follows. Tahiti was destroyed by the sea: no man, nor hog, nor fowl, nor dog survived. The groves of trees and the stones were carried away by the wind. They were destroyed, and the deep was over the land. But two persons, a husband and a wife, were saved. When the flood came, the wife took up her young chicken, her young dog, and her kitten; the husband took up his young pig. [These were all the animals formerly known to the natives; and as the term *fanaua,* "young," is both singular and plural, it may apply to one or more than one chicken, etc.]. The husband proposed that they should take refuge on Mount Orofena, a high mountain in Tahiti, saying that it was lofty and would not be reached by the sea. But his wife said that the sea would reach to Mount Orofena, and that they had better go to Mount O Pitohito, where they would be safe from the flood. So to Mount O Pitohito they went; and she was right, for Orofena was overwhelmed by the sea, but O Pitohito rose above the waste of waters and became their abode. There they watched ten nights, till the sea ebbed, and they saw the little heads of the mountains appearing above the waves. When the sea retired, the land remained without produce, without man, and the fish were putrid in the caves and holes of the rocks. They said, "Dig a hole for the fish in the sea." The wind also died away, and when all was calm, the stones and the trees began to fall from the heavens, to which they had been carried up by the wind. For all the trees of the land had been torn up and whirled aloft by the hurricane. The two looked about, and the woman said, "We two are safe from the sea, but death, or hurt, comes now in these stones that are falling. Where shall we abide?" So the two dug a hole, lined it with grass, and covered it over with stones and earth. Then they crept into the hole, and sitting there they heard with terror the roar and crash of the stones falling down from the sky. By and by the rain of stones abated, till only a few stones fell at intervals, and then they dropped one by one, and finally ceased altogether. The woman said, "Arise, go out, and see whether the stones are still falling." But her husband said, "Nay, I go not out, lest I die." A day and a night he waited, and in the morning he said, "The wind is truly dead, and the stones and the trunks of trees cease to fall, neither is there the sound of the stones."

They went out, and like a small mountain was the heap of fallen stones and tree trunks. Of the land there remained the earth and the rocks, but the shrubs were destroyed by the sea. They descended from the mountain, and gazed with astonishment: there were no houses, nor coco-nuts, nor palm-trees, nor bread-fruit, nor hibiscus, nor grass: all was destroyed by the sea. The two dwelt together. The woman brought forth two children; one was a son, the other a daughter. They grieved that there was no food for their children. Again the mother brought forth, but still there was no food; then the bread-fruit bore fruit, and the coco-nut, and every other kind of food. In three days the land was covered with food; and in time it swarmed with men also, for from those two persons, the father and the mother, all the people are descended.

In Raiatea, one of the Leeward Islands in the Tahitian group, tradition ran that shortly after the peopling of the world by the descendants of Taata, the sea-god Ruahatu was reposing among groves of coral in the depths of ocean, when his repose was rudely interrupted. A fisherman, paddling his canoe overhead, in ignorance or forgetfulness of the divine presence, let down his hooks among the branching corals at the bottom of the clear translucent water, and they became entangled in the hair of the sleeping god. With great difficulty the fisherman wrenched the hooks out of the ambrosial locks and began pulling them up hand-over-hand. But the god, enraged at being disturbed in his nap, came also bubbling up to the surface, and popping his head out of the water upbraided the fisherman for his impiety, and threatened in revenge to destroy the land. The affrighted fisherman prostrated himself before the sea-god, confessed his sin, and implored his forgiveness, beseeching that the judgment denounced might be averted, or at least that he himself might escape. Moved by his penitence and importunity, Ruahatu bade him return home for his wife and child and go with them to Toamarama, a small island situated within the reefs on the eastern side of Raiatea. There he was promised security amid the destruction of the surrounding islands. The man hastened home, and taking with him his wife and child he repaired to the little isle of refuge in the lagoon. Some say that he took with him also a friend, who was living under his roof, together with a dog, a pig, and a pair of fowls; so that the refugees numbered four souls, together with the only domesticated animals which were then known in the islands. They reached the harbour of refuge before the close of day, and as the sun set the waters of the ocean began to rise, and the inhabitants of the adjacent shore left their dwellings and fled to the mountains. All that night the waters rose, and next morning only the tops of the high mountains appeared above the widespread sea. Even these were at last covered, and all the inhabitants of the land perished. Afterwards the waters retired, the fisherman and his companions left their retreat, took up their abode on the mainland, and became the progenitors of the present inhabitants.

The coral islet in which these forefathers of the race found refuge from the great flood is not more than two feet at the highest above the level of the sea, so that it is difficult to understand how it could have escaped the inundation, while the lofty mountains which tower up thousands of feet from the adjacent shore were submerged. This difficulty, however, presents no stumbling-block to the faith of the natives; they usually decline to discuss such sceptical doubts, and point triumphantly for confirmation of their story to the coral, shells, and other marine substances which are occasionally found near the surface of the ground on the tops of their highest mountains. These must, they insist, have been deposited there by the waters of the ocean when the islands were submerged.

It is significant, as we shall see later on, that in these Tahitian legends the flood is ascribed solely to the rising of the sea, and not at all to heavy rain, which is not even mentioned. On this point the Rev. William Ellis, to whom we owe the record of these legends, makes the following observations: "I have frequently conversed with the people on the subject, both in the northern and southern groups, but could never learn that they had any accounts of the windows of heaven having been opened, or the rain having descended. In the legend of Ruahatu, the Toamarama of Tahiti, and the Kai of Kahinárii in Hawaii, the inundation is ascribed to the rising of the waters of the sea. In each account, the anger of the god is considered as the cause of the inundation of the world and the destruction of its inhabitants."

When Mr. Ellis preached in the year 1822 to the natives of Hawaii on the subject of Noah's deluge, they told him of a similar legend which had been handed down among them. "They said they were informed by their fathers, that all the land had once been overflowed by the sea, except a small peak on the top of Mouna-Kea, where two human beings were preserved from the destruction that overtook the rest, but they said they had never before heard of a ship, or of Noah, having been always accustomed to call it *kai a Kahinárii* (sea of Kahinárii)."

The Maoris of New Zealand have a long legend of the deluge. They say that when men multiplied on the earth and there were many great tribes, evil prevailed everywhere, the tribes quarrelled and made war on each other. The worship of the great god Tane, who had created man and woman, was neglected and his doctrines openly denied. Two great prophets, indeed, there were who taught the true doctrine concerning the separation of heaven and earth, but men scoffed at them, saying that they were false teachers and that heaven and earth had been from the beginning just as we see them now. The names of these two wise prophets were Para-whenua-mea and Tupu-nui-a-uta. They continued to preach till the tribes cursed them, saying, "You two can eat the words of your history as food for you, and you can eat the heads of the words of that history." That grieved the prophets, when men said the wicked words "Eat the heads," and they grew angry. So they took their stone axes and cut down trees, and dragged the trunks to the source of the Tohinga River, and bound them together with vines and ropes, and made a very wide raft. Moreover, they built a house on the raft, and put much food in it, fern-root, and sweet potatoes, and dogs. Then they recited incantations and prayed that rain might descend in such abundance as would convince men of the existence and power of the god Tane, and would teach them the need of worship for life and for peace. After that the two prophets embarked on the raft, along with two men called Tiu and Reti and a woman named Wai-puna-hau. But there were other women also on the raft. Now Tiu was the priest on the raft, and he prayed and uttered incantations for rain. So it rained in torrents for four or five days, and then the priest repeated incantations to make the rain cease, and it ceased. But still the flood rose; next day it reached the settlement, and on the following day the raft was lifted up by the waters, and floated down the River Tohinga. Great as a sea was now the inundation, and the raft drifted to and fro on the face of the waters. When they had tossed about for seven moons, the priest Tiu said to his companions, "We shall not die, we shall land on the earth"; and in the eighth month he said moreover, "The sea has become thin; the flood has begun to subside." The two prophets asked him, "By what do you know?" He answered, "By the signs of my staff." For he had kept his altar on one side of the deck, and there he performed his ceremonies, and repeated his incantations, and observed his staff. And he understood the signs of his staff, and he said again to his companions, "The blustering winds of the past moons have fallen, the winds of this month have died away, and the sea is calm." In the eighth month the raft no longer rolled as before; it now pitched as well as rolled, so the priest knew that the sea was shallow, and that they were drawing near to land. He said to his companions, "This is the moon in which we shall land on dry earth, for by the signs of my staff I know that the sea is becoming less deep." All the while they floated on the deep they repeated incantations and performed ceremonies in honour of the god Tane. At last they landed on dry earth at Hawaiki. They thought that they might find some of the inhabitants of the world still alive, and that the earth would look as it had looked before the flood. But all was changed. The earth was cracked and fissured in some places, and in others it had been turned upside down and confounded by reason of the flood. And not one soul was left alive in the world. They who came forth from the raft were the solitary survivors of all the tribes of the earth. When they landed, the first thing they did was to perform ceremonies and repeat incantations. They worshipped

Tane, and the Heaven (Rangi), and Rehua, and all the gods; and as they worshipped them they offered them seaweed, a length of the priest's two thumbs for each god. Each god was worshipped in a different place, and for each there was an altar, where the incantations were recited. The altar was a root of grass, a shrub, a tree, or a flax-bush. These were the altars of the gods at that time; and now, if any of the people of the tribes go near to such altars, the food they have eaten in their stomachs will swell and kill them. The chief priest alone may go to such holy spots. If common folk were to go to these sacred places and afterwards cook food in their village, the food would kill all who ate it. It would be cursed by the sin of the people in desecrating the sanctity of the altars, and the punishment of the eaters would be death. When the persons who were saved on the raft had performed all the ceremonies needful for removing the taboo under which they laboured, they procured fire by friction at one of the sacred places. And with the fire the priest kindled bundles of grass, and he put a bundle of burning grass on each altar beside the piece destined for the god; and the priests presented the seaweed to the gods as a thank-offering for the rescue of the people from the flood and for the preservation of their lives on the raft.

In Micronesia as well as Polynesia the story of a great flood has been recorded. The Pelew Islanders say that once on a time a man went up into the sky, whence the gods with their shining eyes, which are the stars, look down every night upon the earth. The cunning fellow stole one of these bright eyes and brought it home with him, and all the money of the Pelew Islanders has been made out of that starry eye ever since. But the gods were very angry at the theft, and down they came to earth to reclaim their stolen property and to punish the thief. They disguised themselves in the likeness of ordinary men, and begged for food and lodging from door to door. But men were churlish and turned them away without a bite or a sup. Only one old woman received them kindly in her cottage, and set before them the best she had to eat and drink. So when they went away they warned the old woman to make a raft of bamboo ready against the next full moon, and when the night of the full moon came she was to lie down on the raft and sleep. She did as she was bidden. Now with the full moon came a dreadful storm and rain, and the sea rose higher and higher, and flooded the islands, rent the mountains, and destroyed the abodes of men; and people knew not how to save themselves, and they all perished in the rising flood. But the good old dame, fast asleep on the raft, was borne on the face of the waters and drifted till her hair caught in the boughs of a tree on the top of Mount Armlimui. There she lay, while the flood ebbed and the water sank lower and lower down the sides of the mountain. Then the gods came down from the sky to seek for the good old woman whom they had taken under their protection, but they found her dead. So they summoned one of their women-folk from heaven, and she entered into the dead body of the old woman and made her live. After that the gods begat five children by the resuscitated old wife, and having done so they left the earth and returned to heaven; the goddess who had kindly reanimated the corpse of the ancient dame also went back to her mansion in the sky. But the five children of the divine fathers and the human mother repeopled the Pelew Islands, and from them the present inhabitants are descended.

§ 12. *Stories of a Great Flood in South America.*—At the time of their discovery the Indians of Brazil, in the neighbourhood of what was afterwards Rio de Janeiro, had a legend of a universal deluge in which only two brothers with their wives were saved. According to one account, the flood covered the whole earth and all men perished except the ancestors of those Indians, who escaped by climbing up into high trees; others, however, thought that the survivors were saved in a canoe.

As reported by the Frenchman André Thevet, who travelled in Brazil about the middle of the sixteenth century, the story related by the Indians about Cape Frio ran thus. A certain great medicine-man, by name Sommay, had two sons called Tamendonare and Ariconte. Tamendonare tilled the ground and was a good father and husband, and he had a wife and children. But his brother Ariconte cared for none of these things. He busied himself only with war, and his one desire was to subdue neighbouring peoples and even his own righteous brother. One day this truculent warrior, returning from a battle, brought to his peaceful brother the amputated arm of a slain foe, and as he did so he said proudly to his brother, "Away with you, coward that you are. I'll have your wife and children, for you are not strong enough to defend them." The good man, grieved at his brother's pride, answered with stinging sarcasm, "If you are as valiant as you say, why did not you bring the whole carcass of your enemy?" Indignant at the taunt, Ariconte threw the arm at the door of his brother's house. At the same moment the village in which they dwelt was transported to the sky, but the two brothers remained on earth. Seeing that, in astonishment or anger Tamendonare stamped on the ground so forcibly that a great fountain of water sprang from it and rose so high that it out-topped the hills and seemed to mount above the clouds; and the water continued to spout till it had covered the whole earth. On perceiving their danger, the two brothers hastened to ascend the highest mountains, and there sought to save themselves by climbing the trees, along with their wives. Tramendonare climbed one tree, called *pindona,* of which the French traveller saw two sorts, one of them with larger fruit and leaves than the other. In his flight from the rising flood he dragged up one of his wives with him, while his brother with his wife climbed another tree called *geniper.* While they were all perched among the boughs, Ariconte gave some of the fruit of the tree to his wife, saying, "Break off some of the fruit and let it fall." She did so, and they perceived by the splash that the water was still high, and that it was not yet time for them to descend into the valley. The Indians believe that in this flood all men and women were drowned, except the two brothers and their wives, and that from these two pairs after the deluge there came forth two different peoples, to wit, the Tonnasseares, surnamed Tupinambo, and the Tonnaitz Hoyanans, surnamed Tominu, who are at perpetual feud and war with each other. The Tupinambo, wishing to exalt themselves and to make themselves out better than their fellows and neighbours, say, "We are descended from Tamendonare, while you are descended from Ariconte," by which they imply that Tamendonare was a better man than Ariconte.

A somewhat different version of the same legend was recorded by the Jesuit Simon de Vasconcellos. In it only a single family is said to have been saved, and no mention is made of the bad brother. Once upon a time, so runs the tale, there was a clever medicine-man or sorcerer named Tamanduare. To him the great god Tupi revealed the coming of a great flood which would swamp the earth, so that even the high trees and mountains would be submerged. Only one lofty peak would rise above the waters, and on its top would be found a tall palm-tree with a fruit like a coco-nut. To that palm the sorcerer was warned to turn for refuge with his family in the hour of need. Without delay Tamanduare and his family betook themselves to the top of the lofty peak. When they were safely there, it began to rain, and it rained and rained till all the earth was covered. The flood even crept up the mountain and washed over the summit, and the man and his family climbed up into the palm-tree and remained in the branches so long as the inundation lasted, and they subsisted by eating the fruit of the palm. When the water subsided, they descended, and being fruitful they proceeded to repeople the drowned and devastated world.

The Caingangs, or Coroados, an Indian tribe of Rio Grande do Sul, the most southerly province of Brazil, have a tradition of a great flood which covered the whole earth inhabited by their forefathers. Only the top of the coastal range called Serra do Mar still appeared above the water. The members of three Indian tribes, namely the Caingangs, the Cayurucres, and the Cames, swam on the water of the flood toward the mountains, holding lighted torches between their teeth. But the Cayurucres and the Cames grew weary, they sank under the waves and were drowned, and their souls went to dwell in the heart of the mountain. However, the Caingangs and a few of the Curutons made shift to reach the mountain, and there they abode, some on the ground, and some on the branches of trees. Several days passed, and yet the water did not sink, and they had no food to eat. They looked for nothing but death, when they heard the song of the *saracuras,* a species of waterfowl, which flew to them with baskets of earth. This earth the birds threw into the water, which accordingly began slowly to sink.

The people cried to the birds to hurry, so the birds called the ducks to their help, and working together they soon cleared enough room and to spare for all the people, except for such as had climbed up the trees: these latter were turned into monkeys. When the flood subsided, the Caingangs descended and settled at the foot of the mountain. The souls of the drowned Cayurucres and Cames contrived to burrow their way out from the bowels of the mountain in which they were imprisoned; and when they had crept forth they kindled a fire, and out of the ashes of the fire one of the Cayurucres moulded jaguars, and tapirs, and ant-bears, and bees, and animals of many other sorts, and he made them live and told them what they should eat. But one of the Cames imitated him by fashioning pumas, and poisonous snakes, and wasps, all in order that these creatures should fight the other animals which the Cayurucres had made, as they do to this day.

A story of a great flood is told also by the Carayas, a tribe of Brazilian Indians, who inhabit the valley of the Araguaya River, which, with the Tocantins, forms the most easterly of the great southern tributaries of the Amazon. The tribe is said to differ from all its neighbours in manners and customs as well as in physical characteristics, while its language appears to be unrelated to any other known language spoken by the Indians of Brazil. The Caraya story of a deluge runs thus. Once upon a time the Carayas were out hunting wild pigs and drove the animals into their dens. Thereupon they began to dig them out, killing each pig as it was dragged forth. In doing so they came upon a deer, then a tapir, and then a white deer. Digging still deeper, they laid bare the feet of a man. Horrified at the discovery, they fetched a mighty magician, who knew all the beasts of the forest, and he contrived to draw the man out of the earth. The man thus unearthed was named Anatiua, and he had a thin body but a fat paunch. He now began to sing, "I am Anatiua. Bring me tobacco to smoke." But the Carayas did not understand what he said. They ran about the wood, and came back with all kinds of flowers and fruits, which they offered to Anatiua. But he refused them all, and pointed to a man who was smoking. Then they understood him and offered him tobacco. He took it and smoked till he fell to the ground senseless. So they carried him to the canoe and brought him to the village. There he awoke from his stupor and began to dance and sing. But his behaviour and his unintelligible speech frightened the Carayas, and they decamped, bag and baggage. That made Anatiua very angry, and he turned himself into a great *piranha* and followed them, carrying with him many calabashes full of water. He called to the Carayas to halt, but they paid no heed, and in his rage he smashed one of the calabashes which he was carrying. The water at once began to rise, but still the Carayas pursued their flight. Then he broke another calabash, and then another and another, and higher and higher rose the water, till the whole land was inundated, and only the mountains at the mouth of Tapirape River projected above the flood. The Carayas took refuge on the two peaks of that range. Anatiua now called all fish together to drag the people down into the water. The *jahu,* the *pintado,* and the *pacu* tried to do so, but none of them succeeded. At last the *bicudo* (a fish with a long beak-like snout) contrived to scale the mountain from behind and to tear the Carayas down from its summit. A great lagoon still marks the spot where they fell. Only a few persons remained on the top of the mountain, and they descended when the water of the flood had run away. On this story the writer who records it remarks that "though in general regularly recurring inundations, as on the Araguaya, do not give rise to flood stories, as Andree has rightly pointed out, yet the local conditions are here favourable to the creation of such a story. The traveller, who, after a long voyage between endless low river-banks, suddenly comes in sight of the mighty conical mountains on the Tapirape River, towering abruptly from the plain, can easily understand how the Carayas, who suffer much from inundations, came to tell their story of the flood. Perhaps on some occasion when the inundation rose to an unusual height, these mountains may really have served as a last refuge to the inhabitants of the surrounding district." And he adds, "As in most South American legends of a flood, this particular flood is said to have been caused, not by rain, but by the breaking of vessels full of water."

Again, the Pamarys, Abederys, and Kataushys, on the River Purus, relate that once on a time people heard a rumbling above and below the ground. The sun and moon, also, turned red, blue, and yellow, and the wild beasts mingled fearlessly with men. A month later they heard a roar and saw darkness ascending from the earth to the sky, accompanied by thunder and heavy rain, which blotted out the day and the earth. Some people lost themselves, some died, without knowing why; for everything was in a dreadful state of confusion. The water rose very high, till the earth was sunk beneath the water and only the branches of the highest trees still stood out above the flood. Thither the people had fled for refuge, and there, perched among the boughs, they perished of cold and hunger; for all the time it was dark and the rain fell. Then only Uassu and his wife were saved. When they came down after the flood they could not find a single corpse, no, not so much as a heap of bleached bones. After that they had many children, and they said one to the other, "Go to, let us build our houses on the river, that when the water rises, we too may rise with it." But when they saw that the land was dry and solid, they thought no more about it. Yet the Pamarys build their houses on the river to this day.

The Muratos, a branch of the Jibaros in Ecuador, have their own version of the deluge story. They say that once on a time a Murato Indian went to fish in a lagoon of the Pastaza River;

a small crocodile swallowed his bait, and the fishermen killed the young animal. The crocodile's mother, or rather the mother of crocodiles in general, was angry and lashed the water with her tail, till the water overflowed and flooded all the neighbourhood of the lagoon. All the people were drowned except one man, who climbed a palm-tree and stayed there for many days. All the time it was as dark as night. From time to time he dropped a fruit of the palm, but he always heard it splash in the water. At last one day the fruit which he let fall dropped with a simple thud on the ground; there was no splash, so he knew that the flood had subsided. Accordingly he descended from the tree, built a house, and set about to till a field. He was without a wife, but he soon provided himself with one by cutting off a piece of his own body and planting it in the ground; for from the earth thus fertilized there sprang up a woman, whom he married.

The Araucanians of Chili have a tradition of a great deluge, in which only a few persons were saved. These fortunate survivors took refuge on a high mountain called Thegtheg, the thundering, or the sparkling, which had three points and possessed the property of floating on water. "From hence," says the Spanish historian, "It is inferable that this deluge was in consequence of some volcanic eruption, accompanied by terrible earthquakes, and is probably very different from that of Noah. Whenever a violent earthquake occurs, these people fly for safety to those mountains which they fancy to be of a similar appearance, and which of course, as they suppose, must possess the same property of floating on the water, assigning as a reason, that they are fearful after an earthquake that the sea will again return and deluge the world. On these occasions, each one takes a good supply of provisions, and wooden plates to protect their heads from being scorched, provided the Thegtheg, when raised by the waters, should be elevated to the sun. Whenever they are told that plates made of earth would be much more suitable for this purpose than those of wood, which are liable to be burned, their usual reply is, that their ancestors did so before them.

The Ackawois of British Guiana tell a story of the great flood which is enriched by a variety of details. They say that in the beginning of the world the great spirit Makonaima created birds and beasts and set his son Sigu to rule over them. Moreover, he caused to spring from the earth a great and very wonderful tree, which bore a different kind of fruit on each of its branches, while round its trunk bananas, plantains, cassava, maize, and corn of all kinds grew in profusion; yams, too, clustered round its roots; and in short all the plants now cultivated on earth flourished in the greatest abundance on or about or under that marvellous tree. In order to diffuse the benefits of the tree all over the world, Sigu resolved to cut it down and plant slips and seeds of it everywhere, and this he did with the help of all the beasts and birds, all except the brown monkey, who, being both lazy and mischievous, refused to assist in the great work of transplantation. So to keep him out of mischief Sigu set the animal to fetch water from the stream in a basket of open-work, calculating that the task would occupy his misdirected energies for some time to come. In the meantime, proceeding with the labour of felling the miraculous tree, he discovered that the stump was hollow and full of water in which the fry of every sort of fresh-water fish was swimming about. The benevolent Sigu determined to stock all the rivers and lakes on earth with the fry on so liberal a scale that every sort of fish should swarm in every water. But this generous intention was unexpectedly frustrated. For the water in the cavity, being connected with the great reservoir somewhere in the bowels of the earth, began to overflow; and to arrest the rising flood Sigu covered the stump with a closely woven basket. This had the desired effect. But unfortunately the brown monkey, tired of his fruitless task, stealthily returned, and his curiosity being aroused by the sight of the basket turned upside down, he imagined that it must conceal something good to eat. So he cautiously lifted it and peeped beneath, and out poured the flood, sweeping the monkey himself away and inundating the whole land. Gathering the rest of the animals together Sigu led them to the highest point of the country, where grew some tall coco-nut palms. Up the tallest of these trees he caused the birds and climbing animals to ascend; and as for the animals that could not climb and were not amphibious, he shut them up in a cave with a very narrow entrance, and having sealed up the mouth of it with wax he gave the animals inside a long thorn with which to pierce the wax and so ascertain when the water had subsided. After taking these measures for the preservation of the more helpless species, he and the rest of the creatures climbed up the palm-tree and ensconced themselves among the branches. During the darkness and storm which followed, they all suffered intensely from cold and hunger; the rest bore their sufferings with stoical fortitude, but the red howling monkey uttered his anguish in such horrible yells that his throat swelled and has remained distended ever since; that, too, is the reason why to this day he has a sort of bony drum in his throat. Meanwhile Sigu from time to time let fall seeds of the palm into the water to judge of its depth by the splash. As the water sank, the interval between the dropping of the seed and the splash in the water grew longer; and at last, instead of a splash, the listening Sigu heard the dull thud of the seeds striking the soft earth. Then he knew that the flood had subsided, and he and the animals prepared to descend. But the trumpeter-bird was in such a hurry to get down that he flopped straight into an ants' nest, and the hungry insects fastened on his legs and gnawed them to the bone. That is why the trumpeter-bird has still such spindle shanks. The other creatures profited by this awful example and came down the tree cautiously and safely. Sigu now rubbed two pieces of wood together to make fire, but just as he produced the first spark, he happened to look away, and the bush-turkey, mistaking the spark for a fire-fly, gobbled it up and flew off. The spark burned the greedy bird's gullet, and that is why turkeys have red wattles on their throats to this day. The alligator was standing by at the time, doing no harm to anybody; but as he was for some reason an unpopular character, all the other animals accused him of having stolen and swallowed the spark. In order to recover the spark from the jaws of the alligator Sigu tore out the animal's tongue, and that is why alligators have no tongue to speak of down to this very day.

The Arawaks of British Guiana believe that since its creation the world has been twice destroyed, once by fire and once by flood. Both destructions were brought on it by Aiomun Kondi, the great "Dweller on High," because of the wickedness of mankind. But he announced beforehand the coming catastrophe, and men who accepted the warning prepared to escape from the great fire by digging deep into a sand-reef and there making for themselves a subterranean chamber with a roof of timber supported on massive pillars of the same material. Over it all they spread layers of earth and a thick upper coating of sand. Having carefully removed everything combustible from the neighbourhood, they retired to this underground dwelling and there stayed quietly till the roaring torrent of flame, which swept across the earth's surface, had passed over them. Afterwards, when the destruction of the world by a deluge was at hand, a pious and wise chief named Marerewana was informed of the coming flood and saved himself and his family in a large canoe. Fearing to drift away out to sea or far from the home of his fathers, he had made ready a long cable of bush-rope, with which he tied his bark to the trunk of a great tree. So when the waters subsided he found himself not far from his former abode.

The Macusis of British Guiana say that in the beginning the good spirit Makunaima, whose name means "He who works in the night," created the heaven and the earth. When he had stocked the earth with plants and trees, he came down from his celestial mansion, climbed up a tall tree, and chipped off the bark with a big stone axe. The chips fell into the river at the foot of the tree and were changed into animals of all kinds. When he had thus provided for the creation of animals the good spirit next created man; and when the man had fallen into a sound sleep he awoke to find a woman standing at his side. Afterwards the evil spirit got the upper hand on earth; so the good spirit Makunaima sent a great flood. Only one man escaped in a canoe; he sent out a rat to see whether the water had abated, and the rat returned with a cob of maize. When the deluge had retreated, the man repeopled the earth, like Deucalion and Pyrrha, by throwing stones behind him. In this story the special creation of woman, the mention of the evil spirit, and the incident of the rat sent out to explore the depth of the flood, present suspicious resemblaces to the Biblical narrative and may be due to missionary, or at all events European, influence. Further, the mode in which, after the flood, the survivors create mankind afresh by throwing stones behind them, resembles so exactly the corresponding incident in the Greek story of Deucalion and Pyrrha, that it is difficult to regard the two as independent.

Legends of a great flood are current also among the Indians of the Orinoco. On this subject Humboldt observes: "I cannot quit this first chain of the mountains of Encamarada without recalling a fact which was not unknown to Father Gili, and which was often mentioned to me during our stay among the missions of the Orinoco. The aborigines of these countries have preserved a belief that at the time of the great flood, while their fathers were forced to betake themselves to canoes in order to escape the general inundation, the waves of the sea broke against the rocks of Encamarada. This belief is not found isolated among a single people, the Tamanaques; it forms part of a system of historical traditions of which scattered notices are discovered among the Maypures of the great cataracts, among the Indians of the Rio Erevato, which falls into the Caura, and among almost all the tribes the Upper Orinoco. When the Tamanaques are asked how the human race escaped this great cataclysm, 'the Age of Water,' as the Mexicans call it, they say that one man and one woman were saved on a high mountain called Tamanacu, situated on the banks of the Asiveru, and that on casting behind them, over their heads, the fruits of the Mauritia palm, they saw springing from the kernels of these fruits men and women, who repeopled the earth." This they did in obedience to a voice which they heard speaking to them as they descended the mountain full of sorrow at the destruction of mankind by the flood. The fruits which the man threw became men, and the fruits which the woman threw became women.

The Cañaris, an Indian tribe of Ecuador, in the ancient kingdom of Quito, tell of a great flood from which two brothers escaped to a very high mountain called Huaca-yñan. As the waters rose, the hill rose with them, so that the flood never reached the two brothers on the summit. When the water sank and their store of provisions was consumed, the brothers descended and sought their food in the hills and valleys. They built a small house, where they dwelt, eking out a miserable subsistence on herbs and roots, and suffering much from hunger and fatigue. One day, after the usual weary search, they returned home, and there found food to eat and *chicha* to drink without knowing who could have prepared or brought it. This happened for ten days, and after that they laid their heads together to find out who it was that did them so much good in their time of need. So the elder brother hid himself, and presently he saw two macaws approaching, dressed like Cañaris. As soon as the birds came to the house, they began to prepare the food which they had brought with them. When the man saw that they were beautiful and had the faces of women, he came forth from his hiding-place; but at sight of him the birds were angry and flew away, leaving nothing to eat. When the younger brother came home from his search for food, and found nothing cooked and ready as on former days, he asked his elder brother the reason, and they were both very angry. Next day the younger brother resolved to hide and watch for the coming of the birds. At the end of three days the two macaws reappeared and began to prepare the food. The two men waited till the birds had finished cooking and then shut the door on them. The birds were very angry at being thus trapped, and while the two brothers were holding the smaller bird, the larger one escaped. Then the two brothers took the smaller macaw to wife, and by her they had six sons and daughters, from whom all the Cañaris are descended. Hence the hill Huaca-yñan, where the macaw lived as the wife of the brothers, is looked upon as a sacred place by the Indians, and they venerate macaws and value their feathers highly for use at their festivals.

The Indians of Huarochiri, a province of Peru in the Andes to the east of Lima, say that once on a time the world nearly came to an end altogether. It happened thus. An Indian was tethering his llama in a place where there was good pasture, but the animal resisted, showing sorrow and moaning after its manner. The master said to the llama, "Fool, why do you moan and refuse to eat? Have I not put you where there is good food?" The llama answered, "Madman, what do you know about it? Learn that I am not sad without due cause; for within five days the sea will rise and cover the whole earth, destroying all there is upon it." Wondering to hear the beast speak, the man asked whether there was any way in which they could save themselves. The llama bade him take food for five days and to follow him to the top of a high mountain called Villca-coto, between the parish of San Damian and the parish of San Geronimo de Surco. The man did as he was bid, carrying the load of food on his back and leading the llama. On reaching the top of the mountain he found many kinds of birds and animals there assembled. Hardly had he reached this place of refuge when the sea began to rise, and it rose till the water flooded all the valleys and covered the tops of the hills, all but the top of Villa-coto, and even there the waves washed so high that the animals had to crowd together in a narrow space, and some of them could hardly find foothold. The tail of the fox was dipped in the flood, and that is why the tips of foxes' tails are black to this day. At the end of five days the waters began to abate, and the sea returned to its former bounds; but all the people in the world were drowned except that one man, and from him all the nations of the earth are descended.

The Incas of Peru had also a tradition of a deluge. They said that the water rose above the highest mountains in the world, so that all people and all created things perished. No living thing escaped except a man and a woman, who floated in a box on the face of the waters and so were saved. When the flood sub-sided, the wind drifted the box with the two in it to Tiahuanacu, about seventy leagues from Cuzco.

The Peruvian legends of a great flood are told by the Spanish historian Herrera as follows. "The ancient Indians reported, they had received it by tradition from their ancestors, that many years before there were any Incas, at the time when the country was very populous, there happened a great flood, the sea breaking out beyond its bounds, so that the land was covered with water, and all the people perished. To this the Guancas, inhabiting the vale of Xauxa, and the natives of Chiquito in the province of Collao. add, that some persons remained in the hollows and caves of the highest mountains, who again peopled the land. Others of the mountain people affirm, that all perished in the deluge, only six persons being saved on a float, from whom descended all the in-habitants of that country. That there had been some particular flood may be credited, because all the several provinces agree in it."

The Chiriguanos, a once powerful Indian tribe of South-eastern Bolivia, tell the following story of a great flood. They say that a certain potent but malignant supernatural being, named Aguara-Tunpa, declared war against the true god Tunpaete, the Creator of the Chiriguanos. His motive for this declaration of war is unknown, but it is believed to have been pure spite or the spirit of contradic-tion. In order to vex the true god, Aguara-Tunpa set fire to all the prairies at the beginning or middle of autumn, so that along with the plants and trees all the animals perished on which in those days the Indians depended for their subsistence; for as yet they had not begun to cultivate maize and other cereals, as they do now. Thus deprived of food the Indians nearly died of hunger. However, they retreated before the flames to the banks of the rivers, and there, while the earth around still smoked from the great conflagration, they made shift to live on the fish which they caught in the water. Seeing his human prey likely to escape him, the baffled Aguara-Tunpa had recourse to another device in order to accomplish his infernal plot against mankind. He caused torrential rain to fall, hoping to drown the whole Chiriguano tribe in the water. He very nearly succeeded. But happily the Chiri-guanos contrived to defeat his fell purpose. Acting on a hint given them by the true god Tunpaete, they looked out for a large mate leaf, placed on it two little babies, a boy and a girl, the children of one mother, and allowed the tiny ark with its precious inmates to float on the face of the water. Still the rain continued to descend in torrents; the floods rose and spread over the face of the earth to a great depth, and all the Chiriguanos were drowned; only the two babes on the leaf of mate were saved. At last, however, the rain ceased to fall, and the flood sank, leaving a great expanse of fetid mud behind. The children now emerged from the ark, for if they had stayed there, they would have perished of cold and hunger. Naturally the fish and other creatures that live in the water were not drowned in the great flood; on the contrary, they throve on it, and were now quite ready to serve as food for the two babes. But how were the infants to cook the fish which they caught? That was the rub, for of course all fire on earth had been extinguished by the deluge. However, a large toad came to the rescue of the two children. Before the flood had swamped the whole earth, that prudent creature had taken the precaution of secreting himself in a hole, taking with him in his mouth some live coals, which he contrived to keep alight all the time of the deluge by blowing on them with his breath. When he saw that the surface of the ground was dry again, he hopped out of his hole with the live coals in his mouth, and making straight for the two children he bestowed on them the gift of fire. Thus they were able to roast the fish they caught and so to warm their chilled bodies. In time they grew up, and from their union the whole tribe of the Chiriguanos is descended.

The natives of Tierra del Fuego, in the extreme south of South America, tell a fantastic and obscure story of a great flood. They say that the sun was sunk in the sea, that the waters rose tumultuously, and that all the earth was submerged except a single very high mountain, on which a few people found refuge.

§ 13. *Stories of a Great Flood in Central America and Mexico.*— The Indians about Panama "had some notion of Noah's flood, and said that when it happened one man escaped in a canoe with his wife and children, from whom all mankind afterwards proceeded and peopled the world." The Indians of Nicaragua believed that since its creation the world had been destroyed by a deluge, and that after its destruction the gods had created men and animals and all things afresh.

"The Mexicans," says the Italian historian Clavigero, "with all other civilized nations, had a clear tradition, though somewhat corrupted by fable, of the creation of the world, of the universal deluge, of the confusion of tongues, and of the dispersion of the people; and had actually all these events represented in their pictures. They said, that when mankind were overwhelmed with the deluge, none were preserved but a man named Coxcox (to whom others give the name of Teocipactli), and a woman called Xochiquetzal, who saved themselves in a little bark, and having afterwards got to land upon a mountain called by them Colhuacan, had there a great many children; that these children were all born dumb, until a dove from a lofty tree imparted to them languages, but differing so much that they could not understand one another. The Tlascalans pretended that the men who survived the deluge were transformed into apes, but recovered speech and reason by degrees."

In Michoacan, a province of Mexico, the legend of a deluge was also preserved. The natives said that when the flood began to rise, a man named Tezpi, with his wife and children, entered into a great vessel, taking with them animals and seeds of diverse kinds sufficient to restock the world after the deluge. When the waters abated, the man sent forth a vulture, and the bird flew away, but finding corpses to batten on, it did not return. Then the man let fly other birds, but they also came not back. At last he sent forth a humming-bird, and it returned with a green bough in its beak. In this story the messenger birds seem clearly to be reminiscences of the raven and the dove in the Noachin legend, of which the Indians may have heard through missionaries.

The Huichol Indians, who inhabit a mountainous region near Santa Catarina in Western Mexico, have also a legend of a deluge. They say that a Huichol was felling trees to clear a field for planting. But every morning he found, to his chagrin, that the trees which he had felled the day before had grown up again as tall as ever. It was very vexatious and he grew tired of labouring in vain. On the fifth day he determined to try once more and to go to the root of the matter. Soon there rose from the ground in the middle of the clearing an old woman with a staff in her hand. She was no other than Great-grandmother Nakawee, the goddess of earth, who makes every green thing to spring forth from the dark underworld. But the man did not know her. With her staff she pointed to the south, north, west, and east, above and below; and all the trees which the young man had felled immediately stood up again. Then he understood how it came to pass that in spite of all his endeavours the clearing was always covered with trees. So he said to the old woman angrily, "Is it you who are undoing my work all the time?" "Yes," she said, "because I wish to talk to you." Then she told him that he laboured in vain. "A great flood," said she, "is coming. It is not more than five days off. There will come a wind, very bitter, and as sharp as chile, which will make you cough. Make a box from the salate (fig) tree, as long as your body, and fit it with a good cover. Take with you five grains of corn of each colour, and five beans of each colour; also take the fire and five squash-stems to feed it, and take with you a black bitch." The man did as the woman told him. On the fifth day he had the box ready and placed in it the things she had told him to take with him. Then he entered the box with the black bitch; and the old woman put on the cover, and caulked every crack with glue, asking the man to point out any chinks. Having made the box thoroughly water-tight and air-tight, the old woman took her seat on the top of it, with a macaw perched on her shoulder. For five years the box floated on the face of the waters. The first year it floated to the south, the second year it floated to the north, the third year it floated to the west, the fourth year it floated to the east, and in the fifth year it rose upward on the flood, and all the world was filled with water. The next year the flood began to abate, and the box settled on a mountain near Santa Catarina, where it may still be seen. When the box grounded on the mountain, the man took off the cover and saw that all the world was still under water. But the macaws and the parrots set to work with a will: they pecked at the mountains with their beaks till they had hollowed them out into valleys, down which the water all ran away and was separated into five seas. Then the land began to dry, and trees and grass sprang up. The old woman turned into wind and so vanished away. But the man resumed the work of clearing the field which had been interrupted by the flood. He lived with the bitch in a cave, going forth to his labour in the morning and returning home in the evening. But the bitch stayed at home all the time. Every evening on his return the man found cakes baked ready against his coming, and he was curious to know who it was that baked them. When five days had passed, he hid himself behind some bushes near the cave to watch. He saw the bitch take off her skin, hang it up, and kneel down in the likeness of a woman to grind the corn for the cakes. Stealthily he drew near her from behind, snatched the skin away, and threw it on the fire. "Now you have burned my tunic!" cried the woman and began to whine like a dog. But he took water mixed with the flour she had prepared, and with the mixture he bathed her head. She felt refreshed and remained a woman ever after. The two had a large family, and their sons and daughters married. So was the world repeopled, and the inhabitants lived in caves.

The Cora Indians, a tribe of nominal Christians whose country borders that of the Huichols on the west, tell a similar story of a great flood, in which the same incidents occur of the woodman who was warned of the coming flood by a woman, and who after the flood cohabited with a bitch transformed into a human wife. But in the Cora version of the legend the man is bidden to take into the ark with him the woodpecker, the sandpiper, and the parrot, as well as the bitch. He embarked at midnight when the flood began. When it subsided, he waited five days and then sent out the sandpiper to see if it were possible to walk on the ground. The bird flew back and cried, "Ee-wee-wee!" from which the man understood that the earth was still too wet. He waited five days more, and then sent out the woodpecker to see if the trees were hard and dry. The woodpecker thrust his beak deep into the tree, and waggled his head from side to side; but the wood was still so soft with the water that he could hardly pull his beak out again, and when at last with a violent tug he succeeded he lost his balance and fell to the ground. So when he returned to the ark he said, "Chu-ee, chu-ee!" The man took his meaning and waited five days more, after which he sent out the spotted sandpiper. By this time the mud was so dry that, when the sandpiper hopped about, his legs did not sink into it; so he came back and reported that all was well. Then the man ventured out of the ark, stepping very gingerly till he saw that the land was dry and flat.

In another fragmentary version of the deluge story, as told by the Cora Indians, the survivors of the flood would seem to have escaped in a canoe. When the waters abated, God sent the vulture out of the canoe to see whether the earth was dry enough. But the vulture did not return, because he devoured the corpses of the drowned. So God was angry with the vulture, and cursed him, and made him black instead of white, as he had been before; only the tips of his wings he left white, that men might know what their colour had been before the flood. Next God commanded the ring-dove to go out and see whether the earth was yet dry. The dove reported that the earth was dry, but that the rivers were in spate. So God ordered all the beasts to drink the rivers dry, and all the beasts and birds came and drank, save only the weeping dove (*Paloma llorona*), which would not come. Therefore she still goes every day to drink water at nightfall, because she is ashamed to be seen drinking by day; and all day long she weeps and wails. In these Cora legends the incident of the birds, especially the vulture and the raven, seems clearly to reflect the influence of missionary teaching.

§ 14. *Stories of a Great Flood in North America.*—The Papagos of South-western Arizona say that the Great Spirit made the earth and all living creatures before he made man. Then he came down to earth, and digging in the ground found some potter's clay. This he took back with him to the sky, and from there let it fall into the hole which he had dug. Immediately there came out the hero Montezuma, and with his help there also issued forth all the Indian tribes in order. Last of all appeared the wild Apaches, who ran away as fast as they were created. Those first days of the world were happy and peaceful. The sun was then nearer the earth than he is now: his raps made all the seasons equable and clothing superfluous. Men and animals talked together: a common language united them in bonds of brotherhood. But a terrible catastrophe put an end to those golden days. A great flood destroyed all flesh wherein was the breath of life: Montezuma and his friend the coyote alone escaped. For before the waters began to rise, the coyote prophesied the coming of the flood, and Montezuma took warning, and hollowed out a boat for himself, and kept it ready on the top of Santa Rosa. The coyote also prepared an ark for himself; for he gnawed down a great cane by the river bank, entered it, and caulked it with gum. So when the waters rose, Montezuma and the coyote floated on them and were saved; and when the flood retired, the man and the animal met on dry land. Anxious to discover how much dry land was left, the man sent out the coyote to explore, and the animal reported that to the west, the south, and the east there was sea, but that to the north he could find no sea. though he had journeyed till he was weary. Meanwhile the Great Spirit, with the help of Montezuma, had restocked the earth with men and animals.

The Pimas, a neighbouring tribe, related to the Papagos, say that the earth and mankind were made by a certain Chiowotmahke, that is to say Earth-prophet. Now the Creator had a son called Szeukha, who, when the earth began to be tolerably peopled, lived in the Gila valley. In the same valley there dwelt at that time a great prophet, whose name has been forgotten. One night, as the prophet slept, he was awakened by a noise at the door. When he opened, who should stand there but a great eagle? And the eagle said, "Arise, for behold, a deluge is at hand." But the prophet laughed the eagle to scorn, wrapt his robe about him, and slept again. Again, the eagle came and warned him, but again he would pay no heed. A third time the long-suffering bird warned the prophet that all the valley of the Gila would be laid waste with water, but still the foolish man turned a deaf ear to the warning. That same night came the flood, and next morning there was nothing alive to be seen but one man, if man indeed he was; for it was Szeukha, the son of the Creator, who had saved himself by floating on a ball of gum or resin. When the waters of the flood sank, he landed near the mouth of the Salt River and dwelt there in a cave on the mountain; the cave is there to this day, and so are the tools which Szeukha used when he lived in it. For some reason or other Szeukha was very angry with the great eagle, though that bird had warned the prophet to escape for his life from the flood. So with the help of a rope-ladder he climbed up the face of the cliff where the eagle resided, and finding him at home in his eyrie he killed him. In and about the nest he discovered the mangled and rotting bodies of a great multitude of people whom the eagle had carried off and devoured. These he raised to life and sent them away to repeople the earth.

The Acagchemen Indians, near St. Juan Capistrano in California, "were not entirely destitute of a knowledge of the universal deluge, but how, or from whence, they received the same, I could never understand. Some of their songs refer to it; and they have a tradition that, at a time very remote, the sea began to swell and roll in upon the plains, and fill the valleys, until it had covered the mountains; and thus nearly all the human race and animals were destroyed, excepting a few, who had resorted to a very high mountain which the waters did not reach."

The Luiseño Indians of Southern California also tell of a great flood which covered all the high mountains and drowned most of the people. But a few were saved, who took refuge on a little knoll near Bonsall. The place was called Mora by the Spaniards, but the Indians call it Katuta. Only the knoll remained above water when all the rest of the country was inundated. The survivors stayed there till the flood went down. To this day you may see on the top of the little hill heaps of sea-shells and seaweed, and ashes, and stones set together, marking the spot where the Indians cooked their food. The shells are those of the shellfish which they ate, and the ashes and stones are the remains of their fire-places. The writer who relates this tradition adds that "the hills near Del Mar and other places along the coast have many such heaps of sea-shells, of the species still found on the beaches, piled in quantities." The Luiseños still sing a Song of the Flood, in which mention is made of the knoll of Katuta.

An Indian woman of the Smith River tribe in California gave the following account of the deluge. At one time there came a great rain. It lasted a long time and the water kept rising till all the valleys were submerged, and the Indians retired to the high land. At last they were all swept away and drowned except one pair, who escaped to the highest peak and were saved. They subsisted on fish, which they cooked by placing them under their arms. They had no fire and could not get any, as everything was far too wet. At last the water sank, and from that solitary pair all the Indians of the present day are descended. As the Indians died, their spirits took the forms of deer, elks, bears, snakes, insects, and so forth, and in this way the earth was repeopled by the various kinds of animals as well as men.

According to Du Pratz, the early French historian of Louisiana, the tradition of a great flood was current among the Natchez, an Indian tribe of the Lower Mississippi. He tells us that on this subject he questioned the guardian of the temple, in which the sacred and perpetual fire was kept with religious care. The guardian replied that "the ancient word taught all the red men that almost all men were destroyed by the waters except a very small number, who had saved themselves on a very high mountain; that he knew nothing more regarding this subject except that these few people had repeopled the earth." And Du Pratz adds, "As the other nations had told me the same thing, I was assured that all the natives thought the same regarding this event, and that they had not preserved any memory of Noah's ark, which did not surprise me very much, since the Greeks, with all their knowledge, were no better informed, and we ourselves, were it not for the Holy Scriptures, might perhaps know no more than they." Elsewhere he reports the tradition somewhat more fully as follows. "They said that a great rain fell on the earth so abundantly and during such a long time that it was completely covered except a very high mountain where some men save themselves; that all fire being extinguished on the earth, a little bird named Coüy-oüy, which is entirely red (it is that which is called in Louisiana the cardinal bird), brought it from heaven. I understood by that that they had forgotten almost all the history of the deluge."

The Mandan Indians had a tradition of a great deluge in which the human race perished except one man, who escaped in a large canoe to a mountain in the west. Hence the Mandans celebrated every year certain rites in memory of the subsidence of the flood, which they called *Mee-nee-ro-ka-ha-sha*, "the sinking down or settling of the waters." The time for the ceremony was determined by the full expansion of the willow leaves on the banks of the river, for according to their tradition "the twig that the bird brought home was a willow bough and had full-grown leaves on it"; and the bird which brought the willow bough was the mourning- or turtle-dove. These doves often fed on the sides of their earth-covered huts, and none of the Indians would destroy or harm them; even their dogs were trained not to molest the birds. In the Mandan village a wooden structure was carefully preserved to represent the canoe in which the only man was saved from the flood. "In the centre of the Mandan village," says the painter Catlin, "is an open, circular area of a hundred and fifty feet diameter, kept always clear, as a public ground, for the display of all their feasts, parades, etc., and around it are their wigwams placed as near to each other as they can well stand, their doors facing the centre of this public area. In the middle of this ground, which is trodden like a hard pavement, is a curb (somewhat like a large hogshead standing on its end) made of planks and bound with hoops, some eight or nine feet high, which they religiously preserve and protect from year to year, free from mark or scratch, and which they call the "big canoe"; it is undoubtedly a symbolic representation of a part of their traditional history of the Flood; which it is very evident, from this and numerous other features of this grand ceremony, they have in some way or other received, and are here endeavouring to perpetuate by vividly impressing it on the minds of the whole nation. This object of superstition, from its position as the very centre of the village, is the rallying-point of the whole nation. To it their devotions are paid on various occasions of feasts and religious exercises during the year."

On the occasion when Catlin witnessed the annual ceremony commemorative of the flood, the first or only man (*Nu-mohk-muck-a-nah*) who escaped the flood was personated by a mummer dressed in a robe of white wolf-skins, which fell back over his shoulders, while on his head he wore a splendid covering of two ravens' skins and in his left hand he carried a large pipe. Entering the village from the prairie he approached the medicine or mystery lodge, which he had the means of opening, and which had been strictly closed during the year except for the performance of these religious rites. All day long this mummer went through the village, stopping in front of every hut and crying, till the owner of the hut came out and asked him who he was and what was the matter. To this the mummer replied by relating the sad catastrophe which had happened on the earth's surface through the overflowing of the waters, saying that "he was the only person saved from the universal calamity; that he landed his big canoe on a high mountain in the west, where he now resides; that he had come to open the medicine-lodge, which must needs receive a present of some edged tool from the owner of every wigwam, that it may be sacrificed to the water;

for he says, 'If this is not done, there will be another flood, and no one will be saved, as it was with such tools that the big canoe was made.'" Having visited every wigwam in the village during the day, and having received from each a hatchet, a knife, or other edged tool, he deposited them at evening in the medicine lodge, where they remained till the afternoon of the last day of the ceremony. Then as the final rite they were thrown into a deep pool in the river from a bank thirty feet high in presence of the whole village; "from whence they can never be recovered, and where they were, undoubtedly, *sacrificed* to the Spirit of the Water." Amongst the ceremonies observed at this spring festival of the Mandans was a bull dance danced by men disguised as buffaloes and intended to procure a plentiful supply of buffaloes in the ensuing season; further, the young men underwent voluntarily a series of excruciating tortures in the medicine lodge for the purpose of commending themselves to the Great Spirit. But how far these quaint and ghastly rites were connected with the commemoration of the Great Flood does not appear from the accounts of our authorities.

This Mandan festival went by the name of *O-kee-pa* and was "an annual religious ceremony, to the strict observance of which those ignorant and superstitious people attributed not only their enjoyment in life, but their very existence; for traditions, their only history, instructed them in the belief that the singular forms of this ceremony produced the buffaloes for their supply of food, and that the omission of this annual ceremony, with its sacrifices made to the waters, would bring upon them a repetition of the calamity which their traditions say once befell them, destroying the whole human race, excepting one man, who landed from his canoe on a high mountain in the west. This tradition, however, was not peculiar to the Mandan tribe, for amongst one hundred and twenty different tribes that I visited in North and South and Central America, not a tribe exists that has not related to me distinct or vague traditions of such a calamity, in which one, or three, or eight persons were saved above the waters, on the top of a high mountain. Some of these, at the base of the Rocky Mountains and in the plains of Venezuela, and the Pampa del Sacramento in South America, make annual pilgrimages to the fancied summits where the antediluvian species were saved in canoes or otherwise, and, under the mysterious regulations of their *medicine* (mystery) men, tender their prayers and sacrifices to the Great Spirit, to ensure their exemption from a similar catastrophe."

The Cherokee Indians are reported to have a tradition that the water once prevailed over the land until all mankind were drowned except a single family. The coming of the calamity was revealed by a dog to his master. For the sagacious animal went day after day to the banks of a river where he stood gazing at the water and howling piteously. Being rebuked by his master and ordered home, the dog opened his mouth and warned the man of the danger in which he stood. "You must build a boat," said he, "and put in it all that you would save; for a great rain is coming that will flood the land." The animal concluded his prediction by informing his master that his salvation depended on throwing him, the dog, into the water; and for a sign of the truth of what he said he bade him look at the back of his neck. The man did so, and sure enough the back of the dog's neck was raw and bare, the flesh and bone appearing. So the man believed, and following the directions of the faithful animal he and his family were saved, and from them the whole of the present population of the globe is lineally descended.

Stories of a great flood are widely spread among Indians of the great Algonquin stock, and they resemble each other in some details. Thus the Delawares, an Algonquin tribe whose home was about Delaware Bay, told of a deluge which submerged the whole earth, and from which few persons escaped alive. They saved themselves by taking refuge on the back of a turtle, which was so old that his shell was mossy like the bank of a rivulet. As they were floating thus forlorn, a loon flew their way, and they begged him to dive and bring up land from the depth of the waters. The bird dived accordingly, but could find no bottom. Then he flew far away and came back with a little earth in his bill. Guided by him, the turtle swam to the place, where some dry land was found. There they settled and repeopled the country.

The Montagnais, a group of Indian tribes in Canada who also belong to the great Algonquin stock, told an early Jesuit missionary that a certain mighty being, whom they called Messou, repaired the world after it had been ruined by the great flood. They said that one day Messou went out to hunt, and that the wolves which he used instead of hounds entered into a lake and were there detained. Messou sought them everywhere, till a bird told him that he saw the lost wolves in the middle of the lake. So he waded into the water to rescue them, but the lake overflowed, covered the earth, and overwhelmed the world. Greatly astonished, Messou sent the raven to search for a clod of earth out of which he might rebuild that element, but no earth could the raven find. Next Messou sent an otter, which plunged into the deep water, but brought back nothing. Lastly, Messou despatched a musk-rat, and the rat brought back a little soil, which Messou used to refashion the earth on which we live. He shot arrows at the trunks of trees, and the arrows were changed into branches: he took vengeance on those who had detained his wolves in the lake; and he married a musk-rat, by which he had children, who repeopled the world.

In this legend there is no mention of men; and but for the part played in it by the animals we might have supposed that the deluge took place in the early ages of the world before the appearance of life on the earth. However, some two centuries later, another Catholic missionary tells us that the Montagnais of the

Hudson Bay Territory have a tradition of a great flood which covered the world, and from which four persons, along with animals and birds, escaped alive on a floating island. Yet another Catholic missionary reports the Montagnais legend more fully as follows. God, being angry with the giants, commanded a man to build a large canoe. The man did so, and when he had embarked in it, the water rose on all sides, and the canoe with it, till no land was anywhere to be seen. Weary of beholding nothing but a heaving mass of water, the man threw an otter into the flood, and the animal dived and brought up a little earth. The man took the earth or mud in his hand and breathed on it, and at once it began to grow. So he laid it on the surface of the water and prevented it from sinking. As it continued to grow into an island, he desired to know whether it was large enough to support him. Accordingly he placed a reindeer upon it, but the animal soon made the circuit of the island and returned to him, from which he concluded that the island was not yet large enough. So he continued to blow on it till the mountains, the lakes, and the rivers were formed. Then he disembarked. The same missionary reports a deluge legend current among the Crees, another tribe of the Algonquin stock in Canada; but this Cree story bears clear traces of Christian influence, for in it the man is said to have sent forth from the canoe, first a raven, and second a wood-pigeon. The raven did not return and as a punishment for his disobedience the bird was changed from white to black; the pigeon returned with his claws full of mud, from which the man inferred that the earth was dried up; so he landed.

The genuine old Algonquin legend of the flood appears to have been first recorded at full length by a Mr. H. E. MacKenzie, who passed much of his early life with the Salteaux or Chippeway Indians, a large and powerful branch of the Algonquin stock. He communicated the tradition to Lieutenant W. H. Hooper, R.N., at Fort Norman, near Bear Lake, about the middle of the nineteenth century. In substance the legend runs as follows.

Once upon a time there were certain Indians and among them a great medicine-man named Wis-kay-tchach. With them also were a wolf and his two sons, who lived on a footing of intimacy with the human beings. Wis-kay-tchach called the old wolf his brother and the young ones his nephews; for he recognized all animals as his relations. In the winter time the whole party began to starve; so in order to find food the parent wolf announced his intention of separating with his children from the band. Wis-kay-tchach offered to bear him company, so off they set together. Soon they came to the track of a moose. The old wolf and the medicine-man Wis (as we may call him for short) stopped to smoke, while the young wolves pursued the moose. After a time, the young ones not returning, Wis and the old wolf set off after them, and soon found blood on the snow, whereby they knew that the moose was killed.

Soon they came up with the young wolves, but no moose was to be seen, for the young wolves had eaten it up. They bade Wis make a fire, and when he had done so, he found the whole of the moose restored and already quartered and cut up. The young wolves divided the spoil into four portions; but one of them retained the tongue and the others the mouffle (upper lip), which are the chief delicacies of the animal. Wis grumbled, and the young wolves gave up these dainties to him. When they had devoured the whole, one of the young wolves said he would make marrow fat, which is done by breaking up the bones very small and boiling them. Soon this resource was also exhausted, and they all began to hunger again. So they agreed to separate once more. This time Old Wolf went off with one of his sons, leaving Wis and the other young wolf to hunt together.

The story now leaves the old wolf and follows the fortunes of Wis and his nephew, one of the two young wolves. The young wolf killed some deer and brought them home in his stomach, disgorging them as before on his arrival. At last he told his uncle that he could catch no more, so Wis sat up all night making medicine or using enchantments. In the morning he bade his nephew go a-hunting, but warned him to be careful at every valley and hollow place to throw a stick over before he ventured to jump himself, or else some evil would certainly befall him. So away went the young wolf, but in pursuing a deer he forgot to follow his uncle's directions, and in attempting to leap a hollow he fell plump into a river and was there killed and devoured by water-lynxes. What kind of a beast a water-lynx is, the narrator did not know. But let that be. Enough that the young wolf was killed and devoured by these creatures. After waiting long for his nephew, Wis set off to look for him, and coming to the spot where the young wolf had leaped, he guessed rightly that the animal had neglected his warning and fallen into the stream. He saw a kingfisher sitting on a tree and gazing fixedly at the water. Asked what he was looking at so earnestly, the bird replied that he was looking at the skin of Wis's nephew, the young wolf, which served as a door-mat to the house of the water-lynxes; for not content with killing and devouring the nephew, these ferocious animals had added insult to injury by putting his skin to this ignoble use. Grateful for the information, Wis called the kingfisher to him, combed the bird's head, and began to put a ruff around his neck; but before he had finished his task, the bird flew away, and that is why down to this day kingfishers have only part of a ruff at the back of their head. Before the kingfisher flew away, he gave Wis a parting hint, that the water-lynxes often came ashore to lie on the sand, and that if he wished to be revenged on them he must turn himself into a stump close by, but he must be most careful to keep perfectly rigid and on no account to let himself be pulled down by the frogs and snakes, which the water-lynxes would be sure to send to dislodge him. On receiving these directions Wis returned to his camp and resorted to enchantments; also he provided all things necessary, among others a large canoe to hold all the animals that could not swim.

Before daylight broke, he had completed his preparations and embarked all the aforesaid animals in the big canoe. He then paddled quietly to the neighbourhood of the lynxes, and having secured the canoe behind a promontory, he landed, transformed himself into a stump, and awaited, in that assumed character, the appearance of the water-lynxes. Soon the black one crawled out and lay down on the sand; and then the grey one did the same. Last of all the white one, which had killed the young wolf, popped his head out of the water, but espying the stump, he grew suspicious, and called out to his brethren that he had never seen that stump before. They answered carelessly that it must have been always there; but the wary white lynx, still suspicious, sent frogs and snakes to pull it down. Wis had a severe struggle to keep himself upright, but he succeeded, and the white lynx, his suspicious now quite lulled to rest, lay down to sleep on the sand. Wis waited a little, then resuming his natural shape he took his spear and crept softly to the white lynx. He had been warned by the kingfisher to strike at the animal's shadow or he would assuredly be balked; but in his eagerness he forgot the injunction, and striking full at his adversary's body he missed his mark. The creature rushed towards the water, but Wis had one more chance and aiming this time at the lynx's shadow he wounded grievously the beast itself. However, the creature contrived to escape into the river, and the other lynxes with it. Instantly the water began to boil and rise, and Wis made for his canoe as fast as he could run. The water continued flowing, until land, trees, and hills were all covered. The canoe floated about on the surface, and Wis, having before taken on board all animals that could not swim, now busied himself in picking up all that could swim only for a short time and were now struggling for life in the water around him.

But in his enchantments to meet the great emergency, Wis had overlooked a necessary condition for the restoration of the world after the flood. He had no earth, not even a particle, which might serve as a nucleus for the new lands which were to rise from the waste of waters. He now set about obtaining it. Tying a string to the leg of a loon he ordered the bird to try for soundings and to persevere in its descent if it should perish in the attempt; for, said he, "If you are drowned, it is no matter: I can easily restore you to life." Encouraged by this assurance, the bird dropped like a stone into the water, and the line ran out fast. When it ceased to run, Wis hauled it up, and at the end of the line was the loon dead. Being duly restored to life, the bird informed Wis that he had found no bottom. So Wis next despatched an otter on the same errand, but he fared no better than the loon. After that Wis tried a beaver, which after being drowned and resuscitated in the usual way, reported that he had seen the tops of trees, but could sink no deeper. Last of all Wis let down a rat fastened to a stone; down went the rat and the stone, and presently the line slackened. Wis hauled it up and at the end of it he found the rat dead but clutching a little earth in its paws. Wis had now all that he wanted. He restored the rat to life and spread out the earth to dry; then he blew upon it till it swelled and grew to a great extent. When he thought it large enough, he sent out a wolf to explore, but the animal soon returned, saying that the world was small. Thereupon Wis again blew on the earth for a long time, and then sent forth a crow. When the bird did not return, Wis concluded that the world was now large enough for all; so he and the animals disembarked from the canoe.

Another version of the same story has been recorded more briefly, with minor variations, among the Ojibways of South-eastern Ontario. It runs thus. Nenebojo was living with his brother in the woods. Every day he went out hunting, while his brother stayed at home. One evening when he returned he noticed that his brother was not at home; so he went out to look for him. But he could find him nowhere. Next morning he again started in search of his brother. As he walked by the shore of a lake, what should he see but a kingfisher sitting on a branch of a tree that drooped over the water. The bird was looking at something intently in the water below him. "What are you looking at?" asked Nenebojo. But the kingfisher pretended not to hear him. Then Nenebojo said again, "If you will tell me what you are looking at, I will make you fair to see. I will paint your feathers." The bird gladly accepted the offer, and as soon as Nenebojo had painted his feathers, the king-fisher said, "I am looking at Nenebojo's brother, whom the water-spirits have killed and whose skin they are using as a door-flap." Then Nenebojo asked again, "Where do these water-spirits come to the shore to sun themselves?" The kingfisher answered, "They always sun themselves over there at one of the bays, where the sand is quite dry."

Then Nenebojo left the kingfisher. He resolved to go over to the sandy beach indicated to him by the bird, and there to wait for the first chance of killing the water spirits. He first pondered what disguise he should assume in order to approach them unawares. Said he to himself, "I will change myself into an old rotten stump." No sooner said than done; the transformation was effected by a long rod, which Nenebojo always carried with him. When the lions came out of the water to sun themselves, one of them noticed the stump and said to one of his fellows, "I never saw that old stump there before. Surely it can't be Nenebojo." But the lion he spoke to said, "Indeed, I have seen that stump before." Then a third lion came over to peer and make sure. He broke a piece off and saw that it was rotten. So all the lions were easy in their minds and lay down to sleep. When Nenebojo thought they were fast asleep he struck them on their heads with his stick. As he struck them the water rose from the lake. He ran away, but the waves pursued him. As he ran he met a woodpecker, who showed him the way to a mountain where grew a tall pine-tree. Nenebojo climbed up the tree and began to build a raft. By the time he had finished the raft the water reached to his neck. Then he put on the raft two animals of all the kinds that existed, and with them he floated about.

When they had drifted for a while, Nenebojo said, "I believe that the water will never subside, so I had better make land again." Then he sent an otter to dive to the bottom of the water and fetch up some earth; but the otter came back without any. Next he sent the beaver on the same errand, but again in vain. After that Nenebojo despatched the musk-rat to bring up earth out of the water. When the musk-rat returned to the surface his paws were tightly closed. On opening them Nenebojo found some little grains of sand, and he discovered other grains in the mouth of the musk-rat. So he put all the grains together, dried them, and then blew them into the lake with the horn which he used for calling the animals. In the lake the grains of sand formed an island. Nenebojo enlarged the island, and sent out a raven to find out how large it was. But the raven never returned. So Nenebojo decided to send out the hawk, the fleetest of all birds on the wing. After a while the hawk returned, and being asked whether he had seen the raven anywhere, he said he had seen him eating dead bodies by the shore of the lake. Then Nenebojo said, "Henceforth the raven will never have anything to eat but what he steals." Yet another interval, and Nenebojo sent out the caribou to explore the size of the island. The animal soon returned, saying that the island was not large enough. So Nenebojo blew more sand into the water, and when he had done so he ceased to make the earth.

The Blackfoot Indians, another Algonquin tribe, who used to range over the eastern slopes of the Rocky Mountains and the prairies at their foot, tell a similar tale of the great primeval deluge. "In the beginning," they say, "all the land was covered with water, an Old Man and all the animals were floating around on a large raft. One day Old Man told the beaver to dive and try to bring up a little mud. The beaver went down, and was gone a long time, but could not reach the bottom. Then the loon tried, and the otter, but the water was too deep for them. At last the musk-rat dived, and he was gone so long that they thought he had been drowned, but he finally came up, almost dead, and when they pulled him on to the raft, they found, in one of his paws, a little mud. With this, Old Man formed the world, and afterwards he made the people."

Similar stories appear to be widely current among the Indian tribes of North-western Canada. They are not confined to tribes of the Algonquin stock, but occur also among their northern neighbours, the Tinnehs or Dénés, who belong to the great Athapascan family, the most widely distributed of all Indian linguistic families in North America, stretching as it does from the Arctic coast far into

Mexico, and extending from the Pacific to Hudson's Bay, and from the Rio Colorado to the mouth of the Rio Grande. Thus the Crees, who are an Algonquin tribe, relate that in the beginning there lived an old magician named Wissaketchak, who wrought marvels by his enchantments. However, a certain sea monster hated the old man and sought to destroy him. So when the magician was paddling in his canoe, the monster lashed the sea with his tail till the waves rose and engulfed the land. But Wissaketchak built a great raft and gathered upon it pairs of all animals and all birds, and in that way he saved his own life and the lives of the other creatures. Nevertheless the great fish continued to lash his tail and the water continued to rise, till it had covered not only the earth but the highest mountains, and not a scrap of dry land was to be seen. Then Wissaketchak sent the diver duck to plunge into the water and bring up the sunken earth; but the bird could not dive to the bottom and was drowned. Thereupon Wissaketchak sent the musk-rat, which, after remaining long under water, reappeared with its throat full of slime. Wissaketchak took the slime, moulded it into a small disk, and placed it on the water, where it floated. It resembled the nests which the musk-rats make for themselves on the ice. By and by the disk swelled into a hillock. Then Wissaketchak blew on it, and the more he blew on it the more it swelled, and being baked by the sun it became a solid mass. As it grew and hardened, Wissaketchak sent forth the animals to lodge upon it, and at last he himself disembarked and took possession of the land thus created, which is the world we now inhabit. A similar tale is told by the Dogrib and Slave Indians, two Tinneh tribes, except that they give the name of Tchapewi to the man who was saved from the great flood; and they say that when he was floating on the raft with couples of all sorts of animals, which he had rescued, he caused all the amphibious animals, one after the other, including the otter and the beaver, to dive into the water, but none of them could bring up any earth except the musk-rat, who dived last of all and came up panting with a little mud in his paw. That mud Tchapewi breathed on till it grew into the earth as we now see it. So Tchapewi replaced the animals on it, and they lived there as before; and he propped the earth on a stout stay, making it firm and solid.

The Hareskin Indians, another Tinneh tribe, say that a certain Kunyan, which means Wise Man, once upon a time resolved to build a great raft. When his sister, who was also his wife, asked him why he would build it, he said, "If there comes a flood, as I foresee, we shall take refuge on the raft." He told his plan to other men on the earth, but they laughed at him, saying, "If there is a flood, we shall take refuge in the trees." Nevertheless the Wise Man made a great raft, joining the logs together by ropes made of roots. All of a sudden there came a flood such that the like of it had never been seen before. The water seemed to gush forth on every side. Men climbed up in the trees, but the water rose after them, and all were drowned. But the Wise Man floated safely on his strong and well-corded raft. As he floated he thought of the future, and he gathered by twos all the herbivorous animals, and all the birds, and even all the beasts of prey he met with on his passage. "Come up on my raft," he said to them, "for soon there will be no more earth." Indeed, the earth disappeared under the water, and for a long time nobody thought of going to look for it. The first to plunge into the depth was the musk-rat, but he could find no bottom, and when he bobbed up on the surface again he was half drowned. "There is no earth!" said he. A second time he dived, and when he came up, he said, "I smelt the smell of the earth, but I could not reach it." Next it came to the turn of the beaver. He dived and remained a long time under water. At last he reappeared, floating on his back, breathless and unconscious. But in his paw he had a little mud, which he gave to the Wise Man. The Wise Man placed the mud on the water, breathed on it, and said, "I would there were an earth again!" At the same time he breathed on the handful of mud, and lo! it began to grow. He put a small bird on it, and the patch of mud grew still bigger. So he breathed, and breathed, and the mud grew and grew. Then the man put a fox on the floating island of mud, and the fox ran round it in a single day. Round and round the island ran the fox, and bigger and bigger grew the island. Six times did the fox make the circuit of the island, but when he made it for the seventh time, the land was complete even as it was before the flood. Then the Wise Man caused all the animals to disembark and landed them on the dry ground. Afterwards he himself disembarked with his wife and son, saying, "It is for us that this earth shall be repeopled." And repeopled it was, sure enough. Only one difficulty remained with which the Wise Man had to grapple. The floods were still out, and how to reduce them was the question. The bittern saw the difficulty and came to the rescue. He swallowed the whole of the water, and then lay like a log on the bank, with his belly swollen to a frightful size. This was more than the Wise Man had bargained for; if there had been too much water before, there was now too little. In his embarrassment the Wise Man had recourse to the plover. "The bittern," he said, "is lying yonder in the sun with his belly full of water. Pierce it." So the artful plover made up to the unsuspecting bittern. "My grandmother," said he, in a sympathizing tone, "has no doubt a pain in her stomach." And he passed his hand softly over the ailing part of the bittern as if to, soothe it. But all of a sudden he put out his claws and clawed the swollen stomach of the bittern. Such a scratch he gave it! There was a gurgling, gurgling sound, and out came the water from the stomach bubbling and foaming. It flowed away into rivers and lakes, and thus the world became habitable once more.

Some Tinneh Indians affirm that the deluge was caused by a heavy fall of snow in the month of September. One old man alone foresaw the catastrophe and warned his fellows, but all in vain.

"We will escape to the mountains," said they. But they were all drowned. Now the old man had built a canoe, and when the flood came, he sailed about in it, rescuing from the water all the animals he fell in with. Unable long to support this manner of life, he caused the beaver, the otter, the musk-rat, and the arctic duck to dive into the water in search of the drowned earth. Only the arctic duck came back with a little slime on its claws; and the man spread the slime on the water, caused it to grow by his breath, and for six days disembarked the animals upon it. After that, when the ground had grown to the size of a great island, he himself stepped ashore. Other Tinnehs say that the old man first sent forth a raven, which gorged itself on the floating corpses and came not back. Next he sent forth a turtle-dove, which flew twice round the world and returned. The third time she came back at evening, very tired, with a budding twig of fir in her mouth. The influence of Christian teaching on this last version of the story is manifest.

The Sarcees, another Indian tribe belonging to the great Tinneh stock, were formerly a powerful nation, but are now reduced to a few hundreds. Their reserve, a fine tract of prairie land, adjoins that of the Blackfeet in Alberta, a little south of the Canadian Pacific Railway. They have a tradition of a deluge which agrees in its main features with that of the Ojibways, Crees, and other Canadian tribes. They say that when the world was flooded, only one man and woman were left alive, being saved on a raft, on which they also collected animals and birds of all sorts. The man sent a beaver down to dive to the bottom. The creature did so and brought up a little mud, which the man moulded in his hands to form a new world. At first the world was so small that a little bird could walk round it, but it kept growing bigger and bigger. "First," said the narrator, "our father took up his abode on it, then there were men, then women, then animals, and then birds. Our father next created the rivers, the mountains, the trees, and all the things as we now see them." At the conclusion of the story the white man, who reports it, observed to the Sarcees that the Ojibway tradition was very like theirs, except that in the Ojibway tradition it was not a beaver but a musk-rat that brought up the earth from the water. The remark elicited a shout of approval from five or six of the tribe, who were squatting around in the tent. "Yes! yes!" they cried in chorus. "The man has told you lies. It was a musk-rat! it was a musk-rat!"

In the religion and mythology of the Tlingits or Thlinkeets, an important Indian tribe of Alaska, Yehl or the Raven plays a great part. He was not only the ancestor of the Raven clan but the creator of men; he caused the plants to grow, and he set the sun, moon, and stars in their places. But he had a wicked uncle, who had murdered Yehl's ten elder brothers either by drowning them or, according to others, by stretching them on a board and sawing off their heads with a knife. To the commission of these atrocious crimes he was instigated by the passion of jealousy, for he had a young wife of whom he was very fond, and he knew that according to Tlingit law his nephews, the sons of his sister, would inherit his widow whenever he himself should depart from this vale of tears. So when Yehl grew up to manhood, his affectionate uncle endeavoured to dispose of him as he had disposed of his ten elder brothers, but all in vain. For Yehl was not a common child. His mother had conceived him through swallowing a round pebble which she found on the shore at ebb tide; and by means of another stone she contrived to render the infant invulnerable. So when his uncle tried to saw off his head in the usual way, the knife made no impression at all on Yehl. Not discouraged by this failure, the old villain attempted the life of his virtuous nephew in other ways. In his fury he said, "Let there be a flood," and a flood there was which covered all the mountains. But Yehl assumed his wings and feathers, which he could put off and on at pleasure, and spreading his pinions he flew up to the sky, and there remained hanging by his beak for ten days, while the water of the flood rose so high that it lapped his wings. When the water sank, he let go and dropped like an arrow into the sea, where he fell soft on a bank of seaweed and was rescued from his perilous position by a sea otter, which brought him safe to land. What happened to mankind during the flood is not mentioned in this version of the Tlingit legend.

Another Tlingit legend tells how Raven caused a great flood in a different way. He had put a woman under the world to attend to the rising and falling of the tides. Once he wished to learn about all that goes on under the sea, so he caused the woman to raise the water, in order that he might go there dry-shod. But he thoughtfully directed her to heave the ocean up slowly, so that when the flood came people might have time to load their canoes with the necessary provisions and get on board. So the ocean rose gradually, bearing on its surface the people in their canoes. As they rose up and up the sides of the mountains, they could see the bears and other wild beasts walking about on the still unsubmerged tops. Many of the bears swam out to the canoes, wishing to scramble on board; then the people who had been wise enough to take their dogs with them were very glad of it, for the noble animals kept off the bears. Some people landed on the tops of the mountains, built walls round them to dam out the water, and tied their canoes on the inside. They could not take much firewood up with them; there was not room for it in the canoes. It was a very anxious and dangerous time. The survivors could see trees torn up by the roots and swept along on the rush of the waters; large devil-fish, too, and other strange creatures floated past on the tide-race. When the water subsided, the people followed the ebbing tide down the sides of the mountains; but the trees were all gone, and having no firewood they perished of cold. When Raven came back from under the sea, and saw the fish lying high and dry on the mountains and in the creeks, he said to them, "Stay there and be turned to stones." So stones they became. And when he saw people coming down he would say in like manner, "Turn to stones just where you are." And turned to stones they were. After all mankind had been destroyed in this way, Raven created them afresh out of leaves. Because he made this new generation out of leaves, people know that he must have turned into stone all the men and women who survived the great flood. And that, too, is why to this day so many people die in autumn with the fall of the leaf; when flowers and leaves are fading and falling, we also pass away like them.

According to yet another account, the Tlingits or Kolosh, as the Russians used to call them, speak of a universal deluge, during which men were saved in a great floating ark which, when the water sank, grounded on a rock and split in two; and that, in their opinion, is the cause of the diversity of languages. The Tlingits represent one-half of the population, which was shut up in the ark, and all the remaining peoples of the earth represent the other half. This last legend may be of Christian origin, for it exhibits a sort of blend of Noah's ark with the tower of Babel.

The Haida Indians of Queen Charlotte Islands say that "very long ago there was a great flood by which all men and animals were destroyed, with the exception of a single raven. This creature was not, however, exactly an ordinary bird, but—as with all animals in the old Indian stories—possessed the attributes of a human being to a great extent. His coat of feathers, for instance, could be put on or taken off at will, like a garment. It is even related in one version of the story that he was born of a woman who had no husband, and that she made bows and arrows for him. When old enough, with these he killed birds, and of their skins she sewed a cape or blanket. The birds were the little snow-bird with black head and neck, the large black and red, and the Mexican woodpeckers. The name of this being was Ne-kil-stlas. When the flood had gone down Ne-kil-stlas looked about, but could find neither companions nor a mate, and became very lonely. At last he took a cockle (*Cardium Nuttalli*) from the beach, and marrying it, he constantly continued to brood and think earnestly of his wish for a companion. By and by in the shell he heard a very faint cry, like that of a newly born child, which gradually became louder, and at last a little female child was seen, which growing by degrees larger and larger, was finally married by the raven, and from this union all the Indians were produced and the country peopled."

The Thompson Indians of British Columbia say that once there was a great flood which covered the whole country, except the tops of some of the highest mountains. The Indians think, though they are not quite sure, that the flood was caused by three brothers called Qoaqlqal, who in those days travelled all over the country working miracles and transforming things, till the transformers were themselves transformed into stones. Be that as it may, everybody was drowned in the great flood except the coyote and three men; the coyote survived because he turned himself into a piece of wood and so floated on the water, and the men escaped with their lives by embarking in a canoe, in which they drifted to the Nzukeski Mountains. There they were afterwards, with their canoe, transformed into stones, and there you may see them sitting in the shape of stones down to this day. As for the coyote, when the flood subsided, he was left high and dry on the shore in the likeness of the piece of wood into which, at the nick of time, he had cleverly transformed himself. So he now resumed his natural shape and looked about him. He found he was in the Thompson River country. He took trees to him to be his wives, and from him and the trees together the Indians of the present day are descended. Before the flood there were neither lakes nor streams in the mountains, and therefore there were no fish. When the waters of the deluge receded, they left lakes in the hollows of the mountains, and streams began to flow down from them towards the sea. That is why we now find lakes in the mountains, and fish in the lakes. Thus the deluge story of the Thompson River Indians appears to have been invented to explain the presence of lakes in the mountains; the primitive philosopher accounted for them by a great flood which, as it retired, left the lakes behind it in the hollows of the hills, just as the ebbing tide leaves pools behind it in the hollows of the rocks on the sea-shore.

Legends of a great flood appear to have been current among the Indian tribes of Washington State. Thus the Twanas, on Puget Sound, say that once on a time the people were wicked, and to punish them a great flood came, which overflowed all the land except one mountain. The people fled in their canoes to the highest mountain in their country—a peak of the Olympic range—and as the water rose above it they tied their canoes with long ropes to the highest tree, but still the water rose above it. Then some of the canoes broke from their moorings and drifted away to the west, where the descendants of the persons saved in them now live, a tribe who speak a language like that of the Twanas. That, too, they say, is why the present number of the tribe is so small. In their language this mountain is called by a name which means "Fastener," because they fastened their canoes to it at that time. They also speak of a pigeon which went out to view the dead.

When the earliest missionaries came among the Spokanas, Nez Perces, and Cayuses, who, with the Yakimas, used to inhabit the eastern part of Washington State, they found that these Indians had their own tradition of a great flood, in which one man and his wife were saved on a raft. Each of these three tribes, together with the Flathead tribes, had its own separate Ararat on which the survivors found refuge.

The story of a great flood is also told by the Indians of Washington State who used to inhabit the lower course of the Columbia River and speak the Kathlamet dialect of Chinook. In one respect their tale resembles the Algonquin legend. They say that a certain maiden was advised by the blue-jay to marry the panther, who was an elk-hunter and the chief of his town to boot. So away she hied to the panther's town, but when she came there she married the beaver by mistake instead of the panther. When her husband the beaver came back from the fishing, she went down to the beach to meet him, and he told her to take up the trout he had caught. But she found that they were not really trout at all, but only willow branches. Disgusted at the discovery, she ran away from him, and finally married the panther, whom she ought to have married at first. Thus deserted by the wife of his bosom, the beaver wept for five days, till all the land was flooded with his tears. The houses were overwhelmed, and the animals took to their canoes. When the flood reached nearly to the sky, they bethought them of fetching up earth from the depths, so they said to the blue-jay, "Now dive, blue-jay!" So the blue-jay dived, but he did not go very deep, for his tail remained sticking out of the water. After that, all the animals tried to dive. First the mink and next the otter plunged into the vasty deep, but came up again without having found the bottom. Then it came to the turn of the musk-rat. He said, "Tie the canoes together." So they tied the canoes together and laid planks across them. Thereupon the musk-rat threw off his blanket, sang his song five times over, and without more ado dived into the water, and disappeared. He was down a long while. At last flags came up to the surface of the water. Then it became summer, the flood sank, and the canoes with it, till they landed on dry ground. All the animals jumped out of the canoes, but as they did so, they knocked their tails against the gunwale and broke them off short. That is why the grizzly bears and the black bears have stumpy tails down to this day. But the otter, the mink, the musk-rat, and the panther returned to the canoe, picked up their missing tails, and fastened them on the stumps. That is why these animals have still tails of a decent length, though they were broken off short at the flood. In this story little is said of the human race, and how it escaped from the deluge. But the tale clearly belongs to that primitive type of story in which no clear distinction is drawn between man and beast, the lower creatures being supposed to think, speak, and act like human beings, and to live on terms of practical equality with them. This community of nature is implicitly indicated in the Kathlamet story by the marriage of a girl, first to a beaver, and then to a panther; and it appears also in the incidental description of the beaver as a man with a big belly. Thus in describing how the animals survived the deluge, the narrator may have assumed that he had sufficiently explained the survival of mankind also.

In North America legends of a great flood are not confined to the Indian tribes; they are found also among the Eskimo and their kinsfolk the Greenlanders. At Orowiknarak, in Alaska, Captain Jacobsen was told that the Eskimo have a tradition of a mighty inundation which, simultaneously with an earthquake, swept over the land so rapidly that only a few persons were able to escape in their skin canoes to the tops of the highest mountains. Again, the Eskimo of Norton Sound, in Alaska, say that in the first days the earth was flooded, all but a very high mountain in the middle. The water came up from the sea and covered the whole land except the top of this mountain. Only a few animals escaped to the mountain and were saved; and a few people made a shift to survive by floating about in a boat and subsisting on the fish they caught till the water subsided. As the flood sank and the mountains emerged from the water, the people landed from the canoe on these heights, and gradually followed the retreating flood to the coast. The animals which had escaped to the mountains also descended and replenished the earth after their kinds.

Again, the Tchiglit Eskimo, who inhabit the coast of the Arctic Ocean from Point Barrow on the west to Cape Bathurst on the east, tell of a great flood which broke over the face of the earth and, driven by the wind, submerged the dwellings of men. The Eskimo tied several boats together so as to form a great raft, and on it they floated about on the face of the great waters, huddling together for warmth under a tent which they had pitched, but shivering in the icy blast and watching the uprooted trees drifting past on the waves. At last a magician named An-odjium, that is, Son of the Owl, threw his bow into the sea, saying, "Enough, wind, be calm!" After that he threw in his ear-rings; and that sufficed to cause the flood to subside.

The Central Eskimo say that long ago the ocean suddenly began to rise and continued rising until it had inundated the whole land. The water even covered the tops of the mountains, and the ice drifted over them. When the flood had subsided, the ice stranded and ever since forms an ice-cap on the top of the mountains. Many shellfish, fish, seals, and whales were left high and dry, and their shells and bones may be seen there to this day. Many Eskimo were then drowned, but many others, who had taken to their boats when the flood began to rise, were saved.

With regard to the Greenlanders their historian Crantz tells us that "almost all heathen nations know something of Noah's Flood, and the first missionaries found also some pretty plain traditions among the Greenlanders; namely, that the world once overset, and all mankind, except one, were drowned; but some were turned into fiery spirits. The only man that escaped alive, afterwards smote the ground with his stick, and out sprang a woman, and these two repeopled the world. As a proof that the deluge once overflowed the whole earth, they say that many shells, and relics of fishes, have been found far within the land where men could never have lived, yea that bones of whales have been found upon a high mountain." Similar evidence in support of the legend was adduced to the traveller C. F. Hall by the Innuits or Eskimo with whom he lived. He tells us that "they have a tradition of a deluge which they attribute to an unusually high tide. On one occasion when I was speaking with Tookoolito concerning her people, she said, 'Innuits all think this earth once covered with water.' I asked her why they thought so. She answered, 'Did you never see little stones, like clams and such things as live in the sea, away up on mountains?'"

§ 15. *Stories of a Great Flood in Africa.*—It is curious, that while legends of a universal flood are widely spread over many parts of the world, they are hardly to be found at all in Africa. Indeed, it may be doubted whether throughout that vast continent a single genuinely native tradition of a great flood has been recorded. Even traces of such traditions are rare. None have as yet been discovered in the literature of ancient Egypt. In Northern Guinea, we are told, there is "a tradition of a great deluge which once overspread the face of the whole earth; but it is coupled with so much that is marvellous and imaginative, that it can scarcely be identified with the same event recorded in the Bible." As the missionary who reports this gives no details, we cannot judge how far the tradition is native and how far borrowed from Europeans. Another missionary has met with a reference to a great flood in the traditions of the natives of the Lower Congo. "The sun and moon once met together, they say, and the sun plastered some mud over a part of the moon, and thus covered up some of the light, and that is why a portion of the moon is often in shadow. When this meeting took place there was a flood, and the ancient people put their porridge (*luku*) sticks to their backs and turned into monkeys. The present race of people is a new creation. Another statement is that when the flood came the men turned into monkeys, and the women into lizards: and the monkey's tail is the man's gun. One would think from this that the transformation took place, in their opinion, in very recent times; but the Congo native has no legend concerning the introduction of the gun into their country, nor any rumours of the time when hunting and fighting were carried on with spears, shields, bows and arrows, and knives." The Bapedi, a Basuto tribe of South Africa, are said to have a legend of a great flood which destroyed nearly all mankind. The experienced missionary Dr. Robert Moffat made fruitless inquiries concerning legends of a deluge among the natives of South Africa; one native who professed to have received such a legend from his forefathers was discovered to have learned it from a missionary named Schmelen. "Stories of a similar kind," adds Dr. Moffat, "originally obtained at a missionary station, or from some godly traveller, get, in course of time, so mixed up and metamorphosed

by heathen ideas, that they look exceedingly like native traditions."
After recording a legend as to the formation of Lake Dilolo in
Angola, in which a whole village with its inhabitants, its fowls,
and its dogs is said to have perished, Dr. Livingstone remarks,
"This may be a faint tradition of the Deluge, and it is remarkable
as the only one I have met with in this country." My experienced
missionary friend, the Rev. John Roscoe, who spent about twenty-
five years in intimate converse with the natives of Central Africa,
particularly the Uganda Protectorate, tells me that he has found
no native legend of a flood among the tribes with which he is
acquainted.

Traditions of a great flood have, however, been discovered by
German writers among the natives of East Africa, but the stories
are plainly mere variations of the Biblical narrative, which has
penetrated to these savages through Christian or possibly Mohammedan influence. One such tradition has been recorded by a German
officer among the Masai. It runs as follows :—

Tumbainot was a righteous man whom God loved. He married
a wife Naipande, who bore him three sons, Oshomo, Bartimaro,
and Barmao. When his brother Lengerni died, Tumbainot, in
accordance with Masai custom, married the widow Nahaba-logunja,
whose name is derived from her high narrow head, that being a
mark of beauty among the Masai. She bore her second husband
three sons; but in consequence of a domestic jar, arising from her
refusal to give her husband a drink of milk in the evening, she
withdrew from his homestead and set up one of her own, fortifying
it with a hedge of thorn-bushes against the attacks of wild beasts.
In those days the world was thickly peopled, but men were not
good. On the contrary, they were sinful and did not obey God's
commands. However, bad as they were, they refrained from murder.
But at last, one unlucky day, a certain man named Nambija knocked
another man named Suage on the head. This was more than God
could bear, and he resolved to destroy the whole race of mankind.
Only the pious Tumbainot found grace in the eyes of God, who
commanded him to build an ark of wood, and go into it, with his
two wives, his six sons, and their wives, taking with him some
animals of every sort. When they were all safely aboard, and
Tumbainot had laid in a great stock of provisions, God caused it
to rain so heavily and so long that a great flood took place, and all
men and beasts were drowned, except those which were in the
ark; for the ark floated on the face of the waters. Tumbainot
longed for the end of the rain, for the provisions in the ark began
to run short. At last the rain stopped. Anxious to ascertain
the state of the flood, Tumbainot let a dove fly out of the ark. In
the evening she came back tired, so Tumbainot knew that the flood
must still be high, and that the dove could have found no place
to rest. Several days later he let a vulture fly out of the ark,
but before doing so he took the precaution to fasten an arrow to

one of its tail-feathers, calculating that if the bird perched to eat, it would trail the arrow behind it, and that the arrow, hitching on to something as it was dragged over the ground, would stick fast and be lost.   The event answered his expectation, for in the evening the vulture returned to the ark without the arrow and the tail-feather.   So Tumbainot inferred that the bird had lighted on carrion, and that the flood must be abating.   When the water had all run away, the ark grounded on the steppe, and men and animals disembarked.   As he stepped out of the ark, Tumbainot saw no less than four rainbows, one in each of the four quarters of the sky, and he took them as a sign that the wrath of God was over.

Another version of the flood story is reported by a German missionary from the same region.   He obtained it at the mission-station of Mkulwe, on the Saisi or Momba River, about twenty miles from where the river flows into Lake Rukwa.   His informant professed to have had it from his grandfather, and stoutly asserted that it was a genuine old tradition of the country and not borrowed from foreigners.   His statement was corroborated by another truth-loving native, who only differed from his fellow in opining that the African Noah sent out two doves instead of one.   The story runs thus :— ,

Long ago, the rivers came down in flood.   God said to the two men, "Go into the ship.   Also take into it seeds of all sorts and all animals, male and female."   They did so.   The flood rose high, it overtopped the mountains, the ship floated on it.   All animals and all men died.   When the water dried up, the man said, "Let us see. Perhaps the water is not yet dried up."   He sent out a dove, she came back to the ship.   He waited and sent out a hawk, but she did not return, because the water was dried up.   The men went out of the ship, they also let out all animals and all seeds.

§ 16. *The Geographical Diffusion of Flood Stories.*—The fore-going survey of diluvial traditions suffices to prove that this type of story, whether we call it legendary or mythical, has been widely diffused throughout the world.   Before we inquire into the relation in which the traditions stand to each other, and the cause or causes which have given rise to them, it may be well to recapitulate briefly the regions in which they have been found.   To begin with Asia, we have found examples of them in Babylonia, Palestine, Syria, Phrygia, ancient and modern India, Burma, Cochin China, the Malay Peninsula, and Kamtchatka.   Roughly speaking, therefore, the traditions prevail in Southern Asia, and are conspicuously absent from Eastern, Central, and Northern Asia.   It is particularly remarkable that neither of the great civilized people of Eastern Asia, the Chinese and the Japanese, should, so far as I know, have preserved in their voluminous and ancient literatures any native legends of a great flood of the sort we are here considering, that is, of a universal inundation in which the whole or the greater part of the human race is said to have perished.

In Europe native diluvial traditions are much rarer than in Asia, but they occurred in ancient Greece, and have been reported in Wales, and among the Lithuanians, the gipsies of Transylvania, and the Voguls of Eastern Russia. The Icelandic story of an inundation of giant's blood hardly conforms to the general type.

In Africa, including Egypt, native legends of a great flood are conspicuously absent; indeed, no single clear case of one has yet been reported.

In the Indian Archipelago we find legends of a great flood in the large islands of Sumatra, Borneo, and Celebes, and among the lesser islands in Nias, Engano, Ceram, Rotti, and Flores. Stories of the same sort are told by the native tribes of the Philippine Islands and Formosa, and by the isolated Andaman Islanders in the Bay of Bengal.

In the vast islands, or continents, of New Guinea and Australia we meet with some stories of a great flood, and legends of the same sort occur in the fringe of smaller islands known as Melanesia, which sweeps in a great arc of a circle round New Guinea and Australia on the north and east.

Passing still eastward out into the Pacific, we discover diluvial traditions widely spread among the Polynesians who occupy the scattered and for the most part small islands of that great ocean, from Hawaii on the north to New Zealand on the south. Among the Micronesians a flood legend has been recorded in the Pelew Islands.

In America, South, Central, and North, diluvial traditions are very widespread. They have been found from Tierra del Fuego in the south to Alaska in the north, and in both continents from east to west. Nor do they occur only among the Indian tribes; examples of them have been reported among the Eskimo from Alaska on the west to Greenland on the east.

Such being in general the geographical diffusion of the traditions we have next to ask, how are they related to each other? Are they all genetically connected with each other, or are they distinct and independent? In other words, are they all descended from one common original, or have they originated independently in different parts of the world? Formerly, under the influence of the Biblical tradition, inquirers were disposed to identify legends of a great flood, wherever found, with the familiar Noachian deluge, and to suppose that in them we had more or less corrupt and apocryphal versions of that great catastrophe, of which the only true and authentic record is preserved in the Book of Genesis. Such a view can hardly be maintained any longer. Even when we have allowed for the numerous corruptions and changes of all kinds which oral tradition necessarily suffers in passing from generation to generation and from land to land through countless ages, we shall still find it difficult to recognize in the diverse, often quaint, childish, or grotesque stories of a great flood, the human copies of a single divine original.

And the difficulty has been greatly increased since modern research has proved the supposed divine original in Genesis to be not an original at all, but a comparatively late copy, of a much older Babylonian or rather Sumerian version. No Christian apologist is likely to treat the Babylonian story, with its strongly polytheistic colouring, as a primitive revelation of God to man; and if the theory of inspiration is inapplicable to the original, it can hardly be invoked to account for the copy.

Dismissing, therefore, the theory of revelation or inspiration as irreconcilable with the known facts, we have still to inquire, whether the Babylonian or Sumerian legend, which is certainly by far the oldest of all diluvial traditions, may not be the one from which all the rest have been derived. The question is one to which a positive answer can hardly be given, since demonstration in such matters is impossible, and our conclusion must be formed from the consideration of a variety of probabilities which different minds will estimate differently. It is no doubt possible to analyse all the stories into their elements, to classify these elements, to count up the number of them which the various versions have in common, and from the sum of the common elements found in any one narrative to calculate the probability of its being a derivative or original version. This, in fact, has been done by one of my predecessors in this department of research, but I do not propose to repeat his calculations: readers with a statistical and mathematical turn of mind may either consult them in his work or repeat them for themselves from the data submitted to them in the foregoing pages. Here I shall content myself with stating my general conclusion, leaving the reader to verify, correct, or reject it by reference to the evidence with which I have furnished him. Apart, then, from the Hebrew legend, which is unquestionably derived from the Babylonian, and from modern instances which exhibit clear traces of late missionary or at all events Christian influence, I do not think that we have decisive grounds for tracing any of the diluvial traditions to the Babylonian as their original. Scholars of repute have, indeed, maintained that both the ancient Greek and the ancient Indian legends are derived from the Babylonian; they may be right, but to me it does not seem that the resemblances between the three are sufficient to justify us in assuming identity of origin. No doubt in the later ages of antiquity the Greeks were acquainted with both the Babylonian and the Hebrew versions of the deluge legend, but their own traditions of a great flood are much older than the conquests of Alexander, which first unlocked the treasuries of Oriental learning to Western scholars; and in their earliest forms the Greek traditions exhibit no clear marks of borrowing from Asiatic sources. In the Deucalion legend, for example, which comes nearest to the Babylonian, only Deucalion and his wife are saved from the flood, and after it has subsided they are reduced to the necessity of miraculously creating mankind afresh out of stones, while nothing at all is said about the restoration of animals, which must presumably have perished in the waters. This is very different from the Babylonian and Hebrew legend, which provides for the regular propagation of both the human and the animal species after the flood by taking a sufficient number of passengers of both sorts on board the ark.

Similarly a comparison of the ancient Indian with the Babylonian version of the legend brings out serious discrepancies between them. The miraculous fish which figures so prominently in all the ancient Indian versions has no obvious parallel in the Babylonian; though some scholars have ingeniously argued that the deity, incarnate in a fish, who warns Manu of the coming deluge in the Indian legend, is a duplicate of Ea, the god who similarly warns Ut-naphishtim in the Babylonian legend, for there seems to be no doubt that Ea was a water deity, conceived and represented partly in human and partly in fish form. If this suggested parallel between the two legends could be made out, it would certainly forge a strong link between them. On the other hand, in the oldest Indian form of the story, that in the *Satapaha Brahmana,* Manu is represented as the solitary survivor of the great flood, and after the catastrophe a woman has to be miraculously created out of the butter, sour milk, whey and curds of his sacrifice, in order to enable him to continue the species. It is only in the later versions of the story that Manu takes a large assortment of animals and plants with him into the ship; and even in them, though the sage appears on shipboard surrounded by a band of brother sages whom he had rescued from a watery grave, nothing whatever is said about rescuing his wife and children. The omission betrays a lack not only of domestic affection but of common prudence on the part of the philosopher, and contrasts forcibly with the practical foresight of his Babylonian counterpart, who under the like distressing circumstances has at least the consolation of being surrounded by the family circle on the stormy waters, and of knowing that as soon as the flood has subsided he will be able, with their assistance, to provide for the continuance of the human race by the ordinary process of nature. In this curious difference between the two tales is it fanciful to detect the contrast between the worldly prudence of the Semitic mind and the dreamy asceticism of the Indian?

On the whole, then, there is little evidence to prove that the ancient Indian and Greek legends of a flood are derived from the corresponding Babylonian tradition. When we remember that the Babylonians, so far as we know, never succeeded in handing on their story of a deluge to the Egyptians, with whom they were in direct communication for centuries, we need not wonder if they failed to transmit it to the more distant Greeks and Indians, with whom down to the days of Alexander the Great they had but little intercourse. In later ages, through the medium of Christian literature, the Babylonian legend has indeed gone the round of the world and been echoed in tales told under the palms of coral islands, in Indian wigwams, and amid the Arctic ice and snow; but in itself, apart from Christian or Mohammedan agencies, it would seem to have travelled little beyond the limits of its native land and the adjoining Semitic regions.

If, among the many other diluvial traditions which we have passed in review, we look about for evidence of derivation from a common source, and therefore of diffusion from a single centre, we cannot fail to be struck by the manifest tokens of such derivation and diffusion in the Algonquin stories of North America. The many flood legends recorded among different tribes of that widely spread stock resemble each other so closely that we cannot but regard them as mere variations of one and the same tradition. Whether in the original story the incident of the various animals diving into the water to fetch up earth is native or based on a reminiscence of the birds in the Noachian story, which has reached the Indians through white men, may be open to question.

Further, we have seen that according to Humboldt a general resemblance may be traced between the diluvial traditions among the Indians of the Orinoco, and that according to William Ellis a like resemblance prevails among the Polynesian legends. It may be that in both these regions the traditions have spread from local centres, in other words, that they are variations of a common original.

But when we have made allowance for all such cases of diffusion from local centres, it seems probable that there still remain deluge legends which have originated independently.

§ 17. *The Origin of Stories of a Great Flood.*—We have still to ask, What was the origin of diluvial traditions? how did men come so commonly to believe that at some time or other the earth, or at all events the whole inhabited portion of it, had been submerged under the waters of a mighty flood in which almost the entire human race perished? The old answer to the question was that such a catastrophe actually occurred, that we have a full and authentic record of it in the Book of Genesis, and that the many legends of a great flood which we find scattered so widely among mankind embody the more or less imperfect, confused, and distorted reminiscences of that tremendous cataclysm. A favourite argument in support of this view was drawn from the marine shells and fossils, which were supposed to have been left high and dry in deserts and on mountain-tops by the retiring waters of the Noachian deluge. Sea-shells found on mountains were adduced by Tertullian as evidence that the waters had once covered the earth, though he did not expressly associate them with the flood recorded in Genesis. When excavations made in 1517, for repairing the city of Verona, brought to light a multitude of curious petrifactions, the discovery gave rise to much speculation, in which Noah and the ark of course figured conspicuously. Yet they were not allowed to pass unchallenged; for a philosophical Italian naturalist, Fracastoro, was bold enough to point out difficulties in the popular hypothesis. "That inundation, he observed, was too transient: it consisted principally of fluviatile waters; and if it had transported shells to great distances, must have strewed them over the surface, not buried them at vast depths in the interior of mountains. His clear exposition of the evidence would have terminated the discussion for ever, if the passions of mankind had not been enlisted in the dispute." Towards the end of the seventeenth century the field of geology was invaded by an army of theologians, recruited in Italy, Germany, France, and England, who darkened counsel and left confusion worse confounded. "Henceforward, they who refused to subscribe to the position, that all marine organic remains were proofs of the Mosaic deluge, were exposed to the imputation of disbelieving the whole of the sacred writings. Scarcely any step had been made in approximating to sound theories since the time of Fracastoro, more than a hundred years having been lost in writing down the dogma that organised fossils were mere sports of nature. An additional period of a century and a half was now destined to be consumed in exploding the hypothesis, that organised fossils had all been buried in the solid strata by Noah's flood. Never did a theoretical fallacy, in any branch of science, interfere more seriously with accurate observation and the systematic classification of facts. In recent times, we may attribute our rapid progress chiefly to the careful determination of the order of succession in mineral masses, by means of their different organic contents, and their regular superposition. But the old diluvialists were induced by their systems to confound all the groups of strata together, referring all appearances to one cause and to one brief period, not to a variety of causes acting throughout a long succession of epochs. They saw the phenomena only, as they desired to see them, sometimes misrepresenting facts, and at other times deducing false conclusion from correct data. In short, a sketch of the progress of geology, from the close of the seventeenth to the end of the eighteenth century, is the history of a constant and violent struggle of new opinions against doctrines sanctioned by the implicit faith of many generations, and supposed to rest on scriptural authority.

The error thus stigmatized by Sir Charles Lyell died hard. Less than a century ago, when William Buckland was appointed Reader in Geology at Oxford, he could still assure his hearers, in his inaugural address to the University, that "the grand fact of an universal deluge at no very remote period is proved on grounds so decisive and incontrovertible, that had we never heard of such an event from Scripture or any other Authority, Geology of itself must have called in the assistance of some such catastrophe to explain the phenomena of diluvial action." And within our own lifetime another eminent geologist wrote and published as follows: "I have long thought that the narrative in Genesis vii. and viii.

can be understood only on the supposition that it is a contemporary journal or log of an eye-witness incorporated by the author of Genesis in his work. The dates of the rising and fall of the water, the note of soundings over the hill-tops when the maximum was attained, and many other details, as well as the whole tone of the narrative, seem to require this supposition, which also removes all the difficulties of interpretation which have been so much felt." But if the story of the flood in Genesis is the contemporary log-book of an eye-witness, how are we to explain the remarkable discrepancies it contains with regard to the duration of the flood and the number of the animals admitted to the ark? Such a theory, far from solving the difficulties that beset the narrative, would on the contrary render them altogether inexplicable, except on a supposition alike injurious and unjust either to the veracity or to the sobriety of the narrator.

Nor need we linger long over another explanation of flood stories which has of late years enjoyed a good deal of popularity in Germany. On this view the story of the flood has really nothing to do with water or an ark; it is a myth relating to the sun or the moon or the stars, or all three of them together; for the learned men who have made this surprising discovery, while they are united in rejecting the vulgar terrestrial interpretation, are by no means agreed among themselves as to all the niceties of their high celestial theory. Some of them will have it that the ark is the sun; another thinks that the ark was the moon, that the pitch with which it was caulked is a figurative expression for a lunar eclipse; and that by the three stories in which the vessel was built we must understand the phases of the lunar orb. The latest advocate of the lunar theory seeks to reconcile all contradictions in a higher unity by embarking the human passengers on board the moon, while he leaves the animals to do the best they can for themselves among the stars. It would be doing such learned absurdities too much honour to discuss them seriously. I have noticed them only for the sake of the hilarity with which they are calculated to relieve the tedium of a grave and prolonged discussion.

But when we have dismissed these fancies to their appropriate limbo, we are still confronted with the question of the origin of diluvial traditions. Are they true or false? Did the flood, which the stories so persistently describe, really happen or did it not? Now so far as the narartives speak of floods which covered the whole world, submerging even the highest mountains and drowning almost all men and animals, we may pronounce with some confidence that they are false; for, if the best accredited testimony of modern geology can be trusted, no such cataclysm has befallen the earth during the period of man's abode on it. Whether, as some philosophers suppose, a universal ocean covered the whole surface of our planet long before man had appeared upon it, is quite a different question. Leibnitz, for example, imagined the earth "to have been originally a burning luminous mass, which ever since its creation has been undergoing refrigeration. When the outer crust had cooled down sufficiently to allow the vapours to be condensed, they fell, and formed a universal ocean, covering the loftiest mountains, and investing the whole globe." A similar view of a universal primeval ocean, formed by the condensation of aqueous vapour while the originally molten matter of the planet gradually lost its heat, follows almost necessarily from the celebrated Nebular Hypothesis as to the origin of the stellar universe, which was first propounded by Kant and afterwards developed by Laplace. Lamarck, too, "was deeply impressed with a belief prevalent amongst the older naturalists that the primeval ocean invested the whole planet long after it became the habitation of living beings." But such speculations, even if they might have occurred to primitive man, are to be clearly distinguished from stories of a deluge which destroyed the majority of mankind, for these stories presuppose the existence of the human race on the earth and therefore can hardly refer to a time earlier than the Pleistocene period.

But though stories of such tremendous cataclysms are almost certainly fabulous, it is possible and indeed probable that under a mythical husk many of them may hide a kernel of truth; that is, they may contain reminiscenses of inundations which really overtook particular district, but which in passing through the medium of popular tradition have been magnified into world-wide catastrophes. The records of the past abound in instances of great floods which have spread havoc far and wide; and it would be strange indeed if the memory of some of them did not long persist among the descendants of the generation which experienced them. For examples of such disastrous deluges we need go no further than the neighbouring country of Holland, which has suffered from them again and again. In the thirteenth century "the low lands along the Vlie, often threatened, at last sank in the waves. The German Ocean rolled in upon the inland Lake of Flevo. The stormy Zuyder Zee began its existence by engulfing thousands of Frisian villages, with all their population, and by spreading a chasm between kindred peoples. The political, as well as the geographical, continuity of the land was obliterated by this tremendous deluge. The Hollanders were cut off from their relatives in the east by as dangerous a sea as that which divided them from their Anglo-Saxon brethren in Britain." Again, early in the sixteenth century, a tempest blowing from the north, drove the waters of the ocean on the low coast of Zealand more rapidly than they could be carried off through the Straits of Dover. The dykes of South Beveland burst, the sea swept over the land, hundreds of villages were overwhelmed, and a tract of country, torn from the province, was buried beneath the waves. South Beveland became an island, and the stretch of water which divides it from the continent has ever since been known as "the Drowned Land."

On these and other occasions the floods which have laid great tracts of Holland under water have been caused, not by heavy rains, but by risings of the sea. Now it is to be observed that in not a few diluvial traditions the cause alleged for the deluge is in like manner not the fall of rain but an incursion of the ocean. Thus a rising of the sea is assigned as the cause of the flood by the natives of the islands of Nias, Engano, Rotti, Formosa, Tahiti, Hawaii, Rakaanga, and the Pelew Islands, by Indian tribes on the west coast of America from Tierra del Fuego in the south to Alaska in the north, and by Eskimo on the shores of the Arctic Ocean. The occurrence of such stories far and wide on the coasts and among the islands of the Pacific is very significant, for that ocean is subject from time to time to great earthquake-waves, which have often inundated the very coasts and islands where stories of great floods caused by the rising of the sea are told. Are we not allowed, nay compelled, to trace some at least of these stories to these inundations as their true cause? All the probabilities seem to be in favour of a casual rather than of an accidental connexion between the two things.

On coasts where the shock of an earthquake is commonly accompanied or followed by an inroad of the sea, it is natural that the first impulse of the natives, on feeling the concussion, should be to take refuge on a height where they may be safe from the dreaded rush of the water. Now we have seen that the Araucanian Indians of Chili, who have a tradition of a great deluge and fear a repetition of the disaster, fly for safety to a mountain when they feel a violent shock of earthquake; and that the Fijians, who have likewise a tradition of a calamitous flood, used to keep canoes in readiness against the recurrence of a similar inundation. Taking all these facts into account we may accept as reasonable and probable the explanation which the distinguished American ethnologist, Horatio Hale, gave of the Fijian tradition of a deluge. Commenting on the statement that the Fijians formerly kept canoes ready against a repetition of the flood, he writes as follows:

"This statement (which we heard from others in the same terms) may induce us to inquire whether there might not have been some occurrence in the actual history of the islands to give rise to this tradition, and the custom here mentioned. On the 7th of November 1837, the Pacific Ocean was traversed from east to west by an immense wave, which, taking its rise with the shock of an earthquake in Chili, was felt as far as the Bonin Islands. At the Sandwich Islands, according to the account given by Mr. Jarvis in his History, p. 21, the water rose, on the east coast of Hawaii, twenty feet above high-water mark, inundated the low lands, swept away several villages, and destroyed many lives. Similar undulations have been experienced at these islands on several occasions. If we suppose (what is no way improbable) that, at some time within the last three or four thousand years, a wave of twice this height crossed the ocean, and swept over the Vitian [Fijian] Islands, it must have submerged the whole alluvial plain on the east side of Vitilevu, the most populous part of the group. Multitudes would no doubt be destroyed. Others would escape in their canoes, and as Mbengga is a mountainous island, in the neighbourhood of this district, it would naturally be the place of refuge for many."

A similar explanation would obviously apply to the other legends of a great flood recorded in the islands of the Pacific, for all these islands have probably suffered in like manner from the invasion of huge earthquake-waves. At least, in the present state of our knowledge, it seems safer to accept provisionally the view of the eminent American ethnologist than to adopt the theory of an eminent German ethnologist, who would explain all these Polynesian traditions as solar, lunar, and stellar myths.

If some of the traditions of a great flood caused by a rising of the sea may thus rest on an historical basis, there can be no reason why some of the traditions of a great flood caused by heavy rain should not be equally well founded. Here in Fngland we who live in flat parts of the country are familiar with local floods produced by this cause; not many years ago, for example, large tracts of Norfolk, including the city of Norwich, were laid under water by a sudden and violent fall of rain, resembling a cloudburst. A similar cause inundated the low-lying parts of Paris a few years ago, creating anxiety and alarm not only among the inhabitants, but among the friends of the beautiful city in all parts of the world. It is easy to understand how among an ignorant and unlettered population, whose intellectual horizon hardly extends beyond the limits of their vision, the memory of a similar catastrophe, orally transmitted, might in the course of a few generations grow into the legend of a universal deluge, from which only a handful of favoured individuals had contrived in one way or another to escape. Even the tradition of a purely local flood, in which many people had been drowned, might unconsciously be exaggerated into vast dimensions by a European settler or traveller, who received it from savages and interpreted it in the light of the Noachian deluge, with which he himself had been familiar from childhood.

In this manner it has been proposed to explain the Babylonian and Hebrew traditions of a great flood by the inundations to which the lower valley of the Euphrates and Tigris is annually exposed by the heavy rains and melting snows in the mountains of Armenia. "The basis of the story," we are told, "is the yearly phenomenon of the rainy and stormy season which lasts in Babylonia for several months and during which time whole districts in the Euphrates Valley are submerged. Great havoc was caused by the rains and storms until the perfection of canal systems regulated the overflow of the Euphrates and Tigris, when what had been a curse was converted into a blessing and brought about that astonishing fertility for which Babylonia became famous. The Hebrew story of the deluge recalls a particularly destructive season that had made a profound impression, and the comparison with the parallel story found on clay tablets of Ashurbanapal's library confirms this view of the local setting of the tale."

On this hypothesis, the great flood was brought about by an unusually heavy fall of rain and snow; it was only an extraordinary case of an ordinary occurrence, and the widespread devastation which it wrought in the valley imprinted it indelibly on the memory of the survivors and of their descendants. In favour of this view it may be said that in the Babylonian and the oldest form of the Hebrew tradition the only alleged cause of the deluge is heavy rain.

The theory may also be supported by the dangerous inundations to which the country is still yearly liable through the action of the same natural causes. When Loftus, the first excavator of the ancient city of Erech, arrived in Baghdad, on the 5th of May 1849, he found the whole population in a state of the utmost apprehension and alarm. In consequence of the rapid melting of the snows on the Kurdish mountains, and the enormous influx of water from the Euphrates through the Seglawiyya canal, the Tigris had risen that spring to the unprecedented height of twenty-two and a half feet; which was about five feet above its highest level in ordinary years and exceeded the great rise of 1831, when the river broke down the walls and destroyed no less than seven thousand dwellings in a single night, at a time when the plague was committing the most fearful ravages among the inhabitants. A few days before the arrival of the English party, the Turkish pasha of Baghdad had summoned the whole population, as one man, to guard against the general danger by raising a strong high mound completely round the walls. Mats of reeds were placed outside to bind the earth compactly together. The water was thus prevented from devastating the interior of the city, though it filtered through the fine alluvial soil and stood several feet deep in the cellars. Outside the city it reached to within two feet of the top of the bank. On the side of the river the house alone, many of them very old and frail, prevented the ingress of the flood. It was a critical juncture. Men were stationed night and day to watch the barriers. If the dam or any of the foundations had failed, Baghdad must have been bodily washed away. Happily the pressure was withstood, and the inundation gradually subsided. The country on all sides for miles was under water, so that there was no possibility of proceeding beyond the dyke, except in the boats which were established as ferries to keep up communication across the flood. The city was for a time an island in a vast inland sea, and it was a full month before the inhabitants could hide beyond the walls. As the summer advanced, the evaporation from the stagnant water caused malaria to such an extent that, out of a population of seventy thousand, no less than twelve thousand died of fever.

If the flood caused by the melting of the snow in the Armenian

mountains can thus endanger the cities in the river valley down
to modern times, it is reasonable to suppose that they did so in
antiquity also, and that the Babylonian tradition of the destruction
of the City of Shurippak in such an inundation may be well founded.
It is true that the city appears to have ultimately perished by fire
rather than by water; but this is quite consistent with the supposition that at some earlier time it had been destroyed by a flood and
afterwards rebuilt.

On the whole, then, there seems to be good reason for thinking
that some and probably many diluvial traditions are merely exaggerated reports of floods which actually occurred, whether as the
result of heavy rain, earthquake-waves, or other causes. All such
traditions, therefore, are partly legendary and partly mythical: so
far as they preserve reminiscences of floods which really happened,
they are legendary; so far as they describe universal deluges which
never happened, they are mythical. But in our survey of diluvial
traditions we found some stories which appear to be purely mythical,
that is, to describe inundations which never took place. Such,
for example, are the Samothracian and Thessalian stories of great
floods which the Greeks associated with the names of Dardanus
and Deucalion. The Samothracian story is probably nothing but
a false inference from the physical geography of the Black Sea
and its outlets, the Bosphorus and Dardanelles: the Thessalian
story is probably nothing but a false inference from the physical
geography of the mountain-ringed Thessalian basin and its outlet,
the gorge of Tempe. Such stories, therefore, are not legendary
but purely mythical: they describe catastrophes which never
occurred. They are examples of that class of mythical tales which,
with Sir Edward Tylor, we may call myths of observation, since
they are suggested by a true observation of nature, but err in their
interpretation of it.

Another set of diluvial traditions, of which we have found
examples, also falls into the class of myths of observation. These
are the stories of a great flood which rest on the observation of
marine fossils found on mountains or in other places remote from
the sea. Such tales, as we saw, are told by the Mongolians, the
Bare'e-speaking people of Celebes, the Tahitians, and the Eskimo
and Greenlanders. Being based on the false assumption that the
sea must formerly have risen above the heights where the fossils
are now found, they are mistaken inferences, or myths of observation; whereas if they had assumed the former depression of these
heights under the level of the sea, they would have been true
inferences, or anticipations of science.

Thus, while there is reason to believe that many diluvial traditions dispersed throughout the world are based on reminiscences
of catastrophes which actually occurred, there is no good ground
for holding that any such traditions are older than a few thousand
years at most; wherever they appear to describe vast changes in

the physical configuration of the globe, which must be referred to more or less remote epochs of geologic time, they probably embody, not the record of contemporary witnesses, but the speculation of much later thinkers. Compared with the great natural features of our planet, man is but a thing of yesterday, and his memory a dream of the night.

CHAPTER V

THE TOWER OF BABEL

AMONG the problems which beset any inquiry into the early history of mankind the question of the origin of language is at the same time one of the most fascinating and one of the most difficult. The writers whose crude speculations on human origins are embodied in the early chapters of Genesis have given us no hint as to the mode in which they supposed man to have acquired the most important of all the endowments which mark him off from the beasts—the gift of articulate speech. On the contrary, they seem to have assumed that this priceless faculty was possessed by him from the beginning, nay, that it was shared with him by the animals, if we may judge by the example of the talking serpent in Eden. However, the diversity of languages spoken by the various races of men naturally attracted the attention of the ancient Hebrews, and they explained it by the following tale.

In the early days of the world all mankind spoke the same language. Journeying from the east as nomads in one huge caravan, they came to the great plains of Shinar or Babylonia, and there they settled. They built their houses of bricks, bound together with a mortar of slime, because stone is rare in the alluvial soil of these vast swampy flats. But not content with building themselves a city, they proposed to construct out of the same materials a tower so high that its top should reach to heaven; this they did in order to make a name for themselves, and also to prevent the citizens from being scattered over the face of the whole earth. For when any had wandered from the city and lost his way on the boundless plain, he would look back westward and see afar off the outline of the tall tower standing up dark against the bright evening sky, or he would look eastward and behold the top of the tower lit up by the last rays of the setting sun. So he would find his bearings, and guided by the landmark would retrace his steps homeward. Their scheme was good, but they failed to reckon with the jealousy and power of the Almighty. For while they were building away with all their might and main, God came down from heaven to see the city and the tower which men were raising so fast. The sight displeased him, for he said, "Behold, they are one people, and they have all one language; and this is what they begin to do: and now nothing will be withholden from them, which they purpose to do." Apparently he feared that when the tower reached the sky, men would swarm up it and beard him in his den, a thing not to be thought of. So he resolved to nip the great project in the bud. "Go to," said he to himself, or to his heavenly counsellors, "let us go down, and there confound their language, that they may not understand one another's speech." Down he went accordingly and confounded their language and scattered them over the face of all the earth. Therefore they left off to build the city and the tower; and the name of the place was called Babel, that is, Confusion, because God did there confound the language of all the earth.

On the plain stuff of this narrative later Jewish tradition has embroidered a rich band of picturesque details. From them we learn that the enterprise of the tower was flat rebellion against God, though the rebels were not at one in their aims. Some wished to scale heaven and there wage war with the Almighty in person, or set up their idols to be worshipped in his stead; others limited their ambition to the more modest scheme of damaging the celestial vault by showers of spears and arrows. Many, many years was the tower in building. It reached so high that at last a bricklayer took a whole year to ascend to the top with his hod on his back. If he fell down and broke his neck, nobody minded for the man, but everybody wept for the brick, because it would take a whole year to replace it on the top of the tower. So eagerly did they work, that a woman would not interrupt her task of brickmaking even to give birth to a child; she would merely tie the baby in a sheet round her body and go on moulding bricks as if nothing had happened. Day and night the work never slackened; and from their dizzy height they shot heavenward arrows, which returned to them dabbled with blood; so they cried, "We have slain all who are in heaven." At last the long-suffering deity lost patience, and turning to the seventy angels who encompass his throne, he proposed that they should all go down and confound the language of men. No sooner said than done. The misunderstandings which consequently arose were frequent and painful. One man, for example, would ask for mortar, and the other would hand him a brick, whereupon the first, in a rage, would hurl the brick at his mate's head and kill him. Many perished in this manner, and the rest were punished by God according to the acts of rebellion which they had meditated. As for the unfinished tower, a part of it sank into the earth, and another part was consumed by fire; only one-third of it remained standing. The place of the tower has never lost its peculiar quality. Whoever passes it forgets all he knows.

The scene of the legend was laid at Babylon, for Babel is only the Hebrew form of the name of the city. The popular derivation from a Hebrew verb *balal* (Aramaic *balbel*) "to confuse" is erroneous; the true meaning, as shown by the form in which the name is written in inscriptions, seems to be "Gate of God" (*Bāb-il* or *Bābilu*).

The commentators are probably right in tracing the origin of the story to the deep impression produced by the great city on the simple minds of Semitic nomads, who, fresh from the solitude and silence of the desert, were bewildered by the hubbub of the streets and bazaars, dazzled by the shifting kaleidoscope of colour in the bustling crowd, stunned by the din of voices jabbering in strange unknown tongues, and overawed by the height of the buildings, above all by the prodigious altitude of the temples towering up, terrace upon terrace, till their glistening tops of enamelled brick seemed to touch the blue sky. No wonder that dwellers in tents should imagine, that they who scaled the pinnacle of such a stupendous pile by the long winding ramp, and appeared at last like moving specks on the summit, must indeed be near the gods.

Of two such gigantic temples the huge mouldering remains are to be seen at Babylon to this day, and it is probable that to one or other of them the legend of the Tower of Babel was attached. One of them rises among the ruins of Babylon itself, and still bears the name of Babil; the other is situated across the river at Borsippa, some eight or nine miles away to the south-west, and is known as Birs-Nimrud. The ancient name of the temple in the city of Babylon was E-sagil: it was dedicated to Marduk. The ancient name of the temple at Borsippa was E-zida: it was dedicated to Nebo. Scholars are not agreed as to which of these ancient edifices was the original Tower of Babel; local and Jewish tradition identifies the legendary tower with the ruins of Birs-Nimrud at Borsippa. From an inscription found on the spot we learn that the ancient Babylonian king, who began to build the great temple-tower at Borsippa, had left it incomplete, wanting its top. It may have been the sight of the huge edifice in its unfinished state which gave rise to the legend of the Tower of Babel.

However, there were many more such temple-towers in ancient Babylonia, and the legend in question may have been attached to any one of them. For example, the remains of such a temple still exist at Uru, the Ur of the Chaldees, from which Abraham is said to have migrated to Canaan. The place is now known as Mukayyar or Mugeyer; it is situated on the right bank of the Euphrates about a hundred and thirty-five miles south-east of Babylon. A series of low mounds, forming an oval, marks the site of the ancient city. The country all around is so flat that often during the annual flood of the Euphrates, from March till June or July, the ruins form an island in a great marsh and can only be approached by boat. Groves of date-palms here line the banks of the river and extend in unbroken succession along its course till it loses itself in the waters of the Persian Gulf. Near the northern end of the site rise the remains of the temple-tower to a height of about seventy feet. The edifice is a rectangular parallelogram, in two stories, with the larger sides facing north-east and south-west, each of them measuring about two hundred feet in length, while the shorter sides measure only one hundred and thirty-three feet. As in all similar Babylonian buildings, one angle points almost due north. The lower story, twenty-seven feet high, is supported by strong buttresses; the upper story, receding from thirty to forty-seven feet from the edge of the first, is fourteen feet high, surmounted by about five feet of brick rubbish. The ascent was on the north-west. A tunnel driven into the mound proved that the entire edifice was built of sun-dried bricks in the centre, with a thick coating of massive, partially burnt bricks of a light red colour with layers of reeds between them, the whole, to a thickness of ten feet, being cased with a wall of inscribed kiln-burnt bricks. Inscribed cylinders were discovered at the four corners of the building, each standing in a niche formed by the omission of a single brick in the layer. Subsequent excavations seem to prove that commemorative inscriptions, inscribed on cylinders, were regularly deposited by the builders or restorers of Babylonian temples and palaces at the four corners of the edifices.

From one of the inscriptions on the cylinders we learn that the name of the city was Ur, and that the temple was dedicated to Sin, the Babylonian moon-god. Further we are informed that King Ur-uk or Urengur, as his name should rather be spelt, who built the temple-tower, left it unfinished, and that the edifice was completed by his son, King Dungi. The reign of King Ur-uk or Urenger is variously dated about 700 B.C or 2300 B.C. In either case the foundation of the temple preceded, perhaps by hundreds of years, the date which is usually assigned to the birth of Abraham; so that if the patriarch really migrated from Ur to Canaan, as Hebrew tradition relates, this very building, whose venerable ruins exist on the spot to this day, dominating by their superior height the flat landscape through which the Euphrates winds seaward, must have been familiar to Abraham from childhood, and may have been the last object on which his eyes rested when, setting out in search of the Promised Land, he took a farewell look backward at his native city disappearing behind its palm groves in the distance. It is possible that in the minds of his descendants, the conspicuous pile, looming dim and vast through the mists of time and of distance, may have assumed the gigantic proportions of a heaven-reaching tower, from which in days of old the various nations of the earth set out on their wanderings.

The authors of Genesis say nothing as to the nature of the common language which all mankind spoke before the confusion of tongues, and in which our first parents may be supposed to have conversed with each other, with the serpent, and with the deity in the garden of Eden. Later ages took it for granted that Hebrew was the primitive language of mankind. The fathers of the Church appear to have entertained no doubt on the subject; and in modern times, when the science of philology was in its infancy, strenuous, but necessarily abortive, efforts were made to deduce all forms of human speech from Hebrew as their original. In this naïve assumption Christian scholars did not differ from the learned men of other religions, who have seen in the language of their sacred writings the tongue not only of our first forefathers but of the gods themselves. The first in modern times to prick the bubble effectively was Leibnitz, who observed that "there is as much reason for supposing Hebrew to have been the primitive language of mankind, as there is for adopting the view of Goropius, who published a work at Antwerp, in 1580, to prove that Dutch was the language spoken in Paradise." Another writer maintained that the language spoken by Adam was Basque; while others, flying clean in the face of Scripture, introduced the diversity of tongues into Eden itself, by holding that Adam and Eve spoke Persian, that the language of the serpent was Arabic, and that the affable archangel Gabriel discoursed with our first parents in Turkish. Yet another eccentric scholar seriously argued that the Almighty addressed Adam in Swedish, that Adam answered his Maker in Danish, and that the serpent conversed with Eve in French. We may suspect that all such philological theories were biassed by the national prejudices and antipathies of the philologers who propounded them.

Stories which bear a certain resemblance to the legend of the Tower of Babel are reported among several African tribes. Thus, some of the natives of the Zambesi, apparently in the neighbourhood of the Victoria Falls, "have a tradition which may refer to the building of the Tower of Babel, but it ends in the bold builders getting their crowns cracked by the fall of the scaffolding." The story thus briefly referred to by Dr. Livingstone has been more fully recorded by a Swiss missionary. The A-Louyi, a tribe of the Upper Zambesi, say that formerly their god Nyambe, whom they identify with the sun, used to dwell on earth, but that he afterwards ascended up to heaven on a spider's web. From his post up aloft he said to men, "Worship me." But men said, "Come, let us kill Nyambe." Alarmed at this impious threat, the deity fled to the sky, from which it would seem that he had temporarily descended. So men said, "Come, let us make masts to reach up to heaven." They set up masts and added more masts, joining them one to the other, and they clambered up them. But when they had climbed far up, the masts fell down, and all the men on the masts were killed by the fall. That was the end of them. The Bambala of the Congo say "that the Wangongo once wanted to know what the moon was, so they started to go and see. They planted a big pole in the ground, and a man climbed up it with a second pole which he fastened to the end; to this a third was fixed, and so on. When their Tower of Babel had reached a considerable height, so high in fact that the whole population of the village was carrying poles up, the erection suddenly collapsed, and they fell victims to their ill-advised curiosity. Since that time no one has tried to find out what the moon is." The natives of Mkulwe, in East Africa, tell a similar tale. According to them, men one day said to each other, "Let us build high, let us reach the moon!" So they rammed a great tree into the earth, and fixed another tree on the top of it, and another on the top of that, and so on, till the trees fell down and the men were killed. But other men said, "Let us not give up this undertaking," and they piled trees one on the top of the other, till one day the trees again fell down and the men were killed. Then the people gave up trying to climb aloft to the moon. The Ashantees have a tradition that God of old dwelt among men, but that, resenting an affront put on him by an old woman, he withdrew in the high dudgeon to his mansion in the sky. Disconsolate at his departure, mankind resolved to seek and find him. For that purpose they collected all the porridge pestles they could find and piled them up, one on the top of the other. When the tower thus built had nearly reached the sky, they found to their dismay that the supply of pestles ran short. What were they to do? In this dilemma a wise man stood up and said, "The matter is quite simple. Take the lowest pestle of all, and put it on the top, and go on doing so till we arrive at God." The proposal was carried, but when they came to put it in practice, down fell the tower, as indeed you might have expected. However, others say that the collapse of the tower was caused by the white ants, which gnawed away the lowest of the pestles. In whichever way it happened, the communication with heaven was not completed, and men were never able to ascend up to God.

A story like the Biblical narrative of the Tower of Babel is told of the great pyramid of Cholula in Mexico. the vastest work of aboriginal man in all America. This colossal fabric, on which the modern traveller still gazes with admiration, stands near the handsome modern city of Puebla, on the way from Vera Cruz to the capital. In form it resembles, and in dimensions it rivals, the pyramids of Egypt. Its perpendicular height is nearly two hundred feet, and its base is twice as long as that of the great pyramid of Cheops. It had the shape common to the Mexican *teocallis*, that of a truncated pyramid, facing with its four sides the cardinal points and divided into four terraces. Its original outlines, however, have been effaced by time and the weather, while its surface is now covered by an exuberant growth of shrubs and trees, so that the huge pile presents the aspect of a natural hill rather than of a mound reared by human labour. The edifice is built of rows of bricks baked in the sun and cemented together with mortar, in which are stuck quantities of small stones, potsherds, and fragments of obsidian knives and weapons. Layers of clay are interposed between the courses of brick. The flat summit, which comprises more than an acre of ground, commands a superb prospect over the broad fertile valley away to the huge volcanic mountains which encircle it, their lower slopes covered with grand forests, their pinnacles of porphyry bare and arid, the highest of them crowned with eternal snow.

A legend concerning the foundation of this huge monument is recorded by the Spanish historian Duran, who wrote in 1579. "In the beginning," says he, "before the light and sun were created, the earth was in darkness and gloom, void of all created things, quite flat, without hill or dale, encircled by water on every side, without trees and without any other created thing. As soon as the sun and the light were born in the east, some men appeared there, ungainly giants who possessed the land. Wishing to see the rising and the setting of the sun, they agreed to go in search of it; so dividing into two bands they journeyed, the one band toward the west, and the other toward the east. So they journeyed till they were stopped by the sea. Thence they resolved to return to the place from which they had set out; so they came back to the place called *Iztacculin ineminian*. Not knowing how to reach the sun, and charmed with its light and beauty, they decided to build a tower so high that its top should reach the sky. In their search for materials with which to carry out their design they found a clay and a very sticky bitumen with which they began in a great hurry to build the tower. When they had reared it as high as they could, so high that it is said to have seemed to reach the sky, the lord of the heights was angry and said to the inhabitants of heaven, 'Have you seen how the inhabitants of the earth have built a tower so high and so proud to climb up here, charmed as they are with the light and beauty of the sun? Come, let us confound them; for it is not meet that the people of the earth, who live in bodies of flesh, should mix with us.' In a moment, the inhabitants of heaven, setting out towards the four quarters of the world, overthrew as by a thunderbolt the edifice which the men had built. After that, the giants, scared and filled with terror, separated and scattered in all directions over the earth."

In this tradition the traces of Biblical influence appear not only in the dispersal of the builders over the face of the earth, but also in the construction of the tower out of clay and bitumen; for while these are the materials out of which the Tower of Babel is said to have been built, bitumen seems never to have been used by the Mexicans for such a purpose and is not found anywhere near Cholula. "The history of the confusion of tongues seems also to have existed in the country, not long after the Conquest, having very probably been learnt from the missionaries; but it does not seem to have been connected with the Tower-of-Babel legend of Cholula. Something like it at least appears in the Gemelli table of Mexican migrations, reproduced in Humboldt, where a bird in a tree is sending down a number of tongues to a crowd of men standing below." On the strength of these suspicious resemblances Tylor may be right in condemning the legend of Cholulu "as not genuine, or at least as partly of late fabrication."

A similar verdict may perhaps be pronounced on a table told by the Karens of Burma, a tribe who display a peculiar aptitude for borrowing Christian legends and disguising them with a thin coat of local colour. Their edition of the Tower of Babel story, as told by the Gaikho section of the tribe, runs as follows. "The Gaikhos trace their genealogy to Adam, and make thirty generations from Adam, to the building of the Tower of Babel, at which time they say separated from the Red Karens. . . . In the days of Pan-dan-man, the people determined to build a pagoda that should reach up to heaven. The place they suppose to be somewhere in the country of the Red Karens, with whom they represent themselves as associated until this event. When the pagoda was half way up to heaven, God came down and confounded the language of the people, so that they could not understand each other. Then the people scattered, and Than-mau-rai, the father of the Gaikho tribe, came west, with eight chiefs, and settled in the valley of the Sitang."

The Biblical story of the Tower of Babel and the confusion of tongues reappears also among the Mikirs, one of the many Tibeto-Burman tribes of Assam. They say that in days of old the descendants of Ram were mighty men, and growing dissatisfied with the mastery of the earth they aspired to conquer heaven. So they began to build a tower which should reach up to the skies. Higher and higher rose the building, till at last the gods and demons feared lest these giants should become the masters of heaven, as they already were of earth. So they confounded their speech, and scattered them to the four corners of the world. Hence arose all the various tongues of mankind. Again, we find the same old story, in a slightly disguised form among the Admiralty Islanders. They say that the tribe or family of the Lohi numbered one hundred and thirty souls and had for their chief a certain Muikiu. This Muikiu said to his people, "Let us build a house as high as heaven." So they built it, and when it nearly reached the sky, there came to them from Kali a man named Po Awi, who forbade them to go on with the building. Said he to Muikiu, "Who told you to build so high a house?" Muikiu answered, "I am master of our people the Lohi. I said, 'Let us build a house as high as heaven.' If I had my way, our houses should have been as high as heaven. But now, thy will is done, our houses will be low." So saying he took water and sprinkled it on the bodies of his people. Then was their language confounded; they understood not each other and dispersed into different lands. Thus every land has now its own speech. There can be little doubt that this story is merely an echo of missionary teaching.

Not a few peoples have attempted to explain the diversities of human speech without reference to a Tower of Babel or similar structures. Thus the Greeks had a tradition that for many ages men lived at peace, without cities and without laws, speaking one language, and ruled by Zeus alone. At last Hermes introduced diversities of speech and divided mankind into separate nations. So discord first arose among mortals, and Zeus, offended at their quarrels, resigned the sovereignty and committed it to the hands of the Argive hero Phoroneus, the first king of men. The Wa-Sania of British East Africa say that of old all the tribes of the earth knew only one language, but that during a severe famine the people went mad and wandered in all directions, jabbering strange words, and so the different languages arose. A different explanation of the diversities of language is given by the Kachcha Nagas, a hill tribe of Assam. According to them, at the creation all men were of one race, but they were destined soon afterwards to be broken up into different nations. The king of the men then on earth had a daughter named Sitoylê. She was wondrous fleet of foot, and loved to roam the jungle the livelong day, far from home, thereby causing much anxiety to her parents, who feared lest she should be devoured by wild beasts. One day her father conceived a plan for keeping her at home. He sent for a basket of linseed, and upsetting it on the ground he ordered his daughter to put the seeds back, one by one, into the basket, counting them as she did so. Then thinking that the task he had set her would occupy the maiden the whole day, he withdrew. But by sunset his daughter had counted all the seeds and put them back in the basket, and no sooner had she done so than away she hurried to the jungle. So when her parents returned, they could find no trace of their missing daughter. After searching for days and days, however, they at last came across a monster python lying gorged in the shade of the trees. All the men being assembled, they attacked the huge reptile with spear and sword. But even as they struck at the snake, their appearance changed, and they found themselves speaking various dialects. The men of the same speech now drew apart from the rest and formed a separate band, and the various bands thus created became the ancestors of the different nations now existing on earth. But what became of the princess, whether she was restored to her sorrowing parents, or whether she had been swallowed by the python, the story does not relate.

The Kukis of Manipur, another hill race of Assam, account for the diversity of languages in their tribes by saying, that once on a time the three grandsons of a certain chief were all playing together in the house, when their father bade them catch a rat. But while they were busy hunting the animal, they were suddenly smitten with a confusion of tongues and could not understand each other, so the rat escaped. The eldest of the three sons now spoke the Lamyang language, the second spoke the Thado language; and as for the third, some say that he spoke the Waiphie language, but others think it was the Manipur tongue which he spoke. At all events the three lads became the ancestors of three distinct tribes. The Encounter Bay tribe of South Australia trace the origin of languages

to an ill-tempered old woman, who died long ago. Her name was
Wurruri, she lived towards the east, and generally walked about with
a big stick in her hand to scatter the fires round which other people
were sleeping. When at last she died, her people were so glad to be
rid of her, that they sent messengers in all directions to announce the
good news of her death. Men, women, and children accordingly
assembled, not to mourn but to rejoice over the decease and to
celebrate it by cannibal banquet. The Raminjerar were the first
who fell upon the corpse and commenced to devour the flesh; and
no sooner did they do so than they began to speak intelligibly. The
other tribes to the eastward, arriving later, ate the contents of the
intestines, which caused them to speak a language slightly different.
Last of all came the northern tribes, and having consumed the intestines all that remained of the corpse, they spoke a language which
differed still more from that of the Raminjerar.

The Maidu Indians of California say that down to a certain time
everybody spoke the same language. But once, when the people
were having a burning, and everything was ready for the next day,
suddenly in the night everybody began to speak in a different
tongue, except that each husband and wife talked the same language.
That night the Creator, whom they call Earth-Initiate, appeared to
a certain man named Kuksu, told him what had happened, and
instructed him how to proceed next day when the Babel of tongues
would commence. Thus prepared, Kuksu summoned all the people
together, for he could speak all the languages. He taught them the
names of the different animals and so forth in their various dialects,
showed them how to cook and to hunt, gave them their laws, and
appointed the times for their dances and festivals. Then he called
each tribe by name, and sent them off in different directions, telling
them where they were to dwell. We have seen that the Tlingits
of Alaska explain the diversity of tongues by the story of a great
flood, which they may have borrowed from Christian missionaries
or traders. The Quiches of Guatemala told of a time, in the early
ages of the world, when men lived together and spoke but one
language, when they invoked as yet neither wood nor stone, and
remembered naught but the word of the Creator, the Heart of heaven
and of earth. However, as years went on the tribes multiplied, and
leaving their old home came to a place called Tulan. It was there,
according to Quiché tradition, that the language of the tribes changed
and the diversity of tongues originated; the people ceased to understand each other's speech and dispersed to seek new homes in different parts of the world.

These last stories, in attempting to account for the diversities
of language, make no reference to a Tower of Babel, and accordingly
they may, with the possible exception of the Tlingit tale, be accepted
as independent efforts of the human mind to grapple with that difficult problem, however little they succeed in solving it.

PART II

THE PATRIARCHAL AGE

CHAPTER I

THE COVENANT OF ABRAHAM

WITH the story of the Tower of Babel, and the dispersion of the peoples from that centre, the authors of Genesis conclude their general history of mankind in the early ages of the world. They now narrow the scope of their narrative and concentrate it on the Hebrew people alone. The history takes the form of a series of biographies, in which the fortunes of the nation are set forth, not in vague general outlines, but in a series of brilliantly coloured pictures recording the adventures of individual men, the forefathers of the race. The unity which runs through the lives of the patriarchs is not merely genealogical; a community of occupational as well as of blood binds these ancestors of Israel together; all are nomadic shepherds and herdsmen, roaming from place to place with their flocks and herds in search of fresh pasture; they have not yet settled down to the humdrum life of the peasant, who repeats, year after year, the same monotonous round of labour on the same fields on which his father and his father's father had laboured all their days before him. In short, it is the pastoral age which the writers of Genesis have depicted with a clearness of outline and a vividness of colouring which time has not dimmed, and which, under all the changed conditions of modern life, still hold the reader spellbound by their ineffable charm. In this gallery of portraits, painted against a background of quiet landscape, the first place is occupied by the majestic figure of Abraham. After quitting Babylonia, the land of his birth, he is said to have migrated to Canaan and there to have received from God in person the assurance of the future grandeur and glory of his race. To confirm his promise the deity, we are told, condescended to enter into a regular covenant with the patriarch, observing all the legal formalities which were customary on such occasions among men. The narrative of this important transaction affords us an interesting glimpse into the means adopted

153

by covenanters in primitive society for the purpose of creating a
binding obligation on both sides.

We read in Genesis that God commanded Abraham, saying to
him, "Take me an heifer of three years old, and a she-goat of three
years old, and a ram of three years old, and a turtledove, and a
young pigeon." So Abraham took the heifer, the she-goat, and the
ram, cut them in two, and laid each half of the animal over against
the other; but the birds he did not divide. And when the birds
of prey came down on the carcases, Abraham drove them away.
When the sun was going down, Abraham sank into a deep sleep, and
a horror of great darkness fell upon him. And it came to pass that
when the sun had set, and it was dark, behold a smoking furnace and
a flaming torch passed between the pieces of the sacrificial victims,
and God proclaimed his covenant with Abraham.

In this description the horror of great darkness which falls on
Abraham at sunset is a premonition of the coming of God, who in
the darkness of night passes between the pieces of the slaughtered
animals in the likeness of a smoking furnace and a flaming torch. In
doing so the deity only complied with the legal formalities required
by ancient Hebrew law at the ratification of a covenant; for we
know from Jeremiah that it was the custom of the contracting
parties to cut a calf in twain and pass between the pieces. That
this was the regular form observed on such occasions is strongly
suggested by the Hebrew phrase for making a covenant, which is
literally to "cut a covenant," and the inference is confirmed by
analogies in the Greek language and ritual; for the Greeks used
similar phrases and practised similar rites. Thus they spoke of
cutting oaths in the sense of swearing them, and of *cutting* a treaty
instead of making one. Such expressions, like the corresponding
phrases in Hebrew and Latin, are undoubtedly derived from a
custom of sacrificing victims and cutting them in pieces as a mode
of adding solemnity to an oath or a treaty. For example, we are
told that when Agamemnon was about to lead the Greeks to Troy,
the soothsayer Calchas brought a boar into the market-place, and
divided it into two parts, one on the west, and one on the east.
Then each man, with a drawn sword in his hand, passed between the
pieces of the boar, and the blade of his sword was smeared with the
blood. Thus they swore enmity to Priam. But sometimes, and
perhaps more commonly, in Greek ritual, instead of passing between
the pieces of the victims, the person who made an oath stood upon
them. So in trials before the court of the Areopagus at Athens the
accuser made oath standing on the pieces of a boar, a ram, and
a bull, which had been sacrificed by special persons on special days.
Again, when the fair Helen was wooed by many suitors, her father
Tyndareus, fearful of the revenge which the rejected lovers might
take, made them all swear to defend her and the man of her choice,
whoever he might be; and to give solemnity to the oath he sacrificed
a horse, cut it up, and caused the suitors to swear standing on the

pieces. Again, in the council chamber at Olympia there was an image of Zeus surnamed the God of Oaths; and before the Olympian games began, it was customary for the athletes, their fathers and brothers, and also the trainers, to swear on the cut pieces of a boar that they would be guilty of no foul play. In Messenia there was a place called the Boar's Grave, because Hercules was there said to have exchanged oaths with the sons of Neleus over the pieces of a boar.

Similar ceremonies at taking an oath or making peace were observed also by barbarous tribes in antiquity. Thus the Molossians used to cut up oxen into small pieces when they made a treaty and swore to observe it; however, we are not told what use precisely they made of the pieces in the ceremony. Among the Scythians, when a man conceived that he was wronged by another, against whom single-handed he was powerless, he appealed to his friends for help in the following manner. He sacrificed an ox, cut up and boiled the flesh, and having spread out the reeking hide on the ground he sat down on it, with his arms doubled up behind him, as if they were pinioned. This was the most urgent form of supplication known to the Scythians. While the man sat thus on the hide, with the slices of boiled beef beside him, his friends and relations and any one else who chose to help him, would take each of them a slice of the beef, and planting every man his right foot on the hide would promise to furnish so many soldiers, horse or foot, all found and free of charge, to assist the suppliant in avenging himself on his enemy. Some would promise to bring five men, some ten, and some more; while the poorest would offer only their personal services. In this way sometimes a large force would be mustered, and so levied it was deemed very formidable, because every man in it was bound by his oath to stand by his fellow. In Tibetan law-courts to this day, "when the great oath is taken, which is seldom, it is done by the person placing a holy scripture on his head, and sitting on the reeking hide of an ox and eating a part of the ox's heart. The expense of this ceremony is borne by the party who challenges the accused."

Ceremonies of a like kind are still observed at peace-making by savage tribes in Africa and India. Thus among the Kavirondo, of British East Africa, in making peace after a war, the vanquished side takes a dog and cuts it in halves. The delegates from each side then hold respectively the fore-quarters and the hind-quarters of the divided dog, and swear peace and friendship over the half dog which they hold in their hands. A similar ceremony is used to seal a covenant of peace among the Nandi, another tribe of the same region. They cut a dog in halves: the two halves are held by men representing the two sides who have been at war; and a third man says, "May the man who breaks this peace be killed like this dog." Among the Bagesu, a Bantu tribe of Mount Elgon, in British East Africa, when two clans have been at war and wish to make peace, the representatives of the clans hold a dog, one by the head and the other by the hind legs, while a third man cuts the dog through with a large knife at one stroke. The body is then thrown away in the bush and left, and thereafter the members of the two clans may freely intermingle without any fear of trouble or danger.

In the Wachaga tribe of the same region, when two districts have resolved to form a solemn league and covenant of peace, the ceremony observed at the ratification of the treaty is as follows. The warriors of the two districts assemble and sit down crowded together in a circle on some piece of open ground. A long rope is stretched round the assembly and its free ends are knotted together on one side, so that the whole body of warriors from both sides is enclosed within the rope. But before the knot is tied, the rope is moved thrice or seven times round the circle and a kid is carried with it. Finally, on the side of the circle where the ends are knotted together, the rope is passed over the body of the kid, which is held stretched at full length by two men, so that the rope and the kid form parallel lines, the rope being over the kid. These motions of the rope and of the kid round the sitting warriors are carried out by two uncircumcised and therefore childless lads; and the circumstance is significant, because the lads symbolize that infertility or death without offspring which the Wachaga regard as the greatest of curses, and which they commonly refer to the action of the higher powers. In most of their treaties they imprecate this dreaded curse on perjurers, and on the contrary call down the blessing of numerous progeny on him who shall keep his oath. In the ceremony under discussion the employment of uncircumcised youths is intended not merely to symbolize the fate of the perjurer but to effect it by sympathetic magic. For a similar reason the curses and the blessings are recited by old men, because they are past the age of begetting children. The recitation runs as follows, "If after the making of this covenant I do anything to harm thee or devise devices against thee without giving thee warning, may I be split in two like this rope and this kid!" Chorus, "Amen!" "May I split in two like a boy who dies without begetting children!" Chorus, "Amen!" "May my cattle perish, every one!" Chorus, "Amen!" "But if I do not that; if I be true to thee, so may I fare well!" Chorus, "Amen!" "May my children be like the bees in number!" Chorus, "Amen!" And so forth and so forth. When the representatives of the two covenanting districts have sworn the oath, the rope and the kid are cut in two at one stroke, and the spouting blood is sprinkled on the covenanters, while the old men in a comprehensive formula call down curses and blessings impartially on both sides. Afterwards the flesh of the goat is eaten by old men who are past the age of begetting children, and the rope is divided between the two districts, each of which keeps its portion carefully. If epidemics should break out and be attributed by the diviners, who interpret the will of the higher powers, to some breach of the treaty committed wittingly or unwittingly by the inhabitants of the afflicted country, the rope must be expiated or, as the native phrase goes, "cooled." For the magical power with which the covenant invested the rope is now believed to be actively engaged in avenging its violation. The expiation consists in sacrificing a lamb and smearing its blood and dung on the rope, while the following words are spoken: "Those people have done wrong without knowing it. Rope, to-day I expiate thee, that thou mayst harm them no more! Be expiated! Be expiated! Be expiated!" The persons who have committed the breach of faith are expiated by a medicine-man, who sprinkles them with a magical mixture compounded out of the blood of tortoises, rock-badgers, and antelopes, together with portions of certain plants, the whole being administered by means of a bunch of herbs of definite sorts and accompanied by appropriate words.

Somewhat different, though conforming to the same general type, are the ceremonies observed at peace-making among some tribes of South Africa. Thus, in the Barolong tribe, when the chief wished to make a covenant of peace with another chief who had fled to him for protection, he took the paunch of a large ox, and bored a hole through it, and the two chiefs crawled through the hole, the one after the other, in order to intimate by this ceremony that their tribes would thenceforth be one. Similarly among the Bechuanas "in making a public covenant or agreement with one another, two chiefs *tshwaragana moshwang;* that is to say, an animal is slaughtered, and some of the contents of its stomach are laid hold of by both covenanting parties, their hands meeting together and laying hold of each other, while covered over with the contents of the sacrificed animal's stomach. This would seem to be the most solemn form of public agreement known in the country. It was performed more than once at Shoshong while I was there, in the case of chiefs who, with their people, placed themselves under Sekhome's protection."

Equivalent ceremonies are observed at peace-making among some of the hill tribes of Assam. Thus the Nagas "have several ways of taking an oath. The commonest and most sacred is for the two parties to the oath to lay hold of a dog or fowl, one by its head the other by its tail or feet, whilst the animal or bird is cut in two with a *do,* emblematic of the perjurer's fate." According to another authority, among the forms of oaths taken by the Nagas are the following: "When they swear to keep the peace, or to perform any promise, they place the barrel of a gun or a spear between their teeth, signifying by this ceremony that, if they do not act up to their agreement, they are prepared to fall by either of the two weapons. Another simple but equally binding oath is, for two parties to take hold of the ends of a piece of spear-iron, and to have it cut into two pieces, leaving a bit in the hand of each party; but the most sacred oath, it is said, is for each party to take a fowl, one by the head and the other by the legs, and in this manner to pull it asunder, intimating that treachery or breach of agreement would merit the same treatment." Other Naga tribes of Assam have a somewhat different way of settling disputes. "A representative of each of the litigant parties holds an end of a cane basket inside which a cat, alive, is placed, and at a signal a third man hacks the cat in two, and both sides then cut it up with their daos, taking care to stain the weapon with blood. On the occasion when I saw this ceremony I was told that the ceremony was a form of peace-making or treaty, and that therefore the slaughter of the cat bound them in a kind of covenant." Among the Lushei Kuki clans of Assam "an oath of friendship between chiefs is a serious matter. A mithian [a species of bison] is tied up to a post and the parties to the oath, grasping a spear with their right hands, stab it behind the shoulder with sufficient force to draw blood, repeating a formula to the effect that until the rivers run backwards into the earth again they will be friends. The animal is then killed and a little of the blood is smeared on the feet and forehead of the oath takers. To make this oath more binding they both eat a small piece of the liver raw."

We have now to ask, what is the meaning of these sacrifices at making a covenant or swearing an oath? Why should the parties to a covenant or an oath ratify it by killing an animal, cutting it in pieces, standing on the pieces or passing between them, and smearing the blood on their persons? Two different theories have been suggested. The one may be called the *retributive* theory and the other the *sacramental* or purificatory. We will consider the retributive theory first. According to it, the killing and cutting up of the victim is symbolic of the retribution which will overtake the man who breaks the covenant or violates the oath; he, like the animal, will perish by a violent death. This certainly appears to be the interpretation put upon the ceremony by some of the peoples who observe it. Thus the Wachaga say, "May I split in two like this rope and this kid!" and in cutting a dog in two the Nandi say, "May the man who breaks this peace be killed like this dog."

A similar ceremony, accompanied by similar imprecations, used to solemnize the making of peace among the Awome, a people of the Niger delta who are better known to Europeans as New Calabars. When two towns or sub-tribes grew weary of fighting, they would send to the ancient village of Ke, situated near the coast, to the east of the Sombreiro River, where was a fetish or ju-ju called Ke-ni Opu-So. On such occasions the fetish priest was invited to come and preside over the ratification of peace between the belligerents. Accordingly he came in his canoe decked with young palm leaves, and arranged with the former foes to meet on an appointed day and swear to the covenant. When the day came, the people gathered together, and the inhabitants of Ke also came, bringing with them the necessary offerings, which consisted of a sheep, a length of black or dark blue cloth, gunpowder, and grass or grass seed. Over these offerings the old enemies swore peace and friendship, the priest first saying, "To-day we Ke people bring peace to your town. From now on neither of you may have evil mind against the other." With these words he drew forward the sheep and cleft it in two, saying, "Should either town fight again, may it be cleft asunder like this sheep." Then, lifting up the piece of dark cloth, he said, "As this cloth is dark, so may the offending town be darkened." Next, setting fire to the gunpowder, he said, "As this powder is burnt, so may fire burn the guilty town." Lastly, holding out the grass, he said, "Should either town fight again, may that town be covered with grass." On account of the services which the people of Ke rendered as peace-makers, an ancient law of Calabar forbade any other town to wage war on Ke under pain of banishment to be inflicted on the transgressors by all the other members of the tribe in concert. In these Calabar rites the retributive intention of cleaving the sheep in two is expressed without ambiguity, and it is corroborated by the imprecations by which the other symbolic ceremonies are accompanied.

The same explanation is given of the similar rite among the Nagas, and is confirmed by the variations in the form of the oath, which seem best explained as signifying the retribution that will befall the perjurer. The retributive theory can be also supported by evidence drawn from classical antiquity. Thus when the Romans and the Albans made a treaty, which, according to Livy, was the most ancient treaty on record, the representative of the Roman people prayed to Jupiter, saying, "If the Roman people shall knowingly and of set purpose depart from the terms of this treaty, then smite thou them, O Jupiter, on that day, as I smite this boar-pig to-day." So saying, he smote and killed the pig with a flint knife. Again, we read in Homer that at the making of a truce between the Greeks and the Trojans, lambs were slaughtered, and while they lay gasping out their life on the ground, Agamemnon poured a libation of wine, and as he did so, both Greeks and Trojans prayed that whichever side violated their oath, their brains might be dashed out, even as the wine was poured on the ground.

The retributive intention of the sacrifice in such cases comes out very clearly in an Assyrian inscription, which records the solemn oath of fealty taken by Mati'-ilu, prince of Bit-Agusi, to Ashur-nirari, king of Assyria. Part of the inscription runs thus: "This he-goat has not been brought up from its flock for sacrifice, neither to the brave warlike (goddess Ishtar), nor to the peaceful (goddess Ishtar), neither for sickness nor for slaughter, but it has been brought up that Mati'-ilu may swear fealty by it to Ashur-nirari, king of Assyria. If Mati'-ilu sins against his oath, just as this he-goat has been brought up from his flock, so that he returns not to his flock and sets himself no more at the head of his flock, so shall Mati'-ilu be brought up from his land, with his sons, his daughters, and the people of his land, and he shall not return to his land, neither set himself at the head of his land. This head is not the head of the he-goat, it is the head of Mati'-ilu, it is the head of his children, of his nobles, of the people of his land. If Mati'-ilu breaks this oath, as the head of this he-goat is cut off, so shall the head of Mati'-ilu be cut off. This right foot is not the right foot of the he-goat, it is the right hand of Mati'-ilu, the right hand of his sons, of his nobles, of the people of his land. If Mati'-ilu (breaks this covenant), just as the right foot (of this he-goat) is torn off (so shall the right hand of Mati'-ilu, the right hand of) his sons (of his nobles, and of the people of his land), be torn off." Here there is a long gap in the inscription. We may conjecture that in the missing portion the dismemberment of the victim was further described, and that as each limb was lopped off, the sacrificer proclaimed that it was not the limb of the goat that was severed, but the limb of Mati'-ilu, of his sons, his daughters, his nobles, and the people of his land, if they should prove traitors to their liege lord, the king of Assyria.

Similar sacrifices, accompanied and interpreted by similar imprecations, meet us in the ritual of barbarous peoples at the present time. Thus in the island of Nias, by way of ratifying a solemn oath or covenant, a man will cut the throat of a sucking-pig, while at the same time he calls down on his own head a like death if he forswears himself or breaks his engagement. In the island of Timor a common form of giving evidence on oath is this: the witness takes a fowl in one hand and a sword in the other, and says, "Lord God, who art in heaven and on earth, look upon me! If I bear false witness to harm my fellow-men, may I be punished! This day I make my oath, and if I am not speaking the truth, may my head be cut off like the head of this fowl!" So saying, he chops off the bird's head on a wooden block. Among the Bataks of Sumatra, when chiefs are assembled to make peace or enter into a solemn covenant, a pig or a cow is brought forth, and the chiefs stand round it, each with his spear in his hand. Then the gongs are beaten, and the oldest or most respected chief cuts the animal's throat with his knife; afterwards the beast's body is opened, and the still palpitating heart torn out and chopped into as many bits as there are chiefs present. Each chief thereupon puts his morsel on a spit, roasts or warms it at a fire, and holding it up says, "If ever I break my oath, may I be slain like this beast that lies bleeding before me, and may I be eaten as its heart is now eaten." So saying he swallows the morsel. When all the chiefs have observed this rite, the still reeking carcass is divided among the people present and serves them for a feast.

Again, among the Chins, who inhabit the hills on the borders of

Assam and Burma, when two tribes take an oath of friendship, they meet and produce a tame bison. The wise men of each village pour liquors over it and mutter to their respective spirits to note the agreement which is now to be made over blood. The chiefs of either side each take a spear and standing on opposite sides of the bison drive their spears into its heart. If guns and not spears are used, the two chiefs simultaneously fire into the animal's brain or heart. As the bison falls its throat is cut and the blood collected in bowls; the tail of the animal is then cut off and dipped in the blood, and with it the chiefs and elders of its two parties daub the blood on each other's faces, whilst the wise men mutter, "May the party who breaks this agreement die even as this animal has died, and may he be buried outside the village and his spirit never rest; may his family also die and may every bad fortune attend his village."

In the old days, when the Karens of Burma desired to make peace with their enemies, the representatives of the two sides met and proceeded as follows. Filings made from a sword, a spear, a musket barrel, and a stone were mixed in a cup of water with the blood of a dog, a hog, and a fowl, which were killed for the purpose. This mixture of blood, water, and filings was called the "peace-making water." Next the skull of the slaughtered dog was chopped in two, and the representative of one side took the lower jaw of the animal and hung it by a string round his neck, while the representative of the other hung the dog's skull, including the upper jaw, round his neck in like manner. Thereafter the representatives solemnly promised that their people would thenceforth live at peace with each other, and in confirmation of the promise they drank the "peace-making water," and having drunk it they said, "Now that we have made peace, if any one breaks the engagement, if he does not act truly, but goes to war again and stirs up the feud again, may the spear eat his breast, the musket his bowels the sword his head; may the dog devour him, may the hog devour him, may the stone devour him!" Here the sword, the spear, the musket, and the stone, as well as the slain dog and hog, are supposed to assist in bringing down vengeance on the perjurer, who has imbibed portions of them all in the "peace-making water."

In these examples the retributive virtue ascribed to the sacrifice is rendered unmistakable by the accompanying words: the slaughter of the animal symbolizes the slaughter of the perjurer, or rather it is a piece of imitative magic designed to bring down on the transgressor the death which he deserves.

But it may be questioned whether the retributive function of the sacrifice suffices to explain the remarkable feature in the Hebrew and Greek rite which consists in passing between the pieces of the slain animal or standing upon them. Accordingly W. Robertson Smith suggested what we may call the sacramental or purificatory interpretation of the rite. He supposed that "the parties stood between the pieces, come as a symbol that they were taken within the mystical life of the victim"; and in confirmation of this view he pointed to the use of the very same rite in other cases to which the idea of punishment or retribution appears to be inapplicable, but of which some at least can be explained as modes of ceremonial purification. Thus in Boeotia a form of public purification was to cut a dog in two and pass between the pieces. A similar rite was observed at purifying a Macedonian army. A dog was cut in two: the head and fore part were placed on the right, the hinder part, with the entrails, was placed on the left, and the troops in arms marched between the pieces. On the conclusion of the rite the army used to divide into two and engage in a sham fight. Again, it is said that when Peleus sacked Iolcus, he slew the king's wife Astydamia, cut her in pieces, and caused the army to march between the pieces into the city. The ceremony was probably regarded as a form of purification to which a high degree of solemnity was imparted by the use of a human victim. This interpretation is confirmed by the ritual which the Albanians of the Caucasus observed at the temple of the Moon; from time to time they used to sacrifice a sacred slave by stabbing him with a spear, after which the body was carried to a certain place and all the people stepped on it as a purificatory rite. Among the Basutos of South Africa a form of ceremonial purification is this. They slaughter an animal, pierce it through and through, and then cause the person who is to be purified to pass through the hole in the carcass. We have seen that among the Barolong of South Africa a similar rite is observed at making a covenant: the covenanters force themselves through a hole in the stomach of the slaughtered animal. Together, these South African customs suggest that the passage between the pieces of a sacrificial victim is a substitute for passing through the carcass itself.

The purificatory, or better, perhaps, the protective, interpretation of such rites is strongly confirmed by the practice of the Arabs of Moab, who still observe similar ceremonies in times of public calamity, such as drought or epidemic, and explain them as intended to deliver the people from the evil which afflicts or threatens them. If, for example, the tribe is suffering from the ravages of cholera, the sheikh will stand up in the middle of the camp and cry out, "Redeem yourselves, O people, redeem yourselves!" Thereupon every family takes a sheep, sacrifices it, and, having divided it in two, hangs the pieces under the tent or on two posts in front of the door. All the members of the family then pass between the two pieces of the victim; children too young to walk are carried by their parents. Often they pass several times between the bleeding fragments of the sheep, because these are thought to possess the virtue of driving away the evil or the jinn who would injure the tribe. A similar remedy is resorted to in seasons of drought, when the pastures are withered and the cattle dying for lack of rain. The sacrifice is regarded as a ransom for man and beast. The Arabs say, "This is our ransom, for us and for our flocks." Questioned as to the mode in which the ceremony produces this salutary effect, they say that the sacrifice meets and combats the calamity. The epidemic, or drought, or whatever it may be, is conceived as a wind blowing across the plains and sweeping all before it, till it encounters the sacrifice which, like a lion, bestrides the path. A terrific combat ensues; the disease or drought is beaten and retires discomfited, while the victorious sacrifice remains in possession of the field. Here certainly there is no idea of retribution: neither symbolically nor magically is the death of the sheep supposed to entail the death of the people who pass between the joints of mutton; on the contrary, it is believed to save their lives by protecting them against the evil which, in one way or another, threatens their existence.

In the like circumstances a precisely similar custom is observed and similarly explained by the Chins, who inhabit the hill country bordering on Assam and Burma. Among these people, "when a person believes that he is followed by an enraged spirit, such as the spirit of cholera, it is a common practice to cut a dog in half without severing the entrails and to place the fore-quarters on one side of the road and the hind-quarters on the other side and connected by the intestines stretched across the road; this is to appease the spirit and to dissuade him from following any further." So strictly do the Chins personify cholera as a dangerous spirit, that when a party of them visited Rangoon in time of the epidemic, they carried their swords drawn, wherever they went, to scare away the demon, and they spent the day hiding under bushes that he might not find them. Similar means of averting a plague or pestilence used to be employed by the Koryaks of North-eastern Siberia. They slaughtered a dog, wound the guts about two posts, and passed under them. No doubt they also thought in this way to give the slip to the spirit of disease, who would find an insourmountable barrier in dog's guts. Again, women after childbirth are commonly supposed to be unclean and to be exposed to the attacks of malignant supernatural beings. Hence among the gipsies of Transylvania, when a woman in such circumstances leaves her bed of sickness, she is made to pass between the pieces of a cock which has been cut in two, if her child is a boy, but between the pieces of a hen, if her child is a girl; after which the cock is eaten by men, or the hen by women.

In all these cases the passage between the severed pieces of the animal is clearly protective, not retributive, in intention: the flesh and blood of the victim are thought somehow or other to present an obstacle to the powers of evil, and so to prevent them from pursuing and injuring the person who has passed through the narrow way. All such ceremonies may therefore be called purificatory in the wide sense of the word, since they purify or deliver the sufferer from malignant influences.

Returning to the point from which we started, we may now ask whether the ancient Hebrew form of making a covenant, by passing between the severed pieces of a sacrificial victim, was retributive or purificatory in its intention; in other words, was it a symbolic mode of imprecating death on the perjurer? or was it a magical mode of purifying the covenanters from evil influences and so guarding them against certain dangers to which both parties alike were exposed? The other instances which I have cited of passing between the severed pieces of a sacrificial victim seem to support the purificatory or protective explanation of the Hebrew rite; for while none of them require the retributive interpretation, some positively exclude it; and on the other hand some are only explicable on the purificatory or protective hypothesis, which is in fact expressly alleged by certain of the peoples, such as the Arabs and the Chins, who observe the custom. Certainly, in any attempt to explain the ancient Hebrew rite, much weight must be given to the analogy of the modern Arab ceremony; for the two customs are identical in form, and the peoples who practise or have practised them are both members of the Semitic family, speaking kindred Semitic languages and inhabiting the same country; since the land of Moab, where the Arabs still observe the ancient custom, formed part of the land of Israel, where Abraham of old sojourned and covenanted with God in like manner. The inference seems almost inevitable, that the ancient Hebrew and the modern Arab rite are both derived from a common Semitic original, the purificatory or protective intention of which is still clearly borne in mind by the Arabs of Moab.

One question still remains to be asked. In what did the purificatory or protective virtue of such an act consist? why should the passage between the pieces of a slaughtered animal be thought to protect a man against danger? Robertson Smith's answer is given in what may be called the sacramental interpretation of the custom. He supposed that the persons who stood or passed between the pieces of the victim were thought to be thereby united with the animal and with each other by the bond of a common blood; in fact, he held that such a covenant is only a variant of the widespread custom known as the blood covenant, in which the covenanters artificially create a tie of consanguinity between themselves by actually mixing a little of their own blood. On this hypothesis the only material difference between the two forms of covenant is, that the blood of an animal is substituted in the one for the human blood of the covenanters themselves in the other. Much is to be said for this theory. In the first place, as we saw, the South African evidence clearly points to the conclusion that the passage between the several pieces of a sacrificial victim is merely a substitute for the passage through the carcass of the animal. This conclusion is confirmed by observing that the Chins, in cutting the sacrificial dog in two, do not absolutely divide it, but keep the fore-quarters connected with the hind-quarters by the string of the animal's guts, under which the people pass; and the same appears, though less clearly, to have been the practice of the Koryaks. The retention of the string of guts as a bond uniting the otherwise severed halves of the victim seems clearly to be an attempt to combine the theoretical unity of the slain animal with the practical convenience of dividing it, so as to admit of the passage of people through its carcass. But what could be the sense of thus putting people, as it were, into the body of the animal unless it were for the purpose of investing them with some qualities which the animal is believed to possess, and which, it is assumed, can be transferred to anybody who physically identifies himself with the animal by actually entering into it?

That this is indeed the conception at the base of the rite is suggested by the analogy of a custom observed by the Patagonian Indians. Among these people, "in some cases when a child is born, a cow or mare is killed, the stomach taken out and cut open, and into this receptacle while still warm the child is laid. Upon the remainder of the animal the tribe feast. . . . A variation of the foregoing birth-ceremony is yet more savage. If a boy is born, his tribe catch a mare or a colt—if the father be rich and a great man among his people, the former; if not, the latter—a lasso is placed round each leg, a couple round the neck, and a couple round the body. The tribe distribute themselves at the various ends of these lassos and take hold. The animal being thus supported cannot fall. The father of the child now advances and cuts the mare or colt open from the neck downwards, the heart, etc., is torn out, and the baby placed in the cavity. The desire is to keep the animal quivering until the child is put inside. By this means they believe that they ensure the child's becoming a fine horseman in the future." The custom and the reason alleged for it are both significant. If you wish to make a child a good horseman, these Indians argue, the best possible way is to identify him at birth with a horse by putting him into the body of a living mare or colt; surrounded by the flesh and blood of the animal he will be one with it corporeally, he will have the hunting seat of a Centaur, whose human body is actually of a piece with the body of his horse. In short, the placing of the child in the body of the mare or colt is neither more nor less than a piece of sympathetic magic intended to endue a human being with equine properties.

On the same principle, as Robertson Smith pointed out, we can explain the Scythian form of covenant by treading on the hide of a slaughtered ox. All who put their right feet on the hide thereby made themselves one with the animal and with each other, so that all were united by a tie of common blood which ensured their fidelity to each other. For the placing of one foot on the hide was probably an abridged form of wrapping up the man completely in it; as a worshipper at the shrine of the Syrian goddess at Hierapolis used to kneel on the skin of the sheep he had sacrificed, and drawing the sheep's head and trotters over his own head and shoulders prayed, as a sheep, to the goddess to accept his sacrifice of a sheep.

This interpretation of the Scythian custom, proposed by Robertson Smith, is strikingly confirmed by an African parallel. Among the Wachaga of East Africa it is customary for lads to receive what may be called their war-baptism two years after they have been circumcised. They assemble with their fathers and all the grown men at the chief's village. Two oxen and two goats are killed, and their blood is caught in an ox-hide, which is held by several men. The lads strip themselves and go in long rows four times round the blood-filled hide. Then they stand in a row. An old man makes a small cut in each of their lower arms. Thereupon each boy, stepping up to the blood-filled hide, allows some drops of blood from his arm to fall into it, takes up a handful of the mixed blood, swallows it, and puts on his clothes. Then they crouch down round the chief, and after many speeches each lad receives a war-name from his father or, if his father is dead, from an old man who acts in place of his father. Next the chief harangues them, declaring that they are no longer children, but soldiers, and instructing them in their new duties. He also gives them all a common scutcheon for their shields, which marks them out as belonging to one and the same company. Here the lads who are to fight shoulder to shoulder in the same company knit themselves together by a double bond of blood, their own and the blood of the sacrificed animals, which are mixed together in the ox-hide and drunk together from the hide by each of the future warriors. Nothing could well demonstrate more clearly the truth of Robertson Smith's view that the intention of the ox-hide in the Scythian rite was similarly to unite the warriors by the tie of a common blood.

Perhaps this discussion of Abraham's covenant may help to throw light on a very dark spot of Canaanite history. In his excavations at Gezer, in Palestine, Professor Stewart Macalister discovered a burial-place of a very remarkable kind. It is simply a cylindrical chamber about twenty feet deep and fifteen feet wide, which has been hewn out of the rock and is entered from the top by a circular hole cut in the roof. The chamber appears to have been originally a water-cistern and to have been used for that purpose before it was converted into a tomb. On the floor of the chamber were found fifteen skeletons of human beings, or rather fourteen and a half skeletons; for of one body only the upper part was discovered, the lower part was wanting. The half skeleton was that of a girl about fourteen years of age; she had been cut or sawn through the middle "at the eighth thoracic vertebra, and as the front ends of the ribs had been divided at this level, it is plain that the section had been made while as yet the bones were supported by the soft parts." The fourteen other skeletons were all males, two of them immature, aged about eighteen and nineteen years respectively; all the rest were full-grown adults, of fair stature and strongly built. The position of the bodies showed that they had not been thrown in through the hole in the roof but deposited by persons who descended with them into the cave; and a large quantity of charcoal found among the bones is thought to indicate that a funeral feast, sacrifice, or other solemn rite had been observed within the sepulchral chamber. Some fine bronze weapons—spear-heads, an axe, and a knife—deposited with the bodies may be regarded as evidence that the burial took place before the advent of the Israelites, and accordingly that the men belonged to a race who preceded the Hebrews in Palestine. Judged by the shape of their bones, their large capacious skulls, their arched noses, and other anatomical peculiarities, the males are believed to be representative specimens of a race not unlike the Palestinian Arab of to-day. If the corporeal resemblance between these ancient men and the present inhabitants of the country is sufficient to justify us in considering them as members of the same stock, we may perhaps conclude that both belong to that Canaanite race whom the Hebrew invaders found in occupation of Palestine, and whom, though they reduced to bondage, they never succeeded in exterminating. For it is the opinion of competent judges that the modern Fellaheen or Arabic-speaking peasants of Palestine are descendants of the pagan tribes which dwelt there before the Israelite invasion and have clung to the soil ever since, being submerged but never destroyed by each successive wave of conquest which has swept over the land. If that is so, it seems reasonable to suppose that in the half-skeleton of the girl at Gezer we have a relic of that custom of human sacrifice which, as we know alike from the Hebrew prophets and classical writers of antiquity, played a prominent part in Canaanite religion. The supposition is strengthened by the discovery of many skeletons of infants, which were found at Gezer buried in large jars under the floor of the temple area; for these remains are commonly believed to attest a practice of sacrificing firstborn children at birth in honour of the local deity. Similar burials of infants in jars have been discovered round a rock-hewn altar at Taanach in Palestine, and they have been similarly interpreted.

But if the half-skeleton of the girl discovered in the cistern at Gezer is indeed a relic of human sacrifice, we have still to ask, why was she hewn or sawn asunder? The analogy of the covenant of Abraham and the similar rites which we have examined suggests that the bisection of the victim may have been intended either to effect a public purification or to ratify a covenant; or, to be more explicit, we may suppose that the girl was cut in two and that the people passed between the pieces either by way of averting some present or threatened evil, or by way of cementing a solemn treaty of peace. We will consider the purificatory or protective interpretation first.

We have seen that when Peleus captured the city of Iolcus, he is said to have taken the king's wife, cut her in two, and then led his army between the pieces into the city. The tradition is not likely to be a pure invention; it may well embody the reminiscence of a barbarous custom formerly observed by conquerors on entering a conquered city. We know that early man stands in great fear of the magic of strangers, and that he resorts to a variety of ceremonies in order to protect himself against it, either when he admits strangers to his own country, or when he enters the territory of another tribe. A similar dread of hostile magic may induce a conqueror to adopt extraordinary precautions for the purpose of safeguarding himself and his troops against the machinations of their enemies, before he ventures to enter the city which he has won from them by the sword. Such an extraordinary precaution might consist in taking a captive, hewing him or her in two, and then causing the army to defile between the pieces into the city. On the sacramental interpretation of this rite the effect of the passage between the pieces of the victim would be to form a blood covenant between the conquerors and the conquered, and thus to secure the victors from all hostile attempts on the part of the vanquished. This would explain the tradition as to the treatment which Peleus meted out to the captive queen of Iolcus: it was a solemn mode of effecting a union between the invaders and the invaded. If this explanation be accepted, it seems to follow that the purificatory or protective and the covenantal aspects of the rite practically coincide: the invaders purify or protect themselves from the malign influence of their foes by implicitly entering into a blood covenant with them.

It is possible that a similar Semitic custom may explain the severed skeleton of the girl at Gezer. To judge from the human remains that have been found on the site, the city was occupied by different races at different times: in the earliest ages it was the seat of a short, slenderly built, yet muscular people, with long oval heads, who did not belong to the Semitic stock and have not yet been correlated with any known Mediterranean race. If the city was conquered by the Canaanites who afterwards possessed it, these barbarous conquerors may have inaugurated their entrance into the city by putting the queen or another female captive to death, sawing her body in two and marching between the pieces into the city. But in that case, how are we to explain the absence of the lower half of the body? We need not suppose, as the discoverer suggested, that it was either burnt or devoured at a cannibal banquet; it may have been buried elsewhere, perhaps on the opposite side of the town, for the purpose of extending the magical influence of the sacrifice over all the intermediate space, so as to render the whole city secure for the conquerors and at the same time impregnable to the assaults of their enemies. In like manner an ancient king of Burma is said to have rendered his capital impregnable by cutting the body of a traitor into four pieces and

burying the quarters at the four corners of the city. In vain did
the traitor's brother besiege the capital with an army; all his
assaults were fruitless, till the widow of the slain man informed
him that he could never take the city so long as her dead husband
guarded the walls. So the besieger contrived to dig up the mouldering quarters of his dismembered brother, and after that he captured the city without resistance. Similarly among the Lushais of
Assam, when a woman is in hard labour, her friends, in order to
facilitate the birth, will take a fowl, kill it, and cut the carcass in
two equal parts. The portion with the head is then put at the
upper end of the village with seven pieces of cane rolled into bundles,
and the lower portion of the fowl is put at the lower end of the
village with five rolls of cane. Moreover, the woman is given a
little water to drink. This ceremony is called *arte-pumphelna,*
"to open the stomach with a fowl," because it is supposed to enable
the sufferer to bring forth. The mode in which the rite is believed
to produce this salutary effect is not mentioned, but we may conjecture that the severed pieces of the fowl placed at the two ends
of the village are thought to guard the intermediate space from the
incursion of those evil and especial demoniacal powers which had
hitherto prevented the birth of the child.

This theory of purificatory or protective intention of the
sacrifice of the girl at Gezer may perhaps be confirmed by another
discovery made at the same place. Later excavations brought to
light the half-skeleton of a boy about seventeen years of age, who,
like the girl in the cistern, had been cut or sawn through the middle
between the ribs and the pelvis; and, just as in the case of the girl,
only the upper half of the body was found, the lower half was
missing. Along with it were found the complete skeletons of two
men lying at full length, with a number of earthenware vessels above
and around them. These remains were discovered under, though
not directly below, the foundations of a building. Hence Professor
Stewart Macalister plausibly inferred that the skeletons are the
remains of human victims who, in accordance with a widespread
custom, had been sacrificed and buried under the foundations in
order to give strength and stability to the edifice or to guard against
enemies. The custom has been so amply illustrated by examples
drawn from many lands that it would be superfluous to dwell on it.
I will cite only a single instance recorded by an eye-witness, because
it clearly shows the train of thought which led to the institution of
the practice. Between seventy and eighty years ago a runaway
English sailor, by name John Jackson, lived alone for nearly two
years among the still heathen and barbarous Fijians, and he has
left us an artless, but valuable, account of his experiences. While
he was with the savages, it happened that the house of the local
chief or king was rebuilt. One day, being near the place where the
work was going on, Jackson saw men led along and buried alive in
the holes in which the posts of the house were set up. The natives

tried to divert his attention from the scene, but in order not to be deceived he ran up to one of the holes and saw a man standing in it with his arms round the post and his head still clear of the soil. When he asked the Fijians why they buried men alive at the foot of the posts, they answered that the house could not stand long if men did not sit down and continually hold the posts up. When he further inquired how they could hold up the posts after they were dead, the Fijians answered, that if the men sacrificed their lives in endeavouring to keep the posts in position, the virtue of the sacrifice would induce the gods to uphold the house after the men were dead.

Such a train of thought might well explain the position of the two male skeletons under the foundations at Gezer; for one of them was discovered with his bony hand in a bowl, as if helping himself to food and thereby fortifying himself for the weary task of holding up the walls. But it is less easy to understand the half-skeleton of the boy in the same place, and the half-skeleton of the girl in the cistern. If the object was indeed to bear up the foundations, it seems obvious that stalwart men would naturally be selected for so fatiguing a duty; of what use would half a boy and half a girl be for such a purpose? How could walls stand firm on lads and lassies who had no legs? Hence the theory that these victims were slain and bisected as foundation sacrifices can hardly be accepted as satisfactory.

Thus far we have considered the purificatory or protective theory of these mysterious sacrifices at Gezer. Let us now turn to the covenantal theory, and try whether it will not fit the facts better. The theory is that the boy and girl were slain and cut in two, not as a form of purification or mode of protecting the site, but as a ratification of a covenant, and that the covenanters passed between the pieces of the human victims, just as in making a covenant the ancient Hebrews passed between the halves of a slaughtered calf. This view may be confirmed by the following analogy. We have seen that the Wachaga of East Africa solemnize a covenant and league of peace between two districts by cutting a kid and a rope in two at one stroke, while they pray that, if they break their oath, they also may be split in two, like the kid and the rope. But they have another mode of concluding an alliance which is said to have the sanction of great antiquity. They take a boy and a girl and lead them three or seven times round the assembled covenanters, while solemn curses or blessings are pronounced on such as shall break or keep their oath. Then the boy and girl are cut in two through the middle, the four halves are buried at the boundary of the two districts, and the representatives of the two peoples who have made the covenant walk over the grave, and disperse to their homes. The notion, we are told, is an implied curse that the life of such as forswear themselves may be cut in two, like the young victims, and that, like them, they may perish without offspring. In order, it is said, that we may understand the full depth and significance of this curse, it is necessary to know that the religion of the Wachaga consists in the worship of ancestral spirits; so that a man who dies without offspring has no one to offer the sacrifices which alone can ensure him of a favourable reception and a continued maintenance among the dead; a childless man must lead for ever a lonely life in the far country, with no one to stay his hunger for beef and to quench his thirst for beer; for beer and beef, or mutton, are the things which the spirits of the departed chiefly desire to receive at the hands of their surviving relatives.

If this comparison of Wachaga with Semitic rituals is well founded, we can readily understand both why the victims at Gezer were cut in two, and why they were a boy and a girl, not a full-grown man and woman. We need only suppose that they were killed and cleft in two at the making of a solemn covenant; that the covenanters passed between the pieces, and that each side took half a boy or half a girl home with them as a guarantee of the good faith of the other side, exactly as among the Wachaga each side takes home one half of the cut rope as a guarantee of the good faith of the other party. At Gezer we have one half of the girl and one half of the boy, in both cases the upper half. It seems not wholly impossible that further excavations in Palestine may yet bring to light the lower halves of the same bodies which had been carried away and buried at home by the other parties to the covenant. Further, we can now understand why the victims chosen for the sacrifice were a boy and a girl, not a grown man and woman. If the Wachaga parallel holds good, the motive was an implied curse, that if either side broke their oath they might perish without offspring, like the child through whose mangled remains they had passed. When we remember the passionate desire of the Semite for offspring, we can appreciate the full gravity for him of such a curse, and can estimate the strength of the bond which it knit between the covenanters.

Lastly, it is to be observed that the analogy of the Wachaga ritual at making a covenant, whether the victim cut in two is a kid or a human being, strongly supports the retributive explanation of the Hebrew ritual on similar occasions; since in both the Wachaga cases we are given to understand that the cutting of the victim in two symbolizes the fate of the perjurer. Nevertheless it may still be open to us to interpret the passage between the pieces of the victim in the sense advocated by Robertson Smith, namely, as a mode of identifying the persons with the victim for the purpose of endowing them with certain properties which the victim is supposed to possess, and which, it is believed, can be imparted to all who enter into communion with the animal, either by passing through its body or in other ways, such as by smearing themselves with its blood or wearing pieces of its skin. In the making of a covenant the motive for identifying the covenanters with the victim is apparently to ensure, by means of sympathetic magic, that if any of the covenanters forswear themselves they shall share the fate of the victim; it is the magical sympathy thus created between the covenanters and the victim which gives a binding force to the covenant and furnishes the best guarantee of its fulfilment.

Thus if my analysis of the Covenant of Abraham is correct, the rite is composed of two distinct but correlated elements, namely, first, the cutting of the victim in two, and second, the passing of the covenanters between the pieces. Of these two elements the first is to be explained by the retributive, and the second by the sacramental theory. The two theories are complementary to each other, and together furnish a complete explanation of the rite.

CHAPTER II

THE HEIRSHIP OF JACOB OR ULTIMOGENITURE

§ 1. *Traces of Ultimogeniture in Israel.*—The traditions concerning the patriarch Jacob are fuller than those which relate to his father Isaac and his grandfather Abraham, and they are correspondingly richer in folk-lore, that is, in reminiscences of archaic belief and custom. It was natural that memories or fancies should gather thick about the ancestral hero from whom the people of Israel derived their name as well as their blood.

Yet the character of this great ancestor, as it is portrayed for us in Genesis, has little to attract or please a modern reader, and it contrasts unfavourably both with the calm dignity of his grandfather Abraham and with the meditative piety of his father Isaac. If Abraham is the type of the Semitic sheikh, brave and hospitable, dignified and courteous, Jacob is the type of the Semitic trader, supple and acute, fertile in expedients, with a keen eye to gain, compassing his ends not by force but by craft, and not too scrupulous in the choice of means by which to outwit and overreach his rivals and competitors. This unamiable combination of cupidity and cunning reveals itself in the earliest recorded incidents of the patriarch's life, the devices by which he contrived to cheat his elder brother Esau out of his birthright and his father's blessing. For Esau and Jacob were twins, and as the elder of the two Esau was entitled, according to the ordinary rule, to receive the paternal benediction and to succeed to the paternal inheritance. The means by which Jacob managed to supplant his elder brother were, to put it mildly, pieces of very sharp practice: he first took advantage of Esau's hunger to buy from him his birthright for a mess of pottage; and afterwards, by dressing in his brother's clothes and simulating the hairiness of his brother's skin, he palmed himself off as Esau on his blind old father, and so intercepted the blessing which was meant for his twin brother. It is true that in the second of these transactions the trick which the young hopeful played his doddered parent was not of his own devising; he was instigated to it by his mother Rebekah, whose maiden name might have been Sharp, to judge by the skill with which she choused her husband. Yet the readiness with which Jacob lent himself to the hoax proves that it was not the goodwill, but only the quick wit, that was wanting on his part to gull his father.

At a certain stage of moral evolution such frauds excite little or no reprobation except among those who immediately suffer by them; the impartial spectator indeed is apt to applaud them as exhibitions of superior intelligence and dexterity triumphing over mere honest stupidity. However, a time comes when public opinion ranges itself on the side of the honest dullard and against the clever sharper, because experience proves that every fraud, however admirable the ingenuity and foresight it displays, directly injures not only individuals but society as a whole by loosening that bond of mutual confidence by which alone any corporate body of men is held together. When this truth has been generally recognized, the historian comes to judge the doings of men in the past by a moral standard which neither the men themselves nor their contemporaries ever dreamed of applying to their actions; and if the heroic figures of the past seem to fall far below that standard, the charitable critic, instead of frankly acknowledging the gulf which moral progress has created between himself and them, attempts to bridge it over by finding excuses or even justifications for deeds which his own ethical judgment leads him to condemn. The process of whitewashing moral blackamoors, when it is prompted by the charity of a kindly heart and not by the empty vanity of maintaining a paradox, is creditable to the whitewasher and perhaps harmless to other people; therein differing from the contrary practice, which consists in blackening the whitest characters; for that execrable, though popular, practice not merely wounds the innocent by a stab in the back, but inflicts a public wrong by lowering the moral standard, since it robs us of those too rare models of virtue, the contemplation of which is better fitted to touch the heart with the admiration and love of goodness than any number of abstract treatises on moral philosophy.

In recent years the defence of Jacob's moral character has been undertaken by a compatriot and namesake, Mr. Joseph Jacobs, who has essayed to wipe out the blot on the ancestral scutcheon by demonstrating that in virtue of an ancient law Jacob, as the younger son, was really entitled to the inheritance, and that the chicane to which, in the Biblical narrative, he resorts in order to obtain it is merely a gloss put by the historian on a transaction he did not understand. Whether this ingenious apology is sound or not, I will not venture to say; but certain it is that such an ancient law of inheritance as his apologist supposes has prevailed among many peoples, and there seems to be no reason why it should not have obtained at a remote time among the ancestors of Israel. The law or custom in question is known as junior-right or ultimogeniture in contrast to primogeniture, because it gives the inheritance to the youngest son instead of the eldest. In this chapter I propose to illustrate the custom by examples and to inquire into its origin.

Let us begin by looking at other possible traces of junior-right or ultimogeniture which may be detected in the Old Testament. In the first place, then, if Jacob supplanted his elder brother, he only did what his father Isaac had done before him. For Isaac also was a younger son and displaced his elder brother Ishmael in the inheritance of their father Abraham. And the principle, if principle it was, on which Jacob acted in dealing with his father and brother, he appears to have followed in dealing with his own sons and grandsons. For we are told that he loved his son Joseph more than his elder sons "because he was the son of his old age"; and he showed his preference so decidedly that the jealousy of Joseph's elder brothers was aroused, and they plotted against his life. It is true that according to the narrative, as it now stands, Joseph was not the youngest son, he was only the youngest but one, since Benjamin was born after him. But we may surmise that in the original narrative Joseph was actually the youngest; the great affection which his father lavished on him, the coat of many colours, or rather the coat with long sleeves, by which he was distinguished among his brethren, and the position of superiority to them which he attained in the sequel, all point in this direction. Again, the name of Benjamin, the youngest of Jacob's sons, means "the son of the right hand"; and that this title marks him out as the lawful heir appears to be indicated by the remarkable account of the way in which Jacob, in blessing his two grandsons, the sons of Joseph, deliberately preferred the younger to the elder by laying his right hand on the head of the younger (Ephraim) and his left hand on the head of the elder (Manasseh), in spite of the protest of their father Joseph, who had placed his sons before their grandfather in such a position that he would naturally lay his right hand on the elder and his left hand on the younger; so that the old man was obliged to cross his hands over his breast in order to reach the head of the younger with his right hand, and the head of the elder with his left. Thus an apologist for Jacob may say with truth that he was at least consistent through life in his preference for young over elder sons, and that he did not merely resort to that principle when it suited his own selfish interests to do so.

But other witnesses may be called to speak in his favour, in other words, to testify to an ancient custom of junior-right or ultimogeniture in Israel. We read in Genesis that Tamar, the daughter of Judah, brought forth twin sons, named Perez and Zerah, and though Perez was born first, a curious detail as to the birth of the children is related, of which the intention seems to be to prove that Perez was really, like Jacob himself, the younger of the twins, and not, as might have been thought, the elder. The motive for proving

Perez to be the younger son is not obvious on the face of the narrative, but it becomes intelligible when we remember that Perez was the direct ancestor of King David, that David himself was the youngest son of his father, and that he was deliberately promoted by Samuel to the kingdom in preference to all his elder brothers. Thus the purpose of the narrator in giving what might seem needless, if not indecent, details as to the birth of the twins in Genesis, may have been to prove that King David was not only himself a youngest son, but that he was also descended from the younger of Judah's twin grandsons. And David in his turn transmitted the kingdom to one of his younger sons, Solomon, deliberately setting aside one of his elder sons, Adonijah, who claimed the crown. All these facts taken together may be held to raise a presumption that in Israel the custom of primogeniture, or preference for the eldest son, had been preceded by an older custom of ultimogeniture or preference for the youngest son as heir to his father. And the presumption is strengthened when we observe that a similar custom of junior-right or ultimogeniture has prevailed in other parts of the world.

§ 2. *Ultimogeniture in Europe.*—One of the countries in which the custom of ultimogeniture has been observed, and is still observed, is England. Under the title of Borough English this ancient usage is still, or was till lately, the law of the land in many parts of the country. The English name for the custom is taken from a local word used in a trial of the time of Edward the Third. It appears from a report in the Yearbook for the first year of that reign that in Nottingham there were then two tenures of land, called respectively Borough English and Borough French; and that under Borough English all the tenements descended to the youngest son, and that under Borough French all the tenements descended to the eldest son, as at the common law. It is said that as late as 1713 Nottingham remained divided into the English Borough and the French Borough, the customs of descent continuing distinct in each; and even at the present time similar customs are observed in that neighbourhood.

The distribution of Borough English or ultimogeniture in England was roughly as follows. The custom extended along the whole line of the "Saxon Shore" from the Wash to the neighbourhood of the Solent, including the whole of the south-eastern counties. To be more precise, it was most prevalent in Kent, Sussex, and Surrey, in a ring of manors encircling ancient London, and to a less extent in Essex and the East Anglian kingdom. In Sussex it prevails so generally on copyhold lands that it has often been called the common law of the country; and in the Rape of Lewes the custom indeed is almost universal. There are few examples in Hampshire, but farther west a great part of Somerset in one continuous tract was under the rule of ultimogeniture. In the Midland Counties the usage was comparatively rare, at the rate of two or three manors to a county; but it occurred in four out of the five great Danish towns.

namely in Derby, Stamford, Leicester, and Nottingham, as well as in other important boroughs, as Stafford and Gloucester. To the north of a line drawn between the Humber and the Mersey the custom appears to have been unknown.

However, the usage was not confined to the Saxon parts of the country; it existed also in Celtic regions, such as Cornwall, Devon, and Wales. In the ancient laws of Wales it is ordained that, "when brothers share their patrimony the youngest is to have the principal messuage (*tyddyn*), and all the buildings and eight acres of land, and the hatchet, the boiler, and the ploughshare, because a father cannot give these three to any one but his youngest son, and though they are pledged, yet they can never become forfeited." But the Welsh rule applied only to estates comprising at least one inhabited house; when property of any other kind was divided, the youngest son could claim no exceptional privilege. In Scotland there seems to be no evidence that ultimogeniture anywhere prevailed; but in the Shetland Islands it was the practice that the youngest child of either sex should have the dwelling-house, when the property came to be divided.

In old English law ultimogeniture appears to have been commonly associated with servile tenure. On this subject the late Professor F. W. Maitland wrote to me as follows: "As to the prevalence of ultimogeniture, I have seen a great deal of it in English documents of the thirteenth century, and rightly or wrongly it is always regarded as evidence, though not conclusive proof, of servile tenure—the theory being, apparently, that in strictness there is no *inheritance* of servile tenements, but that custom requires the lord to accept one of the family of the dead tenants as a new tenant. Here the choice of the youngest seems not unnatural: there being no inheritance to transmit, the children are sent into the world as they come of age; the youngest is the one most likely to be found at the hearth when the father dies. In several customs which divide the inheritance equally among sons, the youngest keeps the homestead, the *astre* or hearth. I am far from saying that the servile origin of ultimogeniture is proved, but certainly the succession of the youngest was regarded as servile in the thirteenth century. I could give you ample proof of that. It is thus brought into connection with the *merchetum*. Very commonly they are mentioned together: 'You are my villains, for I have talliged you, you paid fine for your daughter's marriage, you were your father's youngest son and succeeded to his tenement.'"

It deserves to be noticed that in England the right of ultimogeniture is not limited to males. There are scores, if not hundreds, of little districts, where the right is extended to females, the youngest of the daughters, or the youngest sister or aunt, being preferred above the other coheiresses.

The custom of ultimogeniture, or the succession of the youngest to the inheritance, also obtained in some parts of France. Thus "in some districts of the county of Cornouailles, in Brittany, the youngest child enjoyed an exclusive right, which is exactly the counterpart of the right of the eldest: the last born, whether son or daughter, succeeded to all the tenure called *quevaise*, to the exclusion of his or her brothers or sisters." This is the right known in French law as *maineté*. Though the custom existed in several extensive lordships of Brittany, we cannot estimate its original prevalence in that country; for when the customs of the province were codified by the feudal lawyers the nobles set their faces against the abnormal usage; and we learn that in the seventeenth century the area within which it survived was almost daily diminishing. The districts where the custom was in vogue included the Duchy of Rohan, the Commandery of Pallacrec, and the domains of the Abbeys of Rellec and Begare. In Brittany, as in England, ultimogeniture was an incident of servile tenure; and in Brittany, as in many parts of England, when a man left no sons, the inheritance went to the youngest daughter. Further, under the names of *Maineté* and *Madelstad*, the custom existed in Picardy, Artois, and Hainault, in Ponthieu and Vivier, in the district around Arras, Douai, Amiens, Lille, and Cassel, and in the neighbourhood of St. Omer. In all these districts the right of ultimogeniture ranged between the descent of the whole inheritance and the privileged succession to articles of household furniture. The same rule of inheritance was also followed at Grimbergthe in Brabant.

Similar customs prevailed in many parts of Friesland. The most notable of these was the *Jus Theelacticum*, or custom of the "Theel-lands," doles or allotable lands, at Norden in East Friesland, not far from the mouth of the Ems. The "Theel-boors" of that district continued down to the nineteenth century to hold their allotments under a complicated system of rules designed to prevent an unprofitable subdivision of estates. An inherited allotment was indivisible: on the death of the father it passed intact to the youngest son, and on his death without issue it became the possession of the whole community.

Other examples of ultimogeniture may be drawn from local customs, now superseded by the Civil Code, in Westphalia and those parts of the Rhine provinces which were under the "Saxon Law," and in the Department of Herford near Minden, the natives of which claim to belong to the purest Saxon race. So strong, we are informed, is the hold of the custom on the peasants that "until quite recently no elder child ever demanded his legal obligatory share: the children acquiesced in the succession of the youngest, even if no portions were left to them, and never dreamed of claiming under the law of indefeasible inheritance; and even if the peasant die without making the usual will the children acquiesce in the passing of the undivided inheritance to the youngest son." A similar practice has grown up in Silesia and in certain parts of Würtemberg, where the modern laws of succession have failed to break down the time-honoured privilege of the youngest, whose rights are guarded by a secret settlement or by the force of the local opinion. Again, in the Forest of the Odenwald, and the thinly peopled district to the north of the Lake of Constance, there are properties called *Hofgüter,* which cannot be divided, but descend to the youngest son or, in default of sons, to the eldest daughter. And many more examples, we are told, might be found in Swabia, in the Grisons of Switzerland, in Alsace and other German or partly German countries, where old customs of this sort have existed and still influence the feelings of the peasantry, though they have ceased to be legally binding.

No evidence of ultimogeniture appears to have been discovered in Denmark, Norway, or Sweden. But the youngest son has his privilege in the Island (once the Kingdom) of Bornholm, an out-lying appendage of the Danish Crown; and traces of a like custom have been recorded in the territory of the old Republic of Lübeck.

In the south and west of Russia it is becoming the practice to break up the old joint families and to establish the children in houses of their own; and it is said that in such cases the youngest son is regarded as the proper successor to the family dwelling-house. On this subject I am indebted to Miss M. A. Czaplicka, the distinguished Polish ethnologist, for the following information: "Junior or Minor right is known to have been the custom of the Russian peasants as early as the time of *Russkaya Pravda,* the first Russian code at the time of Yaroslav the Great. It is even now a very widespread practice in the peasants' customary law, which makes it possible to trace the origin of this law of inheritance. The 'minor right' is not a privilege but a natural course, owing to the fact that the elder sons usually separate from the father and from their own households, while the younger, or youngest, 'never severs from the father's root.' If in addition to the father's house the younger son inherits other property to the disadvantage of the elder sons, he also inherits certain duties: to take care of his enfeebled father and mother, and often also of unmarried sisters. If the elder sons have not separated from the father before his death, the house goes to the youngest son, but it is his duty to help the elder brothers in starting new households for themselves." Further, Miss Czaplicka tells me that "there is no trace of junior right among any other class than that of peasants in Russia, and among the peasants it is restricted to the house, or the house and a piece of personal, not communal land."

Thus far we have considered the prevalence of ultimogeniture among the Aryan peoples of Europe. Passing now to the European peoples who do not belong to the Aryan stock, we learn that "in Hungary it was the law of the country districts that the youngest son should inherit the father's house, making a proper compensation to the other coheirs for the privilege. Among the Northern Tchuds, although the chief of the family can delegate his power to the eldest or youngest son, or even to a stranger if he so pleases, yet the house in which he lives must go to the youngest son at his death."

§ 3. *The Question of the Origin of Ultimogeniture.*—So much for the distribution of ultimogeniture or the preference for youngest sons in Europe. We have now to ask, What was the origin of a custom which nowadays strikes us as so strange and indeed unjust? On this subject speculation has been rife. It may be well to begin by quoting the opinion which the learned and judicious Sir William Blackstone has expressed in his celebrated Commentaries on English Law. Speaking of the tenure of property in boroughs, or towns which had the right of sending members to parliament, he opposes it to military tenure of knight-service, and regards it as a relic of Saxon liberty retained by such persons as had neither forfeited it to the king or been obliged to exchange it "for the more honour-able, as it was called, but at the same time, more burthensome, tenure of knight-service." Saxon liberty, in his opinion, "may also account for the great variety of customs, affecting many of these tenements so held in antient burgage; the principal and most remarkable of which is that called Borough English; so named in contradistinction as it were to the Norman customs, and which is taken notice of by Glanvil, and by Littleton; viz. that the young-est son, and not the eldest, succeeds to the burgage tenement on the death of his father. For which Littleton gives this reason: because the younger son, by reason of his tender age, is not so capable as the rest of his brethren to help himself. Other authors have indeed given a much stranger reason for this custom, as if the lord of the fee had antiently a right of concubinage with his tenant's wife on her wedding-night; and that therefore the tene-ment descended not to the eldest, but the youngest son, who was more certainly the offspring of the tenant. But I cannot learn that ever this custom prevailed in England, though it certainly did in Scotland (under the name of *mercheta or marcheta*), till abolished by Malcolm III. And perhaps a more rational account than either may be fetched (though at a sufficient distance) from the practice of the Tartars; among whom, according to Father Duhalde, this custom of descent to the youngest son also prevails. That nation is composed totally of shepherds and herdsmen; and the eldest sons, as soon as they are capable of leading a pastoral life, migrate from their father with a certain allotment of cattle; and go to seek a new habitation. The youngest son, therefore, who continues latest with his father, is naturally the heir of his house, the rest being already provided for. And thus we find that, among many other northern nations, it was the custom for all the sons but one to migrate from the father, which one became his heir. So that possibly this custom, wherever it prevails, may be the rem-nant of that pastoral state of our British and German ancestors, which Caesar and Tacitus describe."

I have not found the passage of Du Halde to which Blackstone refers, but his statement is confirmed by a modern historian, who tells us that "a still more characteristic feature of ancient law among the Turks and Mongols, and one which sheds a vivid light on their history, is the custom which, for want of another term, I shall call 'inverse adoption.' Turkish custom regulates succession in a very peculiar manner; the permanent heir, who is in a manner attached to his native soil, is the youngest of the sons; it is he who is called the *Ot-dzékine*, as the Mongols say, or the *Tékine*, as the Turks say, 'the guardian of the hearth'; it is to him that the invariable portion of land reverts which is mentioned by Chinese annalists and western travellers. The elder brothers divide among themselves the moveables, above all the principal one, the *mal*, or capital, that is, the flocks and herds." Further, I find the custom of ultimogeniture common in a group of Mongoloid tribes in South-western China and the adjoining parts of Burma and India. An inquiry into their social state may throw light on the problem before us. But at the outset of the inquiry I would observe that, contrary to what we should expect if Blackstone's theory is correct, none of these tribes is pastoral: all are agricultural, depending almost wholly for their subsistence on the produce which they extract from the earth by tillage.

§ 4. *Ultimogeniture in Southern Asia.*—We begin with the Lushais, a tribe who inhabit a large tract of hills in Assam. They are a short, sturdy, muscular people, with broad and almost hairless faces, prominent cheek-bones, short flat noses, small almond-shaped eyes, and a complexion that varies between different shades of yellow and brown. Their Mongolian origin is therefore unmistakeable. And the evidence furnished by their physical appearance is confirmed by their language, which belongs to the Tibeto-Burman branch of the Tibeto-Chinese family of speech. They are an agricultural people and their staple food is rice. Yet in virtue of the mode of cultivation which they follow they are compelled to be migratory, seldom residing many years in any one district. Their system of farming is commonly known to English writers on India as *jhuming* or *jooming*. They fell the timber or bamboos in a piece of the forest or jungle; and when the fallen trees or bamboos have dried, they are burnt, and the ashes serve to manure the ground. The surface of the field thus obtained is lightly hoed, and when the gathering clouds warn the husbandmen that the dry season is nearly over and that the rains are about to begin, every one sallies out with a basket of seed over his shoulder and a long broad-ended knife (*dao*) in his hand. Thus equipped, the whole family sows the field, digging shallow holes in the ground with their knives and dropping a few seeds into each hole. The chief crop is rice, but maize, millet, Job's tears, peas, beans, tobacco, and cotton are also grown. This mode of cultivation is very wasteful, for seldom more than two crops are taken off the same

piece of ground in successive years, and the land is then allowed
to lie fallow till it is again overgrown with jungle or underwood.
If the clearing has been made in a bamboo jungle, three or four
years will elapse before the land is again fit for cultivation; but
if the clearing was made in a forest, a period of from seven to ten
years will pass before the procession of felling the trees is repeated.
Forest land is said to yield better crops than jungle land, but the
labour of clearing and weeding it is much greater. In this way
all the arable land within reach of a large valley is in time used
up, and a migration to another home becomes necessary. The
choice of a new site is a matter of anxious concern; a deputation
of elders is sent to sleep on the ground, and they draw omens
from the crowing of a cock which they take with them for the
purpose. If the fowl crows lustily an hour before daybreak, the
site is adopted. A village may be occupied for four or five years,
and in the old days the new village might be distant two or three
days' journey from the old one. The inhabitants must carry all
their worldly goods on their backs from one place to the other;
and the prospect of frequent and laborious transportations naturally
deters men from multiplying their possessions, and so checks the
growth of wealth and industry. Under such a system of shifting
cultivation, which is common to most of the hill tribes of this
region, the peasants acquire no rights in the soil, and even the chiefs
claim no property in the land and the forest. A chief asserts his
authority only over the men of his tribe, wherever they may wander, and wherever they may temporarily settle. Among some of
the wilder tribes the labour of reclaiming and tilling the ground
used to be performed in great part by slaves, whom the tribesmen
had captured on raids mainly undertaken for the purpose of procuring bondmen to relieve them of such servile toil.

The villages of the Lushais are generally perched on the tops
of ridges and extend down the steep sides of the hills. They are
large, often comprising hundreds of houses; but under the security
for life and property which the British Government has brought to
the country, the need for congregating in large fortified villages
has passed away, and accordingly the size of the villages is steadily
decreasing, and the people are scattering more and more into hamlets and even into lonely houses in the jungle far from other
habitations. A notable feature in a Lushai village is regularly the
zawlbuk or bachelors' hall, in which the unmarried men and lads
from the age of puberty upwards pass the night; for they are not
allowed to sleep in the houses of their parents. Travellers from
other villages also lodge in these halls, of which in a large village
there will be several. The institution is a common one among the
hill tribes of Assam.

Among the Lushais, each village is a separate state, ruled over
by its own chief. "Each son of a chief, as he attained a marriage-
able age, was provided with a wife at his father's expense, and

given a certain number of households from his father's village, and sent forth to a village of his own. Henceforth he ruled as an independent chief, and his success or failure depended on his own talents for ruling. He paid no tribute to his father, but was expected to help him in his quarrels with neighbouring chiefs; but when fathers lived long it was not unusual to find their sons disowning even this amount of subordination. The youngest son remained in his father's village and succeeded not only to the village, but also to all the property." Thus the practice of the Lushais strongly confirms the theoretical explanation of ultimogeniture which was suggested by Blackstone; for among them it would seem that the youngest son inherits simply because he remains at his father's home when all his elder brothers have left it and gone forth into the world to form new homes of their own. If further confirmation of this view were needed it appears to be furnished by a change which is taking place in the tribe at the present day. In the last Census Report on Assam we read that among the Lushais, "the decrease in the size of villages has led to an important modification of the custom under which the youngest son inherits his father's village and property. The *raison d'être* of this system of inheritance is that elder sons established villages of their own on their marriage. In order to enable them to do so, a certain number of headmen or Upas and also of the common people were told off to accompany the young chief and form the nucleus of his new village. When all the elder sons had been established in this way, it is not unnatural that the youngest should inherit his father's village and property, and on him rested the responsibility for his mother's support. But while there has been no tendency for chief's families to decrease, the average size of villages has been decreased by half and there are not enough houses to go round among the sons. Indeed, in some cases none of the sons have been able to start a separate village, and it is obvious that under these circumstances inheritance should pass to the eldest son, and this change has been readily accepted by the people."

Thus it would seem that among these people ultimogeniture is actually passing into primogeniture, because the social causes which led to the adoption of ultimogeniture are ceasing to exist. It is true that so far only the rule of inheritance in chief's families has been referred to; but substantially the same rule obtains as to the inheritance of private property among ordinary people. According to one account "property is divided amongst the sons; the youngest, however, gets the largest share; the rest in equal portions." According to a later account, "the general rule is for the youngest son to inherit, but occasionally the oldest also claims a share." And the reason for the custom in the families of commoners is probably the same as in the families of chiefs; for we have seen that when a chief's son is sent forth to found another village he takes with him a certain number of commoners to be his retainers and subjects in the new home. It is reasonable to suppose that in all such cases the colonists are drawn from the elder sons of families, while the youngest sons remain with their fathers in the old home and inherit the family property.

Among the Angamis, another Mongoloid tribe of Assam, the custom of ultimogeniture is found in a limited form. "During a man's life his sons, as they marry, receive their share of his landed property. Should, however, a man die, leaving several unmarried sons, these will all receive equal shares. As the sons marry, they leave the paternal mansion, and build houses of their own. The youngest son, therefore, in practice nearly always inherits his father's house." Here again, therefore, the inheritance of the paternal mansion by the youngest son depends simply on the accident of his being left last at home after his elder brothers have married and set up separate establishments of their own. If, at the time of their father's death, it should happen that there are several unmarried sons at home, the youngest will have no advantage over his elder brothers.

It deserves to be noted that the Angamis, who are the largest of the Naga tribes of Assam, are not migratory and do not cultivate the soil in the primitive and wasteful manner common to most hill tribes of this region, namely by clearing patches in the forest or jungle, cultivating them for a few years, and then suffering them to relapse into their former state of wild nature. On the contrary, the Angamis raise their crops on permanent terraces excavated with great labour and skill from the hill-sides, and these terraces they irrigate by means of artificial channels carried along the slope of the hills for long distances at easy gradients. Their large fortified villages are also permanent, for the Angamis are strongly attached to their homes and reluctant to change them.

The Meitheis, who constitute the dominant race of Manipur, in Assam, are a Mongoloid people speaking a Tibeto-Burman tongue. Although by blood and language they are akin to the wild hill tribes which surround them, they have advanced to a higher degree of social culture, so as to form a singular oasis of comparative civilization and organized society in the midst of a wilderness of barbarism. They live in settled villages, and subsist chiefly by the rice which they cultivate in permanent fields. They have thus passed beyond the stage of periodical migrations caused by the exhaustion of the arable lands in their neighbourhood. As to the rules of inheritance among the Meitheis, we are told that "the Chronicles of Manipur do not afford us much aid in ascertaining the rules of inheritance for private property, and at the present time the economics of the State are in flux under pressure of new ideas political and social. Land is regarded as held at the will of the ruling power of the State. As regards moveable property the general practice seems to be to provide for the sons during the lifetime of the father, and to regard the youngest son as the heir general if at the time of the father's death he is still living in the ancestral home. If he had separated and was living apart from his father, the property should be equally divided among the sons. Marriage is of course the cause of the separation of the sons from the home, and is the occasion of finding provision for them as well as for the daughters." Thus among the Meitheis, as among the Angamis, of Assam, the heirship of the youngest son depends solely on the accident of his being left last at the paternal home, after his elder brothers have married and settled elsewhere. If like them he should have married and set up house for himself, he will have no preference in the inheritance, but will divide the property equally with his brothers. Further, we see that in Assam, as in England, the custom of ultimogeniture survives in a limited form after the population has ceased to be migratory and has settled down in permanent villages surrounded by fields which remain the same from generation to generation.

The Kachins or, as they call themselves, the Chingpaws or Singphos, are a Mongoloid race who inhabit the northern parts of Upper Burma. Their old settlements were on the head waters of the Irrawaddy River, but they have spread eastward into the Chinese province of Yunnan, and westward into the Indian province of Assam. The name of Chingpaws or Singphos, which they give themselves, means simply "men." The Burmese call them Kachins or Kakhyens. They are wild and savage mountaineers, broken up into a number of small communities or petty tribes, each under its own chief; their raids were much dreaded by the more pacific Burmese and Shans before the English occupation of the country. Yet they cultivate the soil, and indeed are expert at tillage; their fields are often deep down in the valleys, while their villages stand far above them on the hills. Of the Tartar origin of the Kachins, we are told, there cannot be much doubt. Their traditions point to a first home somewhere south of the desert of Gobi, and their movements have always been towards the south. But the diversity of complexion and features which prevails even in tracts where Shan and Burmese influences have apparently never penetrated, seems to point to admixture with aboriginal races whom the Kachins supplanted.

The law of inheritance among the Kachins, as it is often stated, combines the principles of primogeniture and ultimogeniture; for we are told that 'the patrimony is divided between the eldest and the youngest son; while any children that may intervene, are left to push their own fortunes as they best can. The eldest son succeeds to the title and estate, while the youngest, carrying away all the personal and moveable property, goes in quest of a settlement for himself." According to this account, which has been substantially repeated by several writers on the Kachins, the eldest son remains at home in possession of the paternal estate, while the youngest son takes the personal property and goes out to push his way in the world. This is just the contrary of what is commonly said to happen among the kindred Mongoloid tribes of this region, and we may suspect that the account, which appears to have originiated with Captain J. B. Neufville in 1828, rests on a misunderstanding. At all events Sir George Scott, who had ample means of acquainting himself with the customs of the Kachins, has given a different account of their law of inheritance. He says, "There has been a constant tendency to disintegration among the Kachins just as there has been among the Tai, and the hillier character of their country has made the subdivisions very much more minute. This disintegration was also in past times due, no doubt, chiefly to the necessity for migration caused by over-population and the wasteful character of the hill cultivation. It became the custom, on the death of a chief, for the youngest son to succeed: while the elder brothers set out with such following as they could muster and founded fresh settlements, which, if they were successful, in time came to be distinct tribes named after their own founder. The Kentish law of Borough English no doubt is a reminiscence of a similar custom among the Anglian tribes."

Elsewhere Sir George Scott gives us an instructive account of the different systems of ownership, communal and individual, which prevail in the hills and the valleys respectively, the difference in the ownership depending on the difference between the migratory and the permanent systems of agriculture practised in the hills and valleys. He says, "With regard to *taungya* or hill cultivation, individual property is not recognized; the land is regarded as belonging to the whole community as represented by their *Duwa* [chief], and the system of cultivation does not permit of a constant use of the same plot of ground. Where land is owned in the valleys and wet-weather paddy is cultivated, the case is different, and individual ownership is admitted with this restriction, that the land cannot be parted with to an alien. It is as a recognition of his theoretical ownership of all the land that the *Duwa* gets one or two baskets of paddy per house annually. Land descends to a household as a whole, and is worked in common for the benefit of all. Those who leave the household lose all right to participate. When the household breaks up voluntarily, a division is made according to no fixed rules, except that the youngest son gets Benjamin's share, as well as the ancentral homestead."

In this account a sharp distinction appears to be drawn between the uplands, where the cultivation is migratory, and the lowlands, where the cultivation is permanent: on the hills the rice is grown on the dry system, in the valleys it is grown on the wet system. The coincidence of the dry system with migratory cultivation, and of the wet system with permanent cultivation, is not accidental; for while the dry system is compatible with a temporary occupation of the ground, the wet system necessitates its permanent occupation. In Java, for example, where the cultivation of rice is carried to a high pitch of excellence by means of artificial irrigation, there are lands which have produced two crops every year beyond the memory of living man. Now it is very significant that among the Kachins the lands which are under temporary cultivation are held in common, whereas the lands which are under permanent cultivation are owned by individuals. Similarly we saw that among the Lushais, who follow the migratory system of agriculture, there is no private property in the soil. The reason is obvious. Permanent occupation is essential to individual ownership; it is not essential to communal or tribal ownership. And as in human history the nomadic life of the hunter, the herdsman, and the migratory husbandman precedes the settled life of the farmer under the more advanced systems of tillage, it seems to follow that individual ownership of land has been developed later than communal or tribal ownership, and that it cannot be recognized by law until the ground is under permanent cultivation. In short, common lands are older than private lands, and the transition from communal to private ownership of the soil is associated with a greatly improved mode of tillage, which in its turn, like all economic improvements, contributes powerfully to the general advance of society.

Like their brethren of Burma, the Kachins of China practise both the migratory and the permanent modes of agriculture. Viewed from the top of a lofty mountain, their country stretches away on every side like a sea of hills, far as the eye can range, their summits and slopes in great part clothed with forest, except where little clearings mark the sites of villages, or where an opening in the mountains reveals a river winding through a narrow valley far below. The villages are always situated near a perennial mountain stream, generally in a sheltered glen, or straggling with their enclosures up a gentle slope, and covering perhaps a mile of ground. The houses, which usually face eastward, are all built on the same plan. They are constructed of bamboo and usually measure from one hundred and fifty to two hundred feet in length, by forty to fifty feet in breadth. The first room of one of these large communal dwellings is reserved for the reception of strangers; the others are the apartments of several families, connected with each other by blood or marriage, which compose the household community. The projecting eaves, supported by posts, form a verandah, where men and women work or lounge by day, and where the buffaloes, mules, ponies, pigs, and fowls lodge by night.

Near the houses are small enclosures, where white-flowered poppies, plantains, and indigo are cultivated; rice and maize are grown together on the adjacent slopes and knolls, which are carefully scarped in terraces, often presenting the appearance of an amphitheatre. The stream is dammed near the highest point, and directed so as to overflow the terraces and rejoin its bed in the valley below. Sometimes the water is led in bamboo conduits to rice fields or distant houses. Fresh clearings are made every year by felling and burning the forests on the hill-sides. Near every village disused paths may be seen, which have been cut to former clearings, and along which little canals have been carried. The cleared ground is broken up with a rude hoe, but in the cultivated terraces wooden ploughs are used. Excessive rain rather than drought is the evil most dreaded by these rude husbandmen. But generally the natural fertility of the soil more than repays their labours with bountiful crops of rice, maize, cotton, and tobacco, all of excellent quality. Near the villages are orchards, where peaches, pomegranates, and guavas are grown; and the forest abounds with chestnuts, plums, cherries, and various wild brambleberries. On the higher slopes, oaks and birches flourish, and large tracts are covered with *Cinnamomum caudatum* and *C. cassia*, of which the oil is commonly sold as oil of cinnamon. Thousands of these trees are felled annually to clear new ground for cultivation, and their fallen trunks and branches are burned where they lie.

The Mongolian origin of these Chinese Kachins is apparent from their physical features, though two types may be distinguished among them. By far the commoner of the two comprises a short, round face, low forehead, prominent cheek-bones, broad nose, thick protruding lips, broad square chin, and slightly oblique eyes set far apart. The ugliness of the face is only redeemed by its good-humoured expression. The hair and eyes are usually dark brown, the complexion a dirty buff. The other type shows finer-cut features, which recall the womanly faces of the Kacharis and Lepchas of Sikhim. In it the obliqueness of the eyes is very marked, and the face is a longish, rather compressed oval, with pointed chin, aquiline nose, prominent cheek-bones, and a complexion so fair that in some cases it might almost pass for European. This type may point to admixture with Shan or Burmese blood. The stature of the Kachins is rather low; the limbs are slight, but well formed, the legs, however, being disproportionately short. Though not muscular, they are athletic and agile. They bring down from the hill loads of firewood and deal planks, which the ordinary European has much ado in lifting; and the young girls bound like deer along the hill-paths, their loose dark locks streaming behind them on the wind.

Among these mountaineers the patriarchal system of government has hitherto universally prevailed. Each clan is governed by an hereditary chief assisted by lieutenants, whose office is also hereditary; but curiously enough, while the office of lieutenant should in strictness be held only by the eldest son of the family, "the chieftainship descends to the youngest son, or, failing sons, to the youngest surviving brother. The land also follows this law of inheritance, the younger sons in all cases inheriting, while the elder go forth and clear wild land for themselves." Thus among the Kachins, as among the Lushais, the right of ultimogeniture appears to be founded on a custom of sending out the elder sons into the world to fend for themselves, while the youngest remains with his parents in the old home.

A similar rule of succession, based on a similar custom, was found by Dr. John Anderson to prevail among the Shans of China, the neighbours of the Kachins in the province of Yunnan. Among them, he tells us, the chiefs, assisted by a council of headmen, exercise full patriarchal authority in their states, adjudicating on all cases, civil and criminal. The chief (*tsawbwa*) "is the nominal owner of all land, but each family holds a certain extent, which they cultivate, paying a tithe of the produce to the chief. These settlements are seldom disturbed, and the land passes in succession, the youngest son inheriting, while the elder brothers, if the farm is too small, look out for another plot, or turn traders; hence the Shans are willing to emigrate and settle on fertile lands, as in British Burma." Most of these Chinese Shans are engaged in agriculture, and as farmers they may rank with the Belgians. Every inch of ground is cultivated; the principal crop is rice, which is grown in small square fields, shut in by low embankments, with passages and floodgates for irrigation. During the dry weather, the water of the nearest stream is led off and conducted in innumerable channels, so that each field can be irrigated at will. At the beginning of May, the valley, from one end to the other, presents the appearance of an immense watery tract of rice plantations glistening in the sunshine, while the bed of the river is left half bare by the withdrawal of the water.

The Shans or Tai, as they should rather be called, are the most numerous and widely spread race of the Indo-Chinese peninsula, extending from Assam far into the Chinese province of Kwang-si, and from Bangkok to the interior of Yunnan. Siam is now the only independent Shan state. The people are closely akin to the Chinese both in physical appearance and in speech; indeed in grammatical structure as well as vocabulary the Chinese and Shan are sister languages, differing widely from the Burmese and Tibetan, which nevertheless belong to the same general family of speech, now called by philologers the Tibeto-Chinese. Though much of their territory is mountainous, the Shans do not profess to be a hill people, preferring to cling to the flat alluvial valleys or wide straths, which are interposed between the mountains. Everywhere they are diligent cultivators of the soil; the larger plains are intersected with irrigation canals, while in the smaller the streams are diverted by dams into channels which water the slopes, or bamboo wheels are used to raise the water to the fields, where the river-banks are high and there is enough flat land to repay the expense and trouble. However, when holdings are not to be obtained in the plain, young men will sometimes apply for jungle land at a distance from the village on the hill-side. Of such jungle land there is no lack, but it is useless for the cultivation of rice and has to be laid out in orchards or banana-gardens. It is interesting to observe the ancient custom of ultimogeniture surviving among a people so comparatively advanced as the Shans.

The custom of ultimogeniture is also said to be observed by the Chins, who inhabit the hills on the borders of Burma and Assam. Their racial affinities have not yet been exactly determined, but apparently they belong to the great Mongolian family and speak dialects of the Tibeto-Burman speech. Most of the Chins are still in a very wild state, living at enmity with all their neighbours. They are divided into numerous small clans, which make frequent raids on each other or on neighbouring Burmese villages. For their subsistence they depend chiefly on agriculture, raising crops of rice, millet, peas, beans, sessamum, and tobacco. But their country does not lend itself well to tillage, for the hills are over-brown with jungle and underwood and broken up by ravines. Small patches, however, are cleared for cultivation in the neighbourhood of the villages. Among their remarkable laws of marriage and inheritance are the custom which gives a man prior right to marry his cousin, and the rule that "the younger son is the heir of a Chin family, and he is bound to stay at home and take care of his parents and sisters." However, among the Haka Chins at the present time the custom of ultimogeniture seems to have passed, or to be passing, into primogeniture, though in two at least of the families or clans, the Kenlawt and the Klarseowsung, the youngest son still regularly succeeds to the family dwelling, unless he waives his claim, or has quarrelled with his father, or is a leper or insane. Formerly it was the invariable rule in all the Haka clans that the youngest son should inherit the family dwelling; but a certain Lyen Non, of Sangte, bequeathed his house to his eldest instead of to his youngest son, and since his time the change of descent has been adopted by most of the clans. "As regards landed property (*lai ram*), situated within the Maka Tracts, two-thirds is apportioned to the eldest and one-third to the youngest son."

Among the Kamees or Hkamies, a hill tribe of Arakan, on the borders of Burma, the rule of inheritance is that "if a man die leaving two or more sons, the property is divided as follows:—two divide equally; if there be more than two, the eldest and youngest take two shares each, and the others one share each." This rule of inheritance is apparently a compromise between the principles of primogeniture and ultimogeniture, the oldest and the youngest sons being both preferred in equal degrees to their intermediate brothers. Perhaps the compromise marks a transition from ultimogeniture to primogeniture.

The practice of ultimogeniture is reported also to prevail among the Lolos, an important and widespread aboriginal race in the Chinese province of Yuman, who belong to the Mongolian family and speak a branch of the Tibeto-Burman language. Among them, according to an English traveller, "the order of succession to property and chieftainship is curious; the youngest son generally succeeds and after him the eldest."

Thus far we have dealt with Mongoloid tribes in which the

principal heir to property is the youngest son. We have now to consider two tribes in which the principal heir is the youngest daughter. These are the Khasis and Garos of Assam. The origin and racial connexions of the Khasis are still matters of discussion. They certainly speak a language which, unlike that of all the tribes around them, does not belong to the Mongolian family and is apparently related to the Mon-Kmer languages of Indo-China, which in their turn are now believed to constitute a branch of a great Austric family of languages spoken from Madagascar in the west to Easter island in the east, and from New Zealand in the south to the Punjab in the north. However, their possession of a non-Mongolian language is no proof that the Khasis belong to a non-Mongolian race; for when a language has not been fixed by being committed to writing the people who speak it are very ready to drop it and replace it by another borrowed from a dominant race with which they have been brought into contact. Instructive instances of such easy and rapid transitions from one language to another have been observed and recorded in modern times among the tribes of Burma, who speak a variety of languages and dialects. The physical appearance and character of the Khasis seem to point to a Mongolian origin; indeed, according to Sir William Hunter, their Mongolian physiognomy is unmistakeable. They are a short, muscular people, with well-developed calves, broad high cheek-bones, flat noses, little beard, black straight hair, black or brown eyes, eyelids set obliquely, though not so acutely as in the Chinese and some other Mongols, and a complexion, according to locality, varying from a light yellowish-brown to a dark brown. In disposition they are cheerful, light-hearted, good-natured, and thoroughly appreciate a joke. These characteristics certainly favour the view that the Khasis belong to the Mongolian stock rather than to the southern and chiefly tropical family of peoples, with whom they are allied by language.

Be that as it may, in their manner of life and the general level of their culture the Khasis do not differ markedly from the Mongoloid tribes of South-eastern Asia who practise ultimogeniture. They live in settled villages, which they seldom shift, and they subsist chiefly by agriculture, being industrious cultivators, though their modes of tillage are somewhat primitive. Like most hill tribes of this region, they obtain fresh land for tillage by clearing the forest, felling the trees, and burning the fallen timber. Their staple food is rice and dried fish.

The social system of the Khasis is based on mother-kin, that is, on the custom of tracing descent exclusively through women. Each clan claims to be sprung from a common ancestress, not from a common ancestor; and each man reckons his genealogy through his mother, grandmother, and so on, not through his father, grandfather, and so on. And as with blood, so with inheritance, it passes through women only, not through men, and it is the youngest, not the eldest daughter, who inherits; if she dies in her mother's lifetime, she is succeeded by the next youngest daughter, and so on. Failing daughters, a woman's property goes to her sister's youngest daughter, who in her turn is succeeded by her youngest daughter, and so on. It is true that on the mother's death, the other daughters are entitled to a share in her property; but the youngest daughter gets the largest share, including the family jewellery and the family house, together with the greater part of the contents. Still she may not dispose of the house without the unanimous consent of all her elder sisters, who, on the other hand, are bound to repair the dwelling for her at their own charges. As for the landed estate, it belongs to the youngest daughter only, but her elder sisters are entitled to maintenance from the produce. Almost invariably the grandmother, her daughters, and her daughters' daughters live together under one roof or in adjoining houses with the same enclosure; and during her lifetime the grandmother is head of the house. In such a household of women a mere man is nobody. If he is a son or brother, he is of no account, because, when he marries, he will leave the house and go and live with his wife's family. If he is the husband of one of the women, he is still of no account, not being a member of the family, and having no share in the inheritance. He is looked upon as a mere begetter. Any property he may earn by his own exertions will go at his death to his wife, and after her to her children, the youngest daughter as usual getting the largest share. So long as he lives, he is a stranger in his wife's house; and when he dies, even his ashes may not rest beside hers in the family tomb.

The custom of tracing descent and transmitting property through women instead of through men is common among uncivilized races, and may in its origin have been based on the certainty of motherhood compared with the uncertainty of fatherhood in a state of society which allowed great freedom of intercourse between the sexes. But that is a large and difficult problem, the discussion of which would lead us too far. Among the Khasis at the present time, whatever its remote origin may have been, the custom is clearly bound up with the rule which keeps all the daughters at home and sends out all the sons to live with their wives' families. For under such a rule the women are the only lifelong members of the household, and it is therefore natural that the house and its contents should be in their hands rather than in the hands of the males, who leave or enter the house only at marriage, and hence spend only a portion of their life within its walls; and the same reasoning would apply also to landed property, if the lands are near the houses, and the sons on marrying take up their abode with their wives' people in distant villages. Under such circumstances it is easy to understand why daughters rather than sons should succeed to the family property, both real and personal.

But if the preference of daughters to sons as heirs is thus

explained, the reason for preferring the youngest daughter, as heiress, to all her elder sisters is still to seek. The Khasis themselves account for the favoured position of the youngest daughter by the religious duties which she is bound to discharge. She holds the religion, as their phrase is; that is, she is bound to perform the family ceremonies and propitiate the family ancestors; hence it is right that, incurring such heavy obligations to the family, she should receive the largest share of the property. For the same reason, if she changes her religion or commits an act of sacrilege by violating a taboo, she forfeits her privileges and is succeeded in them by her next youngest sister, just as if she had died. This explanation of the privileged position accorded to the youngest daughter is hardly satisfactory; for we have still to ask, why should the youngest daughter be deemed better fitted than her elder sisters to discharge the duty of worshipping the ancestors? To this question no answer seems to be forthcoming. And the reason assigned in other tribes for preferring the youngest son as heir, because he stays at home in the parental house after his elder brothers have gone out into the world, seems inapplicable to the youngest daughter among the Khasis; since in that tribe all the daughters apparently remain all their lives at home in the parental house and there receive their husbands. Yet we should naturally expect the reason for preferring the youngest daughter to be analogous to the reason for preferring the youngest son; and accordingly a theory which explains the one case but not the other, can hardly be regarded as adequate.

The other tribe of Assam who follow the customs of mother-kin and ultimogeniture in favour of the youngest daughter are the Garos, who inhabit the thickly wooded but not lofty hills which take their name from the tribe. They undoubtedly belong to the Mongolian race, for they are a short, stout-limbed, active people, with strongly marked Chinese countenances, and they speak a Tibeto-Burman language of the Tibeto-Chinese family. Indeed, they have a very distinct "story of their migration from Thibet; of their arrival in the plains at the foot of the Himalayas; of their wanderings eastward up the Brahmaputra valley, and of the subsequent retracing of their steps until they came to the plains which lie between that river and the hills they now inhabit. Here they seem to have settled for a time before making the last move into the mountainous country that now forms the home of the tribe." Most of the great virgin forests which formerly covered the Garo Hills have been destroyed to make room for tillage, and their place has been taken by bamboos and small trees; for, fostered by the heavy rainfall, a dense jungle has overspread almost the whole face of the country except where patches of land have been cleared for cultivation. The Garo is essentially a husbandman. To till the soil is the beginning and the end of his life's work, and the occupation to which he devotes all the energy he can muster. His mode of cultivation is rude. A piece of land, generally on a hill-side, is chosen and the jungle on it cut down in the cold weather, which lasts from December to February. The felled trees or bam-boos—for in many parts of the hills the jungle consists of bamboos only—cumber the ground till the end of March, when they are burnt as they lie. The crops are sown in April and May as soon as the first showers have fallen. The land is not hoed, much less ploughed; but holes are made in it with a pointed stick and a few seeds of rice dropped into each. Millet is simply sown broadcast in the ashes of the burnt jungle. Land thus reclaimed is kept under cultivation for two years; then it is abandoned and lies fallow for at least seven years. The villages are usually built in valleys or in hollows on the hill-sides, where there is plenty of running water. Around, on all sides, stretches the limitless jungle. The houses are raised on piles and are very long, often more than a hundred feet in length; being destitute of windows, the interiors are dark and gloomy. The public room of the family occupies the greater part of the building, and there the unmarried women sleep on the floor; but spaces are portioned off in it for married daughters and their husbands, and the householder and his wife have a bed-room to themselves. The bachelors do not sleep in their parents' house, but in a house set apart for the use of all the unmarried men of the village. In this bachelors' hall strangers are lodged, and the village elders hold their meetings. Such dormitories for the unmarried men are a regular institution with the Naga tribes of Assam, but they are not found among the Khasi Uplanders.

Amongst the Garos, as amongst the Khasis, the system of mother-kin prevails. The wife is the head of the family, and through her all the family property descends. The tribe is divided into a great many family groups or "motherhoods," called *machongs*. All the members of a "motherhood" claim to be descended from a common ancestress; and all the children of a family belong to their mother's "motherhood," not to that of their father, whose family is barely recognized. Inheritance also follows the same course and is restricted to the female line. No man may possess property except what he earns by his own exertions; no man may inherit property under any circumstances whatever. "The law of inheritance may be briefly stated to be, that property once in a motherhood, cannot pass out of it. A woman's children are all of her *machong* [motherhood], and therefore it might at first appear that her son would satisfy the rule; but he must marry a woman of another clan, and his children would be of their mother's sept, so that, if he inherited his mother's property, it would pass out of her *machong* [motherhood] in the second generation. The daughter must therefore inherit, and her daughter after her, or, failing issue, another woman of the clan appointed by some of its members." However, although in the eyes of the law the family estate and property belong to the woman, in practice her husband has full use of both during her lifetime, and while he cannot will it away, his authority otherwise over it is unquestioned. For example, the lands of a village belong, strictly speaking, to the wife of the village headman, yet he is always thought of and spoken of as the proprietor; and although he derives his rights exclusively through his wife, she is never considered, unless it is convenient to mention her name in a lawsuit. Practically, therefore, a woman is merely the vehicle by which property descends from generation to generation for the benefit principally of males.

So far we have heard of the legal preference of daughters to sons among the Garos, but nothing has yet been said as to a preference of the youngest daughter to all the rest. Indeed, Major Playfair, who has given us a valuable monograph on the tribe, drops no hint of such a preference; from which we may perhaps infer that the practice of ultimogeniture is obsolete or obsolescent among the Garos at the present day. However, it appears to have existed in the tribe down at least to nearly the end of the eighteenth century; for an Englishman who visited and studied the Garos in 1788 has recorded the custom among them. After describing a Garo marriage which he witnessed, he goes on as follows: "I discovered these circumstances of the marriage ceremony of the Garrows, from being present at the marriage of Lungree, youngest daughter of the chief Oodassey, seven years of age, and Buglun, twenty-three years old, the son of a common Garrow: and I may here observe, that this marriage, disproportionate as to age and rank, is a very happy one for Buglum, as he will succeed to the *Booneahship* [chieftainship] and estate; for among all the Garrows, the youngest daughter is always heiress; and if there be any other children who were born before her, they would get nothing on the death of the *Booneah* [chief]. What is more strange, if Buglun were to die, Lungree would marry one of his brothers; and if all his brothers were dead, she would then marry the father: and if the father afterwards should prove too old, she would put him aside, and take any one else whom she might chuse."

Thus we have found the custom of ultimogeniture observed by a number of tribes of South-western China and the adjoining regions of Burma and Assam. With the doubtful exception of the Khasis, all these tribes are of the Mongolian family. Their original home is believed to have been North-western China, between the upper courses of the Yang-tse-kiang and the Ho-ang-ho, from which they spread out in all directions. Following the river valleys in their migrations, they passed down the Chindwin, Irrawaddy and Salween into Burma, and down the Brahmaputra into Assam. Three successive waves of migration of these Mongoloid peoples have been traced; the latest of them was that of the Kachins or Singphos, which was actually in progress when it was stopped by the British conquest of Upper Burma. The valleys of the great rivers Brahmaputra and Irrawaddy are indeed the gateways through which the hardy northern invaders have poured from their colder, bleaker homes in Central Asia to invade the warmer, richer regions of the south. By means of this natural highway they were able to turn the flank of the long, almost impenetrable barrier which the Himalayas present to a direct invasion of India from the north. Yet in their southward march their hordes would seem never to have advanced beyond the rugged, wooded, rain-drenched mountains of Assam; there they halted, and there they remain to this day, like the vanguard of a great army looking out from their breezy hill-tops and the edge of their high tablelands over the hot valleys and sultry plains, carpeted as with green velvet, which stretch away thousands of feet below, till they melt into the sky-line or are bounded by blue mountains in the far distance. The heat of India probably served on this side as a better shield against the northern invader than the feeble arms of its unwarlike inhabitants. He could breathe freely among the oaks, the chestnuts, and the firs of these mountains: he feared to descend among the palms, the rattans, and the tree-ferns of the vales below.

However, the custom of ultimogeniture, or the preference for the youngest child, whether son or daughter, is not restricted in these regions to Mongoloid tribes. Thus among the Mrus, a small tribe who inhabit the hills between Arakan and Chittagong, "if a man has sons and daughters, and they marry, he will live with his youngest child, who also inherits all property on the death of the father." The Mrus are tall, powerful, dark men, with no traces of the Mongol in their faces. They cultivate rice and drink milk, and eat the flesh of the cow or any other animal. In character they are a peaceable, timid, simple folk, who settle their disputes by an appeal to the spirits rather than by fighting. Among them a young man serves three years for his wife in her father's house, but if he is wealthy, he can compound for this period of servitude by paying two hundred or three hundred ruppees down.

Further, the custom of ultimogeniture prevails among the Hos or Larka Kols (Lurka Coles), who inhabit the district of Singbhum in South-western Bengal. The Hos belong to the dark aboriginal race of India, resembling the Dravidians in physical type, though they speak a totally different language believed to be a branch of that great Southern or Austric family of speech to which the Khasi language in Assam also belongs. The race of which the Kols (Coles) are members, used to be called Kolarian, but it is now generally named Munda after the tribe of that name. The Hos or Larka Kols are a purely agricultural people, and have advanced so far as to use wooden ploughs tipped with iron. Their original home appears to have been Chota Nagpur, the great and isolated tableland to the north of their present country, where their kindred the Mundas, still dwell. The Hos admit their kinship with the Mundas, and preserve a tradition of their migration from Chota Nagpur. According to the Oraons, a still more primitive tribe who inhabit Chota

Nagpur, it was their invasion of the plateau which drove the Hos from it to seek a new home in the south; but it is difficult to believe that the Hos should have given way to so inferior and so unwarlike a race as the Oraons. Whatever the cause of the migration may have been, the Hos now inhabit a country still more wild and mountainous than the romantic hills and valleys of Chota Nagpur which their forefathers abandoned long ago. Their territory, known as Kolhan or Kolehan, is everywhere undulating, traversed by dykes of trap which rise in rugged masses of broken rock; and the views are bounded on all sides by ranges of mountains about three thousand feet high. The most fertile, populous, and highly cultivated parts of the country are the lowlands surrounding the station of Chaibasa. To the west stretches a region of hills and vast jungles interspersed with some fruitful valleys; while the extreme south-west is occupied by a mass of rugged, forest-clad mountains known as "Saranda of the Seven Hundred Hills," where the miserable inhabitants of a few poor solitary hamlets, nestling in deep glens, can hardly struggle for mastery with the tigers which prowl the thick jungle. The Hos of these secluded highlanders are more savage and turbulent than their brethren of the lowlands, and their agriculture is primitive. They clear a few patches in the forest or jungle which surrounds their hamlets; and though the rich black soil yields at first an abundant harvest, it is soon exhausted by the rude mode of cultivation which the Hos practise, and in three or four years they are obliged to make fresh clearings, and build for themselves fresh lodges in another part of the great wilderness. When even these resources failed them in time of famine, the wild highlanders used to raid their neighbours and bring back to their mountain fastness such plunder as they could lay hands on. Things are better with their kinsfolk who inhabit the more open and fertile districts in the north. There the villages are often prettily situated on hills overlooking the flat terraced rice-fields and undulating uplands. Very ancient and noble tamarind trees mark the sites, and, mingled with mango and jack trees and bamboos, add a pleasing feature to an agreeable landscape. The roomy, substantially built houses, with their thatched roofs and neat verandahs, stand each in its own plot of ground, and each is so arranged with outhouses as to form a square with a large pigeon-house in the centre. The village green, carpeted with turf and shaded by grand tamarind trees, contains the great slabs of stone under which "the rude forefathers of the hamlet sleep." There, under the solemn shade of the trees, when the work and heat of the day are over, the elders love to gather, and sitting on the stones to enjoy a gossip and smoke; there, too, in due time they will be laid to their last long rest with their fathers under the stones.

Each Ho village is under the authority of a headman called a *Munda*; and a group of villages, numbering from six to twelve, is governed by a chief called a *Mankie*. Curiously enough, the rule

of inheritance for the chieftainship differs from the rule of inheritance of private property; for while the descent of the chieftainship
is regulated by primogeniture, the descent of property. is regulated
by ultimogeniture. The distinction was ascertained by Dr. William
Dunbar, who tells us that "the custom of the Coles regarding the
inheritance of property is singular, and was first explained to me in
the case of a *Mankie*, as he is termed, whose villages are contiguous
to the cantonments of Chaibassa. Although he ruled over a considerable number of these, and was reckoned a powerful man among
his class, I was surprised to find that his house was a small and poor
one, and that his younger brother resided in the largest building in
the place, which had formerly belonged to the deceased *Mankie*, his
father. On enquiry, I found that on the death of the parent, the
youngest son uniformly receives the largest share of the property
strictly personal; and hence the *Mankie*, though he succeeded to his
father's authority and station as a patriarchal ruler, was obliged
to resign all the goods and chattels to his younger brother." Although
Dr. Dunbar was not aware of it, the same rule of succession to
private property among the Hos or Larka Kols (Lurka Coles) had
been recorded many years before by Lieutenant Tickell in the following terms: "The youngest-born male is heir to the father's property,
on the plea of his being less able to help himself on the death of
the parents than his elder brethren, who have had their father's
assistance in settling themselves in the world, during his lifetime."
The reason for the distinction between the two rules of succession
is perhaps not far to seek; for while on the death of a chief the
enjoyment of his private possessions might safely enough be left
to his youngest son, even should he be a minor, prudence would
generally prescribe that the exercise of his public authority should
be committed to the more experienced hands of his eldest son.

Again, ultimogeniture in a limited form is reported to be practised by the Bhils, a wild indigenous race of Central India. They
are a short dark people, wiry and often thickest, with great powers
of endurance. Their name is said to be derived from the Dravidian
word for bow, the characteristic weapon of the tribe. They have
lost their original language, but it probably belonged either to the
Munda (Kolarian) or to the Dravidian family. Formerly they roved
as huntsmen through the forests of their native mountains, but
they have now had to abandon the indiscriminate slaughter of game
and the free use of the woods, in which they committed destructive
ravages. At present many of them live in the open country and
have become farm servants and field labourers. Some of them are
tenants, but very few own villages. In the Barwani district of Central
India, for example, they are said to be as yet little affected by
civilization and to lead a most primitive life. They have no fixed
villages. The collections of huts, which pass for villages, are
abandoned at the least alarm; the report that a white man is coming often suffices to put the whole population to flight. Even

within what may be called a village the huts are commonly far apart, for each man fears the treachery of his neighbours and their designs upon his wife. The Bhil is an excellent woodsman. He knows the shortest cuts over the hills, and can walk the roughest paths and climb the steepest crags without slipping or feeling distressed. In old Sanscrit works he is often called *Venaputra*, that is "child of the forest," or *Pal Indra*, "lord of the pass." These names well describe his character. For his country is approached through narrow defile (*pāl*), and through these in the olden time none could pass without his permission. On travellers he used always to levy blackmail, and even now natives on a journey find him ready to assert what he deems his just rights. As a huntsman the Bhil is skilful and bold. He knows all the haunts of tigers, panthers, and bears, and will track them down and kill them. Armed only with swords a party of Bhils will attack a leopard and cut him in pieces.

Among the Bhils of Western Malwa and the Vindhyan-Satpura region along the Narbada Valley, in Central India, tribal custom determines inheritance. Of the property half goes to the youngest son, who is bound to defray all the expenses of the funeral feast held usually on the twelfth day after his father's death. He has also to make provision for his sisters. The other half of the property is divided between the elder sons. But if all the sons live together, which very rarely happens, they share the property equally between them. Here again, therefore, the preference for the youngest son in the inheritance apparently depends on his being left alone with his father at the time of his father's death; if all the sons chance to be living together with their father at the time of his death, the youngest enjoys no special privilege, but merely receives an equal share with the rest.

Further, it appears that ultimogeniture in a limited form prevails among the Badagas, an agricultural people who, along with the agricultural Kotas and the purely pastoral Todas, inhabit the Neilgherry Hills of Southern India. On this subject Dr. Rivers reports as follows: " Breeks has stated that the Toda custom is that the house shall pass to the youngest son. It seems quite clear that this is wrong, and that this custom is absolutely unknown among the Todas. It is, however, a Badaga custom, and among them I was told that it is due to the fact that as the sons of a family grow up and marry, they leave the house of the parents and build houses elsewhere. It is the duty of the youngest son to dwell with his parents and support them as long as they live, and when they die he continues to live in the parental home, of which he becomes the owner."

Very few traces of ultimogeniture appear to be reported from the Malay region. In Rembau, one of the States of the Malay Peninsula, all ancestral property vests in women. When there are several daughters in a family, the mother's house is normally inherited by the youngest daughter, who undertakes, in return for the prospective inheritance, to support her mother in old age. The Bataks of Sumatra are an agricultural people living in settled villages. Among them, when a man dies and leaves several sons or brothers, the custom is to divide the inheritance among them, giving the eldest and the youngest a larger share than the rest, generally double the other shares. In the Transcaucasian province of Georgia, according to the provisions of a written but apparently unpublished code, it is the rule that, on the death of a prince or nobleman, the youngest son should get his father's house, with the adjoining buildings and garden; if there is a church tower, the youngest son keeps it also, but it is valued, and he pays his elder brothers a portion of the value. On the death of a peasant his house and meadows go to his eldest son, but his granary to the youngest.

§ 5. *Ultimogeniture in North-eastern Asia.*—So far the peoples amongst whom we have found the practice of ultimogeniture are, with the exception of the Bhils, all agricultural. The custom however prevails to some extent among tribes in the hunting and pastoral stages of society. Thus it is reported to obtain among the Yukaghirs, a Mongolian tribe of North-eastern Siberia, who live partly by hunting and fishing, and partly by their herds of reindeer. The possibility of agriculture is excluded by the extreme rigour of the climate, which is the coldest in all Siberia, indeed one of the coldest on earth. "The Yukaghir who subsist by hunting and fishing near river-banks are so poor, and their mode of life is so primitive, that the private possession in the family of any article, not to speak of food-products, is almost entirely beyond their conception. Whatever is procured through hunting or fishing is turned over by the hunters and the fishermen to the women, the oldest of whom looks after its distribution. . . . Individual ownership is recognized to some extent with reference to articles of clothing and hunting-implements, such as the gun, the bow, etc. Each member of the family has what he calls *his* clothing, and the hunter has *his* gun. . . . The principle of private property holds also in regard to women's ornaments, and to such utensils as needles, thimbles, scissors, and thread. Here also belong the smoking utensils—the pipe, the strike-a-light, the tobacco-pouch, and the tinder—and the canoe. But boats, fishing-nets, house and all household implements are the common property of the whole family. . . . With regard to inheritance of family property, the principle of minority is generally applied. When the older brothers separate from the family, or, after their parents' death, go to live in the families of their wives' parents, the family property remains in the hands of the youngest brother. He also becomes the owner of the father's gun, after the death of the latter, while all the dresses and trinkets of the mother become the property of the youngest daughter. As already stated, the youngest son does not leave the house of his parents to go to live with his father-in-law. He serves for the latter a certain time, in requital for his bride, and then she goes to live with his parents. The Yukaghir explain the custom of minority right to inheritance by saying that the youngest child loves its parents more than do the other children, and is more attached to them than they are."

In spite of the sentimental reason alleged by the Yukaghirs for preferring younger children in the inheritance, we may suspect that among them, as among the other tribes considered above, the preference is really based on the custom of keeping the youngest son at home, after his elder brothers have married and quitted the parental house to live in the houses of their wives' parents. The suspicion is raised to something like certainty when we observe in that branch of the tribe which depends for its subsistence on herds of reindeer, that the sons "do not leave their father's house after marriage, but remain in the family, and share the property in common. The brothers are kept together, on the one hand by ties of kinship, and on the other by the scarcity of reindeer, which makes divided households impracticable." Nothing could well set the true origin of ultimogeniture in a clearer light than the observation that within the narrow limits of the same small tribe—for the Yukaghirs number only a few hundreds all told—the youngest son only succeeds to the whole of the property in that branch of the tribe where he remains alone in his father's house, whereas, in that branch of the tribe where all the sons alike remain in their father's house, the youngest son has no special privilege, but all the sons share alike in the property at the death of their father. On the other hand, among these reindeer-breeding Yukaghirs a married daughter leaves the house of her parents and goes to live in the house of her parents-in-law. Hence she gets no part of the family property on the death of her parents; the mother's personal property, such as clothes, trinkets, and working utensils, passes at her death to her unmarried daughters. Thus among these reindeer-breeding Yukaghirs the social conditions are to some extent directly the reverse of those which prevail among the Khasis. Among the Yukaghirs the sons remain at the parental home all their lives and inherit the parental property, whereas daughters quit the parental home at marriage and inherit nothing. Among the Khasis, on the other hand, daughters remain at the parental home all their lives and inherit the parental property, whereas sons quit the parental home at marriage and inherit nothing. In both cases the inheritance passes, as is natural, to the children who stay at home, whether they are sons or daughters.

Among the reindeer-breeding Chukchee, who inhabit the north-eastern extremity of Asia, great importance is attached to the fire-board, which is a rude figure carved out of wood in human form and used in the kindling of fire by friction. These fire-boards are personified and held sacred: they are supposed to protect the herds of reindeer, and actually to keep watch over them. Many families have several fire-boards, some of them comparatively new, others inherited from preceding generations. In every case the oldest fire-board, as a precious heirloom, descends, with the house and its belongings, to the principal heir, who is usually either the eldest or the youngest son. Apparently the question whether the eldest or the youngest son is to be the principal heir is decided in favour of the one who remains last at home; for we are told that "when the elder brother leaves, the house is then given over to a younger brother, who becomes the principal heir."

The Koryaks of North-eastern Siberia entertain a similar super-stitious reverence for their fire-boards, which they regard as the deities of the household fire, the guardians of the family hearth, and to which they ascribe the magical functions of protecting the herds of reindeer and helping the men to hunt and kill the sea-mammals. "Among the Maritime group, as well as among the Rein-deer Koryak, the sacred fire-board is connected with the family welfare, and therefore it must not be carried into a strange house. But if two families join for the winter and live in one house, in order to obviate the necessity of procuring fuel for two houses, both take their own charms along into the common house, without risk to their effectiveness by so doing. The sacred fire-board is usually transmitted to the younger son,—or to the younger daughter, provided her husband remains in his father-in-law's house and the brothers establish new houses for themselves or raise separate herds." Here again, therefore, ultimogeniture seems to be determined solely by the residence of the youngest child in the parental home after the elder children have quitted it: the right is not affected by sex, for the heir may be either the youngest son or the youngest daughter, whichever happens to remain last in the house.

§ 6. *Ultimogeniture in Africa.*—Among the pastoral tribes of Africa the custom of ultimogeniture seems to be exceedingly rare. It is practised in a limited form by the Bogos, a tribe who subsist chiefly by their herds of cattle, though they also till the ground to a certain extent. They inhabit the outlying spurs of the Abyssinian mountains towards the north; their country lacks woods and flow-ing water, but enjoys a temperate and healthy climate. Almost the whole year the cattle roam the mountains in search of fresh pastures, and about a third of the population migrates with them, dwelling in tents of palm-mats, which, when the camp shifts, are transported on the backs of oxen. The rest of the people live in more or less permanent villages of straw huts; but in case of need they can burn down these frail habitations and decamp with the herds in a night, for land is to be had in plenty everywhere. Among the Bogos the rule of primogeniture prevails. The firstborn is the head of the family; and the chieftainship also descends through the firstborn from generation to generation. Indeed, the firstborn of a great family is regarded as something holy and inviolable;

he is a king without kingly power. On the death of a man his property is divided, and the firstborn gets the best share, including the highly valued white cows and all the furniture and other domestic goods in the house. But the empty house itself belongs of right to the youngest son. Among the Nures, a pastoral people on the White Nile, when the king dies he is succeeded by his youngest son. Among the Suk, a tribe of British East Africa, the eldest son inherits most of his father's property, and the youngest son inherits most of his mother's. The Suk appear to have been originally a purely agricultural people, but for some time past they have been divided into two sections, the one agricultural and the other pastoral. The rule of inheritance just mentioned obtains in both sections of the tribe, and also among the Turkanas, another tribe of the same district.

The custom of ultimogeniture or junior right is observed by some of the Ibos, a settled agricultural people of Southern Nigeria; but among them, curiously enough, the rule applies only to property inherited from women, it does not extend to property inherited from men, and even in this limited form the custom appears to be exceptional rather than general.

§ 7. *The Origin of Ultimogeniture.*—Surveying the instances of ultimogeniture as they meet us among the tribes of Asia and Africa, we may conclude that the custom is compatible with an agricultural as well as with a pastoral life. Indeed, the great majority of peoples who are known to observe ultimogeniture at the present day subsist mainly by agriculture. But the migratory system of agriculture which many of them follow is wasteful, and requires an extent of territory large out of all proportion to the population which it supports. As the sons of a family grow up, they successively quit the parental abode and clear for themselves fresh fields in the forest or jungle, till only the youngest is left at home with his parents; he is therefore the natural support and guardian of his parents in their old age. This seems to be the simplest and most probable explanation of ultimogeniture, so far at least as it relates to the rights of youngest sons. It is confirmed by the present practice of the Russian peasants, among whom both the custom and the reason for it survive to the present time. Further, it is corroborated by the observation that the parental house is the part of the inheritance which oftenest goes to the youngest son; it is his rightful share, even if he gets nothing else. The rule is natural and equitable, if the youngest son is the only child left in the parental house at the time of his parents' death.

Perhaps among tribes like the Khasis and the Garos, who observe the custom of mother-kin, the succession of the youngest daughter can be explained on similar principles. The youngest daughter is naturally the last to marry; indeed in some peoples, including the Garos, she is actually forbidden to marry before her elder sisters. She therefore naturally remains at home longest with her parents and becomes their stay and comfort in life and their heir after death. Even when, as appears to be the custom with the Khasis, the married daughters also remain at home in the old parental dwelling or in adjoining houses, the care of their families will necessarily absorb most of their time and energy, leaving them comparatively little leisure to spare for attending to their parents. In this case also, therefore, the preference for the youngest daughter in the inheritance seems not unnatural.

Among pastoral peoples, as Blackstone long ago perceived, the preference for youngest sons is still more easily intelligible. The wide extent of territory needed to support a tribe of nomadic shepherds or herdsmen leaves ample room for the sons, as they grow up, to go out into the world and push their fortunes with wandering flocks or herds, while the youngest remains to the last with the old folks, to nourish and protect them in the decline of life, and to succeed to their property when in due time they are gathered to their fathers. Among the Bedouins the relation between a father and his sons are such as might easily result in a preference for the youngest son over his elder brothers. On this subject Burckhardt, who was familiar with Bedouin life, writes as follows : "The daily quarrels between parents and children in the desert constitute the worst feature of the Bedouin character. The son, arrived at manhood, is too proud to ask his father for any cattle, as his own arm can procure for him whatever he desires ; yet he thinks that his father ought to offer it to him : on the other hand, the father is hurt at finding that his son behaves with haughtiness towards him ; and thus a breach is often made, which generally becomes so wide that it never can be closed. The young man, as soon as it is in his power, emancipates himself from the father's authority, still paying him some deference as long as he continues in his tent ; but whenever he can become master of a tent himself (to obtain which is his constant endeavour), he listens to no advice, nor obeys any earthly command but that of his own will. A boy, not yet arrived at puberty, shows respect for his father by never presuming to eat out of the same dish with him, nor even before him. It would be reckoned scandalous were any one to say, 'Look at that boy, he satisfied his appetite in the presence of his father.' The youngest male children, till four or five years of age, are often invited to eat by the side of their parents, and out of the same dish." Here again, as in so many other cases, the turning-point in the relations between a father and his sons appears to come at the moment when the sons quit the parental abode to set up dwellings of their own. The haughty spirit of independence, which a Bedouin manifests to his father from the time when he ceases to dwell with his parent in the same tent, might easily alienate the father's affections and lead him, in disposing of his property, to pass over the proud headstrong elder son, who has gone forth from him, and to leave everything to the obsequious deferential youngest son, who has remained with him in the tent. It is true that, under the influence of Mohammedan law, the Arabs now divide the property equally among their sons; but in old days, before the rise of Islam, they may often have yielded to the natural impulse to disinherit their elder in favour of their younger sons.

Thus, whether at the pastoral or the agricultural stage of society, the conditions requisite for the rise and prevalence of ultimogeniture seem to be a wide territory and a sparse population. When through the growth of population or other causes it ceases to be easy for the sons to hive off from the old stock and scatter far and wide, the right of the youngest to the exclusive inheritance is apt to be disputed by his elder brothers, and to fall into abeyance or even to be replaced by primogeniture, as is happening at the present time among the Lushais of Assam. Nevertheless, through sheer force of inherited custom, the old rule may continue to be observed even when the conditions of life in which it originated have passed away. Hence it comes about that ultimogeniture still exists, or existed till lately, side by side with primogeniture in not a few parts of England. Hence, too, to return to the point from which we started, we can understand why among the ancient Hebrews some traces of ultimogeniture should have survived long after the people generally had abandoned it for primogeniture, having exchanged the nomadic life of herdsmen in the desert for the settled life of peasants in Palestine. The historian of a later age, when the old custom of ultimogeniture had long been forgotten, was surprised to find traditions of younger sons inheriting to the exclusion of their elder brothers and, in order to explain cases of succession which violated all his own notions of propriety, he represented them as exceptions due to a variety of fortuitous causes, such as an accident at birth, the arbitrary preference of the father, or the cupidity and cunning of the younger son. On this view, therefore, Jacob did no wrong to his elder brother Esau; he merely vindicated for himself that right of succession which the ancient law had universally conferred on younger sons, though in his own day a new fashion had crept in of transferring the inheritance from the youngest to the eldest son.

CHAPTER III

JACOB AND THE KIDSKINS OR THE NEW BIRTH

§ 1. *The Diverted Blessing.*—In the last chapter we found some reason to think that as a younger son Jacob had, in virtue of an ancient custom, a prior claim to the inheritance of his father Isaac, and that the shifts to which he is said to have resorted for the purpose of depriving his elder brother Esau of his birthright were no more than attempts on the part of the historian to explain that succession of a younger in preference to an elder son which in his own day had long been obsolete and almost incomprehensible. In the light of this conclusion I propose in the present chapter to consider the ruse which Jacob, acting in collusion with his mother Rebekah, is reported to have practised on his father Isaac in order to divert the paternal blessing from his elder brother to himself. I conjecture that this story embodies a reminiscence of an ancient ceremony which in later times, when primogeniture had generally displaced ultimogeniture, was occasionally observed for the purpose of substituting a younger for an elder son as heir to his father. When once primogeniture or the succession of the firstborn had become firmly established as the rule of inheritance, any departure from it would be regarded as a breach of traditional custom that could only be sanctioned by the observance of some extraordinary formality designed either to invert the order of birth between the sons or to protect the younger son against certain dangers to which he might conceivably be exposed through the act of ousting his elder brother from the heritage. We need not suppose that such a formality was actually observed by Jacob for the purpose of serving himself heir to his father; for if the custom of ultimogeniture was still in full vogue in his day, he was the legal heir, and no special ceremony was needed to invest him with those rights to which he was entitled in virtue of his birth. But at a later time, when ultimogeniture had been replaced by primogeniture, Jacob's biographer may have deemed it necessary to justify the traditionary succession of his hero to the estate by attributing to him the observance of a ceremony which, in the historian's day, was occasionally resorted to for the sake of giving a legal sanction to the preference of a younger son. At a still later time the editor of the biography, to whom the ceremony in question was unfamiliar, may have overlooked its legal significance, and represented it as merely a cunning subterfuge employed by Jacob at the instigation of his mother to cheat his elder brother out of the blessing which was his due. It is in this last stage of misunderstanding and misrepresentation that, on the present hypothesis, the narrative in Genesis has come down to us.

The points in this narrative to which I would call attention are first, the displacement of the elder by the younger son, and, second, the means by which the displacement was affected. The younger son pretended to be his elder brother by dressing in his elder brother's clothes and by wearing kidskins on his hands and neck for the purpose of imitating the hairiness of his elder brother's skin; and to this pretence he was instigated by his mother, who actively assisted him in the make-believe by putting his elder brother's garments on his body and the kidskins on his hands and neck. In this way Jacob, the younger son, succeeded in diverting to himself the paternal blessing which was intended for his elder brother, and thus he

served himself heir to his father. It seems possible that in this
story there may be preserved the reminiscence of a legal ceremony
whereby a younger son was substituted for his elder brother as
rightful heir to the paternal inheritance.

§ 2. *Sacrificial Skins in Ritual.*—In Eastern Africa there is a
group of tribes, whose customs present some curious points of
resemblance to those of Semitic peoples, and may help to illustrate
and explain them; for in the slow course of social evolution these
African tribes have lagged far behind the Semitic nations, and have
accordingly preserved, crisp and clear, the stamp of certain primitive
usages which elsewhere has been more or less effaced and worn down
by the march of civilization. The tribes in question occupy what is
called the eastern horn of Africa, roughly speaking from Abyssinia
and the Gulf of Aden on the north to Mount Kilimanjaro and Lake
Victoria Nyanza on the south. They belong neither to the pure
negro stock, which is confined to Western Africa, nor to the pure
Bantu stock, which, broadly speaking, occupies the whole of
Southern Africa from the equator to the Cape of Good Hope. It is
true that among them are tribes, such as the Akamba and Akikuyu,
who speak Bantu languages and perhaps belong in the main to the
Bantu family; but even in regard to them it may be doubted how
far they are true Bantus, and how far they have been transformed
by admixture or contact with tribes of an alien race. On the whole
the dominant race in this part of Africa is the one to which modern
ethnologists give the name of Ethiopian, and of which the Gallas
are probably the purest type. Their farthest outpost to the west
appears to be formed by the pastoral Bahima of Ankole, in the
Uganda Protectorate, to whom the royal families of Uganda, Unyoro,
and Karagwe are believed to be allied. Among the other tribes of
this family the best-known perhaps are the kindred Masai and Nandi,
as to whom we are fortunate enough to possess two excellent
monographs by an English ethnologist, Mr. A. C. Hollis. On the
affinity of these tribes to the Gallas he tells us: "I do not consider
that the part which the Galla have played in building up the Masai,
Nandi-Lumbwa, and other races, such as perhaps the Bahima of
Uganda, has been sufficiently realized or taken into account in the
past. The influence of their Galla ancestors is frequently shown
in the personal appearance, religion, customs, and, in a lesser degree,
in the languages of many of these tribes." Now the home of the
Gallas in Africa is separated only by a narrow sea from Arabia, the
cradle of the Semitic race, and intercourse between the two countries
and the two peoples must have been frequent from a remote antiquity. Hence it is not so surprising as might at first appear, if we
should find resemblances between Semitic and Ethiopian customs.
The cry from Mount Zion to Kilimanjaro is indeed far, but it may
have been passed on through intermediate stations along the coasts
of Arabia and Africa. In saying this I do not wish to imply any
opinion as to the question whether similarities of Semitic and

Ethiopian usage are to be explained by derivation from a common source or by the influence of similar circumstances acting independently on the minds of different races. I only indicate the hypothesis of a common origin as an alternative which should not be lightly rejected.

Having said so much to guard myself against the suspicion of fetching my comparisons from an unreasonable distance, I will now adduce some of the facts which suggest that an ancient legal formality underlies the story of the deceit practised by Jacob on his father.

Among the Gallas it is customary for childless couples to adopt children; and so close is the tie formed by adoption that even if the couple should afterwards have offspring of their own, the adopted child retains all the right of the firstborn. In order to transfer a child from its real to its adoptive parents, the following ceremony is performed. The child, who is commonly about three years old, is taken from its mother and led or carried away into a wood. There the father formally relinquishes all claim to it, by declaring that thenceforth the child is dead to him. Then an ox is killed, its blood is smeared on the child's forehead, a portion of its fat is put around the child's neck, and with a portion of its skin the child's hands are covered. The resemblance of this ceremony to Jacob's subterfuge is obvious: in both cases the hands and neck of the person concerned are covered with the skin or fat of a slain animal. But the meaning of the ceremony is not yet apparent. Perhaps we may discover it by examining some similar rites observed on various occasions by tribes of East Africa.

Among these tribes it is a common practice to sacrifice an animal, usually a goat or a sheep, skin it, cut the skin into strips, and place the strips round the wrists or on the fingers of persons who are supposed in one way or other to benefit thereby; it may be that they are rid of sickness or rendered immune against it, or that they are purified from ceremonial pollution, or that they are invested with mysterious powers. Thus, among the Akamba, when a child is born, a goat is killed and skinned, three strips are cut from the skin, and placed on the wrists of the child, the mother, and the father respectively. Among the Akikuyu, on a like occasion, a sheep is slaughtered, and a strip of skin, taken from one of its fore-feet, is fastened as a bracelet on the infant's wrist, to remove the ill-luck or ceremonial pollution (*thahu*) which is supposed to attach to new-born children. Again, a similar custom is observed by the Akikuyu at the curious rite of "being born again" (*ko-chi-a-rú-o ke-ri*) or "born of a goat" (*ko-chi-a-re-i-rú-o m'bór-i*), as the natives call it, which every Kikuyu child had formerly to undergo before circumcision. The age at which the ceremony is performed varies with the ability of the father to provide the goat or sheep which is required for the due observance of the rite; but it seems that the new birth generally takes place when a child is about ten years or younger. If the child's father or mother is dead, a man or woman acts as proxy on the occasion, and in such a case the woman is thenceforth regarded by the child as its own mother. A goat or sheep is killed in the afternoon and the stomach and intestines are reserved. The ceremony takes place at evening in a hut; none but women are allowed to be present. A circular piece of the goat-skin or sheep-skin is passed over one shoulder and under the other arm of the child who is to be born again; and the animal's stomach is similarly passed over the child's other shoulder and under its other arm. The mother, or the woman who acts as mother, sits on a hide on the floor with the child between her knees. The goat's or sheep's gut is passed round her and brought in front of the child. She groans as if in labour, another woman cuts the gut as if it were the navel-string, and the child imitates the cry of a new-born infant. Until a lad has thus been born again in mimicry, he may not assist at the disposal of his father's body after death, nor help to carry him out into the wilds to die. Formerly the ceremony of the new birth was combined with the ceremony of circumcision; but the two are now kept separate.

Such is the curious custom of the new birth, as it is, or used to be, practised by the Akikuyu, and as it was described to Mr. and Mrs. Routledge by natives who had freed themselves from tradition and come under the influence of Christianity. Yet great reluctance was shown to speak about the subject, and neither persuasion nor bribery availed to procure leave for the English inquirers to witness the ceremony. Yet its general meaning seems plain enough, and indeed is sufficiently declared in the alternative title which the Akikuyu give to the rite, namely, "to be born of a goat." The ceremony, in fact, consists essentially of a pretence that the mother is a she-goat and that she has given birth to a kid. This explains why the child is enveloped in the stomach and skin of a goat, and why the goat's guts are passed around both mother and child. So far as the mother is concerned, this assimilation to an animal comes out perhaps more clearly in an independent account which Mr. C. W. Hobley has given of the ceremony; though in his description the animal which the mother mimics is a sheep and not a goat. The name of the ceremony, he tells us, is *Ku-chiaruo ringi*, the literal translation of which is "to be born again." He further informs us that the Akikuyu are divided into two guilds, the Kikuyu and the Masai, and that the ceremony of being born again differs somewhat as it is observed by the two guilds respectively. When the parents of the child belong to the Masai guild, the rite is celebrated as follows. "About eight days after the birth of the child, be it male or female, the father of the infant kills a male sheep and takes the meat to the house of the mother, who eats it assisted by her neighbours as long as they belong to the Masai guild. At the conclusion of the feast the mother is adorned with the skin from the left fore-leg and shoulder of the sheep, the piece of skin being fastened from her left wrist to left shoulder; she wears this for four days, and it is then taken off and thrown on to her bed and stays there till it disappears. The mother and child have their heads shaved on the day this ceremony takes place; it has no connection with the naming of the child which is done on the day of its birth." Here the intention seems to be to assimilate the mother to a sheep; this is done by giving her sheep's flesh to eat and investing her with the skin of the animal, which is left lying on the bed where, eight days before, she gave birth to the child. For it is to be observed that in this form of the ritual the simulation of the new birth follows the real birth at an interval of only a few days.

But if the parents belong to the Kikuyu guild, the ritual of the new birth is as follows in the south of the Kikuyu country. "The day after the birth a male sheep is killed and some of the fat of the sheep is cooked in a pot and given to the mother and infant to drink. It was not specifically stated that this had a direct connection with the rite referred to, but the description commenced with a mention of this. When the child reaches the age of from three to six years the father kills a male sheep, and three days later the novice is adorned with part of the skin and the skin of the big stomach. These skins are fastened on the right shoulder of a boy or on the left shoulder of a girl. The skin used for a boy has, however, the left shoulder and leg cut out of it, and that for a girl has the right shoulder and leg cut away. The child wears these for three days, and on the fourth day the father cohabits with the mother of the child. There is, however, one important point, and that is that before the child is decorated with the sheep-skin it has to go and lie alongside its mother on her bed and cry out like a newly born infant. Only after this ceremony has been performed is the child eligible for circumcision. A few days after circumcision the child returns to sleep on a bed in its mother's hut, but the father has to kill a sheep before he can return, and the child has to drink some of the blood, the father also has to cohabit with the mother upon the occasion."

In this form of the ritual, as in the one described by Mr. and Mrs. Routledge, the ceremony of the new birth is deferred until several years after the real birth. But the essence of the rite appears to be the same: it is a pretence that the mother is a sheep, and that she has given birth to a lamb. However, we must note the inconsistency of using, for the purpose of this legal fiction, a ram instead of a ewe.

Having described the ceremony of the new birth in the two forms in which it is observed by the two guilds of the Akikuyu, Mr. Hobley proceeds to describe another Kikuyu ceremony, which is similar in form to the rite of the new birth and is designated by a similar, though not identical, name (*Ku-chiaruo kungi* instead of *Ku-chiaruo ringi*). It is a ceremony of adoption and is said to resemble the Skahili rite called *ndugu Kuchanjiana*. "If a person has no brothers or parents he will probably try to obtain the protection of some wealthy man and his family. If such a man agrees to adopt him, he will take a male sheep and slaughter it, and the suppliant takes another one. The elders are assembled and slaughter these sheep, and strips of the skin (*rukwaru*) from the right foot and from the chest of each sheep are tied round each person's hand, each is decorated with strips of skin from the sheep of the other party. The poor man is then considered as the son of the wealthy one, and when the occasion arises the latter pays out live stock to buy a wife for his adopted son." In this ceremony there can hardly be any pretence of a new birth, since both the performers are males; but on the analogy of the preceding customs it seems fair to suppose that the two parties, the adopting father and the adopted son, pretend to be sheep.

Further, a similar ritual is observed before the Kikuyu ceremony of circumcision. On the morning of the day which precedes the rite of circumcision, a he-goat is killed by being strangled; it is then skinned, and the skin having been cut into strips, a strip of the skin is fastened round the right wrist and carried over the back of the hand of each male candidate, after which the second finger of the candidate's hand is inserted through a slit in the strip of skin. A similar custom is observed by the Washamba, another tribe of East Africa. Before the rite of circumcision is performed, they sacrifice a goat to an ancestral spirit, and cut wristlets from its skin for the boys who are to be circumcised, as well as for their parents and kinsfolk. In sacrificing the goat the father of the boy prays to the ancestor, saying, "We are come to tell thee that our son is to be circumcised to-day. Guard the child and be gracious, be not wrathful! We bring thee a goat." Here, by binding strips of the skin on their own bodies, the members of the family seem to identify themselves with the goat which they offer to the ancestral ghost. Among the Wachaga of Mount Kilimanjaro, about two months after circumcision the lads assemble at the chief's village, where the sorcerers or medicine-men are also gathered together. Goats are killed and the newly circumcised lads cut thongs from the hides and insert the middle fingers of their right hands through slits in the thongs. Meantime the sorcerers compound a medicine out of the contents of the stomachs of the goats, mixed with water and magical stuffs. This mixture the chief sprinkles on the lads, perhaps to complete the magical or sacramental identification of the lads with the animal. Next day the father of each lad makes a feast for his relations. A goat is killed, and every guest gets a piece of the goat's skin, which he puts around the middle finger of his right hand. We may compare a ceremony observed among the Bworana Gallas when lads attain their majority. The ceremony is called *ada* or forehead, but this is explained by a word *jara*, which means circumcision. On these occasions the young men, on whose behalf the rite is celebrated, assemble with their parents and elder relatives in a hut built for the purpose. A bullock is there sacrificed, and every person present dips a finger into the blood, which is allowed to flow over the ground; the men dab the blood on their foreheads, and the women on their windpipes. Further, the women smear themselves with fat taken from the sacrificial victim, and wear narrow strips of its hide round their necks till the next day. The flesh of the bullock furnishes a banquet.

A similar use of sacrificial skins is made at marriage in some of these African tribes. Thus among the Wawanga of the Elgon District, in British East Africa, a part of the marriage ceremony is this. A he-goat is killed, and a long strip of skin is cut from its belly. The bridegroom's father, or some other elderly male relative, then slits the skin up lengthwise and passes it over the bride's head, so that it hangs down over her chest, while he says, "Now I have put this skin over your head; if you leave us for any other man, may this skin repudiate you, and may you become barren." Again, among the Wa-giriama, a Bantu tribe of British East Africa, on the day after marriage the husband kills a goat, and cutting off a piece of skin from its forehead makes it into an amulet and gives it to his wife, who wears it on her left arm. The flesh of the goat is eaten by the persons present. In these cases the goat's skin is applied only to the bride, but among the Nandi of British East Africa it is applied to the bridegroom also. On the marriage day a goat, specially selected as a strong, healthy animal from the flock, is anointed and then killed by being strangled. Its entrails are extracted and omens drawn from their condition. Afterwards the animal is skinned, and while the women roast and eat the meat, the skin is rapidly dressed and given to the bride to wear. Moreover, a ring and a bracelet are made out of the skin; the ring is put on the middle finger of the bridegroom's right hand, and the bracelet is put on the bride's left wrist.

Again, rings made from the skin of a sacrificed goat are placed on the fingers of persons who form a covenant of friendship with each other. The custom appears to be common among the tribes of British East Africa. Thus, among the Wachaga "friendships are formed by the *Kiskong'o* ceremony, which consists in taking the skin from the head of a goat, making a slit in it, and putting it upon the middle finger in the form of a ring." Similarly, among the Akamba, the exchange of rings made out of the skin of a sacrificial victim, which has been eaten in common, cements the bond of friendship.

Among the Akikuyu a similar, but somewhat more elaborate, ceremony is observed when a man leaves his own district and formally joins another. He and the representative of the district to which he is about to attach himself each provide a sheep or, if they are well off, an ox. The animal is killed, "and from the belly of each a strip is cut, and also a piece of skin from a leg of each animal. Blood from each of the two animals is put into one leaf and the contents of the two bellies into another leaf. The elders (*ki-á-ma*) slit the two pieces of skin from the leg and the two strips from the belly, and make four wristlets; the two coming from the beast of one party are placed on the right arm of the other party, and *vice versa*. The elders then take the two leaves containing blood, and both parties to the transaction extend their hands; the elders pour a little blood into all the four palms, and this is passed from the palms of the one person to those of the other. All round are called to see that the blood is mingled, and hear the proclamation that the two are now of one blood." This last example is instructive, since it shows clearly that the intention of the rite is to make the two contracting parties of one blood; hence we seem bound to explain on the same principle the custom of encircling their wrists with strips of skin taken from the same animals which furnished the blood for the ceremony.

Among the Wawanga of the Elgon District, in British East Africa, various sacrifices have to be offered before the people are allowed to sow their millet. Among the rest, a black ram is strangled before the hut of the king's mother, after which the carcass is taken into the hut and placed by the bedside facing towards the head of the bed. Next day it is taken out and cut up, and the king, his wives, and children, tie strips of its skin round their fingers. The Njamus, a mixed people of British East Africa, water their plantations by means of ditches cut in the dry season. When the time is come to irrigate the land by opening the dam and allowing the water to flow into the fields, they kill a sheep of a particular colour by smothering it, and then sprinkle its melted fat, dung, and blood at the mouth of the furrow and in the water. Then the dam is opened, and the flesh of the sacrificed sheep is eaten. For two days afterwards the man who performed the sacrifice, and who must belong to one particular clan (the Il Mayek), has to wear the skin of the sheep bound about his head. Later in the season, if the crops are not doing well, recourse is again had to sacrifice. Two elders of the same officiating clan, who may be compared to the Levites of Israel, repair to the plantations along with two elders from any other clan. They take with them a sheep of the same colour as before; and having killed and eaten it, they cut up the skin, and each man binds a strip of it round his head, which he must wear for two days. Then separating, they walk in opposite directions round the plantation, sprinkling fat, honey, and dung on the ground, until they meet on the other side.

The Masai sacrifice to God for the health of man and beast at frequent intervals, in some places almost every month. A great fire is kindled in the kraal with dry wood, and fed with certain leaves, bark, and powder, which yield a fragrant smell and send up a high column of thick smoke. God smells the sweet scent in heaven and is well pleased. Then a large black ram is brought forward, washed with honey beer, and sprinkled with the powder of a certain wood. Next the animal is killed by being stifled; afterwards it is skinned and the flesh cut up. Every person present receives a morsel of the flesh, which he roasts in the ashes and eats. Also he is given a strip of the skin, which he makes into rings, one for himself and the others for the members of his family. These rings are regarded as amulets which protect the wearers from sickness of every kind. Men wear them on the middle finger of the right hand; women wear them fastened to the great spiral-shaped neck-laces of iron wire by which they adorn, or disfigure, their necks.

Again, similar sacrificial customs are observed in cases of sick-ness. For example, among the Wawanga it sometimes happens that a sick man in a state of delirium calls out the name of a departed relative. When he does so, the sickness is at once set down at the door of the ghost, and steps are taken to deal effectually with him. A poor old man is bribed to engage in the dangerous task of digging up the corpse, after which the bones are burnt over a nest of red ants, and the ashes swept into a basket and thrown into a river. Sometimes the mode of giving his quietus to the ghost is slightly different. Instead of digging up his bones, his relatives drive a stake into the head of the grave, and, to make assurance doubly sure, pour boiling water down after it. Having thus disposed of the ghost in a satisfactory manner, they kill a black ram, rub dung from the stomach of the animal on their chests, and tie strips of its skin around their right wrists. Further, the head of the family, in which the sickness occurred, binds a strip of the skin round the second finger of his right hand, and the sick man himself fastens a strip round his neck. In this case we cannot regard the sacrifice of the black ram as intended to soothe and propitiate the ghost who had just had a stake thrust through his head and boiling water poured on his bones. Rather we must suppose that the sacrifice is due to a lingering suspicion that even these strong measures may not be wholly effectual in disarming him; so to be on the safe side the sick man and his friends fortify themselves against ghostly assaults by the skin of a sacrificial victim, which serves them as an amulet. Again, among these same people a man accused of theft will sometimes go with his accuser to a tree of a particular kind (*Erythrina tomentosa*) and the two will thrust their spears into it. After that the guilty party, whether the thief or his wrongful ac-cuser, falls sick. The cause of the sickness is not alleged, but we may suppose that it is the wrath of the tree-spirit, who naturally resents being jabbed with spears and, with a discrimination which does him credit, vents his anguish on the criminal only. So the bad man sickens, and nothing can cure him but to dig up the tree, root and branch; for that, we may suppose, is the only way of settling accounts with the tree-spirit. Accordingly the friends of the sufferer repair to the tree and root it up; at the same time they sacrifice a sheep and eat it on the spot, with some medicinal con-coction. After that every one ties a strip of the sheep's skin round his right wrist; and the sick man, for whose benefit the ceremony is performed, binds a strip of the skin round his neck, and rubs some of the dung of the slaughtered beast on his chest. Here again the sacrifice of the sheep can hardly be regarded as propitiatory; rather it is designed to protect the patient and his friends against the natural indignation of the tree-spirit, in case they should not have succeeded in radically destroying him.

Further, the custom of wearing portions of the skins of sacrificial victims is commonly observed among these East African tribes at expiatory ceremonies. For example, among the Wachaga, if a husband has beaten his wife and she comes back to him, he cuts off a goat's ear and makes rings out of it, which they put on each other's fingers. Till he has done this, she may neither cook for him nor eat with him. Further, like many other African tribes, the Wachaga look upon a smith with superstitious awe as a being invested with mysterious powers, which elevate him above the level of common men. This atmosphere of wonder and mystery extends also to the instruments of his craft, and particularly to his hammer, which is supposed to be endowed with magical or spiritual virtue. Hence he must be very careful how he handles the hammer in presence of other people, lest he should endanger their lives by its miraculous influence. For example, if he merely points at a man with the hammer, they believe that the man will die, unless a solemn ceremony is performed to expiate the injury. Hence a goat is killed, and two rings are made out of its skin. One of the rings is put on the middle finger of the smith's right hand, the other is put on the corresponding finger of the man whose life he has jeopardized, and expiatory formulas are recited. A similar atonement must be made if the smith has pointed at any one with the tongs, or has chanced to hit any one with the slag of his iron.

Expiatory ceremonies of the same kind are performed by the Wawanga, in the Elgon District of British East Africa. For example, if a stranger forces his way into a hut, and in doing so his skin cloak falls to the ground, or if he be bleeding from a fight, and his blood drips on the floor, one of the inmates of the hut will fall sick, unless proper measures are taken to prevent it. The offender must produce a goat. The animal is killed, and the skin, having been removed from its chest and belly, is cut into strips; these strips are stirred round in the contents of the goat's stomach, and every person in the hut puts one of them round his right wrist. If any person in the hut should have fallen sick before this precaution was taken, the strip of skin is tied round his neck, and he rubs some of the goat's dung on his chest. Half of the goat is eaten by the occupants of the hut, and the other half by the stranger in his own village. Again, the Wawanga, like many other savages, believe that a woman who has given birth to twins is in a very parlous state, and a variety of purificatory ceremonies must be performed before she can leave the hut; otherwise there is no saying what might not happen to her. Among other things they catch a mole and kill it by driving a wooden spike into the back of its neck. Then the animal's belly is split open and the contents of the stomach removed and rubbed on the chests of the mother and the twins. Next, the animal's skin is cut up, and strips of it are tied round the right wrist of each of the twins, and round the mother's neck. They are worn for five days, after which the mother goes to the river, washes, and throws the pieces of skin into the water. The mole's flesh is buried in a hole under the veranda of the hut, before the door, and a pot, with a hole knocked in the bottom, is placed upside down over it.

Lastly, it may be noticed that a similar use of sacrificial skins is made by some of these East African tribes at certain solemn festivals which are held by them at long intervals determined by the length of the age grades into which the whole population is divided. For example, the Nandi are divided into seven such age grades, and the festivals in question are held at intervals of seven and a half years. At each of these festivals the government of the country is transferred from the men of one age grade to the men of the age grade next below it in point of seniority. The chief medicine-man attends, and the proceedings open with the slaughter of a white bullock, which is purchased by the young warriors for the occasion. After the meat has been eaten by the old men, each of the young men makes a small ring out of the hide and puts it on one of the fingers of his right hand. Afterwards the transference of power from the older to the younger men is formally effected, the seniors doffing their warroir's skins and donning the fur garments of old men. At the corresponding ceremony among the Akikuyu, which is held at intervals of about fifteen years, every person puts a strip of skin from a male goat round his wrist before he returns home.

On a general survey of the foregoing customs we may conclude that the intention of investing a person with a portion of a sacrificial skin is to protect him against some actual or threatened evil, so that the skin serves the purpose of an amulet. This interpretation probably covers even the cases in which the custom is observed at the ratification of a covenant, since the two covenanters thereby guard against the danger which they apprehend from a breach of contract. Similarly, the strange rite of the new birth, or birth from a goat, which the Akikuyu used to observe as a preliminary to circumcision, may be supposed to protect the performers from some evil which would otherwise befall them. As to the mode in which the desired object is effected by this particular means, we may conjecture that by wearing a portion of the animal's skin the man identifies himself with the sacrificial victim, which thus acts as a sort of buffer against the assaults of the evil powers, whether it be that these powers are persuaded or cajoled into taking the beast for the man, or that the blood, flesh, and skin of the victim are thought to be endowed with a certain magical virtue which keeps malignant beings at bay. This identification of the man with the animal comes out most clearly in the Kikuyu rite of the new birth, in which mother and child pretend to be a shoe-goat and her newborn kid. Arguing from it, we may suppose that in every case the attachment of a piece of sacrificial skin to a person is only an abridged way of wrapping him up in the whole skin for the purpose of identifying him with the beast.

§ 3. *The New Birth.*—The quaint story of the Diverted Blessing, with its implication of fraud and treachery practised by a designing mother and a crafty son on a doting husband and father, wears another and a far more respectable aspect, if we suppose that the discreditable colour it displays has been imported into it by the narrator, who failed to understand the true nature of the transaction which he described. That transaction, if I am right, was neither more nor less than a legal fiction that Jacob was born again as a goat for the purpose of ranking as the elder instead of the younger son of his mother. We have seen that among the Akiyuku of East Africa, a tribe possibly of Arabian, if not of Semitic, descent, a similar fiction of birth from a goat or a sheep appears to play an important part in the social and religious life of the people. It will be some confirmation of our hypothesis if we can show that the pretence of a new birth, either from a woman or from an animal, has been resorted to by other peoples in cases in which, for one reason or another, it has been deemed desirable that a man should, as it were, strip himself of his old personality and, assuming a new one, make a fresh start in life. In short, at an early stage in the history of law the legal fiction of a new birth has often been employed for the purpose of effecting and marking a change of status. The following instances may serve to illustrate this general proposition.

In the first place, then, the fiction of a new birth has been made use of, not unnaturally, in cases of adoption for the sake of converting the adopted child into the real child of his adopting mother. Thus the Sicilian historian Diodorus informs us that when Hercules was raised to the rank of the gods, his divine father Zeus persuaded his wife Hera to adopt the bastard as her own true-born son, and this the complacent goddess did by getting into bed, clasping Hercules to her body, and letting him fall through her garments to the ground in imitation of a real birth; and the historian adds that in his own day the barbarians followed the same procedure in adopting a son. During the Middle Ages a similar form of adoption appears to have been observed in Spain and other parts of Europe. The adopted child was taken under the mantle of his adopting father or mother; sometimes he was passed through the folds of the flowing garment. Hence adopted children were called "mantle children." "In several manuscripts of the *Cronica General* it is told how, on the day when Mudarra was baptized and dubbed a knight, his stepmother put on a very wide shirt over her garments, drew a sleeve of the same over him, and brought him out at the opening for the head,

by which action she acknowledged him for her son and heir."
This procedure is said to have been a regular form of adoption in
Spain, and it is reported to be still in vogue among certain of the
Southern Slavs.   Thus in some parts of Bulgaria the adoptive
mother passed the child under her dress at her feet and brings it
out at the level of her breast; and among the Bosnian Turks it is
said that "the adoption of a son takes place thus: the future adoptive mother pushes the adoptive child through her hose, and in that
way imitates the act of birth."   And of the Turks in general we
are told that "adoption, which is common among them, is carried
out by causing the person who is to be adopted to pass through the
shirt of the person who adopts him.   That is why, to signify adoption in Turkish, the expression is employed, 'to cause somebody to
pass through one's shirt.'"

In Borneo "some of the Klemantans (Barawans and Lelaks in
the Baram) practise a curious symbolic ceremony on the adoption
of a child.   When a couple has arranged to adopt a child, both man
and wife observe for some weeks before the ceremony all the prohibitions usually observed during the later months of pregnancy
Many of these prohibitions may be described in general terms by
saying that they imply abstention from every action that may suggest difficulty or delay in delivery; e.g. the hand must not be
thrust into any narrow hole to pull anything out of it; no fixing of
things with wooden pegs must be done; there must be no lingering
on the threshold on entering or leaving a room.   When the appointed
day arrives, the woman sits in her room propped up and with a cloth
round her, in the attitude commonly adopted during delivery.   The
child is pushed forward from behind between the woman's legs,
and, if it is a young child, it is put to the breast and encouraged to
suck.   Later it receives a new name.   It is very difficult to obtain
admission that a particular child has been adopted and is not the
actual offspring of the parents; and this seems to be due, not so
much to any desire to conceal the facts as to the completeness of
the adoption, the parents coming to regard the child as so entirely
their own that it is difficult to find words which will express the
difference between the adopted child and the offspring.   This is
especially the case if the woman has actually suckled the child."
Here it is to be observed that both the adopting parents participate
in the legal fiction of the new birth, the pretended father and mother
observing the same rules which, among these people, real fathers
and mothers observe for the sake of facilitating the real birth of
children; indeed, so seriously do they play their parts in the little
domestic drama that they have almost ceased to distinguish the
pretense from the reality, and can hardly find words to express the
difference between the child they have adopted and the child they
have begotten.   The force of make-believe could scarcely go farther.

Among the pastoral Bahima of Central Africa, "when a man
inherits children of a deceased brother, he takes the children and

places them one by one in the lap of his chief wife, who receives them and embraces them and thus accepts them as her own children. Her husband afterwards brings a thong, which he uses for tying the legs of restive cows during milking and binds it round her waist in the manner a midwife binds a woman after childbirth. After this ceremony the children grow up with the family and are counted as part of it." In this ceremony we may detect the simulation of childbirth both in the placing of the children on the woman's lap and in tying of a thong round her waist after the manner of mid-wives, who do the same for women in actual childbed.

Further, the pretence of a new birth has been enacted for the benefit of persons who have erroneously been supposed to have died, and for whom in their absence funeral rites have been performed for the purpose of laying their wandering ghosts, who might other-wise haunt and trouble the survivors. The return of such persons to the bosom of their family is embarrassing, since on the principles of imitative magic or make-believe they are theoretically dead, though practically alive. The problem thus created was solved in ancient Greece and ancient India by the legal fiction of a new birth; the returned wanderer had solemnly to pretend to come to life by being born again of a woman before he might mix freely with living folk. Till that pretence had been enacted, the ancient Greeks treated such persons as unclean, refused to associate with them, and excluded them from all participation in religious rites; in particular, they strictly forbade them to enter the sanctuary of the Furies. Before they were restored to the privileges of civil life, they had to be passed through the bosom of a woman's robe, to be washed by a nurse, wrapped in swaddling clothes, and suckled at the breast. Some people thought that the custom originated with a certain Aristinus, for whom in his absence funeral rites had been performed. On his return home, finding himself shunned by all as an outcast, he applied to the Delphic oracle for advice, and was directed by the god to perform the rite of the new birth. Other people, however, with great probability believed that the rite was older than the time of Aristinus and had been handed down from remote antiquity. In ancient India, under the like circumstances, the supposed dead man had to pass the first night after his return in a tub filled with a mixture of fat and water. When he stepped into the tub, his father or next of kin pronounced over him a certain verse, after which he was supposed to have attained to the stage of an embryo in the womb. In that character he sat silent in the tub, with clenched fists, while over him were performed all the sacraments that were regularly celebrated for a woman with child. Next morning he got out of the tub, at the back, and went through all the other sacraments he had formerly partaken of from his youth upwards: in particular he married a wife or espoused his old one over again with due solemnity. This ancient custom appears to be not alto-gether obsolete in India even at the present day. In Kumaon a person supposed to be dying is carried out of the house, and the ceremony of the remission of sins is performed over him by his next of kin. But should he afterwards recover, he must go through all the ceremonies previously performed by him from his birth upwards, such as putting on the sacred thread and marrying wives, though he sometimes marries his old wives over again.

But in ancient India the rite of the new birth was also enacted for a different and far more august purpose. A Brahman householder who performed the regular half-monthly sacrifices was supposed thereby to become himself a god for the time being, and in order to effect this transition from the human to the divine, from the mortal to the immortal, it was necessary for him to be born again. For this purpose he was sprinkled with water as a symbol of seed. He feigned to be an embryo and as such was shut up in a special hut representing the womb. Under his robe he wore a belt, and over it the skin of a black antelope: the belt stood for the navel-string, and the robe and the black antelope skin typified the inner and outer membranes (the amnion and chorion) in which an embryo is wrapped. He might not scratch himself with his nails or a stick, because he was an embryo, and were an embryo scratched with nails or a stick, it would die. If he moved about in the hut, it was because a child moves about in the womb. If he kept his fist clenched, it was because an unborn babe does the same. If in bathing he put off the black antelope skin but retained his robe, it was because the child is born with the amnion but not with the chorion. By these observations he acquired, besides his old natural and mortal body, a new and glorified body, invested with superhuman powers and encircled with an aureole of fire. Thus by a new birth, a regeneration of his carnal nature, the man became a god.

Thus we see that the ceremony of the new birth may serve different purposes, according as it is employed to raise a supposed dead man to life or to elevate a living man to the rank of a deity. In modern India it has been, and indeed still is, occasionally performed as an expiatory rite to atone for some breach of ancestral custom. The train of thought which has prompted this use of the ceremony is obvious enough. The sinner who has been born again becomes thereby a new man and ceases to be responsible for the sins committed by him in his former state of existence; the process of regeneration is at the same time a process of purification, the old nature has been put off and an entirely new one put on. For example, among the Korkus, an aboriginal tribe of the Munda or Kolarian stock in the Central Provinces of India, social offences of an ordinary kind are punished by the tribal council, which inflicts the usual penalties, but "in very serious cases, such as intercourse with a low caste, it causes the offender to be born again. He is placed inside a large earthen pot which is sealed up, and when taken out of this he is said to be born again from his mother's womb.

He is then buried in sand and comes out as a fresh incarnation from the earth, placed in a grass hut which is fired, and from within which he runs out as it is burning, immersed in water, and finally has a tuft cut from his scalp-lock and is fined two and a half rupees." Here the ceremony of the new birth seems clearly intended to relieve the culprit from all responsibility for his former acts by converting him into an entirely new person. With what show of reason could he be held to account for an offence committed by somebody else before he was born?

Far more elaborate and costly is the ceremony of the new birth when the sinner who is to be regenerated is a person of high birth or exalted dignity. In the eighteenth century "when the unfortunate Raghu-Náth-Ráya or Ragoba, sent two Brahmens as embassadors to England, they went by sea as far as Suez, but they came back by the way of Persia, and of course crossed the Indus. On their return they were treated as outcasts, because they conceived it hardly possible for them to travel through countries inhabited by *Mlec'h'has* or impure tribes, and live according to the rules laid down in their sacred books: it was also alleged, that they had crossed the Attaca. Numerous meetings were held in consequence of this, and learned Brahmens were convened from all parts. The influence and authority of Raghu-Náth-Ráya could not save his embassadors. However, the body assembly decreed, that in consideration of their universal good character, and of the motive of their travelling to distant countries, which was solely to promote the good of their country, they might be regenerated and have the sacerdotal ordination renewed. For the purpose of regeneration, it is directed to make an image of pure gold of the female power of nature; in the shape either of a woman or of a cow. In this statue the person to be regenerated is enclosed and dragged through the usual channel. As a statue of pure gold and of proper dimensions would be too expensive, it is sufficient to make an image of the sacred *Yoni*, through which the persons to be regenerated is to pass. Raghu-Náth-Ráya had one made of pure gold and of proper dimensions: his embassadors were regenerated, and the usual ceremonies of ordination having been performed, and immense presents bestowed on the Brahmens, they were re-admitted into the communion of the faithful." Again, "it is on record that the Tanjore Navakar, having betrayed Madura and suffered for it, was told by his Brahman advisers that he had better be born again. So a colossal cow was cast in bronze, and the Nayakar shut up inside. The wife of his Brahman guru [teacher] acted as nurse, received him in her arms, rocked him on her knees, and caressed him on her breast, and he tried to cry like a baby."

In India the fiction of a new birth has further been employed for the purpose of raising a man of low caste into a social rank higher than the one to which his first or real birth had consigned him. For example, the Maharajahs of Travancore belong to the

Sudra caste, the lowest of the four great Indian castes, but they appear regularly to exalt themselves to a level with the Brahmans, the highest caste, by being born again either from a large golden cow or from a large golden lotus-flower. Hence the ceremony is called *Hiranya Garbham,* "the golden womb," or *Patma Garbha Dānam,* "the lotus womb-gift," according as the effigy, from which the Maharajah emerged new-born, represented a cow or a lotus-flower. When James Forbes was at Travancore, the image through which the potentate passed was that of a cow made of pure gold; and after his passage through it the image was broken up and distributed among the Brahmans. But when the ceremony was performed by the Rajah Martanda Vurmah in July 1854, the image was cast in the form of a lotus-flower and was estimated to have cost about £6000. Inside the golden vessel had been placed a small quantity of the consecrated mixture, composed of the five products of the cow (milk, curd, butter, urine, and dung); which suggests that the proper rebirth for the Maharajah is rather from the sacred cow than from the sacred lotus. After entering the vessel, His Highness remained within it for the prescribed time, while the officiating priests repeated prayers appropriate to the occasion.

From later notices of the ceremony we may infer that the Maharajahs have since reverted to the other, and perhaps more orthodox, form of the new birth, namely, the birth from a cow. Thus in the year 1869 it was announced that "another not less curious ceremony, called *Ernjagherpum,* will take place next year, whereat His Highness (the Maharajah of Travancore) will go through a golden cow, which thereupon will also become the property of the priests." Again, we read that "the Maharaja of Travancore, a Native State in the extreme South of India, has just completed the second and last of the costly ceremonies known as 'going through the golden cow,' which he has to perform in order to rank more or less on the same footing as a Brahman—his original caste being that of Sudra. The first of these ceremonies is known as *Thulapurusha danam.*—Sanscrit *Thula,* scales; *purusha,* man; and *danam,* gift of a religious character. The ceremony consists in the Maharaja entering the scales against an equal weight of gold coins, which are afterwards distributed among Brahmans. . . . The second ceremony is known as the *Hirannya garbham*—Sanskrit *hirannya,* gold; and *garbham,* womb—and constitutes the process known as going through the golden cow. A large golden vessel is constructed, ten feet in height and eight feet in circumference. This vessel is half filled with water, mixed with the various products of the cow, and Brahmans perform the prescribed rites over it. The Maharaja next enters the vessel by means of a specially constructed ornamental ladder. The cover is then put on, and the Raja immerses himself five times in the contained fluid, while the Brahmans keep up a chanted accompaniment of prayers and Vedic hyms. The portion of the ceremony lasts about ten minutes,

after which time the Maharaja emerges from the vessel and prostrates himself before the image of the deity of the Travancore kings.
The high priest now places the crown of Travancore on the Raja's
head, and after this he is considered to have rendered himself holy
by having passed through the golden cow. The previous ceremony
of being weighed against gold simply fitted him for performing
the more exalted and more costly ceremony of going through the
golden cow. The cost of these curious ceremonies is very great;
for quite apart from the actual value of the gold, much expenditure
is incurred in feasting the vast concourse of Brahmans who assemble
in Trevandrum on these occasions. From time immemorial, however, the Rajas of Travancore have performed these ceremonies,
and any omission on their part to do so would be regarded as an
offence against the traditions of the country, which is a very strong-
hold of Hindu superstition."

If none could be born again save such as can afford to provide
a colossal cow of pure gold for the ceremony, it seems obvious that
the chances of regeneration for the human race generally would be
but slender, and that practically none but the rich could enter into
the realm of bliss through this singular aperture. Fortunately,
however, the expedient of employing a real cow instead of a golden
image places the rite of the new birth within the reach even of the
poor and lowly, and thus opens to multitudes a gate of paradise
which otherwise would have been barred and bolted against them.
Indeed we may with some probability conjecture, that birth from
a live cow was the original form of the ceremony, and that the substitution of a golden image for the real animal was merely a sop
thrown to the pride of Rajahs and other persons of high degree,
who would have esteemed it a blot on their scutcheon to be born
in vulgar fashion, like common folk, from a common cow. Be that
as it may, certain it is that in some parts of India a real live
cow still serves as the instrument of the new birth. Thus in the
Himalayan districts of the North-Western Provinces "the ceremony
of being born again from the cow's mouth (*gomukhaprasava*) takes
place when the horoscope foretells some crime on the part of the
native or some deadly calamity to him. The child is clothed in
scarlet and tied on a new sieve, which is passed between the hind-legs
of a cow forward through the fore-legs to the mouth and again in
the reverse direction, signifying the new birth. The usual worship,
aspersion, etc., takes place, and the father smells his son as the cow
smells her calf." Here, though it is necessarily impossible to carry
out the simulation of birth completely by passing the child through
the body of the living cow, the next best thing is done by passing
it backwards and forwards between the cow's legs; thus the infant
is assimilated to a calf, and the father acts the part of its dam by
smelling his offspring as a cow smells hers. Similarly in Southern
India, when a man has for grave cause been expelled from his caste,
he may be restored to it after passing several times under the belly

of a cow. Though the writer who reports this custom does not describe it as a ceremony of rebirth, we may reasonably regard it as such in the light of the foregoing evidence. A further extenuation of the original ceremony may perhaps be seen in the practice of placing an unlucky child in a basket before a good milch cow with a calf and allowing the cow to lick the child, "by which operation the noxious qualities which the child has derived from its birth are removed."

If the rite of birth from a cow could thus dwindle down into one of which, without a knowledge of the complete ceremony, we could hardly divine the true meaning, it seems not improbable that the rite of birth from a goat may have similarly dwindled from its full form, such as we find it among the Akikuyu, into a greatly abridged form, such as the practice of putting the animal's skin on the hands of the person who is to be regenerated. Consistently with this hypothesis we see that this latter practice is commonly observed on a variety of occasions by the Akikuyu, the very people who on solemn occasions observe the ceremony of the new birth at full length. Is it not natural to suppose that in the hurry and bustle of ordinary existence, which does not admit of tedious ceremonial, the people have contracted the sovereign remedy of the new birth, with its elaborate details, into a compendious and convenient shape which they can apply without needless delay in the lesser emergencies of life?

§ 4. *Conclusion.*—To return now to the point from which we started, I conjecture that the story of the deception practised by Jacob on his father Isaac contains a reminiscence of an ancient legal ceremony of new birth from a goat, which it was deemed necessary or desirable to observe whenever a younger son was advanced to the rights of the firstborn at the expense of his still living brother; just as in India to this day a man pretends to be born again from a cow when he desires to be promoted to a higher caste or to be restored to the one which he has forfeited through his misfortune or misconduct. But among the Hebrews, as among the Akikuyu, the quaint ceremony may have dwindled into a simple custom of killing a goat and placing pieces of its skin on the person who was supposed to be born again as a goat. In this degenerate form, if my conjecture is well founded, the ancient rite has been reported and misunderstood by the Biblical narrator.

CHAPTER IV

JACOB AT BETHEL

§ 1. *Jacob's Dream.*—The treachery of Jacob to Esau, as it is represented in the Biblical narrative, naturally led to an estrangement between the brothers. The elder brother smarted under a sense of intolerable wrong, and his passionate nature prompted him to avenge it on his crafty younger brother, who had robbed him of his heritage. Jacob therefore went in fear of his life, and his mother, who had been his accomplice in the deceit, shared his fears and schemed to put him in a place of safety till the anger of his hot-tempered, but generous and placable, brother had cooled down. So she hit upon the device of sending him away to her brother, Laban, in Haran. Memories of the far home beyond the great river, from which in the bloom of her youthful beauty she had been brought to be the bride of Isaac, rose up before her mind and perhaps touched her somewhat hard and worldly heart. How well she remembered that golden evening when she lighted from her camel to meet yon solitary figure pacing meditatively in the fields, and found in him her husband! That manly form was now a blind bedridden dotard; and only last evening, when she looked into the well, she saw mirrored there in the water a wrinkled face and grizzled hair—a ghost and shadow of her former self! Well, well, how time slips by! It would be some consolation for the ravages of years if her favourite son should bring back from her native land a fair young wife in whom she might see an image of her own lost youth. This thought may have occurred to the fond mother in parting with her son, though, if we may trust the Jehovistic writer, she said not a word of it to him.

So Jacob departed. From Beer-Sheba, on the verge of the desert in the extreme south of Canaan, he took his journey northward. He must have traversed the bleak uplands of Judea, and still pursuing his northward way by a rough and fatiguing footpath he came at evening, just as the sun was setting, to a place where, weary and footsore, with the darkness closing in upon him, he decided to pass the night. It was a desolate spot. He had been gradually ascending and now stood at a height of about three thousand feet above sea-level. The air was keen and nipping. Around him, so far as the falling shadows permitted him to judge, lay a wilderness of stony fields and grey rocks, some of them piled up in weird forms of pillars, menhirs, or cromlechs, while a little way off a bare hill loomed dimly skyward, its sides appearing to rise in a succession of stony terraces. It was a dreary landscape, and the traveller had little temptation to gaze long upon it. He laid himself down in the centre of a circle of great stones, resting his head on one of them as a pillow, and fell asleep. As he slept, he dreamed a dream. He thought he saw a ladder reaching from earth to heaven and angels plying up and down it. And God stood by him and promised to give all that land to him and to his seed after him. But Jacob woke from his sleep in terror and said, "How dreadful is this place! This is none other but the house of God, and this is the gate of heaven." He lay still, trembling till morning broke over the desolate landscape, revealing the same forbidding prospect of stony fields and grey rocks on which his eyes had rested the evening before. Then he arose, and taking the stone on which he had laid his head he set it up as a pillar, and poured oil on the top of it, and called the place Bethel, that is, the House of God. Overawed though he was by the vision of the night, we may suppose that he pursued his journey that day in better spirits for the divine promise which he had received. As he went on, too, the landscape itself soon began to wear a more smiling and cheerful aspect in harmony with the new hopes springing up in his breast. He left behind him the bleak highlands of Benjamin and descended into the rich lowlands of Ephraim. For hours the path led down a lovely glen where the hill-sides were terraced to the top and planted with fig-trees and olives, the white rocks tapestried with ferns and embroidered with pink and white cyclamens and crocuses, while woodpeckers, jays, and little owls laughed, tapped, or hooted, each after its kind, among the boughs. So with a lighter heart he sped him on his way to the far country.

§ 2. *Dreams of the Gods.*—As critics have seen, the story of Jacob's dream was probably told to explain the immemorial sanctity of Bethel, which may well have been revered by the aboriginal inhabitants of Canaan long before the Hebrews invaded and conquered the land. The belief that the gods revealed themselves and declared their will to mankind in dreams was widespread in antiquity : and accordingly people resorted to temples and other sacred spots for the purpose of sleeping there and holding converse with the higher powers in visions of the night, for they naturally supposed that the deities or the deified spirits of the dead would be most likely to manifest themselves in places specially dedicated to their worship. For example, at Oropus in Attica there was a sanctuary of the dead soothsayer Amphiaraus, where inquirers used to sacrifice rams to him and to other divine beings, whose names were inscribed on the altar ; and having offered the sacrifice they spread the skins of the rams on the ground and slept on them, expecting revelations in dreams. The oracle appears to have been chiefly frequented by sick people who sought a release from their sufferings, and, when they had found it, testified their gratitude by dropping gold or silver coins into the sacred spring. Livy tells us that the ancient temple of Amphiaraus was delightfully situated among springs and brooks, and the discovery of the site in modern times has confirmed his description. The place is in a pleasant little glen, neither wide nor deep, among low hills partially wooded with pine. A brook flows through it and finds its way between banks fringed by plane-trees and oleanders to the sea, distant about a mile. In the distance the high blue mountains of Euboea close the view. The clumps of trees and shrubs, which tuft the sides of the glen and in which the nightingale warbles, the stretch of green meadows at the bottom, the stillness and seclusion of the spot, and its sheltered and sunny aspect, all fitted it to be the resort of invalids, who thronged thither to consult the healing god. So sheltered indeed is the spot that even on a May morning the heat in the airless glen, with the Greek sun beating down out of a cloudless sky, is apt to be felt by a northerner as somewhat overpowering. But to a Greek it was probably agreeable. The oracle indeed appears to have been open only in summer, for the priest was bound to be in attendance at the sanctuary not less than ten days a month from the end of winter till the ploughing season, which fell at the time of the setting of the Pleiades in November; and during these summer months he might not absent himself for more than three days at a time. Every patient who sought the advice of the god had first of all to pay a fee of not less than nine obols (about a shilling) of good silver into the treasury, in presence of the sacristan, who thereupon entered his name and the name of his city in a public register. When the priest was in attendance, it was his duty to pray over the sacrificial victims and lay their flesh on the altar; but in his absence the person who presented the sacrifice might perform these offices himself. The skin and a shoulder of every victim sacrificed were the priest's perquisites. None of the flesh might be removed from the precinct. Every person who complied with these rules was allowed to sleep in the sanctuary for the purpose of receiving an oracle in a dream. In the dormitory the men and women slept apart, divided by the altar, the men on the east and the women on the west.

There was a similar dormitory for the use of patients who came to consult the Good Physician in the great sanctuary of Aesculapius near Epidaurus. The ruins of the sanctuary, covering a wide area, have been excavated in modern times, and together form one of the most impressive monuments of ancient Greek civilization. They stand in a fine open valley encircled by lofty mountains, on the north-west rising into sharp peaks of grey and barren rock, but on the south and east of softer outlines and verdurous slopes. In spring the level bottom of the valley, interspersed with clumps of trees and bushes, is green with corn. The whole effect of the landscape is still and solemn, with a certain pleasing solitariness; for it lies remote from towns. A wild, romantic, densely wooded glen leads down to the ruins of the ancient Epidaurus, beautifully situated on a rocky promontory, which juts out into the sea from a plain covered with lemon groves and backed by high wooded mountains. Patients who had slept in the sanctuary of Aesculapius at Epidaurus, and had been healed of their infirmities through the revelations accorded to them in dreams, used to commemorate the cures on tablets, which were set up in the holy place as eloquent testimonies to the restorative powers of the god and to the saving faith of those who put their trust in him. The sacred precinct was crowded with such tablets in antiquity, and some of them have been discovered in modern times. The inscriptions shed a curious light on institutions which in some respects answered to the hospitals of modern times.

For example, we read how a man whose fingers were all paralysed but one, came as a suppliant to the god. But when he saw the tablets in the sanctuary and the miraculous cures recorded on them, he was incredulous. However, he fell asleep in the dormitory and dreamed a dream. He thought he was playing at dice in the temple, and that, as he was in the act of throwing, the god appeared, pounced on his hand, and stretched out his fingers, one after the other, and, having done so, asked him whether he still disbelieved the inscriptions on the tablets in the sanctuary. The man said no, he did not. "Therefore," answered the god, "because you disbelieved them before, your name shall henceforth be Unbeliever." Next morning the man went forth whole. Again, Ambrosia, a one-eyed lady of Athens, came to consult the god about her infirmity. Walking about the sanctuary she read the cures on the tablets and laughed at some of them as plainly incredible and impossible. "How could it be," said she, "that the lame and the blind should be made whole by simply dreaming a dream?" In this sceptical frame of mind she composed herself to sleep in the dormitory, and as she slept she saw a vision. It seemed to her that the god stood by her and promised to restore the sight of her other eye, on condition that she should dedicate a silver pig in the sanctuary as a memorial of her crass infidelity. Having given this gracious promise, he slit open her ailing eye and poured balm on it. Next day she went forth healed. Again, Pandarus, a Thessalian, came to the sanctuary in order to get rid of certain scarlet letters which had been branded on his brow. In his dream he thought that the god stood by him, bound a scarf about his brow, and commanded him, when he went forth from the dormitory, to take off the scarf and dedicate it in the temple. Next morning Pandarus arose and unbound the scarf from his head, and on looking at it he saw that the infamous letters were transferred from his brow to the scarf. So he dedicated the scarf in the temple and departed. On his way home he stopped at Athens, and despatched his servant Echedorus to Epidaurus with a present of money, which he was to dedicate as a thank-offering in the temple. Now Echedorus, too, had letters of shame branded on his brow, and when he came to the sanctuary, instead of paying the money into the treasury of the god, he kept it and laid himself down to sleep in the dormitory, hoping to rid himself of the marks on his forehead, just as his master had done. In his dream the god stood by him and asked whether he had brought any money from Pandarus to dedicate in the sanctuary. The fellow denied that he had received anything from Pandarus, but promised that, if the god would heal him, he would have his portrait painted and would dedicate it to the deity. The god bade him take the scarf of Pandarus and tie it round his forehead; and when he went out of the dormitory he was to take off the scarf, wash his face in the fountain, and look at himself in the water. So, when it was day, the rascal hurried out of the dormitory, untied the scarf and scanned it eagerly, expecting to see the brand-marks imprinted on it. But they were not there. Next he went to the fountain, and, looking at his face reflected in the water, he saw the red letters of Pandarus printed on his brow in addition to his own.

Again, on the wild ironbound coast of Laconia, where the great range of Taygetus descends in naked crags to the sea, there was an oracular shrine, where a goddess revealed their hearts' desires to mortals in dreams. Different opinions prevailed as to who the goddess was. The Greek traveller Pausanias, who visited the place, thought that she was Ino, a marine goddess; but he acknowledged that he could not see the image in the temple for the multitude of garlands with which it was covered, probably by worshippers who thus expressed their thanks for the revelations vouchsafed to them in sleep. The vicinity of the sea, with the solemn lullaby of its waves, might plead in favour of Ino's claim to be the patroness of the shrine. Others, however, held that she was Pasiphae in the character of the Moon; and they may have supported their opinion, before they retired at nightfall to the sacred dormitory, by pointing to the silvery orb in the sky and her shimmering reflection on the moonlit water. Be that as it may, the highest magistrates of Sparta appear to have frequented this sequestered spot for the sake of the divine counsels which they expected to receive in slumber, and it is said that at a momentous crisis of Spartan history one of them here dreamed an ominous dream.

Ancient Italy as well as Greece had its oracular seats, where anxious mortals sought for advice and comfort from the gods or deified men in dreams. Thus the soothsayer Calchas was worshipped at Drium in Apulia, and persons who wished to inquire of him sacrificed a black ram and slept on the skin. Another ancient and revered Italian oracle was that of Faunus, and the mode of consulting him was similar. The inquirer sacrificed a sheep, spread out its skin on the ground, and sleeping on it received an answer in a dream. If the seat of the oracle was, as there is reason to think, in a sacred grove beside the cascade at Tibur, the solemn shade of the trees and the roar of the tumbling waters might well inspire the pilgrim with religious awe and mingle with his dreams. The little circular shrine, which still overhangs the waterfall, may have been the very spot where the rustic god was believed to whisper in the ears of his slumbering votaries.

§ 3. *The Heavenly Ladder.*—Far different from these oracular seats in the fair landscapes of Greece and Italy was the desolate stony hollow among the barren hills, where Jacob slept and saw the vision of angels ascending and descending the ladder that led from earth to heaven. The belief in such a ladder, used by divine beings or the souls of the dead, meets us in other parts of the world. Thus, speaking of the gods of West Africa, Miss Kingsley tells us that "in almost all the series of native traditions there, you will find accounts of a time when there was direct intercourse between the gods or spirits that live in the sky, and men. That intercourse is always said to have been cut off by some human error; for example, the Fernando Po people say that once upon a time there was no trouble or serious disturbance upon earth because there was a ladder, made like the one you get palm-nuts with, 'only long, long'; and this ladder reached from earth to heaven so the gods could go up and down it and attend personally to mundane affairs. But one day a cripple boy started to go up the ladder, and he had got a long way up when his mother saw him, and went up in pursuit. The gods, horrified at the prospect of having boys and women invading heaven, threw down the ladder, and have since left humanity severely alone."

The Bare'e-speaking Toradjas of Central Celebes say that in the olden time, when all men lived together, sky and earth were connected with each other by a creeper. One day a handsome young man, of celestial origin, whom they call Mr. Sun, appeared on earth, riding a white buffalo. He found a girl at work in the fields, and falling in love with the damsel he took her to wife. They lived together for a time, and Mr. Sun taught people to till the ground and supplied them with buffaloes. But one day it chanced that the child, which Mr. Sun had by his wife, misbehaved in the house and so offended his father that, in disgust at mankind, he returned to heaven by the creeper. His wife attempted to clamber up it after him, but he cut the creeper through, so that it and his wife together fell down to earth and were turned to stone. They may be seen to this day in the form of a limestone hill not far from the river Wimbi. The hill is shaped like a coil of rope and bears the name of Creeper Hill. Further, in Toradia stories we hear of a certain Rolled-up Rattan, by which mortals can ascend from earth to heaven. It is a thorny creeper growing about a fig-tree and adding every year a fresh coil around the bole. Any person who would use it must first waken it from sleep by shattering seven cudgels on its tough fibres. That rouses the creeper from its slumber; it shakes itself, takes a betel-nut, and asks the person what he wants. When he begs to be carried up to the sky, the creeper directs him to seat himself either on its thorns or on its upper end, taking with him seven bamboo vessels full of water to serve as ballast. As the creeper rises in the air, it heels over to right or left, whereupon the passenger pours out some water, and the creeper rights itself accordingly. Arrived at the vault of heaven, the creeper shoots through a hole in the firmament; and, grappling fast by its thorns to the celestial floor, waits patiently till the passenger has done his business up aloft and is ready to return to earth. In this way the hero of the tale makes his way to the upper regions and executes his purpose there, whatever it is, whether it be to recover a stolen necklace, to storm and pillage a heavenly village, or to have a dead man restored to life by the heavenly smith.

The Bataks of Sumatra say that at the middle of the earth there was formerly a rock, of which the top reached up to heaven, and by which certain privileged beings, such as heroes and priests, could mount up to the sky. In heaven there grew a great fig-tree which sent down its roots to meet the rock, thus enabling mortals to swarm up it to the mansions on high. But one day a man out of spite cut down the tree, or perhaps rather severed its roots, because his wife, who had come down from heaven, returned thither and left him forlorn. The Betsimisaraka of Madagascar think that the souls of the dead ascend to the sky by climbing up a silver cable, by which also celestial spirits come and go on their missions to earth.

Different from these imaginary ladders are the real ladders which some people set up to facilitate the descent of gods or spirits from heaven to earth. For example, the natives of Timorlaut, Babar, and the Leti Islands in the Indian Archipelago worship the sun as the chief male god, who fertilizes the earth, regarded as a goddess, every year at the beginning of the rainy season. For this beneficient purpose the deity descends into a sacred fig-tree, and to enable him to alight on the ground the people place under the tree a ladder with seven rungs, the rails of which are decorated with the carved figures of two cocks, as if to announce the arrival of the god of day by their shrill clarion. When the Toradjas of Central Celebes are offering sacrifices to the gods at the dedication of a new house, they set up two stalks of plants, adorned with seven strips of white cotton or barkcloth, to serve the gods as ladders whereby they may descend to partake of the rice, tobacco, betel, and palm-wine provided for them.

Again, some people both in ancient and modern times have imagined that the souls of the dead pass up from earth to heaven by means of a ladder, and they have even placed miniature ladders in the graves in order to enable the ghosts to swarm up them to the abode of bliss. Thus in the Pyramid Texts, which are amongst the oldest literature of the world, mention is often made of the ladder up which dead Egyptian kings climbed to the sky. In many Egyptian graves there has been found a ladder, which may have been intended to enable the ghost to scramble up out of the grave, perhaps even to ascend up to heaven, like the kings of old. The Mangars, a fighting tribe of Nepaul, are careful to provide their dead with ladders up which they may climb to the celestial mansions. "Two bits of wood, about three feet long, are set up on either side of the grave. In the one are cut nine steps or notches forming a ladder for the spirit of the dead to ascend to heaven; on the other every one present at the funeral cuts a notch to show that he has been there. As the maternal uncle steps out of the grave, he bids a solemn farewell to the dead and calls upon him to ascend to heaven by the ladder that stands ready for him." However, lest the ghost should decline to avail himself of this opportunity of scaling the heights of heaven, and should prefer to return to his familiar home, the mourners are careful to barricade the road against him with thorn bushes.

§ 4. *The Sacred Stone.*—In spite of its dreary and inhospitable surroundings, Bethel became in later times the most popular sanctuary of the northern kingdom. Jeroboam instituted there the worship of one of the two golden calves which he had made to be the gods of Israel; he built an altar and created a priesthood. In the age of the prophet Amos the sanctuary was under the special patronage of the king and was regarded as a royal chapel; it was thronged with worshippers; the altars were multiplied; the ritual was elaborate; the expenses of maintenance were met by the tithes levied at the shrine; the summer and winter houses of the noble and wealthy in the neighbourhood were numerous and luxurious. To account for the odour of sanctity which, from time immemorial, had hung round this naturally desolate and uninviting spot and had gradually invested it with all this splendour and refinement of luxury, the old story of Jacob and his dream was told to the worshippers. As often as they paid their tithes to the priests, they understood that they were fulfilling the vow made long ago by the patriarch when, waking in fright from his troubled sleep in the circle of stones, he promised to give to God a tenth of all that the deity should give to him. And the great standing-stone or pillar, which doubtless stood beside the principal altar, was believed to be the very stone on which the wanderer had laid his weary head that memorable night, and which he had set up next morning as a monument of his dream. For such sacred stones or monoliths were regular features of Canaanite and Hebrew sanctuaries in days of old; many of them have been discovered in their original positions by the excavators who have laid bare these ancient "high places" in modern times. Even the prophet Hosea appears to have regarded a standing-stone or pillar as an indispensable adjunct of a holy place dedicated to the worship of Jehovah. It was not only in later times that the progressive spirit of Israelitish religion condemned these rude stone monuments as heathenish, decreed their destruction, and forbade their erection. Originally the deity seems to have been conceived as actually resident in the stones; it was his awful presence which conferred on them their sanctity. Hence Jacob declared that the stone which he erected at Bethel should be God's house.

The idea of a stone tenanted by a god or other powerful spirit was not peculiar to ancient Israel; it has been shared by many peoples in many lands. The Arabs in antiquity worshipped stones, and even under Islam the Black Stone at Mecca continues to occupy a principal place in their devotions at the central shrine of their religion. As commonly understood, the prophet Isaiah, or the later writer who passed under his name, denounced the idolatrous Israelites who worshipped the smooth, water-worn boulders in the dry rocky gullies, pouring libations and making offerings to them. We are told that in the olden time all the Greeks worshipped unwrought stones instead of images. In the market-place of Pharae, in Achaia, there were thirty square stones, to each of which the people gave the name of a god. The inhabitants of Thespiae, in Boeotia, honoured Love above all the gods; and the great sculptors Lysippus and Praxiteles wrought for the city glorious images of the amorous deity in bronze and marble. Yet beside these works of refined Greek art the people paid their devotions to an uncouth idol of the god in the shape of a rough stone. The Aenianes of Thessaly worshipped a stone, sacrificing to it and covering it with the fat of victims.

The worship of rude stones has been practised all over the world, nowhere perhaps more systematically than in Melanesia. Thus, for example, in the Banks Islands and the Northern New Hebrides the spirits to whom food is offered are almost always connected with stones on which the offerings are made. Certain of these stones have been sacred to some spirit from ancient times, and the knowledge of the proper way of propitiating the spirit has been handed down, generation after generation, to the particular man who is now the fortunate possessor of it. "But any man may find a stone for himself, the shape of which strikes his fancy, or some other object, an octopus in his hole, a shark, a snake, an eel, which seems to him something unusual, and therefore connected with a spirit. He gets money and scatters it about the stone, or on the place where he has seen the object of his fancy; then he goes home to sleep. He dreams that some one takes him to a place and shews him the pigs or money he is to have because of his connexion with the thing that he has found. This thing in the Banks Islands becomes his *tano-oloolo,* the place of his offering, the objects in regard to which offering is made to get pigs or money. His neighbours begin to know that he has it, and that his increasing wealth has its origin there; they come to him, therefore, and obtain through him the good offices of the spirit he has come to know. He hands down the knowledge of this to his son or nephew. If a man is sick he gives another who is known to have a stone of power—the spirit connected with which it is suggested that he has offended—a short string of money, and a bit of the pepper root, *gea,* that is used for kava; the sick man is said to *oloolo* to the possessor of the stone. The latter takes the things offered to his sacred place and throws them down, saying, 'Let So-and-So recover.' When the sick man recovers he pays a fee. If a man desires to get the benefit of the stone, or whatever it is, known to another, with a view to increase of money, pigs, or food, or success in fighting, the possessor of the stone will take him to his sacred place, where probably there are many stones, each good for its own purpose. The applicant will supply money, perhaps a hundred strings a few inches long. The introducer will shew him one stone and say, 'This is a big yam,' and the worshipper puts money down. Of another he says it is a boar, of another that it is a pig with tusks, and money is put down. The notion is that the spirit, *vui,* attached to the stone likes the money, which is allowed to remain upon or by the stone. In case the *oloolo,* the sacrifice, succeeds, the man benefited pays the man to whom the stones and spirits belong."

From this instructive account we learn that in these islands a regular sanctuary may originate in the fancy of a man who, having noticed a peculiar-looking stone and dreamed about it, concludes that the stone must contain a powerful spirit, who can help him, and whom he and his descendants henceforth propitiate with offerings. Further, we see how such a sanctuary, as it rises in reputation, may attract more and more worshippers, and so grow wealthy through the offerings which the gratitude or the cupidity of the devotees may lead them to deposit at the shrine. Have we not here a Melanesian counterpart of the history of Bethel? An older mode of interpretation might see in it a diabolical counterfeit of a divine original.

In one of the Samoan Islands the god Turia had his shrine in a very smooth stone, which was kept in a sacred grove. The priest was careful to weed all round about, and covered the stone with branches to keep the god warm. When prayers were offered on account of war, drought, famine, or epidemic, the branches were carefully renewed. Nobody dared to touch the stone, lest a poisonous and deadly influence should radiate from it on the transgressor. In another Samoan village two oblong smooth stones, standing on a platform, were believed to be the parents of Saato, a god who controlled the rain. When the chiefs and people were ready to go off for weeks to the bush for the sport of pigeon-catching, they laid offerings of cooked taro and fish on the stones, accompanying them with prayers for fine weather and no rain. Any one who refused an offering to the stones was frowned upon; and if rain fell, he was blamed and punished for bringing down the wrath of the fine-weather god and spoiling the sport of the season. Moreover, in time of scarcity, when people were on their way to search for wild yams, they would give a yam to the two stones as a thank-offering, supposing that these gods caused the yams to grow, and that they could lead them to the best places for finding such edible roots. Any person casually passing by with a basket of food would also stop and lay a morsel on the stone. When such offerings were eaten in the night by dogs or rats, the people thought that the god became temporarily incarnate in these animals in order to consume the victuals.

The natives of Timor, an island of the Indian Archipelago, are much concerned about earth-spirits, which dwell in rocks and stones of unusual and striking shape. Not all such rocks and stones, however, are haunted, and when a man has found one of them he must dream upon it, in order to ascertain whether a spirit dwells in it or not. If in his dream the spirit appears to him and demands a sacrifice of man, or beast, or betel, he has the stone removed and set up near his house. Such stones are worshipped by whole families or villages and even districts. The spirit who resides in the stone cares for the welfare of the people, and requires to receive in return betel and rice, but sometimes also fowls, pigs, and buffaloes. Beside the stone there often stand pointed stakes, on which hang the skulls of slain foes.

In Busoga, a district of Central Africa, to the north of Lake Victoria Nyanza, "each piece of rock and large stone is said to have its spirit, which is always active in a district either for good or for evil. Various kinds of diseases, especially plague, are attributed to the malevolence of rock-spirits. When sickness or plague breaks out, the spirit invariably takes possession of some person of the place, either a man or a woman; and, under the influence of the spirit, the person mounts the rock and calls from it to the people. The chief and the medicine-men assemble the people, make an offering of a goat or a fowl to the spirit, and are then told how to act in order to stay the disease. After making known its wishes to the people, the spirit leaves the person and returns to the rock, and the medium goes home to his or her ordinary pursuits and may possibly never be used again by the spirit." Hence there are many sacred rocks and stones in Busoga. They are described as local deities; and to them the people go under all manner of circumstances to pray for help. The Menkieras of the French Sudan, to the south of the Niger, offer sacrifices to rocks and stones. For example, at Sapo the village chief owns a great stone at the door of his house. Any man who cannot procure a wife, or whose wife is childless, will offer a fowl to the stone, hoping that the stone will provide him with a wife or child. He hands over the bird to the chief, who sacrifices and eats it. If his wishes are granted, the man will present another fowl to the stone as a thank-offering.

The great oracle of the Mandan Indians was a thick porous stone some twenty feet in circumference, whose miraculous utterances were believed with implicit confidence by these simple savages. Every spring, and on some occasions during the summer, a deputation waited on the holy stone and solemnly smoked to it, alternately taking a whiff themselves and then passing the pipe to the stone. That ceremony duly performed, the deputies retired to an adjoining wood for the night, while the stone was supposed to be left to his unassisted meditations. Next morning the ripe fruit of his reflections was visible in the shape of certain white marks on the stone, which some members of the deputation had the less difficulty in deciphering because they had themselves painted them there during the hours of darkness, while their credulous brethren were plunged in sleep. Again, we are told of the Dacota Indians that a man "will pick up a round stone, of any kind, and paint it, and go a few rods from his lodge, and clean away the grass, say from one to two feet in diameter, and there place his stone, or god, as he would term it, and make an offering of some tobacco and some feathers, and pray to the stone to deliver him from some danger that he has probably dreamed of" or imagined.

The Highlanders of Scotland used to believe in a certain fairy called the Gruagach, sometimes regarded as male and sometimes as female, who looked after the herds and kept them from the rocks, haunting the fields where the cattle were at pasture. A Gruagach was to be found in every gentleman's fold, and milk had to be set apart for him every evening in the hollow of a particular stone, which was kept in the byre and called the Gruagach stone. If this were not done, the cows would yield no milk, and the cream would not rise to the surface in the bowls. Some say that milk was poured into the Gruagach stone only when the people were going to or returning from the summer pastures, or when some one was passing the byre with milk. At Holm, East-Side, and Scorrybreck, near Portree in Skye, the stones on which the libations were poured may still be seen. However, these stones are perhaps to be regarded rather as the vessels from which the Gruagach lapped the milk than as the houses in which he lived. Generally he or she was conceived as a well-dressed gentleman or lady with long yellow hair. In some mountain districts of Norway down to the end of the eighteenth century the peasant used to keep round stones, which they washed every Thursday evening, and, smearing them with butter or some other grease before the fire, laid them on fresh straw in the seat of honour. Moreover, at certain seasons of the year they steeped the stones in ale, believing that they would bring luck and comfort to the house.

This Norwegian custom of smearing the stones with butter reminds us of the story that Jacob poured oil on the stone which he set up to commemorate his vision at Bethel. The legend is the best proof of the sanctity of the stone, and probably points to an ancient custom of anointing the sacred stone at the sanctuary. Certainly the practice of anointing holy stones has been widespread. At Delphi, near the grave of Neoptolemus, there was a small stone on which oil was poured every day; and at every festival unspun wool was spread on it. Among the ancient Greeks, according to Theophrastus, it was characteristic of the superstitious man that when he saw smooth stones at cross-roads he would pour oil on them from a flask, and then falling on his knees worship them before going his way. Similarly Lucian mentions a Roman named Rutillianus, who, as often as he spied an anointed or crowned stone, went down on his knees before it, and after worshipping the dumb deity remained standing in prayer beside it for a long time. Elsewhere, the same sceptical writer refers scornfully to the oiled and wreathed stones which were supposed to give oracles. Speaking of the blind idolatry of his heathen days, the Christian writer Arnobius says, "If ever I perceived an anointed stone, greasy with oil, I used to adore it, as if there were some indwelling power in it, I flattered it, I spoke to it, I demanded benefits from the senseless block."

The Waralis, a tribe who inhabits the jungles of Northern Konkan, in the Bombay Presidency, worship Waghia, the lord of tigers, in the form of a shapeless stone smeared with red lead and clarified butter. They give him chickens and goats, break coco-nuts on his head, and pour oil on him. In return for these attentions he preserves them from tigers, gives them good crops, and keeps disease from them. And generally in the Bombay Presidency, particularly in the Konkan districts, fetish stones are worshipped by the ignorant and superstitious for the purpose of averting evil or curing disease. In every village such stones are to be seen. The villagers call each of them by the name of some god or spirit, of whom they stand in great fear, believing that he has control over all demons or ghosts. When an epidemic prevails in a village people offer food, such as fowls, goats, and coco-nuts, to the fetish stones. For example, at Poona there is such a sacred stone which is coloured red and oiled. Among the Todas of the Neilgherry Hills, in Southern India, the sacred buffaloes migrate from place to place in the hills at certain seasons of the year. At the sacred dairies there are stones on which milk is poured and butter rubbed before the migration begins. For example, at Modr there are four such stones, and they are rounded and worn quite smooth, probably through the frequent repetition of the ceremony.

In the Kei Islands, to the south-west of New Guinea, every householder keeps a black stone at the head of his sleeping-place; and when he goes out to war or on a voyage or on business, he anoints the stone with oil to secure success. With regard to the Betsileo, a tribe in Central Madagascar, we are told that "in many parts of the country are large stones, which strike the eye of every traveller, owing to the fact that they present the appearance of having been greased all over, or at any rate of having had fat or oil poured on the top. This has given rise to a belief among strangers that these stones were gods worshipped by the Betsileo. I think it can scarcely be said that they were reverenced or treated as divinities, but that they were connected with superstitious beliefs there can be no shadow of a doubt. There are two kinds of single stones in the country looked upon thus superstitiously by the people. One kind, called *vatobétròka,* is resorted to by women who have had no children. They carry with them a little fat or oil with which they anoint the stone, at the same time apostrophising it, they promise that if they have a child, they will return and re-anoint it with more oil. These same stones are also resorted to by traders, who promise that, if their wares are sold at a good price and quickly, they will return to the stone and either anoint it with oil, or bury a piece of silver at its base. These stones are sometimes natural but curious formations, and sometimes, but more rarely, very ancient memorials of the dead." At a certain spot in a mountain pass, which is particularly difficult for cattle, every man of the Akamba tribe, in British East Africa, stops and anoints a particular rock with butter or fat.

In the light of these analogies it is reasonable to suppose that there was a sacred stone at Bethel, on which worshippers from time immemorial had been accustomed to pour oil, because they believed it to be in truth a "house of God" (*Beth-el*), the domicile of a divine spirit. The belief and the practice were traced to a revelation vouchsafed to the patriarch Jacob on the spot long before his descendants had multiplied and taken possession of the land. Whether the story of that revelation embodies the tradition of a real event, or was merely invented to explain the sanctity of the place in harmony with the existing practice, we have no means of deciding. Probably there were many such sacred stones or Bethels in Canaan, all of which were regarded as the abodes of powerful spirits and anointed accordingly. Certainly the name of Beth-el or God's House would seem to have been a common designation for sacred stones of a certain sort in Palestine; for in the form *baityl-os* or *baityl-ion* the Greeks adopted it from the Hebrews and applied it to stones which are described as round and black, as living or animated by a soul, as moving through the air and uttering oracles in a whistling voice, which a wizard was able to interpret. Such stones were sacred to various deities, whom the Greeks called Cronus, Zeus, the Sun, and so forth. However, the description of these stones suggests that as a rule they were small and portable; one of them is said to have been a perfect sphere, measuring a span in diameter, though it miraculously increased or diminished in bulk and changed in colour from whitish to purple; letters, too, were engraved on its surface and picked out in vermilion. On the other hand the holy stone at Bethel was probably one of those massive standing-stones or rough pillars which the Hebrews called *masseboth*, and which, as we have seen, were regular adjuncts of Canaanite and early Israelitish sanctuaries. Well-preserved specimens of these standing-stones or pillars have been recently discovered in Palestine, notably at the sanctuaries of Gezer and Taanach. In some of them holes are cut, either on the top or on the side of the pillar, perhaps to receive offerings of oil or blood. Such we may suppose to have been the sacred stone which Jacob is said to have set up and anointed at Bethel, and for which his descendants probably attested their veneration in like manner for many ages.

CHAPTER V

JACOB AT THE WELL

CHEERED by the vision of angels and by the divine promise of protection which he had received at Bethel, the patriarch went on his way and came in time to the land of the children of the East. There he met his kinsfolk; there he found his wives; and there, from being a poor homeless wanderer, he grew rich in flocks and herds. The land where these events, so momentous in the history of Jacob and his descendants, took place is not exactly defined. The historian, or rather the literary artist, is content to leave the geography vague, while at the same time he depicts the meeting of the exile with his first love in the most vivid colours. Under his pen the scene glows as intensely as it does under the brush of Raphael, who has conferred a second immortality on it in the panels of the Vatican. It is a picture not of urban but of pastoral life. The lovers met, not in the throng and bustle of the bazaar, but in the silence and peace of green pastures on the skirts of the desert, with a great expanse of sky overhead and flocks of sheep lying around, waiting patiently to be watered at the well. The very hour of the day when the meeting took place is indicated by the writer; for he tells us that it was not yet high noon, he allows us, as it were, to inhale the fresh air of a summer morning before the day had worn on to the sultry heat of a southern afternoon. What more fitting time and place could have been imagined for the first meeting of youthful lovers? Under the charm of the hour and of the scene even the hard mercenary character of Jacob melted into something like tenderness; he forgot for once the cool calculations of gain and gave way to an impulse of love, almost of chivalry: for at sight of the fair damsel approaching with her flocks, he ran to the well and rolling away the heavy stone which blocked its mouth he watered the sheep for her. Then he kissed his cousin's pretty face and wept. Did he remember his dream of angels at Bethel and find the vision come true in love's young dream? We cannot tell. Certainly for a time the selfish schemer appeared to be transformed into the impassioned lover. It was the one brief hour of poetry and romance in a prosaic and even sordid life.

The commentators on Genesis are a little puzzled to explain why Jacob, on kissing his pretty cousin Rachel, should have burst into tears. They suppose that his tears flowed for joy at the happy termination of his journey, and they account for this mode of manifesting pleasure by the greater sensibility of Oriental peoples, or by the less degree of control which they exercise over the expression of their feelings. The explanation perhaps contains a measure of truth; but the commentators have apparently failed to notice that among not a few races weeping is a conventional mode of greeting strangers or friends, especially after a long absence, and that as such it is often a simple formality attended with hardly more emotion than our custom of shaking hands or raising the hat. Examples of the custom will make this clear.

In the Old Testament itself we meet wtih other examples of thus saluting relations or friends. When Joseph revealed himself to his brethren, in Egypt, he kissed them and wept so loudly that the Egyptians in another part of the house heard him. But his tears on that occasion were probably a natural, not a mere conventional, expression of his feelings. Indeed this is rendered almost certain by the touching incident at his first meeting with Benjamin, when, moved beyond his power of control by the sight of his long-lost and best-loved brother, he hastily quitted the audience chamber and retiring to his own room wept there alone, till he could command himself again; then he washed his red eyes and tear-wetted cheeks, and returned with a steady face to his brethren. Again, when Joseph met his aged father Jacob at Goshen, he fell on the old man's neck and wept a good while. But here too his tears probably welled up from the heart when he saw the grey head bent humbly before him, and remembered all his father's kindness to him in the days of his youth so long ago. Again, when the two dear friends David and Jonathan met in a dark hour for the last time, with a presentiment perhaps that they should see each other no more, they kissed one another and wept one with another, till David exceeded Here also we may well believe that the emotion was unfeigned. Once more we read in the Book of Tobit how when Tobias was come as a stranger to the house of his kinsman Raguel in Ecbatana, and had revealed himself to his host, "then Raguel leaped up, and kissed him and wept." Even here, however, the outburst of tears may have been an effect of joyous surprise rather than a mere conformity to social custom.

But however it may have been with the Hebrews, it seems certain that among races at a lower level of culture the shedding of tears at meeting or parting is often little or nothing more than a formal compliance with an etiquette prescribed by polite society. One of the peoples among whom this display of real or artificial emotion was rigorously required of all who had any claim to good breeding, were the Maoris of New Zealand. "The affectionate disposition of the people," we are told "appears more, however, in the departure and return of friends. Should a friend be going a short voyage to Port Jackson, or Van Dieman's Land, a great display of outward feeling is made: it commences with a kind of ogling glance, then a whimper, and an affectionate exclamation; then a tear begins to glisten in the eye; a wry face is drawn; then they will shuffle nearer to the individual, and at length cling round his neck. They then begin to cry outright, and to use the flint about the face and arms; and, at last, to roar most outrageously, and almost to smother with kisses, tears, and blood, the poor fellow who is anxious to escape all this. On the return of friends, or when visited by them from a distance, the same scene, only more universally, is gone through: and it is difficult to keep your own tears from falling at the melancholy sight they present, and the miserable howlings and discordant noises which they make. There is much of the cant of affection in all this; for they can keep within a short distance of the person over whom they know they must weep, till they have prepared themselves by thinking and have worked themselves up to the proper pitch; when, with a rush of pretended eagerness, they grasp their victim (for that is the best term to use), and commence at once to operate upon their own bodies, and upon his patience. There is one thing worthy of observation, that, as they can command tears to appear, upon all occasions, at a moment's warning, so they can cease crying when told to do so, or when it becomes inconvenient to continue it longer. I was once much amused at a scene of this kind, which happened at a village called Kaikohi, about ten miles from the Waimate. Half-a-dozen of their friends and relations had returned, after an absence of six months, from a visit to the Thames. They were all busily engaged in the usual routine of crying; when two of the women of the village, suddenly, at a signal one from the other, dried up their tears, closed the sluices of their affection, and very innocently said to the assembly: 'We have not finished crying yet: we will go and put the food in the oven, cook it, and make the baskets for it, and then we will come and finish crying; perhaps we shall not have done when the food is ready; and if not, we can cry again at night.' All this, in a canting, whining tone of voice, was concluded with a 'Shan't it be so? he! shan't it be so? he!' I spoke to them about their hypocrisy, when they knew they did not care, so much as the value of a potato, whether they should ever see those persons again, over whom they had been crying. The answer I received was, 'Ha! a New Zealander's love is all outside; it is in his eyes, and his mouth.'" The navigator Captain P. Dillon frequently fell a victim to these uproarious demonstrations of affection, and he tells us how he contrived to respond to them in an appropriate manner. "It is the custom," he says, "in New Zealand, when friends or relations meet after long absence, for both parties to touch noses and shed tears. With this ceremony I have frequently complied out of courtesy; for my failure in this respect would have been considered a breach of friendship, and I should have been regarded as little better than a barbarian, according to the rules of New Zealand politeness. Unfortunately, however, my hard heart could not upon all occasions readily produce a tear, not being made of such melting stuff as those of the New Zealanders; but the application of a pocket handkerchief to my eyes for some time, accompanied with an occasional howl in the native language, answered all the purposes of real grief. This ceremony is dispensed with from strange Europeans; but with me it was indispensable, I being a *Thongata moury;* that is, a New Zealander, or countryman, as they were pleased to term me." Again, we read that "emotion characterised the meeting of New Zealanders, but parting was generally unattended by any outward display. At meeting men and women pressed their noses together, during which, in a low lachrymose whine, they repeated amidst showers of tears circumstances which had occurred mutually interesting since they last met. Silent grief is unknown among them. When the parties meeting are near relatives and have been long absent, the pressing of noses and

crying were continued for half an hour; when the meeting was
between accidental acquaintances, it was merely nose to nose and
away. This salutation is called *hongi,* and is defined as a smelling
Like the Eastern custom of eating salt, it destroyed hostility
between enemies. During the *hongi* the lips never met, there was
no kissing."

Again, among the aborigines of the Andaman Islands "relatives
after an absence of a few weeks or months, testify their joy at meeting by sitting with their arms round each other's necks, and weeping
and howling in a manner which would lead a stranger to suppose
that some great sorrow had befallen them; and, in point of fact,
there is no difference observable between their demonstrations of
joy and those of grief at the death of one of their number. The
crying chorus is started by women, but the men speedily chime in,
and groups of three or four may thus be seen weeping in concert
until, from sheer exhaustion, they are compelled to desist." Among
the people of Mungeli Tahsil, in the Bilaspore district of India, "it
is an invariable practice when relatives come together who have
not met for a long while, for the womenfolk to weep and wail loudly.
A son has been away for months and returns to his parents' house.
He will first go and touch the feet of his father and mother. When
he has been seated the mother and sisters come to him and each
in turn, placing both hands on his shoulders, weeps loudly and in
a wailing tone narrates anything special that has taken place in
his absence." Among the Chauhans of the Central Provinces in
India etiquette requires that women should weep whenever they
meet relatives from a distance. "In such cases when two women
see each other they cry together, each placing her head on the other's
shoulder and her hands at her sides. While they cry they change
the positions of their heads two or three times, and each addresses
the other according to their relationship, as mother, sister, and so
on. Or if any member of the family has recently died, they call
upon him or her exclaiming 'O my mother! O my sister! O my
father! Why did not I, unfortunate one, die instead of thee?'
A woman when weeping with a man holds to his sides and rests her
head against his breast. The man exclaims at intervals, 'Stop
crying, do not cry.' When two women are weeping together it is
a point of eitquette that the elder should stop first and then beg
her companion to do so, but if it is doubtful which is the elder,
they sometimes go on crying for an hour at a time, exciting the
younger spectators to mirth, until at length some elder steps forward
and tells one of them to stop."

The custom of shedding floods of tears as a sign of welcome seems
to have been common among the Indian tribes of both South and
North America. Among the Tupis of Brazil, who inhabited the
country in the neighbourhood of Rio de Janeiro, etiquette required
that when a stranger entered the hut where he expected to receive
hospitality, he should seat himself in the hammock of his host and

remain there for some time in pensive silence. Then the women of the house would approach, and sitting down on the ground about the hammock, they would cover their faces with their hands, burst into tears, and bid the stranger welcome, weeping and paying him compliments in the same breath. While these demonstrations were proceeding, the stranger on his part was expected to weep in sympathy, or if he could not command real tears, the least he could do was to heave deep sighs and to look as lugubrious as possible. When these formalities, exacted by the Tupi code of good manners, had been duly complied with, the host, who had hitherto remained an apparently indifferent and unconcerned spectator, would approach his guest and enter into conversation with him. The Lenguas, an Indian tribe of the Chaco, "employ among themselves a singular form of politeness when they see again any one after some time of absence. It consists in this: the two Indians shed some tears before they utter a word to each other; to act otherwise would be an insult, or at least a proof that the visit was not welcome."

In the sixteenth century the Spanish explorer, Cabeça de Vaca, describes a similar custom observed by two tribes of Indians who inhabited an island off what seems to be now the coast of Texas. "On the island," he says, "there dwell two peoples speaking different languages, of whom the one are called Capoques and the other Han. They have a custom that when they know each other and see each other from time to time, they weep for half an hour before they speak to one another. Then the one who receives the visit rises first and gives all he possesses to the other, who accepts it and soon afterwards goes away; sometimes even, after the gift has been accepted, they go away without speaking a word." A Frenchman, Nicolas Perrot, who lived among the Indians for many years in the latter part of the seventeenth century, describes how a party of Sioux, visiting a village of their friends the Ottawas, "had no sooner arrived than they began, in accordance with custom, to weep over all whom they met, in order to signify to them the sensible joy they felt at having found them." Indeed, the Frenchman himself was more than once made the object, or rather the victim, of the like doleful demonstrations. Being sent by the governor of New France to treat with the Indian tribes beyond the Mississippi, he took up his quarters on the banks of that river, and there received an embassy from the Ayeos, the neighbours and allies of the Sioux, whose village lay some days to the westward, and who wished to enter into friendly relations with the French. A French historian has described the meeting of these Indian ambassadors with poor Perrot. They wept over him till the tears ran down their bodies; they beslobbered him with the filth which exuded from their mouths and their noses, smearing it on his head, his face, and his clothes, till he was almost turned sick by their caresses, while all the time they shrieked and howled most lamentably. At last the present of a few knives and awls had the effect of checking these noisy effusions; but having no interpreter with them, they were quite unable to make themselves intelligible, and so had to return the way they came without effecting their purpose. A few days later four other Indians arrived, one of whom spoke a language understood by the French. He explained that their village was nine leagues up the river, and he invited the French to visit it. The invitation was accepted. At the approach of the strangers the women fled to the woods and the mountains, weeping and stretching out their arms to the sun. However, twenty of the chief men appeared, offered Perrot the pipe of peace, and carried him on a buffalo's skin into the chief's hut. Having deposited him there, they and the chief proceeded to weep over him in the usual way, bedewing his head with the moisture which dripped from their eyes, their mouths, and their noses. When that indispensable ceremony was over, they dried their eyes and their noses, and offered him the pipe of peace once more. "Never in the world," adds the French historian, "were seen such people for weeping; their meetings are accompanied by tears, and their partings are equally tearful."

CHAPTER VI

THE COVENANT ON THE CAIRN

WHEN Jacob had served his father-in-law Laban for many years, and had acquired great store of sheep and goats by his industry and craft, he grew weary of the long service and resolved to return, with his wives and his children and all that he had, to the land of his fathers. We may surmise that it was not a simple feeling of homesickness which moved him to take this resolution. The morning of life was long over with him, and the warm impulses of youth, if he had ever known them, had ceased to sway his essentially cool and sober temperament. A calm calculation of profit had probably more to do in determining him to this step than any yearning for the scenes of his childhood and any affection for his native country. By a happy combination of diligence and cunning he had contrived in the course of years to draft the flower of the flocks from his father-in-law's fold to his own; he saw that there was little more to be got in that quarter: he had drained the old man as dry as a squeezed lemon, and it was high time to transfer his talents to a more profitable market. But foreseeing that his relative might possibly raise some objection to his walking off with the greater part of the flocks, he prudently resolved to avoid all painful family disputes by a moonlight flitting. For this purpose it was necessary to let his wives into the secret. Apparently he had some doubts how they would receive the communication he was about to make to them, so he broke the subject gently. In an insinuating voice he began by referring to the changed demeanour of their father towards himself; next with unctuous piety he related how God had been on his side and had taken away their father's cattle and given them to himself; finally, to clinch matters, he told them, perhaps with a twinkle in his eye, how last night he had dreamed a dream, in which the angel of God had appeared to him and bidden him depart to the land of his nativity. But he soon found that there was no need to beat about the bush, for his wives entered readily into the project, and avowed their purely mercenary motives with cynical frankness. They complained that their spendthrift parent had wasted all he had received as the price of their marriage, so that he had nothing left to give or bequeath to them. Hence they were quite ready to turn their backs on him and to follow their husband to the strange far-away land beyond the great river. But before they went off, bag and baggage, the sharp-witted Rachel fortunately remembered, that though their father had been stripped of most of his goods, he still had his household gods about him, who might be expected to resent and punish any injury done to their proprietor. So she contrived to steal and hide them among her baggage, without, however, informing her husband of what she had done, probably from a fear lest a relic of masculine conscience might induce him to restore the stolen deities to their own owner.

The preparations of the worthy family for flight were now complete. All that remained was to await a moment when they might be able to steal away unobserved. It came when Laban went off for some days to the sheep-shearing. Now was the chance. The great caravan set out, the women and children riding on camels and preceded or followed by an endless procession of bleating flocks. Their progress was necessarily slow, for the sheep and goats could not be hurried, but they had a full two days' start, for it was not till the third day that Laban got wind of their departure. With his brethren he hastened in pursuit, and after a forced march of seven days he came up with the long lumbering train of fugitives among the beautiful wooded mountains of Gilead, perhaps in a glade of the forest where the sheep were nibbling the greensward, perhaps in a deep glen where the camels were crashing through the cane-brakes, or the flocks splashing across the ford. An angry altercation ensued between the two kinsmen. Laban opened the wordy war by loudly reproaching Jacob with having stolen his gods and carried off his daughters as if they were captives of the sword. To this Jacob, who knew nothing about the gods, retorted warmly that he was neither a thief nor a resetter of stolen goods; that Laban was free to search his baggage, and that if the missing deities were found in the luggage of any of Jacob's people, Laban was welcome to put the thief to death. So Laban ransacked the tents, one after the other, but found nothing; for the crafty Rachel had hidden the images in the camel's palanquin and sat on it, laughing in her sleeve while her father rummaged about in her tent.

This failure to discover the stolen property completely restored the self-confidence of Jacob, who at first had probably been somewhat abashed on being confronted by the kinsman whom he had outwitted and left in the lurch. He now felt that he even occupied a position of moral elevation, and he proceeded to turn the tables on his crestfallen adversary with great volubility and a fine show of virtuous indignation. He dismissed with withering scorn the trumped-up charge of theft which had just been brought against him: he declared that he had honestly earned his wives and his flocks by many years of diligent service: he enlarged pathetically on the many hardships he had endured and the nice sense of honour he had ever displayed in his office of shepherd; and in a glowing peroration he wound up by asserting that if it had not been for God's good help his rascally father-in-law would have turned his faithful servant adrift without a rag on his back or a penny in his pocket. To this torrent of eloquence his father-in-law had little in the way of argument to oppose; he would seem to have been as inferior to his respectable son-in-law in the gift of the gab as he was in the refinements of cunning. A man would need to have a very long spoon to sup with Jacob, and so Laban found to his cost. He contented himself with answering sullenly that the daughters were his daughters, the children his children, the flocks his flocks, in fact that everything Jacob had in the world really belonged to his father-in-law. The answer was something more than the retort courteous, it even bordered on the lie circumstantial; but neither of the disputants had any stomach for fighting, and without going so far as to measure swords they agreed to part in peace, Jacob to resume his journey with his whole caravan, and Laban to return empty-handed to his people. But before they separated, they set up a large stone as a pillar, gathered a cairn of smaller stones about it, and sitting or standing on the cairn ate bread together. The cairn was to mark the boundary which neither party should pass for the purpose of harming the other, and, more than that, it was to serve as a witness between them when they were far from each other; wherefore they called it in the Hebrew and Syrian tongues the Heap of Witness. The covenant was sealed by a sacrifice and a common meal, after which the adversaries, now reconciled, at least in appearance, retired to their tents—Jacob no doubt well content with the result of his diplomacy, Laban probably less so, but still silenced, if not satisfied. However, he put the best face he could on the matter, and rising betimes next morning he kissed his sons and his daughters and bade them farewell. So he departed to his own place, but Jacob went on his way.

The whole drift of the preceding narrative tends to show that the erection of the cairn by the two kinsmen on the spot where they parted was a monument, not of their friendship and affection, but

of their mutual suspicion and distrust: the heap of stones furnished
a material guarantee of the observance of the treaty: it was as it
were a deed or document in stone, to which each of the contracting
parties set his hand, and which in case of a breach of faith was
expected to testify against the traitor. For apparently the cairn
was conceived not simply as a heap of stones, but as a personality,
a powerful spirit or deity, who would keep a watchful eye on both
the covenanters and hold them to their bond. This is implied in
the words which Laban addressed to Jacob on the completion of
the ceremony. He said, "The Lord watch between me and thee,
when we are absent one from another. If thou shalt afflict my
daughters, and if thou shalt take wives beside my daughters, no
man is with us; see, God is witness betwixt me and thee." Hence
the cairn was called the Watch-tower (*Mizpah*), as well as the Heap
of Witness, because it acted as watchman and witness in one.

The pillar and cairn of which this picturesque legend was told
doubtless belonged to the class of rude stone monuments which
are still frequent in the region beyond Jordan, including Mount
Gilead, where tradition laid the parting of Jacob and Laban.
Speaking of the land of Moab, the late ·Canon Tristram observes:
"Part of our route was by the side of the Wady 'Atabeiyeh, which
runs down south to the Zerka, a short and rapidly deepening valley.
Here, on a rocky upland bank, we came for the first time upon a
dolmen, consisting of four stones, rough and undressed; three set
on end, so as to form three sides of a square; and the fourth, laid
across them, forming the roof. The stones were each about eight
feet square. From this place northwards, we continually met with
these dolmens, sometimes over twenty in a morning's ride, and all
of exactly similar construction. They were invariably placed on
the rocky sides, never on the tops, of hills; the three large blocks
set on edge, at right angles to each other, and supporting the massive
stone laid across them, which was from six to ten feet square. They
are favourite stations for the Arab herdsmen, whom we frequently
saw stretched at full length upon the top of them, watching their
flocks. The dolmens appear to be confined to the district between
the Callirrhoe and Heshbon: in similar districts to the south of
that region, they never occurred. I have, however, in former
visits to Palestine, seen many such in the bare parts of Gilead,
between Jebel Osha and Gerash. It is difficult to understand why
they were erected on these hill-sides. I never found one with a
fourth upright stone, and in many instances the edifice had fallen,
but in such cases the heap always consisted of four blocks, neither
more nor less. From the shallowness of the soil, there could have
been no sepulture here underground; and there are no traces of
any cairns or other sepulchral erections in the neighbourhood. It
is possible that the primaeval inhabitants erected these dolmens in
many other situations, but that they have been removed by the
subsequent agricultural races, who left them undisturbed only on

these bare hill-sides, which can never have been utilized in any degree for cultivation. Still it is worthy of notice that the three classes of primaeval monuments in Moab—the stone circles, dolmens, and cairns—exist, each in great abundance, in three different parts of the country, but never side by side: the cairns exclusively in the east, on the spurs of the Arabian range; the stone circles south of the Callirrhoe; and the dolmens, north of that valley. This fact would seem to indicate three neighbouring tribes, co-existent in the prehistoric period, each with distinct funeral or religious customs. Of course the modern Arab attributes all these dolmens to the jinns."

We have seen that when Jacob and Laban had raised a cairn, they ate together, sitting on the stones.[1] The eating of food upon the stones was probably intended to ratify the covenant. How it was supposed to do so may perhaps be gathered from a Norse custom described by the old Danish historian, Saxo Grammaticus. He tells us that "the ancients, when they were to choose a king, were wont to stand on stones planted in the ground, and to proclaim their votes, in order to foreshadow from the steadfastness of the stones that the deed would be lasting." In fact, the stability of the stones may have been thought to pass into the person who stood upon them and so to confirm his oath. Thus we read of a certain mythical Rajah of Java, who bore the title of Raja Sela Perwata, "which in the common language is the same as Wátu Gúnung, a name conferred upon him from his having rested on a mountain like a stone, and obtained his strength and power thereby, without other aid or assistance." At a Brahman marriage in India the bridegroom leads the bride thrice round the fire, and each time he does so he makes her tread with her right foot on a millstone, saying, "Tread on this stone; like a stone be firm. Overcome the enemies: tread the foes down." This ancient rite, prescribed by the ritual books of the Aryans in Northern India, has been adopted in Southern India outside the limits of the Brahman caste. The married couple "go round the sacred fire, and the bridegroom takes up in his hands the right foot of the bride, and places it on a millstone seven times. This is known as *saptapadi* (seven feet), and is the essential and binding portion of the marriage ceremony. The bride is exhorted to be as fixed in constancy as the stone on which her foot has been thus placed." Similarly at initiation a Brahman boy is made to tread with his right foot on a stone, while the words are repeated, "Tread on this stone; like a stone be firm. Destroy those who seek to do thee harm; overcome thy enemies."

---

[1] In Genesis xxxi. 46 the Revised Version translates "and they did eat there by the heap," where the Authorized Version renders "and they did eat there upon the heap." The parallels which I adduce in the text make it probable that the Authorized Version is here right and the Revised Version wrong. The primary sense of the preposition in question (על) is certainly "upon," and there is no reason to depart from it in the present passage.

Among the Kookies of Northern Cachar at marriage "the young couple place a foot each upon a large stone in the centre of the village, and the Ghalim [headman] sprinkles them with water, and pronounces an exhortation to general virtue and conjugal fidelity, together with a blessing and the expression of hopes regarding numerous progeny." In Madagascar it is believed that you can guard against the instability of earthly bliss by burying a stone under the main post or under the threshold of your house.

On the same principle we can explain the custom of swearing with one foot or with both feet planted on a stone. The idea seems to be that the solid enduring quality of the stone will somehow pass into the swearer and so ensure that the oath will be kept. Thus there was a stone at Athens on which the nine archons stood when they swore to rule justly and according to the laws. A little to the west of St. Columba's tomb in Iona "lie the black stones, which are so called, not from their colour, for that is grey, but from the effects that tradition says ensued upon perjury, if any one became guilty of it after swearing on these stones in the usual manner; for an oath made on them was decisive in all controversies. Mac-Donald, King of the Isles, delivered the rights of their lands to his vassals in the isles and continent, with uplifted hands and bended knees, on the black stones; and in this posture, before many witnesses, he solemnly swore that he would never recall those rights which he then granted: and this was instead of his great seal. Hence it is that when one was certain of what he affirmed, he said positively, I have freedom to swear this matter upon the black stones." Again, in the island of Fladda, another of the Hebrides, there was formerly a round blue stone on which people swore decisive oaths. At the old parish church of Lairg, in Sutherlandshire, there used to be built into an adjoining wall a stone called the Plighting Stone. "It was known far and wide as a medium—one might almost say, as a sacred medium—for the making of bargains, the pledging of faith, and the plighting of troth. By grasping hands through this stone, the parties to an agreement of any kind bound themselves with the inviolability of a solemn oath."

Similar customs are observed by rude races in Africa and India. When two Bogos of Eastern Africa, on the border of Abyssinia, have a dispute, they will sometimes settle it at a certain stone, which one of them mounts. His adversary calls down the most dreadful curses on him if he forswears himself, and to every curse the man on the stone answers "Amen!" Among the Akamba of British East Africa solemn oaths are made before an object called a kitichto, which is believed to be endowed with a mysterious power of killing perjurors. In front of the object are placed seven stones, and the man who makes oath stands so that his heels rest on two of them. At Naimu, a village of the Tangkhuls of Assam, there is a heap of peculiarly shaped stones upon which the people swear solemn oaths. At Ghosegong, in the Garo hills of Assam, there is a stone on which the natives swear their most solemn oaths. In doing so they first salute the stone, then with their hands joined and uplifted, and their eyes steadfastly fixed on the hills, they call on Mahadeva to witness to the truth of what they affirm. After that they again touch the stone with all the appearance of the utmost fear, and bow their heads to it, calling again on Mahadeva. And while they make their declaration they look steadfastly to the hills and keep their right hand on the stone. The Garos also swear on meteoric stones, saying, "May Goera (the god of lightning) kill me with one of these if I have told a lie." In this case, however, the use of the stone is retributive rather than confirmatory; it is designed, not so much to give to the oath the stability of the stone, as to call down the vengeance of the lightning-god on the perjurer. The same was perhaps the intention of a Samoan oath. When suspected thieves swore to their innocence in the presence of chiefs, they "laid a handful of grass on the stone, or whatever it was, which was supposed to be the representative of the village god, and, laying their hand on it, would say, 'In the presence of our chiefs now assembled, I lay my hand on the stone. If I stole the thing may I speedily die.'"

In this last case, and perhaps in some of the others, the stone appears to be conceived as instinct with a divine life which enables it to hear the oath, to judge of its truth, and to punish perjury. Oaths sworn upon stones thus definitely conceived as divine are clearly religious in character, since they involve an appeal to a supernatural power who visits transgressors with his anger. But in some of the preceding instances the stone is apparently supposed to act purely through the physical properties of weight, solidity, and inertia; accordingly in these cases the oath, or whatever the ceremony may be, is purely magical in character. The man absorbs the valuable properties of the stone just as he might absorb electrical force from a battery; he is, so to say, petrified by the stone in the one case just as he is electrified by the electricity in the other. The religious and the magical aspects of the oath on a stone need not be mutually exclusive in the minds of the swearers. Vagueness and confusion are characteristic of primitive thought, and must always be allowed for in our attempts to resolve that strange compound into its elements.

These two different strains of thought, the religious and the magical, seem both to enter into the Biblical account of the covenant made by Jacob and Laban on the cairn. For on the one hand the parties to the covenant apparently attribute life and consciousness to the stones by solemnly calling them to witness their agreement, just as Joshua called on the great stone under the oak to be a witness, because the stone had heard all the words that the Lord spake unto Israel. Thus conceived, the cairn, or the pillar which stood in the midst of it, was a sort of Janus-figure with heads facing both ways for the purpose of keeping a sharp eye on both the parties to the covenant. And on the other hand the act of eating food together on the cairn, if I am right, is best explained as an attempt to establish a sympathetic bond of union between the covenanters by partaking of a common meal, while at the same time they strengthened and tightened the bond by absorbing into their system the strength and solidity of the stones on which they were seated.

If any reader, afflicted with a sceptical turn of mind, still doubts whether the ground on which a man stands can affect the moral quality of his oath, I would remind him of a passage in Procopius which should set his doubts at rest. That veracious historian tells how a Persian king contrived to wring the truth from a reluctant witness who had every motive and desire to perjure himself. When Pacurius reigned over Persia, he suspected that his vassal, Arsaces, king of Armenia, meditated a revolt. So he sent for him and taxed him to his face with disloyalty. The king of Armenia indignantly repelled the charge, swearing by all the gods that such a thought had never entered his mind. Thereupon the king of Persia, acting on a hint from his magicians, took steps to unmask the traitor. He caused the floor of the royal pavilion to be spread with muck, one half of it with muck from Persia, and the other half of it with muck from Armenia. Then on the floor so prepared he walked up and down with his vassal, reproaching him with his treacherous intentions. The replies of the culprit were marked by the most extraordinary discrepancies. So long as he trod the Persian muck he swore with the most dreadful oaths that he was the faithful slave of the Persian king; but as soon as he trod the Armenian muck his tone changed, and he turned fiercely on his liege-lord, threatening him with vengeance for his insults, and bragging of what he would do when he regained his liberty. Yet the moment he set foot again on the Persian muck he cringed and fawned as before, entreating the mercy of his suzerain in the most pitiful language. The ruse was successful: the murder was out: the traitor stood self-revealed. Yet being one of the blood-royal, for he was an Arsacid, he might not be put to death. So they did to him what was regularly done to erring princes. They shut him up for life in a prison called the Castle of Oblivion, because whenever a prisoner has passed within its gloomy portal, and the door had grated on its hinges behind him, his name might never again be mentioned under the pain of death. There traitors rotted, and there the perjured king of Armenia ended his days.

The custom of erecting cairns as witnesses is apparently not extinct in Syria even now. One of the most famous shrines of the country is that of Aaron on Mount Hor. The prophets' tomb on the mountain is visited by pilgrims, who pray the saint to intercede the recovery of sick friends, and pile up heaps of stones as witness (*mashhad*) of the vows they make on behalf of the sufferers.

CHAPTER VII

JACOB AT THE FORD OF THE JABBOK

AFTER parting from Laban at the cairn, Jacob, with his wives and children, his flocks and his herds, pursued his way southward. From the breezy, wooded heights of the mountains of Gilead he now plunged down into the profound ravine of the Jabbok thousands of feet below. The descent occupies several hours, and the traveller who accomplishes it feels that, on reaching the bottom of the deep glen, he has passed into a different climate. From the pine-woods and chilly winds of the high uplands he descends first in about an hour's time to the balmy atmosphere of the village of Burmeh, embowered in fruit-trees, shrubs, and flowers, where the clear, cold water of a fine fountain will slake his thirst at the noonday rest. Still continuing the descent, he goes steeply down another two thousand feet to find himself breathing a hothouse air amid luxuriant semi-tropical vegetation in the depths of the great lyn of the Jabbok. The gorge is, in the highest degree, wild and picturesque. On either hand the cliffs rise almost perpendicularly to a great height; you look up the precipices or steep declivities to the sky-line far above. At the bottom of this mighty chasm the Jabbok flows with a powerful current, its blue-grey water fringed and hidden, even at a short distance, by a dense jungle of tall oleanders, whose crimson blossoms add a glow of colour to the glen in early summer. The Blue River, for such is its modern name, runs fast and strong. Even in ordinary times the water reaches to the horses' girths, and sometimes the stream is quite unfordable, the flood washing grass and bushes high up the banks on either hand. On the opposite or southern side the ascent from the ford is again exceedingly steep. The path winds up and up; the traveller must dismount and lead his horse. It was up that long ascent that Jacob, lingering alone by the ford in the gloaming, watched the camels labouring, and heard the cries of the drivers growing fainter and fainter above him, till sight and sound of them alike were lost in the darkness and the distance.

The scene may help us to understand the strange adventure which befell Jacob at the passage of the river. He had sent his wives, his handmaids, and his children, riding on camels, across the river, and all his flocks and herds had preceded or followed them. So he remained alone at the ford. It was night, probably a moonlight summer night; for it is unlikely that with such a long train he would have attempted to ford the river in the dark or in the winter when the current would run fast and deep. Be that as it may, in the moonlight or in the dark, beside the rushing river, a man wrestled with him all night long, till morning flushed the wooded crests of the ravine high above the struggling pair in the shadows below. The stranger looked up and saw the light and said, "Let me go, for the day breaketh." So Jupiter tore himself from the arms of the fond Alcmena before the peep of dawn; so the ghost of Hamlet's father faded at cockcrow; so Mephistopheles in the prison warned Faust, with the hammering of the gallows in his ears, to hurry for the day —Gretchen's last day—was breaking. But Jacob clung to the man and said, "I will not let thee go, except thou bless me." The stranger asked him his name, and when Jacob told it he said, "Thy name shall be called no more Jacob, but Israel, for thou hast striven with God and with men, and hast prevailed." But when Jacob inquired of him, "Tell me, I pray thee, thy name," the man refused to mention it, and having given the blessing which Jacob had extorted, he vanished. So Jacob called the name of the place Peniel, that is, the Face of God; "For," said he, "I have seen God face to face, and my life is preserved." Soon afterwards the sun rose and shone on Jacob, and as it did so he limped; for in the struggle his adversary had touched him on the hollow of the thigh. "Therefore the children of Israel eat not the sinew of the hip which is upon the hollow of the thigh, unto this day: because he touched the hollow of Jacob's thigh in the sinew of the hip."

The story is obscure, and it is probable that some of its original features have been slurred over by the compilers of Genesis because they savoured of heathendom. Hence any explanation of it must be to a great extent conjectural. But taking it in connexion with the natural features of the place where the scene of the story is laid, and with the other legends of a similar character which I shall adduce, we may, perhaps, provisionally suppose that Jacob's mysterious adversary was the spirit or jinnee of the river, and that the struggle was purposely sought by Jacob for the sake of obtaining his blessing. This would explain why he sent on his long train of women, servants, and animals, and waited alone in the darkness by the ford. He might calculate that the shy river-god, scared by the trampling and splashing of so great a caravan through the water, would lurk in a deep pool or a brake of oleanders at a safe distance, and that when all had passed and silence again reigned, except for the usual monotonous swish of the current, curiosity would lead him to venture out from his lair and inspect the ford, the scene of all this hubbub and disturbance. Then the subtle Jacob, lying in wait, would pounce out and grapple with him until he had obtained the coveted blessing. It was thus that Menelaus caught the shy sea-god Proteus sleeping at high noon among the seals on the yellow sands, and compelled him reluctantly to say his sooth. It was thus that Peleus caught the sea-goddess Thetis and won her, a Grecian Undine, for his wife. In both these Greek legends the supple, slippery water-spirit writhes in the grip of his or her captor, slipping through his hands again and again, and shifting his or her shape from lion to serpent, from serpent to water, and so forth, in the effort to escape; not till he is at the end of all his shifts and sees no hope of evading his determined adversary does he at last consent to grant the wished-for boon. So, too, when Hercules wrestled with the river-god Achelous for the possession of the fair Dejanira, the water-sprite turned himself first into a serpent and then into a bull in order to give the brawny hero the slip; but all in vain.

These parallels suggest that in the original form of the tale Jacob's adversary may in like manner have shifted his shape to evade his importunate suitor. A trace of such metamorphoses, perhaps, survives in the story of God's revelation of himself to Elijah on Mount Horeb; the wind, the earthquake, and the fire in that sublime narrative may in the first version of it have been disguises assumed, one after the other, by the reluctant deity until, vanquished by the prophet's perseverance, he revealed himself in a still small voice. For it is to be observed that water-spirits are not the only class of supernatural beings for whom men have laid wait in order to wring from them a blessing or an oracle. Thus the Phrygian god Silenus is said, in spite of his dissipated habits, to have possessed a large stock of general information which, like Proteus, he only imparted on compulsion. So Midas, king of Phrygia, caught him by mixing wine with the water of a spring from which, in a moment of weakness, the sage had condescended to drink. When he woke from his drunken nap, Silenus found himself a prisoner, and he had to hold high discourse on the world and the vanity of human life before the king would let him go. Some of the gravest writers of antiquity have bequeathed to us a more or less accurate report of the sermon which the jolly toper preached beside the plashing wayside spring, or, according to others, in a bower of roses. By a stratagem like that of Midas it is said that Numa caught the rustic deities Picus and Faunus, and compelled them to draw down Jupiter himself from the sky by their charms and spells.

The view that Jacob's adversary at the ford of the Jabbok was the river-god himself may perhaps be confirmed by the observation that it has been a common practice with many peoples to propitiate the fickle and dangerous spirits of the water at fords. Hesiod says that when you are about to ford a river you should look at the running water and pray and wash your hands; for he who wades through a stream with unwashed hands incurs the wrath of the gods. When the Spartan king Cleomenes, intending to invade Argolis, came with his army to the banks of the Erasinus, he sacrificed to the river, but the omens were unfavourable to his crossing. Thereupon the king remarked that he admired the patriotism of the river-god in not betraying his people, but that he would invade Argolis in spite of him. With that he led his men to the seashore, sacrificed a bull to the sea, and transported his army in ships to the enemy's country. When the Persian host under Xerxes came to the river Strymon in Thrace, the Magians sacrificed white horses and performed other strange ceremonies before they crossed the stream. Lucullus, at the head of a Roman army, sacrificed a bull to the

Euphrates at his passage of the river. "On the river-bank, the Peruvians would scoop up a handful of water and drink it, praying the river-deity to let them cross or to give them fish, and they threw maize into the stream as a propitiatory offering; even to this day the Indians of the Cordilleras perform the ceremonial sip before they will pass a river on foot or horseback." Old Welsh people "always spat thrice on the ground before crossing water after dark. to avert the evil influences of spirits and witches."

In the belief of the Bantu tribes of Soutn-east Africa "rivers are inhabited by demons or malignant spirits, and it is necessary to propitiate these on crossing an unknown stream, by throwing a handful of corn or some other offering, even if it is of no intrinsic value, into the water." When the Masai of East Africa cross a stream they throw a handful of grass into the water as an offering; for grass, the source of life to their cattle, plays an important part in Masai superstition and ritual. Among the Baganda of Central Africa, before a traveller forded any river, he would ask the spirit of the river to give him a safe crossing, and would throw a few coffee-berries as an offering into the water. When a man was carried away by the current his friends would not try to save him, because they feared that the river-spirit would take them also, if they helped the drowning man. They thought that the man's guardian spirit had left him to the mercy of the river-spirit, and that die he must. At certain spots on the Rivers Nakiza and Sezibwa, in Uganda, there was a heap of grass and sticks on either bank, and every person who crossed the river threw a little grass or some sticks on the one heap before crossing, and on the other heap after crossing; this was his offering to the spirit of the river for a safe passage through the water. From time to time more costly offerings were made at these heaps; the worshipper would bring beer, or an animal, or a fowl, or some bark-cloth, tie the offering to the heap, and leave it there, after praying to the spirit. The worship of each of these rivers was cared for by a priest, but there was no temple. The Bean Clan was especially addicted to the worship of the River Nakiza, and the father of the clan was the priest. When the river was in flood no member of the clan would attempt to ford it; the priest strictly forbade them to do so under pain of death.

At a place on the Upper Nile, called the Karuma Falls, the flow of the river is broken by a line of high stones, and the water rushes down a long slope in a sort of sluice to a depth of ten feet. The native tradition runs, that the stones were placed in position by Karuma, the agent or familiar of a great spirit, who, pleased with the barrier thus erected by his servant, rewarded him by bestowing his name on the falls. A wizard used to be stationed at the place to direct the devotions of such as crossed the river. When Speke and his companions were ferried over the Nile at this point, a party of Banyoro, travelling with them, sacrificed two kids, one on either side of the river, flaying them with one long cut each down their breasts and bellies. The slaughtered animals were then laid, spread-eagle fashion, on their backs upon grass and twigs, and the travellers stepped over them, that their journey might be prosperous. The place of sacrifice was chosen under the directions of the wizard of the falls.

The Ituri River, one of the upper tributaries of the Congo, forms the dividing-line between the grass land and the great forest. "When my canoe had almost crossed the clear, rapid waters, a hundred and fifty yards wide, I noticed on the opposite bank two miniature houses built close to the edge and resembling in every feature the huts of the villagers. The old chief was loth to explain the object of these houses, but at length I was told that they were erected for the shade of his predecessor, who was told that he must recompense them for their labours by guarding the passage of those crossing the river. From that time, whenever a caravan was seen to approach the bank, a little food would be carried down to the ghost-houses, as a warning that the shade's protection was needed for the caravan about to cross." Among the Ibos of the Awka district, in Southern Nigeria, when a corpse is being carried to the grave and the bearers have to cross water, a she-goat and a hen are sacrificed to the river.

The Badagas, a tribe of the Neilgherry Hills in Southern India, believe in a deity named Gangamma, "who is supposed to be present at every stream, and especially so at the Koondé and Pykaré rivers, into which it was formerly the practice for every owner of cattle, which had to cross them at their height, to throw a quarter of a rupee, because their cattle used frequently to be carried away by the current and destroyed. It is enumerated amongst the great sins of every deceased Badaga, at his funeral, that he had crossed a stream without paying due adoration to Gangamma." Again, the Todas, another smaller but better-known tribe of the same hills, regard two of their rivers, the Teipakh (Paikara) and the Pakhwar (Avalanche), as gods or the abodes of gods. Every person in crossing one of these streams must put his right arm outside of his cloak in token of respect. Formerly these rivers might only be crossed on certain days of the week. When two men who are sons of a brother and a sister respectively pass in company over either of the sacred streams they have to perform a special ceremony. As they approach the river they pluck and chew some grass, and each man says to the other, "Shall I throw the river (water)? Shall I cross the river?" Then they go down to the bank, and each man dips his hand in the river and throws a handful of water away from him thrice. After that they cross the river, each of them with his arm outside of his cloak in the usual way.

A certain famous chief of the Angoni, in British Central Africa, was cremated near a river; and even now, when the Angoni cross the stream, they greet it with the deep-throated manly salutation which they accord only to royalty. And when the Angoni ferry over any river in a canoe they make a general confession of any sins of infidelity of which they may have been guilty towards their consorts, apparently from a notion that otherwise they might be drowned in the river. The Toradjas of Central Celebes believe that water-spirits, in the shape of snakes, inhabit the deep pools and rapids of rivers. Men have to be on their guard against these dangerous beings. Hence when a Toradja is about to make a voyage down a river, he will often call out from the bank, "I am not going today, I will go to-morrow." The spirits hear the announcement, and if there should be amongst them one who is lying in wait for the voyager, he will imagine that the voyage has been postponed and will defer his attack accordingly till the following day. Meantime the cunning Toradja will drop quietly down the river, laughing in his sleeve at the simplicity of the water-sprite whom he has bilked.

Though the exact reasons for observing many of these customs in regard to rivers may remain obscure, the general motive appears to be the awe and dread of rivers conceived either as powerful personal beings or as haunted by mighty spirits. The conception of a river as a personal being is well illustrated by a practice which is in vogue among the Kakhyeen of Upper Burma. When one of the tribe has been drowned in crossing a river the avenger of blood repairs once a year to the banks of the guilty stream, and filling a vessel full of water he hews it through with his sword, as if he were despatching a human foe. It is said that once on a time, when the Nile had flooded the land of Egypt to a depth of eighteen cubits, and the waters were lashed into waves by a strong wind, the Egyptian king Pheron seized a dart and hurled it into the swirling current; but for this rash and impious act he was punished by the loss of his eyesight. Again, we read that when Cyrus, marching against Babylon, crossed the River Gyndes, one of the sacred white horses, which accompanied the march of the army, was swept away by the current and drowned. In a rage at this sacrilege, the king threatened the river to bring its water so low that a woman would be able to wade through them without wetting her knees. Accordingly he employed his army in digging channels by which the water of the river was diverted from its bed, and in this futile labour the whole summer, which should have been devoted to the siege of Babylon, was wasted to gratify the childish whim of a superstitious despot.

Nor are the spirits of rivers the only water-divinities which bold men have dared to fight or punish. When a storm swept away the first bridge by which Xerxes spanned the Hellespont for the passage of his army, the king in a rage sentenced the straits to receive three hundred lashes and to be fettered with chains. And as the executioners plied their whips on the surface of the water, they said, "O bitter water, thy master inflicts this punishment on thee because thou has wronged him who did no wrong to thee. But King

Xerxes will cross thee, willy-nilly. And it serves thee right that no man sacrifices to thee, because thou art a treacerous and a briny river." The ancient Celts are said to have waded into the billows as they rolled in upon the shore, hewing and stabbing them with swords and spears, as if they could wound or frighten the ocean itself. The Toradjas of Central Celebes relate that one of their tribes, which is proverbial for stupidity, once came down to the sea-shore when the tide was out. Immediately they built a hut on the beach below high-water mark. When the tide rose and threatened to wash away the hut, they regarded it as a monster trying to devour them, and sought to appease it by throwing their whole stock of rice into the waves. As the tide still continued to advance, they next hurled their swords, spears, and chopping-knives into the sea, apparently with the intention of wounding or frightening the dangerous creature and so compelling him to retreat. Once on a time, when a party of Arafoos, a tribe of mountaineers on the northern coast of Dutch New Guinea, were disporting them-selves in the surf, three of them were swept out to sea by a refluent wave and drowned. To avenge the death their friends fired on the inrolling billows for hours with guns and bows and arrows. Such personifications of the water as a personal being who can be cowed or overcome by physical violence, may help to explain the weird story of Jacob's adventure at the ford of the Jabbok.

The tradition that a certain sinew in Jacob's thigh was strained in the struggle with his nocturnal adversary is clearly an attempt to explain why the Hebrews would not eat the corresponding sinew in animals. Both the tradition and the custom have their parallels among some tribes of North American Indians, who regularly cut out and throw away the hamstrings of the deer they kill. The Cherokee Indians assign two reasons for the practice. One is that "this tendon, when severed, draws up into the flesh; ergo, any one who should unfortunately partake of the hamstring would find his limbs draw up in the same manner." The other reason is that if, instead of cutting out the hamstring and throwing it away the hunter were to eat it, he would thereafter easily grow tired in travel-ling. Both reasons assume the principle of sympathetic magic, though they apply it differently. The one supposes that, if you eat a sinew which shrinks, the corresponding sinew in your own body will shrink likewise. The other seems to assume that if you destroy the sinew without which the deer cannot walk, you yourself will be incapacitated from walking in precisely the same way. Both reasons are thoroughly in keeping with savage philosophy. Either of them would suffice to account for the Hebrew taboo. On this theory the narrative in Genesis supplies a religious sanction for a rule which was originally based on sympathetic magic alone.

The story of Jacob's wrestling with the nocturnal phantom and extorting a blessing from his reluctant adversary at the break of dawn has a close parallel in the superstition of the ancient Mexicans.

They thought that the great god Tezcatlipoca used to roam about at night in the likeness of a gigantic man wrapt in an ash-coloured sheet and carrying his head in his hand. When timid people saw this dreadful apparition they fell to the ground in a faint and died soon afterwards, but a brave man would grapple with the phantom and tell him that he would not let him go till the sun rose. But the spectre would beg his adversary to release him, threatening to curse him if he did not. Should the man, however, succeed in holding the horrible being fast till day was just about to break, the spectre changed his tune and offered to grant the man any boon he might ask for, such as riches or invincible strength, if only he would unhand him and let him go before the dawn. The human victor in this tussel with a superhuman foe received from his vanquished enemy four thorns of a certain sort as a token of victory. Nay, a very valiant man would wrench the heart from the breast of the phantom, wrap it up in a cloth, and carry it home. But when he undid the cloth to gloat over the trophy, he would find nothing in it but some white feathers, or a thorn, or it might be only a cinder or an old rag.

CHAPTER VIII

JOSEPH'S CUP

WHEN his brethren came to Egypt to procure corn during the famine, and were about to set out on their homeward journey to Palestine, Joseph caused his silver drinking-cup to be hidden in the mouth of Benjamin's sack. Then when the men were gone out of the city and were not yet far off, he sent his steward after them to tax them with theft in having stolen his cup. A search was accordingly made in the sacks, and the missing cup was found in Benjamin's sack. The steward reproached the brethren with their ingratitude to his master, who had treated them hospitably, and whose kindness they had repaid by robbing him of the precious goblet. "Wherefore have ye rewarded evil for good?" he asked. "Is not this it in which my lord drinketh, and whereby he indeed divineth? ye have done evil in so doing." And when the brethren were brought back and confronted with Joseph, he repeated these reproaches, saying, "What deed is this that ye have done? know ye not that such a man as I can indeed divine?" Hence we may infer that Joseph piqued himself in particular on his power of detecting a thief by means of his divining cup.

The use of a cup in divination has been not uncommon both in ancient and modern times, though the particular mode of employing it for that purpose has not always been the same. Thus in the life of the Neoplatonic philosopher Isidorus we read that the sage fell in with a sacred woman, who possessed a divine talent of a remarkable kind. She used to pour clean water into a crystal cup, and from the appearances in the water she predicted the things that should come to pass. Such predictions from appearances in water formed a special branch of divination, on which the Greeks bestowed the name of *hydramantia*; sometimes a particular sort of gem was put in the water for the sake of evoking the images of the gods. King Numa is said to have divined by means of the images of the gods which he saw in water, but we are not told that he used a cup for the purpose; more probably he was supposed to have beheld the divine figures in a pool of the sacred spring Egeria, to the spirit of which he was wedded. When the people of Tralles, in Caria, desired to ascertain what would be the result of the Mithridatic war, they employed a boy, who, gazing into water, professed to behold in it the image of Mercury and, under the inspiration of the divine manifestation, chanted the coming events in a hundred and sixty verses. The Persians are related to have been adepts in the art of water-divination; indeed the art is said to have been imported into the West from Persia.

How Joseph used his magic cup for the detection of a thief or for other purposes of divination we do not know, but we may conjecture that he was supposed to draw his inferences from figures which appeared to him in the water. Certainly this mode of divination is still practised in Egypt, and it may have been in vogue in that conservative country from remote antiquity. Its modern name is the Magic Mirror. "The magic mirror is much employed. A pure innocent boy (not more than twelve years of age) is directed to look into a cup filled with water and inscribed with texts, while under his cap is stuck a paper, also with writing on it, so as to hang over his forehead; he is also fumigated with incense, while sentences are murmured by the conjuror. After a little time, when the boy is asked what he sees, he says that he sees persons moving in the water, as if in a mirror. The conjuror orders the boy to lay certain commands on the spirit, as for instance to set up a tent, or to bring coffee and pipes. All this is done at once. The conjuror asks the inquisitive spectators to name any person whom they wish to appear on the scene, and some name is mentioned, no matter whether the person is living or dead. The boy commands the spirit to bring him. In a few seconds he is present, and the boy proceeds to describe him. The description, however, according to our own observation, is always quite wide of the mark. The boy excuses himself by saying that the person brought before him will not come right into the middle, and always remains half in the shade; but at other times he sees the persons really and in motion. When a theft is committed the magic mirror is also sometimes questioned, as we ourselves were witnesses on one occasion. (This is called *darb el mandel*.) The accusations of the boy fell upon a person who was afterwards proved to be quite innocent, but whom the boy, as it appeared, designedly charged with the crime out of malevolence. For this reason such experiments, formerly much in vogue, were strictly prohibited by the government, though they are still practised."

Sometimes in Egypt the magic mirror used in divination is formed, not by water in a cup, but by ink poured into the palm of the diviner's hand, but the principle and the mode of procedure are the same in both cases. The divine professes to see in the ink the figures of the persons, whether alive or dead, whom the inquirer desires him to summon up. The magic mirror of ink, like the magic mirror of water, is resorted to for the detection of a thief and other purposes. The persons who can see in it are a boy under puberty, a virgin, a black female slave, and a pregnant woman, but apparently a boy under puberty is most commonly employed. A magic square is drawn with ink in the palm of his hand, and in the centre of the square a little pool of ink serves as the magic mirror. While the diviner is gazing into it, incense is burnt, and pieces of paper with charms written on them are consumed in the fire. When Kinglake was in Cairo he sent for a magician and invited him to give a specimen of his skill. The magician, a stately old man with flowing beard, picturesquely set off by a vast turban and ample robes, employed a boy to gaze into a blot of ink in his palm and there to descry the image of such a person as the Englishman might name. Kinglake called for Keate, his old headmaster at Eton, a ferocious dominie of the ancient school, short in figure and in temper, with shaggy red eyebrows and other features to match. In response to this call the youthful diviner professed to see in the inky mirror the image of a fair girl, with golden hair, blue eyes, pallid face, and rosy lips. When Kinglake burst into a roar of laughter, the discomfited magician declared that the boy must have known sin, and incontinently kicked him down stairs.

Similar modes of divination have been practised in other parts of the world. Thus, in Scandinavia people used to go to a diviner on a Thursday evening in order to see in a pail of water the face of the thief who had robbed them. The Tahitians "have a singular mode of detecting a thief, in any case of stolen goods, by applying to a person possessing the spirit of divination, who, they observe, is always sure to show them the face of the thief reflected from a calabash of clear water." Some diviners in South-eastern New Guinea profess to describe the face of a culprit in a pool of water into which coco-nut oil has been squeezed. Among the Eskimo, when a man has gone out to sea and has not returned in due time, a wizard will undertake to ascertain by means of the magic mirror whether the missing man is alive or dead. For this purpose he lifts up the head of the nearest relation of the missing man with a stick; a tub of water stands under, and in this mirror the wizard professes to behold the image of the absent mariner either overset in his canoe or sitting upright and rowing. Thus he is able either to comfort the anxious relative with an assurance of the safety of their friend or to confirm their worst fears by the tidings of his death.

But the magic mirror is not the only form of divination in which the material instrument employed for the discovery of truth is a vessel of water. An Indian mode of detecting a thief is to inscribe the names of all the suspected persons on separate balls of paste or wax, and then to throw the balls into a vessel of water. It is believed that the ball which contains the name of the thief will float on the surface, and that all the others will sink to the bottom. In Europe young people used to resort to many forms of divination on Midsummer Eve in order to ascertain their fortune in love. Thus in Dorsetshire a girl on going to bed would write the letters of the alphabet on scraps of paper and drop them in a basin of water with the letters downwards; and next morning she would expect to find the first letter of her future husband's name turned up, but all the other letters still turned down.

Sometimes the fates ascertained by dropping substances of one kind or another in a vessel of water and judging of the issue by the position or configuration which the substance assumes in the water. Thus among the Bahima or Banyankole, a pastoral tribe of Central Africa, in the Uganda Protectorate, a medicine-man would sometimes take a pot of water and cast certain herbs into it, which caused a froth to rise; then he dropped four coffee-berries into the water, marked the positions which they took up, and inferred the wishes of the gods according to the direction in which the berries pointed or the side which they turned up in floating. Among the Garos of Assam a priest will sometimes divine by means of a cup of water and some grains of uncooked rice. Holding the cup of water in his left hand, he drops the rice into it, grain by grain, calling out the name of a spirit as each grain falls. The spirit who chances to be named at the moment when two grains, floating in the water, collide with each other, is the one who must be propitiated. In the Highlands of Scotland the art of divining by the tea-leaves or sediment in a tea-cup was carried out in great detail. Even yet, we are told, young women resort in numbers to fortune-tellers of this class, who, for the simple reward of the tea, spell out to them most excellent matches. The prediction is made from the arrangement of the sediment or tea-leaves in the cup after the last of the liquid has been made to wash the sides of the cup in the *deiseal* or right-hand-turn direction and then poured out. In England similar prophecies are hazarded from tea-leaves and coffee-grounds left at the bottom of cups. So in Macedonia people divine by coffee. "One solitary bubble in the centre of the cup betokens that the person holding it possesses one staunch and faithful friend. If there are several bubbles forming a ring close to the edge of the cup, they signify that he is fickle in his affections, and that his heart is divided between several objects of worship. The grounds of coffee are likewise observed and variously explained according to the forms which they assume: if they spread round the cup in the shape of rivulets and streams money is prognosticated, and so forth."

In Europe a favourite mode of divination is practised by pouring molten lead or wax into a vessel of water and watching the forms which the substance assumes as it cools in the water. This way of prying into the future has been resorted to in Lithuania, Sweden, Scotland, and Ireland. Again, in Ireland a certain disease called *esane* was supposed to be sent by the fairies, and in order to prognosticate its course or prescribe for its treatment diviners used to inspect coals which they had dropped into a pot of clean water.

In one or other of these ways Joseph may be supposed to have divined by means of his silver cup.

PART III

THE TIMES OF THE JUDGES AND THE KINGS

CHAPTER I

MOSES IN THE ARK OF BULRUSHES

With the life of Joseph the patriarchal age of Israel may be said to end. A brilliant series of biographical sketches, vivid in colouring and masterly in the delineation of character, has described the march of the patriarchs from the banks of the Euphrates to the banks of the Nile. There the historian leaves them for a time. The curtain descends on the first act of the drama, and when it rises again on the same scene, some four hundred years are supposed to have elapsed, and the patriarchal family has expanded into a nation. From this point the national history begins, and the first commanding figure in it is that of Moses, the great leader and lawgiver, who is said to have delivered his people from bondage in Egypt, to have guided them in their wanderings across the Arabian desert, to have moulded their institutions, and finally to have died within sight of the Promised Land, which he was not to enter. There seems to be no sufficient reason to doubt that in these broad outlines the tradition concerning him is correct. In the story of his exploits, as in that of so many national heroes, later ages unquestionably embroidered the sober tissue of fact with the gay threads of fancy; yet the change thus wrought in the web has not been so great as to disguise the main strands beyond recognition. We can still trace the limbs of the man under the gorgeous drapery of the magician who confronted Pharaoh and wrought plagues on all the land of Egypt; we can still perceive the human features through the nimbus of supernatural glory which shone on the features of the saint and prophet as he descended from the mountain, where he had conversed with God and had received from the divine hands a new code of law for his people. It is indeed remarkable that, though Moses stands so much nearer than the patriarchs to the border line of history, the element of the marvellous and the miraculous enters much more deeply into his story than into theirs. While from time to time they are said to have commune with the

263

deity, either face to face or in visions, not one of them is represented as a worker of those signs and wonders which occur so frequently in the career of Moses. We see them moving as men among men, attending to the common business and sharing the common joys and sorrows of humanity. Moses, on the other hand, from the beginning to the end of his life is represented as set apart for a great mission and moving accordingly on a higher plane than ordinary mortals, with hardly any traces of those frailties which are incidental to all men, and which, touched in by a delicate brush, add so much life-like colour to the portraits of the patriarchs. That is why the simple humanity of Abraham, Isaac, and Jacob touches us all so much more nearly than the splendid but solitary figure of Moses.

Like all the events of his life, the birth of Moses is encircled in tradition with a halo of romance. After the death of Joseph and his brethren, their descendants, the children of Israel, are said to have multiplied so fast in Egypt that the Egyptians viewed them with fear and distrust, and attempted to check their increase by putting them to hard service. When this harsh treatment failed to produce the desired effect, the king of Egypt issued orders that all male Hebrew children should be killed at birth, and when the cruel command was evaded by the humane subterfuge of the mid-wives who were charged to carry it out, he commanded all his people to fling every Hebrew man child at birth into the river. Accordingly, on the birth of Moses, his mother hid him at first for three months, and when she could hide him no longer she made an ark of bulrushes, or rather of papyrus, daubed it with slime and pitch, and put the child therein. Then she carried the ark out sadly and laid it in the flags by the river's brink. But the child's elder sister stood afar off to know what should become of her little brother. Now it chanced that the daughter of Pharaoh, the king of Egypt, came down to bathe at the river, and spying the ark among the flags she sent one of her maidens to fetch it. When the ark was brought and opened, the princess saw the child in it, and behold, the babe wept. So she had compassion on him and said, "This is one of the Hebrews' children." While she was looking at him, the child's sister, who had been watching and had seen all that had happened, came up and said to the princess, "Shall I go and call thee a nurse of the Hebrew women, that she may nurse the child for thee?" And Pharaoah's daughter said, "Go." And the maid went and called the child's mother. And Pharaoh's daughter said to her, "Take this child away, and nurse it for me, and I will give thee thy wages." So the mother took her child and nursed it. And the child grew, and she brought him to Pharaoah's daughter, and he became her son. And she called his name Moses, "Because," she said, "I drew him out of the water."

While this story of the birth and upbringing of Moses is free from all supernatural elements, it nevertheless presents features which may reasonably be suspected of belonging to the realm of

folk-lore rather than of history.   In order, apparently, to enhance
the wonder of his hero's career; the story-teller loves to relate how
the great man or woman was exposed at birth, and was only rescued
from imminent death by what might seem to vulgar eyes an accident,
but what really proved to be the finger of Fate interposed to preserve the helpless babe for the high destiny that awaited him or her.
Such incidents are probably in most cases to be regarded as embel-
lishments due to the invention of the narrator, picturesque touches
added by him to heighten the effect of a plain tale which he deemed
below the dignity of his subject.

According to Roman tradition, the founder of Rome himself
was exposed in his infancy and might have perished, if it had not
been for the providential interposition of a she-wolf and a woodpecker.   The story ran thus.   On the slope of the Alban Mountains
stood the long white city of Alba Longa, and a dynasty of kings
named the Sylvii or the Woods reigned over it, while as yet shepherds
fed their flocks on the hills of Rome, and wolves prowled in the
marshy hollows between them.   It so chanced that one of the kings
of Alba, by name Proca, left two sons, Numitor and Amulius,
of whom Numitor was the elder and was destined by his father to
succeed him on the throne.   But his younger brother, ambitious
and unscrupulous, contrived to oust his elder brother by violence
and to reign in his stead.   Not content with that he plotted to
secure his usurped power by depriving his injured brother of an
heir.   For that purpose he caused the only son of Numitor to be
murdered, and he persuaded or compelled his brother's daughter,
Rhea Silvia by name, to dedicate herself to the worship of Vesta
and thereby to take the vow of perpetual virginity.   But the vow
was broken.   The Vestal virgin was found to be with child, and in
due time she gave birth to twin boys.   She fathered them on the
god Mars, but her hard-hearted uncle refused to admit the plea, and
ordered the two babes to be thrown into the river.   It happened
that the Tiber had overflowed its banks, and the servants who were
charged with the task of drowning the infants, unable to approach
the main stream, were obliged to deposit the ark containing the
children in shoal water at the foot of the Palatine hill.   There they
abandoned the babes to their fate, and there a she-wolf, attracted
by their cries, found and suckled them and licked their bodies clean
of the slime with which they were covered.   Down to imperial
times the bronze statue of a wolf suckling two infants stood on the
spot to commemorate the tradition, and the statue is still preserved
in the Capitoline Museum at Rome.   Some said that a woodpecker
assisted the wolf in feeding and guarding the forsaken twins; and
as both the wolf and the woodpecker were creatures sacred to Mars,
people drew from this circumstance a fresh argument in favour of
the divine parentage of Romulus and Remus.

Such marvellous tales appear to have been told particularly of
the founders of dynasties or of kingdoms, whose parentage and

upbringing were forgotten, the blank thus left by memory being supplied by the fancy of the story-teller. Oriental history furnishes an instance of a similar glamour thrown over the dark beginning of a powerful empire. The first Semitic king to reign over Babylonia was Sargon the Elder, who lived about 2600 B.C. A redoubtable conqueror and an active builder, he made a great name for himself, yet apparently he did not know the name of his own father. At least we gather as much from an inscription which is said to have been carved on one of his statues, a copy of the inscription was made in the eighth century before our era and deposited in the royal library at Nineveh, where it was discovered in modern times. In this document the king set forth his own early history as follows :—

> *"Sargon, the mighty king, the king of Agade, am I,*
> *My mother was lowly, my father I knew not,*
> *And the brother of my father dwells in the mountain.*
> *My city is Azuripanu, which lies on the banks of the Euphrates.*
> *My lowly mother conceived me, in secret she brought me forth.*
> *She set me in a basket of rushes, with bitumen she closed my door:*
> *She cast me into the river, which rose not over me.*
> *The river bore me up, unto Akki, the irrigator, it carried me.*
> *Akki, the irrigator, with . . . lifted me out,*
> *Akki, the irrigator, as his own son . . . reared me,*
> *Akki, the irrigator, as his gardener appointed me.*
> *While I was a gardener, the goddess Ishtar loved me,*
> *And for . . . four years I ruled the kingdom.*
> *The black-headed peoples I ruled, I governed."*

This story of the exposure of the infant Sargon in a basket of rushes on the river closely resembles the story of the exposure of the infant Moses among the flags of the Nile, and as it is to all appearance very much older than the Hebrew tradition, the authors of Exodus may perhaps have been acquainted with it and may have modelled their narrative of the episode on the Babylonian original. But it is equally possible that the Babylonian and the Hebrew tales are independent offshoots from the common root of popular imagination. In the absence of evidence pointing conclusively in the one direction or the other, dogmatism on the question would be out of place.

The theory of the independent origin of the Babylonia and Hebrew stories is to some extent confirmed by the occurence of a parallel legend in the great Indian epic the *Mahabharata*, since it is hardly likely that the authors of that work had any acquaintance with Semitic traditions. The poet relates how the king's daughter Kunti or Pritha was beloved by the Sun-god and bore him a son "beautiful as a celestial," "clad in armour, adorned with brilliant golden ear-rings, endued with leonine eyes and bovine shoulders." But ashamed of her frailty, and dreading the anger of her royal father and mother, the princess, "in consultation with her nurse, placed her child in a waterproof basket, covered all over with sheets, made of wicker-work, smooth, comfortable and furnished with a beautiful pillow. And with tearful eyes she consigned it to (the waters of) the river Asva." Having done so, she returned to the palace, heavy at heart, lest her angry sire should learn her secret. But the basket containing the babe floated down the river till it came to the Ganges and was washed ashore at the city of Champa in the Suta territory. There it chanced that a man of the Suta tribe and his wife, walking on the bank of the river, saw the basket, drew it from the water, and on opening it beheld a baby boy "(beautiful) as the morning sun, clad in a golden armour, and with a beautiful face adorned with brilliant ear-rings." Now the pair were childless, and when the man looked upon the fair infant, he said to his wife, "Surely, considering that I have no son, the gods have sent this child to me." So they adopted him, and brought him up, and he became a mighty archer, and his name was Karna. But his royal mother had news of him through her spies.

A similar story is told of the exposure and upbringing of Trakhan, king of Gilgit, a town situated at a height of about five thousand feet above the sea in the very heart of the snowy Himalayas. Enjoying a fine climate, a central position, and a considerable stretch of fertile land, Gilgit seems to have been from ancient times the seat of a succession of rulers, who bore more or less undisputed sway over the neighbouring valleys and states. Among them Trakhan, who reigned about the beginning of the thirteenth century, was particularly famous. He is said to have been the strongest and the proudest king of Gilgit, and tradition still busies itself with his fortunes and doings. The story of his birth and exposure runs thus. His father Tra-Trakhan, king of Gilgit, had married a woman of a wealthy family at Darel. Being passionately devoted to polo, the king was in the habit of going over to Darel every week to play his favourite game with the seven brothers of his wife. One day, so keen were they all on the sport, they agreed to play on condition that the winner should put the losers to death. The contest was long and skilful, but at last the king won the match, and agreeably to the compact he, like a true sportsman, put his seven brothers-in-law to death. When he came home, no doubt in high spirits, and told the queen the result of the match, with its painful but necessary sequel, she was so far from sharing in his glee that she actually resented the murder, or rather the execution, of her seven brothers and resolved to avenge it. So she put arsenic in the king's food, which soon laid him out, and the queen reigned in his stead. Now so it was that, at the time when she took this strong step, she was with child by the king, and about a month afterwards she gave birth to a son and called his name Trakhan. But so deeply did she mourn the death of her brothers, that she could not bear to look on the child of their murderer; hence she locked the infant in a wooden box and secretly threw it into the river. The current swept the box down the river as far as Hodar, a village in the Chilas District. Now it chanced that, as it floated by, two poor brothers were gathering sticks on the bank; and, thinking that the chest might contain treasure, one of them plunged into the water and drew it ashore. In order not to excite the covetousness of others by a display of the expected treasure, they hid the chest in a bundle of faggots and carried it home. There they opened it, and what was their surprise to discover in it a lovely babe still alive. Their mother brought up the little foundling with every care; and it seemed as if the infant brought a blessing to the house, for whereas they had been poor before, they now grew richer and richer, and set down their prosperity to the windfall of the child in the chest. When the boy was twelve years old, he conceived a great longing to go to Gilgit, of which he had heard much. So he went with his two foster-brothers, but on the way they stayed for a few days at a place called Baldas, on the top of a hill. Now his mother was still queen of Gilgit, but she had fallen very ill, and as there was none to succeed her in Gilgit the people were searching for a king to come from elsewhere and reign over them. One morning, while things were in this state and all minds were in suspense, it chanced that the village cocks crew, but instead of saying as usual "Cock-a-doodle-do" they said *"Beldas tham bayi,"* which being interpreted means, "There is a king at Baldas." So men were at once sent to bring down any stranger they might find there. The messengers found the three brothers and brought them before the queen. As Trakhan was handsome and stately the queen addressed herself to him, and in course of conversation elicited from him his story. To her surprise and joy she learned that this goodly boy was her own lost son, whom on a rash impulse of grief and resentment she had cast into the river. So she embraced him and proclaimed him the rightful heir to the kingdom of Gilgit.

It has been conjectured that in stories like that of the exposure of the infant Moses on the water we have a reminiscence of an old custom of testing the legitimacy of children by throwing them into the water and leaving them to swim or sink, the infants which swam being accepted as legitimate and those which sank being rejected as bastards. In the light of this conjecture it may be significant that in several of these stories the birth of the child is represented as supernatural, which in this connexion cynics are apt to regard as a delicate synonym for illegitimate. Thus in Greek legend the child Perseus and the child Telephus were fathered upon the god Zeus and the hero Hercules respectively; in Roman legend the twins Romulus and Remus were gotten on their virgin mother by the god Mars; and in the Indian epic the princess ascribed the birth of her infant to the embrace of the Sungod. In the Babylonian story, on the other hand, King Sargon, less fortunate or more honest than his Greek, Roman, and Indian compeers, frankly confessed that his father was unknown. The Biblical narrative of the birth of Moses drops no hint that his legitimacy was doubtful; but when we remember that his father Amram married his paternal aunt, that Moses was the

offspring of the marriage, and that later Jewish law condemned all
such marriages as incestuous, we may perhaps, without being uncharitable, suspect that in the original form of the story the mother
of Moses had a more particular reason for exposing her babe on the
water than a general command of Pharaoh to cast all male children
of the Hebrews into the river. Be that as it may, it appears that
the water ordeal has been resorted to by peoples far apart for the
purpose of deciding whether an infant is legitimate or not, and therefore whether it is to be saved or destroyed. Thus the Celts are said
to have submitted the question of the legitimacy of their offspring
to the judgment of the Rhine; they threw the infants into the
water, and if the babes were bastards the pure and stern river
drowned them, but if they were true-born, it graciously bore them
up on its surface and wafted them gently ashore to the arms of their
trembling mothers. Similarly in Central Africa the explorer Speke
was told "about Ururi, a province of Unyoro, under the jurisdiction
of Kiméziri, a noted governor, who covers his children with bead
ornaments, and throws them into the N'yanza, to prove their
identity as his own true offspring; for should they sink, it stands to
reason some other person must be their father; but should they
float, then he recovers them."

CHAPTER II

SAMSON AND DELILAH

AMONG the grave judges of Israel the burly hero Samson cuts a
strange figure. That he judged Israel for twenty years we are
indeed informed by the sacred writer, but of the judgments which
he delivered in his judicial character not one has been recorded, and
if the tenor of his pronouncements can be inferred from the nature
of his acts, we may be allowed to doubt whether he particularly
adorned the bench of justice. His talent would seem to have lain
rather in the direction of brawling and fighting, burning down
people's corn-ricks, and beating up the quarters of loose women;
in short, he appears to have shone in the character of a libertine
and a rake-hell rather than in a strictly judicial capacity. Instead
of a dull list of his legal decisions we are treated to an amusing, if
not very edifying, narrative of his adventures in love and in war,
or rather in filibustering; for if we accept, as we are bound to do,
the scriptural account of this roystering swashbuckler, he never
levied a regular war or headed a national insurrection against the
Philistines, the oppressors of his people; he merely sallied forth
from time to time as a solitary paladin or knight-errant, and mowed
them down with the jawbone of an ass or any other equally serviceable weapon that came to his hand. And even on these predatory

expeditions (for he had no scruple about relieving his victims of their clothes and probably of their purses) the idea of delivering his nation from servitude was to all appearance the last thing that would have occurred to him. If he massacred the Philistines, as he certainly did in great profusion and with hearty good will, it was from no high motive of patriotism or policy, but purely from a personal grudge which he bore them for the wrongs which they had done to himself, to his wife, and to his father-in-law. From first to last his story is that of an utterly selfish and unscrupulous adventurer, swayed by gusts of fitful passion and indifferent to everything but the gratification of his momentary whims. It is only redeemed from the staleness and vulgarity of commonplace rascality by the elements of supernatural strength, headlong valour, and a certain grim humour which together elevate it into a sort of burlesque epic after the manner of Ariosto. But these features, while they lend piquancy to the tale of his exploits, hardly lessen the sense of incongruity which we experience on coming across the grotesque figure of this swaggering, hectoring bully side by side with the solemn effigies of saints and heroes in the Pantheon of Israel's history. The truth seems to be that in the extravagance of its colouring the picture of Samson owes more to the brush of the story-teller than to the pen of the historian. The marvellous and diverting incidents of his disreputable career probably floated about loosely as popular tales on the current of oral tradition long before they crystallized around the memory of a real man, a doughty highlander and borderer, a sort of Hebrew Rob Roy, whose choleric temper, dauntless courage, and prodigious bodily strength marked him out as the champion of Israel in many a wild foray across the border into the rich lowlands of Philistia. For there is no sufficient reason to doubt that a firm basis of fact underlies the flimsy and transparent superstructure of fancy in the Samson saga. The particularity with which the scenes of his life, from birth to death, are laid in definite towns and places, speaks strongly in favour of a genuine local tradition, and as strongly against the theory of a solar myth, into which some writers would dissolve the story of the brawny hero.

The hand of the storyteller reveals itself most clearly in the account of the catastrophe which befell his hero through the wiles of a false woman, who wormed from him the secret of his great strength and then betrayed him to his enemies. The account runs as follows :—

"And it came to pass afterward, that he loved a woman in the valley of Sorek, whose name was Delilah. And the lords of the Philistines came up unto her, and said unto her, 'Entice him, and see wherein his great strength lieth, and by what means we may prevail against him, that we may bind him to afflict him : and we will give thee every one of us eleven hundred pieces of silver.' And Delilah said to Samson, 'Tell me, I pray thee, wherein thy great strength lieth, and wherewith thou mightest be bound to afflict thee.' And Samson said unto her, 'If they bind me with seven green withes that were never dried, then shall I become weak, and be as another man.' Then the lords of the Philistines brought up to her seven green withes which had not been dried, and she bound him with them. Now she had liers in wait abiding in the inner chamber. And she said unto him, 'The Philistines be upon thee, Samson.' And he brake the withes, as a string of tow is broken when it toucheth the fire. So his strength was not known. And Delilah said unto Samson, 'Behold, thou hast mocked me, and told me lies: now tell me, I pray thee, wherewith thou mightest be bound.' And he said unto her, 'If they only bind me with new ropes wherewith no work hath been done, then shall I become weak, and be as another man.' So Delilah took new ropes, and bound him therewith, and said unto him, 'The Philistines be upon thee, Samson.' And the liers in wait were abiding in the inner chamber. And he brake them from off his arms like a thread. And Delilah said unto Samson, 'Hitherto thou hast mocked me, and told me lies: tell me wherewith thou mightest be bound. And he said unto her, 'If thou weavest the seven locks of my head with the web, *and makest (the whole) fast with the pin, then shall I become weak and like any other man.' And Delilah made him sleep, and wove the seven locks of his head with the web,*[1] and she fastened it with the pin, and said unto him, 'The Philistines be upon thee, Samson.' And he awaked out of his sleep, and plucked away the pin of the beam, and the web. And she said unto him, 'How canst thou say, I love thee, when thine heart is not with me? thou hast mocked me these three times, and hast not told me wherein thy great strength lieth.' And it came to pass, when she pressed him daily with her words, and urged him, that his soul was vexed unto death. And he told her all his heart, and said unto her, 'There hath not come a razor upon mine head; for I have been a Nazirite unto God from my mother's womb: if I be shaven, then my strength will go from me, and I shall become weak, and be like any other man.' And when Delilah saw that he had told her all his heart, she sent and called for the lords of the Philistines, saying, 'Come up this once, for he hath told me all his heart.' Then the lords of the Philistines came up unto her, and brought the money in their hand. And she made him sleep upon her knees; and she called for a man, and shaved off the seven locks of his head; and she began to afflict him, and his strength went from him. And she said, 'The Philistines be upon thee, Samson.' And he awoke out of his sleep, and said, 'I will go out as at other times, and shake myself.' But he wist not that the Lord was departed from him. And the Philistines laid hold on him, and put out his eyes; and they brought him down to Gaza, and bound him with fetters of brass; and he did grind in the prison house."

[1] The words printed in italics have been accidentally omitted from the Hebrew text, but they can be restored from the Greek versions.

Thus it was supposed that Samson's great strength resided in his hair, and that to shave the long shaggy locks, which flowed down on his shoulders and had remained unshorn from infancy, would suffice to rob him of his superhuman vigour and reduce him to impotence. In various parts of the world a similar belief has prevailed as to living men and women, especially such as lay claim, like Samson, to powers above the reach of common mortals. Thus the natives of Amboyna, an island in the East Indies, used to think that their strength was in their hair and would desert them if their locks were shorn. A criminal under torture in a Dutch court of that island persisted in denying his guilt till his hair was cut off, when he immediately confessed. One man, who was tried for murder, endured without flinching the utmost ingenuity of his torturers till he saw the surgeon standing by with a pair of shears. On asking what they were for, and being told that it was to shave his hair, he begged that they would not do it, and made a clean breast. In subsequent cases, when torture failed to wring a confession from a prisoner, the Dutch authorities made a practice of cutting off his hair. The natives of Ceram, another East Indian Island, still believe that if young people have their hair cut they will be weakened and enervated thereby.

Here in Europe it used to be thought that the maleficent powers of witches and wizards resided in their hair, and that nothing could make any impression on these miscreants so long as they kept their hair on. Hence in France it was customary to shave the whole bodies of persons charged with sorcery before handing them over to the tormentor. Millaeus witnessed the torture of some persons at Toulouse, from whom no confession could be wrung until they were stripped and completely shaven, when they readily acknowledged the truth of the charge. A woman also, who apparently led a pious life, was put to the torture on suspicion of witchcraft, and bore her agonies with incredible constancy, until complete depilation drove her to admit her guilt. The noted inquisitor Sprenger contended himself with shaving the head of the suspected witch or warlock; but his more thoroughgoing colleague Cumanus shaved the whole bodies of forty-one women before committing them all to the flames. He had high authority for this rigorous scrutiny, since Satan himself in a sermon preached from the pulpit of North Berwick church, comforted his many servants by assuring them that no harm could befall them "sa lang as their hair wes on, and sould newir latt ane teir fall fra thair ene." Similarly in Bastar, a province of India, "if a man is adjudged guilty of witchcraft, he is beaten by the crowd, his hair is shaved, the hair being supposed to constitute his power of mischief, his front teeth are knocked out, in order, it is said, to prevent him from muttering incantations. . . . Women suspected of sorcery have to undergo the same ordeal; if found guilty, the same punishment is awarded, and after being shaved, their hair is attached to a tree in some public place." So among the Bhils, a rude race of Central India, when a woman was convicted of witch-craft and had been subjected to various forms of persuasion, such as hanging head downwards from a tree and having pepper rubbed into her eyes, a lock of hair was cut from her head and buried in the ground, "that the last link between her and her former powers of mischief might be broken." In like manner among the Aztecs of Mexico, when wizards and witches "had done their evil deeds, and the time came to put an end to their detestable life, some one laid hold of them and cropped the hair on the crown of their heads, which took from them all their power of sorcery and enchantment, and then it was that by death they put an end to their odious existence."

It is no wonder that a belief so widespread should find its way into fairy tales which, for all the seeming licence of fancy, reflect as in a mirror the real faith once held by the people among whom the stories circulated. The natives of Nias, an island off the west coast of Sumatra, relate that once upon a time a certain chief named Laubo Maros was driven by an earthquake from Macassar, in Celebes, and migrated with his followers to Nias. Among those who followed his fortunes to the new land were his uncle and his uncle's wife. But the rascally nephew fell in love with his uncle's wife and con-trived by a stratagem to get possession of the lady. The injured husband fled to Malacca and besought the Sultan of Johore to assist him in avenging his wrongs. The sultan consented, and declared war on Laubo Maros. Meanwhile, however, that un-scrupulous chief had fortified his settlement with an impenetrable hedge of prickly bamboo, which defied all the attempts of the Sultan and his troops to take it by storm. Defeated in open battle, the wily Sultan now had recourse to stratagem. He returned to Johore and there laded a ship with Spanish mats. Then he sailed back to Nias, and anchoring off his enemy's fort he loaded his guns with the Spanish mats instead of with shot and shell, and so opened fire on the place. The mats flew like hail through the air and soon were lying thick on the prickly hedge of the fort and on the shore in its neighbourhood. The trap was now set and the Sultan waited to see what would follow. He had not long to wait. An old woman, prowling along the beach, picked up one of the mats and saw the rest spread out temptingly around her. Overjoyed at the discovery she passed the good news among her neighbours, who hastened to the spot, and in a trice the prickly hedge was not only stripped bare of the mats but torn down and levelled with the ground. So the Sultan of Johore and his men had only to march into the fort and take possession. The defenders fled, but the wicked chief himself fell into the hands of the victors. He was condemned to death, but great difficulty was experienced in executing the sentence. They threw him into the sea, but the water would not drown him; they laid him on a blazing pyre, but the fire would not burn him; they hacked at every part of his body with swords, but steel would not pierce him. Then they perceived that he was an enchanter, and they consulted his wife to learn how they might kill him. Like Delilah, she revealed the fatal secret. On the chief's head grew a hair as hard as a copper wire, and with this wire his life was bound up. So the hair was plucked out, and with it his spirit fled. In this and some of the following tales it is not merely the strength but the life of the hero which is supposed to have it seat in his hair, so that the loss of the hair involves his death.

Tales like that of Samson and Delilah were current in the legendary lore of ancient Greece. It is said that Nisus, king of Megara, had a purple or golden hair on the middle of his head, and that he was doomed to die whenever that hair should be plucked out. When Megara was besieged by the Cretans, the king's daughter Scylla fell in love with Minos, their king, and pulled out the fatal hair from her father's head. So he died. According to one account it was not the life but the strength of Nisus that was in his golden hair; when it was pulled out, he grew weak and was slain by Minos. In this form the story of Nisus resembles still more closely the story of Samson. Again, Poseidon is said to have made Pterelaus immortal by giving him a golden hair on his head. But when Taphos, the home of Pterelaus, was besieged by Amphitryo, the daughter of Pterelaus fell in love with Amphitryo and killed her father by plucking out the golden hair with which his life was bound up. In a modern Greek folk-tale a man's strength lies in three golden hairs on his head. When his mother pulls them out, he grows weak and timid and is slain by his enemies. Another Greek story, in which we may perhaps detect a reminiscence of Nisus and Scylla, relates how a certain king, who was the strongest man of his time, had three long hairs on his breast. But when he went to war with another king, and his own treacherous wife had cut off the three hairs, he became the weakest of men.

The story how Samson was befooled by his false leman Delilah into betraying the secret of his strength has close parallels in Slavonic and Celtic folk-lore, with this difference, however, that in the Slavonic and Celtic tales the strength or the life of the hero is said to reside, not in his hair, but in some external object such as an egg or a bird. Thus a Russian story relates how a certain warlock called Kashtshei or Koshchei the Deathless carried off a princess and kept her prisoner in his golden castle. However, a prince made up to her one day as she was walking alone and disconsolate in the castle garden, and cheered by the prospect of escaping with him she went to the warlock and coaxed him with false and flattering words, saying, "My dearest friend, tell me, I pray you, will you never die?" "Certainly not," says he. "Well," says she, "and where is your death? Is it in your dwelling?" "To be sure it is," says he; "it is in the broom under the threshold." Thereupon the princess seized the broom and threw it on the fire, but although the broom burned, the deathless Koshchei remained alive; indeed not so much as a hair of him was singed. Balked in her first attempt, the artful hussy pouted and said, "You do not love me true, for you have not told me where your death is; yet I am not angry, but love you with all my heart." With these fawning words she besought the warlock to tell her truly where his death was. So he laughed and said, "Why do you wish to know? Well, then, out of love I will tell you where it lies. In a certain field there stand three green oaks, and under the roots of the largest oak is a worm, and if ever this worm is found and crushed, I shall die." When the princess heard these words, she went straight to her lover and told him all; and he searched till he found the oaks and dug up the worm and crushed it. Then he hurried to the warlock's castle, but only to learn that the warlock was still alive. Then the princess fell to wheedling and coaxing Koshchei once more, and this time, overcome by her wiles, he opened his heart to her and told her the truth. "My death," said he, "is far from here and hard to find, on the wide ocean. In that sea is an island, and on the island grows a green oak, and beneath the oak is an iron chest, and in the chest is a small basket, and in the basket is a hare, and in the hare is a duck, and in the duck is an egg; and he who finds the egg and breaks it, kills me at the same time." The prince naturally procured the fateful egg and with it in his hands he confronted the deathless warlock. The monster would have killed him, but the prince began to squeeze the egg. At that the warlock shrieked with pain, and turning to the false princess, who stood smirking and smiling, "Was it not out of love for you," said he, "that I told you where my death was? And is this the return you make to me?" With that he grabbed at his sword, which hung from a peg on the wall; but before he could reach it the prince had crushed the egg, and sure enough the deathless warlock found his death at the same moment.

In another version of the same story, when the cunning warlock deceives the traitress by telling her that his death is in the broom, she gilds the broom, and at supper the warlock sees it shining under the threshold and asks her sharply, "What's that?" "Oh," says she, "you see how I honour you." "Simpleton!" says he, "I was joking. My death is out there fastened to the oak fence." So next day, when the warlock was out, the prince came and gilded the whole fence; and in the evening, when the warlock was at supper, he looked out of the window and saw the fence glistening like gold. "And pray what may that be?" said he to the princess. "You see," said she, "how I respect you. If you are dear to me, dear too is your death. That is why I have gilded the fence in which your death resides." The speech pleased the warlock, and in the fullness of his heart he revealed to her the fatal secret of the egg. When the prince, with the help of some friendly animals, obtained possession of the egg, he put it in his bosom and repaired to the warlock's house. The warlock himself was sitting at the window in a very gloomy frame of mind; and when the prince appeared and showed him the egg, the light grew dim in the warlock's eyes, and he became all of a sudden very meek and mild. But when the prince began to play with the egg and to throw it from one hand to the other, the deathless Koshchei staggered from one corner of the room to the other, and when the prince broke the egg Koshchei the Deathless fell down and died.

A Serbian story relates how a certain warlock called True Steel carried off a prince's wife and kept her shut up in his cave. But the prince contrived to get speech of her, and told her that she must persuade True Steel to reveal to her where his strength lay. So when True Steel came home, the prince's wife said to him, "Tell me, now, where is your great strength?" He answered, "My wife, my strength is in my sword." Then she began to pray and turned to his sword. When True Steel saw that, he laughed and said, "O foolish woman! my strength is not in my sword, but in my bow and arrows." Then she turned towards the bow and arrows and prayed. But True Steel said, "I see, my wife, you have a clever teacher who has taught you to find out where my strength lies. I could almost say that your husband is living, and it is he who teaches you." But she assured him that nobody had taught her. When she found he had deceived her again, she waited for some days and then asked him again about the secret of his strength. He answered, "Since you think so much of my strength, I will tell you truly where it is. Far away from here there is a very high mountain; in the mountain there is a fox; in the fox there is a heart; in the heart there is a bird, and in this bird is my strength. It is no easy task, however, to catch the fox, for she can transform herself into a multitude of creatures." Next day, when True Steel went forth from the cave, the prince came and learned from his wife the true secret of the warlock's strength. So away he hied to the mountain, and there, though the fox, or rather the vixen, turned herself into various shapes, he contrived, with the help of some friendly eagles, falcons, and dragons, to catch and kill her. Then he took out the fox's heart, and out of the heart he took the bird and burned it in a great fire. At that very moment True Steel fell down dead.

In another Serbian story we read how a dragon resided in a water-mill and ate up two king's sons, one after the other. The third son went out to seek his brothers, and coming to the water-mill he found nobody in it but an old woman. She revealed to him the dreadful character of the being that kept the mill, and how he had devoured the prince's two elder brothers, and she implored him to go away home before a like fate should overtake him. But he was both brave and cunning, and he said to her, "Listen well to what I am going to say to you. Ask the dragon whither he goes and where his great strength is; then kiss all that place where he tells you his strength is, as if you loved it dearly, till you find it out, and afterwards tell me when I come." So when the dragon came home the old woman began to question him, "Where in God's name have you been? Whither do you go so far? You will never tell me whither you go." The dragon replied, "Well, my dear old woman, I do go far." Then the old woman coaxed him, saying, "And why do you go so far? Tell me where your strength is. If I knew where your strength is, I don't know what I should do for love; I would kiss all that place." Thereupon the dragon smiled and said to her, "Yonder is my strength in that fireplace." Then the old woman began to kiss and fondle the fireplace; and the dragon on seeing it burst into a laugh. "Silly old woman," he said, "my strength is not there. It is in the tree-fungus in front of the house." Then the old woman began to fondle and kiss the tree; but the dragon laughed again and said to her, "Away, old woman! my strength is not there." "Then where is it?" asked the old woman. "My strength," said he, "is a long way off, and you cannot go thither. Far in another kingdom under the king's city is a lake; in the lake is a dragon; in the dragon is a boar; in the boar is a pigeon, and in the pigeon is my strength." The secret was out; so next morning, when the dragon went away from the mill to attend to his usual business of gobbling people up, the prince came to the old woman and she led him into the mystery of the dragon's strength. Needless to say that the prince contrived to make his way to the lake in the far country, where after a terrible tussel he slew the water-dragon and extracted the pigeon, in which was the strength of the other unscrupulous dragon who kept the mill. Having questioned the pigeon, and ascertained from it how to restore his two murdered brothers to life, the prince wrung the bird's neck, and no doubt the wicked dragon perished miserably the very same moment, though the story-teller has omitted to mention the fact.

Similar incidents occur in Celtic stories. Thus a tale, told by a blind fiddler in the island of Islay, relates how a giant carried off a king's wife and his two horses, and kept them in his den. But the horses attacked the giant and mauled him so that he could hardly crawl. He said to the queen, "If I myself had my soul to keep, those horses would have killed me long ago." "And where, my dear," said she, "is thy soul? By the books I will take care of it." "It is in the Bonnach stone," said he. So on the morrow when the giant went out, the queen set the Bonnach stone in order exceedingly. In the dusk of the evening the giant came back, and he said to the queen, "What made thee set the Bonnach stone in order like that?" "Because thy soul is in it," quoth she. "I perceive," said he, "that if thou didst know where my soul is, thou wouldst give it much respect." "That I would," said she. "It is not there," said he, "my soul is; it is in the threshold." On the morrow she set the threshold in order finely, and when the giant returned he asked her, "What brought thee to set the threshold in order like that?" "Because thy soul is in it," said she. "I perceive," said he, "that if thou knewest where my soul is, thou wouldst take care of it." "That I would," said she. "It is not there that my soul is," said he. "There is a great flagstone under the threshold. There is a wether under the flag: there is a duck in the wether's belly, and an egg in the belly of the duck, and it is in the egg that my soul is." On the morrow when the giant was gone, they raised the flagstone and out came the wether. They opened the wether and out came the duck. They split the duck and out came the egg. And the queen took the egg and crushed it in her hands, and at that very moment the giant, who was coming home in the dusk, fell down dead.

Once more, in an Argyleshire story we read how a big giant, King of Sorcha, stole away the wife of the herdsman of Cruachan, and hid her in the cave in which he dwelt. But by the help of some obliging animals the herdsman contrived to discover the cave and his own lost wife in it. Fortunately the giant was not at home; so after giving her husband food to eat, she hid him under some clothes at the upper end of the cave. And when the giant came home he sniffed about and said, "The smell of a stranger is in the cave." But she said no, it was only a little bird she had roasted. "And I wish you would tell me," said she," "where you keep your life, that I might take good care of it." "It is in a grey stone over there," said he. So next day when he went away, she took the grey stone and dressed it well, and placed it in the upper end of the cave. When the giant came home in the evening he said to her, "what is it that you have dressed there?" "Your own life,". she said, "and we must be careful of it." "I perceive that you are very fond of me, but it is not there," said he. "Where is it?" said she. "It is in a grey sheep on yonder hillside," said he. On the morrow, when he went away, she got the grey sheep, dressed it well, and placed it in the upper end of the cave. When he came home in the evening, he said, "What is it that you have dressed there?" "Your own life, my love," said she. "It is not there as yet," said he. "Well!" said she, "you are putting me to great trouble taking care of it, and you have not told me the truth these two times." He then said, "I think that I may tell it to you now. My life is below the feet of the big horse in the stable. There is a place down there in which there is a small lake. Over the lake are seven grey hides, and over the hides are seven sods from the heath, and under all these are seven oak planks. There is a trout in the lake, and a duck in the belly of the trout, an egg in the belly of the duck, and a thorn of blackthorn inside of the egg, and till that thorn is chewed small I cannot be killed. Whenever the seven grey hides, the seven sods from the heath, and the seven oak planks are touched, I shall feel it wherever I shall be. I have an axe above the door, and unless all these are cut through with one blow of it, the lake will not be reached; and when it will be reached I shall feel it." Next day, when the giant had gone out hunting on the hill, the herdsman of Cruachan contrived, with the help of the

same friendly animals which had assisted him before, to get possession of the fateful thorn, and to chew it before the giant could reach
him; and no sooner had he done so than the giant dropped stark
and stiff, a corpse.

A story of the same sort is told by the natives of Gilgit in the
highlands of North-western India.   They say that once on a time
Gilgit was ruled by an ogre king named Shri Badat, who levied a
tax of children on his subjects and had their flesh regularly served
up to him at dinner.   Hence he went by the surname of the Man-
Eater.   He had a daughter called Sakina or Miyo Khai, who used
to spend the summer months at a pleasant spot high up in the
mountains, while Gilgi sweltered in the sultry heat of the valley
below.   One day it chanced that a handsome prince named Shamsher
was hunting in the mountains near the summer quarters of the
princess, and being fatigued by the chase he and his men lay down
to sleep beside a bubbling spring under the grateful shade of trees;
for it was high noon and the sun was hot.   As chance or fate would
have it, a handmaid of the princess came just then to draw water
at the spring, and seeing the strangers sleeping beside it she returned
and reported the matter to her mistress.   The princess was very
angry at this intrusion on her chace, and caused the intruders to be
brought before her.   But at sight of the handsome prince, her
anger fled; she entered into conversation with him, and though
the day wore on to afternoon and evening, and the prince requested
to be allowed to descend the mountains, the princess detained him,
hanging on his lips as he recountered to her his adventures and deeds
of valour.   At last she could hide her feelings no longer; she told
her love and offered him her hand.   He accepted it, not without
hesitation, for he feared that her cruel father the king would never
consent to her union with a stranger like himself.   So they resolved
to keep their marriage secret, and married they were that very
night.

But hardly had the prince won the hand of the princess than
his ambition took a higher flight, and he aimed at making himself
master of the kingdom. For that purpose he instigated his wife
to murder her father and to raise a rebellion against him.   Infatu-
ated by her love of her husband, the princess consented to plot
against her royal father's life.   But there was an obstacle to the
accomplishment of their design; for Shri Badat, the king, was a
descendant of the giants, and as such had no fear of being attacked
by sword or arrow, because these weapons could make neither
scratch nor dint on his body, and nobody knew what his soul was
made of.   Accordingly the first thing the ambitious prince had to
do was to learn the exact nature of his father-in-law's soul; and
who so well able to worm the king's secret from him as his daughter?
So one day, whether to gratify a whim or to prove his wife's fidelity,
he told her that no sooner should the leaves of a certain tree fade
and turn yellow than she should see her father no more.   Well, that

autumn—for summer was now passing—it chanced that the leaves
of the tree faded and turned yellow earlier than usual; and at sight
of the yellow leaves the princess, thinking that her father's last
hour was come, and touched perhaps with remorse for the murder
she had been revolving in her heart, went down the hill lamenting,
and so returned to Gilgit. But in the castle, to her surprise, she
found her royal sire in the enjoyment of his usual robust health and
cannibal appetite. Taken somewhat aback, she excused her abrupt
and unexpected return from her summer quarters in the hills by
saying that a holy man had foretold how with the fading leaves of
a certain tree her dear father also would fade and die. "This very
day," she said, "the leaves turned yellow, and I feared for you, and
came to throw myself at your feet. But I thank God that the
omen has not come true, and that the holy man has proved a false
prophet." The paternal heart of the ogre was touched by this
proof of filial affection, and he said, "O my affectionate daughter,
nobody in the world can kill me, for nobody knows of what my soul
is made. How can it be injured until some one knows its nature?
It is beyond a man's power to inflict harm on my body." To this
his daughter replied that her happiness depended on his life and
safety, and as she was dearest to him in all the wide world, he ought
not to fear to tell her the secret of his soul. If she only knew it,
she would be able to forestall any evil omens, to guard against any
threatened danger, and to prove her love by devoting herself to
the safety of her kind father. Yet the wary ogre distrusted her,
and, like Samson and the giants of the fairy tales, tried to put her
off by many false or evasive answers. But at last, overcome by
her importunity or mollified by her cajoleries, he revealed the fatal
secret. He told her that his soul was made of butter, and that
whenever she should see a great fire burning in or around the castle,
she might know that his last day was come; for how could the
butter of his soul hold out against the heat of the conflagration?
Little did he wot that in saying this he was betraying himself into
the hands of a weak woman and an ungrateful daughter who was
plotting against his life.

After passing a few days with her too confiding sire, the traitress
returned to her abode in the hills, where she found her beloved
spouse Shamsher anxiously expecting her. Very glad was he to
learn the secret of the king's soul, for he was resolved to spare no
pains in taking his father-in-law's life, and he now saw the road
clear to the accomplishment of his design. In the prosecution of
the plot he counted on the active assistance of the king's own
subjects, who were eager to rid themselves of the odious ogre and
so to save the lives of their remaining children from his ravening
maw. Nor was the prince deceived in his calculation; for on learning that a deliverer was at hand, the people readily gave in their
adhesion to him, and in collusion with them the plot was laid for
bearding the monster in his den. The plan had the merit of extreme

simplicity. A great fire was to be kindled round about the royal castle, and in the heat of it the king's soul of butter was expected to melt away and dissolve. A few days before the plot was to be put into execution, the prince sent down his wife to her father at Gilgit, with strict injunctions to keep their secret and so to lull the doating ogre into a sense of false security. All was now ready. At dead of night the people turned out of their homes with torches and bundles of wood in their hands. As they drew near the castle, the king's soul of butter began to feel uneasy; a restlessness came over him, and late as the hour was he sent out his daughter to learn the source of his uneasiness. The undutiful and faithless woman accordingly went out into the night, and after tarrying a while, to let the rebels with their torches draw nearer, she returned to the castle and attempted to reassure her father by telling him that his fears were vain, and that there was nothing the matter. But now the presentiment of coming evil in the king's mind was too strong to be reasoned away by his wheedling daughter; he went out from his chamber himself only to see the darkness of night lit up by the blaze of fires surrounding the castle. There was no time to hesitate or loiter. His resolution was soon taken. He leaped into the air and winged his way in the direction of Chotur Khan, a region of snow and ice among the lofty mountains which encircle Gilgit. There he hid himself under a great glacier, and there, since his butter soul could not melt in ice, he remains down to this day. Yet still the people of Gilgit believe that he will come back one day to rule over them and to devour their children with redoubled fury; hence every year on a night in November—the anniversary of the day when he was driven from Gilgit—they keep great fires burning all through the hours of darkness in order to repel his ghost, if he should attempt to return. On that night no one would dare to sleep; so to while away the time the people dance and sing about the blazing bonfires.

The general conformity of this Indian story to the Samson legend and the Slavonic and Celtic tales is sufficiently obvious. Its resemblance to them would probably be still closer if the story-teller had recorded the false or evasive answers which the ogre gave to his daughter in regard to the secret of his soul; for on the analogy of the Hebrew, Slavonic, and Celtic parallels we may suppose that the wily monster attempted to deceive her by pretending that his soul was stowed away in things with which in reality it had no connexion. Perhaps one of his answers was that his soul was in the leaves of a certain tree, and that when they turned yellow it would be a sign of his death, though as the story now runs this false prediction is put in the mouth of a third person instead of in that of the ogre himself.

While these Slavonic, Celtic, and Indian tales resemble the story of Samson and Delilah in their general scheme or plot, they differ from it in at least one important respect. For in the Samson story the reader's sympathy is all enlisted on the side of the betrayed warlock, who is represented in an amiable light as a patriot and champion of his people; we admire his marvellous feats; we pity his sufferings and death; we abhor the treachery of the artful hussy whose false protestations of affection have brought these un-merited calamities on her lover. On the other hand, in the Slavonic, Celtic, and Indian stories the dramatic interest of the situation is exactly reversed. The betrayed warlock is represented in a very unamiable light as a wretch who abuses his great power for wicked purposes; we detest his crimes, we rejoice at his downfall, and we applaud or condone the cunning of the woman who betrays him to his doom, because in doing so she merely avenges a great wrong which he has done to her or to a whole people. Thus in the two different renderings of the same general theme the parts of the villain and the victim are transposed: in the one rendering the part of the innocent victim is taken by the warlock, and the part of the artful villain by the woman; in the other rendering it is the warlock who figures as the artful villain, and it is the woman who plays the part of the innocent victim, or at all events, as in the Indian tale, of the fond wife and natural deliverer. There can be little doubt that if we had the Philistine version of the story of Samson and Delilah, we should find in it the parts of the villain and the victim transposed; we should see Samson figuring as the unscrupulous villain who robbed and murdered the defenceless Philistines, and we should see Delilah appearing as the innocent victim of his brutal violence, who by her quick wit and high courage contrived at once to avenge her own wrongs and to deliver her people from the monster who had so long and so cruelly afflicted them. It is thus that in the warfare of nations and of factions the parts of the hero and the villain are apt to shift according to the standpoint from which we view them: seen from one side the same man will appear as the whitest of heroes; seen from the other side he will appear as the blackest of villains; from the one side he will be greeted with showers of roses, from the other side he will be pelted with volleys of stones. We may almost say that every man who has made a great figure in the turbulent scenes of history is a harlequin, whose parti-coloured costume differs according as you look at him from the front or the back, from the right or the left. His friends and his foes behold him from opposite sides, and they naturally see only that particular hue of his coat which happens to be turned towards them. It is for the impartial historian to contemplate these harlequins from every side and to paint them in their coats of many colours, neither altogether so white as they appeared to their friends nor altogether so black as they seemed to their enemies.

CHAPTER III

THE BUNDLE OF LIFE

THE traveller who, quitting the cultivated lands of central Judea, rides eastwards towards the Dead Sea, traverses at first a series of rolling hills and waterless valleys covered by broom and grass. But as he pursues his way onward the scenery changes; the grass and thistles disappear, and he gradually passes into a bare and arid region, where the wide expanse of brown or yellow sand, of crumbling limestone, and of scattered shingle is only relieved by thorny shrubs and succulent creepers. Not a tree is to be seen; not a human habitation, not a sign of life meets the eye for mile after mile. Ridge follows ridge in monotonous and seemingly endless succession, all equally white, steep, and narrow, their sides furrowed by the dry beds of innumerable torrents, and their crests looming sharp and ragged against the sky above him as the traveller ascends from the broad flats of soft white marl, interspersed with flints, which divide each isolated ridge from the one beyond it. The nearer slopes of these desolate hills look as if they were torn and rent by waterspouts; the more distant heights present the aspect of gigantic dustheaps. In some places the ground gives out a hollow sound under the horse's tread; in others the stones and sand slip from beneath the animal's hoofs; and in the frequent gullies the rocks glow with a furnace heat under the pitiless sun which beats down on them out of the cloudless firmament. Here and there, as we proceed eastward, the desolation of the landscape is momentarily lightened by a glimpse of the Dead Sea, its waters of a deep blue appearing in a hollow of the hills and contrasting refreshingly with the dull drab colouring of the desert foreground. When the last ridge is surmounted and he stands on the brink of the great cliffs, a wonderful panorama bursts upon the spectator. Some two thousand feet below him lies the Dead Sea, visible in its whole length from end to end, its banks a long succession of castellated crags, bastion beyond bastion, divided by deep gorges, with white capes running out into the calm blue water, while beyond the lake rise the mountains of Moab to melt in the far distance into the azure of the sky. If he has struck the lake above the springs of Engedi, he finds himself on the summit of an amphitheatre of nearly vertical cliffs, down which a rugged winding track, or rather staircase, cut in the face of the precipice, leads to a little horse-shoe shaped plain sloping to the water's edge. It is necessary to dismount and lead the horses carefully down this giddy descent, the last of the party picking their steps very warily, for a single slip might dislodge a stone, which, hurtling down the crag, and striking on the travellers below, would precipitate them to the bottom. At the foot of the cliffs the copious warm fountain of Engedi, "the spring of the kid," bursts in a foaming cascade from the rock amid a verdurous oasis of luxuriant semi-tropical vegetation, which strikes the wayfarer all the more by contrast with the dreary waterless wilderness through which he has been toiling for many hours. That wilderness is what the ancient Hebrews called Jeshimmon, or desolation, the wilderness of Judea. From the bitter but brilliant water of the Dead Sea it stretches right up into the heart of the country, to the roots of the Mount of Olives, to within two hours of the gates of Hebron, Bethlehem, and Jerusalem.

To these dismal wilds the hunted David fled for refuge from the pursuit of his implacable enemy Saul. While he was in hiding there with the band of broken men he had gathered round him, he was visited by Abigail, the wise and beautiful wife of the rich sheep-farmer Nabal, whom the gallant outlaw had laid under a deep obligation by not stealing his sheep. Insensible of the services thus rendered to him by the caterans, the surly boor refused with contumely a request, couched in the most polite terms, which the captain of the band had sent in for the loan of provisions. The insult touched the captain's nice sense of honour to the quick, and he was marching over the hills at the head of four hundred pretty fellows, every man of them with his broadsword buckled at his side, and was making straight for the farm, when the farmer's wife met him on the moor. She had soft words to soothe the ruffled pride of the angry chieftain, and, better perhaps than words, a train of asses laden with meat and drink from the sharp-set brigands. David was melted. The beauty of the woman, her gentle words, the sight of the asses with their panniers, all had their effect. He received the wife, pleading for her husband, with the utmost courtesy, promised his protection, not without dark hints of the sight that the sun would have seen at the farm next morning if she had not met him, and so dismissed her with a blessing. The word was given. The outlaws faced to the right-about, and, followed no doubt by the asses with their panniers, marched off the way they had come. As she watched those stalwart, sunburnt figures stepping out briskly till the column disappeared over the nearest ridge, Abigail may have smiled and sighed. Then, turning homeward, she hastened with a lighter heart to the house where her boorish husband and his hinds, little wotting of what had passed on the hills, were drinking deep and late after the sheepshearing. That night over the wine she wisely said nothing. But next morning, when he was sober, she told him, and his heart died within him. The shock to his nervous system, or perhaps something stronger, was too much for him. Within ten days he was a dead man, and after a decent interval the widow was over the hills and far away with the captain of the brigands.

Among the compliments which the charming Abigail paid to the susceptible David at their first meeting, there is one which deserves our attention. She said, "And though man be risen up to pursue thee, and to seek thy soul, yet the soul of my lord shall be bound in the bundle of life with the Lord thy God; and the souls of thine enemies, them shall he sling out, as from the hollow of a sling." No doubt the language is metaphorical, but to an English writer the metaphor is strange and obscure. It implies that the souls of living people could be tied up for safety in a bundle, and that, on the contrary, when the souls were those of enemies, the bundle might be undone and the souls scattered to the winds. Such an idea could hardly have occurred to a Hebrew even as a figure of speech, unless he were familiar with an actual belief that souls could thus be treated. To us, who conceive of a soul as immanent in its body so long as life lasts, the idea conveyed by the verse in question is naturally preposterous. But it would not be so to many peoples whose theory of life differs widely from ours. There is in fact a widespread belief among savages that the soul can be, and often is, extracted from the body during the lifetime of its owner without immediately causing his death. Commonly this is done by ghosts, demons, or evil-disposed persons, who have a grudge at a man and steal his soul for the purpose of killing him; for if they succeed in their fell intent and detain the truant soul long enough, the man will fall ill and die. For that reason people who identify their souls with their shades or reflections are often in mortal terror of a camera, because they think that the photographer who has taken their likeness has abstracted their souls or shades along with it. To take a single instance out of a multitude. At a village on the lower Yukon River, in Alaska, an explorer had set up his camera to get a picture of the Eskimo as they were moving about among their houses. While he was focussing the instrument, the headman of the village came up and insisted on peeping under the cloth. Being allowed to do so he gazed agog for a minute at the moving figures on the ground-glass; then jerking his head from under the cloth he bellowed out to his people, "He has got all your shades in this box." A panic ensued among the group, and in a twinkling they disappeared helter-skelter into their houses. On this theory a camera or a packet of photographs is a box or bundle of souls, packed ready for transport like sardines in a tin.

But sometimes souls are extracted from their bodies with a kindly intention. The savage seems to think that nobody can die properly so long as his soul remains intact, whether in the body or out of the body; hence he infers that if he can contrive to draw out his soul and stow it away in some place where nothing can injure it, he will be for all practical purposes immortal so long as his soul remains unharmed and undisturbed in its haven of refuge. Hence in time of danger the wary savage will sometimes carefully extract his own soul or the soul of a friend and leave it, so to say, at deposit account in some safe place till the danger is past and he can reclaim his spiritual property. For example, many people regard the removal to a new house as a crisis fraught with peril to their souls; hence in Minahassa, a district of Celebes, at such critical times a priest collects the souls of the whole family in a bag, and keeps them there till the danger is over, when he restores them to their respective owners. Again, in Southern Celebes, when a woman's time is near, the messenger who goes to fetch the doctor or midwife takes with him a chopping-knife or something else made of iron. The thing, whatever it is, represents the woman's soul, which at this dangerous time is believed to be safer outside of her body than in it. Hence the doctor must take great care of the thing, for were it lost the woman's soul would with it be lost also. So he keeps it in his house till the confinement is over, when he gives back the precious object in return for a fee. In the Kei Islands a hollowed-out coco-nut, split in two and carefully pieced together, may sometimes be seen hanging up. This is a receptacle in which the soul of a newly-born infant is kept lest it should fall a prey to demons. For in those parts the soul does not permanently lodge in its tabernacle of clay, until the clay has taken a firm consistency. The Eskimo of Alaska adopt a similar precaution for the soul of a sick child. The medicine-man conjures it into an amulet and then stows the amulet in his medicine-bag, where, if anywhere, the soul should be out of harm's way. In some parts of South-eastern New Guinea, when a woman walks abroad carrying her baby in a bag, she "must tie a long streamer of vine of some kind to her skirt, or better still to the baby's bag, so that it trails behind her on the ground. For should, by chance, the child's spirit wander from the body it must have some means of crawling back from the ground, and what so convenient as a vine trailing on the path?

But perhaps the closest analogy to the "bundle of life" is furnished by the bundles of *churinga*, that is, flattened and elongated stones and sticks, which the Arunta and other tribes of Central Australia keep with the greatest care and secrecy in caves and crevices of the rocks. Each of these mysterious stones or sticks is intimately associated with the spirit of a member of the clan, living or dead; for as soon as the spirit of a child enters into a woman to be born, one of these holy sticks or stones is dropped on the spot where the mother felt her womb quickened. Directed by her, the father searches for the stick or stone of his child, and having found it, or carved it out of the nearest hard-wood tree, he delivers it to the headman of the district, who deposits it with the rest in the sacred store-house among the rocks. These precious sticks and stones, closely bound up with the spirits of all the members of the clan, are often carefully tied up in bundles. They constitute the most sacred possession of the tribe, and the places where they are deposited are skilfully screened from observation, the entrance to the caves being blocked up with stones arranged so naturally as to disarm suspicion. Not only the spot itself but its surroundings are sacred. The plants and trees that grow there are never touched: the wild animals that find their way thither are never molested. And if a man fleeing from his enemies or from the avenger of blood succeeds in reaching the sanctuary, he is safe so long as he remains within its bounds. The loss of their *churinga,* as they call the sacred sticks and stones thus associated with the spirits of all the living and all the dead members of the community, is the most serious evil that can befall a tribe. Robbed of them by inconsiderate white men, the natives have been known to stay in camp for a fortnight, weeping and wailing over their loss and plastering their bodies with white pipeclay, the emblem of mourning for the dead.

In these beliefs and practices of the Central Australians with regard to the *churinga* we have, as Messrs. Spencer and Gillen justly observe, "a modification of the idea which finds expression in the folklore of so many peoples, and according to which primitive man, regarding his soul as a concrete object, imagines that he can place it in some secure spot apart, if needs be, from his body, and thus, if the latter be in any way destroyed, the spirit part of him still persists unharmed." Not that the Arunta of the present day believe these sacred sticks and stones to be the actual receptacles of their spirits in the sense that the destruction of one of the sticks or stones would of necessity involve the destruction of the man, woman, or child whose spirit is associated with it. But in their traditions we meet with clear traces of a belief that their ancestors did really deposit their spirits in these sacred objects. For example, we are told that some men of the Wild Cat totem kept their spirits in their *churinga,* which they used to hang up on a sacred pole in the camp when they went out to hunt; and on their return from the chase they would take down the *churinga* from the pole and carry them about as before. The intention of thus hanging up the *churinga* on a pole when they went out hunting may have been to put their souls in safe keeping till they came back.

Thus there is fair ground to think that the bundles of sacred sticks and stones, which are still treasured so carefully in secret places by the Arunta and other tribes of Central Australia, were formerly believed to house the souls of every member of the community. So long as these bundles remained securely tied up in the sanctuary, so long, might it be thought, was it well with the souls of all the people; but once open the bundles and scatter their precious contents to the winds, and the most fatal consequences would follow. It would be rash to assert that the primitive Semites ever kept their souls for safety in sticks and stones which they deposited in caves and crannies of their native wilderness; but it is not rash to affirm that some such practice would explain in an easy and natural way the words of Abigail to the hunted outlaw, "And though man be risen up to pursue thee, and to seek thy soul, yet the soul of my lord shall be bound in the bundle of life with the Lord thy God; and the souls of thine enemies, them shall he sling out, as from the hollow of a sling."

Be that as it may, the Hebrews would seem even down to comparatively late times to have been familiar with a form of witchcraft which aimed at catching and detaining the souls of living persons with the intent to do them grievous hurt. The witches who practised this black art were formally denounced by the prophet Ezekiel in the following terms:—

"And thou, son of man, set thy face against the daughters of thy people, which prophesy out of their own heart; and prophesy thou against them, and say, Thus saith the Lord God: Woe to the women that sew fillets upon all elbows, and make kerchiefs for the head of *persons* of every stature to hunt souls! Will ye hunt the souls of my people, and save souls alive for yourselves? And ye have profaned me among my people for handfuls of barley and for pieces of bread, to slay the souls that should not die, and to save the souls alive that should not live, by your lying to my people that hearken unto lies. Wherefore thus saith the Lord God: Behold I am against your fillets, wherewith ye hunt the souls, and I will tear them from your arms; and I will let the souls which ye hunt go free like birds. Your kerchiefs also will I tear, and deliver my people out of your hand, and they shall be no more in your hand to be hunted; and ye shall know that I am the Lord." [1]

The nefarious practices of these women, which the prophet denounces, apparently consisted in attempts to catch stray souls in fillets and cloths, and so to kill some people by keeping their souls in durance vile, and to save the lives of others, probably of sick people, by capturing their vagabond souls and restoring them to their bodies. Similar devices have been and still are adopted for the same purpose by sorcerers and witches in many parts of the world. For example, Fijian chiefs used to whisk away the souls of criminals in scarves, whereupon the poor wretches, deprived of this indispensable part of their persons, used to pine and die. The sorcerers of Danger Island, in the Pacific, caught the souls of sick people in snares, which they set up near the houses of the sufferers, and watched till a soul came fluttering into the trap and was entangled in its meshes, after which the death of the patient was, sooner or later, inevitable. The snares were made of stout cinet with loops of various sizes adapted to catch souls of all sizes, whether

---

[1] Ezekiel xiii. 17-21. Many years ago my friend W. Robertson Smith suggested to me the true interpretation of this passage, which seems to have escaped the commentators. Robertson Smith's explanation is accepted by A. Lods, *La Croyance à la Vie Future et le Culte des Morts dans l'Antiquité Israélite* (Paris, 1906), i. 47 *sq.* In verse 20, following I. W. Rothstein (in R. Kittel's *Biblia Hebraica*, ii. 761), I read פֹּה for שָׁם ("there") and omit the first לִפְרֹחוֹת ("like birds") as a doublet of the second, if indeed both should not be omitted as a gloss. The word (פֹּרְחוֹת) is Aramaic, not Hebrew. Further, for אֶת נְפָשִׁים ("the souls," an unheard-of plural of נֶפֶשׁ) I read אֹתָם חָפְשִׁים ("them free") with Cornill and other critics.

large or small, whether fat or thin. Among the negroes of West Africa "witches are continually setting traps to catch the soul that wanders from the body when a man is sleeping; and when they have caught this soul, they tie it up over the canoe fire and its owners sickens as the soul shrivels. This is merely a regular line of business, and not an affair of individual hate or revenge. The witch does not care whose dream-soul gets into the trap, and will restore it on payment. Also witch-doctors, men of unblemished professional reputation, will keep asylums for lost souls, *i.e*, souls who have been out wandering and found on their return to their body that their place had been filled up by a Sisa, a low-class soul. . . . These doctors keep souls, and administer them to patients who are short of the article." Among the Baoules of the Ivory Coast it happened once that a chief's soul was extracted by the magic of an enemy, who succeeded in shutting it up in a box. To recover it, two men held a garment of the sufferer, while a witch performed certain enchantments. After a time she declared that the soul was now in the garment, which was accordingly rolled up and hastily wrapped about the invalid for the purpose of restoring his spirit to him. Malay wizards catch the souls of women whom they love in the folds of their turbans, and then go about with the dear souls in their girdles by day and sleep with them under their pillows by night. Among the Toradjas of Central Celebes the priest who accompanied an armed force on an expedition used to wear a string of sea-shells hanging down over his breast and back for the purpose of catching the souls of the enemy; the shells were branched and hooked, and it was supposed that, once the souls were conjured into the shells, the branches and hooks would prevent them from escaping. The way in which the priest set and baited this soul-trap was as follows. When the warriors had entered the hostile territory, the priest went by night to the village which they intended to attack, and there, close by the entrance, he laid down his string of shells on the path so as to form a circle, and inside of the circle he buried an egg and the guts of a fowl, from which omens had been drawn before the troop set out from their own land. Then the priest took up the string of shells and waved it seven times over the spot, calling quietly on the souls of the enemy and saying, "Oh, soul of So-and-So," mentioning the name of one of the inhabitants of the village, "come, tread on my fowl; thou are guilty, thou hast done wrong, come!" Then he waited, and if the string of shells gave out a tinkling sound, it was a sign that the soul of an enemy had really come and was held fast by the shells. Next day the man, whose soul had thus been ensnared, would be drawn, in spite of himself, to the spot where the foes who had captured his soul were lying in wait, and thus he would fall an easy prey to their weapons.

Such practices may serve to explain those proceedings of the Hebrew witches against which Ezekiel fulminated. These abandoned women seem to have caught vagrant souls in kerchiefs which they threw over the heads of their victims, and to have detained their spiritual captives in fillets which they sewed to their own elbows.

Thus the Hebrews apparently retained down to historical times the conception of the soul as a separable thing, which can be removed from a man's body in his lifetime, either by the wicked art of witches, or by the owner's voluntary act in order to deposit it for a longer or shorter time in a place of safety. If one great prophet reveals to us the Hebrew witch at her infernal business of decoying the souls of others, another great prophet perhaps affords us a glimpse of a fine lady of Jerusalem carrying her own soul about with her in a little casket. After describing, in a strain of Puritan invective and scorn, the haughty daughters of Zion who tripped about with languishing eyes, mincing steps, and tinkling feet, Isaiah proceeds to give a long catalogue of the jewels and trinkets, the robes and shawls, the veils and turbans, all the finery and frippery of these fashionable and luxurious dames. In his list of feminine gauds he mentions "houses of the soul." The expression thus literally translated is unique in the Old Testament. Modern translators and commentators, following Jerome, render it "perfume boxes," "scent-bottles," or the like. But it may well be that these "houses of the soul were amulets in which the soul of the wearer was supposed to lodge. The commentators on the passage recognize that many of the trinkets in the prophet's list were probably charms, just as personal ornaments often are in the East to the present day. The very word which follows "houses of the souls" in the text is rendered "amulets" in the English Revised Version; it is derived from a verb meaning 'to whisper," "to charm."

But this view of the "houses of the soul" does not necessarily exclude their identification with scent-bottles. In the eyes of a people who, like the Hebrews, identified the principle of life with the breath, the mere act of smelling a perfume might easily assume a spiritual aspect; the scented breath inhaled might seem an accession of life, an addition made to the essence of the soul. Hence it would be natural to regard the fragrant object itself, whether a scent-bottle, incense, or a flower, as a centre of radiant spiritual energy, and therefore as a fitting place into which to breathe out the soul whenever it was deemed desirable to do so for a time. Far-fetched as this idea may appear to us, it may seem natural enough to the folk and to their best interpreters the poets :—

> "I sent thee late a rosy wreath,
>   Not so much honouring thee
> As giving it a hope that there
>   It could not wither'd be;
> But thou thereon didst only breathe
>   And sent'st it back to me;
> Since when it grows, and smells, I swear,
>   Not of itself but thee!"

Or again:

"Ihr vebluhet, susse Rosen,
Meine Liebe trug euch nicht."

But if beauty can thus be thought to give of her life, her soul, to the soul of the rose to keep it fadeless, it is not extravagant to suppose that she can breathe her soul also into her scent-bottle. At all events these old-world fancies, if such indeed they are, would explain very naturally why a scent-bottle should be called a "house of the soul." But the folk-lore of scents has yet to be studied. In investigating it, as every other branch of folk-lore, the student may learn much from the poets, who perceive by intuition what most of us have to learn by a laborious collection of facts. Indeed, without some touch of poetic fancy, it is hardly possible to enter into the heart of the people. A frigid rationalist will knock in vain at the magic rose-wreathed portal of fairyland. The porter will not open to Mr. Gradgrind.

CHAPTER IV

THE WITCH OF ENDOR

ONE of the most tragic figures in the history of Israel is that of Saul, the first king of the nation. Dissatisfied with the rule of pontiffs who professed to govern them in the name and under the direct guidance of the deity, the people had clamoured for a civil king, and the last of the pontiffs, the prophet Samuel, had reluctantly yielded to their importunity and anointed Saul king of Israel. The revolution thus effected was such as might have taken place in the Papal States, if ever the inhabitants, weary of ecclesiastical oppression and misgovernment, had risen against the Popes, and compelled the reigning pontiff, while he still clutched the heavenly keys, to resign the earthly sceptre into the hands of a secular monarch. A shrewd man of affairs as well as an ecclesiastic of the most rigid type, Samuel had dexterously contrived not only to anoint but to nominate the new king on whom the hopes of Israel now centered.

The man of his choice was well fitted to win the admiration and attract the homage of the crowd. His tall and stately form, his gallant bearing, his skilful generalship and dauntless courage on the field of battle, all marked him out as a natural leader of men. Yet, under a showy exterior, this dashing and popular soldier concealed some fatal infirmities—a jealous and suspicious disposition, a choleric temper, a weakness of will, a vacillation of purpose, and, above all, a brooding melancholy under which his intellect, never of a high order, sometimes trembled on the verge of insanity. In such dark hours the profound dejection which clouded his brain could only be lightened and dispelled by the soothing strains of solemn music; and one of the most graphic pictures painted for us by the Hebrew historian is that of the handsome king sitting sunk in gloom, while the minstrel boy, the ruddy-cheeked David, stood before him discoursing sweet music on the trembling strings of the harp, till the frown passed from the royal brow and the sufferer found a truce to his uneasy thoughts.

Perhaps with his keen eye Samuel had detected and even counted on these weaknesses when, bowing to the popular will, he ostensibly consented to be superseded in the supreme direction of affairs. He may have reckoned on setting up Saul as an ornamental figure-head, a florid mask, which, under the martial features of the brave but pliable soldier, should conceal the stern visage of the inflexible prophet; he may have expected to treat the king as a crowned and sceptred puppet, who would dance on the national stage to the tune played by his ghostly adviser behind the scenes. If such were his calculations when he raised Saul to the throne, they were fully justified by the event. For so long as Samuel lived, Saul was little more than a tool in hands far stronger than his own. The prophet was indeed one of those masterful natures, those fanatics cast in an iron mould, who, mistaking their own unbending purpose for the will of heaven, march forward unswervingly to their goal, trampling down all opposition, their hearts steeled against every tender emotion of humanity and pity. While Saul was content to do the bidding of this imperious mentor, committing his conscience to him as to a father confessor, he was graciously permitted to strut before the eyes of the vulgar wearing his shadowy crown; but no sooner did he dare to diverge by a hair's breadth from the ruthless commands laid on him by his spiritual director, than Samuel broke his puppet king and threw him away as an instrument that had ceased to serve his purpose. The prophet secretly appointed a successor to Saul in the person of the minstrel David, and indignantly turning his back on the now repentant and conscience-stricken king, he refused to see him again and continued to mourn over him as dead till the end of his life.

After that, things went ill with Saul. Deprived of the strong arm on which he had long trustfully leaned, he followed a course even more wayward and erratic. His melancholy deepened. His suspicions multiplied. His temper, always uncertain, became uncontrollable. He gave way to outbursts of fury. He attempted the life, not only of David, but of his own son Jonathan, and though these fits of passionate anger were sometimes followed by fits of as passionate remorse, the steady deterioration of his once noble nature was unmistakable.

While the clouds thus gathered thick about his setting sun, it happened that the Philistines, against whom he had waged a lifelong war, invaded the land in greater force than ever. Saul mustered the militia of Israel to oppose them, and the two armies encamped on opposite hill-slopes with the broad valley of Jezreel lying between them. It was the eve of battle. The morrow would decide the

fate of Israel. The king looked forward to the decisive struggle
with deep misgiving. A weight like lead hung on his drooping
spirits. He deemed himself forsaken of God, for all his attempts to
lift the veil and pry into the future by means of the legitimate forms
of divination had proved fruitless. The prophets were silent: the
oracles were dumb; no vision of the night brightened with a ray of
hope his heavy and dreamless sleep. Even music, which once
could charm away his cares, was no longer at his command. His
own violence had banished the deft musician, whose cunning hand
had so often swept the strings and wakened all their harmonies to
lap his troubled soul in momentary forgetfulness of sorrow. In
his despair the king's mind reverted irresistibly to Samuel, the
faithful counsellor to whom in happier days he had never looked in
vain for help. But Samuel was in his grave at Ramah. Yet a
thought struck the king. Might he not summon up the dead seer
from the grave and elicit words of hope and comfort from his ghostly
lips? The thing was possible, but difficult; for he had himself
driven into exile all the practitioners of the black art. He inquired
of his servants, and learned from them that a witch still lived at the
village of Endor, not many miles away to the north, among the hills
on the farther side of the valley. The king resolved to consult her
and, if possible, to set his harassing doubts and fears at rest. It was
a hazardous enterprise, for between him and the witch's home lay
the whole army of the Philistines. To go by day would have been
to court death. It was necessary to wait for nightfall.

Having made all his dispositions for battle, the king retired to
his tent, but not to sleep. The fever in his blood forbade repose,
and he impatiently expected the hour when he could set out under
cover of darkness. At last the sun went down, the shadows deepened,
and the tumult of the camp subsided into silence. The king now
laid aside the regal pomp in which he had but lately shown himself to
the army, and muffling his tall figure in a common robe he lifted the
flap of the tent and, followed by two attendants, stole out into the
night. Around him in the starlight lay the slumbering forms of
his soldiers, stretched in groups on the bare ground about their
piled arms, the dying embers of the fires casting here and there a
fitful gleam on the sleepers. On the opposite hillside, far as the eye
could see, twinkled the watch-fires of the enemy, and the distant
sounds of revelry and music, borne across the valley on the night
wind, told of the triumph which the insolent foe anticipated on the
morrow.

Striking straight across the plain the three adventurers came to
the foot of the hills, and giving a wide berth to the last outpost of
the Philistine camp, they began the ascent. A desolate track led
them over the shoulder of the hill to the miserable village of Endor,
its mud-built hovels stuck to the side of the rocks on the bare stony
declivity. Away to the north Mount Tabor loomed up black and
massive against the sky, and in the farthest distance the snowy top

of Herman showed pale and ghost-like in the starlight. But the travellers had neither leisure nor inclination to survey the nocturnal landscape. The king's guide led the way to a cottage; a light was burning in the window, and he tapped softly at the door. It seemed that the party was expected, for a woman's voice from within bade them enter. They did so, and closing the door behind them, they stood in the presence of the witch. The sacred writer has not described her appearance, so we are free to picture her according to our fancy. She may have been young and fair, with raven locks and lustrous eyes, or she may have been a wizened, toothless hag, with meeting nose and chin, blear eyes and grizzled hair, bent double with age and infirmity. We cannot tell, and the king was doubtless too preoccupied to pay much attention to her aspect. He bluntly told her the object of his visit. "Divine unto me," he said, "I pray thee, by the familiar spirit, and bring me up whomsoever I shall name unto thee." But the beldame protested, and reminded her visitor, in whom she did not recognize the king, of the royal proclamation against witches and warlocks, asserting that it was as much as her life was worth to comply with the request. Only when the tall stranger, with an air between entreaty and command, assured her on his honour that no harm should befall her, did she at last consent to exert her uncanny powers on his behalf. She asked, "Whom shall I bring up unto thee?" And he said, "Bring me up Samuel." The demand startled the necromancer, and looking hard at her visitor she discerned him to be the king. In great alarm, believing she had been caught in a trap, she cried out, "Why hast thou deceived me? for thou art Saul." But the king pacified her with an assurance of his royal clemency and bade her proceed with her incantations. She settled herself to her task accordingly, and gazing intently into what seemed to her visitors mere vacancy, it was soon manifest by her wild and haggard look that she saw something invisible to them. The king asked her what she saw. "I see," said she, "a god coming up out of the earth." Saul asked, "What form is he of?" And she answered, "An old man cometh up; and he is covered with a robe." So the king perceived that it was the ghost of Samuel, and he bowed with his face to the ground, and did obeisance. But the ghost asked sternly, 'Why hast thou disquieted me, to bring me up?" The king replied, "I am sore distressed; for the Philistines make war against me, and God is departed from me, and answereth me no more, neither by prophets, nor by dreams: therefore I have called thee, that thou mayest make known unto me what I shall do." But the unhappy monarch found the ghost as hard and implacable as the living prophet had been when he turned his back in anger on the king who had presumed to disobey his behest. In pitiless tones the inexorable old man demanded of the trembling suppliant how he dared, he the forsaken of God, to consult him, the prophet of God? He upbraided him once more with his disobedience: he reminded him of his prophecy that the

kingdom should be rent from him and given to David : he announced
the fulfilment of the prediction ; and he wound up his fierce invective
by declaring that to-morrow should witness the defeat of Israel by
the Philistines, and that before another sun had set Saul and his
sons should be with him in the nether world. With these dreadful
words the grim spectre sank into the earth, and Saul fell to the
ground in a faint.

From this graphic narrative we learn that the practice of necromancy, or the evocation of the spirits of the dead for the purpose of
consulting them oracularly, was familiar in ancient Israel, and that
severe legislative prohibitions were unable wholly to suppress it.
How deeply rooted the custom was in the popular religion or superstition of the people we can see from the behaviour of Saul, who in
his dire distress did not hesitate to call in the services of the very
same necromancers whom in the days of his prosperity he had laid
under a ban. His example is typical of that tendency to relapse
into heathenism which the prophets of Israel observed and deplored
in their countrymen, and which always manifested itself most
prominently in seasons of extraordinary calamity or danger when
the ordinances of the orthodox religion appeared to be unavailing.
A law of Israel, which in its existing form is probably much later than
the time of Saul but may nevertheless embody a very ancient usage,
denounced the penalty of death by stoning against all who had
familiar spirits or were wizards, that is, apparently, against all who
professed to evoke the souls of the dead for the sake of consulting
them oracularly. Yet among the pagan practices revived long
after the days of Saul by King Manasseh was that of necromancy ;
from the holes and corners into which the practitioners of that black
art had been driven by the terror of the law, the superstitious
monarch brought them forth and established them publicly in the
light of day. However, in his sweeping reformation of the national
religion the pious King Josiah soon afterwards relegated all
necromancers, witches, and wizards to the criminal classes, from
which they had for a short period emerged.

The account of the interview of Saul with the ghost of Samuel
clearly implies that the phantom was visible only to the witch, but
that the king, though he did not see it, was able to hear its voice
and to answer it directly. We may safely conclude that this was
one of the regular ways in which Israelitish witches and wizards
professed to hold converse with the dead ; they pretended to conjure
up and to see the ghost, while their dupes saw nothing but heard
a voice speaking, which, in their simplicity, they took to be that of
the spirit, though in reality it would commonly be the voice either
of the wizard himself or of a confederate. In such cases, whatever
the source of the sound, it appeared to proceed not from the mouth
of the wizard, but from a point outside him, which the credulous
inquirer supposed to be the station of the invisible ghost. Such
audible effects could easily be produced by ventriloquism, which

has the advantage of enabling the necromancer to work without the assistance of a confederate, and so to lessen the chance of detection.

The witch told Saul that the ghost of Samuel rose out of the earth, and through the exertion of her vocal talent she may have caused to issue apparently from the ground a hollow and squeaky voice which the king mistook for the accents of the deceased seer; for in such hollow, squeaky tones were ghosts commonly supposed to discourse from the ground. However, the necromancer did not always take the trouble of projecting his voice out of himself; he was often content to bring it up from his own inside and to palm it off on his gullible hearers as the voice of his familiar spirit or of the worshipful ghost. Hence the familiar spirit or the ghost was said to be inside the necromancer: the supernatural accents appeared to issue from his stomach. But wherever the voice may have seemed to come from, whether from the bowels of the earth or from the bowels of the conjurer, it is probable that the ghost himself always modestly kept in the background; for we can hardly suppose that in the rudimentary state of Hebrew art Hebrew wizards were able, like their brethren of a later age, to astonish and terrify believers by exhibiting to them in a dark room the figures of hobgoblins, which, painted in inflammable pigments on the walls, and ignited at the proper moment by the application of a torch, suddenly burst out from the gloom in lurid splendour to confirm the mysteries of faith by the demonstrations of science.

The practice of necromancy was probably common to the Hebrews with other branches of the Semitic race. A clear reference to it appears to be contained in the twelfth canto of the Gilgamesh epic. There the hero Gilgamesh is represented mourning for his dead friend Eabani. In his sorrow he appeals to the gods to bring up for him the soul of his departed comrade from the nether world. But one after another the deities confess themselves powerless to grant his request. At last he prays to Nergal, the god of the dead, saying, "Break open the chamber of the grave *and open the ground*, that the spirit of Eabani, like a wind, may rise out of the ground." The deity graciously listened to his prayer. "He broke open the chamber of the grave and opened the ground; and caused the spirit of Eabani to rise out of the ground like a wind." With the ghost thus summoned from the vasty deep Gilgamesh converses, and learns from him the mournful state of the dead in the nether world, where is the devouring worm and all things are cloaked in dust. However, the gloominess of the picture is a little relieved by the information which the apparition vouchsafes as to the solace which the rites of burial afford to the souls of warriors fallen in battle, compared with the deplorable condition of those whose corpses have been suffered to welter unburied on the field.

The ancient Greeks were familiar with the practice of evoking the souls of the dead in order either to obtain information from them or to appease their wrath. The first instance of necromancy in Greek literature occurs in the famous passage of the *Odyssey*, where Ulysses sails to the gloomy land on the utmost verge of Ocean, and there summons up the ghosts from the underworld. In order that he may get speech of them, he has to dig a trench and sacrifice sheep over it, allowing their blood to drain into its depth. Thereupon the weak and thirsty ghosts gather at the trench, and, after quaffing the blood, say their sooth to the hero, who sits beside it, drawn sword in hand, keeping order among the shades and suffering none to gulp the precious liquid out of his turn.

In ancient Greece it would seem that the practice of calling up the shades from the nether regions was not carried on by necromancers at any place indiscriminately, but was restricted to certain definite spots which were supposed to communicate directly with the underworld by passages or apertures, through which the spirits could come up and go down as they were summoned or dismissed. Such spots were called oracles of the dead, and at them alone, so far as appears, could legitimate business with the shades of the departed be transacted.

Of these oracles of the dead there was one at Aornum in Thesprotis, where the legendary musician Orpheus is said to have called up, but called in vain, the soul of his loved and lost Eurydice. In a later age the tyrant Periander of Corinth sent to the same oracle to consult the ghost of his dead wife Melissa about a deposit which a stranger had left in his charge, and which had been mislaid. But the ghost refused to answer his question, declaring that she was cold and naked, because the clothes which he had buried with her body were of no use to her, not having been burnt. On receiving this answer Periander issued a proclamation that all the women of Corinth should assemble in the sanctuary of Hera. They did so accordingly in all their finery as for a festival; but no sooner were they gathered than the tyrant surrounded the gay assembly with his guards, and caused every woman in it, mistress and maid alike, to be stripped of her clothes, which he thereupon piled up in a pit and burned for the benefit of his deceased spouse. Transmitted by the medium of fire, the garments reached their address; for when Periander afterwards sent again to the oracle and repeated his question about the deposit, his wife's ghost, now warm and comfortable, answered readily. The whole vicinity of this oracular seat would seem to have been associated with, if not haunted by, the spirits of the dead; for the names of the infernal rivers were given to the neighbouring waters. Beside it ran the Acheron, and not far off flowed the Cocytus, "named of lamentation loud heard on the rueful stream." The exact spot where this commerce with the other world was maintained is perhaps to be identified with a hamlet now called Glyky, where some fragments of granite columns and pieces of a white marble cornice may mark the site of an ancient temple. The river Acheron, now called the Suliotiko or Phanariotiko river, here issues from the wild and barren mountains of the once famous Suli, to wander, a sluggish, turbid, weedy stream, through a wide stretch of swampy plain till it falls into the sea. Before entering the plain from the mountains, which stand up behind it like a huge grey wall, the river traverses a profound and gloomy gorge, one of the darkest and deepest of the glens of Greece. On either side precipices rise sheer from the water's edge to a height of hundreds of feet, their ledges and crannies tufted with dwarf oaks and shrubs. Higher up, where the sides of the glen recede from the perpendicular, the mountains soar to a height of over three thousand feet, the black pine-woods which cling to their precipitous sides adding to the sombre magnificence of the scene. A perilous foot-path leads along a narrow ledge high up on the mountain side, from which the traveler gazes down into the depths of the tremendous ravine, where the rapid river may be seen rushing and foaming along, often plunging in a cascade into a dark abyss, but so far below him that even the roar of the waterfall is lost in mid-air before it can reach his ear. The whole landscape combines the elements of grandeur, solitude, and desolation in a degree that is fitted to oppress the mind with a sense of awe and gloom, and thereby to predispose it for communion with supernatural beings. No wonder that in these rugged mountains, these dreary fens, these melancholy streams, the ancients fancied they beheld the haunts of the spirits of the dead.

Another oracle of the dead was established at Heraclea in Bithynia. The Spartan King Pausanias, who defeated the Persians in the battle of Plataea, resorted to this oracle, and there attempted to summon up and propitiate the ghost of a Byzantine maiden named Cleonice, whom he had accidentally killed. Her spirit appeared to him and announced in ambiguous language that all his troubles would cease when he should return to Sparta. The prophecy was fulfilled by the king's speedy death.

We have no information as to the mode in which the ghosts were supposed to appear and reply to questions at these places; hence we cannot say whether the phantoms revealed themselves to the inquirer himself or only to the wizard who conjured them up; nor again do we know whether the person who was favoured with these manifestations beheld them awake or in dreams. However, at some Greek oracles of the dead the communication with the souls of the departed is known to have taken place in sleep. Such, for example, was the custom at the oracle of the soothsayer Mopsus in Cilicia. Plutarch tells us that on one occasion the governor of Cilicia, a sceptic in religion and a friend of Epicurean philosophers, who derided the supernatural, resolved to test the oracle. For that purpose he wrote a question on a tablet, and without revealing what he had written to anybody he sealed up the tablet and entrusted it to a freedman, with orders to submit the question to the ghostly seer. Accordingly the man slept that

night, according to custom, in the shrine of Mopsus, and next
morning he reported to the governor that he had dreamed a dream.
He thought he saw a handsome man standing by him, who opened
his mouth, and, having uttered the single work "Black," immediately vanished.   The friends of the governor, who had assembled
to hear and to quiz the messenger from the other world, were at a
loss what to make of this laconic message, but no sooner did the
governor himself receive it than he fell on his knees in an attitude
of devotion.   The reason for this very unusual posture was revealed
when the seal of the tablet was broken and its contents read aloud.
For the question which the governor had written therein was this,
"Shall I sacrifice a white bull or a black?"   The appropriateness
of the answer staggered even the incredulous Epicurean philosophers,
and as for the governor himself, he sacrificed the black bull and
continued to revere the dead soothsayer Mopsus to the end of his
days.

The pious Plutarch, who reports with obvious satisfaction this
triumphant refutation of shallow infidelity, has related another
incident of the same sort which was said to have occurred in Italy.
A certain very rich man named Elysius, a native of the Greek city
of Terina in Bruttium, lost his son and heir, Euthynus, by a sudden
and mysterious death.   Fearing that there might have been foul
play in this loss of the heir to all his riches, the anxious father had
recourse to an oracle of the dead.   There he offered a sacrifice, and
then, in accordance with the custom of the sanctuary, he fell asleep
and dreamed a dream.   It seemed to him that he saw his own father,
and begged and prayed him to help in tracking down the author of
his son's death.   "For that very purpose am I come," answered
the ghost, "and I beg you will accept my message from this young
man," pointing, as he said so, to a youth who followed at his heels,
and who resembled to the life the son whose loss Elysius mourned.
Startled by the likeness, Elysius asked the young man, "And who
are you?" to which the phantom answered, "I am your son's
genius.   Take that."   So saying, he handed to Elysius a tablet
inscribed with some verses, which declared that his son had died a
natural death, because death was better for him than life.

In antiquity the Nasamones, a tribe of northern Libya, used to
seek for oracular dreams by sleeping on the tombs of their ancestors;
probably they imagined that the souls of the departed rose from
their graves to advise and comfort their descendants.   A similar
custom is still practised by some of the Tuaregs of the Sahara.
When the men are away on distant expeditions, their wives, dressed
in their finest clothes, will go and lie on ancient tombs, where they
call up the soul of one who will give them news of their husbands.
At their call a spirit named Idebni appears in the form of a man.
If the woman contrives to please this spirit, he tells her all that has
happened on the expedition; but if she fails to win his favour, he
strangles her.   Similarly, "near the Wady Augidit, in the Northern

Sahara, is a group of great elliptical tombs. The Azgar woman, when desiring news of an absent husband, brother, or lover, goes to these graves and sleeps among them. She is thought to be sure to receive visions which will give her the news she seeks." So, too, the Toradjas of Central Celebes will sometimes go and sleep upon a grave in order to receive advice from the ghost in a dream.

The most elaborate description of the evocation of a ghost in Greek literature is to be found in Aeschylus's tragedy, *The Persians*. The scene of the play is laid at the tomb of King Darius, where Queen Atossa, the wife of Xerxes, is anxiously waiting for news of her husband and the mighty host which he had led against Greece. A messenger arrives with tidings of the total defeat of the Persians at Salamis. In her grief and consternation the queen resolves to summon up the ghost of Darius from the grave, and to seek counsel of him in the great emergency. For that purpose she offers libations of milk, honey, water, wine, and olive oil at the tomb, while at the same time the chorus chants hymns calling on the gods of the nether world to send up the soul of the dead king to the light of day. The ghost accordingly emerges from the earth, and learning of the disaster that has befallen the Persian arms, he gives advice and warning to his afflicted people. In this account it is clearly implied that the ghost appears in broad daylight, and not merely in a dream, to those who have evoked it; but whether the poet is describing a Greek or a Persian form of necromancy, or is simply drawing on his own imagination, we cannot say for certain. Probably the description is based on rites commonly performed by Greek necromancers, either at the regular oracles of the dead, or at the graves of the particular persons whose ghosts they desired to consult. The Pythagorean philosopher Apollonius of Tyana is reported by his biographer Philostratus to have conjured up the soul of Achilles from his grave in Thessaly. The hero appeared from the barrow in the likeness of a tall and handsome young man, and entered into conversation with the sage in the most affable manner, complaining that the Thessalians had long since ceased to bring offerings to his tomb, and begging him to remonstrate with them on their negligence. In Pliny's youth a certain grammarian named Apion professed to have evoked the shade of Homer and questioned the poet as to his parents and his native land, but he refused to reveal the answers which he received from the ghost; hence later ages have not benefitted by this bold attempt to solve the Homeric problem at the fountain head.

The poet Lucan has given us, in his usual tawdry bombastic style, a tedious report of an interview which, according to the bard, Sextus Pompeius, son of Pompey the Great, had with a Thessalian witch before the battle of Pharsalia. Anxious to learn the issue of the war, the unworthy son of a great father, as Lucan calls him, has recourse, not to the legitimate oracles of the gods, but to the vile arts of witchcraft and necromancy. At his request a foul hag, whose dwelling is among the tombs, restores an unburied corpse to life, and the soul thus temporarily replaced in its earthly tabernacle tells of the commotion which it has witnessed among the shades at the prospect of the catastrophe so soon to befall the Roman world. Having delivered his message, the dead man requests as a particular favour to be allowed to die a second time for good and all. The witch grants his request, and considerately erects a pyre for his convenience, to which the corpse walks unassisted and is there comfortably burnt to ashes. Thessalian witches were certainly notorious in antiquity, and it is likely enough that necromancy was one of the black arts which they professed; but no reliance can be placed on Lucan's highly coloured description of the rites which they observed in evoking the ghosts. More probable is the account which Horace gives of the proceedings of two witches, whom he represents as pouring the blood of a black lamb into a trench for the purpose of calling up ghosts to answer questions. Tibullus speaks of a witch who conjured up the shades from their tombs by her chants; and in the reign of Tiberius a high-born but feeble-minded youth, named Libo, who dabbled in the black art, requested a certain Junius to evoke the spirits of the dead for him by incantations.

More than one of the wicked Roman emperors are said to have had recourse to necromancy in the hope of allaying those terrors with which the memory of their crimes, like avenging spirits, visited their uneasy consciences. We are told that the monster Nero never knew peace of mind again after he had murdered his mother Agrippina: he often confessed that he was haunted by her spectre and by the Furies with whips and burning torches, and it was in vain that by magic rites he conjured up her ghost and attempted to appease her anger. Similarly, the crazed and bloody tyrant Caracalla imagined that the phantoms of his father Severus and of his murdered brother Geta pursued him with drawn swords, and to obtain some alleviation of these horrors he called in the help of wizards. Among the ghosts which they evoked for him were those of the emperor's father and the Emperor Commodus. But of all the shades thus summoned to his aid none deigned to hold converse with the imperial assassin except the kindred spirit of Commodus, and even from him no words of consolation or hope could be elicited, nothing but dark hints of a fearful judgment to come, which only served to fill the guilty soul of Caracalla with a fresh access of terror.

The art of necromancy has been practised by barbarous as well as civilized peoples. In some African tribes the practice has prevailed of consulting the ghosts of dead kings or chiefs as oracles through the medium of a priest or priestess, who professed to be inspired by the soul of a deceased ruler and to speak in his name. For example, among the Baganda of Central Africa a temple was built for the ghost of each dead king, and in its lower jawbone was reverently preserved; for curiously enough the part of his body to which the ghost of a dead Baganda man clings most persistently is his jawbone. The temple, a large conical hut of the usual pattern, was divided into two chambers, an outer and an inner, and in the inner chamber or holy of holies the precious jawbone was kept for safety in a cell dug in the floor. The prophet or medium, whose business it was from time to time to be inspired by the ghost of the dead monarch, dedicated himself to his holy office by drinking a draught of beer and a draught of milk out of the royal skull. When the ghost held a reception, the jawbone, wrapt in a decorated packet, was brought forth from the inner shrine and set on a throne in the outer chamber, where the people assembled to hear the oracle. On such occasions the prophets stepped up to the throne, and addressing the spirit informed him of the business in hand. Then he smoked one or two pipes of homegrown tobacco, and the fumes bringing on the prophetic fit he began to rave and speak in the very voice and with the characteristic turns of speech of the departed monarch; for the king's soul was now supposed to be in him. However, his rapid utterances were hard to understand, and a priest was in attendance to interpret them to the inquirer. The living king thus consulted his dead predecessors periodically on affairs of state, visiting first one and then another of the temples in which their sacred relics were preserved with religious care.

Among the Bantu tribes who inhabit the great tableland of Northern Rhodesia the spirits of dead chiefs sometimes take possession of the bodies of live men or women and prophesy through their mouths. When the spirit thus comes upon a man, he begins to roar like a lion, and the women gather together and beat the drums, shouting that the chief has come to visit the village. The possessed person will predict future wars, and warn the people of approaching visitations by lions. While the inspiration lasts, the medium may eat nothing cooked by fire, but only unfermented dough. However, this gift of prophecy usually descends on women rather than on men. Such prophetesses give out that they are possessed by the soul of some dead chief, and when they feel the divine afflatus they whiten their faces to attract attention, and they smear themselves with flour, which has a religious and sanctifying potency. One of their number beats a drum, and the others dance, singing at the same time a weird song, with curious intervals. Finally, when they have worked themselves up to the requisite pitch of religious exaltation, the possessed woman drops to the ground, and bursts out into a low and almost inarticulate chant, which amid the awestruck silence of the bystanders is interpreted by the medicine-men as the voice of the spirit.

Among the Ewe-speaking negroes of South Togoland, when the funeral celebration is over, it is customary to summon up the soul of the deceased. His relations take cooked food to the priest and tell him that they wish to bring water for the spirit of their departed

brother. The priest accordingly receives food, palm-wine, and
cowry-shells at their hands, and with them retires into his room and
shuts the door behind him. Then he evokes the ghost, who on his
arrival begins to weep and to converse with the priest, sometimes
making some general observations on the difference between life
in the upper and in the under world, sometimes entering into
particulars as to the manner of his own death; often he mentions
the name of the wicked sorcerer who has killed him by his enchantments. When the dead man's friends outside hear the lamentations
and complaints of his ghost proceeding from the room, they are
moved to tears and cry out, "We pity you!" Finally, the ghost
bids them be comforted and takes his departure. Among the Kissi,
a tribe of negroes on the border of Liberia, the souls of dead chiefs
are consulted as oracles by means of the statuettes which are erected
on their graves. For the purpose of the consultation the statuettes
are placed on a board, which is carried by two men on their heads;
if the bearers remain motionless, the answer of the spirit is assumed
to be "No"; if they sway to and fro, the answer is "Yes." In the
island of Ambrym, one of the New Hebrides, wooden statues representing ancestors are similarly employed as a means of communicat-
ing with the souls of the dead. When a man is in trouble, he blows a
whistle at nightfall near the statue of an ancestor, and if he hears
a noise he believes that the soul of the dead kinsman has entered into
the image; thereupon he recounts his woes to the effigy and prays
the spirit to help him.

The Maoris of New Zealand feared and worshipped the spirits
of their dead kinsfolk, especially dead chiefs and warriors, who were
believed to be constantly watching over the living tribesmen, protecting them in war and marking any breach of the sacred law of
taboo. These spirits dwelt normally below the earth, but they
could return to the upper air at pleasure and enter into the bodies
of men or even into the substance of inanimate objects. Some
tribes kept in their houses small carved images of wood, each of which
was dedicated to the spirit of an ancestor, who was supposed to
enter into the image on particular occasions in order to hold converse
with the living. Such an ancestral spirit (*atua*) might communicate
with the living either in dreams or more directly by talking with
them in their waking hours. Their voice, however, was not like
that of mortals, but a mysterious kind of sound, half whistle, half
whisper. The English writer, to whom we owe these particulars,
was privileged thus to converse with the souls of two chiefs who had
been dead for several years. The interview took place through the
agency of an old woman, a Maori witch of Endor, at whose bidding
the ancestral spirits of the tribe were supposed to appear.

In Nukahiva, one of the Marquesas Islands, the priests and
priestesses claimed to possess the power of evoking the spirits of the
dead, who took up their abode for the time being in the bodies of
the mediums and so conversed with their surviving relatives. The

occasion for summoning up a ghost was usually the sickness of a member of the family, on whose behalf his friends desired to have the benefit of ghostly advice. A French writer, who lived in the island in the first half of the nineteenth century, was present at one of these interviews with a departed spirit and has described it. The meeting took place at night in the house of a sick man, for the purpose of ascertaining the issue of his illness. A priestess acted as medium, and by her direction the room was darkened by the extinction of the fires. The spirit invoked was that of a lady who had died a few years before, leaving no less than twelve widowed husbands to mourn her loss. Of these numerous widowers the sick man was one; indeed he had been her favourite husband, but her ghost now announced to him his approaching death without the least ambiguity or circumlocution. Her voice appeared at first to come from a distance and then to approach nearer and nearer, till it settled on the roof of the house.

At the initiation ceremonies, which they observe every year, the Marindineeze, a tribe on the southern coast of Dutch New Guinea, summon up the souls of their forefathers from the underworld by knocking hard on the ground with the lower ends of coconut leaves for an hour together. The evocation takes place by night. Similarly at their festivals the Bare'e-speaking Toradjas of Central Celebes evoke the souls of dead chiefs and heroes, the guardian spirits of the village, by beating on the floor of the temple with a long stick.

Among the Kayans of Borneo, when a dispute has arisen concerning the division of a dead man's property, recourse is sometimes had to a professional wizard or witch, who summons up the ghost of the deceased and questions him as to his intentions in the disposal of his estate. The evocation, however, cannot take place until after the harvest which follows upon the death. When the time comes for it, a small model of a house is made for the temporary accommodation of the ghost and is placed in the gallery of the common house, beside the door of the dead man's chamber. For the refreshment of the spirit, moreover, food, drink, and cigarettes are laid out in the little house. The wizard takes up his post beside the tiny dwelling and chants his invocation, calling upon the soul of the deceased to enter the soul-house, and mentioning the names of the members of his family. From time to time he looks in, and at last announces that all the food and drink have been consumed. The people believe that the ghost has now entered the soul-house; and the wizard pretends to listen to the whispering of the soul within the house, starting and clucking from time to time. Finally, he declares the will of the ghost in regard to the distribution of the property, speaking in the first person and mimicking the mode of speech and other peculiarities of the dead man. The directions so obtained are usually followed, and thus the dispute is settled.

The Bataks of Central Sumatar believe that the souls of the

dead, being incorporeal, can only communicate with the living
through the person of a living man, and for the purpose of such
communication they choose an appropriate medium, who, in serving
as a vehicle for the ghostly message, imitates the voice, the manner,
the walk, and even the dress of the deceased so closely, that his
surviving relations are often moved to tears by the resemblance.
By the mouth of the medium the spirit reveals his name, mentions
his relations, and describes the pursuits he followed on earth. He
discloses family secrets which he had kept during life, and the dis-
closure confirms his kinsfolk in the belief that it is really the ghost
of their departed brother who is conversing with them. When a
member of the family is sick, the ghost is consulted as to whether
the patient will live or die. When an epidemic is raging, the ghost
is evoked and sacrifices are offered to him, that they may guard the
people against the infection. When a man is childless, he inquires
of a ghost, through a medium, how he can obtain offspring. When
something has been lost or stolen, a ghost is conjured up to tell
whether the missing property will be recovered. When any one
has missed his way in the forest or elsewhere and has not returned
home, it is still to a ghost, through the intervention of a medium,
that the anxious friends apply in order to learn where the strayed
wayfarer is to be sought. If a medium is questioned as to how
the ghost takes possession of him, he says that he sees the ghost
approaching and feels as if his body were being dragged away, his
feet grow light and leap about, human beings seem small and reddish
in colour, the houses appear to be turning round. But the possession
is not continuous; from time to time during the fit the ghost leaves
the medium and plays about. When the fit is over, the medium is
often sick and sometimes dies.

    Necromancy has been practised by man amid Arctic snow and
ice as well as in tropical forests and jungles. Among the Eskimo
of Labrador we read of a shaman who used to oblige his friends by
calling up the spirits of the dead, whenever the living desired to
inquire concerning the welfare of the departed, or the whereabouts
of absent relatives at sea. He would first blindfold the questioner,
and then rap thrice on the ground with a stick. On the third rap
the spirit appeared and answered the shama's questions. Having
supplied the information that was wanted, the ghost would be
dismissed to his own place by three more raps on the ground.
This sort of necromancy was called "conjuring with a stick."
A similar method of evoking the souls of the dead is employed by
the Eskimo of Alaska. They believe that the spirits ascend from
the under world and pass through the body of the shaman, who
converses audibly with them and, having learned all he desires, sends
them back to their subterranean abode by a stamp of his foot. The
answers of the ghosts to his questions are supposed by sceptics to be
produced by ventriloquism.

    In China, where the worship of the dead forms a principal **part**

of the national religion, the practice of necromancy is naturally
common, and the practitioners at the present day appear to be
chiefly old women. Such necromancers, for example, abound in
Canton and Amoy. During his residence at Canton, Archdeacon
Gray witnessed many exhibitions of their skill.

The practice of calling up the spirits of the dead for consultation
is said to be very common in Amoy, where the necromancers are
professional women. Among the male sex the reputation of those
ladies for strict veracity seems not to stand very high, for to tell
a man, in common parlance, that he is "bringing up the dead" is
almost equivalent to saying that he is telling a lie. Hence these
female necromancers often prefer to confine their ministrations to
their own sex, lest they should expose their high mysteries to the
derision of masculine sceptics. In that case the session is held with
closed doors in the private apartments of the women; otherwise it
takes place in the main hall, at the domestic altar, and all inmates of
the house are free to attend. Many families, indeed, make a rule to
question, by means of these witches, every deceased relation at least
once not long after his or her death, in order to ascertain whether
the souls are comfortable in the other world, and whether anything
can be done by family affection to ameliorate their condition. An
auspicious day having been chosen for the ceremony, the apartment
is swept and watered, because spirits entertain an aversion to dirt
and dust. To allure the ghost, food and dainties, together with
burning incense, are placed on the domestic altar, or, should the
conference take place in a secluded room, on an ordinary table. In
the latter case, when the medium has come, it is necessary for one of
the women to go to the altar, where the tablets are deposited in
which the souls of the dead membrs of the family are believed to
reside. Having lighted two candles and three incense-sticks at the
altar, she invites the ghost to leave its tablet and follow her. Then,
with the incense between her fingers, she slowly walks back into the
room, and plants the sticks in a bowl or cup with some uncooked
rice. The medium now goes to work, chanting conjurations, while
she trums a lyre or beats a drum. In time her movements grow
convulsive, she rocks to and fro, and sweat bursts from her body.
These things are regarded as evidence that the ghost has arrived.
Two women support the medium and place her in a chair, where she
falls into a state of distraction or slumber, with her arms resting on
the table. A black veil is next thrown over her head, and in her
mesmeric state she can now answer questions, shivering, as she does
so, rocking in her seat, and drumming the table nervously with her
hands or with a stick. Through her mouth the ghost informs his
relations of his state in the other world and what they can do to
improve it or even to redeem him entirely from his sufferings. He
mentions whether the sacrifices which are offered to him reach their
destination intact or suffer loss and damage in process of transmission through the spiritual post; he states his preferences and

he enumerates his wants. He also favours his kinsfolk with his advice on domestic affairs, though his language is often ambiguous and his remarks have sometimes little or no bearing on the questions submitted to him. Now and then the medium holds whispered monologues, or rather conversations with the ghost. At last she suddenly shivers, awakes, and raising herself up declares that the ghost has gone. Having pocketed the rice and the incense-sticks in the bowl, she receives her fee and takes her departure. "The various phases in the condition of the medium during the conference are of course taken by the onlookers for the several moments of her connection with the other world. Yet we remain entitled to consider them to be symptoms of psychical aberration and nervous affection. Her spasms and convulsions pass for possession, either by the ghost which is consulted, or by the spirit with which she usually has intercourse, and which thus imparts to her the faculty of second sight by which she sees that ghost. And her mesmeric fits confessedly are the moments when her soul leaves her, in order to visit the other world, there to see the ghost and speak with it. Her whispering lips indicate conversation with her spirit, or with the ghost which is consulted. It may be asked why, since this ghost dwells in its tablet on the altar, her soul should travel to the other world to see it. We can give no answer."

From this account it appears that a Chinese witch sometimes calls up the souls of the dead, not directly, but through the mediation of a familiar spirit which she has at her command. Similarly Archdeacon Gray tells us that "in China, as in other lands, there are persons—always old women—who profess to have familiar spirits, and who pretend that they can call up the spirits of the dead to converse with the living." In this respect Chinese witches resemble the ancient Hebrew witches, who would seem to have depended on the help of familiar spirits for the evocation of ghosts; for when Saul desired the witch of Endor to summon up the ghost of Samuel, he said to her, "Divine unto me, I pray thee, by the familiar spirit, and bring me up whomsoever I shall name unto thee."

These examples may serve to show how widely spread the practice of necromancy has been among the races of mankind.

CHAPTER V

THE SIN OF A CENSUS

From two well-known narratives in the Books of Samuel and Chronicles we learn that at one period of his career Jehovah cherished a singular antipathy to the taking of a census, which he appears to have regarded as a crime of even deeper dye than boiling milk or jumping on a threshold.[1] We read that Jehovah, or Satan, inspired King David with the unhappy idea of counting his people. Whatever the precise source of the inspiration may have been—for on that point the sacred writers differ—the result, or at least the sequel, was disastrous. The numbering of the people was immediately followed by a great pestilence, and popular opinion viewed the calamity as a righteous retribution for the sin of the census. The excited imagination of the plague-stricken people even beheld in the clouds the figure of the Destroying Angel with his sword stretched out over Jerusalem, just as in the Great Plague of London, if we may trust Defoe, a crowd in the street fancied they saw the same dreadful apparition hovering in the air. It was not till the contrite king had confessed his sin and offered sacrifice to appease the angry deity, that the Angel of Death put up his sword and the mourners ceased to go about the streets of Jerusalem.

The objection which Jehovah, or rather the Jews, entertained to the taking of a census appears to be simply a particular case of the general aversion which many ignorant people feel to allowing themselves, their cattle, or their possessions to be counted. This curious superstition—for such it is—seems to be common among the black races of Africa. For example, among the Bakongo, of the Lower Congo, "it is considered extremely unlucky for a woman to count her children one, two, three, and so on, for the evil spirits will hear and take some of them away by death. The people themselves do not like to be counted; for they fear that counting will draw to them the attention of the evil spirits, and as a result of the counting some of them will soon die. In 1908 the Congo State officials, desiring to number the people for the purpose of levying a tax, sent an officer with soldiers to count them. The natives would have resisted the officer, but he had too many soldiers with him; and it is not improbable that fights have taken place between whites and blacks in other parts of Africa, not that they resisted the taxation, but because they objected to be counted for fear the spirits would hear and kill them." Similarly among the Boloki or Bangala of the Upper Congo, "the native has a very strong superstition and prejudice against counting his children, for he believes that if he does so, or if he states the proper number, the evil spirits will hear it and some of his children will die; hence when you ask him such a simple question as, 'How many children have you?' you stir up his superstitious fears, and he will answer: 'I don't know.' If you press him, he will tell you sixty, or one hundred children, or any other number that jumps to his tongue; and even then he is thinking of those who, from the native view of kinship, are regarded as his children; and desiring to deceive not you, but those ubiquitous and prowling evil spirits, he states a large number that leaves a wide margin."

Again, the Masai of East Africa count neither men nor beasts, believing that if they did so the men or beasts would die. Hence

[1] As to these two latter enormities, see below, pp. 330, 360 sq.

they reckon a great multitude of people or a large herd of cattle only in round numbers; of smaller groups of men or beasts they can reckon the totals with tolerable accuracy without numbering the individuals of the groups. Only dead men or dead beasts may be counted one by one, because naturally there is no risk of their dying again in consequence of the numeration. The Wa-Sania of British East Africa "most strongly object to being counted, as they believe that one of those who were counted would die shortly afterwards." To the Akamba, another tribe of the same region, the welfare of the cattle is a matter of great concern; hence the people observe certain superstitious rules, the breach of which is believed to entail misfortune on the herds. One of these rules is that the cattle may never be counted; so when the herd returns to the village the owner will merely cast his eye over it to discover if a beast is missing. And in this tribe the unluckiness of counting is not limited to cattle; it extends to all living creatures, and particularly to girls. On the other hand, another authority on the Akamba tells us that "there does not appear to be any superstition against counting stock; if a man has a large herd he does not know the number, but he or his wives when milking would quickly notice if a beast with certain markings was not present. A man, however, knows the number of his children but is averse to telling any one outside his family. There is a tradition that a man named Munda wa Ngola, who lived in the Ibeti Hills, had many sons and daughters, and boasted of the size of his family, saying that he and his sons could resist any attack from the Masai; one night, however, the Masai surprised him and killed him and his people, and the countryside considered that this was a judgment on him." Again, among the Akikuyu, another tribe of British East Africa, "it is difficult to arrive at figures, even approximately correct, with regard to the size of the families. The natural method of conversing with the mothers as to the number of their children is soon found to be, to say the least, a tactless proceeding. It is considered most unlucky to give such figures, a sentiment similar, no doubt, to the aversion felt in the Old Testament days to the numbering of the people. The inquiry is politely waived, with a request to 'come and see.'" The Gallas of East Africa think that to count cattle is an evil omen, and that it impedes the increase of the herd. To count the members of a community or company is reckoned by the Hottentots to be of very evil augury, for they believe that some member of the company will die. A missionary who once, in ignorance of this superstition, counted his work-people, is said to have paid for his rashness with his life.

The superstitious objection to numbering people seems to be general in North Africa; in Algeria the opposition offered by the natives to all French regulations which require an enumeration of the inhabitants is said to be based in great measure on this aversion to be counted. Nor is this repugnance limited to the counting persons; it is exhibited also in the counting of measures of grain, an operation which has a sacred character. For example, at Oran the person who counts the measures of grain should be in a state of ceremonial purity, and instead of counting one, two, three, and so on, he says "In the name of God" for "one"; "two blessings" for "two"; "hospitality of the Prophet" for "three"; "we shall gain, please God" for "four"; "in the eye of the Devil" for "five"; "in the eye of his son" for "six"; "it is God who gives us our fill" for "seven"; and so on, up to "twelve," for which the expression is "the perfection for God." So in Palestine, at counting the measures of grain, many Mohammedans say for the first one, "God is one," and for the next, "He has no second," then simply "Three," "Four," and so on. But "there are several unlucky numbers, the first being five, and therefore, instead of saying the number, they often say 'Your hand,' five being the number of the fingers; seven is another unlucky number, strange to say, and is passed over in silence, or the word 'A blessing' is used instead; at nine Moslems often say, 'Pray in the name of Mohammed'; eleven also is not unfrequently omitted, the measurer saying, 'There are ten,' and then passing on to twelve." Perhaps such substitutes for the ordinary numbers are intended to deceive evil spirits, who may be lying in wait to steal or harm the corn, and who are presumably too dull-witted to comprehend these eccentric modes of numeration.

In the Shortlands group of islands, in the Western Pacific, the building of a chief's house is attended by a variety of ceremonies and observances. The roof is heavily thatched at each gable with thatch made of the leaves of the ivory-nut palm. In collecting these leaves the builders are not allowed to count the number, as the counting would be deemed unlucky; yet if the number of leaves collected should fall short of the number required, the house, though nearing completion, would be at once abandoned. Thus the loss entailed by a miscalculation may be heavy, and from its possible extent we can judge how serious must, in the opinion of the natives, be the objection to counting the leaves, since rather than count them they are prepared to sacrifice the fruit of their labour. Among the Cherokee Indians of North America it is a rule that "melons and squashes must not be counted or examined too closely, while still growing upon the vine, or they will cease to thrive." Once on a time the officer in charge of Fort Simpson, in British Columbia, took a census of the Indians in the neighbourhood, and very soon afterwards great numbers of them were swept away by measles. Of course the Indians attributed the calamity to their having been numbered, just as the Hebrews in King David's time ascribed the wasting pestilence to the sin of the census. The Omaha Indians "preserve no account of their ages; they think that some evil will attend the numbering of their years."

Similar superstitions are to be found in Europe and in our **own** country to this day. The Lapps used to be, and perhaps still are, unwilling to count themselves and to declare the number, because they feared that such a reckoning would both forebode and cause a great mortality among their people. In the Highlands of Scotland "it is reckoned unlucky to number the people or cattle belonging to any family, but more particularly upon Friday. The cowherd knows every creature committed to his charge by the colour, size, and other particular marks, but is perhaps all along ignorant of the sum total of his flock. And fishermen do not care to confess the number of salmon or other fish which they have taken at a draught or in a day, imagining that this discovery would spoil their luck." Though this account is derived from a writer of the eighteenth century, similar superstitions are known to have prevailed in Scotland far into the nineteenth century, and it is probable that they are not extinct at the present time. In Shetland, we are told, "counting the number of sheep, of cattle, of horses, of fish, or of any of a man's chattels, whether animate or inanimate, has always been considered as productive of bad luck. There is also said to have been an idea prevalent at one time, that an outbreak of small-pox always followed the census being taken." Among the fisher-folk on the north-east coast of Scotland on no account might the boats be counted when they were at sea, nor might any gathering of men, women, or children be numbered. Nothing aroused the indignation of a company of fisherwomen trudging along the road to sell their fish more than to point at them with a finger, and begin to number them aloud :

> "Ane, twa, three,
> Faht a fishers I see
> Gyain our the brigg o' Dee,
> Deel pick their muckle greethy ee."

So the fishwives of Auchmithie, a village on the coast of Forfarshire, used to be irritated by mischievous children who counted them with extended forefingers, repeating the verse :

> "Ane, twa, three!
> Ane, twa, three!
> Sic a lot o' fisher-wifies
> I do see!"

And the unluckiness extended to counting the fish caught or the boats in the herring-fleet.

In Lincolnshire "no farmer should count his lambs too closely during the lambing season. This idea is, it may be guessed, con-nected with the notion that to reckon very accurately gives the powers of evil information which they can use against the objects under consideration. 'Brebis comptées, le loup les mange.' I have seen a shepherd in obvious embarrassment because his employer knew so little of his own business that, though usually the most easy of masters, he would insist on learning every morning the exact number of lambs his flock had produced. For a cognate reason, it may be, some people when asked how old they are reply, 'As old as my tongue, and a little bit older than my teeth.' M. Gaidoz remarks in *Melusine* (ix 35) that old people ought not to tell their age, and when importuned to reveal it they should answer that they are as old as their little finger. Inhabitants of Godarville, Hainault, reply, "I am the age of a calf, every year twelve months." In England the superstitious objection to counting lambs is not confined to Lincolnshire. A friend, whose home is in a village of south Warwickshire, wrote to me some years ago: "Superstitions die hard. Yesterday I asked a woman how many lambs her husband had. She said she didn't know; then, perceiving the surprise in my face, added, 'You know, sir, it's unlucky to count them.' Then she went on, 'However, we haven't lost any yet.' And her husband is postmaster and keeps the village shop, and, in his own esteem, stands high above a peasant."

In Denmark they say that you should never count the eggs under a brooding hen, else the mother will tread on the eggs and kill the chickens. And when the chickens are hatched, you ought not to count them, or they will easily fall a prey to the glede or the hawk. So, too, blossoms and fruit should not be counted, or the blossoms will wither and the fruit will fall untimely from the bough. In North Jutland people have a notion that if you count any mice which the cat has caught, or which you chance to discover, the mice will increase in number; and if you count lice, fleas, or any other vermin, they also will multiply in like manner. It is said to be a Greek and Armenian superstition that if you count your warts they will increase in number. On the other hand, it is a popular German belief that if you count your money often it will steadily decrease. In the Upper Palatinate, a district of Bavaria, people think that loaves in the oven should not be counted, or they will not turn out well. In Upper Franconia, another district of Bavaria, they say that when dumplings are being cooked you should not count them, because if you do, the Little Wood Women, who like dumplings, could not fetch any away, and deprived of that form of nutriment they would perish, with the necessary consequence that the forest would dwindle and die. Therefore to prevent the country from being stripped bare of its woods, you are urged not to count dumplings in the pan. In the north-east of Scotland a similar rule used to be observed for a somewhat different reason. "When bread was baked in a family the cakes must not be counted. Fairies always ate cakes that had been counted; they did not last the ordinary time."

On the whole we may assume, with a fair degree of probability, that the objection which the Jews in King David's time felt to the taking of a census rested on no firmer foundation than sheer superstition, which may have been confirmed by an outbreak of plague immediately after the numbering of the people. To this day the same repugnance to count or be counted appears to linger among the Arabs of Syria, for we are told that an Arab is averse to counting the tents, or horsemen, or cattle of his tribe, lest some misfortune befall them.

At a later time the Jewish legislator so far relaxed the ban upon a census as to permit the nation to be numbered, on condition that every man paid half a shekel to the Lord as a ransom for his life, lest a plague should break out among the people. On receipt of that moderate fee the deity was apparently assumed to waive the scruples he felt at the sin of a census.

CHAPTER VI

THE KEEPERS OF THE THRESHOLD

In the temple at Jerusalem there were three officials, apparently priests, who bore the title of Keepers of the Threshold.[1] What precisely was their function? They may have been mere door-keepers, but their title suggests that they were something more; for many curious superstitions have gathered round the threshold in ancient and modern times. The prophet Zephaniah represents Jehovah himself saying, "And in that day I will punish all those that leap on the threshold, which fill their master's house with violence and deceit."[2] From this denunciation it would appear that to jump on a threshold was viewed as a sin, which, equally with violence and deceit, drew down the divine wrath on the jumper. At Ashdod the Philistine god Dagon clearly took a similar view of the sinfulness of such jumps, for we read that his priests and wor-shippers were careful not to tread on the threshold when they entered his temple. The same scruple has persisted in the same regions to this day. Captain Conder tells us of a Syrian belief "that it is unlucky to tread on a threshold. In all mosques a wooden bar at the door obliges those who enter to stride across the sill, and the same custom is observed in the rustic shrines." These rustic shrines are the chapels of the saints which are to be found in almost every village of Syria, and form the real centre of the peasant's religion. "The greatest respect is shown to the chapel, where the invisible presence of the saint is supposed always to

[1] Jeremiah xxxv. 4, lii. 24; 2 Kings xii. 9, xxii. 4, xxiii. 4, xxv. 18. In all these passages the English Versian, both Authorized and Revised, wrongly substitutes "door" for "threshold."

[2] Zephaniah i. 9. The Revised Version wrongly renders "over the threshold." The phrase is rightly translated in the Authorized Version. The English revisers and E. Kautsch in his German translation of the Bible (Freiburg i. B. and Leipsic, 1894) have done violence to the proper sense of the preposition על ("upon"), apparently for the purpose of harmonizing the passage with 1 Samuel v. 5.

abide. The peasant removes his shoes before entering, and takes care not to tread on the threshold."

This persistence of the superstition in Syria down to modern times suggests that in the temple at Jerusalem the Keepers of the Threshold may have been warders stationed at the entrance of the sacred edifice to prevent all who entered from treading on the threshold. The suggestion is confirmed by the observation that elsewhere Keepers of the Threshold have been employed to discharge a similar duty. When Marco Polo visited the palace at Peking in the days of the famous Kublai Khan, he found that "at every door of the hall (or, indeed, wherever the Emperor may be) there stand a couple of big men like giants, one on each side, armed with staves. Their business is to see that no one steps upon the threshold in entering, and if this does happen they strip the offender of his clothes, and he must pay a forfeit to have them back again; or in lieu of taking his clothes they give him a certain number of blows. If they are foreigners ignorant of the order, then there are Barons appointed to introduce them and explain it to them. They think, in fact, that it brings bad luck if any one touches the threshold. Howbeit, they are not expected to stick at this in going forth again, for at that time some are like to be the worse for liquor and incapable of looking to their steps." From the account of Friar Odoric, who travelled in the East in the early part of the thirteenth century, it would appear that sometimes these Keepers of the Threshold at Peking gave offenders no choice, but laid on lustily with their staves whenever a man was unlucky enough to touch the threshold. When the monk de Rubruquis, who went as ambassador to China for Louis IX., was at the court of Mangu-Khan, one of his companions happened to stumble at the threshold in going out. The warders at once seized the delinquent and caused him to be carried before "the Bulgai, who is the chancellor, or secretary of the court, who judgeth those who are arraigned of life and death." However, on learning that the offence had been committed in ignorance, the chancellor pardoned the culprit, but would never afterwards let him enter any of the houses of Mangu-Khan. The monk was lucky to get off with a whole skin. Even sore bones were by no means the worst that could happen to a man under these circumstances in that part of the world. Plano Carpini, who travelled in Tartary about the middle of the thirteenth century, a few years before the embassy of de Rubruquis, tells us that any one who touched the threshold of the hut or tent of a Tartar prince used to be dragged out through a hole made for the purpose under the hut or tent, and then put to death without mercy. The feeling on which these restrictions were based is tersely expressed in a Mongol saying, "Step not on the threshold; it is sin."

But in the Middle Ages this respect for the threshold was not limited to Tartar or Mongol peoples. The caliphs of Baghdad "obliged all those who entered their place to prostrate themselves on the threshold of the gate, where they had inlaid a piece of the black stone of the temple at Meccah, in order to render it more venerable to the peoples who had been accustomed to press their foreheads against it. The threshold was of some height, and it would have been a crime to set foot upon it." At a later time, when the Italian traveller Pietro della Valle visited the palace of the Persian kings at Ispahan early in the seventeenth century, he observed that "the utmost reverence is shewn to the gate of entrance, so much so, that no one presumes to tread on a certain step of wood in it somewhat elevated, but, on the contrary, people kiss it occasionally as a precious and holy thing." Any criminal who contrived to pass this threshold and enter the palace was in sanctuary and might not be molested. When Pietro della Valle was in Ispahan, there was a man of rank living in the palace whom the king wished to put to death. But the offender had been quick enough to make his way into the palace, and there he was safe from every violence, though had he stepped outside of the gate he would instantly have been cut down. "None is refused admittance to the palace, but on passing the threshold, which he kisses, as I have before remarked, he has claim of protection. This threshold, in short, is in such veneration, that its name of Astane is the denomination for the court and the royal palace itself."

A similar respect for the threshold and a reluctance to touch it are found among barbarous as well as civilized peoples. In Fiji, "to sit on the threshold of a temple is *tabu* to any but a chief of the highest rank. All are careful not to tread on the threshold of a place set apart for the gods: persons of rank stride over; others pass over on their hands and knees. The same form is observed in crossing the threshold of a chief's house. Indeed, there is very little difference between a chief of high rank and one of the second order of deities. The former regards himself very much as a god, and is often spoken of as such by his people, and, on some occasions, claims for himself publicly the right of divinity." In West Africa "at the entrance to a village the way is often barred by a temporary light fence, only a narrow arched gateway of saplings being left open. These saplings are wreathed with leaves or flowers. That fence, frail as it is, is intended as a bar to evil spirits, for from those arched saplings hang fetich charms. When actual war is coming, this street entrance is barricaded by logs, behind which real fight is to be made against human, not spiritual, foes. The light gateway is sometimes further guarded by a sapling pinned to the ground horizontally across the narrow threshold. An entering stranger must be careful to tread over and not on it. In an expected great evil the gateway is sometimes sprinkled with the blood of a sacrificed goat or sheep." Among the Nandi of British East Africa, nobody may sit at the door or on the threshold of a house; and a man may not even touch the threshold of his own house or anything in it, except his own bed, when his wife has a child that has not been weaned. In Morocco similarly nobody is allowed to sit down on the threshold of a house or at the entrance of a tent; should any person do so, it is believed that he would fall ill or would bring ill luck on the house. The Korwas, a Dravidian tribe of Mirzapur, will not touch the threshold of a house either on entering or on leaving it. The Kurmis, the principal class of cultivators in the Central Provinces of India, say that "no one should ever sit on the threshold of a house; this is the seat of Lakshmi, the goddess of wealth, and to sit on it is disrespectful to her." The Kalmuks think it a sin to sit on the threshold of a door.

In most of these cases the prohibition to touch or sit on a threshold is general and absolute; nobody, so far as appears, is ever allowed to touch or sit on it at any time or under any circumstances. Only in one case is the prohibition temporary and conditional. Among the Nandi it seems that a man is only forbidden to touch the threshold of his own house when his wife has a child at the breast; but in that case the prohibition is not confined to the threshold but extends to everything in the house except the man's own bed. However, there are other cases in which the prohibition expressly refers only to certain particular circumstances, though it might be unsafe to infer that its scope is really so limited, and that under all other circumstances people are free to use the threshold at their discretion. For example, at Tangier, when a man has returned from a pilgrimage to Mecca it is customary for his friends to carry him over the threshold and deposit him on his bed. But from this usage it would be wrong to infer that in Morocco, at all other times and under all other circumstances, a man or a woman may be freely deposited, or may seat himself or herself, on the threshold of a house; for we have seen that in Morocco nobody is ever allowed under any circumstances to sit down on the threshold of a house or at the entrance of a tent. Again, in Morocco a bride at marriage is carried across the threshold of her husband's house, her relatives taking care that she shall not touch it. This practice of carrying a bride across the threshold on her first entrance into her new home has been observed in many parts of the world, and the custom has been discussed and variously interpreted both in ancient and modern times. It may be well to give some instances of it before we inquire into its meaning.

In Palestine at the present time "a bride is often carried over the threshold that her feet may not touch it, to do so being considered unlucky." The Chinese precautions to prevent a bride's feet from touching the threshold are more elaborate. Among the Hakkas, for example, when the bride arrives at the door of her husband's house, she "is assisted from her chair by an old woman acting in the man's interest, and is handed by her over the threshold, where is placed a red-hot coulter steeped in vinegar." The usage perhaps varies somewhat in different parts of China. According to another account, which probably applies to Canton and the

neighbourhood, when the bride alights from her sedan-chair at the
door of the bridegroom's house, "she is placed on the back of a
female servant, and carried over a slow charcoal fire, on each side
of which are arranged the shoes which were borne in the procession
as a gift to her future husband. Above her head, as she is conveyed
over the charcoal fire, another female servant raises a tray containing several pairs of chop-sticks, some rice, and betel-nuts." Among
the Mordvins of Russia the bride is, or used to be, carried into the
bridegroom's house in the arms of some of the wedding party. In
Java and other of the Sunda Islands the bridegroom himself carries
his bride in his arms into the house. In Sierra Leone, when the
bridal party approaches the bridegroom's town, the bride is taken
on the back of an old woman and covered with a fine cloth, "for
from this time she is not allowed to be seen by any male person, till
after consummation. Mats are spread on the ground, that the
feet of the person who carries her may not touch the earth ; in this
manner she is carried to the house of her intended husband."
Among the Atonga, a tribe of British Central Africa, to the west
of Lake Nyasa, a bride is conducted by young girls to the bridegroom's house, where he awaits her. At the threshold she stops,
and will not cross it until the bridegroom has given her a hoe. She
then puts one foot over the threshold of the doorway, and her
husband gives her two yards of cloth. After that, the bride puts
both feet within the house and stands near the doorway, whereupon
she receives a present of beads or some equivalent.

In these latter accounts the avoidance of the threshold at the
bride's entrance into her new home is implied rather than expressed.
But among Aryan peoples from India to Scotland it has been
customary for the bride on such occasions carefully to shun contact
with the threshold, either by stepping over it or by being carried
over it. Thus, for example, in ancient India it was the rule that
the bride should cross the threshold of her husband's house with
her right foot foremost, but should not stand on the threshold.
Exactly the same rule is said to be still followed by the southern
Slavs at Mostar in Herzegovina and the Bocca di Cattaro. Among
the Albanians, when the bridal party arrives at the bridegroom's
house, the members of it take care to cross the thresholds of the
rooms, especially that of the room in which the bridal crowns are
deposited, with the right foot foremost. In Slavonia the bride is
carried into the bridegroom's house by the best man. Similarly,
in modern Greece, the bride may not touch the threshold, but is
lifted over it. So in ancient Rome, when the bride entered her
new home, she was forbidden to touch the threshold with her feet,
and in order to avoid doing so she was lifted over it. In some parts
of Silesia the bride is carried over the threshold of her new home.
Similarly, in country districts of the Altmark it is, or used to be,
customary for the bride to drive in a carriage or cart to her husband's
house ; on her arrival the bridegroom took her in his arms, carried

her into the house without allowing her feet to touch the ground, and set her down on the hearth. In French Switzerland the bride used to be met at the door of her husband's house by an old woman who threw three handfuls of wheat over her. Then the bridegroom took her in his arms, and so assisted her to leap over the threshold, which she might not touch with her feet. The custom of carrying the bride over the threshold into the house is said to have been formerly observed in Lorraine and other parts of France. In Wales "it was considered very unlucky for a bride to place her feet on or near the threshold, and the lady, on her return from the marriage ceremony, was always carefully lifted over the threshold and into the house. The brides who were lifted were generally fortunate, but trouble was in store for the maiden who preferred walking into the house." In some parts of Scotland, as late as the beginning of the nineteenth century, when the wedding party arrived at the bridegroom's house, "the young wife was lifted over the threshold, or first step of the door, lest any witchcraft or *ill e'e* should be cast upon and influence her."

What is the meaning of this custom of lifting a bride over the threshold of her husband's house? Plutarch suggested that at Rome the ceremony might be a reminiscence of the rape of the Sabine women, whom the early Romans carried off to be their wives. Similarly some modern writers have argued that the rite is a relic or survival of an ancient custom of capturing wives from a hostile tribe and bringing them by force into the houses of their captors. But against this view it may be observed that the custom of lifting the bride over the threshold can hardly be separated from the custom which enjoins the bride to step over the threshold without touching it. In this latter custom there is no suggestion of violence or constraint; the bride walks freely of her own accord into the bridegroom's house, only taking care that in doing so her feet should not touch the threshold; and, so far as we know, this custom is at least as old as the other, since it is the one prescribed in the ancient Indian law-books, which say nothing about lifting the bride over the threshold. Accordingly we may conclude that the practice of carrying a wife at marriage into her husband's house is simply a precaution to prevent her feet from coming into contact with the threshold, and that it is therefore only a particular instance of that scrupulous avoidance of the threshold which we have found to prevail among many races of mankind. If any further argument were needed against bride-capture as an explanation of the practice, it would seem to be supplied by the marriage customs of Salsette, an island near Bombay, where the bridegroom is first himself carried by his maternal uncle into the house, and afterwards lifts his bride over the threshold. As no one, probably, will interpret the carrying of the bridegroom into the house as a relic of a custom of capturing husbands, so neither should the parallel lifting of the bride over the threshold be interpreted as a relic of a custom of capturing wives.

But we have still to ask, What is the reason for this reluctance to touch the threshold? Why all these elaborate precautions to avoid contact with that part of the house? It seems probable that all these customs of avoidance are based on a religious or superstitious belief in some danger which attaches to the threshold and can affect those who tread or sit upon it. The learned Varro, one of the fathers of folk-lore, held that the custom of lifting the bride over the threshold was to prevent her committing a sacrilege by treading on an object which was sacred to the chaste goddess Vesta. In thus referring the rite to a religious scruple the Roman antiquary Varro was much nearer the truth than the Greek antiquary Plutarch, who proposed to deduce the ceremony from a practice, or at all events a case, of capturing wives by force. Certainly in the opinion of the Romans the threshold appears to have been invested with a high degree of sanctity; for not only was it sacred to Vesta, but it enjoyed the advantage of a god all to itself, a sort of divine door-keeper or Keeper of the Threshold, named Limentinus, who was roughly handled by the Christian Fathers, his humble station in life laying him open to the gibes of irreverent witlings.

Elsewhere the threshold has been supposed to be haunted by spirits, and this belief of itself might suffice to account for the reluctance to tread or sit upon it, since such acts would naturally disturb and annoy the supernatural beings who have their abode on the spot. Thus in Morocco people believe that the threshold is haunted by jinn, and this notion is apparently the reason why in that country the bride is carried across the threshold of her new home. In Armenia the threshold is deemed the resort of spirits, and as newly wedded people are thought to be particularly exposed to evil influences, they are attended by a man who carries a sword for their protection and who makes a cross with it on the wall over every door. In heathen Russia the spirits of the house are said to have had their seat at the threshold; and consistently with this tradition "in Lithuania, when a new house is being built, a wooden cross, or some article which has been handed down from past generations, is placed under the threshold. There, also, when a newly-baptized child is being brought back from church, it is customary for its father to hold it for a while over the threshold, 'so as to place the new member of the family under the protection of the domestic divinities.' . . . A man should always cross himself when he steps over a threshold, and he ought not, it is believed in some places, to sit down on one. Sick children, who are supposed to have been afflicted by an evil eye, are washed on the threshold of their cottage, in order that with the help of the Penates who reside there, the malady may be driven out of doors." A German super-stition forbids us to tread on the threshold in entering a new house, since to do so "would hurt the poor souls"; and it is an Icelandic belief that he who sits on the threshold of a courtyard will be at-tacked by spectres.

Sometimes, though not always, the spirits who haunt the threshold are probably believed to be those of the human dead. This will naturally happen whenever it is customary to bury the dead, or some of them, at the doorway of the house. For example, among the Wataveta of East Africa "men who have issue are as a rule interred at the door of the hut of their eldest surviving wife, whose duty it is to see that the remains are not disturbed by a stray hyena. The Muinjari family and the Ndighiri clan, however, prefer making the grave inside the wife's hut. Women are buried near the doors of their own houses. People who are not mourned by a son or a daughter are cast into a pit or trench which is dug some little distance from the cluster of huts, and no notice is taken even if a beast of prey should exhume and devour the corpse." Again, in Russia the peasants bury still-born children under the threshold; hence the souls of the dead babes may be thought to haunt the spot. Similarly in Bilaspore, a district of the Central Provinces of India, "a still-born child, or one who has passed away before the *Chhatti* (the sixth day, the day of purification) is not taken out of the house for burial, but is placed in an earthen vessel (a *gharā*) and is buried in the doorway or in the yard of the house. Some say that this is done in order that the mother may bear another child." So in the Hissar District of the Punjab, "Bishnois bury dead infants at the threshold, in the belief that it would facilitate the return of the soul to the mother. The practice is also in vogue in the Kangra District, where the body is buried in front of the back door." And with regard to Northern India generally, we read that "when a child dies it is usually buried under the house threshold, in the belief that as the parents tread daily over its grave, its soul will be reborn in the family." A similar belief in reincarnation may explain the custom, common in Central Africa, of burying the afterbirth at the doorway or actually under the threshold of the hut; for the afterbirth is supposed by many peoples to be a personal being, the twin brother or sister of the infant whom it follows at a short interval into the world. By burying the child or the afterbirth under the threshold the mother apparently hopes that, as she steps over it, the spirit of the child or of its supposed twin will pass into her womb and be born again.

Curiously enough in some parts of England down to modern times a similar remedy has been applied to a similar evil among cows, though probably the persons who practise or recommend it have no very clear notion of the way in which the cure is effected. In the Cleveland district of Yorkshire "it is alleged as a fact, and by no means without reason or as contrary to experience, that if one of the cows in a dairy unfortunately produces a calf prematurely —in local phrase 'picks her cauf'—the remainder of the cows in the same building are only too likely, or too liable, to follow suit; of course to the serious loss of the owner. The old-world prophylactic or folklore-prescribed preventative in such a contingency used to be to remove the threshold of the cowhouse in which the mischance had befallen, dig a deep hole in the place so laid bare, deep enough, indeed, to admit of the abortive calf being buried in it, on its back, with its four legs all stretching vertically upwards in the rigidity of death, and then to cover all up as before." A shrewd Yorkshireman, whom Dr. Atkinson questioned as to the continued observance of this quaint custom, replied, "Ay, there's many as dis it yet. My au'd father did it. But it's sae mony years syne, it must be about wore out by now, and I shall have to dee it again." Clearly he thought that the salutary influence of the buried calf could not reasonably be expected to last for ever, and that it must be reinforced by a fresh burial. Similarly the manager of a large farm near Cambridge wrote not many years ago, "A cowman (a Suffolk man) lately said to me that the only cure for cows when there was an epidemic of abortion was to bury one of the premature calves in a gateway through which the herd passed daily." The same remedy was recorded more than a hundred years ago by an English antiquary : "A slunk or abortive calf buried in the highway over which cattle frequently pass, will greatly prevent that misfortune happening to cows. This is commonly practised in Suffolk." Perhaps the old belief may have been that the spirit of the buried calf entered into one of the cows which passed over its body and was thus born again ; but it seems hardly probable that so definite a notion as to the operation of the charm should have survived in England to modern times.

Thus the glamour which surrounds the threshold in popular fancy may be in part due to an ancient custom of burying dead infants or dead animals under the doorway. But this custom cannot completely account for the superstition, since the superstition, as we saw, attaches to the thresholds of tents as well as of houses, and so far as I am aware there is no evidence or probability of a custom of burying the dead in the doorway of a tent. In Morocco it is not the spirits of the dead, but the jinn, who are supposed to haunt the threshold.

The sacredness of the threshold, whatever may be the exact nature of the spiritual beings by whom it is supposed to be enforced, is well illustrated by the practice of slaying animals in sacrifice at the threshold and obliging persons who enter the house to step over the flowing blood. Such a sacrifice often takes place at the moment when a bride is about to enter her husband's house for the first time. For example, among the Brahuis of Baluchistan, "if they are folk of means, they take the bride to her new home mounted on a camel in a *kajāva* or litter, while the bridegroom rides along astride a horse. Otherwise they must needs trudge along as best they may. And as soon as they reach the dwelling, a sheep is slaughtered on the threshold, and the bride is made to step on the blood that is sprinkled, in such wise that one of the heels of her shoe is marked therewith. A little of the blood is caught in a cup, and a bunch of green grass is dropped therein, and the mother of the groom stains the bride's forehead with the blood as she steps over the threshold." So at marriages at Mehardeh, in Syria, they sacrifice a sheep outside the door of the house, and the bride steps over the blood of the animal while it is still flowing. This custom is apparently observed both by Greeks and Protestants. Similarly "in Egypt, the Copts kill a sheep as soon as the bride enters the bridegroom's house, and she is obliged to step over the blood flowing upon the threshold, at the doorway." Among the Bambaras of the Upper Niger sacrifices to the dead are generally offered on the threshold of the house, and the blood is poured on the two side-walls of the entrance. It is on the threshold, too, that the shades of ancestors are saluted by the child who is charged with the duty of carrying the seed-corn from the house to the field at the ceremony of sowing. These customs seem to show that in the opinion of the Bambaras the souls of their dead dwell especially at the threshold of the old home.

All these various customs are intelligible if the threshold is believed to be haunted by spirits, which at critical seasons must be propitiated by persons who enter or leave the house. The same belief would explain why in so many lands people under certain circumstances have been careful to avoid contact with the threshold, and why in some places that avoidance has been enforced by warders stationed for the purpose at the doorway. Such warders may well have been the Keepers of the Threshold in the temple at Jerusalem, though no notice of the duties which they discharged has been preserved in the Old Testament.

CHAPTER VII

SACRED OAKS AND TEREBINTHS

AMONG the sacred trees of the ancient Hebrews the oak and the terebinth seem to have held a foremost place. Both are still common in Palestine. The two trees are very different in kind, but their general similarity of appearance is great, and accordingly they appear to have been confused, or at least classed together, by the ancient Hebrews, who bestowed very similar names upon them. In particular passages of the Old Testament it is not always easy to determine whether the reference is to an oak or to a terebinth.

Three species of oaks are common in Palestine at the present time. Of these the most abundant is the prickly evergreen oak (*Quercus pseudo-cocifera*). In general appearance and in the colour of its leaves this oak closely resembles the holm oak of our own country, but the leaves are prickly and very different in shape, being more like holly leaves. The natives call it *sindian*, while *ballout* is their generic name for all the species of oak. This prickly evergreen oak "is by far the most abundant tree throughout Syria, covering the rock hills, of Palestine especially, with a dense brush-wood of trees 8-12 feet high, branching from the base, thickly covered with small evergreen rigid leaves, and bearing acorns copiously. On Mount Carmel it forms nine-tenths of the shrubby vegetation, and it is almost equally abundant on the west flanks of the Anti-Lebanon and many slopes and valleys of Lebanon. Even in localities where it is not now seen, its roots are found in the soil, and dug up for fuel, as in the valleys to the south of Bethlehem. Owing to the indiscriminate destruction of the forests in Syria, this oak rarely attains its full size."

The second species of oak in Palestine is the Valonia oak (*Quercus aegilops*). It is deciduous and very much resembles our English oak in general appearance and growth, never forming a bush or undergrowth, but rising on a stout gnarled trunk, from three to seven feet in girth, to a height of from twenty to thirty feet. The foliage is dense, and the trees, occurring for the most part in open glades, give a park-like appearance to the landscape. Rare in the south, it is very common in the north. It is scattered over Carmel, abounds on Tabor, and forms a forest to the north of that mountain. In Bashan it almost supplants the prickly-leaved evergreen oak, and is no doubt the oak of Bashan to which the Hebrew prophets refer as a type of pride and strength; for in that country the tree attains a magnificent size, especially in the lower valleys. Its very large acorns are eaten by the natives, while the acorn cups are used by dyers under the name of Valonia and are largely exported.

The third species of oak in Palestine (*Quercus infectoria*) is also deciduous; its leaves are very white on the under surface. It is not so common as the other two species, but it grows on Carmel and occurs plentifully near Kedes, the ancient Kedesh Naphtali. The abundance of spherical galls, of a deep red-brown colour and shining viscid surface, make the tree very conspicuous. Canon Tristram saw no large specimens of this oak anywhere and none at all south of Samaria.

The oaks which thus abound in many parts of Palestine are still often regarded with superstitious veneration by the peasantry. Thus, speaking of a fine oak grove near the Lake of Phiala in northern Palestine, Thomson remarks, "These oaks under which we now sit are believed to be inhabited by Jân and other spirits. Almost every village in these wadys and on these mountains has one or more of such thick oaks, which are sacred from the same superstition. Many of them in this region are believed to be inhabited by certain spirits, called *Benât Ya'kôb*—daughters of Jacob—a strange and obscure notion, in regard to which I could never obtain an intelligible explanation. It seems to be a relic of ancient idolatry, which the stringent laws of Muhammed banished in form, but could not entirely eradicate from the minds of the multitude. Indeed, **the**

Moslems are as stupidly given to such superstitions as any class of
the community. Connected with this notion, no doubt, is the
custom of burying their holy men and so-called prophets under
those trees, and erecting *muzârs* [domed shrines] to them there.
All non-Christian sects believe that the spirits of these saints love
to return to this world, and especially to visit the place of their
tombs."

At the romantic village of Bludan, a favourite retreat of the
people of Damascus in the heat of summer, there are "remains of
an old temple of Baal; and the grove of aged oaks on the slope
beneath it is still a place held in superstitious veneration by the
villagers." "In the *W. Barado,* near Damascus, where certain
heathenish festival customs do yet remain amongst the Moslemin, I
have visited two groves of evergreen oaks, which are *wishing-places*
for the peasantry. If anything fall to them for which they vowed,
they will go to the one on a certain day in the year to break a crock
there; or they lay up a new stean in a little cave which is under a
rock at the other. There I have looked in, and saw it full to the
entry of their yet whole offering-pots: in that other grove you will
see the heap of their broken potsherds." Another sacred grove of
oaks is at Beinu in Northern Syria. A ruined Greek church stands
among the trees. Again, we are told that "in a Turkish village in
northern Syria, there is a large and very old oak-tree, which is
regarded as sacred. People burn incense to it, and bring their
offerings to it, precisely in the same way as to some shrine. There
is no tomb of any saint in its neighbourhood, but the people
worship the tree itself."

Very often these venerated oaks are found growing singly or in
groves beside one of those white-domed chapels or supposed tombs
of Mohammedan saints, which may be seen from one end of Syria
to the other. Many such white domes and green groves crown the
tops of hills. "Yet no one knows when, by whom, or for what
special reason they first became consecrated shrines. Many of
them are dedicated to the patriarchs and prophets, a few to Jesus
and the apostles; some bear the names of traditional heroes, and
others appear to honour persons, places, and incidents of merely
local interest. Many of these 'high places' have probably come
down from remote ages, through all the mutations of dynasties and
religions, unchanged to the present day. We can believe this the
more readily because some of them are now frequented by the
oldest communities in the country, and those opposed to each other
—Arabs of the desert, Muhammedans, Metawileh, Druses, Christians,
and even Jews. We may have, therefore, in those 'high places
under every green tree upon the high mountains and upon the hills,'
not only sites of the very highest antiquity, but existing monuments,
with their groves and domes, of man's ancient superstitions; and
if that does not add to our veneration, it will greatly increase the
interest with which we examine them. There is one of these 'high

places,' with its groves of venerable oak-trees, on the summit of Lebanon, east of this village of Jezzin. The top of the mountain is of an oval shape, and the grove was planted regularly around it."

To the same effect another writer, who long sojourned in the Holy Land, observes, "The traveller in Palestine will often see a little clump of trees with the white dome of a low stone building peeping out of the dark-green foliage, and on inquiring what it is will be told that it is a *Wely*, or saint—that is, his reputed tomb. These buildings are usually, though not invariably, on the tops of hills, and can be seen for many miles round, some of them, indeed, forming landmarks for a great distance. Who these *Ouliah* were is for the most part lost in obscurity; but the real explanation is that they mark the site of some of the old Canaantish high places, which we know, from many passages in the Old Testament, were not all destroyed by the Israelites when they took possession of the land, becoming in subsequent ages a frequent cause of sin to them. There is generally, but not always, a grove of trees round the Wely. The oak is the kind most commonly found in these groves at the present day, as would appear to have been also the case in Bible times, especially in the hill country. Besides the oak—which is invariably the evergreen kind, and not the deciduous species of our English woods—the terebinth, tamarisk, sidr, or nubk (the *Zizyphus-spina-Christi*, sometimes called *Dôm* by Europeans), and other trees, are to be seen as well. Occasionally the grove is represented by one large solitary tree under whose shade the Wely nestles. The shrine itself usually consists of a plain stone building, for the most part windowless, but having a *Mihrâb*, or prayer-niche. It is kept in fair repair as a rule, and whitewashed from time to time both inside and out. Occasionally a grave is to be found inside, under the dome, an ugly erection of stone plastered over, about three feet high, and frequently of abnormal length; that of the so-called grave of Joshua, near Es Salt, east of the Jordan, is over thirty feet in length."

In like manner Captain Conder, speaking of the real, not the nominal, religion of the Syrian peasantry at the present day, writes as follows: "The professed religion of the country is Islam, the simple creed of 'one God, and one messenger of God'; yet you may live for months in the out-of-the-way parts of Palestine without seeing a mosque, or hearing the call of the Muedhen to prayer. Still the people are not without a religion which shapes every action of their daily life. . . . In almost every village in the country a small building surmounted by a whitewashed dome is observable, being the sacred chapel of the place; it is variously called *Kubbeh*, 'dome'; *Mazâr*, 'shrine'; or *Mukam*, 'station,' the latter being a Hebrew word, used in the Bible for the 'places' of the Canaanites, which Israel was commanded to destroy 'upon the high mountains, and upon the hills, and under every green tree' (Deut. xxi. 2). Just as in the time of Moses, so now, the position chosen for the

Mukâm is generally conspicuous. On the top of a peak, or on the back of a ridge, the little white dome gleams brightly in the sun; under the boughs of the spreading oak or terebinth; beside the solitary palm, or among the aged lotus-trees at a spring, one lights constantly on the low buildings, standing isolated, or surrounded by the shallow graves of a small cemetery. The trees besides the *Mukâms* are always considered sacred, and every bough which falls is treasured within the sacred building.

"The *Mukâms* are of very various degrees of importance; sometimes, as at Neby Jibrîn, there is only a plot of bare ground, with a few stones walling it in; or again, as at the Mosque of Abu Harîreh (a Companion of the Prophet), near Yebnah, the building has architectural pretensions, with inscriptions and ornamental stone-work. The typical *Mukâm* is, however, a little building of modern masonry, some ten feet square, with a round dome, carefully whitewashed, and a *Mihrab* or prayer-niche on the south wall. The walls round the door, and the lintel-stone are generally adorned with daubs of orange-coloured henna, and a pitcher for water is placed beside the threshold to refresh the pilgrim. There is generally a small cenotaph within, directed with the head to the west, the body beneath being supposed to lie on its right side facing Mecca. A few old mats sometimes cover the floor, and a plough, or other object of value, is often found stored inside the *Mukâm*, where it is quite safe from the most daring thief, as none would venture to incur the displeasure of the saint in whose shrine the property has thus been deposited on trust.

"This *Mukâm* represents the real religion of the peasant. It is sacred as the place where some saint is supposed once to have 'stood' (the name signifying 'standing-place'), or else it is consecrated by some other connection with his history. It is the central point from which the influence of the saint is supposed to radiate, extending in the case of a powerful Sheikh to a distance of perhaps twenty miles all round. If propitious, the Sheikh bestows good luck, health, and general blessings on his worshippers; if enraged, he will inflict palpable blows, distraction of mind, or even death. If a man seems at all queer in his manner, his fellow-villagers will say, 'Oh, the Sheikh has struck him!' and it is said that a peasant will rather confess a murder, taking his chance of escape, than forswear himself on the shrine of a reputed Sheikh, with the supposed certainty of being killed by spiritual agencies.

"The *cultus* of the *Mukâm* is simple. There is always a guardian of the building; sometimes it is the civil Sheikh, or elder of the village, sometimes it is a Derwîsh, who lives near, but there is always some one to fill the water-pitcher, and to take care of the place. The greatest respect is shown to the chapel, where the invisible presence of the saint is supposed always to abide. The peasant removes his shoes before entering, and takes care not to tread on the threshold; he uses the formula, 'Your leave, O blessed one,' as he approaches, and he avoids any action which might give offence to the *numen* of the place. When sickness prevails in a village, votive offerings are brought to the *Mukâm*, and I have often seen a little earthenware lamp brought down by some poor wife or mother, whose husband or child was sick, to be burnt before the shrine. A vow to the saint is paid by a sacrifice called *Kôd*, or 'requital,' a sheep being killed close to the *Mukâm*, and eaten at a feast in honour of the beneficent Sheikh."

The fallen branches of the sacred trees, whether oaks, terebinths, tamarisks, or others, which grow beside these local sanctuaries, may not be used as fuel; the Mohammedans believe that were they to turn the sacred wood to such base uses, the curse of the saint would rest on them. Hence at these spots it is a curious sight, in a country where firewood is scarce, to see huge boughs lie rotting on the ground. Only at festivals in honour of the saints do the Moslems dare to burn the sacred lumber. The Christian peasants are less scrupulous; they sometimes surreptitiously employ the fallen branches to feed the fire on the domestic hearth.

Thus the worship at the high places and green trees, which pious Hebrew kings forbade and prophets thundered against thousands of years ago, persists apparently in the same places to this day. So little is an ignorant peasantry affected by the passing of empires, by the moral and spiritual revolutions which change the face of the civilized world.

To take, now, some particular examples of these local sanctuaries. On a ridge near the lake of Phiala in northern Palestine, there is a knoll "covered with a copse of noble oak trees, forming a truly venerable grove, with a deep religious gloom." In the midst of the grove stands the *wely* or shrine of Sheikh 'Othmân Hâzûry; it is merely a common Moslem tomb surrounded by a shabby stone wall. Just below, on one side of the knoll, is a small fountain which takes its name from the saint. Again, on the summit of Jebel Osh'a, the highest mountain in Gilead, may be seen the reputed tomb of the prophet Hosea, shaded by a magnificent evergreen oak. The tomb is venerated alike by Moslems, Christians, and Jews. People used to come on pilgrimage to the spot to sacrifice, pray, and feast. The prospect from the summit is esteemed the finest in all Palestine, surpassing in beauty, though not in range, the more famous view from Mount Nebo, whence Moses just before death gazed on the Promised Land, which he was not to enter, lying spread out in purple lights and shadows across the deep valley of the Jordan.

Again, the reputed tomb of Abel, high up a cliff beside the river Abana in the Lebanon, is surrounded by venerable oak trees. It is a domed structure of the usual sort, and is a place of Mohammedan pilgrimage. A similar association of tombs with trees is to be found at Tell el Kadi, "the mound of the judge," the ancient

Dan, where the lower springs of the Jordan take their rise. The place is a natural mound of limestone rock some eighty feet high and half a mile across. It rises on the edge of a wide plain, below a long succession of olive yards and oak glades which slope down from Banias, where are the upper sources of the Jordan. The situation is very lovely. On the western side of the mound an almost impenetrable thicket of reeds, oaks, and oleanders is fed by the lower springs of the river, a wonderful fountain like a large bubbling basin, said to be the largest single fountain not only in Syria but in the world. On the eastern side of the mound, overhanging another bright feeder of the Jordan, stand side by side two noble trees, a holm oak and a terebinth, shading the graves of Moslem saints. Their branches are hung with rags and other trumpery offerings.

Even when the hallowed oaks do not grow beside the tombs or shrines of saints they are often thus decorated with rags by the superstitious peasantry. Thus at Seilûn, the site of the ancient Shiloh "is a large and noble oak tree called Balûtat-Ibrahîm, Abraham's oak. It is one of the 'inhabited trees' so common in this country, and the superstitious peasants hang bits of rags on the branches to propitiate the mysterious beings that are supposed to 'inhabit' it." "Some distance back we passed a cluster of large oak trees, and the lower branches of one of them were hung with bits of rag of every variety of shape and colour. What is the meaning of this ornamentation? That was one of the haunted or 'inhabited trees,' supposed to be the abode of evil spirits; and those bits of rags are suspended upon the branches to protect the wayfarer from their malign influence. There are many such trees in all parts of the country, and the superstitious inhabitants are afraid to sleep under them." One of these haunted trees may be seen on the site of Old Beyrout. It is a venerable evergreen oak growing near the edge of a precipice. The people hang strips of their garments on its boughs, believing that it has the power to cure sickness. One of its roots forms an arch above ground, and through this arch persons who suffer from rheumatism and lumbago crawl to be healed of their infirmities. Expectant mothers also creep through it to obtain an easy delivery. On the twenty-first of September men and women dance and sing all night beside the tree, the sexes dancing separately. This oak is so sacred that when a sceptic dared to cut a branch of it, his arm withered up.

In various parts of the upper valley of the Jordan there are groves of oaks and shrines dedicated to the daughters of Jacob. One of these shrines may be seen at the town of Safed. It is a small mosque containing a tomb in which the damsels are supposed to live in all the bloom of beauty. Incense is offered at the door of the tomb. A gallant and afterwards highly distinguished officer, then engaged in the survey of Palestine, searched the tomb carefully for the ladies, but without success. The association of the daughters of Jacob with oak-trees may perhaps point to a belief in Dryads or nymphs of the oak.

The Hebrew words commonly rendered "oak" and "terebinth" are very similar, the difference between them being in part merely a difference in the vowel points which were added to the text by the Massoretic scribes in the Middle Ages. Scholars are not agreed as to the correct equivalents of the words, so that when we meet with one or other of them in the Old Testament it is to some extent doubtful whether the tree referred to is an oak or a terebinth. The terebinth (*Pistacia terebinthus*) is still a common tree in Palestine, occurring either singly or in clumps mingled with forests of oak. The natives call it the *butm* tree. The terebinth "is a very common tree in the southern and eastern part of the country, being generally found in situations too warm or dry for the oak, whose place it there supplies, and which it much resembles in general appearance at a distance. It is seldom seen in clumps or groves, never in forests, but stands isolated and weird-like in some bare ravine or on a hillside, where nothing else towers above the low brushwood. When it sheds its leaves at the beginning of winter, it still more recalls the familiar English oak, with its short and gnarled trunk, spreading and irregular limbs, and small twigs. The leaves are pinnate, the leaflets larger than those of the lentisk, and their hue is a very dark reddish-green, not quite so sombre as the locust tree. . . . Towards the north this tree becomes more scarce, but in the ancient Moab and Ammon, and in the region round Heshbon, it is the only one which relieves the monotony of the rolling downs and boundless sheep-walks; and in the few glens south of the Jabbok we noticed many trees of a larger size than any others which remain west of Jordan."

Yet if we may judge from the comparative frequence of allusions to the two trees in the descriptions of travellers, the terebinth is less common in Palestine than the oak, and is apparently less often the object of superstitious regard. However, instances of such veneration for the tree are not uncommon. Canon Tristram tells us that "many terebinth remain to this day objects of veneration in their neighbourhood; and the favourite burying-place of the Bedouin sheikh is under a solitary tree. Eastern travellers will recall the 'Mother of Rags' on the outskirts of the desert, a terebinth covered with the votive offerings of superstition or affection"; and elsewhere the same writer mentions a terebinth hung with rags at the source of the Jordan. In Moab "the sacred trees—oak, evergreen oak, terebinth, locust-tree, olive, the particular kind is unimportant—are found under a double aspect, either attached to a sanctuary or isolated. In the first case they appear not to have an origin independent of the holy place which they shade, nor to have any function distinct from the influence ascribed to the saint (*wely*) who caused them to grow, and who vivifies and protects them. . . . The second sort of sacred trees does not enjoy the benefit of a sanctuary in the neighbourhood; they grow solitary, near a spring, on a hill, or at the top of a mountain. . . . Near Taibeh, not far from Hanzireh, to the south-west of Kerak, I passed near a sacred terebinth, with thick green foliage, covered with rags and much honoured by the Arabs of the district. I asked where was the tomb of the saint (*wely*). 'There is no tomb here,' replied an Arab who was finishing his devotions. 'But then,' I continued, 'why do you come here to pray?' 'Because there is a saint,' he answered promptly. 'Where is he?' 'All the ground shaded by the tree serves as his abode; but he dwells also in the tree, in the branches, and in the leaves.'" Again, among the ruins of a Roman fortress called Rumeileh, in Moab, there grows a verdurous terebinth, of which no Arab would dare to cut a bough, lest he should be immediately struck by the spirit of the saint (*wely*), who resides in the tree and has made it his domain. On being asked whether the saint lived in the tree, some Arabs answered that it was his spirit which lent its vigour to the tree, others thought that he dwelt beneath it, but their ideas on the subject were vague, and they agreed that "God knows." Father Jauseen, to whom we owe these accounts of sacred terebinths in Moab, informs us that "the spirit or *wely* who is worshipped in the tree has his abode circumscribed by the tree; he cannot quit it, he lives there as in prison. His situation thus differs from that of the saint (*wely*), properly so called, and from the ancestor, who are not confined to one spot, but can transport themselves to the places where they are invoked by their worshippers. When from motives of devotion a Bedouin, to obtain a cure, sleeps under one of the sacred trees, the spirit or the saint (*wely*) often appears to him by night and charges him with a commission or incites him to offer a sacrifice. He is always obeyed."

In these latter cases the saint in the tree is probably neither more nor less than an old heathen tree-spirit, who has survived, in a hardly disguised form, through all the ages of Christian and Mohammedan supremacy. This is confined by the account which Father Jauseen gives of the superstitious veneration entertained by the Arabs for these trees. "The magnificent group of trees," he says, "called Meïseh, to the south of Kerak, enjoys the same renown and the same worship. Similarly, the tree of ed-De 'al does not cover any tomb of a saint (*wely*), nevertheless its reputation is very great and its power considerable. I found it impossible to ascertain whether there is a saint (*wely*); to the thinking of the persons with whom I conversed it is the tree itself that is to be feared. Woe to the Arab who would dare to cut a branch, a bough, or even a leaf! The spirit or the virtue of the tree would punish him at once, perhaps it might cause his death. A Bedouin had deposited a bag of barley, for a few hours only, under its protection. Two goats, straying from a flock in the neighbourhood, found the bag and ate up the barley. The tree sent a wolf after them, which devoured them that evening. It is indeed the tree itself with punishes, as it is the tree itself which bestows its benefits. In the touch of its leaves there is healing. At Meïseh, at ed-De 'al the Bedouins never fail to pass a green bough over their faces or arms in order either to rid themselves of a malady or to acquire fresh vigour. The mere touch communicates to them the virtue of the tree. It is under its shade that the sick go and sleep to be healed of their infirmities. It is to its branches that the rags are tied which can be seen in such number and variety. The day that the cloth is tied to the tree the sickness must pass out of the body of the patient, because, as they have assured me, the sickness is thus fastened to the tree. Others, with a dash of rationalism, hold that the rag is nothing but a memorial of a visit paid to the tree. Sometimes an Arab, passing near a tree, ties a piece of cloth or leaves his staff under the tree, in token of respect, or to secure its favour for himself in time to come. It is not, in fact, uncommon to meet with Arabs who knot a scrap of red or green cloth (never black, rarely white) to the boughs of a sacred tree for the purpose of ensuring the health of a favourite child. . . . At Meïseh I found, fastened to a branch, several locks of hair. My companion gave me the following explanation: 'It is a sick woman who has paid a visit to the tree; she has shorn her hair in token of veneration for the tree.' "

In the warm and dry climate of Moab the terebinth is the principal tree, while the oak flourishes more in the cooler and rainier districts of Gilead and Galilee in the north. It is, therefore, natural that the terebinth should be predominantly the sacred tree of the south and the oak of the north; but throughout Palestine as a whole, if we may judge by the accounts of travellers, the oak appears to be the commoner tree, and consequently, perhaps, the more frequently revered by the peasants. Accordingly, when we consider the tenacity and persistence of identical forms of superstition through the ages, we seem justified in concluding that in antiquity also the oak was more generally worshipped by the idolatrous inhabitants of the land. From this it follows that when a doubt exists as to whether in the Old Testament the Hebrew word for a sacred tree should be rendered "oak" or "terebinth," the preference ought to be given to the rendering "oak." This conclusion is confirmed by the general practice of the old Greek translators and of St. Jerome, who, in translating these passages, commonly render the doubtful word by "oak," and not by "terebinth." On the whole, then, the revisers of our English Bible have done well to translate all the words in question by "oak" instead of by "terebinth," except in the two passages where two of these words occur in the same verse. In these two passages the revisers render 'allōn by "oak," but 'elāh by "terebinth." Elsewhere they render 'elāh by "oak"; but in the margin they mention "terebinth," as an alternative rendering. I shall follow their example and cite the Revised Version in the sequel.

That the idolatrous Hebrews of antiquity revered the oak tree is proved by the evidence of the prophets who denounced the superstition. Thus Hosea says, "They sacrifice upon the tops of the mountains, and burn incense upon the hills, under oaks and poplars and terebinths, because the shadow thereof is good: therefore your daughters commit whoredom, and your brides commit adultery. I will not punish your daughters when they commit whoredom, nor your brides when they commit adultery, for they themselves go apart with whores, and they sacrifice with the harlots." The prophet here refers to a custom of religious prostitution which was carried on under the shadow of the sacred trees. Referring to the sacred groves of his heathenish countrymen, Ezekiel says, "And ye shall know that I am the Lord, when their slain men shall be among their idols round about their altars, upon every high hill, in all the tops of the mountains, and under every green tree, and under every thick oak, the place where they did offer sweet savour to all their idols." Again, Isaiah, speaking of the sinners who have forsaken the Lord, says, "For they shall be ashamed of the oaks which ye have desired, and ye shall be confounded for the gardens that ye have chosen." Again, the author of the later prophecy which passes under the name of Isaiah, in denouncing the idolatry of his day, says, "Ye that inflame yourselves among the oaks, under every green tree; that slay the children in the valleys, under the clefts of the rocks." The sacrifice here referred to is, no doubt, the sacrifice of children to Moloch. Jeremiah alludes to the same practice in a passionate address to sinful Israel: Also in thy skirts is found the blood of the souls of the innocent poor: I have not found it at the place of breaking in, but upon every oak."[1] Thus it would seem that the blood of the sacrificed children was smeared on, or at least offered in some form to, the sacred oaks. In this connexion it should be remembered that the victims were slaughtered before being burned in the fire, so that it would be possible to use their blood as an unguent or libation. The Gallas of East Africa pour the blood of animals at the foot of their sacred trees in order to prevent the trees from withering, and sometimes they smear the trunks and boughs with blood, butter, and milk. The Masai of East Africa revere a species of parasitic fig which gradually envelops the whole trunk of the original tree in glistening whitish coils of glabrous root and branch. Such trees the Masai propitiate by killing a goat and pouring its blood at the base of the

---

[1] Jeremiah ii. 34, where the meaningless אֵלֶּה ("these") of the "Massoretic text should be corrected into אֵלָה or אַלָּה ("oak" or "terebinth") in accordance with the readings of the Septuagint (ἐπὶ πάσῃ δρυΐ) and of the Syriac Version. The change is merely one of punctuation; the original Hebrew text remains unaffected. The vague sense of the preposition עַל leaves it uncertain whether the blood was smeared on the trees or poured out at their foot. However, Professor Kennett writes to me that he believes the textual corruption in Jeremiah ii. 34 to be too deep to be healed by the slight emendation I have adopted. He conjectures that the last clause of the verse is defective through the omission of a word or words.

trunk. When the Nounoumas of the French Sudan are sacrificing to Earth for good crops, they pour the blood of fowls on tamarinds and other trees. The Bambaras, of the Upper Niger, sacrifice sheep, goats, and fowls to their baobabs or other sacred trees, and apply the blood of the victims to the trunks, accompanying the sacrifice with prayers to the indwelling spirit of the tree. In like manner the old Prussians sprinkled the blood of their sacrifices on the holy oak at Romove; and Lucan says that in the sacred Druidical grove at Marseilles every tree was washed with human blood.

But if, in the later times of Israel, the worship of the oak or the terebinth was denounced by the prophets as a heathenish rite, there is a good deal of evidence to show that at an earlier period sacred oaks or terebinths played an important part in the popular religion, and that Jehovah himself was closely associated with them. At all events, it is remarkable how often God or his angel is said to have revealed himself to one of the old patriarchs or heroes at an oak or terebinth. Thus the first recorded appearance of Jehovah to Abraham took place at the oracular oak or terebinth of Shechem, and there Abraham built him an altar. Again, we are told that Abraham dwelt beside the oaks or terebinths of Mamre at Hebron, and that he built there also an altar to the Lord. And it was there, beside the oaks or terebinths of Mamre, as he sat at the door of his tent in the heat of the day, that God appeared to him in the likeness of three men, and there under the shadow of the trees the Deity partook of the flesh, the milk, and the curds which the hospitable patriarch offered him. So, too, the angel of the Lord came and sat under the oak or terebinth of Ophrah, and Gideon, who was busy threshing the wheat, brought him the flesh and broth of a kid and unleavened cakes to eat under the oak. But the angel, instead of eating the food, bade Gideon lay the flesh and cakes on a rock and pour out the broth; then with a touch of his staff he drew fire from the rock, and the flame consumed the flesh and the cakes. After that the heavenly, or perhaps the arboreal, visitor vanished, and Gideon, like Abraham, built an altar on the spot.

There was an oracular oak or terebinth near Shechem as well as at Mamre; whether it was the same tree under which God appeared to Abraham, we do not know. Its name, "the oak or terebinth of the augurs," seems to show that a set of wizards or Druids, if we may call them so, had their station at the sacred tree in order to interpret to inquirers the rustling of the leaves in the wind, the cooing of the wood-pigeons in the branches, or such other omens as the spirit of the oak vouchsafed to his worshippers. The beautiful vale of Shechem, embosomed in olives, orange-groves, and palms, and watered by plenteous rills, still presents perhaps the richest landscape in all Palestine, and of old it would seem to have been a great seat of tree-worship. At all events in its history we meet again and again with the mention of oaks or terebinths which from the context appear to have been sacred. Thus Jacob took the idols or "strange gods" of his household, together with the earrings which had probably served as amulets, and buried them under the oak or terebinth at Shechem. According to Eustathius, the tree was a terebinth and was worshipped by the people of the neighbourhood down to his own time. An altar stood beside it on which sacrifices were offered. Again, it was under the oak by the sanctuary of the Lord at Shechem that Joshua set up a great stone as a witness, saying to the Israelites, "Behold, this stone shall be a witness against us; for it hath heard all the words of the Lord which he spake unto us: it shall be therefore a witness against you, lest ye deny your God." And it was at "the oak of the pillar" in Shechem that the men of the city made Abimelech king. The oak or terebinth may have been supposed to stand in some close relation to the king; for elsewhere we read of a tree called "the king's oak" on the borders of the tribe Asher; and according to one account the bones of Saul and of his sons were buried under the oak or terebinth at Jabesh. So when Rebekah's nurse Deborah died, she was buried below Bethel under the oak, and hence the tree was called the Oak of Weeping. The Oak of Weeping may perhaps have been the very oak at which, according to the directions of Samuel the prophet, Saul shortly before his coronation was to meet three men going up to sacrifice to the Lord at Bethel, who would salute him and give him two of their loaves. This salutation of the future king by three men at the oak reminds us of the meeting of Abraham with God in the likeness of three men under the oaks of Mamre. In the original story the greeting of the three men at the oak may have had a deeper meaning than transpires in the form in which the narrative has come down to us. Taken along with the coronation of Abimelech under an oak, it suggests that the spirit of the oak, perhaps in triple form, was expected to bless the king at his inauguration. In the light of this suggestion the burial of Saul's bones under an oak seems to acquire a fresh significance. The king, who at the beginning of his reign had been blessed by the god of the oak, was fittingly laid to his last rest under the sacred tree.

But of all the holy trees of ancient Palestine by far the most famous and the most popular was apparently the oak or terebinth of Mamre, where God revealed himself to Abraham, the founder of the Israelitish nation, in the likeness of three men. Was the tree an oak or a terebinth? The ancient testimonies are conflicting, but the balance of evidence is in favour of the terebinth. Josephus tells us that in his day many monuments of Abraham, finely built of beautiful marble, were shown at Hebron, and that six furlongs from the town grew a very large terebinth, which was said to have stood there since the creation of the world. Though he does not expressly say so, we may assume that this terebinth was the one under which Abraham was believed to have entertained the angels.

Again Eusebius affirms that the terebinth remained down to his own time in the early part of the fourth century A.D., and that the spot was still revered as divine by the people of the neighbourhood. A holy picture represented the three mysterious guests who partook of Abraham's hospitality under the tree; the middle of the three figures excelled the rest in honour, and him the good bishop identified with "Our Lord Himself, our Saviour, whom even they who know Him not adore." All three angels were worshipped by the people of the neighbourhood. They curiously remind us of the three gods whose images were worshipped in the holy oak at Romove, the religious centre of the heathen Prussians. Perhaps both at Hebron and at Romove the tree-god was for some reason conceived in triple form. A pilgrim of Bordeaux, author of the oldest *Itinerary of Jerusalem*, writing in the year 333 A.D., tells us that the terebinth was two miles from Hebron, and that a fine basilica had been built there by order of Constantine. Yet from the manner of his reference to it we gather that "the terebinth" was in his time merely the name of a place, the tree itself having disappeared, Certainly Jerome, writing later in the same century, seems to imply that the tree no longer existed. For he says that the oak of Abraham or Mamre was shown down to the reign of Constantine, and that "the place of the terebinth" was worshipped superstitiously by all the people round about, because Abraham had there entertained the angels.

When Constantine determined to build a church at the sacred tree, he communicated his intention in a letter to Eusebius, bishop of Caesarea, who has fortunately preserved a copy of the letter in his life of the emperor. I will extract from it the passage which relates to the holy tree: "The place which is called 'at the Oak of Mamre,' where we learn that Abraham had his home, is said to be polluted by certain superstitious persons in various ways; for it is reported that most damnable idols are set up beside it, and that an altar stands hard by, and that unclean sacrifices are constantly offered. Wherefore, seeing that this appears to be foreign to the present age and unworthy of the holiness of the place, I wish your Grace to know that I have written to the right honourable Count Acacius, my friend, commanding that without delay all the idols found at the aforesaid place shall be committed to the flames, and the altar overturned; and any one who after this decree may dare to commit impiety in such a place shall be deemed liable to punishment. We have ordered that the spot shall be adorned with the pure building of a basilica, in order that it may be made a meeting-place worthy of holy men."

In this letter it will be observed that the emperor speaks of the sacred tree as an oak, not as a terebinth, and it is called an oak also by the Church historians Socrates and Sozomenus. But little weight can be given to their testimony since all three probably followed the reading of the Septuagint, which calls the tree an oak, not a terebinth. It is probably in deference to the authority of the Septuagint that Eusebius himself speaks of "the oak of Abraham" in the very passage in which he tells us that the terebinth existed to his own time. The Church historian Sozomenus has bequeathed to us a curious and valuable description of the festival, which down to the time of Constantine, or even later, was held every summer at the sacred tree. His account runs thus:—

"I must now relate the decree which the Emperor Constantine passed with regard to what is called the oak of Mamre. This place, which they now call Terebinth, is fifteen furlongs north of Hebron and about two hundred and fifty furlongs from Jerusalem. It is a true tale that with the angels sent against the people of Sodom the Son of God appeared to Abraham and told him of the birth of his son. There every year a famous festival is still held in summer time by the people of the neighbourhood as well as by the inhabitants of the more distant parts of Palestine and by the Phoenicians and Arabians. Very many also assemble for trade, to buy and sell; for every one sets great store on the festival. The Jews do so because they pride themselves on Abraham as their founder; the Greeks do so on account of the visit of the angels; and the Christians do so also because there appeared at that time to the pious man One who in after ages made himself manifest through the Virgin for the salvation of mankind. Each, after the manner of his faith, does honour to the place, some praying to the God of all, some invoking the angels and pouring wine, or offering incense, or an ox, or a goat, or a sheep, or a cock. For every man fattened a valuable animal throughout the year, vowing to keep it for himself and his family to feast upon at the festival on the spot. And all of them here refrain from women, either out of respect to the place or lest some evil should befall them through the wrath of God, though the women beautify and adorn their persons specially, as at a festival, and show themselves freely in public. Yet there is no lewd conduct, though the sexes camp together and sleep promiscuously. For the ground is ploughed and open to the sky, and there are no houses except the ancient house of Abraham at the oak and the well that was made by him. But at the time of the festival no one draws water from the well. For, after the Greek fashion, some set burning lamps there; others poured wine on it, or threw in cakes, money, perfumes, or incense. On that account, probably, the water was rendered unfit to drink by being mixed with the things thrown into it. The performance of these ceremonies according to Greek ritual was reported to the Emperor Constantine by his wife's mother, who had gone to the place in fulfilment of a vow."

Thus it appears that at Hebron an old heathen worship of the sacred tree and the sacred well survived in full force down to the establishment of Christianity. The fair which was held along with the summer festival appears to have drawn merchants together from many quarters of the Semitic world. It played a melancholy part in the history of the Jews; for at this fair, after the suppression of the last Jewish rebellion by the Romans in the year 119 A.D., a vast multitude of captive men, women, and children was sold into slavery. So the Jewish nation came to an end on the very spot where it was traditionally said to have been founded by Abraham, at the sacred oak or terebinth of Mamre. The tree, or rather its successor, is shown to this day in a grassy field a mile and a half to the west of Hebron. It is a fine old evergreen oak (*Quercus pseudo-coccifera*), the noblest tree in southern Palestine. The trunk is twenty-three feet in girth, and the span of its spreading boughs measures ninety feet. Thus in the long rivalry between the oak and the terebinth for the place of honour at Mamre the oak has won. There is not a single large terebinth in the neighbourhood of Hebron.

CHAPTER VIII

THE HIGH PLACES OF ISRAEL

FROM many passages in the Old Testament we learn that in ancient Israel the regular seats of religious worship were situated on natural heights, which were often, perhaps generally, shaded by the thick foliage of venerable trees. For the most part these sanctuaries appear to have been unenclosed and open to the sky, though sometimes perhaps gay canopies of many colours were spread to protect the sacred emblems, a wooden pole and a stone pillar, from the fierce rays of the summer sun or the driving showers of winter rain. Thither for many ages after the Israelites had settled in Palestine the people resorted to offer sacrifice, and there, under the shadow of ancient oaks or terebinths, their devotions were led by pious prophets and kings, not only without offence, but with an inward persuasion of the divine approbation and blessing. But the multiplication of sanctuaries is apt to foster in ignorant worshippers a belief in a corresponding multiplication of the deities who are worshipped at the shrines; and thus the doctrine of the unity of God, dear to the higher minds in Israel, tended to be frittered away into a tacit acknowledgment of many gods or Baalim, each the lord of his own wooded height, each dispensing the boons of sunshine and rain, of fruitfulness and fecundity, to a little circle of hamlets, which looked to him, as Italian villages look to their patron saints, to bless and prosper them in their flocks and herds, their fields and vineyards and oliveyards. The facility with which a theoretical monotheism could thus insensibly slide into a practical polytheism excited the apprehension of the prophets, and the anxiety with which they viewed this theological decadence was quickened into a fiery glow of moral indignation by some of the lewd rites of which these fair scenes, though consecrated, as it might seem, by nature herself to purity and peace, to heavenly thoughts and pensive contemplations, were too often the silent and, we may almost add, the ashamed and reluctant witnesses.   And these religious and ethical considerations were reinforced by others which we might call political, though to the ancient Hebrew mind, which beheld all things through a golden haze of divinity, they wore the aspect of judgments threatened or executed by the supreme disposer of events against sinners and evil-doers.   The rising power of the great Assyrian and Babylonian empires first menaced and then extinguished the liberties of the little Palestine kingdoms; and the coming catastrophe was long foreseen and predicted by the higher intelligences in Israel, who clothed their forecasts and pre-dictions in the poetical rhapsodies of prophecy.   Musing on the dangers which thus threatened their country, they thought that they discovered a principal source of the peril in the religious worship of the high places, which by their polytheistic tendencies infringed the majesty, and by their immoral seductions insulted the purity, of the one true God.   The root of the evil they believed to be religious, and the remedy which they proposed for it was religious also.   It was to sweep away the worship of the high places, with all their attendant debaucheries, and to concentrate the whole religious ceremonials of the country at Jerusalem, where a more regular and solemn ritual, cleansed from every impurity, was by its daily intercession, its savoury sacrifices and sweet psalmody, to ensure the divine favour and protection for the whole land.   The scheme, bred in the souls and hearts of the great prophets, took practical shape in the memorable reformation of King Josiah; but the measure, so fondly planned and so hopefully executed, proved unavailing to stay the decline and avert the downfall of the kingdom of Judah.   From the day when the high places were abolished and the temple on Mount Zion was constituted the one legitimate national sanctuary, hardly a generation passed before Jerusalem opened her gates to the enemy and the flower of her sons was led away captive to Babylon.

Our knowledge of the local sanctuaries on which, according to the religious interpretation of Jewish history, the destiny of the nation was believed in great measure to turn, is partly drawn from the denunciations of them by the prophets, in whose invectives the frequent association of high places with green trees suggests that the presence of trees, especially perhaps of evergreen trees, was a characteristic feature of these sacred eminences.   Thus Jeremiah, speaking of the sin of Israel, says that "their children remember their altars and their sacred poles (*asherim*) by the green trees upon the high hills."   And again, "Moreover the Lord said unto me in the days of Josiah the king, Hast thou seen that which backsliding Israel hath done? she is gone up upon every high mountain and under every green tree, and there hath played the harlot."   And Ezekiel, speaking in the name of God, writes as follows: "For when I

had brought them into the land, which I lifted up mine hand to give
unto them, then they saw every high hill, and every thick tree, and
they offered there their sacrifices, and there they presented the provocation of their offering, there also they made their sweet savour,
and they poured out there their drink offerings." And in Deuteronomy, which is generally believed to be substantially the "book of
the law" on which King Josiah founded his reformation, the doom
of the high places and their idolatrous appurtenances is pronounced
in these words: "Ye shall surely destroy all the places, wherein
the nations which ye shall possess served their gods, upon the high
mountains, and upon the hills, and under every green tree: and ye
shall break down their altars, and dash in pieces their pillars, and
burn their sacred poles (*asherim*) with fire; and ye shall hew down
the graven images of their gods; and ye shall destroy their name out
of that place." At an earlier period, when these verdant hilltops
had not yet fallen into disrepute, we hear of King Saul seated on
one of them under the shade of a tamarisk tree, grasping his spear
as the symbol of royalty and surrounded by a circle of courtiers
and councillors.

We have seen that in Palestine down to the present time many
such heights, crowned by clumps of venerable trees, particularly
evergreen oaks, still receive the religious homage of the surrounding
peasantry, though their old heathen character is thinly disguised
by the tradition that a Mohammedan saint sleeps under their solemn
shade. It is reasonable to suppose with some modern writers, who
have long sojourned in the Holy Land, that many at least of these
shady hilltops are the identical spots where the ancient Israelites
sacrificed and burned incense, and that in spite of the zeal of
reformers and the hammers of iconoclasts the immemorial sanctuaries
on these belvederes have continued through all the ages to be the
real centre of the popular religion. Perhaps we may go a step
farther and conjecture that these wooded eminences, standing out
conspicuously from the broad expanse of brown fields and grey-blue
oliveyards, are the last surviving representatives of the old primeval
forests which once clothed the country-side for miles and miles,
till the industry of man had cleared them from the lowlands to
make room for tilth, while his superstition suffered their scanty
relics to linger on the heights, as the last retreat of the sylvan
deities before the axe of the woodman. At least sacred groves
appear to have originated in this fashion elsewhere, and their
analogy supports the conjecture that a similar cause may have
produced a similar effect in Palestine.

For example, the Akikuyu of British East Africa "are essentially
an agricultural people, and have but few cattle, but there are goats
in every village, and often sheep too. To make their fields, acres
of forest land must have been cut down, the burning of which has
made the soil so fertile. At one time probably the forests of Kenya
joined those of the Aberdares and the whole of this area was forest

land. The only sign of this now extant are various little tree-topped hills dotted all over the country. Such hills are sacred, and the groves on their top must not be cut. It is this that has preserved them from the fate of the rest of the forest." The hill Kahumbu "is one of the hills topped by sacred groves, of which there are so many in Kikuyu-land. As neither the trees nor the undergrowth may be cut, for fear of sickness visiting the land, these hills are generally surmounted by large trees arising out of a dense mass of undergrowth. This undergrowth is at Kahumbu the retreat of a number of hyenas to whom the surrounding bare and cultivated country affords little other cover. At the top of the hill is a flat spot surrounded by a thicket. This is the sacrificial place, and is called *athuri aliakuru*. When there is a famine or want of rain it will be decided that a sacrifice should be resorted to. Everybody remains in their huts, there being no leave to go out, with the exception of fourteen old men (*wazuri*). These, the elected priests of the hill, ascend with a sheep; goats are not acceptable to Ngai (God) on such an occasion. At the top they light a fire, and then kill the sheep by holding its mouth and nose till it dies of suffocation. It is then skinned, the skin being subsequently given to and worn by one of the old men's children. The sheep is then cooked, a branch is plucked and dipped into the fat which is sprinkled on to the leaves of the surrounding trees. The old men then eat some of the meat; should they not do this the sacrifice is not acceptable. The rest of the flesh is burnt in the fire, and Ngai comes to eat it afterwards. Directly this function is completed, even while the old men are descending the hill, thunder rolls up and hail pours down with such force that the old men have to wrap their clothes round their heads and run for their houses. Water then bursts forth from the top of the hill and flows down the side." So on the wooded top of Mount Carmel the sacrifice offered by the prophet Elijah is said to have ended the drought which had parched the land of Israel for years; hardly was the rite accomplished when a cloud rose from the sea and darkened all the sky, and the idolatrous king, who had witnessed the discomfiture of the false prophets, had to hurry in his chariot down the hill and across the plain to escape the torrents of rain that descended like a waterspout from the angry heaven.

Two Mundas of Chota Nagpur, in Bengal "make no images of their gods, nor do they worship symbols, but they believe that though invisible to mortal eyes, the gods may, when propitiated by sacrifice, take up for a time their abode in places especially dedicated to them. Thus they have their 'high places' and 'their groves' —the former, some mighty mass of rock to which man has added nothing and from which he takes nothing, the latter, a fragment of the original forest, the trees in which have been for ages, carefully protected, left when the clearance was first made, lest the sylvan gods of the places, disquieted at the wholesale felling of the trees, that sheltered them, should abandon the locality. Even now if a tree is destroyed in the sacred grove (*Jáhirá* or *Sarna*) the gods evince their displeasure by withholding seasonable rain." Every Munda village "has in its vicinity a grove reputed to be a remnant of the primeval forest left intact for the local gods when the clearing was originally made. Here Desauli, the tutelary deity of the village, and his wife, Jhár-Era or Mabúrú, are supposed to sojourn when attending to the wants of their votaries. There is a Desauli for every village, and his authority does not extend beyond the boundary of the village to which his grove belongs; if a man of that village cultivates land in another village, he must pay his devotions to the Desauli of both. The grove deities are held responsible for the crops, and are especially honoured at all the great agricultural festivals. They are also appealed to in sickness." To the same effect another writer tells us that "although the greater portion of the primeval forest, in clearings of which the Munda villages were originally established, have since disappeared under the axe or under the *jārā*-fire,[1] many a Munda village still retains a portion or portions of the original forest to serve as Sarnas or sacred groves. In some Mundari villages, only a small clump of ancient trees now represents the original forest and serves as the village-Sarna. These Sarnas are the only temples the Mundas know. Here the village-gods reside, and are periodically worshipped and propitiated with sacrifices."

We may suppose that these local Desaulis, who reside in sacred groves, the remnants of the primeval forest, and are held responsible for the crops, answer closely to the Baalim of Canaan, who in like manner dwelt among the trees on the hilltops adjoining the villages, and there received the first-fruits of the earth, which the peasants of the neighbourhood brought them in gratitude for bountiful harvests and the refreshing rain of heaven.

Again, on the borders of Afghanistan and India "the frontier hills are often bare enough of fields or habitations, but one cannot go far without coming across some *zyarat*, or holy shrine, where the faithful worship and make their vows. It is very frequently situated on some mountain top or inaccessible cliff, reminding one of the 'high places' of the Israelites. Round the grave are some stunted trees of tamarisk or her (*Zizyphus jujuba*). On the branches of these are hung innumerable bits of rag and pieces of coloured cloth, because every votary who makes a petition at the shrine is bound to tie a piece of cloth on as the outward symbol of his vow." One famous shrine of this sort is on the Suliman Range. "Despite its inaccessibility, hundreds of pilgrims visit this yearly, and sick people are carried up in their beds, with the hope that the blessing of the saint may cure them. Sick people are often carried on beds, either strapped on camels or on the shoulders of their friends, for

---

[1] "By the *jara* system, land is prepared for cultivation by burning down portions of jungles." As to this mode of cultivation, see above, pp. 180 *sqq.*

considerably more than a hundred miles to one or other of these *zyarats*. . . . Another feature of these shrines is that their sanctity is so universally acknowledged that articles of personal property may be safely left by the owners for long periods of time in perfect confidence of finding them untouched on their return, some months later, exactly as they left them. One distinct advantage of these shrines is that it is a sin to cut wood from any of the trees surrounding them. Thus it comes about that the shrines are the only green spots among the hills which the improvident vandalism of the tribes has denuded of all their trees and shrubs."

These Afghan *zyarats*, or mountain shrines, clearly bear a close resemblance to the modern *welys* of Palestine. Both sets of sanctuaries are commonly situated on hilltops and surrounded by trees which may not be felled or lopped; both are supposed to derive their sanctity from the graves of Mohammedan saints; at both it is customary to deposit property in perfect assurance that it will remain inviolate; and at both it is common for pilgrims to leave memorials of their visit in the shape of rags attached to the branches of the trees.

Once more, among the Cheremiss of Russia "at the present time isolated groves serve as places of sacrifice and prayer: these groves are known under the name of *kjus-oto*. But in former days it was in the depths of the forest that the Cheremiss sacrificed to their gods. Some manifestation of the divine will, for example the sudden welling-up of a spring, generally marked out the places of prayer to be selected by the people. The Cheremiss of Ufa sought out by preference heights in the neighbourhood of brooks; and even after the axe of the woodman had stripped the surrounding country of its trees, these heights continued to be sacred."

To judge by these analogies the sacred groves of Palestine in antiquity, which gave so much offence to the later prophets, may well have been remnants of a primeval forest, green islets left standing on solitary heights as refuges for the rustic divinities, whom the husbandman had despoiled of their broad acres, and to whom, as the true owners or Baalin of the land, he still believed himself bound to pay tribute for all the produce he drew from the soil. The sacred pole itself (*asherah*), which was a regular adjunct of the local sanctuaries, may have been no more than the trunk of one of the holy trees stripped of its boughs either by the hand of man or by natural decay. To this day we can detect such religious emblems in process of formation among the Kayans of Borneo. These savages believe in the existence of certain dangerous spirits whom they call *Toh*; and when they clear a patch of jungle in which to sow rice, "it is usual to leave a few trees standing on some high point of the ground in order not to offend the *Toh* of the locality by depriving them of all the trees, which they are vaguely supposed to make use of as resting-places. Such trees are sometimes stripped of all their branches save a few at the top; and sometimes a pole is lashed across the stem at a height from the ground and bunches of palm leaves hung upon it; a 'bull-roarer,' which is used by boys as a toy, is sometimes hung upon such a cross-piece to dangle and flicker in the breeze."

CHAPTER IX

THE SILENT WIDOW

AMONG many, if not all, peoples of the world the occurrence of a death in the family has entailed on the survivors the obligation of observing certain rules, the general effect of which is to limit in various directions the liberty enjoyed by persons in ordinary life; and the nearer the relationship of the survivor to the deceased, the more stringent and burdensome are usually the restrictions laid on his or her freedom. Though the reasons for imposing these trammels are often unknown to the people who submit to them, a large body of evidence points to the conclusion that many, perhaps most, of them originated in a fear of the ghost and a desire to escape his unwelcome attentions by eluding his observation, repelling his advances, or otherwise inducing or compelling him to acquiesce in his fate, so far at least as to abstain from molesting his kinsfolk and friends. The ancient Hebrews observed many restrictions on the occurrence of a death, which are either expressly enjoined or incidentally referred to in the Old Testament. To the list of rules for the conduct of mourners, which can thus be collected from Scripture, may perhaps be added one which, though it is neither inculcated nor alluded to by the sacred writers, is suggested by etymology and confirmed by the analogous usages of other peoples.

The Hebrew word for a widow is perhaps etymologically connected with an adjective meaning "dumb." [1] If this etymology is correct, it would seem that the Hebrew name for a widow is "a silent woman." Why should a widow be called a silent woman? I conjecture, with all due diffidence, that the epithet may be explained by a widespread custom which imposes the duty of absolute silence on a widow for some time, often a long time, after the death of her husband.

Thus among the Kutus, a tribe on the Congo, widows observe mourning for three lunar months. They shave their heads, strip themselves almost naked, daub their bodies all over with white clay, and pass the whole of the three months in the house without speaking. Among the Sihanaka in Madagascar the observances

---

[1] *Alemanah,* "a widow," perhaps connected with *illem,* "dumb." The etymology appears to be favoured by the authors of the Oxford Hebrew dictionary, since they class both words together as derived from the same root. See *Hebrew and English Lexicon of the Old Testament,* by Fr. Brown, S. R. Driver, and Ch. A. Briggs (Oxford, 1906), p. 48.

are similar, but the period of silence is still longer, lasting for at least eight months, and sometimes for a year. During the whole of that time the widow is stripped of all her ornaments and covered up with a coarse mat, and she is given only a broken spoon and a broken dish to eat out of. She may not wash her face or her hands, but only the tips of her fingers. In this state she remains all day long in the house and may not speak to any one who enters it. Among the Nandi, of British East Africa, as long as a widow is in mourning she is considered unclean and may not speak above a whisper, though she is not absolutely forbidden to speak at all. In describing the Nishinam tribe of California Indians, a writer who knew these Indians well, as they were in the third quarter of the nineteenth century, mentions that "around Auburn, a devoted widow never speaks, on any occasion or upon any pretext, for several months, sometimes a year or more, after the death of her husband. Of this singular fact I had ocular demonstration. Elsewhere, as on the American River, she speaks only in a whisper for several months. As you go down towards the Cosumnes this custom disappears." Among the Kwakiutl Indians of British Columbia, for four days after the death of her husband a widow must sit motionless, with her knees drawn up to her chin. For sixteen days after that she is bound to remain on the same spot, but she enjoys the privilege of stretching her legs, though not of moving her hands. During all that time nobody may speak to her. It is thought that if any one dared to break the rule of silence and speak to the widow, he would be punished by the death of one of his relatives. A widower has to observe precisely the same restrictions on the death of his wife. Similarly among the Bella Coola Indians of the same region a widow must fast for four days, and during that time she may not speak a word; otherwise they think that her husband's ghost would come and lay a hand on her mouth, and she would die. The same rule of silence has to be observed by a widower on the death of his wife, and for a similar reason. Here it is to be noted that the reason assigned for keeping silence is a fear of attracting the dangerous and indeed fatal attention of the ghost.

But by no people is this curious custom of silence more strictly observed than by some of the savage tribes of Central and Northern Australia. Thus, among the Waduman and Mudburra, two tribes on the Victoria River in the Northern Territory, not only a man's widows but also the wives of his brothers are under a ban of silence for three or four weeks after his death. In the interval the body is placed on a platform of boughs built in a tree, and there it remains till all the flesh has disappeared from the bones. Then the bones are wrapt in bark and carried to a special camp, where the members of the tribe sit round them and weep. When this ceremony of mourning has been performed, the bones are taken back to the tree and left there finally. During the whole time which elapses from the death to the final disposition of the bones in the tree, no one may

eat the animal or plant which was the totem of the deceased. But
when the bones have been laid in their last resting-place among the
boughs, one or two old men go out into the bush and secure some of
the animals or plants which were the dead man's totem. If, for
example, the deceased had the flying fox for his totem, then the
old men will catch some flying foxes and bring them into the camp.
There a fire is kindled and the flying foxes are laid on it to cook.
While they are cooking, the women who have been under a ban of
silence, that is to say, the widows of the dead man and his brothers'
wives, go up to the fire and, after calling out *"Yakai! Yakai!"*
put their heads in the smoke. An old man then hits them lightly
on the head and afterwards holds out his hand for them to bite a
finger. This ceremony removes the ban of silence under which the
women had hitherto laboured; they are now free to use their
tongues as usual. Afterwards the cooked flying foxes are eaten by
some of the male relatives of the deceased; and when that has been
done, all the people are free to partake of the flesh.

Again, in the Arunta tribe of Central Australia a man's widows
smear their hair, faces, and breasts with white pipeclay and remain
silent for a certain time, until a ceremony has been performed which
restores to them the use of their tongues. The ceremony is as
follows. When a widow wishes the ban of silence to be removed,
she gathers a large wooden vessel full of some edible seed or small
tuber, and smears herself with white pipeclay at the women's camp,
where she has been living ever since her husband's death. Carrying
the vessel, and accompanied by the women whom she has collected
for the purpose, she walks to the centre of the general camp, midway
between the two sections occupied by the two halves of the tribe.
There they all sit down and cry loudly, whereupon the men, who
stand to them either in the actual or in the classificatory relationship
of sons and younger brothers of the dead man, come up and join
the party. Next, these men take the vessel of seeds or tubers from
the hands of the widow, and as many as possible laying hold of it,
they shout loudly, *"Wah! wah! wah!"* All the women, except the
widow, stop crying and join in the shout. After a short time the
men hold the vessel of seeds or tubers close to, but not touching,
the widow's face, and make passes to right and left of her cheeks,
while all again shout *"Wah! wah! wah!"* The widow now stops
her crying and utters the same shout, only in subdued tones. After
a few minutes the vessel of seeds or tubers is passed to the rear of
the men, who now, squatting on the ground and holding their
shields in both hands, strike them heavily on the ground in front of
the women, who are standing. When that has been done the men
disperse to their camps and eat the food brought in the vessel by
the widow, who is now free to speak to them, though she still continues to smear herself with pipeclay.

The significance of this curious rite, by which an Arunta widow
recovers her freedom of speech, is explained as follows by Messrs.

Spencer and Gillen: "The meaning of this ceremony, as symbolised by the gathering of the tubers or grass seed, is that the widow is about to resume the ordinary occupations of a woman's life, which have been to a large extent suspended while she remained in camp in what we may call deep mourning. It is in fact closely akin in feeling to the transition from deep to narrow black-edged paper amongst certain more highly civilised peoples. The offering to the sons and younger brothers is intended both to show them that she has properly carried out the first period of mourning, and to gain their good will, as they, especially the younger brothers, are supposed to be for some time displeased with a woman when her husband is dead and she is alive. In fact a younger brother meeting the wife of a dead elder brother, out in the bush performing the ordinary duties of a woman, such as hunting for 'yams,' within a short time of her husband's death, would be quite justified in spearing her. The only reason that the natives give for this hostile feeling is that it grieves them too much when they see the widow, because it reminds them of the dead man. This, however, can scarcely be the whole reason, as the same rule does not apply to the elder brothers, and very probably the real explanation of the feeling is associated, in some way, with the custom according to which the widow will, when the final stage of mourning is over, become the wife of one of these younger brothers whom at first she has carefully to avoid."

Again, among the Unmatjera and Kaitish, two other tribes of Central Australia, a widow's hair is burnt off close to her head with a firestick, and she covers her body with ashes from the camp fire. This covering of ashes she renews from time to time during the whole period of mourning. If she did not do so, it is believed that the spirit of her dead husband, who constantly follows her about, would kill her and strip all the flesh from her bones. Moreover, her late husband's younger brother would be justified in severely thrashing or even killing her, if at any time he were to meet her during the period of deep morning without this emblem of sorrow. Further, she must also observe the ban of silence until, usually many months after her husband's death, she is released from it by her husband's younger brother. When this takes place she makes an offering to him of a very considerable quantity of food, and with a fragment of it he touches her mouth, thus indicating to her that she is once more free to talk and to take part in the ordinary duties of a woman.

But among the Warramunga, another tribe of Central Asutralia, the command of silence imposed on women after a death is much more comprehensive and extraordinary. With them it is not only the dead man's widow who must be silent during the whole time of mourning, which may last for one or even two years; his mother, his sisters, his daughters, his mother-in-law or mothers-in-law, must all equally be dumb and for the same protracted period. More than that, not only his real wife, real mother, real sisters, and real mothers-in-law are subjected to this rule of silence, but a great many more women whom the natives, on the classificatory principle, reckon in these relationships, though we should not do so, are similarly bound over to hold their tongues, it may be for a year, or it may be for two years. As a consequence it is no uncommon thing in a Warramunga camp to find the majority of women prohibited from speaking. Even when the period of mourning is over, some women prefer to remain silent and to use only the gesture language, in the practice of which they become remarkably proficient. Not seldom, when a party of women are in camp, there will be almost perfect silence, and yet a brisk conversation is all the while being conducted among them on their fingers, or rather with their hands and arms, for many of the signs are made by putting the hands or elbows in varying positions. At Tennant's Creek some years ago there was an old woman who had not opened her mouth, except to eat or drink, for more than twenty-five years, and who has probably since then gone down to her grave without uttering another syllable. When, however, after a longer or a shorter interval of absolute silence, a Warramunga widow desires to recover her liberty to speak, she applies to the men who stand to her in the classificatory or tribal relationship of sons, to whom, as is customary in such cases, she has to make a present of food. The ceremony itself is a very simple one; the woman brings the food, usually a large cake of grass seed, and in turn bites the finger of each of the men who are releasing her from the ban of silence. After that she is free to talk as much as she likes. It only remains to add that in the Warramunga tribe a widow crops her hair short, cuts open the middle line of her scalp, and runs a burning firestick along the gaping wound. The consequences of this horrible mutilation are sometimes serious.

Again, in the Dieri tribe of Central Australia a widow was not allowed to speak until the whole of the white clay, which she had smeared on her body in token of mourning, had crumbled and fallen away of itself. During this intermediate period, which might last for months, she might communicate with others only by means of the gesture language.

But why should a widow be bound over to silence for a longer or a shorter time after the death of her spouse? The motive for observing the custom is probably a dread of attracting the dangerous attentions of her late husband's ghost. This fear is indeed plainly alleged as the reason by the Bella Coola Indians, and it is assigned by the Unmatjera and Kaitish as the motive for covering the widow's body with ashes. The whole intention of these customs is apparently either to elude or to disgust and repel the ghost. The widow eludes him by remaining silent; she disgusts and repels him by discarding her finery, shaving or burning her hair, and daubing herself with clay or ashes. This interpretation is confirmed by certain particularities of the Australian usages.

In the first place, among the Waduman and Mudburra the custom of silence is observed by the widow only so long as the flesh adheres to her late husband's bones; as soon as it has quite decayed and the bones are bare, she is made free of the use of her tongue once more. But it appears to be a common notion that the ghost lingers about his mouldering remains while any of the flesh is left, and that only after the flesh has wholly vanished does he take his departure for the more or less distant spirit-land. Where such a belief prevails it is perfectly natural that the widow should hold her tongue so long as the decomposition of her husband's body is still incomplete, for so long may his spirit be supposed to haunt the neighbourhood and to be liable at any moment to be attracted by the sound of her familiar voice.

In the second place, the relation in which among the Arunta, the Unmatjera, and the kaitish the widow stands to her late husband's younger brother favours the supposition that the motive of the restrictions laid on her is the fear of the ghost. In these tribes the younger brother of her late husband appears to exercise a special superintendence over the widow during the period of mourning; he sees to it that she strictly observes the rules enjoined by custom at such times, and he has the right severely to punish or even to kill her for breaches of them. Further, among the Unmatjera and Kaitish it is the younger brother of the deceased who finally releases the widow from the ban of silence, and thereby restores her to the freedom of ordinary life. Now this special relationship in which the widow stands to her late husband's younger brother is quite intelligible on the supposition that at the end of mourning she is to become his wife, as regularly happens under the common form of the levirate which assigns a man's widow to one of his younger brothers. This custom actually obtains in all the three tribes—the Arunta, the Unmatjera, and the Kaitish—in which the widow observes the rule of silence and stands in this special relation to the younger brothers of her late husband. In the Arunta it is the custom that on the conclusion of mourning the widow becomes the wife of one of her deceased husband's younger brothers; and with regard to the Unmatjera and Kaitish we are told that "this passing on of the widow to a younger, but never to an elder, brother is a very characteristic feature of these tribes." Similarly in the Dieri tribe, which enforced the rule of silence on widows during the period of mourning, a man's widow passed at his death to his brother, who became her husband, and her children called him father. But among rude races, who believe that a man's ghost haunts his widow and pesters her with his unwelcome attentions, marriage with a widow is naturally thought to involve the bridegroom in certain risks arising from the jealousy of his deceased rival, who is loth to resign his spouse to the arms of another. Examples of such imaginary dangers attendant on marriage with a widow have been cited by me elsewhere. They may help us to understand why, among the Australian tribes in question, a man keeps such a vigilant watch over the conduct of his deceased elder brother's widow. The motive is probably not so much a disinterested respect for the honour of his dead brother as a selfish regard for his own personal safety, which would be put in jeopardy if he were to marry the widow before she had completely got rid of her late husband's ghost by strictly observing all the precautions usually taken for that purpose, including the rule of silence.

Thus the analogy of customs observed among widely separated peoples supports the conjecture that among the ancient Hebrews also, at some early time of their history, a widow may have been expected to keep silence for a certain time after the death of her husband for the sake of giving the slip to his ghost; and further, perhaps, that the observance of this precaution may have been particularly enforced by her late husband's younger brother, who, in accordance with the custom of the levirate, proposed to marry her when the days of her mourning were over. But it should be observed that, apart from analogy, the direct evidence for such an enforced silence of widows among the Hebrews is no more than a doubtful etymology; and as all inferences from etymology to custom are exceedingly precarious, I cannot claim any high degree of probability for the present conjecture.

PART IV

THE LAW

CHAPTER I

THE PLACE OF THE LAW IN JEWISH HISTORY

BEFORE we pass to an examination of some particular Jewish laws, it may be well briefly to consider the place which the Law as a whole occupies in the history of Israel, so far as that place has been determined by the critical analysis of modern scholars.

The most important and the best attested result of linquistic and historical criticism applied to the Old Testament is the proof that the Pentateuchal legislation, in the form in which we now possess it, cannot have been promulgated by Moses in the desert and in Moab before the entrance of the Israelites into Palestine, and that it can only have assumed its final shape at some time after the capture of Jerusalem by Nebuchadnezzar in the year 586 B.C., when the Jews were carried away into exile. In short, the legal portion of the Pentateuch, as we now have it, belongs not to the earliest but to a late date in the history of Israel; far from having been promulgated before the nation took possession of the Promised Land, very little of it appears to have been written and published till near the end of the national independence, and the bulk of it, comprising what the critics call the Priestly Code, seems to have been composed for the first time in its present form and committed to writing either during or after the captivity.

But it is necessary to distinguish carefully between the age of the laws themselves and the dates when they were first given to the world in the shape of written codes. A very little thought will satisfy us that laws in general do not spring armed cap-à-pie into existence like Athena from the head of Zeus, at the moment when they are codified. Legislation and codification are two very different things. Legislation is the authoritative enactment of certain rules of conduct which have either not been observed or have not been legally binding before the acts enforcing them were passed by the supreme authority. But even new laws are seldom or never complete innovations; they nearly always rest upon and presuppose a basis of existing custom and public opinion which harmonize more or less with the new laws, and have long silently prepared for their reception in the minds of the people. The most despotic monarch in the world could not force upon his subjects an absolutely new law, which should run counter to the whole bent and current of their natural disposition, outraging all their hereditary opinions and habits, flouting all their most cherished sentiments and aspirations. Even in the most seemingly revolutionary enactment there is always a conservative element which succeeds in securing the general assent and obedience of a community. Only a law which in some measure answers to a people's past has any power to mould that people's future. To reconstruct human society from the foundations upward is a visionary enterprise, harmless enough so long as it is confined to the Utopias of philosophic dreamers, but dangerous and possibly disastrous when it is attempted in practice by men, whether demagogues or despots, who by the very attempt prove their ignorance of the fundamental principles of the problem they rashly set themselves to solve. Society is a growth, not a structure; and though we may modify that growth and mould it into fairer forms, as the gardener by his art has evolved blooms of lovelier shape and richer hue from the humbler flowers of the field and the meadow, the hedgerow and the river-bank, we can as little create society afresh as the gardener can create a lily or a rose. Thus in every law, as in every plant, there is an element of the past, an element which, if we could trace it to its ultimate source, would lead us backwards to the earliest stages of human life in the one case and of plant life in the other.

And when we pass from legislation to codification, the possible antiquity of the laws codified is so obvious that it seems almost superfluous to insist upon it. The most famous of all codes, the *Digest* or *Pandects* of Justinian, is a compilation of extracts from the works of older Roman jurists in the very words of the writers, all of whom are carefully named in every separate citation; thus the code is not a series of new laws, it is simply a new collection of the old laws which had obtained in the Roman Empire for centuries. Of modern codes the most celebrated is the French code issued by Napoleon, but though it superseded that immense number of separate local systems of jurisprudence, of which it was observed that a traveller in France changed laws oftener than he changed horses, it by no means formed an entirely novel body of legislation; on the contrary, it is "the product of Roman and customary law, together with the ordinances of the kings and the laws of the Revolution." But to multiply modern instances would be superfluous.

In the Semitic world the course of legislation has probably been similar. The most ancient code in the world which has come down to us is that of Hammurabi, king of Babylon, who reigned about 2100 B.C.; but there is no reason to suppose that the enactments

which it contains were all brand-new creations of the royal legislator; on the contrary, probability and evidence alike favour the
view that he merely erected his structure of law upon an old
foundation of immemorial custom and usage, which had come down
to him, at least in part, from the ancient predecessors of the Semites
in Babylonia, the Sumerians, and had for long ages been consecrated
by popular prejudice, sanctioned by kings, and administered by
judges. Similarly the critics who assign the great bulk of the so-
called Mosaic legislation to the ages immediately preceding or following at no long intervals the loss of national independence, fully
recognize that even in its latest form the Law not only records but
enforces customs and ceremonial institutions, of which many, and
among them the most fundamental, are undoubtedly far older than
the time when the Pentateuch received its final form in the fifth
century before our era. This conclusion as to the great antiquity
of the chief ceremonial institutions of Israel is amply confirmed by
a comparison of them with the institutions of other peoples; for
such a comparison reveals in Hebrew usage not a few marks of
barbarism and even of savagery, which could not possibly have
been imprinted on it for the first time at the final codification of the
law, but must have adhered to it from ages which probably long
preceded the dawn of history. A few such marks will be pointed
out in the sequel; but the number of them might easily be much
enlarged. Such customs, for example, as circumcision, the ceremonial uncleanness of women, and the employment of scapegoats
have their analogues in the customs of savage tribes in many parts
of the world.

What I have said may suffice to dissipate the misapprehension
that, in assigning a late date to the final codification of Hebrew law,
Biblical critics implicitly assume a late origin for all the laws
embodied in the code. But it may be well before going farther to
correct another possible misconception which might arise in regard
to the critical doctrine. Because little or nothing of the so-called
Mosaic legislation in the Pentateuch can be proved to have emanated
from Moses, it by no means follows that the great lawgiver was a
mere mythical personage, a creation of popular or priestly fancy,
invented to explain the origin of the religious and civil constitution
of the nation. Any such inference would do violence, not only to
the particular evidence which speaks in favour of the historical
reality of Moses, but to the general laws of probability; for great
religious and national movements seldom or never occur except
under the driving force of great men. The origin of Israel and
Judaism without Moses would be hardly more intelligible than the
origin of Buddhism without Buddha, the origin of Christianity
without Christ, or the origin of Mohammedanism without Mohammed. There is, indeed, a tendency in some quarters at the present
day to assume that history is made by the blind collective impulses
of the multitude without the initiative and direction of extraordinary

minds; but this assumption, born of or fostered by the false and pernicious doctrine of the natural equality of men, contradicts both the teaching of history and the experience of life. The multitude needs a leader, and without him, though it possesses a large faculty of destruction, it possesses little or none of construction. Without men great in thought, in word, in action, and in their influence over their fellows, no great nation ever was or ever will be built up. Moses was such a man, and he may justly rank as the real founder of Israel. Stripped of the miraculous features, which gather round the memory of popular heroes, as naturally as moss and lichens gather round stones, the account given of him in the earlier Hebrew histories is probably in substance correct: he rallied the Israelites against their oppressors in Egypt, led them to freedom in the wilderness, moulded them into a nation, impressed on their civil and religious institutions the stamp of his own remarkable genius, and having guided them to Moab, he died in sight of the Promised Land, which he was not to enter.

In the complex mass of laws which compose a large part of the Pentateuch critics now generally distinguish at least three separate groups or bodies of law, which differ from each other in character and date. These are, in chronological order, the Book of the Covenant, the Deuteronomic Code, and the Priestly Code. A brief notice of these documents may help the reader to understand the place which each of them occupies in the history of Jewish legislation, so far as it has been determined by the investigations of the critics. The arguments in support of these conclusions are too numerous and complex to be cited here; the reader who desires to acquaint himself with them will find them fully stated in many easily accessible works on the subject.

The oldest code in the Pentateuch is generally acknowledged to be what is called the Book of the Covenant, comprising Exodus xx. 22-xxxiii. 33. This has been named the First Legislation. Closely related to it is Exodus xxxiv. 11-27, which is sometimes called the Little Book of the Covenant. The Book of the Covenant is embedded in the Elohistic document, which is generally believed to have been written in northern Israel not later than the early part of the eighth century B.C. The Little Book of the Covenant is embedded in the Jehovistic Document, which is generally believed to have been written in Judea somewhat earlier than the Elohistic document, perhaps in the ninth century B.C. But the laws themselves probably existed as a separate code or codes long before they were incorporated in these documents; and even before they had been codified the laws may be assumed to have been generally observed as customary regulations, many of them perhaps from a time beyond the memory of man. As a whole the Book of the Covenant reflects life in the days of the early kings and judges. "The society contemplated in this legislation is of very simple structure. The basis of life is agricultural. Cattle and agricultural produce are the elements of wealth, and the laws of property deal almost exclusively with them. The principles of civil and criminal justice are those still current among the Arabs of the desert. They are two in number, retaliation and pecuniary compensation. Murder is dealt with by the law of blood-revenge, but the innocent manslayer may seek asylum at God's altar. With murder are ranked man-stealing, offences against parents, and witchcraft. Other injuries are occasions of self-help or of private suits to be adjusted at the sanctuary. Personal injuries fall under the law of retaliation, just as murder does. Blow for blow is still the law of the Arabs, and in Canaan no doubt, as in the desert, the retaliation was usually sought in the way of self-help."

The second code which critics distinguish in the Pentateuch is the Deuteronomic. It includes the greater part of our present book of Deuteronomy, with the exception of the historical intro-duction and the closing chapters. Modern critics appear in general to agree that the Deuteronomic Code is substantially the "book of the law" which was found in the temple at Jerusalem in the year 621 B.C., and which King Josiah took as the basis of his religious reformation. The main features of the reform were, first, the sup-pression of all the local sanctuaries or "high places" throughout the land, and, second, the concentration of the ceremonial worship of Jehovah at the temple in Jerusalem alone. These measures are strongly inculcated in Deuteronomy; and from the lessons of that book the reforming king appears to have derived both the ideals which he set himself to convert into realities and the warm religious zeal which animated and sustained him in his arduous task. For the deep impression made on his mind by the reading of the book is easily accounted for by the blessings which the writer of Deuteron-omy promises as the reward of obedience to the law, and by the curses which he denounces as the punishment of disobedience.

The reformation thus inaugurated by Josiah was of great impor-tance not only for the measures which it enforced but for the manner in which they were promulgated. It was the first time, so far as we know, in the history of Israel that a written code was ever published with the authority of the government to be the supreme rule of life of the whole nation. Hitherto law had been customary, not statutory; it had existed for the most part merely as usages, with which every one complied in deference to public opinion and from force of habit; its origin was either explained by ancient tradition or altogether lost in the mists of antiquity. It is true that some of the customs had been reduced to writing in the form of short codes; at least one such volume is known to us in the Book of the Covenant. But it does not appear that these works received any official sanction; they were probably mere manuals destined for private circulation. The real repositories of the laws were apparently the priests at the local sanctuaries, who handed down orally from generation to generation the ordinances of ritual and religion, with which in primitive society the rules of morality are almost inseparably united. On all points of doubtful usage, in all legal disputes, the priests were consulted by the people and gave their decisions, not so much in the capacity of ordinary human judges, as in that of the mouthpieces of the deity, whose will they consulted and interpreted by means of the lots or other oracular machinery. These oral decisions of the priests were the original law of the land; they were the *Torah* in its proper significance of authoritative direction or instruction, long before the application of that word came to be narrowed down, first to law in general, and afterwards to the written law of the Pentateuch in particular. But in its original sense of direction or teaching, the Torah was not limited to the lessons given by the priests; it included also the instructions and warnings which the prophets uttered under impulses which they and their hearers believed to be divine. There was thus a prophetic as well as a priestly Torah, but in the beginning and for long ages afterwards the two agreed in being oral and not written.

The publication of the Deuteronomic Code in written form marked an era in the history not only of the Jewish people but of humanity. It was the first step towards the canonization of Scripture and thereby to the substitution of the written for the spoken word as the supreme and infallible rule of conduct. The accomplishment of the process by the completion of the Canon in the succeeding centuries laid thought under shackles from which in the Western world it has never since wholly succeeded in emancipating itself. The spoken word before was free, and therefore thought was free, since speech is nothing but thought made vocal and articulate. The prophets enjoyed full freedom both of thought and of speech, because their thoughts and words were believed to be inspired by the deity. Even the priests were far from being hide-bound by tradition; though God was not supposed to speak by their lips, they no doubt allowed themselves considerable latitude in working the oracular machinery of lots and other mechanical devices through which the deity vouchsafed to manifest his will to anxious inquirers. But when once the oracles were committed to writing they were stereotyped and immovable; from the fluid they had solidified into the crystalline form with all its hardness and durability; a living growth had been replaced by a dead letter; the scribe had ousted the prophet and even the priest, so far as the functions of the priest were oracular and not sacrificial. Henceforth Israel became the "people of the book"; the highest wisdom and knowledge were to be obtained not by independent observation, not by the free investigation of man and of nature, but by the servile interpretation of a written record. The author must make room for the commentator; the national genius, which had created the Bible, accommodated itself to the task of writing the Talmud.

While we can ascertain with a fair degree of assurance the date when the Deuteronomic Code was published, we have no information as to the date when it was composed. It was discovered and promulgated in the eighteenth year of Josiah's reign (621 B.C.), and it must have been written either in the preceding part of the king's reign under his predecessor Manasseh; for internal evidence proves that the book cannot be older, and that its composition must therefore have fallen some time within the seventh century before our era. On the whole, the most probable hypothesis appears to be that Deuteronomy was written in the reign of Manasseh, and that under the oppressive and cruel rule of that bad king it was concealed for safety in the temple, where it lay hid till it came to light during the repairs of the sacred edifice instituted by the devout Josiah. It has, indeed, sometimes been suspected that the book was a forgery of the temple priests, who contrived by a devout fraud to palm it off as a work of hoar antiquity on the guileless young king. But that the suspicion is as unjust as it is uncharitable will perhaps appear to any one who candidly considers the liberal provision which the new code made for the reception at Jerusalem of the rural clergy whom the destruction of the local sanctuaries had stripped of their benefices. These disestablished and disendowed priests, reduced to the level of homeless landlopers, had only to come up to the capital to be put on a level with their urban colleagues and enjoy all the dignity and emoluments of the priesthood. We shall probably be doing no more than justice to the city clergy by supposing that they held firmly to the good old maxim *Beati possidentes,* and that except under the cruel compulsion of the law they were not very likely to open their arms and their purses to their needy brethren from the country.

Whoever was the unknown author of Deuteronomy, there can be no question that he was a disinterested patriot and reformer, animated by a true love of his country and an honest zeal for pure religion and morality, which he believed to be imperilled by the superstitious practices and lascivious excesses of the local sanctuaries. Whether he was a priest or a prophet, it is difficult to judge, for the book exhibits a remarkable fusion of priestly, or at all events legal, matter with the prophetic spirit. That he wrote under the inspiring influence of the great prophets of the eighth century, Amos, Hosea, and Isaiah, seems certain; accepting their view of the superiority of the moral to the ritual law, he propounds a system of legislation which he bases on religious and ethical principles, on piety and humanity, on the love of God and of man; and in recommending these principles to his hearers and readers he falls naturally into a strain of earnest and even pathetic pleading, which is more akin to the warmth and animation of the orator than to the judicial calm and gravity of the lawgiver. The impression which he makes on a modern reader is that of a preacher rolling out the stream of his impassioned eloquence to a rapt audience in the resounding aisles of some vast cathedral. We seem almost to see the kindling eyes and the eager gestures of the speaker, to catch the ring of his sonorous accents echoing along the vaulted roof and thrilling his hearers with alternate emotions of comfortable assurance and hope, of poignant remorse and repentance, of overwhelming terror and despair. And it is on a high note of awful warning, of fierce denunciation of the wrath to come on the sinful and disobedient, that the voice of the preacher finally dies away into silence. In sustained declamatory power, as has been well observed by an eminent critic, the orator's peroration stands unrivalled in the Old Testament.

Yet though the reform was unquestionably advocated from the purest motives and carried through on a wave of genuine enthusiasm, the philosophic student of religion may be allowed to express a doubt whether, contemplated from the theoretical standpoint, the centralization of worship at a single sanctuary did not mark rather a retrogression than an advance; and whether, regarded from the practical standpoint, it may not have been attended by some inconveniences which went a certain way to balance its advantages. On the one hand, to modern minds, habituated to the idea of God as bounded by no limits either of space or of time, and therefore as equally accessible to his worshippers everywhere and always, the notion that he could be properly worshipped only at Jerusalem appears childish, if not absurd. Certainly the abstract conception of an omnipresent deity finds a fitter expression in a multitude of sanctuaries scattered over the length and breadth of the land than in one solitary sanctuary at the capital. And on the other hand, considered from the side of practical convenience, the old unreformed religion possessed some obvious advantages over its rival. Under the ancient system every man had, so to speak, his God at his own door, to whom he could resort on every occasion of doubt and difficulty, of sorrow and distress. Not so under the new system. To reach the temple at Jerusalem the peasant might often have to travel a long way, and with the engrossing occupations of his little farm he could seldom afford time for the journey. No wonder, therefore, if under the new dispensation he sometimes sighed for the old; no wonder if to him the destruction of the local sanctuaries should have appeared as shocking a sacrilege as to our own peasantry might seem the demolition of all the village churches in England, and the felling of the ancient elms and immemorial yews under whose solemn shade "the rude forefathers of the hamlet sleep." How sadly would our simple rustic folk miss the sight of the familiar grey tower or spire embosomed among trees or peeping over the shoulder of the hills! How often would they listen in vain for the sweet sound of Sabbath bells chiming across the fields and calling them to the house of prayer, where they and their forefathers had so often gathered to adore the common Father of all! We may suppose that it was not essentially different with the peasant of Judea when the reformation swept like a hurricane over the country-side.

With a heavy heart he may have witnessed the iconoclasts at their work of destruction and devastation. It was there, on yonder hilltop, under the shade of that spreading thick-leaved oak that he and his fathers before him had brought, year after year, the first yellow sheaves of harvest and the first purple clusters of the vintage. How often had he seen the blue smoke of sacrifice curling up in the still air above the trees, and how often had he imagined God himself to be somewhere not far off—perhaps in yon rifted cloud through which the sunbeams poured in mysty glory—there are somewhere near, inhaling the sweet savour and blessing him and his for the gift! And now the hilltop was bare and desolate; the ancient trees that had so long shaded it were felled, and the grey old pillar, on which he had so often poured his libation of oil, was smashed and its fragments littered the ground. God, it seems, had gone away; he had departed to the capital, and if the peasant would find him, he must follow him thither. A long and a weary journey it might be, and the countryman could only undertake it at rare intervals, trudging over hill and dale with his offerings to thread his way through the narrow crowded streets of Jerusalem and to mingle in the noisy jostling throng within the temple precincts, there to wait with his lamb in a long line of footsore, travel-stained worshippers, while the butcher-priest, with tucked-up sleeves, was despatching the lambs of all in front of him; till his turn came at last, and his lamb's spurtling blood added a tiny rivulet to the crimson tide which flooded the courtyard. Well, they told him it was better so, and perhaps God really did prefer to dwell in these stately buildings and spacious courts, to see all that blood, and to hear all that chanting of the temple choir; but for his own part his thoughts went back with something like regret to the silence of the hilltop, with the shade of its immemorial trees and the far prospect over the peaceful landscape. Yet no doubt the priests were wiser than he; so God's will be done! Such may well have been the crude reflections of many a simple country soul on his first pilgrimage to Jerusalem after the reformation. Not a few of them, perhaps, then beheld the splendour and squalor of the great city for the first time; for we may suppose that the rustics of Judea were as stay-at-home in those days as the rural population in the remoter districts of England is now, of whom many live and die without ever having travelled more than a few miles from their native village.

But in the kingdom of Judea the reformation had a very short course to run. From the time when Josiah instituted his measures for the religious and moral regeneration of the country, a generation hardly passed before the Babylonian armies swept down on Jerusalem, captured the city, and carried off the king and the flower of his people into captivity. The completion of the reforms was prevented by the same causes which had hastened their inception. For we cannot doubt that the growing fear of foreign conquest was one of the principal incentives which quickened the consciences

and nerved the arms of the best Jews to set their house in order
before it was too late, lest the same fate should overtake the Southern
Kingdom at the hands of the Babylonians which had overtaken the
Northern Kingdom a century before at the hands of the Assyrians.
The cloud had been gradually rising from the east and now darkened
the whole sky of Judea. It was under the shadow of the coming
storm and with the muttering of its distant thunder in their ears
that the pious king and his ministers had laboured at the reformation
by which they hoped to avert the threatened catastrophe. For
with that unquestioning faith in the supernatural which was the
strength, or the weakness, of Israel's attitude towards the world,
they traced the national danger to national sin, and believed that
the march of invading armies could be arrested by the suppression
of heathen worship and a better regulation of the sacrificial ritual.
Menaced by the extinction of their political independence, it
apparently never occurred to them to betake themselves to those
merely carnal weapons to which a less religious people would
instinctively turn in such an emergency. To build fortresses, to
strengthen the walls of Jerusalem, to arm and train the male population, to seek the aid of foreign allies,—these were measures which
to the Gentile mind common sense might seem to dictate, but which
to the Jew might appear to imply an impious distrust of Jehovah,
who alone could save his people from their enemies. In truth the
ancient Hebrew as little conceived the action of purely natural
causes in the events of history as in the fall of the rain, the course
of the wind, or the changes of the seasons; alike in the affairs of
man and in the processes of nature he was content to trace the finger
of God, and this calm acquiescence in supernatural agency as the
ultimate explanation of all things presented almost as great an
obstacle to the cool concerting of political measures in the council-
chamber as to the dispassionate investigation of physical forces
in the laboratory.

Nor was the faith of the Jews in their religious interpretation
of history in the least shaken by the complete failure of Josiah's
reformation to avert the national ruin. Their confidence in the
virtue of religious rites and ceremonies as the prime necessity of
national welfare, far from being abated by the collapse of reformation and kingdom together, was to all appearance rather strengthened than weakened by the catastrophe. Instead of being led to
doubt the perfect wisdom of the measures which they had adopted,
they only concluded that they had not carried them out far enough;
and accordingly no sooner were they settled as captives in Babylonia
than they applied themselves to devise a far more elaborate system
of religious ritual, by which they hoped to ensure a return of the
divine favour and a restoration of the exiles to their own land. The
first sketch of the new system was drawn up by Ezekiel in his
banishment by the river Chebar. Himself a priest as well as a
prophet, he must have been familiar with the ritual of the first

temple, and the scheme which he propounded as an ideal programme of reform for the future was no doubt based on his experience of the past. But while it embraced much that was old, it also advocated much that was new, including ampler, more regular, and more solemn sacrifices, a more awful separation of the clergy from the laity, and a more rigid seclusion of the temple and its precincts from contact with the profane. The contrast between Ezekiel, who followed, and the great prophets who preceded, the exile, is extraordinary. While they had laid all the emphasis of their teaching on moral virtue, and scouted the notion of rites and ceremonies as the best or the only means by which man can commend himself to God, Ezekiel appears to invert the relation between the two things, for he has little to say of morality, but much to say of ritual. The programme which he published in the early years of the captivity was developed by later thinkers and writers of the priestly school among the exiles, till after a period of incubation, which lasted more than a century, the full-blown system of the Levitical law was ushered into the world by Ezra at Jerusalem in the year 444 B.C. The document which embodied the fruit of so much labour and thought was the Priestly Code, which forms the framework of the Pentateuch. With it the period of Judaism began, and the transformation of Israel from a nation into a church was complete. The Priestly Code, which set the coping-stone to the edifice, is the third and last body of law which critics distinguish in the Pentateuch. The lateness of its date is the fundamental doctrine of modern criticism applied to the Old Testament.

CHAPTER II

NOT TO SEETHE A KID IN ITS MOTHER'S MILK

A MODERN reader is naturally startled when among the solemn commandments professedly given by God to ancient Irael he finds the precept, "Thou shalt not seethe a kid in its mother's milk." And his surprise is not lessened but greatly increased by an attentive study of one of the three passages in which the command is recorded; for the context of the passage seems to show, as some eminent critics, from Goethe downwards, have pointed out, that the injunction not to seethe a kid in its mother's milk was actually one of the original Ten Commandments. The passage occurs in the thirty-fourth chapter of Exodus. In this chapter we read an account of what purports to be the second revelation to Moses of the Ten Commandments, after that, in his anger at the idolatry of the Israelites, he had broken the tables of stone on which the first version of the commandments was written. What is professedly given us in the chapter is therefore a second edition of the Ten

Commandments. That this is so appears to be put beyond the reach of doubt by the verses which introduce and which follow the list of commandments. Thus the chapter begins, "And the Lord said unto Moses, Hew thee two tables of stone like unto the first: and I will write upon the tables the words that were on the first tables, which thou brakest." Then follows an account of God's interview with Moses on Mount Sinai and of the second revelation of the commandments. And at the close of the passage we read, "And the Lord said unto Moses, Write thou these words : for after the tenor of these words I have made a covenant with thee and with Israel. And he was there with the Lord forty days and forty nights; he did neither eat bread nor drink water. And he wrote upon the tables the words of the covenant, the ten commandments." Thus unquestionably the writer of the chapter regarded the commandments given in it as the Ten Commandments.

But here a difficulty arises; for the commandments recorded in this chapter agree only in part with the commandments contained in the far more familiar version of the Decalogue which we read in the twentieth chapter of Exodus, and again in the fifth chapter of Deuteronomy. Moreover, in that professedly second version of the Decalogue, with which we are here concerned, the commandments are not enunciated with the brevity and precision which characterize the first version, so that it is less easy to define them exactly. And the difficulty of disengaging them from the context is rather increased than diminished by the occurrence of a duplicate version in the Book of the Covenant, which, as we saw, is generally recognized by modern critics as the oldest code in the Pentateuch. At the same time, while it adds to the difficulty of disentangling the commandments from their setting, the occurrence of a duplicate version in the ancient Book of the Covenant furnishes a fresh guarantee of the genuine antiquity of that version of the Decalogue which includes the commandment, "Thou shalt not seethe a kid in its mother's milk."

As to the great bulk of this ancient version of the Decalogue critics are agreed; they differ only with regard to the identification of one or two of the ordinances, and with regard to the order of others. The following is the enumeration of the commandments which is given by Professor K. Budde in his *History of Ancient Hebrew Literature*. It is based on the version of the Decalogue in the thirty-fourth chapter of Exodus, but in respect of one commandment it prefers the parallel version of the Decalogue in the Book of the Covenant :—

1. Thou shalt worship no other god.
2. Thou shalt make thee no molten gods.
3. All the firstborn are mine.
4. Six days shalt thou work, but on the seventh day thou shalt rest.

5. The feast of unleavened bread shalt thou keep in the month when the corn is in ear.
6. Thou shalt observe the feast of weeks, even of the first-fruits of wheat harvest, and the feast of ingathering at the year's end.
7. Thou shalt not offer the blood of my sacrifice with leavened bread.
8. The fat of my feast shall not remain all night until the morning.
9. The first of the firstfruits of thy ground thou shalt bring unto the house of the Lord thy God.
10. Thou shalt not seethe a kid in its mother's milk.

The enumeration of the commandments proposed by Wellhausen is similar, except that he omits "Six days shalt thou work, but on the seventh day thou shalt rest," and inserts instead of it, "Thou shalt observe the feast of ingathering at the year's end" as a separate ordinance instead of as part of another commandment.

In general agreement with the enumerations of Budde and Wellhausen is the list of commandments adopted by Professor R. H. Kennett; but he differs from Budde in treating the command of the feast of ingathering as a separate commandment; he differs from Wellhausen in retaining the command of the seventh day's rest; and he differs from both of them in omitting the command to make no molten gods. His reconstruction of the Decalogue, like theirs, is based mainly on the version of it in the thirty-fourth chapter of Exodus, departures from that version being indicated by italics. It runs as follows:—

1. *I am Jehovah thy God,* thou shalt worship no other God (*v.*14).
2. The feast of unleavened cakes thou shalt keep: seven days thou shalt eat unleavened cakes (*v.* 18).
3. All that openeth the womb is mine; and all thy cattle that is male, the firstlings of ox and sheep (*v.* 19).
4. *My sabbath shalt thou keep;* six days shalt thou work, but on the seventh day thou shalt rest (*v.* 21).
5. The feast of weeks thou shalt celebrate, even the firstfruits of wheat harvest (*v.* 22).
6. The feast of ingathering *thou shalt celebrate* at the end of the year (*v.* 22).
7. Thou shalt not sacrifice (*lit.* slay) my sacrificial blood upon leavened bread (*v.* 25).
8. *The fat of my feast shall not remain all night until the morn-*
law to the Passover.
9. The first of the firstfruits of thy ground thou shalt bring into the house of the Lord thy God (*v.* 26).
10. Thou shalt not seethe a kid in its mother's milk (*v.* 26).

Whichever of these reconstructions of the Decalogue we adopt, its difference from that version of the Decalogue with which we are familiar is sufficiently striking. Here morality is totally absent. The commandments without exception refer purely to matters of ritual. They are religious in the strict sense of the word, for they define with scrupulous, almost niggling, precision the proper relation of man to God. But of the relations of man to man, not a word. The attitude of God to man in these commandments is like that of a feudal lord to his vassals. He stipulates that they shall render him his dues to the utmost farthing, but what they do to each other, so long as they do not interfere with the payment of his feu-duties, is seemingly no concern of his. How different from the six concluding commandments of the other version: "Honour thy father and thy mother. Thou shalt do no murder. Thou shalt not commit adultery. Thou shalt not steal. Thou shalt not bear false witness against thy neighbour. Thou shalt not covet thy neighbour's house, thou shalt not covet thy neighbour's wife, nor his manservant, nor his maidservant, nor his ox, nor his ass, nor any thing that is thy neighbour's."

If we ask which of these two discrepant versions of the Decalogue is the older, the answer cannot be doubtful. It would happily be contrary to all analogy to suppose that precepts of morality, which had originally formed part of an ancient code, were afterwards struck out of it to make room for precepts concerned with mere points of ritual. Is it credible that, for example, the command, "Thou shalt not steal," was afterwards omitted from the code and its place taken by the command, "The fat of my feast shall not remain all night until the morning"? or that the command, "Thou shalt do no murder," was ousted by the command, "Thou shalt not seethe a kid in its mother's milk"? The whole course of human history refutes the supposition. All probability is in favour of the view that the moral version of the Decalogue, if we may call it so from its predominant element, was later than the ritual version, because the general trend of civilization has been, still is, and we hope always will be, towards insisting on the superiority of morality to ritual. It was this insistence which lent force to the teaching, first, of the Hebrew prophets, and afterwards of Christ himself. We should probably not be far wrong in surmising that the change from the ritual to the moral Decalogue was carried out under prophetic influence.

But if we may safely assume, as I think we may, that the ritual version of the Decalogue is the older of the two, we have still to ask, Why was the precept not to seethe a kid in its mother's milk deemed of such vital importance that it was assigned a place in the primitive code of the Hebrews, while precepts which seem to us infinitely more important, such as the prohibitions of murder, theft, and adultery, were excluded from it? The commandment has proved a great stumbling-block to critics, and has been interpreted in many different ways. In the whole body of ritual legislation, it has been said, there is hardly to be found a law which God more frequently inculcated or which men have more seriously perverted than the prohibition to boil a kid in its mother's milk. A precept which the deity, or at all events the lawgiver, took such particular pains to impress on the minds of the people must be well worthy of our attentive study, and if commentators have hitherto failed to ascertain its true meaning, their failure may be due to the stand-point from which they approached the question, or to the incompleteness of their information, rather than to the intrinsic difficulty of the problem itself. The supposition, for example, which has found favour both in ancient and modern times, that the precept is one of refined humanity, conflicts with the whole tenor of the code in which the command is found. A legislator who, so far as appears from the rest of the primitive Decalogue, paid no attention to the feelings of human beings, was not likely to pay much to the maternal feelings of goats. More plausible is the view that the prohibition was directed against some magical or idolatrous rite which the lawgiver reprobated and desired to suppress. This theory has been accepted as the most probable by some eminent scholars from Maimonides to W. Robertson Smith, but it rests on no positive evidence; for little or no weight can be given to the unsupported statement of an anonymous mediaeval writer, a member of the Jewish Karaite sect, who says that "there was a custom among the ancient heathen, who, when they had gathered all the crops, used to boil a kid in its mother's milk, and then, as a magical rite, sprinkle the milk on trees, fields, gardens, and orchards, believing that in this way they would render them more fruitful the following year." So far as this explanation assumes a superstition to lie at the root of the prohibition, it may well be correct; and accordingly it may be worth while to inquire whether analogous prohibitions, with the reasons for them, can be discovered among rude pastoral tribes in modern times, for on the face of it the rule is likely to be observed rather by people who depend on their flocks and herds than by such as subsist on the produce of their fields and gardens.

Now among pastoral tribes in Africa at the present day there appears to be a widely spread and deeply rooted aversion to boil the milk of their cattle, the aversion being founded on a belief that a cow whose milk has been boiled will yield no more milk, and that the animal may even die of the injury thereby done to it. For example, the milk and butter of cows form a large part of the diet of the Mohammedan natives of Sierra Leone and the neighbourhood; but "they never boil the milk, for fear of causing the cow to become dry, nor will they sell milk to any one who should practise it. The Bulloms entertain a similar prejudice respecting oranges, and will not sell them to those who throw the skins into the fire, 'lest it occasion the unripe fruit to fall off.'" Thus it appears that with these people the objection to boil milk is based on the principle of sympathetic magic. Even after the milk has been drawn from the cow it is supposed to remain in such vital connexion with the animal that any injury done to the milk will be sympathetically felt by the cow. Hence to boil the milk in a pot is like boiling it in the cow's udders; it is to dry up the fluid at its source. This explanation is confirmed by the beliefs of the Mohammedans of Morocco, though with them the prohibition to boil a cow's milk is limited to a certain time after the birth of the calf. They think that "if milk boils over into the fire the cow will have a diseased udder, or it will give no milk, or its milk will be poor in cream; and if biestings happen to fall into the fire, the cow or the calf will probably die. Among the Ait Wäryâgäl the biestings must not be boiled after the third day and until forty days have passed after the birth of the calf; if they were boiled during this period, the calf would die or the milk of the cow would give only a small quantity of butter." Here the prohibition to boil milk is not absolute but is limited to a certain time after the birth of the calf, during which the cow may be thought to stand in a closer relation of sympathy than ever afterwards both to her calf and to her milk. The limitation of the rule is therefore significant and rather confirms than invalidates the explanation of the prohibition here suggested. A further confirmation is supplied by the superstition as to the effect on the cow of allowing its milk to fall into the fire; if such an accident should happen at ordinary times, the cow or its milk is believed to suffer, but if it should happen shortly after the birth of its calf, when the thick curdy milk bears the special English name of biestings, the cow or the calf is expected to die. Clearly the notion is that if at such a critical time the biestings were to fall into the fire, it is much the same thing as if the cow or the calf were to fall into the fire and to be burnt to death. So close is the sympathetic bond then supposed to be between the cow, her calf, and her milk. The train of thought may be illustrated by a parallel superstition of the Toradjas in Central Celebes. These people make much use of palm-wine, and the lees of the wine form an excellent yeast in the baking of bread. But some Toradjas refuse to part with the lees of the wine for that purpose to Europeans, because they fear that the palm-tree from which the wine was extracted would soon yield no more wine and would dry up, if the lees were brought into contact with the heat of the fire in the process of baking. This reluctance to subject the lees of palm-wine to the heat of fire lest the palm-tree from which the wine was drawn should thereby be desiccated, is exactly parallel to the reluctance of African tribes to subject milk to the heat of fire lest the cow from which the milk was extracted should dry up or actually perish. Exactly parallel, too, is the reluctance of the Bulloms to allow orange-skins to be thrown into the fire, lest the tree from which the oranges were gathered should be baked by the heat, and its fruit should consequently drop off.

The objection to boil milk for fear of injuring the cows is shared by pastoral tribes of Central and Eastern Africa. When Speke and Grant were on their memorable journey from Zanzibar to the source of the Nile, they passed through the district of Ukuni, which lies to the south of the Victoria Nyanza. The king of the country lived at the village of Nunda and "owned three hundred milch cows, yet every day there was a difficulty about purchasing milk, and we were obliged to boil it that it might keep, for fear we should have none the following day. This practice the natives objected to, saying, 'The cows will stop their milk if you do so.'" Similarly Speke tells us that he received milk from some Wahuma (Bahima) women whom he had treated for ophthalmia, but he adds, "The milk, however, I could not boil excepting in secrecy, else they would have stopped their donations on the plea that this process would be an incantation or bewitchment, from which their cattle would fall sick and dry up." Among the Masai of East Africa, who are, or used to be, a purely pastoral tribe depending for their sustenance on their herds of cattle, to boil milk "is a heinous offence, and would be accounted a sufficient reason for massacring a caravan. It is believed that the cattle would cease to give milk." Similarly the Baganda, of Central Africa, believed that to boil milk would cause the cow's milk to cease, and among them no one was ever permitted to boil milk except in a single case, which was this: "When the cow that had calved was milked again for the first time, the herdboy was given the milk and carried it to some place in the pasture, where according to custom he showed the cow and calf to his fellow-herdsmen. Then he slowly boiled the milk until it became a cake, when he and his companions partook of the milk cake together." Among the Bahima or Banyankole, a pastoral tribe of Central Africa, both the rule and the exception are similar. "Milk must not be boiled for food, as the boiling would endanger the health of the herd and might cause some of the cows to die. For ceremonial use it is boiled when the umbilical cord falls from a calf, and the milk which has been sacred becomes common. Milk from any cow that has newly calved is taboo for several days, until the umbilical cord falls from the calf; during this time some member of the family is set apart to drink the milk, but he must then be careful to touch no milk from any other cow." So, too, among the Thonga, a Bantu tribe of South-eastern Africa, "the milk of the first week after a cow has calved is taboo. It must not be mixed with other cows' milk, because the umbilical cord of the calf has not yet fallen. It can, however, be boiled and consumed by children as they do not count! After that milk is never boiled: not that there is any taboo to fear, but it is not customary. Natives do not give any clear reason for these milk taboos." It is possible that the Thonga have forgotten the original reasons for these customary restrictions on the use of milk; as their lands are situated on and near Delagoa Bay in Portuguese territory, the tribe has for centuries been in contact with Europeans and is naturally in a less primitive state than the tribes of Central Africa, which till about the middle of the nineteenth century lived absolutely secluded from all European influence.   On the analogy, therefore, of those pastoral peoples who in their long seclusion have preserved their primitive ideas and customs with little change, we may safely conclude that with the Thonga also the original motive for refusing to boil milk was a fear of sympathetically injuring the cows from which the milk had been extracted.

To return to the Bahima of Central Africa, they even say that "if a European puts his milk into tea it will kill the cow which gave the milk."   In this tribe "strange notions prevail as to the knowingness of cows as to the disposition of their milk; one gets quite used to being told by one's cow-herd such fables as that a certain cow refuses to be milked any more because you have been boiling the milk!"   This last statement probably implies a slight misunderstanding of native opinion on the subject; to judge by analogy, the flow of milk is supposed to cease, not because the cow will not yield it, but because she cannot, her udders being dried up by the heat of the fire over which her milk has been boiled. Among the Banyoro, again, another pastoral tribe of Central Africa, it is a rule that "no milk may be cooked nor may it be warmed by fire, because of the harm likely to happen to the herd."   Similarly among the Somali of East Africa "camel's milk is never heated, for fear of bewitching the animal."   The same prohibition to boil milk is observed, probably for the same reason, by the Southern Gallas of the same region, the Nandi of British East Africa, and the Wagogo, the Wamegi, and the Wahumba, three tribes of what till lately was German East Africa.   And among the tribes of the Anglo-Egyptian Sudan "the majority of the Hadendoa will not cook milk, and in this the Artega and the Ashraf resemble them."

Relics of a similar belief in a sympathetic relation between a cow and the milk that has been drawn from her are reported to exist among some of the more backward peoples of Europe down to the present time.   Among the Esthonians, when the first fresh milk of a cow after calving is to be boiled, a silver ring and a small saucer are laid under the kettle before the milk is poured into it. This is done "in order that the cow's udder may remain healthy, and that the milk may not be bad."   Further, the Esthonians believe that "if, in boiling, the milk boils over into the fire, the cow's dugs will be diseased."   Bulgarian peasants in like manner think that "when the milk, in boiling, runs over into the fire, the cow's supply of milk is diminished and may even cease entirely." In these latter cases, though no scruple seems to be felt about boiling milk, there is a strong objection to burning it by letting it fall into the fire, because the burning of the milk is supposed to harm the cow from which the milk was extracted, either by injuring her dugs or by checking the flow of her milk.   We have seen that the Moors of Morocco entertain precisely similar notions as to the harmful effect of letting the milk in a pot boil over into the fire. We need not suppose that the superstition has spread from Morocco through Bulgaria to Esthonia, or in the reverse direction from Esthonia through Bulgaria to Morocco. In all three regions the belief may have originated independently in those elementary laws of the association of ideas which are common to all human minds, and which lie at the foundation of sympathetic magic. A like train of thought may explain the Eskimo rule that no water should be boiled inside a house during the salmon fishery, because "it is bad for the fishery." We may conjecture, though we are not told, that the boiling of the water in the house at such a time is supposed sympathetically to injure or frighten the salmon in the river and so to spoil the catch.

A similar fear of tampering with the principal source of subsistence may well have dictated the old Hebrew commandment, "Thou shalt not seethe a kid in its mother's milk." On this theory an objection will be felt to seething or boiling a kid in any milk, because the she-goat from which the milk had been drawn would be injured by the process, whether she was the dam of the boiled kid or not. The reason why the mother's milk is specially mentioned may have been either because as a matter of convenience the mother's milk was more likely to be used than any other for that purpose, or because the injury to the she-goat in such a case was deemed to be even more certain than in any other. For being linked to the boiling pot by a double bond of sympathy, since the kid, as well as the milk, had come from her bowels, the mother goat was twice as likely as any other goat to lose her milk or to be killed outright by the heat and ebullition.

But it may be asked, "If the objection was simply to the boiling of milk, why is the kid mentioned at all in the commandment?" The practice, if not the theory, of the Baganda seems to supply the answer. Among these people it is recognized that flesh boiled in milk is a great dainty, and naughty boys and other unprincipled persons, who think more of their own pleasure than of the welfare of the herds, will gratify their sinful lusts, whenever they can do so on the sly, heedless of the sufferings which their illicit banquet inflicts on the poor cows and goats. Thus the Hebrew commandment, "Thou shalt not seethe a kid in its mother's milk," may have been directed against miscreants of this sort, whose surreptitious joys were condemned by public opinion as striking a fatal blow at the staple food of the community. We can therefore understand why in the eyes of a primitive pastoral people the boiling of milk should seem a blacker crime than robbery and murder. For whereas robbery and murder harm only individuals, the boiling of milk, like the poisoning of wells, seems to threaten the existence of the whole tribe by cutting off its principal source of nourishment. That may be why in the first edition of the Hebrew Decalogue we miss the commandments, "Thou shalt not steal" and "Thou shalt do no murder," and find instead the commandment, "Thou shalt not boil milk."

The conception of a sympathetic bond between an animal and the milk that has been drawn from it, appears to explain certain other rules observed by pastoral peoples, for some of which no sufficient explanation has yet been suggested. Thus milk is the staple food of the Damaras or Herero of South-west Africa, but they never cleanse the milk-vessels out of which they drink or eat, because they firmly believe that, were they to wash out the vessels, the cows would cease to give milk. Apparently their notion is that to wash out the sediment of the milk from the pot would be to wash out the dregs of the milk from the cow's udders. With the Masai it is a rule that "the milk must be drawn into calabashes specially reserved for its reception, into which water is not allowed to enter—cleanliness being ensured by wood-ashes."

As the pastoral Hereros refrain from washing the milk-vessels with water out of regard for their cows, so the pastoral Bahima abstain for a similar reason from washing themselves. "Neither men nor women wash, as it is considered to be detrimental to the cattle. They therefore use a dry bath for cleansing the skin, smearing butter and a kind of red earth over the body instead of water, and, after drying the skin, they rub butter well into the flesh." Water applied by a man to his own body "is said to injure his cattle and also his family."

Moreover, some pastoral tribes believe their cattle to be sympathetically affected, not only by the nature of the substance which is employed to clean the milk-vessels, but also by the material of which the vessels are made. Thus among the Bahima "no vessel of iron is allowed to be used for milk, only wooden bowls, gourds, or earthen pots. The use of other kinds of vessels would be injurious, they believe, to the cattle and might possibly cause the cows to fall ill." So among the Banyoro the milk-vessels are almost all of wood or gourds, though a few earthen pots may be found in a kraal for holding milk. "No metal vessels are used; pastoral peoples do not allow such vessels to have milk poured into them lest the cows should suffer." Similarly among the Baganda "most milk-vessels were made of pottery, a few only being made of wood; the people objected to tin or iron vessels, because the use of them would be harmful to the cows"; and among the Nandi "the only vessels that may be used for milk are the gourds or calabashes. If anything else were employed, it is believed that it would be injurious to the cattle." The Akikuyu often think "that to milk an animal into any vessel other than the usual half calabash, e.g. into a European white enamelled bowl, is likely to make it go off its milk."

The theory that a cow remains in direct physical sympathy with her milk, even after she has parted with it, is carried out by some pastoral tribes to the length of forbidding the milk to be brought into contact either with flesh or with vegetables, because any such contact is believed to injure the cow from which the milk was drawn. Thus the Masai are at the utmost pains to keep milk from touching flesh, because it is a general opinion among them that such contact would set up a disease in the udders of the cow which had yielded the milk, and that no more milk could be extracted for the animal. Hence they can seldom be induced, and then only most reluctantly, to sell their milk, lest the purchaser should make their cows ill by allowing it to touch flesh. For the same reason they will not suffer milk to be kept in a pot in which flesh has been cooked, nor flesh to be put in a vessel which has contained milk, and consequently they have two different sets of pots set apart for the two purposes. The belief and practice of the Bahima are similar. Once when a German officer, encamped in their country, offered them one of his cooking-pots in exchange for one of their milk-pots, they refused to accept it, alleging that if milk were poured into a pot in which flesh had been boiled, the cow that had yielded the milk would die.

But it is not merely in a pot that milk and flesh may not come into contact with each other; they may not meet in a man's stomach, because contact there would be equally dangerous to the cow whose milk was thus contaminated. Hence pastoral tribes who subsist on the milk and flesh of their cattle are careful not to eat beef and milk at the same time; they allow a considerable interval to elapse between a meal of beef and a meal of milk, and they sometimes even employ an emetic or purgative in order to clear their stomach entirely of the one food before it receives the other. For example, "the food of the Masai consists exclusively of meat and milk; for the warriors cow's milk, while goat's milk is drunk by the women. It is considered a great offence to partake of milk (which is never allowed to be boiled) and meat at the same time, so that for ten days the Masai lives exclusively on milk, and then ten days solely on meat. To such an extent is this aversion to bringing these two things into contact entertained, that before a change is made from the one kind of food to the other, a Masai takes an emetic." These rules of diet are particularly incumbent on Masai warriors. Their practice is to eat nothing but milk and honey for twelve or fifteen days, and then nothing but meat and honey for twelve or fifteen days more. But before they pass from the one diet to the other they take a strong purgative, consisting of blood mixed with milk, which is said to produce vomiting as well as purging, in order to make sure that no vestige of the previous food remains in their stomachs; so scrupulous are they not to bring milk into contact with flesh or blood. And we are expressly told that they do this, not out of regard to their own health, but out of regard to their cattle, because they believe that the cows would yield less milk if they omitted to observe the precaution. If, contrary to custom, a Masai should be tempted to eat beef and

drink milk on the same day, he endeavours to avert the ill consequences of the act by tickling his throat with a stalk of grass so
as to produce vomiting before he passes from the one article of
diet to the other. Similarly the Washamba of East Africa never
drink milk and eat meat at the same meal; they believe that
if they did so, it would infallibly cause the death of the cow from
which the milk was obtained. Hence many of them are unwilling
to dispose of the milk of their cows to Europeans, for fear that the
ignorant or thoughtless purchaser might kill the animals by mixing
their milk with flesh meat in his stomach. Again, the Bahima are
a pastoral people and live chiefly on the milk of their cattle, but
chiefs and wealthy men add beef to their milk diet. But "beef or
other flesh is eaten in the evening only, and beer is drunk afterwards.
They do not eat any kind of vegetable food with the beef, and milk
is avoided for some hours: usually the night intervenes after a
meal of beef and beer before milk is again drunk. There is a firm
belief that the cows would sicken should milk and meat or vegetable
meet in the stomach." So, too, the pastoral Banyoro abstain from
drinking milk for about twelve hours after a meal of meat and beer;
they say that such a period of abstinence is necessary, because
"food eaten indiscriminately will cause sickness among the cattle."
Among the Nandi of British East Africa "meat and milk may not
be taken together. If milk is drunk, no meat may be eaten for
twenty-four hours. Boiled meat in soup must be eaten first, after
which roast meat may be taken. When meat has been eaten, no
milk may be drunk for twelve hours, and then only after some salt
and water has been swallowed. If no salt, which is obtained from
the salt-licks, is near at hand, blood may be drunk instead. An
exception to this rule is made in the case of small children, boys
and girls who have recently been circumcised, women who have a
short while before given birth to a child, and very sick people.
These may eat meat and drink milk at the same time, and are called
pitorik. If anybody else breaks the rule he is soundly flogged."
Among the pastoral Suk of British East Africa it is forbidden to
partake of milk and meat on the same day. Although no reason
is assigned for the prohibition by the writers who report the Suk
and Nandi rules on this subject, the analogy of the preceding tribes
allows us to assume, with great probability, that among the Suk
and Nandi also the motive for interdicting the simultaneous consumption of meat and milk is a fear that the contact of the two
substances in the stomach of the consumer might be injurious, if
not fatal to the cows.

Similar, though somewhat less stringent, rules as to the separation of flesh and milk are observed by the Israelites to this day.
A Jew who has eaten flesh or broth ought not to taste cheese or
anything made of milk for an hour afterwards; strait-laced people
extend the period of abstinence to six hours. Moreover, flesh and
milk are carefully kept apart. There are separate sets of vessels

for them, each bearing a special mark, and a vessel used to hold milk may not be used to hold flesh. Two sets of knives are also kept, one for cutting flesh, the other for cutting cheese and fish. Moreover, flesh and milk are not cooked in the oven together nor placed on the table at the same time; even the table-cloths on which they are set ought to be different. If a family is too poor to have two table-cloths, they should at least wash their solitary table-cloth before putting milk on it after meat. These rules, on which Rabbinical subtlety has embroidered a variety of fine distinctions, are professedly derived from the commandment not to seethe a kid in its mother's milk; and in view of all the evidence collected in this chapter we can hardly doubt that the rules and the commandment in question do belong together as parts of a common inheritance transmitted to the Jews from a time when their forefathers were nomadic herdsmen subsisting mainly on the milk of their cattle, and as afraid of diminishing the supply of it as are the pastoral tribes of Africa at the present day.

But the contamination of milk with meat is not the only danger against which the pastoral tribes of Africa, in the interest of their cattle, seek to guard themselves by rules of diet. They are equally solicitous not to suffer milk to be contaminated by vegetables; hence they abstain from drinking milk and eating vegetables at the same time, because they believe that the mixture of the two things in their stomachs would somehow be harmful to the herd. Thus among the pastoral Bahima, or Ankole, "various kinds of vegetables, such as peas, beans, and sweet potatoes, may not be eaten by any member of the clans, unless he fasts from milk for some months after a meal of vegetables. Should a man be forced by hunger to eat vegetables, he must fast some time after eating them; by preference he will eat plantains, but even then he must fast ten or twelve hours before he again drinks milk. To drink milk while vegetable food is still in the stomach is believed to endanger the health of the cows." So the Bairo of Ankole, "who eat sweet potatoes and ground-nuts, are not allowed to drink milk, as it would then injure the cattle." When Speke was travelling through the country of the Bahima or Wahuma, as he calls them, he experienced the inconvenience of this scruple; for though cattle were plentiful, the people "could not sell their milk to us because we ate fowls, and a bean called *maharagué*." "Since we had entered Karagué we never could get one drop of milk either for love or for money, and I wished to know what motive the Wahuma had for withholding it. We had heard they held superstitious dreads; that any one who ate the flesh of pigs, fish, or fowls, or the bean called *maharagué*, if he tasted the products of their cows, would destroy their cattle." Questioned by Speke, the king of the country replied that "it was only the poor who thought so; and as he now saw we were in want, he would set apart one of his cows expressly for our use." Among the Banyoro "the middle classes who keep cows and also cultivate are most careful in their diet not to eat vegetables and to drink milk near together. Persons who drink milk in the morning do not eat other food until the evening, and those who drink milk in the evening eat no vegetables until the next day. Sweet potatoes and beans are the vegetables they avoid most of all, and each person, after eating such food, is careful to abstain from drinking milk for a period of two days. The precaution is taken to prevent milk from coming into contact with either meat or vegetables in the stomach; it is believed that food eaten indiscriminately will cause sickness among the cattle." Hence in this tribe "no stranger is offered milk when visiting a kraal, because he may have previously eaten some kind of food which they consider would be harmful to the herd, should he drink milk without a fast to clear his system of vegetable food; their hospitality is shown by giving the visitor some other food such as beef and beer, which will prepare him for a meal of milk on the following morning. Should there be insufficient milk to supply the needs of the men in the kraal, some of them will be given vegetables in the evening and fast until the following morning. Should there be no plantains and the people be reduced to eating sweet potatoes, it will be necessary to abstain from milk for two days after eating them, until the system is quite clear, before they may again drink milk." Indeed in this tribe vegetable food is entirely forbidden to herdsmen, because "it is said to be dangerous to the health of the herd for them to partake of such food." Coming as he does perpetually into contact with the herd, the herdsman is clearly much more liable than ordinary folk to endanger the health of the animals by the miscellaneous contents of his stomach; common prudence, therefore, appears to dictate the rule which cuts him off entirely from a vegetarian diet.

Among the Baganda "no person was allowed to eat beans or sugar-cane, or to drink beer, or to smoke Indian hemp, and at the same time to drink milk; the person who drank milk fasted for several hours before he might eat or drink the tabooed foods, and he might not drink milk for a similar period after partaking of such food." Among the Suk any man who chews raw millet is forbidden to drink milk for seven days. No doubt, though this is not stated, in both tribes the prohibition is based on the deleterious influence which a mixed diet of the people is supposed to exercise on their cattle. Similarly among the Masai, who are so solicitous for the welfare of their cattle and so convinced of the sufferings inflicted on the animals by boiling milk or drinking it with meat, warriors are strictly prohibited from partaking of vegetables at all. A Masai soldier would rather die of hunger than eat them; merely to offer them to him is the deepest insult; should he so far forget himself as to taste the forbidden food, he would be degraded, no woman would have him for her husband.

Pastoral peoples who believe that the eating of vegetable food may imperil the prime source of their subsistence by diminishing or stopping the supply of milk are not likely to encourage the practice of agriculture; accordingly it is not surprising to learn that "in Bunyoro cultivation is avoided by the pastoral people: it is said to be harmful for a wife of a man belonging to a pastoral clan to till the land as, by doing so, she may injure the cattle." Among the pastoral clans of that country "women do no work beyond churning and washing milk-pots. Manual work has always been regarded as degrading, and cultivation of the ground as positively injurious to their cattle." Even among the Baganda, who, while they keep cattle, are diligent tillers of the soil, a woman might not cultivate her garden during the first four days after one of her husband's cows had been delivered of a calf; and though the reason of the prohibition is not mentioned, we may, in the light of the foregoing evidence, surmise that the motive for this compulsory abstinence from agricultural labour was a fear lest, by engaging in it at such a time, the woman should endanger the health or even the life of the new-born calf and its dam.

Moreover, some pastoral tribes abstain from eating certain wild animals on the ground, expressed or implied, that if they ate of the flesh of such creatures, their cattle would be injured thereby. For example, among the Suk of British East Africa "there certainly used to be a superstition that to eat the flesh of a certain forest pig called *kiptorainy* would cause the cattle of the man who partook of it to run dry, but since the descent into the plains, where the pig does not exist, it remains as a tradition only." And in the same tribe it is believed that "if a rich man eats fish, the milk of his cows will dry up." Among the Nandi "certain animals may not be eaten if it is possible to obtain other food. These are waterbuck, zebra, elephant, rhinoceros, Senegal hartebeest, and the common and blue duiker. If a Nandi eats the meat of any of these animals, he may not drink milk for at least four months afterwards, and then only after he has purified himself by taking a strong purge made from the *segetet* tree, mixed with blood." Only one Nandi clan, the Kipasiso, is so far exempt from this restriction that members of it are free to drink milk the day after they have eaten game. Among the animals, which, under certain limitations, the Nandi are allowed to eat, the waterbuck is considered an unclean animal; it is often alluded to by a name (*chemakimwa*) which means "the animal which may not be talked about." And among wild fowl the francolin or spur-fowl is viewed with much the same disfavour as the waterbuck; its flesh may indeed be eaten, but the eater is forbidden to drink milk for several months afterwards. The reasons for these restrictions are not mentioned, but in the light of the foregoing evidence we may assume with some confidence that the abstinence from milk for months after eating certain wild animals or birds is dictated by a fear of harming the cows through bringing their milk into contact with game in the stomach of the eater. The same fear may underlie the rule observed by the Wataturu of East Africa, that a man who has eaten the flesh of a certain antelope (called *povu* in Swahili) may not drink milk on the same day.

Further, it may be worth while to consider whether the aversion, which some pastoral tribes entertain to the eating of game in general, may not spring from the same superstitious dread of injuring the cattle by contaminating their milk with the flesh of wild animals in the process of digestion. For example, the Masai in their native state are a purely pastoral people, living wholly on the flesh, blood, and milk of their cattle, and they are said to despise every sort of game, including fish and fowl. "The Masai," we are told, "ate the flesh of no wild animals when in olden days they all had cattle; but some of those who have lost all their cattle are now beginning to eat venison." As they did not eat game, and only hunted such fierce carnivorous beasts as preyed on their cattle, the herds of wild graminivorous animals grew extraordinarily tame all over the Masai country, and it was no uncommon sight to see antelopes, zebras, and gazelles grazing peacefully, without a sign of fear, among the domestic cattle near the Masai kraals. Yet while in general the Masai neither hunted nor ate wild animals, they made two exceptions to the rule, and these exceptions are significant. "The eland," we are told, "is one of the few game animals hunted by the Masai. It is driven, and then run down and speared. Strangely enough, the Masai also eat its flesh, since it is considered by them to be a species of cow. Another wild animal which the Masai both hunted and ate was the buffalo, which they valued both for its hide and its flesh; but we are informed that "the buffalo is not regarded as game by the Masai. Probably they regard the buffalo, like the eland, but with much better reason, as a species of cow; and if that is so, the reason why they kill and eat buffaloes and elands is the same, namely, a belief that these animals do not differ essentially from cattle, and that they may therefore be lawfully killed and eaten by cattle-breeders. The practical conclusion is probably sound, though the system of zoology from which it is deduced leaves something to be desired. The Bahima, another pastoral tribe, who subsist chiefly on the milk of their cattle, have adopted similar rules of diet based on a similar classification of the animal kingdom; for we learn that "there are a few kinds of wild animals they will eat, though these are limited to such as they consider related to cows, for example buffalo and one or two kinds of antelope, waterbuck, and hartebeest." On the other hand, "the meat of goats, sheep, fowls, and all kinds of fish is deemed bad and is absolutely forbidden to any member of the tribe," apparently because these creatures cannot, on the most liberal interpretation of the bovine genus, be regarded as a species of cows. Hence, being allowed to eat but few wild animals, the pastoral Bahima pay little attention to the chase, though they hunt down beasts of prey whenever these become troublesome; "other game is left almost entirely to men of agricultural clans who keep a few dogs and hunt game for food." Similarly the flesh of most wild animals is forbidden to the pastoral clans of the Banyoro, and accordingly members of these clans hardly engage in hunting, except when it becomes necessary to attack and kill the lions and leopards which prey on the herds; "hunting is therefore in the main limited to members of agricultural clans and is engaged in by them for the sake of meat."

In all such cases it may well be that the aversion of pastoral tribes to the eating of game is derived from a belief that cows are directly injured whenever their milk comes into contact with the flesh of wild animals in the stomachs of the tribesmen, and that the consequent danger to the cattle can only be averted, either by abstaining from game altogether, or at all events by leaving a sufficient interval between the consumption of game and the consumption of milk to allow of the stomach being completely cleared of the one food before it receives the other. The remarkable exceptions which some of these tribes make to the general rule, by permitting the consumption of wild animals that bear a more or less distant resemblance to cattle, suggests a comparison with the ancient Hebrew distinction of clean and unclean animals. Can it be that the distinction in question originated in the rudimentary zoology of a pastoral people, who divided the whole animal kingdom into creatures which resembled, and creatures which differed from, their own domestic cattle, and on the basis of that fundamental classification laid down a law of capital importance, that the first of these classes might be eaten and that the second might not? The actual law of clean and unclean animals, as it is set forth in the Pentateuch, is probably too complex to admit of resolution into elements so simple and so few; yet its leading principle is curiously reminiscent of the practice of some African tribes which we have been discussing: "These are the beasts which ye shall eat: the ox, the sheep, and the goat, the hart, and the gazelle, and the roebuck, and the wild goat, and the pygarg, and the antelope, and the chamois. And every beast that pareth the hoof and hath the hoof cloven in two, and cheweth the cud among the beasts, that ye shall eat." Here the test of an animal's fitness to serve as human food is its zoological affinity to domestic ruminants, and judged by that test various species of deer and antelopes are, correctly enough, included among the edible animals, exactly as the Masai and Bahima, on similar grounds, include various kinds of antelopes within their dietary. However, the Hebrew scale of diet is a good deal more liberal than that of the Masai, and even if it originated, as seems possible, in a purely pastoral state, it has probably been expanded by successive additions to meet the needs and tastes of an agricultural people.

Thus far I have attempted to trace certain analogies between

Hebrew and African usages in respect to the boiling of milk, the regulation of a mixed diet of milk and flesh, and the distinction drawn between animals as clean and unclean, or edible and inedible. If these analogies are well founded, they tend to prove that the Hebrew usages in all these matters took their rise in the pastoral stage of society, and accordingly they confirm the native tradition of the Israelites that their ancestors were nomadic herdsmen, roaming with their flocks and herds from pasture to pasture, for many ages before their descendants, swarming across the fords of the Jordan from the grassy uplands of Moab, settled down to the stationary life of husbandmen and vine-dressers in the fat land of Palestine.

CHAPTER III

CUTTINGS FOR THE DEAD

In ancient Israel mourners were accustomed to testify their sorrow for the death of friends by cutting their own bodies and shearing part of their hair so as to make bald patches on their heads. Fore-telling the desolation which was to come upon the land of Judah, the prophet Jeremiah describes how the people would die, and how there would be none to bury them or to perform the usual rites of mourning. "Both great and small shall die in this land: they shall not be buried, neither shall men lament for them, nor cut themselves, nor make themselves bald for them." Again, we read in Jeremiah how, after the Jews had been carried away into cap-tivity by King Nebuchadnezzar, "there came certain from Shechem, from Shiloh, and from Samaria, even fourscore men, having their beards shaven and their clothes rent, and having cut themselves, with oblations and frankincense in their hand, to bring them to the house of the Lord." To mark their sorrow for the great calamity which had befallen Judah and Jerusalem, these pious pilgrims assumed the garb and attributes of the deepest mourning. The practice of making bald the head, though not that of cutting the body, is mentioned also by earlier prophets among the ordinary tokens of grief which were permitted and even enjoined by religion. Thus Amos, the earliest of the prophets whose writings have come down to us, proclaims the doom of Israel in the name of the Lord, "I will turn your feasts into mourning, and all your songs into lamentation; and I will bring up sackcloth upon all loins, and baldness upon every head; and I will make it as the mourning for an only son, and the end thereof as a bitter day." Again, we read in Isaiah that "in that day did the Lord, the Lord of hosts, call to weeping, and to mourning, and to baldness, and to girding with sackcloth." And Micah, prophesying the calamities which were to overtake the southern kingdom, bids the inhabitants anticipate their woes by shaving themselves like mourners: "Make thee bald, and poll thee for the children of thy delight: enlarge thy baldness as the eagle; for they are gone into captivity from thee." The comparison is here not with the eagle, as the English Version has it, but with the great griffon-vulture, which has the neck and head bald and covered with down, a characteristic which no eagle shares with it. And even after these prophecies had been fulfilled by the Baylonian conquest of Judah, the prophet Ezekiel could still write in exile that "they shall also gird themselves with sackcloth, and horror shall cover them; and shame shall be upon all faces, and baldness upon all their heads."

The same customs of cutting the flesh and shaving part of the head in mourning appear to have been common to the Jews with their neighbours, the Philistines and the Moabites. Thus Jeremiah says, "Baldness is come upon Gaza; Ashkelon is brought to nought. the remnant of their valley; how long wilt thou cut thyself?" And, speaking of the desolation of Moab, the same prophet declares, "Every head is bald, and every beard clipped; upon all the hands are cuttings, and upon the loins sackcloth. On all the housetops of Moab and in the streets thereof there is lamentation everywhere." To the same effect Isaiah writes that "Moab howleth over Nebo, and over Medeba; on all their heads is baldness, every beard is cut off. In their streets they gird themselves with sackcloth: on their housetops, and in their broad places, every one howleth, weeping abundantly."

Yet in time these observances, long practised without offence by Israelites in mourning, came to be viewed as barbarous and heathenish, and as such they were forbidden in the codes of law which were framed near the end of the Jewish monarchy, and during or after the Babylonian captivity. Thus in the Deuteronomic code, which was promulgated at Jerusalem in 621 B. C., about a generation before the conquest, we read that "Ye are the children of the Lord your God: ye shall not cut yourselves, nor make any baldness between your eyes for the dead. For thou art an holy people unto the Lord thy God, and the Lord hath chosen thee to be a peculiar people unto himself, above all peoples that are upon the face of the earth." Here the prohibition is based upon the peculiar religious position which Israel occupies as the chosen people of Jehovah, and the nation is exhorted to distinguish itself by abstinence from certain extravagant forms of mourning, in which it had hitherto indulged without sin, and which were still observed by the pagan nations around it. So far as we can judge, the reform originated in a growing refinement of sentiment, which revolted against such extravagant expressions of sorrow as repugnant alike to good taste and to humanity; but the reformer clothed his precept, as usual, in the garb of religion, not from any deliberate considerations of policy, but merely because, in accordance with the ideas of his time, he could conceive no other ultimate sanction for human conduct than the fear of God.

In the Levitical code, composed during or after the Exile, the same prohibitions are repeated. "Ye shall not round the corners of your heads, neither shalt thou mar the corners of thy beard. Ye shall not make any cuttings in your flesh for the dead, nor print any marks upon you: I am the Lord." Yet the lawgiver seems to have felt that it might not be easy by a stroke of the pen to eradicate practices which were deeply ingrained in the popular mind and had long been regarded as innocent; for a little farther on, as if hopeless of weaning the whole people from their old fashion of mourning, he insists that at least the priests shall absolutely renounce it: "And the Lord said unto Moses, Speak unto the priests, the sons of Aaron, and say unto them, There shall none defile himself for the dead among his people, except for his kin. . . . He shall not defile himself, being a chief man among his people, to profane himself. They shall not make baldness upon their head, neither shall they shave off the corner of their beard, nor make any cuttings in their flesh. They shall be holy unto their God, and not profane the name of their God." Any doubts which the lawgiver may have entertained as to the complete efficacy of the remedy which he applied to the evil were justified by the event; for many centuries after his time Jerome informs us that some Jews still made cuttings in their arms and bald places on their heads in token of mourning for the dead.

The customs of cropping or shaving the hair and cutting or mutilating the body in mourning have been very widespread among mankind. I propose now to illustrate both practices and to inquire into their meaning. In doing so I shall pay attention chiefly to the custom of wounding, scarifying, or lacerating the body as the more remarkable and mysterious of the two.

Among Semitic peoples the ancient Arabs, like the ancient Jews, practised both customs. Arab women in mourning rent their upper garments, scratched their faces and breasts with their nails, beat and bruised themselves with their shoes, and cut off their hair. When the great warrior Chalid ben al Valid died, there was not a single woman of his tribe, the Banu Mugira, who did not shear her locks and lay them on his grave. To this day similar practices are in vogue among the Arabs of Moab. As soon as a death has taken place, the women of the family scratch their faces to the effusion of blood and rend their robes to the waist. And if the deceased was a husband, a father, or other near relation, they cut off their long tresses and spread them out on the grave or wind them about the headstone. Or they insert two stakes in the earth, one at the head and the other at the foot of the grave, and join them by a string, to which they attach their shorn locks.

Similarly in ancient Greece women in mourning for near and dear relatives cut off their hair and scratched their cheeks, and sometimes their necks, with their nails till they bled. Greek men also shore their hair as a token of sorrow and respect for the dead. Homer tells how the Greek warriors before Troy covered the corpse of Patroclus with their shorn tresses, and how Achilles laid in the hand of his dead friend the lock of hair which his father Peleus had vowed that his son should dedicate to the river Sperchius whenever he returned home from the war. So Orestes is said to have laid a lock of his hair on the tomb of his murdered father Agamamnon. But the humane legislation of Solon at Athens, like the humane legislation of Deuteronomy at Jerusalem, forbade the barbarous custom of scratching and scarifying the person in mourning; and though the practice of shearing the hair in honour of the dead appears not to have been expressly prohibited by law, it perhaps also fell into abeyance in Greece under the influence of advancing civilization; at least it is significant that both these modes of manifesting distress for the loss of relations and friends are known to us chiefly from the writings of poets who depicted the life and manners of the heroic age, which lay far behind them in the past.

Assyrian and Armenian women in antiquity were also wont to scratch their cheeks in token of sorrow, as we learn from Xenophon, who may have witnessed these demonstrations of grief on that retreat of the Ten Thousand which he shared as a soldier and immortalized as a writer. The same custom was not unknown in ancient Rome; for one of the laws of the Ten Tables, based on the legislation of Solon, forbade women to lacerate their cheeks with their nails in mourning. The learned Roman antiquary Varro held that the essence of the custom consisted in an offering of blood to the dead, the blood drawn from the cheeks of the women being an imperfect substitute for the blood of captives or gladiators sacrificed at the grave. The usages of modern savages, as we shall see presently, confirm to some extent this interpretation of the rite. Virgil represents Anna disfiguring her face with her nails and beating her breasts with her fists at the tidings of the death of her sister Dido on the pyre; but whether in this description the poet had in mind the Carthaginian or the old Roman practice of mourners may be doubted.

When they mourned the death of a king, the ancient Scythians cropped their hair all round their heads, made incisions in their arms, lacerated their foreheads and noses, cut off pieces of their ears, and thrust arrows through their left hands. Among the Huns it was customary for mourners to gash their faces and crop their hair; it was thus that Attila was mourned, "not with womanish lamentations and tears, but with the blood of men." "In all Slavonic countries great stress has from time immemorial been laid on loud expressions of grief for the dead. These were formerly attended by laceration of the faces of the mourners, a custom still preserved among some of the inhabitants of Dalmatia and Monte-

negro." Among the Mingrelians of the Caucasus, when a death has taken place in a house, the mourners scratch their faces and tear out their hair; according to one account they shave their faces entirely, including their eyebrows. However, from another report it would seem that only the women indulge in these demonstrations of grief. Assembled in the chamber of death, the widow and the nearest female relations of the deceased abandon themselves to the vehemence, or at all events to the display, of their sorrow, wrenching out their hair, rending their faces and breasts, and remonstrating with the dead man on his undutiful conduct in dying. The hair which the widow tears from her head on this occasion is afterwards deposited by her in the coffin. Among the Ossetes of the Caucasus on similar occasions the relatives assemble: the men bare their heads and hips, and lash themselves with whips till the blood streams forth; the women scratch their faces, bite their arms, wrench out their hair, and beat their breasts with lamentable howls.

In Africa the custom of cutting the body in mourning, apart from the reported practice of lopping off finger-joints, appears to be comparatively rare. Among the Abyssinians, in deep mourning for a blood relation, it is customary to shear the hair, strew ashes on the head, and scratch the skin of the temples till the blood flows. When a death has taken place among the Wanika of East Africa, the relations and friends assemble, lament loudly, poll their heads, and scratch their faces. Among the Kissi, a tribe on the border of Liberia, women in mourning cover their bodies, and especially their hair, with a thick coating of mud, and scratch their faces and their breasts with their nails. In some Kafir tribes of South Africa a widow used to be secluded in a solitary place for a month after her husband's death, and before she returned home at the expiration of that period she had to throw her clothes away, wash her whole body, and lacerate her breast, arms, and legs with sharp stones.

On the other hand, the laceration of the body in mourning, if rarely practised in Africa, was common among the Indian tribes of North America. Thus on the death of a relative the Tinneh or Déné Indians of North-western America used to make incisions in their flesh, cut off their hair, rend their garments, and roll in the dust. Again, on the occasion of a death among the Knisteneaux or Crees, who ranged over a vast extent of territory in Western Canada, "great lamentations are made, and if the departed person is very much regretted the near relations cut off their hair, pierce the fleshy part of their thighs and arms with arrows, knives, etc., and blacken their faces with charcoal." Among the Kyganis, a branch of the Thlinkeet or Tlingit Indians of Alaska, while a body was burning on the funeral pyre, the assembled kinsfolk used to torture themselves mercilessly, slashing and lacerating their arms, thumping their faces with stones, and so forth. On these self-inflicted torments they prided themselves not a little. Other

Thlinkeet Indians on these melancholy occasions contented themselves with burning or singeing their hair by thrusting their heads into the flames of the blazing pyre; while others, still more discreet or less affectionate, merely cut their hair short and blackened their faces with the ashes of the deceased.

Among the Flathead Indians of Washington State it was customary for the bravest of the men and women ceremonially to bewail the death of a warrior by cutting out pieces of their own flesh and casting them with roots into the fire. And among the Indians of this region, "in case of a tribal disaster, as the death of a prominent chief, or the killing of a band of warriors by a hostile tribe, all indulge in the most frantic demonstrations, tearing the hair, lacerating the flesh with flints, often inflicting serious injury." With the Chinooks and other Indian tribes of the Oregon or Columbia River it was customary for the relations of a deceased person to destroy his property, to cut their hair, and to disfigure and wound their bodies. "To have seen those savages streaming all over with blood, one would suppose they could never have survived such acts of cruelty inflicted on themselves; but such wounds, although bad, are not dangerous. To inflict these wounds on himself, the savage takes hold of any part of his skin, between his forefinger and thumb, draws it out to the stretch, and then runs a knife through it, between the hand and the flesh, which leaves, when the skin resumes its former place, two unsightly gashes, resembling ball holes, out of which the blood issues freely. With such wounds, and sometimes others of a more serious nature, the near relations of the deceased completely disfigure themselves."

Among the Indians of the California peninsula, when a death has taken place, those who want to show the relations of the deceased their respect for the latter lie in wait for these people, and if they pass they come out from their hiding-place, almost creeping, and intonate a mournful, plainful *hu, hu, hu!* wounding their heads with pointed, sharp stones, until the blood flows down to their shoulders. Although this barbarous custom has frequently been interdicted, they are unwilling to discontinue it." Among the Gallinomeras, a branch of the Pomo Indians, who inhabit the valley of the Russian River in California, "as soon as life is extinct they lay the body decently on the funeral pyre, and the torch is applied. The weird and hideous scenes which ensue, the screams, the blood-curdling ululations, the self-lacerations they perform during the burning are too terrible to be described. Joseph Fitch says he has seen an Indian become so frenzied that he would rush up to the blazing pyre, snatch from the body a handful of burning flesh and devour it." In some tribes of Californian Indians the nearest relations cut off their hair and throw it on the burning pyre, while they beat their bodies with stones till they bleed.

To testify their grief for the death of a relative or friend the Snake Indians of the Rocky Mountains used to make incisions in all the fleshy parts of their bodies, and the greater their affection for the deceased, the deeper they cut into their own persons. They assured a French missionary that the pain which they felt in their minds escaped by these wounds. The same missionary tells us how he met groups of Crow women in mourning, their bodies so covered and disfigured by clotted blood that they presented a spectacle as pitiable as it was horrible. For several years after a death the poor creatures were bound to renew the rites of mourning every time they passed near the graves of their relations; and so long as a single clot of blood remained on their persons, they were forbidden to wash themselves. Among the Comanches, a famous tribe of horse Indians in Texas, a dead man's horses were generally killed and buried, that he might ride them to the Happy Hunting Grounds; and all the best of his property was burnt in order that it might be ready for his use on his arrival in the better land. His widows assembled round the dead horses, and with a knife in one hand and a whetstone in the other they uttered loud lamentations, while they cut gashes in their arms, legs, and bodies, till they were exhausted by the loss of blood. In token of grief on such occasions the Comanches cut off the manes and tails of their horses, cropped their own hair, and lacerated their own bodies in various ways. Among the Arapaho Indians women in mourning gash themselves lightly across the lower and upper arms and below the knees. Mourners in that tribe unbraid their hair and sometimes cut it off; the greater their love for their departed friend, the more hair they cut off. The severed locks are buried with the corpse. Moreover, the tail and mane of the horse which bore the body to its last resting-place are severed and strewn over the grave. After a bereavement the Sauks and Foxes, another tribe of Indians, "make incisions in their arms, legs, and other parts of the body; these are not made for the purposes of mortification, or to create a pain, which shall, by diverting their attention, efface the recollection of their loss, but entirely from a belief that their grief is internal, and that the only way of dispelling it is to give it a vent through which to escape." The Dacotas or Sioux in like manner lacerated their arms, thighs, legs, breasts, and so on, after the death of a friend; and the writer who reports the custom thinks it probable that they did so for the purpose of relieving their mental pain, for these same Indians, in order to cure a physical pain, used frequently to make incisions in their skin and suck up the blood, accompanying the operation with songs, or rather incantations, which were no doubt supposed to assist the cure. Among the Kansas or Konzas, a branch of the Siouan stock who have given their name to a State of the American Union, a widow after the death of her husband used to scarify herself and rub her body with clay; she also became negligent of her dress, and in this melancholy state she continued for a year, after which the eldest surviving brother of her deceased husband took her to wife without ceremony.

The custom in regard to the mourning of widows was similar among the Omahas of Nebraska, another branch of the Siouan family. "On the death of the husband, the squaws exhibit the sincerity of their grief by giving away to their neighbours every thing they possess, excepting only a bare sufficiency of clothing to cover their persons with decency. They go out from the village, and build for themselves a small shelter of grass or bark; they mortify themselves by cutting off their hair, scarifying their skin, and, in their insulated hut, they lament incessantly. If the deceased has left a brother, he takes the widow to his lodge after a proper interval, and considers her as his wife, without any preparatory formality." But among the Omahas it was not widows only who subjected themselves to these austerities in mourning. "The relatives bedaub their persons with white clay, scarify themselves with a flint, cut out pieces of their skin and flesh, pass arrows through their skin; and, if on a march, they walk barefoot at a distance from their people, in testimony of the sincerity of their mourning." Among these Indians, "when a man or woman greatly respected died, the following ceremony sometimes took place. The young men in the prime of life met at a lodge near that of the deceased, and divested themselves of all clothing except the breech-cloth; each person made two incisions in the upper left arm, and under the loop of flesh thus made thrust a small willow twig having on its end a spray of leaves. With the blood dripping on the leaves of the sprays that hung from their arms, the men moved in single file to the lodge where the dead lay. There, ranging themselves in a line shoulder to shoulder facing the tent, and marking the rhythm of the music with the willow springs they sang in unison the funeral song—the only one of its kind in the tribe. . . . At the close of the song a near relative of the dead advanced toward the singers and, raising a hand in the attitude of thanks, withdrew the willow twigs from their arms and threw them on the ground." Further, as a token of grief at the death of a relative or friend, the Omahas used to cut off locks of their hair and cast them on the corpse. Similarly among the Indians of Virginia the women in mourning would sometimes sever their tresses and throw them on the grave.

Among the Indians of Patagonia, when a death took place, mourners used to pay visits of condolence to the widow or other relations of the deceased, crying, howling, and singing in the most dismal manner, squeezing out tears, and pricking their arms and thighs with sharp thorns to make them bleed. For these demonstrations of woe they were paid with glass beads and other baubles. As soon as the Fuegians learn of the death of a relative or friend, they break into vehement demonstrations of sorrow, weeping and groaning; they lacerate their faces with the sharp edges of shells and cut the hair short on the crowns of their heads. Among the Onas, a Fuegian tribe, the custom of lacerating the face in mourning is confined to the widows or other female relations of the deceased.

The Turks of old used to cut their faces with knives in mourning for the dead, so that their blood and tears ran down their cheeks together. Among the Orang Sakai, a primitive pagan tribe, who subsist by agriculture and hunting in the almost impenetrable forests of Eastern Sumatra, it is customary before a burial for the relations to cut their heads with knives and let the flowing blood drip on the face of the corpse. Again, among the Roro-speaking tribes, who occupy a territory at the mouth of St. Joseph River in British New Guinea, when a death has taken place, the female relations of the deceased cut their skulls, faces, breasts, bellies, arms, and legs with sharp shells, till they stream with blood and fall down exhausted. In the Koiari and Toaripi tribes of British New Guinea mourners cut themselves with shells or flints till the blood flows freely. So in Vate or Efate, an island of the New Hebrides, a death was the occasion of great wailing, and the mourners scratched their faces till they streamed with blood. Similarly in Malekula, another island of the New Hebrides, gashes are or were cut in the bodies of mourners.

The Galelareeze of Halmahera, an island to the west of New Guinea, make an offering of their hair to the soul of a deceased relative on the third day after his or her death, which is the day after burial. A woman, who has not recently suffered any bereavement in her own family, operates on the mourners, snipping off merely the tips of their eyebrows and of the locks which overhang their temples. After being thus shorn, they go and bathe in the sea and wash their hair with grated coco-nuts in order to purify themselves from the taint of death; for to touch or go near a corpse is thought to render a person unclean. A seer, for example, is supposed to lose his power of seeing spirits if he incurs this pollution or so much as eats food which has been in a house with a dead body. Should the survivors fail to offer their hair to the deceased and to cleanse themselves afterwards, it is believed that they do not get rid of the soul of their departed brother or sister. For instance, if some one has died away from home, and his family has had no news of his death, so that they have not shorn their hair nor bathed on the third day, the ghost (*soso*) of the dead man will haunt them and hinder them in all their work. When they crush coco-nuts, they will get no oil: when they pound sago, they will obtain no meal: when they are hunting, they will see no game. Not until they have learned of the death, and shorn their hair, and bathed, will the ghost cease thus to thwart and baffle them in their undertakings. The well-informed Dutch missionary who reports these customs believes that the offering of hair is intended to delude the simple ghost into imagining that his friends have followed him to the far country; but we may doubt whether even the elastic credulity of ghosts could be stretched so far as to mistake a few snippets of hair for the persons from whose heads they had been severed.

Customs of the same sort appear to have been observed by all the widely spread branches of the Polynesian race in the Pacific. Thus in Otaheite, when a death occurred, the corpse used to be conveyed to a house or hut, called *tupapow,* built specially for the purpose, where it was left to putrefy till the flesh had wholly wasted from the bones. "As soon as the body is deposited in the *tupapow,* the mourning is renewed. The women assemble, and are led to the door by the nearest relation, who strikes a shark's tooth several times into the crown of her head; the blood copiously follows, and is carefully received upon pieces of linen, which are thrown into the bier. The rest of the women follow this example, and the ceremony is repeated at the interval of two or three days, as long as the zeal and sorrow of the parties hold out. The tears also which are shed upon these occasions, are received upon pieces of cloth, and offered as oblations to the dead; some of the younger people cut off their hair, and that is thrown under the bier with the other offerings. This custom is founded upon a notion that the soul of the deceased, which they believe to exist in a separate state, is hovering about the place where the body is deposited: that it observes the actions of the survivors, and is gratified by such testimonies of their affection and grief." According to a later writer the Tahitians in mourning "not only wailed in the loudest and most affecting tone, but tore her hair, rent their garments, and cut themselves with shark's teeth or knives in a shocking manner. The instrument usually employed was a small cane, about four inches long, with five or six shark's teeth fixed in, on opposite sides. With one of these instruments every female provided herself after marriage, and on occasions of death it was unsparingly used. With some this was not sufficient; they prepared a short instrument, something like a plumber's mallet, about five or six inches long, rounded at one end for a handle, and armed with two or three rows of shark's teeth fixed in the wood, at the other. With this, on the death of a relative or a friend, they cut themselves unmercifully, striking the head, temples, cheek, and breast, till the blood flowed profusely from the wounds. At the same time they uttered the most deafening and agonizing cries; and the distortion of their countenances, their torn and dishevelled hair, the mingled tears and blood that covered their bodies, their wild gestures and unruly conduct, often gave them a frightful and almost inhuman appearance. This cruelty was principally performed by females, but not by them only; the men committed on these occasions the same enormities, and not only cut themselves, but came armed with clubs and other deadly weapons." At these doleful ceremonies the women sometimes wore short aprons, which they held up with one hand to receive the blood, while they cut themselves with the other. The blood-drenched apron was afterwards dried in the sun and given in token of affection to the bereaved family, who preserved it as a proof of the high esteem in which the departed had been held. On the death of a king or principal chief, his subjects assembled, tore their hair, lacerated their bodies till they were covered with blood, and often fought with clubs and stones till one or more of them were killed. Such fights at the death of a great man may help us to understand how the custom of gladiatorial combats arose at Rome; for the ancients themselves inform us that these combats first took place at funerals and were a substitute for the slaughter of captives at the tomb. At Rome the first exhibition of gladiators was given by D. Junius Brutus in 264 B.C. in honour of his dead father.

Among the women of Otaheite the use of shark's teeth as a lancet to draw blood from their heads was not limited to occasions of death. If any accident befell a woman's husband, his relations or friends, or her own child, she went to work on herself with the shark's teeth; even if the child had only fallen down and hurt itself, the mother mingled her blood with its tears. But when a child died, the whole house was filled with kinsfolk, cutting their heads and making loud lamentations. "On this occasion, in addition to other tokens of grief, the parents cut their hair short on one part of their heads, leaving the rest long. Sometimes this is confined to a square patch on the forehead; at others they leave that, and cut off all the rest: sometimes a bunch is left over both ears, sometimes over one only; and sometimes one half is clipped quite close, and the other left to grow long; and these tokens of mourning are sometimes prolonged for two or three years." This description may illustrate the Israelitish practice of making bald places on the head in sign of mourning.

In Hawaii or the Sandwich Islands, when a king or great chief died, the people expressed their grief "by the most shocking personal outrages, not only by tearing off their clothes entirely, but by knocking out their eyes and teeth with clubs and stones, and pulling out their hair, and by burning and cutting their flesh." Of these various mutilations, that of knocking out teeth would seem to have been on these occasions the most prevalent and popular. It was practised by both sexes, though perhaps most extensively by men. On the death of a king or important chief the lesser chiefs connected with him by ties of blood or friendship were expected to display their attachment by knocking out one of their front teeth with a stone; and when they had done so, their followers felt bound to follow their example. Sometimes a man broke out his own tooth; more frequently, however, the friendly office was discharged for him by another, who, planting one end of a stick against the tooth, hammered the other end with a stone, till the tooth was either knocked out or broken off. If the men shrank from submitting to this operation, the women would often perform it on them while they slept. More than one tooth was seldom extracted at one time; but the mutilation being repeated on the death of every chief of rank or authority, few adult men were to be seen with an entire set of teeth, and many had lost the front teeth on both the upper and lower jaw, which, apart from other inconveniences, caused a great defect in their speech. Some, however, dared to be singular and to retain most of their teeth.

Similarly the Tongans in mourning beat their teeth with stones, burned circles and scars on their flesh, struck shark's teeth into their heads until the blood flowed in streams, and thrust spears into the inner parts of their thighs, into their sides below the arm-pits, and through their cheeks into their mouths. When the cast-away English seaman, William Mariner, resided among the Tongans early in the nineteenth century, he witnessed and has graphically described the extravagant mourning for Finow, king of Tonga. The assembled chiefs and nobles on that occasion, he tells us, evinced their grief by cutting and wounding themselves with clubs, stones, knives, or sharp shells; one at a time, or two or three together, would run into the middle of the circle formed by the spectators to give these proofs of their extreme sorrow for the death and their great respect for the memory, of their departed lord and friend. Thus one would cry, "Finow! I know well your mind; you have departed to Boloton,[1] and left your people under suspicion that I, or some of those about you, were unfaithful; but where is the proof of infidelity? where is a single instance of disrespect?" So saying, he would inflict violent blows and deep cuts on his head with a club, stone, or knife, exclaiming at intervals, "Is this not a proof of my fidelity? does this not evince loyalty and attachment to the memory of the departed warrior?" Another, after parading up and down with a wild and agitated step, spinning and whirling a club, would strike himself with the edge of it two or three times violently on the top or back of the head; then stopping suddenly and gazing steadfastly at the blood-bespattered implement, he would cry, "Alas! my club, who could have said that you would have done this kind office for me, and have enabled me thus to evince a testimony of my respect for Finow! Never, no, never, can you again tear open the brains of his enemies! Alas! what a great and mighty warrior has fallen! Oh! Finow, cease to suspect my loyalty; be convinced of my fidelity!" Some, more violent than others, cut their heads to the skull with such strong and frequent blows that they reeled and lost for a time the use of their reason. Other men during the mourning for Finow shaved their heads and burned their cheeks with lighted rolls of cloth, and rubbing the wounds with astringent berries caused them to bleed. This blood they smeared about the wounds in circles of nearly two inches in diameter, giving themselves a very unseemly appearance; and they repeated the friction with the berries daily, making the blood to flow afresh. To show their love for their deceased master, the king's fishermen beat and bruised their heads with the paddles of their canoes. Moreover, each of them had three arrows stuck

[1] The land of the dead.

through each cheek in a slanting direction, so that, while the points were within the mouth, the heads of the arrows projected over the shoulders and were kept in that position by another arrow tied to both sets of heads at the fisherman's back, so as to form a triangle. With this strange accoutrement the fishermen walked round the grave, beating their faces and heads with their paddles, or pinching up the skin of the breast and sticking a spear quite through it, all to prove their affection for the deceased chief.

In the Samoan islands it was in like manner customary for mourners to manifest their grief by frantic lamentations and wailing, by rending the garments, tearing out the hair, burning their flesh with firebrands, bruising their bodies with stones, and gashing themselves with sharp stones, shells, and shark's teeth, till they were covered with blood. This was called an "offering of blood" (*taulanga toto*); but according to Dr. George Brown, the expression did not imply that the blood was presented to the gods, it signified no more than affection for the deceased and sorrow for his loss. Similarly in Mangaia, one of the Hervey Islands, no sooner did a sick person expire than the near relatives blackened their faces, cut off their hair, and slashed their bodies with shark's teeth so that the blood streamed down. At Raratonga it was usual to knock out some of the front teeth in token of sorrow. So, too, in the Marquesas Islands, "on the death of a great chief, his widow and the women of the tribe uttered piercing shrieks, whilst they slashed their foreheads, cheeks, and breasts with splinters of bamboo. This custom has disappeared, at least in Nuka-Hiva; but in the south-eastern group the women still comply with this usage, and, with faces bleeding from deep wounds, abandon themselves to demonstrations of despair as the funeral of their relations."

Among the Maoris of New Zealand the mourning customs were similar. "The wives and near relations, especially the female ones, testified their grief by cutting the face and forehead with shells or pieces of obsidian, until the blood flowed plentifully, suffering the streamlets to dry on the face, and the more perfectly it was covered with clotted gore the greater the proof of their respect for the dead; the hair was always cut as a sign of grief, the men generally cut it only on one side, from the forehead to the neck." According to another account, the cuttings for the dead among the Maoris were by no means confined to the face and fore-head. "All the immediate relatives and friends of the deceased, with the slaves, or other servants or dependants, if he possessed any, cut themselves most grievously, and present a frightful picture to a European eye. A piece of flint (made sacred on account of the blood which it has shed, and the purpose for which it has been used) is held between the third finger and the thumb; the depth to which it is to enter the skin appearing beyond the nails. The operation commences in the middle of the forehead; and the cut extends, in a curve, all down the face, on either side: the legs, arms, and chest are then most miserably scratched; and the breasts of the women, who cut themselves more extensively and deeper than the men, are sometimes wofully gashed."

Nowhere, perhaps, has this custom of cutting the bodies of the living in honour of the dead been practised more systematically or with greater severity than among the rude aborigines of Australia. who stand at the foot of the social ladder. Thus among the tribes of Western Victoria a widower mourned his wife for three moons. Every second night he wailed and recounted her good qualities, and lacerated his forehead with his nails till the blood flowed down his cheeks; also he covered his head and face with white clay. If he loved her very dearly and wished to express his grief at her loss, he would burn himself across the waist in three lines with a red-hot piece of bark. A widow mourned for her husband for twelve moons. She cut her hair quite close, and burned her thighs with hot ashes pressed down on them with a piece of bark till she screamed with agony. Every second night she wailed and recounted his good qualities, and lacerated her forehead till the blood flowed down her cheeks. At the same time she covered her head and face with white clay. This she must do for three moons on pain of death. Children in mourning for their parents lacerated their brows. Among the natives of Central Victoria the parents of the deceased were wont to lacerate themselves fearfully, the father beating and cutting his head with a tomahawk, and the mother burning her breasts and belly with a firestick. This they did daily for hours until the period of mourning was over. Widows in these tribes not only burned their breasts, arms, legs, and thighs with firesticks, but rubbed ashes into their wounds and scratched their faces till the blood mingled with the ashes. Among the Kurnai of South-eastern Victoria mourners cut and gashed themselves with sharp stones and tomahawks until their heads and bodies streamed with blood. In the Mukjarawaint tribe of Western Victoria, when a man died, his relatives cried over him and cut themselves with tom- ahawks and other sharp instruments for a week.

Among the tribes of the Lower Murray and Lower Darling rivers mourners scored their backs and arms, sometimes even their faces, with red-hot brands, which raised hideous ulcers; afterwards they flung themselves prone on the grave, tore out their hair by handfuls, rubbed earth over their heads and bodies in great profusion, and ripped up their green ulcers till the mingled blood and grime presented a ghastly spectacle. Among the Kamilaroi, a large tribe of Eastern New South Wales, the mourners, especially the women, used to plaster their heads and faces with white clay, and then cut gashes in their heads with axes, so that the blood flowed down over the clay to their shoulders, where it was allowed to dry. Speaking of a native burial on the Murray River, a writer says that "around the bier were many women, relations of the deceased, wailing and lamenting bitterly, and lacerating their thighs, backs, and breasts with shells or flint, until the blood flowed copiously from the gashes."

In the Kabi and Wakka tribes of South-eastern Queensland, about the Mary River, mourning lasted approximately six weeks. "Every night a general, loud wailing was sustained for hours, and was accompanied by personal laceration with sharp flints or other cutting instruments. The men would be content with a few incisions on the back of the head, but the women would gash themselves from head to foot and allow the blood to dry upon the skin." In the Boulia district of Central Queensland women in mourning score their thighs, both inside and outside, with sharp stones or bits of glass, so as to make a series of parallel cuts; in neighbouring districts of Queensland the men make a single large and much deeper cruciform cut in the corresponding part of the thigh. Members of the Kakadu tribe, in the Northern Territory of Australia, cut their heads in mourning till the blood flows down their faces on to their bodies. This is done by men and women alike. Some of the blood is afterwards collected in a piece of bark and apparently deposited in a tree close to the spot where the person died.

In the Kariera tribe of Western Australia, when a death has occurred, the relations, both male and female, wail and cut their scalps until the blood trickles from their heads. The hair of the deceased is cut off and preserved, being worn by the relatives in the form of string. Among the Narriyeri, a tribe of South Australia, the bodies of the dead used to be partially dried over a slow fire, then skinned, reddened with ochre, and set up naked on stages. "A great lamentation and wailing is made at this time by all the relations and friends of the dead man. They cut their hair off close to the head, and besmear themselves with oil and pounded charcoal. The women besmear themselves with the most disgusting filth; they all beat and cut themselves, and make violent demonstrations of grief. All the relatives are careful to be present and not to be wanting in the proper signs of sorrow, lest they should be suspected of complicity in causing the death."

In the Arunta tribe of Central Australia a man is bound to cut himself on the shoulder in mourning for his father-in-law; if he does not do so, his wife may be given away to another man in order to appease the wrath of the ghost at his undutiful son-in-law. Arunta men regularly bear on their shoulders the raised scars which show that they have done their duty by their dead fathers-in-law. The female relations of a dead man in the Arunta tribe also cut and hack themselves in token of sorrow, working themselves up into a sort of frenzy as they do so, yet in all their apparent excitement they take care never to wound a vital part, but vent their fury on their scalps, their shoulders, and their legs. In the Warramunga tribe of Central Australia widows crop their hair short, and, after cutting open the middle line of the scalp, run firesticks along the wounds, often with serious consequences. Other female relations of the deceased among the Warramunga content themselves with cutting their scalps open by repeated blows of yamsticks till the blood streams down over their faces; while men gash their thighs more or less deeply with knives. These wounds on the thigh are made to gape as widely as possible by tying strings tightly round the leg on both sides of the gash. The scars so made are permanent. A man has been seen with traces of no less than twenty-three such wounds inflicted at different times in mourning. In addition, some Warramunga men in mourning cut off their hair closely, burn it, and smear their scalps with pipeclay, while other men cut off their whiskers. All these things are regulated by very definite rules. The gashing of the thighs, and even the cutting of the hair and of the whiskers, are not left to chance or to the caprice of the mourners; the persons who perform these operations on themselves must be related to the deceased in certain definite ways and in no other; and the relationships are of that classificatory or group order which is alone recognized by the Australian aborigines. In this tribe, "if a man, who stands in a particular relationship to you, happens to die, you must do the proper thing, which may be either gashing your thigh or cutting your hair, quite regardless of whether you were personally acquainted with the dead man, or whether he was your dearest friend or greatest enemy."

It deserves to be noticed that in these cuttings for the dead among the Australians the blood drawn from the bodies of the mourners is sometimes applied directly to the corpse, or at least allowed to drop into the grave. Thus among some tribes on the Darling River several men used to stand by the open grave and cut each other's heads with a boomerang; then they held their bleeding heads over the grave, so that the blood dripped on the corpse lying in it. If the deceased was held in high esteem, the bleeding was repeated after some earth had been thrown on the corpse. Similarly in the Milya-uppa tribe, which occupied the country about the Torrowotta Lake in the north-west of New South Wales, when the dead man had been a warrior, the mourners cut each other's heads and let the blood fall on the corpse as it lay in the grave. Again, in the Bahkunjy tribe at Bourke, on the Darling River, "I was present at a burial, when the widower (as the chief mourner chanced to be) leapt into the grave, and, holding his hair apart with the fingers of both hands, received from another black, who had leapt after him, a smart blow with a boomerang on the 'parting.' A strong jet of blood followed. The widower then performed the same duty by his comrade. This transaction took place, I fancy, on the bed of leaves, before the corpse had been deposited." Among the Arunta of Central Australia the female relations of the dead used to throw themselves on the grave and there cut their own and each other's heads with fighting-clubs or digging-sticks till the blood, streaming down over the pipeclay with which their bodies were whitened, dripped upon the grave.

Again, at a burial on the Vasse River, in Western Australia, a writer describes how, when the grave was dug, the natives placed the corpse beside it, then "gashed their thighs, and at the flowing of the blood they all said, "I have brought blood,' and they stamped the foot forcibly on the ground, sprinkling the blood around them; then wiping the wounds with a wisp of leaves, they threw it, bloody as it was, on the dead man."

Further, it is deserving of notice that the Australian aborigines sometimes apply their severed hair, as well as their spilt blood, to the bodies of their dead friends. Thus, Sir George Grey tells us that "the natives of many parts of Australia, when at a funeral, cut off portions of their beards, and singeing these, throw them upon the dead body; in some instances they cut off the beard of the corpse, and burning it, rub themselves and the body with the singed portions of it." Comparing the modern Australian with the ancient Hebrew usages in mourning, Sir George Grey adds, "The native females invariably cut themselves and scratch their faces in mourning for the dead; they also literally make a baldness between their eyes, this being always one of the places where they tear the skin with the finger nails."

Among the rude aborigines of Tasmania the mourning customs appear to have been similar. "Plastering their shaven heads with pipeclay, and covering their faces with a mixture of charcoal and emu fat, or mutton-bird grease, the women not only wept, but lacerated their bodies with sharp shells and stones, even burning their thighs with a firestick. Flowers would be thrown on the grave, and trees entwined to cover their beloved ones. The hair cut off in grief was thrown upon the mound."

The customs of cutting the body and shearing the hair in token of mourning for the dead have now been traced throughout a considerable portion of mankind, from the most highly civilized nations of antiquity down to the lowest savages of modern times. It remains to ask, What is the meaning of these practices? The Nicobarese shave their hair and eyebrows in mourning for the alleged purpose of disguising themselves from the ghost, whose unwelcome attentions they desire to avoid, and whom they apparently imagine to be incapable of recognizing them with their hair cut. Can it be, then, that both customs have been adopted in order either to deceive or to repel the ghost by rendering his surviving relations either unrecognizable or repulsive in his eyes? On this theory both customs are based on a fear of the ghost; by cutting their flesh and cropping their hair the mourners hope that the ghost will either not know them, or that knowing them he will turn away in disgust from their cropped heads and bleeding bodies, so that in either case he will not molest them.

How does this hypothesis square with the facts which we have passed in review? The fear of the ghost certainly counts for something in the Australian ceremonies of mourning; for we have seen that among the Arunta, if a man does not cut himself properly in mourning for his father-in-law, the old man's ghost is supposed to be so angry that the only way of appeasing his wrath is to take away his daughter from the arms of his undutiful son-in-law. Further, in the Unmatjera and Kaitish tribes of Central Australia a widow covers her body with ashes and renews this token of grief during the whole period of mourning, because, if she failed to do so, "the *atnirinja,* or spirit of the dead man, who constantly follows her about, will kill her and strip all the flesh off her bones." In these customs the fear of the ghost is manifest, but there is apparently no intention either to deceive or to disgust him by rendering the person of the mourner unrecognizable or repulsive. On the contrary, the Australian practices in mourning seem to aim rather at obtruding the mourners on the attention of the ghost, in order that he may be satisfied with their demonstrations of sorrow at the irreparable loss they have sustained through his death. The Arunta and other tribes of Central Australia fear that if they do not display a sufficient amount of grief, the spirit of the dead man will be offended and do them a mischief. And with regard to their practice of whitening the mourner's body with pipe-clay, we are told that "there is no idea of concealing from the spirit of the dead person the identity of the mourner; on the other hand, the idea is to render him or her more conspicuous, and so to allow the spirit to see that it is being properly mourned for." In short, the Central Australian customs in mourning appear designed to please or propitiate the ghost rather than to elude his observation or excite his disgust. That this is the real intention of the Australian usages in general is strongly suggested by the practices of allowing the mourner's blood to drop on the corpse or into the grave, and depositing his severed locks on the lifeless body; for these acts can hardly be interpreted otherwise than as tribute paid or offerings presented to the spirit of the dead in order either to gratify his wishes or to avert his wrath. Similarly we saw that among the Orang Sakai of Sumatra mourners allow the blood dripping from their wounded heads to fall on the face of the corpse, and that in Otaheite the blood flowing from the self-inflicted wounds of mourners used to be caught in pieces of cloth, which were then laid beside the dead body on the bier. Further, the custom of depositing the shorn hair of mourners on the corpse or in the grave has been observed in ancient or modern times by Arabs, Greeks, Mingrelians, North American Indians, Tahitians, and Tasmanians, as well as by the aborigines of Australia. Hence we seem to be justified in concluding that the desire to benefit or please the ghost has been at least one motive which has led many peoples to practise those corporeal mutilations with which we are here concerned. But to say this is not to affirm that the propitiation of the ghost has been the sole intention with which these austerities have been practised. Different peoples may well have inflicted these sufferings or disfigurements on themselves from different motives, and amongst these various motives the wish to elude or deceive the dangerous spirit of the dead may sometimes have been one.

We have still to inquire how the offering of blood and hair is supposed to benefit or please the ghost? Is he thought to delight in them merely as expressions of the unfeigned sorrow which his friends feel at his death? That certainly would seem to have been the interpretation which the Tahitians put upon the custom; for along with their blood and hair they offered to the soul of the deceased their tears, and they believed that the ghost "observes the actions of the survivors, and is gratified by such testimonies of their affection and grief." Yet even when we have made every allowance for the selfishness of the savage, we should probably do injustice to the primitive ghost if we supposed that he exacted a tribute of blood and tears and hair from no other motive than a ghoulish delight in the sufferings and privations of his surviving kinsfolk. It seems likely that originally he was believed to reap some more tangible and material benefit from these demonstrations of affection and devotion. Robertson Smith suggested that the intention of offering the blood of the mourners to the spirit of the departed was to create a blood covenant between the living and the dead, and thus to confirm or establish friendly relations with the spiritual powers. In support of this view he referred to the practice of some Australian tribes on the Darling River, who, besides wounding their heads and allowing the blood from the wounds to drop on the corpse, were wont to cut a piece of flesh from the dead body, dry it in the sun, cut it in small pieces, and distribute the pieces among the relatives and friends, some of whom sucked it to get strength and courage, while others threw it into the river to bring a flood and fish, when both were wanted. Here the giving of blood to the dead and the sucking of his flesh undoubtedly appear to imply a relation of mutual benefit between the survivors and the deceased, whether that relation is to be described as a covenant or not. Similarly among the Kariera of Western Australia, who bleed themselves in mourning, the hair of the deceased is cut off and worn by the relatives in the form of string. Here, again, there seems to be an exchange of benefits between the living and the dead, the survivors giving their blood to their departed kinsman and receiving his hair in return.

However, these indications of an interchange of good offices between the mourners and the mourned are too few and slight to warrant the conclusion that bodily mutilations and wounds inflicted on themselves by bereaved relatives are always or even generally intended to establish a covenant of mutual help and protection with the dead. The great majority of the practices which we have surveyed in this chapter can reasonably be interpreted as benefits supposed to be conferred by the living on the dead, but few or none of them, apart from the Australian practices which I have just cited, appear to imply any corresponding return of kindness made by the ghost to his surviving kinsfolk. Accordingly the hypothesis which would explain the cuttings for the dead as attempts to institute a blood covenant with them must apparently be set aside on the ground that it is not adequately supported by the evidence at our disposal.

A simpler and more obvious explanation of the cuttings is suggested by the customs of some of the savages who inflict such wounds on themselves. Thus we have seen that the practice of wounding the heads of mourners and letting the blood drip on the corpse was prevalent among the Australian tribes of the Darling River. Now among these same tribes it is, or rather used to be, the custom that on undergoing the ceremony of initiation into manhood "during the first two days the youth drinks only blood from the veins in the arms of his friends, who willingly supply the required food. Having bound a ligature round the upper part of the arm they cut a vein on the under side of the forearm, and run the blood into a wooden vessel, or a dish-shaped piece of bark. The youth, kneeling on his bed, made of the small branches of a fuchsia shrub, leans forward, while holding his hands behind him, and licks up the blood from the vessel placed in front of him with his tongue, like a dog. Later he is allowed to eat the flesh of ducks as well as the blood." Again, among these same tribes of the Darling River, "a very sick or weak person is fed upon blood which the male friends provide, taken from their bodies in the way already described. It is generally taken in a raw state by the invalid, who lifts it to his mouth like jelly between his fingers and thumb. I have seen it cooked in a wooden vessel by putting a few red-hot ashes among it." Again, speaking of the same tribes, the same writer tells us that "it sometimes happens that a change of camp has to be made, and a long journey over a dry country undertaken, with a helpless invalid, who is carried by the strong men, who willingly bleed themselves until they are weak and faint, to provide the food they consider is the best for a sick person." But if these savages gave their own blood to feed the weak and sickly among their living friends, why should they not have given it for the same purpose to their dead kinsfolk? Like almost all savages, the Australian aborigines believed that the human soul survives the death of the body; what more natural accordingly than that in its disembodied state the soul should be supplied by its loving relatives with the same sustaining nourishment with which they may have often strengthened it in life? On the same principle, when Ulysses was come to deadland in the far country of Cimmerian darkness, he sacrificed sheep and caused their blood to flow into a trench, and the weak ghosts, gathering eagerly about it, drank the blood and so acquired the strength to speak with him.

But if the blood offered by mourners was designed for the refreshment of the ghost, what are we to say of the parallel offering of their hair? The ghost may have been thought to drink the blood, but we can hardly suppose that he was reduced to such extremities of hunger as to eat the hair. Still it is to be remembered that in the opinion of some peoples the hair is the special seat of its owner's strength, and that accordingly in cutting their hair and presenting it to the dead they may have imagined that they were supplying him with a source of energy not less ample and certain than when they provided him with their blood to drink. If that were so, the parallelism which runs through the mourning customs of cutting the body and polling the hair would be intelligible. That this is the true explanation of both practices, however, the evidence at our command is hardly sufficient to enable us to pronounce with confidence.

So far as it goes, however, the preceding inquiry tends to confirm the view that the widespread practices of cutting the bodies and shearing the hair of the living after a death were originally designed to gratify or benefit in some way the spirit of the departed; and accordingly, wherever such customs have prevailed, they may be taken as evidence that the people who observed them believed in the survival of the human soul after death and desired to maintain friendly relations with it. In other words, the observance of these usages implies a propitiation or worship of the dead. Since the Hebrews appear to have long cut both their bodies and their hair in honour of their departed relations, we may safely include them among the many tribes and nations who have at one time or another been addicted to that worship of ancestors which, of all forms of primitive religion, has probably enjoyed the widest popularity and exerted the deepest influence on mankind. The intimate connexion of these mourning customs with the worship of the dead was probably well remembered in Israel down to the close of the monarchy, and may have furnished the religious reformers of that age with their principal motive for prohibiting extravagant displays of sorrow which they justly regarded as heathenish.

CHAPTER IV

THE OX THAT GORED

In the Book of the Covenant, the oldest code of laws embodied in the Pentateuch, it is laid down that "if an ox gore a man or a woman, that they die, the ox shall be surely stoned, and his flesh shall not be eaten; but the owner of the ox shall be quit. But if the ox were wont to gore in time past, and it hath been testified to his owner, and he hath not kept him in, but that he hath killed a man or a woman; the ox shall be stoned, and his owner also shall be put to death." In the much later Priestly Code the rule regulating the punishment of homicidal animals is stated more comprehensively as part of the general law of blood-revenge which was revealed by God to Noah after the great flood: "And surely your blood, the blood of your lives, will I require; at the hand of every beast will I require it; and at the hand of man, even at the hand of every man's brother, will I require the life of man. Whoso sheddeth man's blood, by man shall his blood be shed."

The principle of blood-revenge has been carried out in the same rigorous manner by savage tribes; indeed some of them have pushed the principle of retaliation yet further by destroying even inanimate objects which have accidentally caused the death of human beings. For example, the Kookies or Kukis of Chittagong, in North-eastern India, "like all savage people, are of a most vindictive disposition: blood must always be shed for blood; if a tiger even kills any of them, near a village, the whole tribe is up in arms, and goes in pursuit of the animal; when, if he is killed, the family of the deceased gives a feast of his flesh, in revenge of his having killed their relation. And should the tribe fail to destroy the tiger, in this first general pursuit of him, the family of the deceased must still continue the chase; for until they have killed either this, or some other tiger, and have given a feast of his flesh, they are in disgrace in the village, and not associated with by the rest of the inhabitants. In like manner, if a tiger destroys one of a hunting party, or of a party of warriors on a hostile excursion, neither the one nor the other (whatever their success may have been) can return to the village, without being disgraced, unless they kill the tiger. A more striking instance still of this revengeful spirit of retaliation is that if a man should happen to be killed by an accidental fall from a tree, all his relations assemble, and cut it down; and however large it may be, they reduce it to chips, which they scatter in the winds, for having, as they say, been the cause of the death of their brother."

Similarly the Ainos or Ainu, a primitive people of Japan, take vengeance on any tree from which a person has fallen and been killed. When such an accident happens, "the people become quite angry, and proceed to make war upon the tree. They assemble and perform a certain ceremony which they call *niokeush rorumbe*. Upon asking about this matter the Ainu said: 'Should a person climb a tree and then fall out of it and die, or should a person cut the tree down and the tree fall upon him and kill him, such a death is called *niokeush*, and it is caused by the multitude of demons inhabiting the various parts of the trunk and branches and leaves. The people ought therefore to meet together, cut the tree down, divide it up into small pieces and scatter them to the winds. For unless that tree be destroyed it will always remain dangerous, the demons continuing to inhabit it. But if the tree is too large to be cut up fine, it may be left there, the place being clearly marked, so that people may not go near it.'" Among the aborigines of

Western Victoria the spear or other weapon of an enemy which had killed a friend was always burnt by the relatives of the deceased. Similarly some of the natives of Western Australia used to burn the point of a spear which had killed a man; and they explained the custom by saying that the soul of the slain man adhered to the point of the weapon and could only depart to its proper place when that point had been burnt. When a murder has been committed among the Akikuyu of British East Africa, the elders take the spear or sword with which the crime was perpetrated, beat it quite blunt, and then throw it into a deep pool in the nearest river. They say that if they omitted to do so the weapon would continue to be the cause of murder. To the same effect a writer who has personally investigated some of the tribes of British East Africa tells us that "the weapon which has destroyed human life is looked upon with awe and dread. Having once caused death it retains an evil propensity to carry death with it for ever. Among the Akikuyu and Atheraka, therefore, it is blunted and buried by the elders. The Akamba pursue a different method, more typical of their crafty character. The belief among them is that the arrow which has killed a man can never lose its fateful spirit, which abides with the one who possesses it. The bow also is possessed of the same spirit, and hence as soon as a Mkamba [1] has killed any one he will induce another by deceitful means to take it. The arrow is at first in possession of the relatives of the person killed; they will extract it from the wound and hide it at night near the murderer's village. The people there make search for it, and, if found, either return it to the other village, or lay it somewhere on a path, in the hopes that some passer-by will pick it up and thus transfer to himself the curse. But people are wary of such finds, and thus mostly possession of the arrow remains with the murderer."

In the Malay code of Malacca there is a section dealing with vicious buffaloes and cattle, and herein it is ordained that "if the animal be tied in the forest, in a place where people are not in the habit of passing, and there gore anybody to death, it shall be put to death." Among the Bare'e-speaking Toradjas of Central Celebes "blood-revenge extends to animals: a buffalo that has killed a man must be put to death." This is natural enough, for "the Toradja conceives an animal to differ from a man only in outward appearance. The animal cannot speak, because its beak or snout is different from the mouth of a man; the animal runs on all fours, because its hands (fore-paws) are different from human hands; but the inmost nature of the animal is the same as that of a man. If a crocodile kills somebody, the family of the victim may thereupon kill a crocodile, that is to say, the murderer or some member of his family; but if more crocodiles than men are killed, then the right of revenge reverts to the crocodiles, and they are sure to exercise their right on somebody or other. If a dog does not

[1] Mkamba is the singular form of Akamba, the plural.

receive his share of the game, he will refuse next time to join in the hunt, because he feels himself aggrieved. The Toradja is much more sensible than we are of the rights of animals; in particular he deems it highly dangerous to make fun of a beast. He would utter a lively protest and predict heavy storms and floods of rain if, for instance, he saw anybody dress up an ape in human clothes. And nobody can laugh at a cat or dog with impunity." Among the Bogos, a tribe on the northern outskirts of Abyssinia, a bull, or a cow, or any head of cattle that kills a human being is put to death.

At the entrance of a Bayaka village, in the valley of the Congo, Mr. Torday saw a roughly constructed gallows, on which hung a dead dog. He learned that as a notorious thief, who had been in the habit of making predatory raids among the fowls, the animal had been strung up to serve as a public example. Among the Arabs of Arabia Petraea, when an animal has killed a man, its owner must drive it away, crying after it "Scabby, scabby!" He may never afterwards recover possession of the beast, under pain of being compelled to pay the bloodwit for the homicide committed by the brute. Should the death have been caused by a sheep or a goat in a flock, as by sending a heavy stone hurtling down a steep slope, but the particular animal which set the stone rolling be unknown, then the whole flock must be driven away with the cry, "Away from us, ye scabby ones!"

Similar principles of retributive justice were recognized in antiquity by other nations than the Jews. In the *Zend-Avesta*, the ancient lawbook of the Persians, it is laid down that if "the mad dog, or the dog that bites without barking, smite a sheep or wound a man, the dog shall pay for it as for wilful murder. If the dog shall smite a sheep or wound a man, they shall cut off his right ear. If he shall smite another sheep or wound another man, they shall cut off his left ear. If he shall smite a third sheep or wound a third man, they shall cut off his right foot. If he shall smite a fourth sheep or wound a fourth man, they shall cut off his left foot. If he shall for the fifth time smite a sheep or wound a man, they shall cut off his tail. Therefore they shall tie him to the post; by the two sides of the collar they shall tie him. If they shall not do so, and the mad dog, or the dog that bites without barking, smite a sheep or wound a man, he shall pay for it as for wilful murder." It will be generally admitted that in this enactment the old Persian lawyer treats a worrying dog with great forbearance; for he gives him no less than five distinct chances of reforming his character before he exacts from the irreclaimable culprit the extreme penalty of the law.

At Athens, the very heart of ancient civilization in its finest efflorescence, there was a court specially set apart for the trial of animals and of lifeless objects which had injured or killed human beings. The court sat in the town-hall (*prytaneum*), and the

judges were no less than the titular king of all Attica and the four
titular kings of the separate Attic tribes. As the town-hall was
in all probability the oldest political centre in Athens, if we except
the fortress of the Acropolis, whose precipitous crags and frowning battlements rose immediately behind the law-court, and as the
titular tribal kings represented the old tribal kings who bore sway
for ages before the inhabitants of Attica overthrew the monarchial
and adopted the republican form of government, we are justified
in assuming that the court held in this venerable building, and
presided over by these august judges, was of extreme antiquity;
and the conclusion is confirmed by the nature of the cases which
here came up for judgment, since to find complete parallels to them
we have had to go to the rude justice of savage tribes in the wilds
of India, Africa, and Celebes. The offenders who were here placed
at the bar were not men and women, but animals and implements
or missiles of stone, wood, or iron which had fallen upon and cracked
somebody's crown, when the hand which had hurled them was
unknown. What was done to the animals which were found guilty,
we do not know; but we are told that lifeless objects, which had
killed anybody by falling on him or her, were banished by the
tribal kings beyond the boundaries. Every year the axe or the
knife which had been used to slaughter an ox at a festival of Zeus
on the Acropolis was solemnly tried for murder before the judges
seated on the bench of justice; every year it was solemnly found
guilty, condemned, and cast into the sea. To ridicule the Athenian
passion for sitting on juries, the comic poet Aristophanes has
described in one of his plays a crazy old juryman trying a dog,
with all legal formalities, for stealing and eating a cheese. Perhaps
the idea of the famous scene, which was copied by Racine in his
only comedy, *Les Plaideurs*, may have occurred to the Athenian
poet as he whiled away an idle hour among the spectators in the
court-house, watching with suppressed amusement the trial of a
canine, bovine, or asinine prisoner at the bar charged with mali-
ciously and feloniously biting, goring, kicking, or otherwise assaulting a burgess of Athens.

Strangely enough the great philosopher of idealism, Plato
himself, cast the mantle of his authority over these quaint relics
of a barbarous jurisprudence by proposing to incorporate them in
the laws of that ideal state which he projected towards the end of
his life. Yet it must be confessed that, when he came to compose
The Laws, the tremulous hand of the aged artist had lost much of
its cunning, and that, large as is the canvas on which his latest
picture is painted, its colours pale beside the visionary glories of
The Republic. Few books bear more visibly impressed upon them
the traces of faded imaginative splendour and of a genius declined
into the vale of years. In this his latest work the sun of Plato
shines dimly through the clouds that have gathered thick about
its setting. The passage, in which the philosopher proposed to

establish a legal procedure modelled on that of the Athenian town-hall, runs as follows: "If a beast of burden or any other animal shall kill any one, except it be while the animal is competing in one of the public games, the relations of the deceased shall prosecute the animal for murder; the judges shall be such overseers of the public lands as the kinsman of the deceased may appoint; and the animal, if found guilty, shall be put to death and cast beyond the boundaries of the country. But if any lifeless object, with the exception of a thunderbolt or any such missile hurled by the hand of God, shall deprive a man of life either by falling on him or through the man's falling on it, the next of kin to the deceased shall, making expiation for himself and all his kin, appoint his nearest neighbour as judge; and the thing, if found guilty, shall be cast beyond the boundaries, as hath been provided in the case of the animals."

The prosecution of inanimate objects for homicide was not peculiar to Athens in ancient Greece. It was a law of the island of Thasos that any lifeless thing which fell down and killed a person should be brought to trial, and, if found guilty, should be cast into the sea. Now in the middle of the city of Thasos there stood the bronze statute of a celebrated boxer named Theagenes, who in his lifetime had won a prodigious number of prizes in the ring, and whose memory was accordingly cherished by the citizens as one of the most shining ornaments of their native land. However, a certain base fellow, who had a spite at the deceased bruiser, came and thrashed the statue soundly every night. For a time the statue bore this treatment in dignified silence, but at last, unable to put up with it any longer, it toppled over, and, falling flat on its cowardly assailant, crushed him to death. The relations of the slain man took the law of the statue, and indicting it for murder, had it convicted, sentenced, and thrown into the sea. A similar law prevailed, or at all events a similar scruple was felt, concerning homicidal statues at Olympia. One day a little boy was playing there under the bronze image of an ox which stood within the sacred precinct; but suddenly rising up, the little fellow knocked his head against the hard metallic stomach of the animal, and, after lingering a few days, died from the impact. The authorities at Olympia decided to remove the ox from the precincts on the ground that it was guilty of wilful murder; but the Delphic oracle took a more lenient view of the case, and, considering that the statue had acted without malice prepense, brought in a verdict of manslaughter. The verdict was accepted by the authorities, and in compliance with the direction of the oracle they performed over the bronze ox the solemn rites of purification which were customary in cases of involuntary homicide. It is said that when Scipio Africanus died, a statue of Apollo at Rome was so much affected that it wept for three days. The Romans considered this grief excessive, and, acting on the advice of the augurs, they had the too sensitive statue cut up small and sunk into the sea. Nor were animals at Rome always exempted from the last severity of the law. An ancient statute or custom, which tradition ascribed to the royal legislator and reformer Numa, directed that if any man ploughed up a boundary stone, not only he himself but the oxen which had aided and abetted him in the commission of the sacrilege should be sacred to the God of Boundaries; in other words, both the man and his beasts were placed outside the pale of the law, and anybody might slay them with impunity.

Such ideas and the practices based on them have not been limited to savage tribes and the civilized people of pagan antiquity. On the continent of Europe down to comparatively recent times the lower animals were in all respects considered amenable to the laws. Domestic animals were tried in the common criminal courts, and their punishment on conviction was death; wild animals fell under the jurisdiction of the ecclesiastical courts, and the penalty they suffered was banishment or death by exorcism and excommunication. Nor was that penalty by any means a light one, if it be true that St. Patrick exorcized the reptiles of Ireland into the sea or turned them into stones, and that St. Bernard, by excommunicating the flies that buzzed about him, laid them all out dead on the floor of the church. The prerogative of trying domestic animals was built, as on a rock, upon the Jewish law in the Book of the Covenant. In every case advocates were assigned to defend the animals, and the whole proceedings, trial, sentence, and execution, were carried out with the strictest regard for the forms of justice and the majesty of the law. The researches of French antiquaries have brought to light the records of ninety-two processes which were tried in French courts from the twelfth to the eighteenth century. The last victim to suffer in that country under what we may call the Jewish dispensation was a cow, which underwent the extreme penalty of the law in the year of our Lord one thousand seven hundred and forty. On the other hand, the title of the ecclesiastical authorities to exercise jurisdiction over wild animals and vermin, such as rats, locusts, caterpillars, and the like, was not altogether, at least at first sight, so perfectly clear and unambiguous on Scriptural grounds, and it had accordingly to be deduced from Holy Writ by a chain of reasoning in which the following appear to have formed the most adamantine links. As God cursed the serpent for beguiling Eve; as David cursed Mount Gilboa on account of the deaths of Saul and Jonathan; and as our Saviour cursed the fig-tree for not bearing figs in the off season; so in like manner it clearly follows that the Catholic Church has full power and authority to exorcize, excommunicate, anathematize, execrate, curse, and damn the whole animate and inanimate creation without any exception whatsoever. It is true that some learned canonists, puffed up with the conceit of mere human learning and of philosophy falsely so-called, presumed to cavil at a line of argument which to plain

men must appear irrefragable. They alleged that authority to try
and punish offences implies a contract, pact, or stipulation between
the supreme power which administers the law and the subjects
which submit to it, that the lower animals, being devoid of intelligence, had never entered into any such contract, pact, or
stipulation, and that consequently they could not legally be punished for acts which they had committed in ignorance of the law.
They urged, further, that the Church could not with any show of
justice ban those creatures which she refused to baptize; and they
laid great stress on the precedent furnished by the Archangel
Michael, who in contending with Satan for possession of the body
of Moses, did not bring any railing accusation against the Old
Serpent, but left it to the Lord to rebuke him. However, such
quibbles and chicane, savouring strongly of rationalism, were of no
avail against the solid strength of Scriptural authority and traditional usage on which the Church rested her jurisdiction. The
mode in which she exercised it was generally as follows.

When the inhabitants of a district suffered from the incursions
or the excessive exurbance of noxious animals or insects, they laid
a complaint against the said animals or insects, in the proper ecclesiastical court, and the court appointed experts to survey and
report upon the damage that had been wrought. An advocate was
next appointed to defend the animals and show cause why they
should not be summoned. They were then cited three several
times, and not appearing to answer for themselves, judgment was
given against them by default. The court after that served a
notice on the animals, warning them to leave the district within a
specified time under pain of adjuration; and if they did not take
their departure on or before the date appointed, the exorcism was
solemnly pronounced. However, the courts seem to have been
extremely reluctant to push matters to extremity by proclaiming
the ban, and they resorted to every shift and expedient for evading
or at least deferring the painful necessity. The motive for this long
delay in launching the ecclesiastical thunder may have been a
tender regard for the feelings of the creatures who were to be
blasted by it; though some sceptics pretended that the real reason
was a fear lest the animals should pay no heed to the interdict, and,
instead of withering away after the anathema, should rather be
fruitful and multiply under it, as was alleged to have happened in
some cases. That such unnatural multiplication of vermin under
excommunication had actually taken place the advocates of the
ecclesiastical courts were not prepared to deny, but they attributed
it, with every show of reason, to the wiles of the Tempter, who, as
we know from the case of Job, is permitted to perambulate the earth
to the great annoyance and distress of mankind.

Nor again, could the curse be reasonably expected to operate
for the benefit of parishioners whose tithes were in arrear. Hence
one of the lights of the law on this subject laid it down as

a first principle that the best way of driving off locusts is to pay
tithes, and he supported this salutary doctrine by the high authority
of the prophet Malachi, who represents the deity as remonstrating
in the strongest terms with the Jews on their delay in the payment
of his tithes, painting in the most alluring colours the blessings
which he would shower down upon them, if only they would pay
up, and pledging his word that, on receipt of the arrears, he would
destroy the locusts that were devouring the crops. The urgency of
this appeal to the pockets as well as to the piety of his worshippers
is suggestive of the low ebb to which the temple funds were reduced
in the days of the prophet. His stirring exhortation may have
furnished the text of eloquent sermons preached under similar circumstances from many a pulpit in the Middle Ages.

So much for the general principles on which animals were
formerly tried and condemned in Europe. A few samples of these
cases, both civil and ecclesiastical, will help to set the sagacity of
our ancestors in a proper light, if not to deepen our respect for the
majesty of the law.

A lawsuit between the inhabitants of the commune of St. Julien
and a coleopterous insect, now known to naturalists as the *Rhynchites
auratus*, lasted with lucid intervals for more than forty-two years.
At length the inhabitants, weary of litigation, proposed to compromise the matter by giving up, in perpetuity, to the insects a
fertile part of the country for their sole use and benefit. The
advocate of the animals demurred to the proposal, which would
have greatly restricted the natural liberty of his clients; but the
court, overruling the demurrer, appointed assessors to survey the
land, and as it proved to be well wooded and watered, and in every
way suitable to the insects, the ecclesiastical authorities ordered the
conveyance to be engrossed in due form and executed. The people
now rejoiced at the happy prospect of being rid both of the insects
and of the lawsuit; but their rejoicings were premature. Inquiry
disclosed the melancholy truth that in the land conveyed to the
insects there existed a mine or quarry of an ocherous earth, used
as a pigment, and though the quarry had long since been worked
out and exhausted, somebody possessed an ancient right-of-way to
it which he could not exercise without putting the new proprietors
to great inconvenience, not to speak of the risk they would run of
bodily injury by being trodden under foot. The obstacle was fatal:
the contract was vitiated; and the whole process began afresh.
How or when it ended will perhaps never be known, for the record
is mutilated. All that is quite certain is, that the suit began in
the year 1445, and that it, or another of the same sort, was still in
process in the year 1487; from which we may infer with great
probability that the people of St. Julien obtained no redress, and
that the coleopterous insects remained in possession of the field.

Another lawsuit carried on against the rats of the diocese of
Autun in the early part of the sixteenth century acquired great

celebrity through the part taken in it by Bartholomew de Chasse-neux, or Chassenée, as he is more commonly named, a famous lawyer and jurisconsult, who has been called the Coke of France, and who laid the foundation of his fame on this occasion by his brilliant advocacy of the rats. It happened that the rats had committed great depredations on the crops, devouring the harvest over a large part of Burgundy. The inhabitants lodged their complaint, and the rats were cited to appear in court to answer to it. The summonses were perfectly regular in form: to prevent all mistakes they described the defendants as dirty animals, of a greyish colour, residing in holes; and they were served in the usual way by an officer of the court, who read out the summons at the places most frequented by the rats. Nevertheless, on the day appointed the rats failed to put in an appearance in court. Their advocate pleaded on behalf of his clients that the summons was of too local and individual a character; that as all the rats in the diocese were interested, all should be summoned from every part of the diocese. The plea being allowed, the curate of every parish in the diocese was instructed to summon every rat for a future day. The day arriving, but still no rats, Chasseneux urged that, as all his clients were summoned, young and old, sick and healthy, great preparations had to be made, and certain arrangements carried into effect, and accordingly he begged for an extension of time. This also being granted, another day was fixed, but still no rats appeared. Their advocate now objected to the legality of the summons, under certain circumstances. A summons from that court, he argued with great plausibility, implied a safe-conduct to the parties summoned both on their way to it and on their return home; but his clients, the rats, though most anxious to appear in obedience to the summons, did not dare to stir out of their holes, being put in bodily fear by the many evil-disposed cats kept by the plaintiffs. "Let the plaintiffs," he continued, "enter into bonds, under heavy pecuniary penalties, that their cats shall not molest my clients, and the summons will be at once obeyed." The court acknowledged the validity of the plea; but the plaintiffs declining to be bound over for the good behaviour of their cats, the period for the attendance of the rats was adjourned *sine die*.

Again, in the year 1519 the commune of the Stelvio in the Tyrol instituted criminal proceedings against the moles or field-mice (*Lutmäuse*), which damaged the crops "by burrowing and throwing up the earth, so that neither grass nor green thing could grow." But "in order that the said mice may be able to show cause for their conduct by pleading their exigencies and distress," an advocate, Hans Grienebner by name, was charged with their defence, "to the end that they may have nothing to complain of in these proceedings." The counsel who appeared for the prose-cution was Schwarz Mining, and the evidence which he led, by the mouths of many witnesses, proved conclusively the serious injury done by the defendants to the lands of the plaintiffs. The counsel for the defence, indeed, as in duty bound, made the best of a bad case on behalf of his clients. He urged in their favour the many benefits they had conferred on the community, and particularly on the agricultural interest, by destroying noxious insects and grubs, and by stirring up and enriching the soil, and he wound up his plea by expressing a hope that, should his clients lose their case and be sentenced to depart from their present quarters, another suitable place of abode might be assigned to them. He demanded, furthermore, as a simple matter of justice, that they should be granted a safe-conduct securing them against harm or annoyance from cat, dog, or other foe. The judge acknowledged the reasonableness of this last request, and with great humanity not only granted the safe-conduct, but allowed a further respite of fourteen days to all such mice as were either with young or still in their infancy.

Again, in the year 1478 the authorities of Berne took legal proceedings against the species of vermin popularly known as *inger,* which seems to have been a coleopterous insect of the genus *Brychus,* and of which we are told, and may readily believe, that not a single specimen was to be found in Noah's ark. The case came on before the Bishop of Lausanne, and dragged out for a long time. The defendants, who had proved very destructive to the fields, meadows, and gardens, were summoned in the usual way to appear and answer for their conduct through their advocate before His Grace the Bishop of Lausanne at Wifflisburg on the sixth day after the issue of the summons, at one of the clock precisely. However, the insects turned a deaf ear to the summons, and their advocate, a certain Jean Perrodet of Freiburg, appears to have displayed but little ability or energy in defence of his clients. At all events, sentence was given against them, and the ecclesiastical thunder was launched in the following terms: "We, Benedict of Mont-ferrand, Bishop of Lausanne, etc., having heard the entreaty of the high and mighty lords of Berne against the *inger* and the ineffectual and rejectable answer of the latter, and having thereupon fortified ourselves with the Holy Cross, and having before our eyes the fear of God, from whom alone all just judgments proceed, and being advised in this cause by a council of men learned in the law, do therefore acknowledge and avow in this our writing that the appeal against the detestable vermin and *inger,* which are harmful to herbs, vines, meadows, grain and other fruits, is valid, and that they be exorcized in the person of Jean Perrodet, their defender. In conformity therewith we charge and burden them with our curse, and command them to be obedient, and anathematize them in the name of the Father, the Son and the Holy Ghost, that they turn away from all fields, grounds, enclosures, seeds, fruits, and produce, and depart. By virtue of the same sentence I declare and affirm that you are banned and exorcized, and through the power of Almighty God shall be called accursed and shall daily decrease withersoever you may go, to the end that of you nothing shall remain save for the use and profit of man." The verdict had been awaited by the people with great anxiety, and the sentence was received with corresponding jubilation. But their joy was short-lived, for, strange to say, the contumacious insects appeared to set the ecclesiastical thunder at defiance: and we are told that they continued to plague and torment the Bernese for their sins, until the sinners had recourse to the usual painful, but effectual, remedy of paying their tithes.

In the thirteenth century the inhabitants of Coire, the capital of the Grisons in Switzerland, instituted proceedings against the green beetles called Spanish flies in the Electorate of Mayence. The judge before whom the insects were cited, out of compassion for the minuteness of their bodies and their extreme youth, granted them a guardian and advocate, who pleaded their cause and obtained for them a piece of land to which they were banished. "And to this day," adds the historian, "the custom is duly observed; every year a definite portion of land is reserved for the beetles, and there they assemble, and no man is subjected to inconvenience by them." Again, in a process against leeches, which was tried at Lausanne in 1451, a number of leeches were brought into court to hear the notice served against them, which admonished all leeches to leave the district within three days. The leeches, however, proving contumacious and refusing to quit the country, they were solemnly exorcized. But the form of exorcism adopted on this occasion differed slightly from one which was in ordinary use; hence it was adversely criticized by some canonists, though stoutly defended by others. The doctors of Heidelberg in particular, then a famous seat of learning, not only expressed their entire and unanimous approbation of the exorcism, but imposed silence on all impertinent meddlers who presumed to speak against it. And though they candidly acknowledged that it deviated somewhat from the recognized formula made and provided for such purposes, yet they triumphantly appealed to its efficacy as proved by the result; for immediately after its delivery the leeches had begun to die off day by day, until they were utterly exterminated.

Among the animal pests against which legal proceedings were taken, a plague of caterpillars would seem to have been one of the most frequent. In the year 1516 an action was brought against these destructive insects by the inhabitants of Villenose, and the case was tried by the Provost of Troyes, who, in giving judgment, admonished the caterpillars to retire within six days from the vineyards and lands of Villenose, threatening them with his solemn curse and malediction if they failed to obey the admonition. In the seventeenth century the inhabitants of Strambino, in Piedmont, suffered much at the hands of caterpillars, or *gatte*, as they called them, which ravaged the vineyards. When the plague had lasted several years, and the usual remedies of prayers, processions, and holy water had proved of no avail to stay it, the insects were summoned in due form by the bailiff to appear before the podesta or mayor in order to answer the claim against them for the damages they had done in the district. The trial took place in the year 1633, and the original record of it is still preserved in the municipal archives of Strambino. The following is a translation of the document:

"In A.D. 1633 on the 14th February judicially before the most illustrious Signor Gerolamo San Martino dei Signori and the Signori Matteo Reno, G. M. Barberis, G. Merlo, Consuls of Strambino on behalf of everybody. Whereas for several years in March and during the spring of each year certain small animals come out in the shape of small worms, called *gatte,* which, from their birth onwards, corrode and consume the branches of the budding grapes in the vineyards of the said Signori and of commoners also. And whereas every power comes from God, whom all creatures obey, even unreasonable ones, and in divine piety recur to the remedy of temporal justice when other human aid is of no avail. We claim, therefore, to appeal to the office of your Excellency in this emergency against these destroying animals, that you may compel them to desist from the said damage, to abandon the vineyards, and summon them to appear before the bench of reason to show cause why they should not desist from corroding and destroying, under penalty of banishment from the place and confiscation. And a declaration of execution is to be proclaimed with shouts and a copy to be affixed to the court.

"Whereas these things having been proved, the Signor Podestà has ordered the said offending animals to appear before the bench to show cause why they should not desist from the aforesaid damage. We, Girolamo di San Martino, Podesta of Strambino, with these presents, summon and assign the animals called *gatte* judicially to appear on the 5th instant before us to show cause why they should not desist from the damage, under penalty of banishment and confiscation in a certain spot. Declaring the execution of the presents to be made by publication and a copy to be affixed to the bench to be made valid on the 14th February 1633.

(Signed)   SAN MARTINO (Podestà)."

In the neighbouring province of Savoy, from the sixteenth century onwards, "there was one very curious old custom, whereby, when caterpillars and other insects were doing serious damage, they were excommunicated by the priests. The cure went to the ruined fields and two advocates pleaded, the one for the insects, the other against them. The former advanced the argument that as God created animals and insects before man, they had the first right to the produce of the field, and the latter answered him that so much damage had been done the peasants could not afford the depredations, even if the insects had the first right. After a lengthy trial, they were solemnly excommunicated by the priest, who ordered that they should stay on a particular piece of ground which was to be allotted to them."

The practice of taking legal proceedings against destructive vermin survived into the first half of the eighteenth century, and was transported by the Church to the New World. In the year 1713 the Friars Minor of the province of Piedade no Maranhao, in Brazil, brought an action against the ants of the said territory, because the said ants did feloniously burrow beneath the foundations of the monastery and undermine the cellars of the said Brethren, thereby weakening the walls of the said monastery and threatening its total ruin. And not content with sapping the foundations of the sacred edifice, the said ants did moreover burglariously enter the stores and carry off the flour which was destined for the consumption of the Brethren. This was most intolerable and not to be endured, and accordingly after all other remedies had been tried in vain, one of the friars gave it as his opinion that, reverting to the spirit of humility and simplicity which had so eminently distinguished their seraphic founder, who termed all creatures his brethren or his sisters, as Brother Sun, Brother Wolf, Sister Swallow, and so forth, they should bring an action against their sisters the ants before the divine tribunal of Providence, and should name counsel for defendants and plaintiffs; also that the bishop should, in the name of supreme Justice, hear the case and give judgment.

This sapient proposal was approved of, and after all arrangements had been made for the trial, an indictment was presented by the counsel for the plaintiffs. As it was contested by the counsel for the defendants, the counsel for the plaintiffs opened his case, showing cause why his clients should receive the protection of the law. He showed that his virtuous clients, the friars, lived upon the public charity, collecting alms from the faithful with much labour and personal inconvenience; whereas the ants, whose morals and manner of life were clearly contrary to the Gospel precepts and were therefore regarded with horror by St. Francis, the founder of the confraternity, did subsist by pillage and fraud; for that, not content with acts of petty larceny, they did go about by open violence to bring down the house about the ears of his clients, the friars. Consequently the defendants were bound to show cause or in default to be sentenced to the extreme penalty of the law, either to be put to death by a pestilence or drowned by a flood, or at all events to be exterminated from the district.

On the other hand, the counsel for the ants argued that, having received from their Maker the gift of life, they were bound by a law of nature to preserve it by means of the natural instincts implanted in them; that in the observance of these means they served Providence by setting men an example of prudence, charity, piety, and other virtues, in proof of which their advocate quoted passages from the Scriptures, St. Jerome, the Abbot Absalon, and even Pliny; that the ants worked far harder than the monks, the burdens which they carried being often larger than their bodies, and their courage greater than their strength; that in the eyes of the Creator men themselves are but worms; that his clients were in possession of the ground long before the plaintiffs established themselves there; that consequently it was the monks, and not the ants, who ought to be expelled from lands to which they had no other claim than a seizure by main force; finally, that the plaintiffs ought to defend their house and meal by human means, which the defendants would not oppose, while they, the defendants, continued their manner of life, obeying the law imposed on their nature and rejoicing in the freedom of the earth, in as much as the earth belongs not to the plaintiffs but to the Lord, for "the earth is the Lord's and the fulness thereof."

This answer was followed by replies and counter-replies, in the course of which the counsel for the prosecution saw himself constrained to admit that the debate had very much altered his opinion of the criminality of the defendants. The upshot of the whole matter was that the judge, after carefully revolving the evidence in his mind, gave sentence that the Brethren should appoint a field in the neighbourhood suitable for the habitation of the ants, and that the insects should immediately shift their quarters to the new abode on pain of suffering the major excommunication. By such an arrangement, he pointed out, both parties would be content and reconciled; for the ants must remember that the monks had come into the land to sow there the seed of the Gospel, while the ants could easily earn their livelihood elsewhere and at even less cost. This sentence having been delivered with judicial gravity, one of the friars was appointed to convey it to the ants, which he did by reading it aloud at the mouths of their burrows. The insects loyally accepted it; and dense columns of them were seen leaving the ant-hills in all haste and marching in a straight line to the residence appointed for them.

Again, in the year 1733 the rats and mice proved very troublesome in the village and lands of Bouranton. They swarmed in the houses and barns, and they ravaged the fields and vineyards. The villagers accordingly brought an action against the vermin, and the case was tried before the judge, Louis Gublin, on the seventeenth day of September 1733. The plaintiffs were represented by the procurator-fiscal, and the defendants by a certain Nicolas Gublin, who pleaded on behalf of his clients that they too were God's creatures and therefore entitled to live. To this the counsel for the prosecution replied that he desired to place no obstacle in the way of the said animals' life; on the contrary, he was ready to point out to them a place to which they could retire and where they could take up their abode. The counsel for the rats and mice thereupon demanded three days' grace to allow his clients to effect their retreat.

Having heard both sides, the judge summed up and pronounced sentence. He said that, taking into consideration the great damage done by the said animals, he condemned them to retire within three days from the houses, barns, tilled fields, and vineyards of Bouranton, but that they were free to betake themselves, if they thought fit, to deserts, uncultivated lands, and highroads, always provided they did no manner of harm to fields, houses, and barns; otherwise he would be compelled to have recourse to God by means of the censures of the Church and the process of excommunication to be pronounced against them. This sentence, engrossed in due form, was signed by the judge, Louis Gublin, with his own hand.

It is easy to understand why in all such cases the execution of the sentence was entrusted to the ecclesiastical rather than to the civil authorities. It was physically impossible for a common executioner, however zealous, active and robust, to hang, decapitate, or otherwise execute all the rats, mice, ants, flies, mosquitoes, caterpillars, and other vermin of a whole district; but what is impossible with man is possible and indeed easy with God, and accordingly it was logically and reasonably left to God's ministers on earth to grapple with a problem which far exceeded the capacity of the civil magistrate and his minister the hangman. On the other hand, when the culprits were not wild but tame animals, the problem of dealing with them was much simplified and was indeed well within the reach of the civil power. In all such cases, therefore, justice took its usual course; there was no difficulty at all in arresting the criminals and in bringing them, after a fair trial, to the gallows, the block, or the stake. That is why in those days vermin enjoyed the benefit of clergy, while tame animals had to submit to all the rigour of the secular arm.

For example, a sow and her litter of six, belonging to a certain Jehan Bailli, *alias* Valot, were indicted at Savigny in 1457 on a charge that they had "committed murder and homicide on the person of Jehan Martin, aged five years, son of Jehan Martin of the said Savigny." On a full consideration of the evidence the judge gave sentence "that the sow of Jehan Bailli, *alias* Valot, by reason of the murder and homicide committed and perpetrated by the said sow on the person of Jehan Martin of Savigny, be confiscated to the justice of Madame de Savigny, in order to suffer the extreme penalty of the law and to be hanged by the hind feet to a bent tree." The sentence was carried out, for in the record of the case, which is still preserved. we read that, "We, Nicolas Quaroillon, judge aforesaid, make known to all, that immediately after the aforesaid proceedings, we did really and in fact deliver the said sow to Mr. Etienne Poinceau, minister of high justice, resident at Chalons-sur-Saône, to be executed according to the form and tenor of our said sentence, which deliverance of that sow having been made by us, as hath been said, immediately the said Mr. Estienne did bring on a cart the said sow to a bent tree within the justice of the said

Madame de Savigny, and on that bent tree Mr. Estienne did hang the said sow by the hind feet, executing our said sentence, according to its form and tenor." As for the six little pigs, though they were found to be stained with blood, yet "as it did by no means appear that these little pigs did eat the said Jehan Martin," their case was deferred, their owner giving bail for their reappearance at the bar of justice in case evidence should be forthcoming, that they had assisted their homicidal parent in devouring the said Jehan Martin. On the resumption of the trial, as no such evidence was forthcoming, and as their owner refused to be answerable for their good conduct thereafter, the judge gave sentence, that "these little pigs do belong and appertain, as vacant property, to the said Madame de Savigny, and we do adjudge them to her as reason, usage, and the custom of the country doth ordain."

Again, in the year 1386 a sow tore the face and arm of a boy at Falaise in Normandy, and on the principle of "an eye for an eye," was condemned to be mutilated in the same manner and afterwards hanged. The criminal was led to the place of execution attired in a waistcoat, gloves, and a pair of drawers, with a human mask on her head to complete the resemblance to an ordinary criminal. The execution cost ten sous, ten deniers, and a pair of gloves to the executioner, that he might not soil his hands in the discharge of his professional duty. Sometimes the execution of animals was a good deal more expensive. Here is the bill for the execution of a sow which had eaten a child at Meulan, near Paris, in 1403 :—

To the expenditure made for her whilst in jail . . .	6 sols
Item. To the executioner, who came from Paris to Meulan to carry out the said execution by command and order of the bailiff and the King's Procurator . .	54 sols
Item. To a cart for conducting her to execution . .	6 sols
Item. To cords to tie and bind her . . .	2 sols, 8 deniers
Item. To gloves	2 deniers

In 1266 a sow was burned at Fontenay-aux Roses, near Paris, for having devoured a child; the order for its execution was given by the officers of justice of the monastery of Sainte-Geneviève.

But sows, though they seem to have frequently suffered the extreme penalty of the law, were by no means the only animals that did so. In 1389 a horse was tried at Dijon, on information given by the magistrates of Montbar, and was condemned to death for having killed a man. Again, in the year 1499, the authorities of the Cistercian Abbey of Beaupré, near Beauvais, condemned a bull "to the gallows, unto death inclusively," because it "did furiously kill a young lad of fourteen or fifteen years, in the lordship of Cauroy, a dependency of this abbey." On another occasion a farmer at Moisy, in 1314, allowed a mad bull to escape. The animal gored a man so severely that he only survived a few hours. Hearing of the accident, Charles, Count de Valois, ordered the bull to be seized and committed for trial. This was accordingly done.

The officers of the Count gathered all requisite information, received the affidavits of witnesses, and established the guilt of the bull, which was accordingly condemned to death and hanged on the gibbet of Moisy-le-Temple. An appeal against the sentence of the Count's officers was afterwards lodged with the parliament; but parliament rejected the appeal, deciding that the bull had got its desserts, though the Count de Valois had exceeded his rights by meddling in the affair. As late as the year 1697 a mare was burned by decree of the Parliament of Aix.

At Bale in the year 1474 an aged cock was tried and found guilty of laying an egg. The counsel for the prosecution proved that cock's eggs were of priceless value for mixing in certain magical preparations; that a sorcerer would rather possess a cock's egg than be master of the philosopher's stone; and that in heathen lands Satan employs witches to hatch such eggs, from which proceed animals most injurious to Christians. These facts were too patent and notorious to be denied, nor did the counsel for the prisoner attempt to dispute them. Admitting to the full the act charged against his client, he asked what evil intent had been proved against him in laying an egg? What harm had he done to man or beast? Besides, he urged that the laying of an egg was an involuntary act and, as such, not punishable by law. As for the charge of sorcery, if that was brought again his client, he totally repudiated it, and he defied the prosecution to adduce a single case in which Satan had made a compact with any of the brute creation. In reply the public prosecutor alleged, that though the devil did not make compacts with brutes, he sometimes entered into them, in confirmation of which he cited the celebrated case of the Gadarene swine, pointing out with great cogency that though these animals, being possessed by devils, were involuntary agents, like the prisoner at the bar when he laid an egg, nevertheless they were punished by being made to run violently down a steep place into the lake, where they perished. This striking precedent apparently made a great impression on the court; at all events, the cock was sentenced to death, not in the character of a cock, but in that of a sorcerer or devil who had assumed the form of the fowl, and he and the egg which he had laid were burned together at the stake with all the solemnity of a regular execution. The pleadings in this case are said to be voluminous.

If Satan thus afflicted animals in the Old World, it could not reasonably be expected that he would spare them in the New. Accordingly we read without surprise that in New England "a dog was strangely afflicted at Salem, upon which those who had the spectral sight declared that a brother of the justices afflicted the poor animal, by riding upon it invisibly. The man made his escape, but the dog was very unjustly hanged. Another dog was accused of afflicting others, who fell into fits the moment it looked upon them, and it also was killed."

In Savoy it is said that animals sometimes appeared in the witness-box as well as in the dock, their testimony being legally valid in certain well-defined cases. If a man's house was broken into between sunset and sunrise, and the owner killed the intruder, the act was considered a justifiable homicide. But it was deemed just possible that a wicked man, who lived all alone, might decoy another into spending the evening with him, and then, after murdering him, might give it out that his victim was a burglar, whom he had slain in self-defense. To guard against this contingency, and to ensure the conviction of the murderer, the law sagaciously provided that when anybody was killed under such circumstances, the solitary householder should not be held innocent, unless he produced a dog, cat, or cock, an inmate of his house, which had witnessed the homicide and could from personal knowledge attest the innocence of its master. The householder was compelled to make his declaration of innocence before the animal, and if the beast or bird did not contradict him, he was considered to be guiltless, the law taking it for granted that the Deity would directly interpose and open the mouth of the cat, dog, or cock, just as he once opened the mouth of Balaam's ass, rather than allow a murderer to escape from justice.

In modern Europe, as in ancient Greece, it would seem that even inanimate objects have sometimes been punished for their misdeeds. After the revocation of the edict of Nantes, in 1685, the Protestant chapel at La Rochelle was condemned to be demolished, but the bell, perhaps out of regard for its value, was spared. However, to expiate the crime of having rung heretics to prayers, it was sentenced to be first whipped, and then buried and disinterred, by way of symbolizing its new birth at passing into Catholic hands. Thereafter it was catechized, and obliged to recant and promise that it would never again relapse into sin. Having made this ample and honourable amends, the bell was reconciled, baptized, and given, or rather sold, to the parish of St. Bartholomew. But when the governor sent in the bill for the bell to the parish authorities, they declined to settle it, alleging that the bell, as a recent convert to Catholicism, desired to take advantage of the law lately passed by the king, which allowed all new converts a delay of three years in paying their debts.

In English law a relic of the same ancient mode of thought survived till near the middle of the nineteenth century in the doctrine and practice of deodand. It was a rule of the common law that not only a beast that killed a man, but any inanimate object that caused his death, such as a cart-wheel which ran over him, or a tree that fell upon him, was *deodand* or given to God, in consequence of which it was forfeited to the king and sold for the benefit of the poor. Hence in all indictments for homicide the instrument of death used to be valued by the grand jury, in order that its money value might be made over to the king or his grantee for pious uses. Thus in practice all deodands came to be looked on as mere forfeitures to the king. Regarded in that light they were very unpopular, and in later times the juries, with the connivance of the judges, used to mitigate the forfeitures by finding only some trifling thing, or part of a thing, to have been the occasion of the death. It was not till the year 1846 that this curious survival of primitive barbarism was finally abolished by statute. So long as it lingered in the courts it naturally proved a stumbling-block in the path of philosophical lawyers, who attempted to reduce all rules of English law to the first principles of natural reason and equity, little wotting of the bottomless abyss of ignorance, savagery, and superstition on which the thin layer of modern law and civilization precariously rests. Thus Blackstone supposed that the original intention of forfeiting the instrument of death was to purchase masses for the soul of the person who had been accidentally killed; hence he thought that the deodands ought properly to have been given to the church rather than to the king. The philosopher Reid opined that the aim of the law was not to punish the animal or thing that had been instrumental in killing a human being, but "to inspire the people with a sacred regard to the life of man."

With far greater probability the practice of deodand and all the customs of punishing animals or things for injuries inflicted by them on persons, have been deduced by Sir Edward Tylor from the same primitive impulse which leads the savage to bite the stone he has stumbled over or the arrow that has wounded him, and which prompts the child, and even at times the grown man, to kick or beat the lifeless object from which he has suffered. The principle, if we may call it so, of this primitive impulse is set forth by Adam Smith with all his customary lucidity, insight, and good sense. "The cause of pain and pleasure," he says, "whatever they are, or however they operate, seem to be the objects, which in all animals, immediately excite those two passions of gratitude and resentment. They are excited by inanimated, as well as by animated objects. We are angry, for a moment, even at the stone that hurts us. A child beats it, a dog barks at it, a choleric man is apt to curse it. The least reflection, indeed, corrects this sentiment, and we soon become sensible, that what has no feeling is a very improper object of revenge. When the mischief, however, is very great, the object which caused it becomes disagreeable to us ever after, and we take pleasure to burn or destroy it. We should treat, in this manner, the instrument which had accidentally been the cause of the death of a friend, and we should often think ourselves guilty of a sort of inhumanity, if we neglected to vent this absurd sort of vengeance upon it."

Modern researches into the progress of mankind have rendered it probable that in the infancy of the race the natural tendency to personify external objects, whether animate or inanimate, in other words, to invest them with the attributes of human beings, was either not corrected at all, or corrected only in a very imperfect degree, by reflection on the distinctions which more advanced thought draws, first, between the animate and the inanimate creation, and second, between man and the brutes. In that hazy state of the human mind it was easy and almost inevitable to confound the motives which actuate a rational man with the impulses which direct a beast, and even with the forces which propel a stone or a tree in falling. It was in some such mental confusion that savages took deliberate vengeance on animals and things that had hurt or offended them; and the intellectual fog in which such actions were possible still obscured the eyes of the primitive legislators who, in various ages and countries, have consecrated the same barbarous system of retaliation under the solemn forms of law and justice.

CHAPTER V

THE GOLDEN BELLS

In the Priestly Code it is ordained that the priest's robe should be made all of violet, and that the skirts of it should be adorned with a fringe of pomegranates wrought of violet and purple and scarlet stuff, with a golden bell between each pair of pomegranates. This gorgeous robe the priest was to wear when he ministered in the sanctuary, and the golden bells were to be heard jingling both when he entered into the holy place and when he came forth, lest he should die.[1]

Why should the priest in his violet robe, with the fringe of gay pomegranates dangling at his heels, fear to die if the golden bells were not heard to jingle, both when he went into, and when he came forth from the holy place? The most probable answer seems to be that the chiming of the holy bells was thought to drive far off the envious and wicked spirits who lurked about the door of the sanctuary, ready to pounce on and carry off the richly apparelled minister as he stepped across the threshold in the discharge of his sacred office. At least this view, which has found favour with some modern scholars, is strongly supported by analogy; for it has been a common opinion, from the days of antiquity downwards, that demons and ghosts can be put to flight by the sound of metal, whether it be the musical jingle of little bells, the deep-mouthed clangour of great bells, the shrill clash of cymbals, the booming of gongs, or the simple clink and clank of plates of bronze or iron knocked together or struck with hammer or sticks. Hence in

---

[1] Exodus xxviii, 31-35. The Hebrew word (תְּכֵלֶת) which in the English Version is regularly translated "blue," means a blue-purple, as distinguished from another word (אַרְגָּמָן) which means red-purple, inclining to crimson, as the other shades into violet.

rites of exorcism it has often been customary for the celebrant either to ring a bell which he holds in his hand, or to wear attached to some part of his person a whole nest of bells, which jingle at every movement he makes. Examples will serve to illustrate the antiquity and the wide diffusion of such beliefs and practices.

Lucian tells us that spectres fled at the sound of bronze and iron, and he contrasts the repulsion which the clank of these metals exerted on spirits with the attraction which the chink of silver money wielded over women of a certain class. At Rome, when the ghosts of the dead had paid their annual visit to the old home in the month of May, and had been entertained with a frugal repast of black beans, the householder used to show them the door, bidding them, "Ghosts of my fathers, go forth!" and emphasizing his request or command by the clash of bronze. Nor did such notions as to the dislike which spirits entertain for the tinkle of metal expire with expiring paganism. They survived in full force under Christianity into the Middle Ages and long afterwards. The learned Christian scholiast, John Tzetzes, tells us that the clash of bronze was just as effective to ban apparitions as the barking of a dog, a proposition which few reasonable men will be inclined to dispute.

But in Christian times the sound deemed above all others abhorrent to the ear of fiends and goblins has been the sweet and solemn music of church bells. The first Provincial Council of Cologne laid it down as an opinion of the fathers that at the sound of the bells summoning Christians to prayer demons are terrified and depart, and the spirits of the storm, the powers of the air, are laid low. However, the members of the Council themselves apparently inclined to attribute this happy result rather to the fervent intercession of the faithful than to the musical clangour of the bells. Again, the service book known as the Roman Pontifical recognizes the virtue of a church bell, wherever its sound is heard, to drive far off the powers of evil, the gibbering and mowing spectres of the dead, and all the spirits of the storm. A great canonist of the thirteenth century, Durandus, in his once famous and popular treatise on the divine offices, tells us that "bells are rung in processions that demons may fear and flee. For when they hear the trumpets of the church militant, that is, the bells, they are afraid, as any tyrant is afraid when he hears in his land the trumpets of a powerful king, his foe. And that, too, is the reason why, at the sight of a storm rising, the Church rings its bells, in order that the demons, hearing the trumpets of the eternal king, that is, the bells, may be terrified and flee away and abstain from stirring up the tempest." On this subject the English antiquery, Captain Francis Grose, the friend of the poet Burns, writes as follows: "The passing-bell was anciently rung for two purposes: one, to bespeak the prayers of all good Christians for a soul just departing; the other, to drive away the evil spirits who stood at the bed's foot, and about the house, ready to seize their prey, or at least to molest

and terrify the soul in its passage: but by the ringing of that bell
(for Durandus informs us, evil spirits are much afraid of bells),
they were kept aloof; and the soul, like a hunted hare, gained the
start, or had what is by sportsmen called Law.   Hence, perhaps,
exclusive of the additional labour, was occasioned the high price
demanded for toiling the greatest bell of the church; for that being
louder, the evil spirits must go farther off, to be clear of its sound,
by which the poor soul got so much more the start of them: besides,
being heard farther off, it would likewise procure the dying man a
greater number of prayers.   This dislike of spirits to bells is
mentioned in the Golden Legend, by W. de Worde.   'It is said,
the evil spirytes that ben in the regyon of th' ayre, doubte moche
when they here the belles rongen: and this is the cause why the
belles ben rongen whan it thondreth, and when grete tempeste and
outrages of wether happen, to the ende that the fiendes and wycked
spirytes should be abashed and flee, and cease of the movynge of
tempeste.' "

In his poetical version of *The Golden Legend* Longfellow has
introduced this picturesque superstition with good effect.   In the
prologue he represents the spire of Strassburg Cathedral in night
and storm, with Lucifer and the powers of the air hovering round
it, trying in vain to tear down the cross and to silence the importunate clangour of the bells.

> "LUCIFER.   *Lower! lower!*
> *Hover downward!*
> *Seize the loud vociferous bells, and*
> *Clashing, clanging, to the pavemenet*
> *Hurl them from their window tower,*
>   VOICES.   *All thy thunders*
> *Here are harmless!*
> *For these bells have been anointed,*
> *And baptized with holy water!*
> *They defy our utmost power."*

And above all the tumult of the storm and the howling of the
infernal legion is heard the solemn voice of the bells:—

> "*Defunctos ploro!*
> *Pestem fugo!*
> *Festa decoro!"*

And again,

> "*Funera plango*
> *Fulgura frango*
> *Sabbata pango,"*

until the baffled demons are fain to sweep away in the darkness,
leaving behind them unharmed the cathedral, where through the
gloom the Archangel Michael with drawn sword is seen flaming in
gold and crimson on the panes of the lighted windows, while, as
they recede into the distance, they are pursued in their flight by
the pealing music of the organ and the voices of the choir chanting

"Nocte surgentes
Vigilemus omnes!"

Of the two reasons which Grose assigns for the ringing of the Passing Bell we may surmise that the intention of driving away evil spirits was the primary and original one, and that the intention of bespeaking the prayers of all good Christians for the soul just about to take its flight was secondary and derivative. In any case the ringing of the bell seems formerly to have regularly begun while the sufferer was still in life, but when his end was visibly near. This appears from not a few passages which antiquarian diligence has gleaned from the writings of old authors. Thus in his *Anatomie of Abuses* Stubbes tells of the dreadful end of a profane swearer down in Lincolnshire: "At the last, the people perceiving his ende to approche, caused the bell to toll; who, hearing the bell to toll for him, rushed up in his bed very vehemently, saying, 'God's bloud, he shall not have me yet'; with that his bloud gushed out, some at his toes endes, some at his fingers endes, some at hys wristes, some at his nose and mouth, some at one joynt of his body, some at an other, never ceasing till all the bloud in his body was streamed forth. And thus ended this bloudy swearer his mortal life." Again, when Lady Catherine Grey was dying a captive in the Tower, the Governor of the fortress, perceiving that his prisoner was about to be released from his charge, without any royal warrant, said to Mr. Bokeham, "Were it not best to send to the church, that the bell may be rung?" And she, feeling her end to be near, entered into prayer, saying, "O Lord! into thy hands I commend my soul: Lord Jesus, receive my spirit!" Thus for her, as for many, the sound of the Passing Bell was the *Nunc dimittis*. Once more, a writer in the first half of the eighteenth century, speaking of the dying Christian who has subdued his passions, says that, "if his senses hold out so long, he can hear even his passing-bell without disturbance."

That the real purpose of the Passing Bell was to dispel maleficent beings hovering invisible in the air rather than to advertise persons at a distance and invite their prayers, is strongly suggested by the apparently primitive form in which the old custom has here and there been kept up down to modern times. Thus in some parts of the Eifel Mountains, a district of Rhenish Prussia, when a sick person was at the point of death, the friends used to ring a small hand-bell, called a Benedictus bell, "in order to keep the evil spirits away from the dying man." Again, at Neusohl, in Northern Hungary, it is said to have been usual to ring a small hand-bell softly when a dying man was near his end, "in order that the parting soul, lured away by death, may still linger for a few moments on earth near its stiffening body." When death had taken place, the bell was rung a little farther off, then farther and farther from the body, then out at the door, and once round the house "in order to accompany the soul on its parting way." After that,

word was sent to the sexton that the bell of the village church
might begin to toll. A similar custom is said to have prevailed in
the Böhmerwald mountains, which divide Bohemia from Bavaria.
The motive assigned for it—the wish to detain the parting soul for
a few moments by the sweet sound of the bell—is too sentimental
to be primitive; the true original motive was doubtless, as in the
case of the similar custom in the Eifel Mountains, to banish the
demons that might carry off the poor soul at the critical moment.
Only when the little bell has performed this kindly office, tinkling
for the soul at its setting out, does the big bell in the steeple begin
to toll, that its sonorous tones may follow, like guardian angels, the
fugitive on its long journey to the spirit land.

In a famous passage of the *Purgatory* Dante has beautifully
applied the conception of the Passing Bell to the sound of the
Vesper Bell heard afar off by voyagers at sea, as if the bell were
tolling for the death of day or of the sun then sinking in the crimson
west. Hardly less famous is Byron's imitation of the passage :—

> *"Soft hour! which makes the wish and melts the heart*
> *Of those who sail the seas, on the first day*
> *When they from their sweet friends are torn apart;*
> *Or fills with love the pilgrim on his way*
> *As the far bell of vesper makes him start,*
> *Seeming to weep the dying day's decay."*

And the same thought has been no less beautifully applied by our
own poet Gray to the curfew bell heard at evening among the
solemn yews and elms of an English churchyard :—

> *"The curfew tolls the knell of parting day."*

There is, indeed, something peculiarly solemnizing and affecting
in the sound of church bells heard at such times and places; it
falls upon the ear, in the language of Froude, like the echo of a
vanished world. The feeling was well expressed by the American
poet Bret Harte, when he heard, or rather imagined that he heard,
the Angelus rung at evening on the site of the long-abandoned
Spanish mission at Dolores in California :—

> *"Bells of the Past, whose long-forgotten music*
> *Still fills the wide expanse,*
> *Tingeing the sober twilight of the Present*
> *With colour of Romance!*

> *"I hear your call and see the sun descending*
> *On rock and wave and sand,*
> *As down the coast the Mission voices, blending,*
> *Girdle the heathen land.*

> *"Within the circle of your incantation*
> *No blight nor mildew falls;*
> *Nor fierce unrest, nor lust, nor low ambition*
> *Passes those airy walls.*

"Borne on the swell of your long waves receding,
I touch the farther past,—
I see the dying glow of Spanish glory,
The sunset dream and last.

"O solemn bells! whose consecrated masses
Recall the faith of old,—
O tinkling bells! that lulled with twilight music
The spiritual fold!"

A like sense of the power of bells to touch the heart and attune the mind to solemn thought is conveyed in a characteristic passage of Renan, in whom the austere convictions of the religious sceptic were happily tempered by the delicate perceptions of the literary artist. Protesting against the arid rationalism of the German theologian Feuerbach, he exclaims, "Would to God that M. Feuerbach had steeped himself in sources of life richer than those of his exclusive and haughty Germanism! Ah! if, seated on the ruins of the Palatine or the Coelian Mount, he had heard the sound of the eternal bells lingering and dying over the deserted hills were Rome once was; or if, from the solitary shore of the Lido, he had heard the chimes of Saint Mark's expiring across the lagoons; if he had seen Assisi and its mystic marvels, its double basilica and the great legend of the second Christ of the Middle Ages traced by the brush of Cimabue and Giotto; if he had gazed his fill on the sweet far-away look of the Virgins of Perugino, or if, in San Domenico at Sienna, he had seen Saint Catherine in ecstasy, no, M. Feuerbach would not thus have cast reproach on one half of human poetry, nor cried aloud as if he would repel from him the phantom of Iscariot!"

Such testimonies to the emotional effect of church bells on the hearer are not alien from the folk-lore of the subject; we cannot understand the ideas of the people unless we allow for the deep colour which they take from feeling and emotion, least of all can we sever thought and feeling in the sphere of religion. There are no impassable barriers between the conceptions of the reason, the sensations of the body, and the sentiments of the heart; they are apt to melt and fuse into each other under waves of emotion, and few things can set these waves rolling more strongly than the power of music. A study of the emotional basis of folk-lore has hardly yet been attempted; inquirers have confined their attention almost exclusively to its logical and rational, or, as some might put it, is illogical and irrational elements. But no doubt great discoveries may be expected from the future exploration of the influence which the passions have exerted in moulding the institutions and destiny of mankind.

Throughout the Middle Ages and down to modern times the sound of church bells was also in great request for the purpose of routing witches and wizards, who gathered unseen in the air to play their wicked pranks on man and beast. There were certain

days of the year which these wretches set apart more particularly
for their unhallowed assemblies or Sabbaths, as they were called,
and on such days accordingly the church bells were specially rung,
sometimes the whole night long, because it was under cover of
darkness that witches and warlocks were busiest at their infernal
tasks. For example, in France witches were thought to scour the
air most particularly on the night of St. Agatha, the fifth of
February; hence the bells of the parish churches used to be set
ringing that night to drive them away, and the same custom is
said to have been observed in some parts of Spain. Again, one of
the most witching times of the whole year was Midsummer Eve;
and accordingly at Rottenburg in Swabia the church bells rang all
that night from nine o'clock till break of day, while honest folk
made fast their shutters, and stopped up even chinks and crannies,
lest the dreadful beings should insinuate themselves into the houses.
Other witches' Sabbaths used to be held at Twelfth Night and the
famous Walpurgis Night, the eve of May Day, and on these days
it used to be customary in various parts of Europe to expel the
baleful, though invisible, crew by making a prodigious racket, to
which the ringing of hand-bells and the cracking of whips contributed
their share.

But though witches and wizards chose certain seasons of the
year above all others for the celebration of their unholy revels,
there was no night on which they might not be encountered abroad
on their errands of mischief by belated wayfarers, none on which
they might not attempt to force their way into the houses of honest
folk who were quiet, but by no means safe, in bed. Something,
therefore, had to be done to protect peaceable citizens from these
nocturnal alarms. For this purpose the watchmen, who patrolled
the streets for the repression of common crime, were charged with
the additional duty of exorcizing the dreaded powers of the air and
of darkness, which went about like roaring lions seeking what they
might devour. To accomplish this object the night watchman
wielded spiritual weapons of two different sorts but of equal power;
he rang a bell, and he chanted a blessing, and if the sleepers in the
neighbourhood were roused and exasperated by the jingle of the
one, they were perhaps soothed and comforted by the drone of the
other, remembering, as they sank back to sleep, that it was only,
in the words of Milton,

> "the bellman's drowsy charm
> To bless the doors from mighty harm."

The benediction which thus broke the stillness of night was usually
cast in a poetical form of such unparalleled atrocity that a bellman's
verses have been proverbial ever since. Their general tenor may
be gathered from the lines which Herrick puts in the mouth of one of
those public guardians, from whose nightly orisons the poet, like
Milton himself, must have often suffered:—

"THE BELL-MAN.

From noise of scare-fires rest ye free,
From murders Benedicitie;
From all mischances that may fright
Your pleasing slumbers in the night;
Mercie secure ye all, and keep
The goblin from ye, while ye sleep.
Past one aclock, and almost two,
My masters all, 'Good day to you.' "

Addison tells us how he heard the bellman begin his midnight homily with the usual exordium, which he had been repeating to his hearers every winter night for the last twenty years,

"Oh! mortal man, thou that art born in sin!"

And though this uncomplimentary allocution might excite pious reflexions in the mind of an Addison, it seems calculated to stir feelings of wrath and indignation in the breasts of more ordinary people, who were roused from their first sleep only to be reminded, at a very unseasonable hour, of the doctrine of original sin.

We have seen that according to medieval authors church bells used to be rung in thunderstorms for the purpose of driving away the evil spirits who were supposed to be causing the tempest. To the same effect an old German writer of the sixteenth century, who under the assumed name of Naogeorgus composed a satirical poem on the superstitions and abuses of the Catholic Church, has recorded that

"If that the thunder chaunce to rore, and stormie tempest shake,
A wonder is it for to see the wretches howe they quake,
Howe that no fayth at all they have, nor trust in any thing,
The clarke doth all the belles forthwith at once in steeple ring;
With wondrous sound and deeper farre, than he was woont before,
Till in the loftie heavens darke, the thunder bray no more.
For in these christened belles they thinke, doth lie such power and might,
As able is the tempest great, and storme to vanquish quight.
I sawe my self at Numburg once, a town in Toring coast,
A bell that with this title bolde, hir self did prowdly boast,
'By name I Mary called am, with sound I put to flight
The thunder crackes, and hurtfull stormes, and every wicket spright.'
Such things whenas these belles can do, no wonder certainlie
It is, if that the Papistes to their tolling alwayes flie,
When haile, or any raging storme, or tempest comes in sight,
Or thunder boltes, or lightning fierce that every place doth smight."

In the Middle Ages, we are told, all over Germany the church bells used to be rung during thunderstorms; and the sexton received a special due in corn from the parishioners for his exertions in pulling the bell-rope in these emergencies. These dues were paid in some places as late as the middle of the nineteenth century. For example, at Jubar in the Altmark, whenever a thunderstorm burst, the sexton was bound to ring the church bell, and he received from every farmer five "thunder-sheaves" of corn for the pains he had been at to rescue the crops from destruction. Writing as to the custom in Swabia about the middle of the nineteenth century, a German author tells us that "in most Catholic parishes, especially in Upper Swabia, the bells are rung in a thunderstorm to drive away hail and prevent damage by lightning. Many churches have special bells for the purpose; for instance, the monastery of Weingarten, near Altdorf, has the so-called 'holy Blood-bell,' which is rung during a thunderstorm. In Wurmlingen they ring the bell on Mount Remigius, and if they only do it soon enough, no lightning strikes any place in the district. However, the neighbouring villages, for example Jesingen, are often discontented at the ringing of the bell, for they believe that with the thunderstorm the rain is also driven away." With regard to the town of Constance in particular we read that, when a thunderstorm broke, the bells of all the parish churches not only in the city but in the neighbourhood were set a-ringing; and as they had been consecrated, many persons believed that the sound of them furnished complete protection against injury by lightning. Indeed, in their zeal not a few people assisted the sexton to pull the bell-ropes, tugging at them with all their might to make the bells swing high. And though some of these volunteers, we are informed, were struck dead by lightning in the very act of ringing the peal, this did not prevent others from doing the same. Even children on such occasions rang little hand-bells made of lead or other metals, which were adorned with figures of saints and had been blessed at the church of Maria Loretto in Steiermerk or at Einsiedeln. Under certain feudal tenures the vassals were bound to ring the church bells on various occasions, but particularly during thunderstorms.

The bells were solemnly consecrated and popularly supposed to be baptized by the priests; certainly they received names and were washed, blessed, and sprinkled with holy oil "to drive away and repel evil spirits." Inscriptions engraved on church bells often refer to the power which they were supposed to possess of dispelling storms of thunder, lightning, and hail; some boldly claim such powers for the bells themselves, others more modestly pray for deliverance from these calamities; for instance, a bell at Haslan bears in Latin the words, "From lightning, hail, and tempest, Lord Jesus Christ deliver us!" Speaking of St. Wenefride's Well, in Flintshire, the traveller and antiquary Pennant in the eighteenth century tells us that "a bell belonging to the church was also christened in honour of her. I cannot learn the names of the gossips, who, as usual, were doubtless rich persons. On the ceremony they all laid hold of the rope; bestowed a name on the bell; and the priest, sprinkling it with holy water, baptised it in the name of the Father, etc.; he then clothed it with a fine garment. After this the gossips gave a grand feast, and made great presents, which the priest received in behalf of the bell. Thus blessed, it was endowed with great powers; allayed (on being rung) all storms;

diverted the thunderbolt; drove away evil spirits. These consecrated bells were always inscribed. The inscription on that in
question ran thus:

> *'Sancta Wenefreda, Deo hoc commendare memento.*
> *Ut pietate sua nos servet ab hoste cruento.'*

And a little lower was another address:

> *'Protege prece pia quos convoco, Virgo Maria.'* "

However, the learned Jesuit Father, Martin Delrio, who published an elaborate work on magic early in the seventeenth century,
indignantly denied that bells were baptized, though he fully admitted
that they were named after saints, blessed, and anointed by ecclesiastical authority. That the ringing of church bells laid a wholesome
restraint on evil spirits, and either averted or allayed the tempests
wrought by these enemies of mankind, was, in the opinion of the
learned Jesuit, a fact of daily experience too patent to be denied;
but he traced these happy results purely to the consecration or
benediction of the bells, and not at all to their shape or to the
nature of the metal of which they were founded. He spurned as
a pagan superstition the notion that the sound of brass sufficed of
itself to put demons to flight, and he ridiculed the idea that a church
bell lost all its miraculous virtue when it was named—he will not
allow us to say baptized—by the priest's concubine. Bacon condescended to mention the belief that "great ringing of bells in
populous cities hath chased away thunder, and also dissipated
pestilent air"; but he suggested a physical explanation of the
supposed fact by adding, "All which may be also from the concussion of the air, and not from the sound."

While all holy bells no doubt possessed in an exactly equal
degree the marvellous property of putting demons and witches to
flight, and thereby of preventing the ravages of thunder and lightning, some bells were more celebrated than others for the active
exertion of their beneficent powers. Such, for instance, was St.
Adelm's Bell at Malmesbury Abbey and the great bell of the Abbey
of St. Germains in Paris, which were regularly rung to drive away
thunder and lightning. In old St. Paul's Cathedral there was a
special endowment for "ringing the hallowed belle in great tempestes
and lighteninges." However, the feats of European bells in this
respect have been thrown into the shade by the bells of Caloto in
South America; though probably the superior fame of the bells
of Caloto is to be ascribed, not so much to any intrinsic superiority
of their own, as to the extraordinary frequency of thunderstorms
in that region of the Andes, which has afforded the bells of the city
more frequent opportunities for distinguishing themselves than fall
to the lot of ordinary church bells. On this subject I will quote
the testimony of an eminent Spanish scholar and sailor, who travelled
in South America in the first half of the eighteenth century. The

jurisdiction of Popayan, he informs us, is more subject to tempests of thunder and lightning and earthquakes than even Quito; "but of all the parts in this jurisdiction Caloto is accounted to be the most subject to tempests of thunder and lightning; this has brought into vogue Caloto bells, which not a few persons use, being firmly persuaded that they have a special virtue against lightning. And indeed, so many stories are told on this head, that one is at a loss what to believe. Without giving credit to, or absolutely rejecting all that is reported, leaving every one to the free decision of his own judgment, I shall only relate the most received opinion here. The town of Caloto, the territory of which contains a great number of Indians, of a nation called Paezes, was formerly very large, but those Indians suddenly assaulting it, soon forced their way in, set fire to the houses, and massacred the inhabitants; among the slain was the priest of the parish, who was particularly the object of their rage, as preaching the gospel, with which they were sensible their savage manner of living did not agree, exposing the folly and wickedness of their idolatry, and laying before them the turpitude of their vices. Even the bell of the church could not escape their rancour, as by its sound it reminded them of their duty to come and receive divine instruction. After many fruitless endeavours to break it, they thought they could do nothing better than bury it under ground, that, by the sight of it, they might never be put in mind of the precepts of the gospel, which tended to abridge them of their liberty. On the news of their revolt, the Spaniards in the neighbourhood of Caloto armed; and, having taken a smart revenge of the insurgents in a battle, they rebuilt the town, and having taken up the bell, they placed it in the steeple of the new church; since which the inhabitants, to their great joy and astonishment, observed that, when a tempest appeared brooding in the air, the tolling of the bell dispersed it; and if the weather did not everywhere grow clear and fair, at least the tempest discharged itself in some other part. The news of this miracle spreading everywhere, great solicitations were made for procuring pieces of it to make clappers for little bells, in order to enjoy the benefit of its virtue, which, in a country where tempests are both so dreadful and frequent, must be of the highest advantage. And to this Caloto owes its reputation for bells."

The great discovery that it is possible to silence thunder and extinguish the thunderbolt by the simple process of ringing a bell, has not been confined to the Christian nations of Europe and their descendants in the New World; it has been shared by some at least of the pagan savages of Africa. "The Teso people," we are informed, "make use of bells to exorcise the storm fiend; a person who has been injured by a flash or in the resulting fire wears bells round the ankles for weeks afterwards. Whenever rain threatens, and rain in Uganda almost always comes in company with thunder and lightning, this person will parade the village for an hour, with the jingling bells upon his legs and a wand of papyrus in his hand, attended by as many of his family as may happen to be at hand and not employed in necessary duties. Any one killed outright by lightning is not buried in the house according to the usual custom, but is carried to a distance and interred beside a stream in some belt of forest. Upon the grave are put all the pots and other household utensils owned by the dead person, and at the door of the hut upon which the stroke fell, now of course a smoking ruin, is planted a sacrifice of hoes which is left for some days. It is interesting to note the efficacy attributed to bells and running water, as in some old European superstitions."

As it seems improbable that the Bateso learned these practices from the missionaries, we may perhaps give them the undivided credit of having invented for themselves the custom of exorcizing the storm-fiend by bells and mollifying him by presents of pots and hoes laid on the scene of his devastation and the grave of his victim. The Chinese also resort to the use of gongs, which for practical purposes may be regarded as equivalent to bells, with a view of combating the ill effects of thunder; but the circumstances under which they do so are peculiar. When a person has been attacked by smallpox, and the pustules have come out, but before the end of the seventh day, whenever it thunders, some member of the family is deputed to beat on a gong or drum, which is kept in readiness for the emergency. The beater has the assistance of another member of the family to inform him when the thunder has ceased, for the operator himself makes far too much noise to be able to distinguish between the peals of thunder and the crash of his gong or the roll of his drum. The object, we are told, of this gonging or drumming is to prevent the pustules of the smallpox from breaking or bursting; but the explanations which the Chinese give of the way in which this result is effected by the beating of a gong or a drum can hardly be regarded as satisfactory. On the analogy of the European theory we may conjecture that originally the bursting of the pustules was supposed to be brought about by the demon of thunder, who could be driven away by the banging of a gong or the rub-a-dub of a drum.

But while savages seem quite able of themselves to hit on the device of scaring evil spirits by loud noises, there is evidence to show that they are also ready to adopt from Europeans any practices which, in their opinion, are likely to serve the same purpose. An instance of such borrowing is recorded by two missionaries, who laboured among the natives of Port Moresby, in British New Guinea. "One night during a thunderstorm," they say, "we heard a terrible noise in the village; the natives were beating their drums and shouting lustily in order to drive away the storm-spirits. By the time their drumming and vociferation ceased, the storm *had* passed away, and the villagers were well satisfied. One Sabbath night, in a similar way, they expelled the sickness-producing spirits who had occasioned the death of several natives! When the church bell was first used, the natives thanked Mr. Lawes for having—as they averred—driven away numerous bands of ghosts from the interior. In like manner they were delighted at the bark of a fine dog domesticated at the mission house (the dingo cannot bark), as they felt certain that all the ghosts would now be compelled to rush back to the interior. Unfortunately, the ghosts got used to the bell and the dog! So the young men had to go about at night —often hiding in terror behind trees and bushes—well armed with bows and arrows, to shoot down these obnoxious spirits." Thus the savages of Port Moresby entirely agree with the opinion of the learned Christian scholiast, John Tzetzes, that for the banning of evil spirits there is nothing better than the clangour of bronze and the barking of a dog.

Some of the Pueblo Indians of Arizona exorcize witches by the sound of bells; but probably they borrowed the practice from the old Spanish missionaries, for before the coming of the Europeans the use of all metals, except gold and silver, and hence the making of bells, was unknown among the aborigines of America. An American officer has described one of these scenes of exorcism as he witnessed it at a village of the Moquis, perched, like many Pueblo villages, on the crest of a high tableland overlooking the fruitful grounds in the valley below :—

"The Moquis have an implicit belief in witches and witchcraft, and the air about them is peopled with maleficent spirits. Those who live at Oraybe exorcise the malign influences with the chanting of hymns and ringing of bells. While with General Crook at that isolated and scarcely-known town, in the fall of 1874, by good luck I had an opportunity of witnessing this strange mode of incantation. The whole village seemed to have assembled, and after shouting in a loud and defiant tone a hymn or litany of musical sound, emphasised by an energetic ringing of a bell, advanced rapidly, in single file, down the trail leading from the crest of the precipice to the peach orchards below. The performers, some of the most important of whom were women, pranced around the boundaries of the orchard, pausing for a brief space of time at the corners, all the while singing in a high key and getting the worth of their money out of the bell. At a signal from the leader a rush was made for the trees, from which, in less than an hour, the last of the delicious peaches breaking down the branches were pulled and carried by the squaws and children to the village above." The motive for thus dancing round the orchard, to the loud chanting of hymns and the energetic ringing of a bell, was no doubt to scare away the witches, who were supposed to be perched among the boughs of the peach-trees, battening on the luscious fruit.

However, the use of bells and gongs for the purpose of exorcism has been familiar to many peoples, who need not have borrowed either the instruments or the application of them from the Christian

nations of Europe. In China "the chief instrument for the pro-
duction of exorcising noise is the gong. This well-known circular
plate of brass is actually a characteristic feature of China, resounding throughout the empire every day, especially in summer, when
a rise in the death-rate induces an increase in devil-expelling activity.
Clashing of cymbals of brass, and rattling of drums of wood and
leather, intensify its useful effects. Very often small groups of
men and even women are beating on gongs, cymbals, and drums
for a succession of hours. No protest is heard from their neighbours, no complaint that they disturb their night's rest; such savage music then must either sound agreeable to Chinese ears, or be
heard with gratitude as a meritorious work, gratuitously performed
by benevolent folks who have at heart the private and public weal
and health." In Southern China these solemn and public ceremonies of exorcism take place chiefly during the heat of summer,
when cholera is rampant and its ravages are popularly attributed
to the malice of demons hovering unseen in the air. To drive these
noxious beings from house and home is the object of the ceremonies.
The whole affair is arranged by a committee, and the expenses are
defrayed by subscription, the local mandarins generally heading
the list of subscribers with goodly sums. The actual business of
banishing the devils is carried out by processions of men and boys,
who parade the streets and beat the bounds in the most literal
sense, striking at the invisible feos with swords and axes, and
stunning them with the clangour of gongs, the jangle of bells, the
popping of crackers, the volleys of matchlocks, and the detonation
of blunderbusses.

In Annam the exorcizer, in the act of banning the demons of
sickness from a private house, strums a lute and jingles a chain of
copper bells attached to his big toe, while his assistants accompany
him on stringed instruments and drums. However, the chime of
the bells is understood by the hearers to proceed from the neck of
an animal on which a deity is galloping to the aid of the principal
performer. Bells play a great part in the religious rites of Burma.
Every large pagoda has dozens of them, and the people seem to be
much attached to their sweet and sonorous music. At the present
day their use is said to be, not so much to drive away evil spirits,
as to announce to the guardian spirits that the praises of Buddha
have been chanted; hence at the conclusion of his devotions the
worshipper proclaims the discharge of his pious duty by three
strokes on a bell. However, we may conjecture that this interpretation is one of those afterthoughts by which an advanced religion justifies and hallows the retention of an old barbaric rite that
was originally instituted for a less refined and beautiful purpose.
Perhaps in Europe also the ringing of church bells, the sound of
which has endeared itself to so many pious hearts by its own
intrinsic sweetness and its tender associations, was practised to
banish demons from the house of prayer before it came to be

regarded as a simple means of summoning worshippers to their devotions in the holy place.

However, among ruder peoples of Asia the use of bells in exorcism, pure and simple, has lingered down to modern times. At a funeral ceremony observed by night among the Michemis, a Tibetan tribe near the northern frontier of Assam, a priest, fantastically bedecked with tiger's teeth, many-coloured plumes, bells and shells, executed a wild dance for the purpose of exorcising the evil spirits, while the bells jingled and the shells clattered about his person. Among the Kirantis, a tribe of the Central Himalayas, who bury their dead on hill-tops, "the priest must attend the funeral, and as he moves along with the corpse to the grave he from time to time strikes a copper vessel with a stick, and, invoking the soul of the deceased, desires it to go in peace, and join the souls that went before it." This beating of a copper vessel at the funeral may have been intended, either to hasten the departure of the ghost to his own place, or to drive away the demons who might molest his passage. It may have been for one or other of these purposes that in antiquity, when a Spartan king died, the women used to go about the streets of the city beating a kettle. Among the Bantu tribes of Kavirondo, in Central Africa, when a woman has separated from her husband and gone back to her own people, she deems it nevertheless her duty on his death to mourn for him in his village. For that purpose "she fastens a cattle bell to her waist at the back, collects her friends, and the party proceeds to the village at a trot, the bell clanking in a melancholy manner the whole way." Here, again, the sound of the bell may be intended to keep the husband's ghost at a safe distance, or perhaps to direct his attention to the dutifulness of his widow in sorrowing for his death. In the south-eastern districts of Dutch Borneo it is customary with the Dyaks to sound gongs day and night so long as a corpse remains in the house. The melancholy music begins as soon as a dying man has breathed his last. The tune is played on four gongs of different tones, which are beaten alternately at regular intervals of about two seconds. Hour after hour, day after day the melody is kept up; and we are told that nothing, not even the Passing Bell of Catholic Europe, is more weird and affecting to a listener than the solemn notes of these death-gongs sounding monotonously and dying away over the broad rivers of Borneo.

Though we are not informed why the Dyaks in this part of Borneo beat the gongs continuously after a death, we may conjecture that the intention is to keep off evil spirits rather than simply to announce the bereavement to friends at a distance; for if the object was merely to convey the intelligence of the decease to the neighbourhood, why sound the gongs continuously day and night so long as the body remains in the house? On the other hand we know that in Borneo the sound of metal instruments is sometimes employed expressly for the purpose of exorcising demons. An English traveller in North Borneo describes how on one occasion he lodged in a large house of the Dusuns, which was inhabited by about a hundred men with their families: "As night came on they struck up a strange kind of music on metal tambourines. A mysterious rhythm and tune was apparent in it, and when I asked if this was *main-main* (*i.e.* larking), they said no, but that a man was sick, and they must play all night to keep away evil spirits." Again, the Dusuns of North Borneo solemnly expel all evil spirits from their villages once a year, and in the expulsion gongs are beaten and bells rung to hasten the departure of the demons. While the men beat gongs and drums, the women go in procession from house to house, dancing and singing to the measured clash of brass castanets, which they hold in their hands, and to the jingle of little brass bells, of which bunches are fastened to their wrists. Having driven the demons from the houses, the women chase or lead them down to the bank of the river, where a raft has been prepared to convey them beyond the territories of the village. Figures of men, women, animals, and birds, made of sago-palm leaf, adorn the raft, and to render it still more attractive offerings of food and cloth and cooking pots are deposited on the planks. When the spiritual passengers are all aboard, the moorings are loosed, and the bark floats away down stream, till it rounds the farthest reach of the river and disappears from sight in the forest. Thus the demons are sent away on a long voyage to return, it is fondly hoped, no more.

When Sir Hugh Low visited a village of the Sebonogh Hill Dyaks, in August 1845, he was received with much ceremony as the first European who had ever been seen in the place. Good-naturedly joining in a prayer to the sun, the moon, and the Rajah of Sarawak, that the rice harvest might be plentiful, the pigs prolific, and the women blessed with male children, the Englishman punctuated and emphasized these petitions by throwing small portions of yellow rice towards heaven at frequent intervals, presumably for the purpose of calling the attention of the three deities to the humble requests of their worshippers. Having engaged in these edifying devotions on a public stage in front of the house, Sir Hugh returned to the verandah, where the chief of the village, in the visitor's own words, "tied a little hawk-bell round my wrist, requesting me at the same time to tie another, with which he furnished me for the purpose, round the same joint of his right hand. After this, the noisy gongs and tomtoms began to play, being suspended from the rafters at one end of the verandah, and the chief tied another of the little bells round my wrist: his example was this time followed by all the old men present, each addressing a few words to me, or rather mumbling them to themselves, of which I did not understand the purport. Every person who now came in, brought with him several bamboos of cooked rice; and each, as he arrived, added one to the number of my bells, so that they had now become inconveniently numerous, and I requested, as a favour, that the remainder might be tied upon my left wrist, if it made no difference to the ceremony. Those who followed, accordingly did as I had begged of them in this particular." Though Sir Hugh Low does not explain, and probably did not know, the meaning of thus belling an honoured visitor, we may conjecture that the intention was the kindly one of keeping evil spirits at bay.

The Patâri priest in Mirzapur and many classes of ascetics throughout India carry bells and rattles made of iron, which they shake as they walk for the purpose of scaring demons. With a like intent, apparently, a special class of devil priests among the Gonds, known as Ojhyâls, always wear bells. It seems probable that a similar motive everywhere underlies the custom of attaching bells to various parts of the person, particularly to the ankles, wrists, and neck, either on special occasions or for long periods of times: originally, we may suppose, the tinkle of the bells was thought to protect the wearer against the assaults of bogies. It is for this purpose that small bells are very commonly worn by children in the southern provinces of China and more sparingly by children in the northern provinces; and silver ornaments, with small bells hanging from them, are worn by Neapolitan women on their dresses as amulets to guard them against the Evil Eye. The Yezidis, who have a robust faith in the devil, perform at the conclusion of one of their pilgrimage festivals a ceremony which may be supposed to keep that ravening wolf from the fold of the faithful. An old man is stripped and dressed in the skin of a goat, while a string of small bells is hung round his neck. Thus arrayed, he crawls round the assembled pilgrims emitting sounds which are intended to mimic the bleating of a he-goat. The ceremony is believed to sanctify the assembly, but we may conjecture that it does so by encircling believers with a spiritual fence which the arch enemy is unable to surmount. With a like intention, probably, a Badaga priest in Southern India ties bells to his legs before he essays to walk barefoot across the glowing embers of a fire-pit at a solemn ceremony which is apparently designed to secure a blessing on the crops.

In Africa bells are much used by the natives for the purpose of putting evil spirits to flight, and we need not suppose that the custom has always or even generally been borrowed by them from Europeans, since the blacks have believed in spirits and have been acquainted with the metals, particularly with iron, from time immemorial. For example, the Yoruba-speaking people of the Slave Coast believe that there are certain wicked spirits called *abikus*, which haunt the forests and waste places and, suffering much from hunger, are very desirous of taking up their abode in human bodies. For that purpose they watch for the moment of conception and insinuate themselves into the embryos in the wombs of women. When such children are born, they peak and pine, because the hungry demons within them are consuming the better part of the nourishment destined for the support of the real infant. To rid the poor babe of its troublesome occupant, a mother will offer a sacrifice of food to the demon, and while he is devouring it, she avails herself of his distraction to attach small bells and iron rings to her child's ankles and iron rings to its neck. The jingling of the iron and the tinkling of the bells are thought to keep the demons at a distance; hence many children are to be seen with their feet weighed down by iron ornaments. Among the Baganda and Banyoro of Central Africa young children learning to walk used to have small bells attached to their feet, and the reason alleged for the custom was that the bells helped the child to walk or strengthened its legs; but perhaps the original motive was to deliver the little one at this critical time from the unwelcome attentions of evil spirits. With the same intention, possibly among the Baganda parents of twins wore bells at their ankles during the long and elaborate ceremonies which the superstitious beliefs of their country imposed upon husband and wife in such cases; and special drums, one for the father and another for the mother, were beaten continually both by day and by night.

Among the Bogos, to the north of Abyssinia, when a woman has been brought to bed, her female friends kindle a fire at the door of the house, and the mother with her infant walks slowly round it, while a great noise is made with bells and palm-branches for the purpose, we are told, of frightening away the evil spirits. It is said that the Gonds of India "always beat a brass dish at a birth so that the noise may penetrate the child's ears, and this will remove any obstruction there may be to its hearing." The reason here assigned for the custom is not likely to be the original one; more probably the noise of the beaten brass was primarily intended, like the sound of bells among the Bogos, to protect the mother and her newborn babe against the assaults of demons. So in Greek legend the Curetes are said to have danced round the infant Zeus, clashing their spears against their shields, to drown the child's squalls, lest they should attract the attention of his unnatural father Cronus, who was in the habit of devouring his offspring as soon as they were born. We may surmise that this Greek legend embodies a reminiscence of an old custom observed for the purpose of protecting babies against the many causes of infantile mortality which primitive man explains by the agency of malevolent and dangerous spirits. To be more explicit, we may conjecture that in former times, when a Greek child was born, the father and his friends were wont to arm themselves with spear or sword and shield and to execute a war dance round the child, clashing their spears or swords against their shields, partly in order to drown the cries of the infant, lest they should attract the attention of the prowling spirits, but partly also to frighten away the demons by the din; while in order to complete the discomfiture of the invisible foes they brandished their weapons, cutting and thrusting vigorously with them in the empty air. At least this conjecture is supported by the following analogies.

A Spanish priest, writing towards the beginning of the eighteenth century, has described as follows the practices observed by the Tagalogs of the Philippine Islands at the birth of a child. "The *patianak,* which some call goblin (if it be not fiction, dream, or their imagination), is the genius or devil who is accustomed to annoy them. . . . To him they attribute the ill result of childbirth, and say that to do them damage, or to cause them to go astray, he places himself in a tree, or hides in any place near the house of the woman who is in childbirth, and there sings after the manner of those who go wandering, etc. To hinder the evil work of the *patianak,* they make themselves naked, and arm themselves with cuirass, bolo, lance, and other arms, and in this manner place themselves on the ridgepole of the roof, and also under the house, where they give many blows and thrusts with the bolo, and make many gestures and motions ordered to the same intent." According to another version of the account, the husband and his friends arm themselves with sword, shield, and spear, and thus equipped hew and slash furiously in the air, both on the roof of the house and underneath it (the houses being raised above the ground on poles), for the purpose of frightening and driving away the dangerous spirit who would injure the mother and child. These armed men, repelling the demon from the newborn babe by cut and thrust of their weapons, appear to be the savage counterpart of the ancient Greek Curetes.

Similar beliefs concerning the danger to which infants are exposed from spiritual enemies have led the wild Kachims of Burma to adopt very similar precautions, for the sake of guarding a mother and her offspring. "At the instant of birth the midwife says 'the child is named so-and-so.' If she does not do this, some malignant *nat* or spirit will give the child a name first, and so cause it to pine away and die. If mother and child do well, there is general drinking and eating, and the happy father is chaffed. If, however, childbirth is attended with much labour, then it is evident that *nats* are at work and a *tumsa* or seer is called into requisition. This man goes to another house in the village and consults the bamboos (*chippawt*) to discover whether it is the house-*nat* who is averse, or whether a jungle *nat* has come and driven the guardian *nat* away. These jungle *nats* are termed *sawn,* and are the spirits of those who have died in childbirth or by violent deaths. They naturally wish for companions, and so enter the house and seize the woman and child. If the bamboo declares that it is the house-*nat* who is angry, he is propitiated by offerings of spirits or by sacrifice in the ordinary manner. If, however, it appears that a *sawn* has taken possession, then prompt action is necessary. Guns are fired all round the house and along the paths leading into the village, arrows are shot under the floor of the house, *dhas* [swords or large knives] and torches are brandished over the body of the woman, and finally old rags, chillies, and other materials likely to produce a sufficiently noisome smell are piled under the raised flooring and set fire to, thereby scaring away any but the most obstinate and pertinacious spirits." To the same effect a Catholic missionary among the Kachins tells us that in the case of a difficult birth these savages "accuse the *sawn* (ghosts of women who died in childbed) of wishing to kill the mother, and they make a regular hunt after them. They rummage in every corner of the house, brandishing spears and knives, making all sorts of noises, of which the least inodorous are the most effectual; they even strip themselves beside the sufferer in order to horrify the evil spirits. In and outside the house they burn stinking leaves, with rice, pepper, and everything that can produce a foul smell; on every side they raise cries, fire muskets, shoot arrows, strike blows with swords, and continue this uproar along the principal road in the forest, as far as the nearest torrent, where they imagine that they put the *sawn* to flight."

When a Kalmuk woman is in travail, her husband stretches a net round the tent, and runs to and fro beating the air with a club and crying, "Devil avaunt!" until the child is born: this he does in order to keep the foul fiend at bay. Among the Nogais, a tribe of Tartars, "when a boy is born, everybody goes to the door of the house with kettles. They make a great noise, saying that they do so in order to put the devil to flight, and that he will have no more power over the spirit of that child." In Boni or Bone, a princedom of Southern Celebes, when a woman is in hard labour, the men "sometimes raise a shout or fire a gun in order, by so doing, to drive away the evil spirits who are hindering the birth"; and at the birth of a prince, as soon as the infant has been separated from the afterbirth, all the metal instruments used for expelling demons are struck and clashed "in order to drive away the evil spirits." For the same purpose drums are beaten in the Aru islands, to the south-west of New Guinea, when a delivery is unduly delayed. The spirit of a certain stream, which flows into Burton Gulf, on Lake Tanganyika, is believed by the natives of the neighbourhood to be very unfriendly to women with child, whom he prevents from bringing forth. When a woman believes herself to be suffering from his machinations, she orders sacrifices to be offered and certain ceremonies to be performed. All the inhabitants of the village assemble, beat drums near the hut where the patient is confined, and shout and dance "to drive away the evil spirit." Among the Singhalese of Ceylon, when a birth has taken place, "the cries of the babe are drowned by those of the nurse, lest the spirits of the forest become aware of its presence and inflict injury on it." So the ancient Romans believed that a woman after childbirth was particularly liable to be attacked by the forest god Silvanus, who made his way into the house by night on purpose to vex and harry her. Hence during the night three men used to go round the thresholds of the house, armed respectively with an axe, a pestle, and a besom; at every threshold they stopped, and while the first two men smote it with the axe and the pestle, the third man swept it with his broom. In this way they thought to protect the mother from the attacks of the woodland deity.

Similarly we may suppose that in ancient Greece it was formerly customary for armed men to protect women in childbed from their spiritual foes by dancing round them and clashing their spears or swords on their shields, and even when the old custom had long fallen into abeyance among men, legend might still tell how the rite had been celebrated by the Curetes about the cradle of the infant Zeus.

But from this digression we must return to the use of bells as a means of repelling the assaults of ghosts and demons. Among the Sunars, who are the goldsmiths and silversmiths of the Central Provinces in India, children and young girls wear hollow anklets with tinkling bells inside; but when a married woman has had several children, she leaves off wearing the hollow anklet and wears a solid one instead. "It is now said that the reason why girls wear sounding anklets is that their whereabouts may be known, and they may be prevented from getting into mischief in dark corners. But the real reason was probably that they served as spirit scarers." Among the Nandi of British East Africa, when a girl is about to be circumcised, she receives from her sweethearts and admirers the loan of large bells, which they usually wear on their legs, but which for this solemn occasion they temporarily transfer to the damsel. A popular girl will frequently receive as many as ten or twenty bells, and she wears them all when the painful operation is performed upon her. As soon as it is over, she stands up and shakes the bells over her head, then goes to meet her lover, and gives him back the borrowed bells. If we knew why Nandi warriors regularly wear bells on their legs, we should probably know why girls wear the very same bells at circumcision. In the absence of positive information we may surmise that the bells are regarded as amulets, which protect both sexes against the supernatural dangers to which each, in virtue of its special functions, is either permanently or temporarily exposed.

In the Congo region the natives fear that demons may enter their bodies through the mouth when they are in the act of drinking; hence on these occasions they make use of various contrivances in order to keep these dangerous beings at a distance, and one of the devices is to ring a bell before every draught of liquid. A chief has been observed to drink ten pots of beer at a sitting in this fashion, shaking his magic bell every time before he raised the beaker to his lips, while by way of additional precaution a boy brandished the chief's spear in front of that dignitary to prevent the demons from insinuating themselves into his stomach with the beer. In this region, also, bells which have been enchanted by the fetish-man are worn as amulets, which can avert fever, bullets, and locusts, and can render the wearer invisible. Among the Bakerewe, who inhabit Ukerewe, the largest island in Lake Victoria Nyanza, it is customary to fasten a bell immediately over the door of every house, and every person on entering the dwelling is careful to ring the bell by knocking his head against it, not, as in Europe, to warn the inmates of his arrival, but to ward off evil spirits and to dispel the enchantments of sorcerers. In West Africa the jangling of bells helps to swell the general uproar which accompanies the periodic banishment of bogies from the haunts of men.

But in Africa the carrying or wearing of bells is particularly characteristic of priests, prophets, and medicine-men in the perform-ance of their solemn ceremonies, whether for the expulsion of demons, the cure of sickness, or the revelation of the divine will to mortals. For example, among the Akamba of British East Africa magicians carry iron cattle-bells attached to a leathern thong, and they ring them when they are engaged in telling fortunes; the sound of the bell is supposed to attract the attention of the spirits. One of these medicine-men told Mr. Hobley that he had dreamed how God told him to get a bell; so he made a special journey to Kikuyu to buy the bell, and on his return he gave a feast of beer and killed a bullock to propitiate the spirits. Among the Gallas of East Africa the class of priests (*Lubas*) is distinct from the class of exorcists (*Kalijos*), but both priests and exorcists carry bells in the celebration of their peculiar rites; and the exorcist is armed in addition with a whip, which he does not hesitate to lay on smartly to the patient for the purpose of driving out the devil by whom the sick man is supposed to be possessed. Again, among the Fans of the Gaboon a witch-doctor, engaged in the detection of a sorcerer, wears a number of little bells fastened to his ankles and wrists, and he professes to be guided by the sound of the bells in singling out the alleged culprit from the crowd of anxious and excited onlookers. The Hos Togoland, in West Africa, believe in the existence of a sort of "drudging goblin" or "lubber fiend," who miraculously multiplies the cowry-shells in a man's treasure-chamber and the crops in his field. The name of this serviceable spirit is Sowlui, and curiously enough the Hos bestow the very same name on the sound of the little bells which Ho priests, like Jewish priests of old, bind on the lower hem of their robes. Among the Banyoro of Central Africa the god of Lake Albert communicated with mortals by the intervention of a prophetess, who wore a fringe of cowry-shells and small iron bells on her leather garment, and as she walked the fringe undulated like the waves of the lake. In the same tribe the god of plenty, by name Wamala, who gave increase of man and cattle and crops, was represented by a prophet, who uttered oracles in the name of the deity. When the prophetic fit was on him, this man wore bells on his ankles and two white calf-skins round his waist, with a row of little iron bells dangling from the lower edge of the skins.

These instances may suffice to show how widespread has been the use of bells in magical or religious rites, and how general has been the belief that their tinkle has power to banish demons. From a few of the examples which I have cited it appears that sometimes the sound of bells is supposed, not so much to repel evil spirits, as to attract the attention of good or guardian spirits, but on the whole the attractive force of these musical instruments in primitive ritual is far less conspicuous than the repulsive. The use of bells for the purpose of attraction rather than of repulsion may correspond to that more advanced stage of religious consciousness when the fear of evil is outweighed by trust in the good, when the desire of pious hearts is not so much to flee from the Devil as to draw near to God. In one way or another the practices and beliefs collected in this chapter may serve to illustrate and perhaps to explain the Jewish custom from which we started, whether it be that the priest in his violet robe, as he crossed the threshold of the sanctuary, was believed to repel the assaults of demons or to attract the attention of the deity by the chime and jingle of the golden bells.

INDEX

Aaron, shrine of, on Mount Hor, 250

Abana, the river, 327

Abederys of Brazil, their story of a great flood, 100

Abel, the reputed tomb of, 327

—— and Cain, 33

Abigail and David, 284 *sq.*

Abimelech made king at an oak, 334

Abortive calves buried under the threshold of the cowhouse, 320 *sq.*

Abraham, his negotiations with the sons of Heth, 59; his migration from Ur, 145, 146; the Covenant of, 153 *sqq.*; his migration to Canaan, 153; his interview with three men at the oaks of Mamre, 333, 334, 335; in relation to oaks or terebinths, 333, 334 *sq.*

Abraham's oak, 328

Abu-Habbah, site of the ancient city of Sippar, 54

Abyssinians, their mourning customs, 381

Acagchemem Indians of California, their story of the creation of man, 11; their story of a great flood, 111

Achelous, the river-god, and Hercules, 253

Acheron, the river, 297 *sq.*

Achilles, his ghost evoked by Apollonius of Tyana, 300; his offering of hair to the dead Patroclus, 380

Ackawois of British Guiana, their story of a great flood, 101

Adam, man, 3; made of red clay, 14

Adamah, ground, 3, 14

Addison, on the bell-man, 424

Admiralty Islanders their story like that of the Tower of Babel, 150

—— Islands, story of the origin of death in the, 28

Adonai substituted for Jehovah in reading the Scriptures, 60

Adonijah, set aside by David, 175

Adoption, ceremony of, among the Gallas, 207; among the Kikuyu, 209 *sq.*; fiction of a new birth at, 216

Aenianes of Thessaly, their worship of a stone, 232

Aeschylus on the murder of Agamemnon, 36; his description of the evocation of the ghost of Darius, 300

Aesculapius at Epidaurus, cures effected in dreams at the sanctuary of, 226 *sqq.*

Afghans, sacred groves among the, 341 *sq.*

Africa, stories of the creation of man in, 10; the tribal mark in, 33; stories of a great flood in, 129 *sqq.*; no clear case of flood story in, 132; stories like that of the Tower of Babel in, 147 *sq.*; peace-making ceremonies in, 155 *sqq.*, 158 *sq.*; ultimogeniture in, 201 *sq.*; oaths on stones in, 248; aversion to count or be counted, 308; respect for the threshold in, 315; sacrifices to sacred trees in, 332 *sq.*; pastoral tribes of object to boil milk, 364 *sq.*; laceration of the body and shearing the hair in mourning in, 381; use of bells to put evil spirits to flight in, 427, 433 *sq.*, 437

——, Central, sacred rocks and stones in, 234

——, East, tribes of, whose customs resemble those of Semitic peoples, 206 *sq.*; their use of skins of sacrificial victims at transference of government, 215

——, West, stories of heavenly ladders in, 228; traps set for souls by witches in, 289

African tribes, their superstitious awe of smiths, 214

Africanus, Julius, on the date of the flood of Ogyges, 71

Afterbirth buried at the doorway, 320; supposed to be the infant's twin, 320

Agamemnon, murder of, 36; his mode of swearing the Greeks, 154; his libation, 159; offering of hair at his tomb, 380

Age, people reluctant to tell their, 312

Age-grades of the Nandi, 215

Agriculture discouraged by pastoral peoples, 374

441

Agrippina, her ghost evoked by Nero, 301

Ainos of Japan, cut down trees which have caused deaths, 398

Ait Wäryâgäl of Morocco, their rule in regard to biestings, 365

Aix, the Parliament of, orders the execution of a mare, 414

Akamba of British East Africa, their language and affinity, 206; birth ceremony among the, 207; their use of sacrificial skins in covenants, 211; their custom of anointing a certain stone, 236; their mode of swearing on stones, 248; their reluctance to count their cattle or tell the number of their children, 309; their disposal of weapons which have killed people, 399; iron cattle bells worn by magicians among the, 438

Akikuyu of British East Africa, their notice of the pollution caused by homicide, 35, 38; their language and affinity, 206; their ceremony of the new birth, 207 sqq.; birth ceremony among the, 207, 215, 216; their two guilds, 208; their ceremony at adoption, 209; circumcision among the, 210; their use of sacrificial skins at covenants, 215 sq.; their use of goatskins at ceremonies, 215; think it unlucky to tell the number of their children, 309; their sacred groves, 339 sq.; their rule as to milk-vessels, 369; blunt the weapons which have killed people, 399

Alaska, stories of the creation of man in, 11; stories of a great flood in, 128; the Tlingkits of, 152; the Eskimo of, 285

Alba Longa, 265

Albanians, their custom in regard to crossing thresholds, 317

—— of the Caucasus, their rite of purification, 162

Albans, their treaty with the Romans, 159

Alcmaeon, the matricide, pursued by his mother's ghost, 36

Alcmena and Jupiter, 252

Algeria, aversion to count or to be counted in, 309

Algonquin Indians, stories of a great flood among the, 115 sqq.; stories of a flood, their wide diffusion, 135

Alopen, the historian, 84

A-Louyi of the Upper Zambesi, their story like that of the Tower of Babel, 147

Alsace, ultimogeniture in, 178

Altars at sacred oaks or terebinths, 333

Altmark, bride carried into her husband's house in the, 317

Amboyna, belief as to a person's strength being in his hair, 272

Ambrym, dead ancestors consulted oracularly by means of their images in, 303

America, stories of the creation of man in, 11 sq.; stories of a great flood in, 97 sqq.; diluvial traditions widespread in, 132

American Indians, their stories of the creation of man, 11 sqq.; traditions of a great flood among the, 114; weeping as a salutation among the, 141 sq. See also North American Indians.

Amiens, ultimogeniture in districts about, 177

Ammizaduga, king of Babylon, 54

Amos, on rites of mourning, 377

Amoy, evocation of the dead in, 306

Amphiaraus, sanctuary of, at Oropus, 225 sq.

Amphitro, how he overcame Pterelaus, king of Taphos, 274

Amram, father of Moses, 268

Amulets, souls of children conjured into, 286; ornaments as, 290

Amulius, king of Alba Longa, 265

Anals of Assam, their story of a great flood, 80 sq.

Ancestral spirits, consulted in China, 306 sq.

Andaman Islands, their story of a great flood, 87 sq.; weeping as a salutation among the, 241

Anderson, Dr. John, on ultimogeniture among the Shans, 188

Andree, Richard, on flood stories, 46

Angamis, ultimogeniture among the, 183; their permanent system of agriculture, 183

Angel of the Lord, his interview with Gideon, 333

——, the Destroying, seen over Jerusalem in the time of plague, 308

Angelius, Bret Harte on the, 421 sq.

Angoni, their ceremonies at crossing rivers, 255 sq. See also Ngoni

Animals, in the ark, discrepancy as to clean and unclean, 61; cut in pieces at ratification of covenants and oaths, 154 sqq.; sacrificed at the threshold, 321 sq.; punished for killing or injuring persons, 397 sq., 399 sqq.; personified, 399; as witnesses in trials for murder, 415

Ankole, the Bahima of, 206

Anna, her mourning for Dido, 380

Annam, story of the origin of death in, 32; the use of bells at exorcisms in, 430

Anointing sacred stones, 235 sqq.

Ant-hill in story of creation, 9

Ants prosecuted by the Friars Minor in Brazil, 410

Anu, Babylonian Father of the gods, 51, 52, 56

Anunnaki, Babylonian mythical personages, 52

Aornum, in Thesprotis, oracle of the dead at, 297

Apamea Cibotos in Phrygia, legend of a flood at, 70

Apion, a grammarian, said to have evoked the ghost of Homer, 300

Apollo, his wrath at Hercules, 73; statue of, punished at Rome, 402 sq.

Apollodorus, his story of Deucalion's flood, 67

Apollonius of Tyana, his evocation of the ghost of Achilles, 300

Arab women, their custom of scratching their faces and shearing their hair in mourning, 379

Arabs, their worship of stones, 231

—— of Arabia Petraea, their treatment of animals that have killed persons, 400

—— of Moab, their ceremony of redeeming the people, 162 sq.; their veneration for terebinths, 330; their mourning customs, 379

—— of Syria, averse to counting their tents, horsemen, or cattle, 313

Arafoos of Dutch New Guinea, their attack on the sea, 257

Araguaya River, 99, 100

Arakan, the Kumis of, 9; the Kamees of, 189

Arapaho Indians, their mourning customs, 383

Araucanians of Chili, their story of a great flood, 101, 139

Arawaks of British Guiana, their story of the origin of death, 27; their story of a great flood, 103

Arcadian legend of a flood, 72 sq.

Archons at Athens, their oath on a stone, 248

Areopagus, the oath before the, 154

Argyleshire story of the king of Sorcha and the herdsman of Cruachan, 278

Ariconte, hero of a Brazilian flood story, 97 sq.

Aristinus, his pretence of being born again, 218

Aristophanes, in Plato, his account of the primitive state of man, 14; on the trial of a dog, 401

Aristotle on Deucalion's flood, 67

Arizona, the Hopi or Moqui Indians of, 13; the Pima Indians of, 13; stories of a great flood in, 110 sq.

Ark in story of the great flood, 64, 65 sq.

—— of bulrushes, Moses in the, 265 sqq.

Armed men repel demons from women in childbed, 434 sq.

Armenia, 49; threshold thought to be haunted by spirits in, 319

Armenian women scratched their faces in mourning, 380

Armenians, their superstition about counting warts, 312

Arnobius on worship of stones, 235

Arras, ultimogeniture in districts about, 177

Arsaces, king of Armenia, his treason detected, 250

Artega, their objection to boil milk, 367

Artois, ultimogeniture in, 177

Aru Islands, women in childbed protected from demons in the, 436

Arunta of Central Australia, 286, 287; their precautions against the ghosts of the slain, 43 sq.; silence of widows among the, 345, 348; their bodily lacerations in mourning, 391, 392, 394

Aryan peoples of Europe, ultimogeniture among the, 17b

Aryans, their settlement in the Punjab, 78; practice of carrying a bride over the threshold of her husband's house among the, 17

Ashantee story of the origin of death, 23

—— story like that of the Tower of Babel, 148

Ashdod, Dagon at, 313

Asherah (singular), Asherim (plural), sacred poles at the "high places" of Israel, 338, 339, 342

Ashes smeared on body in sign of mourning, 394

Ashraf, their objection to boil milk, 367

Ashurbanipal, his library at Nineveh, 49, 53, 141

Ashur-nirari, king of Assyria, 159

Asia, Eastern, stories of a great flood in, 81 sqq.

——, North-eastern, ultimogeniture in, 199 sqq.

——, Southern, ultimogeniture in, 180 sqq.

Assam, story of the creation of man in, 9; the Anals of, their story of a great flood, 80 sq.; story like that of the Tower of Babel in, 150; stories of the origin of the diversity of languages in, 151; peace-making ceremonies in, 157 sq.; the Lushais of, 169; ultimogeniture in, 180; oaths on stones in, 249

Assisi, its basilica, 422

Association of ideas, sympathetic magic based on the, 368

Assyrian oath of fealty, 159 sq.

—— women scratched their faces in mourning, 380

Astarte at Hierapolis, 68

Astydamia, slain by Peleus, 162, 168

Athapascan family of American Indian languages, 120 sq.

Athens, grave of Deucalion at, 67, 68; sanctuary of Olympian Zeus at, 68; the Festival of the Water-bearing at, 68; stone used to swear on, at, 248;

trial and punishment of animals and inanimate objects in, 400 sq.

Atheraka of British East Africa, blunt the weapons which have killed people, 399

Athletes at Olympia, their oath, 155

Atkinson, Rev. J. C., on the burial of abortive calves under the threshold in Yorkshire, 321

Atonga, their ceremony at the passage of a bride over the threshold, 317

Atossa, wife of Xerxes, her evocation of the ghost of Darius, 300

Atrakasis, hero of Babylonian flood story, 53, 54

Attic law concerning homicides, 34, 35

Attila, the mourning for, 380

Auchmithie in Forfarshire, the fishwives of, their objection to being counted, 311

"Augurs, the oak or terebinth of the," 333

Australia, stories of a great flood in, 88 sqq.

——, aborigines of, bodily lacerations in mourning among the, 390 sqq.

——, Central, story of resurrection from the dead in, 30; the churinga or sacred sticks and stones of the aborigines of, 285 sq.; Central and Northern, silence of widows and other women after a death among the tribes of, 344

——, Western, natives of, burn spears which have killed men, 399

Australian story of the creation of man, 4

Austric family of speech, 195

Autun, lawsuit against rats in the diocese of, 405

Aversion of people to count or be counted, 308 sqq.

Awome of Calabar, their ceremonies at peace-making, 158 sq.

Axe, or knife, sacrificial, annually punished at Athens, 401

Aztecs, their customs of cropping the hair of witches and wizards, 273

Baalim, the lords of wooded heights, 337, 341, 342

Babel, the Tower of, 143 sqq.; later Jewish legends concerning, 144

Babil, temple mound at Babylon, 145

Babylon, ruined temples at, 145

Babylonian, annual floods at, 140

Babylonian captivity, 57, 338, 358, 360

—— conception of the creation of man, 3

—— story of a great flood, 48 sqq.; Hebrew legend derived from the, 133

Bachelors' halls among the tribes of Assam, 193

Bacon, Lord, on the ringing of bells in thunderstorms, 426

Badaga priest wears bells at fire-walk, 433

Badagas of the Neilgherry Hills, ultimo-

geniture among the, 198; their offerings to rivers at crossing them, 255

Baganda, their ceremonies at crossing rivers, 254; their worship of rivers, 254; ghosts of dead kings consulted as oracles among the, 301 sq.; their objection to boil milk, 366; practice of boiling flesh in milk on the sly among the, 368; their rule as to milkvessels, 369; do not eat vegetables and milk together, 373; discourage agriculture from fear of injuring their cattle, 374; bells worn by children among the, 434; bells worn by parents of twins among the, 434. See also Uganda

Bagesu of British East Africa, their customs in regard to homicide, 38; their ceremony at peace-making, 155

Baghdad, flood at, 141; the Caliphs of, reverence for the threshold of their palace, 314 sq.

Bagobos of Mindanao, their story of the creation of man, 9

Bahima, or Banyankole, of Ankole, their ethical affinity, 206; their form of adoption, 217 sq.; their divination by water, 261; their objection to boil milk, 366, 367; will not wash themselves for fear of injuring the cows, 369; their rule as to milk-vessels, 369; their rule to keep milk and flesh apart, 370; do not eat meat and milk together, 371; do not eat vegetables and milk together, 372; eat only a few wild animals, 375.

Bahkunjy tribe, mourning custom in the, 392

Bahnars of Cochin China, their story of the origin of death, 30 sq.; their story of a great flood, 82

Bairo of Ankole, do not drink milk with vegetables, 372

Baitylos, baitylion, 237

Bakerewe, their use of bells to ward off evil spirits, 438

Bakongo of the Lower Congo, their dislike to being counted or counting their children, 308

Baldness, artificial, in sign of mourning, 377 sq., 387, 393

Bâle, cock tried and executed at, 414

Baluchistan, bride stepping over blood at threshold in, 321

Bambala of the Congo, their story like that of the Tower of Babel, 147

Bambaras of the Upper Niger, offer sacrifices to the dead on the threshold, 322; their sacrifices to sacred trees, 333

Bangala. See Boloki

Banias, the Syrian Tivoli, 328

Banks Islands, story of the creation of man in the, 6; story how men used not to die in the, 28; worship of stones in the, 232

Bantu tribes of Africa, their story of the origin of death, 25; their belief that rivers are inhabited by demons or malignant spirits, 254; of Rhodesia, spirits of dead chiefs consulted as oracles among the, 302

—— Kavirondo. See Kavirondo

Banyoro, their sacrifice at crossing a river, 254 sq.; their objection to boil milk, 367; their rule as to milk-vessels, 369; do not eat vegetables and milk together, 372 sq.; the pastoral, abstain from the flesh of most wild animals, 376; bells worn by children among the, 434; iron bells worn by prophetess among the, 438

Baobabs, sacrifices to, 333

Baoules of the Ivory Coast, chief's soul shut up in a box among the, 289

Bapedi of South Africa, their story of a great flood, 129

Bare'e-speaking Toradjas. See Toradjas

Baris, Mount, 49

Barolong of South Africa, their mode of making peace, 157, 162

Baronga, blame the chamelon for having brought death into the world, 25

Barricading the road against the souls of the dead, 230

Bashan, the oak of, 323

Bastar, the shaving and torture of witches in, 272

Basutos, 25; purification of manslayers among the, 41; their form of ceremonial purification, 162

Bataks of Sumatra, their story of a great flood, 84 sq.; their mode of ratifying a covenant, 160; their rule of inheritance, 199; their story of former connexion between earth and heaven, 229; their evocation of the dead, 304 sq.

Bateso, their customs in regard to persons who have been struck by lightning, 428

Bavaria, superstition as to counting loaves and dumplings in, 312

Ba-Yaka, in the Congo Valley, their precaution against ghosts of the slain, 41; their execution of a thieving dog, 400

Beans, black, offered to ghosts at Rome, 418

Beaupré, near Beauvais, bull condemned by the authorities of the Cistercian Abbey of, 413

Beaver, in stories of a great flood, 118, 120, 121, 122, 123

Bechuanas, 25; their mode of making a covenant, 157

Bedel Tartars of Siberia, their story of the creation of man, 6

Bedouins, their tribal badges, 33; strained relations of a father to his grown sons among the, 203

Beef not to be eaten with milk, 370 sq.

Beetle creates man out of clay, 14

Beetles supposed to renew their youth, 26

Bel, or Marduk, Babylonian god, 3, 56

Bell of Protestant chapel of La Rochelle punished for heresy, 415. See also Bells

——, the Curfew, 421

——, the Passing, 449 sqq.

——, the Vesper, 421

Bell-man, the, 424 sq.

Bella Coola Indians, silence of widows and widowers among the, 344

Bells, the golden, 417 sqq.; golden, attached to robes of Jewish priests, 417, 439; thought to drive away demons, 417; used in exorcism, 418, 422 sqq., 427 sqq.; worn as a protection against lightning, 427 sq.; fastened to person of honoured visitor, 432 sq.; worn by ascetics and priests in India, 433; by Neapolitan women, 433; by children in China, 433; by children in Africa, 434; worn by children among the Sunars, 437; rung to prevent demons from entering the body, 437; worn by priests, prophets, and medicine-men in Africa, 438; their repulsive and attractive force in religious ritual, 439. See also Church bells

Ben Jonson's "rosy wreath," 290

Benât Ya'kôb, the daughters of Jacob, 323

Benedictus bell, 420

Benjamin, "son of the right hand," 174; his meeting with Joseph, 239

Benua-Jakun of the Malay Peninsula, their story of a great flood, 82 sq.

Berne, the authorities of, prosecute a species of vermin called inger, 407

Berosus, his account of the creation of man, 3; on the flood, 48, 49, 56, 62

Bethel, Jacob at, 223 sqq.; the sanctuary at, 231; "the house of God," 237; the oak at, 334

Bethels in Canaan, 237

Beetsileo, their sacred stones, 236

Betsimisaraka, the, of Madagascar, their story of a cable between earth and heaven, 230

Beyrout, Old, haunted tree at, 328

Bhils of Central India; their story of a great flood, 79 sq.; their mode of life, 197; ultimogeniture among the, 198; their custom of torturing witches and shearing their hair, 272 sq.

Biestings, rules in regard to, 365

Bila-an, their story of the creation of man, 8

Bilaspore, India, weeping as a salutation in 241; still-born children buried in the doorway in, 320

Birs-Nimrud, ruined temple at Borsippa, 145

Birth, supernatural, in legend, 268

——, the new, among the Akikuyu, 207 sqq., 215, 216; rite of, 216; fiction of, at adoption, 216 sq.; fiction of, enacted by Brahman householder, 219; fiction of, as expiation for breach of custom, 219; enacted by Maharajahs of Travancore, 220 sqq. See also Born again

Birth ceremonies among the Patagonian Indians, 165

Bisection, of sacrifical victims at covenants, oaths, and purifications, 154, 155 sq., 157, 158 sq., 162 sqq.; of human victims, 166 sqq.

Bishnois bury dead infants at the threshold, 320

Bismarck Archipelago, story of the origin of death in the, 26

Bison, sacrificial, in oath of friendship, 161

Bitch as wife of man, 109

Bittern in flood story, 122

Black antelope skin, in fiction of new birth, 219

—— beans offered to ghosts at Rome, 418

—— bull sacrificed to the dead, 299

—— lamb sacrificed at evocation of ghosts, 301

—— ram as sacrificial victim, 212, 213; its skin used to sleep on, 228

—— Sea, flood said to have been caused by the bursting of the, 74 sq.

—— stone at Mecca, 231

—— stones anointed, 236; in Iona, used to swear on, 248

Blackening the face in mourning, 381, 389, 391, 393

—— faces or bodies of man-slayers, 43 sq.

Blackfoot Indians, their story of a great flood, 120

Blackstone, Sir William, on ultimogeniture, 179, 203; on mercheta, 179; on the law of deodand, 416

Blessing of Isaac, how secured by Jacob, 204 sqq.

Blood, of gods used in creation of man, 3; of murdered man cries for vengeance, 34; of murdered man supposed to poison the ground, 34; given to ghosts to drink, 297; of sheep on threshold, bride stepping over, at entering her new home, 321 sq.; offered to the dead, 380, 385, 392 sq., 394, 395, 396; of mourners allowed to drip on corpses, 385, 392 sq., 394; of friends drunk by youths at initiation, 396; of friends drunk by sick or weak persons, 396; offered to ghosts to strengthen them, 396.

Blood covenant, 164, 165 sq., 168; with the dead, theory of a, 395

Blood revenge, the law of, revealed to Noah, 398

—— -wit, custom of the Yabim in regard to, 40

Bloody sacrifices to sacred trees, 332 sq.

Bludan, village near Damascus, 324

Blue River, modern name of the Jabbok, 251

Boar, use of, in oaths, 154 sq., 159

Bobos of Senegal, their customs in regard to bloodshed and homicide, 37

Bocca di Cattaro, custom in regard to bride crossing the threshold on the, 317

Bodies of dead dried over a slow fire, 391

Boeotia, form of public purification in, 162

Bogos, their mode of life, 201; their rules of succession, 201 sq.; their custom of swearing on a stone, 248; kill cattle that have killed persons, 400; bells rung to frighten away evil spirits from women after childbirth among the, 434

Böhmerwald Mountains, the Passing Bell in the, 421

Boiling the milk supposed to injure the cows, 364 sqq.

Bokor, a creator, 6

Bolivia, a story of a great flood in, 106 sq.

Boloki, or Bangala, of the Upper Congo, their custom in regard to homicide, 39; their dislike to counting their children, 308

Bombay, Presidency, sacred stones in the, 236

Bone, woman created out of a man's bone, 5

Bones of dead deposited in trees, 344 sq.; ghost supposed to linger while flesh adheres to his, 348

Boni or Bone, in Celebes, evil spirits kept from women in childbed by clash of metal instruments in, 436

Bonnach stone in Celtic story, 277

Book of the Covenant, 353, 354, 361, 397

Borâna Gallas. See Gallas

Born again, ceremony of being, among the Akikuyu, 206; persons supposed to have died pretend to be, 218 sq.; from a cow, ceremony of being, 220

"Born of a goat," ceremony among the Akikuyu, 207, 223

Borneo, the Dyaks of, 7; stories of a great flood in, 84 sq.; form of adoption in, 217; the Kayans of, 304, 342; the use of gongs, bells, and other metal instruments at exorcisms in, 431 sq.

Bornholm, privilege of the youngest son in, 178

Borough English, 175 sq., 185; Sir William Blacksone on, 179

Borsippa, ruins of Birs-Nimrud at, 145

Bosphorus, flood said to have been caused by the opening of the, 74 sq.

Boulia district of Queensland, mourning custom in the, 391
Boundary stones, Roman law concerning the removal of, 403
Bouranton, the inhabitants of, prosecute rats and mice, 411
Bourke, John G., on the exorcism of witches by bells among the Pueblo Indians, 429
Bowditch Island, story of the creation of man in, 5
Box, soul caught in a, 289
Boy and girl cut in two at making a covenant, 170 sq.
Brabant, ultimogeniture in, 177
Brahman householder, his fiction of a new birth, 219
—— marriage ceremony, use of a stone in, 247
Brahmaputra, its valley a line of migration, 194
Brahuis of Baluchistan, their custom of making a bride step over blood on threshold of her new home, 321
Brazil, stories of a great flood among the Indians of, 97 sqq.; the Tupi Indians of, 241
Breach of treaty, mode of expiating, 157
Bret Harte, on the Angelus, 421 sq.
Bride, carried over threshold, 316 sqq., 319; stepping over blood of sheep at threshold of her husband's house, 321 sq.
Bride-capture, supposed relic of, 318
Bridegroom carried over threshold at marriage, 318
British Central Africa, the Atonga of, 317
—— Columbia, story of a great flood in, 125 sq.; Indians of, their objection to a census, 310; silence of widows and widowers among the Indians of, 344
Brittany, ultimogeniture in, 177
Bronze, the clash of, used to drive away spirits, 418
Bronze Age, 67
—— weapons in Palestine, 167
Brothers, younger, of dead man, in special relation to his widow, 345 sq., 348
Brown, Dr. George, on the "offering of blood" in mourning, 389
Brutus, D. Junius, his exhibition of gladiators, 387
Buckland, William, on evidence of a universal deluge, 136
Budde, Professor K., on the original Ten Commandments, 362
Buddha, bells in the worship of, 430
Bulgaria, form of adoption in, 217
Bulgaria, their superstition as to boiling milk, 367
Bull, its use in oaths, 154; sacrificed to river, 253 sq.; sacrificed to the dead, 299; mad, tried and hanged, 413 sq.

Bull dance, 114
Bullooms, their objection throw orange skins into the fire, 364, 365
Bundle of life, the, 283 sqq.
Bunyoro, cultivation avoided by pastoral people in, 374. See also Banyoro
Burckhardt, J. L., on relations of grown-up sons to their father among the Bedouins, 203
Burial of the dead at doorway of house, 320
Burma, the Karens of, their version of the creation of man, 6; stories of a great flood in, 81 sq.; story like that of the Tower of Babel in, 150; capital of, rendered impregnable by human sacrifices, 168; bells in religious rites in, 430; the Kachins of, 435
Burton Gulf, in Lake Tanganyika, women in childbed protected from evil spirit by natives of, 436
Bushmen, their stories of the origin of death, 20 sq., 22
Bush-turkey, why it has red wattles, 103
Busoga in Central Africa, worship of rocks and stones in, 234
Butm tree, the terebinth, 329
Butter, an ogre whose soul was made of, 280
Bworana Gallas, ceremony at attainment of majority among the, 210
Byron on the vesper bell, 421

Cable connecting earth and heaven, 230
Cain, the mark of, 33 sqq.
Caingangs, or Coroados, their story of a great flood, 98 sq.
Cairn, the covenant on the, 243 sqq.; personified as guarantor of covenant, 246
Cairns as witnesses in Syria, 250
Calabars, the New, their ceremonies at peace-making, 158 sq.
Calchas, the soothsayer, 154; his dream oracle, 228
California, stories of the creation of man in, 11; stories of a great flood in, 111 sq.; the Maidu Indians of, 152
Californian Indians, silence of widows among the, 344; laceration of the body in mourning among the, 382
Caliphs of Baghdad, reverence for the threshold of their palace, 314 sq.
Callirrhoe, the modern Zerka Ma'in, in Moab, 246, 247
Caloto in South America, its church bell famous for driving away thunder-storms, 426 sq.
Calves, abortive, buried under the threshold of the cowhouse, 321
——, golden worship of, 231
Calves of the legs, birth from, in legend, 83
Cames, Brazilian Indians, 98, 99
Canaanite race, 167

Canaanite sanctuaries, sacred stones at, 231, 237

Canada, the Indians of, stories of a great flood among, 115

Canal system in Babylonia, 140

Cañaris of Ecuador, their story of a great flood. 104

Canoes kept ready against a flood, 91, 139

Canon, completion of the, 355

Canton, necromancy at, 306; custom of handing a bride over a charcoal fire at, 317

Capitoline Museum, bronze statue of wolf in the, 265

Captivity, the Babylonian, 57, 338, 358, 360

Capturing wives, supposed relic of a custom of. 318

Caracalla evokes the ghosts of Severus and Commodus, 301

Carayas of Brazil, their story of a great flood, 99 sq.

Carmel, Mount, its oak woods, 323; Elijah's sacrifice for rain on, 340

Caroline Islands, story of the origin of death in the, 29

Carpini, Plano, as to touching the threshold of a Tartar prince, 314

Cassel, ultimogeniture in districts about, 177

Cast skin, story of the, 26 sqq., 31 sqq.

Castle of Oblivion, 250

Cat killed at peace-making, 158

Caterpillars, lawsuits against, 408 sq.

Catholic Church, its authority to exorcise animals, 403

Catlin, George, on the Mandan story of the great flood, 113; on stories of a great flood among the American Indians, 114

Cattle, unlucky to count, 308, 309, 311, 313; killed for killing people, 399. See also Cow, Cows

Caucasus, the Albanians of the, 162; mourning customs in the, 381; the Mingrelians of the, 381; the Ossetes of the, 381

Cayurucres, Brazilian Indians, 98, 99

Cayuses, their story of a great flood, 126

Celebes, story of the creation of man in, 6; stories of the origin of death in, 26, 29; story of a great flood in, 86; the Toradjas of, 229, 230, 256, 257, 289, 300, 304, 365, 399; woman's soul at childbirth stowed away for safety in, 286

——, Minahassa, a district of, 286

Celtic parallels to the story of Samson and Delilah, 277 sq.

Celts, the ancient, said to have attacked the waves of the sea, 257; said to have tested the legitimacy of their children by throwing them into the Rhine, 269

Census, the sin of a, 307 sqq.; superstitious objections to, 308, 310, 311, 312; permitted by Jewish legislator on payment of half a shekel a head, 313

Central America, stories of a great flood in. 107 sqq.

Centralization of the worship at the one sanctuary, its theoretical inadequacy and practical inconvenience, 357

Cephissus, the Boeotian, 4

Ceram, belief in, as to a person's strength being in his hair, 272

Ceremonial institutions of Israel, their great antiquity, 352

—— use of rings made from skins of sacrificial animals in East Africa, 207 sq.

Chaco, the Lenguas of the, 242

Chaeronean plain, 4

Chaibasa (Chaibassa), in India, 196, 197

Chameleon charged with message of immortality to men, 25; hated and killed by some African tribes, 25 sq.

—— and lizard, story of the, 25

Chasseneux, or Chassenée, Bartholomew de, his defence of rats, 406

Chauhans of India, weeping as a salutation among the, 241

Cheremiss, their story of the creation of man, 10; their sacred groves, 342

Cherokee Indians, their story of a great flood, 114 sq.; their reasons for cuting out the hamstrings of deer, 257; their unwillingness to count fruit, 310

Chief of the Earth, a priest in Upper Senegal, 37

Chiefs, ghosts of dead, consulted as oracles in Africa, 301 sq.

Chieftanship, descent of, regulated by primogeniture, 197

Childbirth, protection of women after, 163; ceremonies to facilitate, 169; woman's soul extracted and stowed away for safety at, 286; women at, protected from demons by bells, armed men, etc., 434 sqq.

Childless women, stones anointed by, in order to procure offspring, 236

Children, their souls stowed away foi safety in receptacles, 286; superstitious dislike of counting, 308; buried under the threshold to ensure their rebirth, 320; sacrificed to Moloch, 332

Chili, story of a great flood in, 101

China, Nestorian Christianity in, 84; the Kachins of, 186; the Shans of, 188; migration of Mongoloid tribes from, 194; necromancy and evocation of the dead in, 305 sqq.; the use of gongs at exorcisms in, 428, 430

——, South-western, ultimogeniture in, 180

Chinese have no tradition of a universal flood, 131; their precautions to prevent bride's feet from touching the threshold, 316

Chinese Encyclopedia, 84

Chingpaws. *See* Singphos, Kachins

Chinigchinich. a Californian deity, 11

Chinook Indians, customs observed by manslayers among the, 43; their mourning customs, 382

Chins, their ceremony at taking an oath of friendship, 160 *sq.*; their sacrifice of a dog in time of cholera, 163; their personification of cholera, 163; ultimogeniture among the, 189

Chiowotmahke, a creator, 111

Chippeway or Salteaux Indians, their story of a great flood, 116 *sqq.*

Chiriguanos of Bolivia, their story of a great flood, 106 *sq.*

Chittagong, the Kumis of, 9; the Kookies or Kukis of, 398

Cholera personified, 163

Cholula, in Mexico, the pyramid at, 148; story like that of the Tower of Babel told concerning, 149

Chota Nagpur, 10, 195, 196; the Mundas of, 340

Christianity, Nestorian, in China, 84

Chukchee, their fire-boards, 200; ultimogeniture among the, 201

Church bells, rung to drive away thunderstorms, 418 *sq.*, 424 *sq.*; used to drive away evil spirits, 418 *sqq.*; rung to drive away witches and wizards, 422 *sq.*; the consecration of, 425 *sq.*

Churinga, sacred sticks and stones of the Central Australian aborigines, 286 *sq.*

Cinnamomum cassia, 187
—— caudatum, 187

Circumcision among the Akikuyu and Wachaga, 210; among the Nandi, 437

Clavigero, F. S., on Mexican story of a great flood, 107

Clay, men fashioned out of, 4 *sqq.*; bodies of manslayers coated with, 42; daubed on bodies of mourners, 383, 384, 390, 393
——, white, smeared on body in sign of mourning, 345, 347

Clean and unclean animals in the ark, 61; suggested explanation of the Hebrew distinction between, 376

Cleomenes, king of Sparta, his sacrifices to a river and the sea, 253

Cleonice, her ghost evoked by Pausanias, 298

Cleveland district of Yorkshire, burial of abortive calves under the threshold in the, 320 *sq.*

Cochin China, the Bahnars of, 30; story of a great flood in, 82

Cock, sacrifice of, after childbirth, 163; tried and executed for laying an egg, 414

Cock's eggs, their value in magic, 414

Cockle married by raven, 125

Coco-nut oil, used in divination, 260

Code of Napoleon, 351

Codification and legislation distinguished, 350

Coffee-grounds, divination by, 261

Coire, lawsuit brought against Spanish flies by the inhabitants of, 408

Cologne, Provincial Council of, on the spiritual power of bells, 418

Columbia River, 127, 382

Comanches, their mourning customs, 383

Commodus, his ghost evoked by Caracalla, 301

Communal houses, 186
—— ownership of land among the Kachins, 185

Concubinage with tenant's wife, supposed right of, 179

Conder, Captain C. R., as to unluckiness of treading on a threshold, 313; on the shrines (*Mukâms*) of Mohammedan saints in Syria, 325 *sq.*

Confession of sins at crossing a river, 256

Confusion of tongues, stories of the, 144, 149 *sqq.*

Congo, story of the origin of death among the Upotos of the, 30; bells rung to prevent demons from entering the body at drinking in the region of the, 437
——, the Lower, tradition of a great flood on, 129
—— the Upper, 39

Congo peoples, their aversion to count or being counted, 308

Consecration of church bells, 425

Constance, church bells run during thunderstorms at, 425

Constantine, the Emperor, his church at the oak of Mamre, 335; his letter to Eusebius, 335 *sq.*

Continence at religious festival, 336

Copaic Lake, 4; its annual vicissitudes, 71 *sq.*

Copts, their custom of making a bride step over sheep's blood on entering her new home, 322

Cora Indians, their story of a great flood, 109 *sq.*

Cornwall, Borough English in, 176

Coroadas. *See* Caingangs

Counting grain, modes of, in Algeria and Palestine, 310
—— people or things, superstitious aversion to, 308 *sqq.*

Covenant, ratified by cutting sacrificial victim in two, 154 *sqq.*
—— of Abraham, 153
——, the Book of the, 353, 354, 361, 397
—— on the cairn, 243 *sqq.*

Covenants, use of sacrificial skins at, 211 sq.

Cow, ceremony of being born again from a, 220

——, golden or bronze, in fiction of new birth, 220

Cows, supposed to be injured by the boiling of their milk, 364 sqq.; believed to be injured if their milk is brought into contact with flesh or vegetables, 370 sqq.

Coyote, in story of the creation of man, 12; prophesies of the coming of a great flood, 110; in story of great flood, 126

Crab in story of a great flood, 82

Crabs in story of the origin of death, 27; supposed to renew their youth by casting their skins, 27 sq.

Crantz, D., on Greenlanders' story of a great flood, 128

Creation of man, 1 sqq.

Creator in the shape of a beetle, 14

Creeper connecting earth and heaven, 229

Crees, or Knisteneaux, their story of a great flood, 116, 121; their mourning customs, 381

Cronus, warns Xisuthrus that all men would be destroyed by a flood, 48; his habit of devouring his offspring, 434

Crossing rivers, ceremonies at, 253 sqq.

—— the threshold right foot foremost, 317

Crow Indians, bodily lacerations of women in mourning among the, 383

Cultivation, the migratory system of, 180, 185 sq.; the permanent system of, 183, 184, 185 sq.

—— of rice, the dry system and the wet system of the, 185

Cumanus, his shaving of witches, 272

Cup, Joseph's, 258 sqq.; as instrument of divination, 258, 259

Cures revealed in dreams at sanctuaries, 225

Curetes protect the infant Zeus, 434, 437

Curfew bell, 421

Curses at concluding treaties, swearing allegiance, etc., 156, 158 sq.

Customary law in Israel, 354

"Cutting a covenant," "cutting oaths," 154

Cuttings of the body in mourning for the dead, 377 sqq.

Cynus, home of Deucalion, 67

Cyrus, his revenge on the river Gyndes, 256

Czaplicka, Miss M. A., on ultimogeniture in Russia, 178

Dacota Indians, their worship of stones, 234. See also Sioux

Daesius, Macedonian month, 48

Dagon, worshippers not to tread on the threshold of his temple, 313

Dalmatia, laceration of the face in mourning in, 380

Damaras (Hereros) refrain from cleansing their milk-vessels, 369

Damascus, 324

Dan, the ancient, 328

Dance, the Bull, 114

Danger Island, souls of sick people caught in snares in, 288 sq.

Dante on the vesper bell, 421

Dardanelles flood said to have been caused by the opening of the, 74 sq.

Dardania, or Troy, founded by Dardanus, 73

Dardanus, the great flood in his time, 70, 72, 73, 78; born at Phenus, 72; migrates to Samothrace, 72, 73; drifts to Mount Ida and founds Troy, 73

Darius, his ghost evoked by Atossa, 300

Darling River, mourning customs of the aborigines on the, 390, 392, 395, 396

Daughters preferred in inheritance under mother-kin, 191

—— of Jacob, oak spirits in Palestine, 323, 328

Daulis, its ruins, 4

David, King, a youngest son, 175; and Jonathan, their meeting, 239; and Abigail, 284; his sin in taking a census, 308

Dawson, Sir J. W., on flood story in Genesis, 136 sq.

Dead, ladders for the use of souls of the, 230; evocation of the, in ancient and modern times, 296 sqq.; oracles of the, 297, 301 sq.; represented by their images, which are employed at consulting their spirits, 303; buried at doorway of house, 320; sacrifices offered to the, on the threshold, 322; cuttings for the, 377 sq.; hair offered to the, 379 sq., 381, 383, 384, 385, 393, 394, 396 sq.; blood offered to the, 380, 385, 392 sq., 394, 395, 396; destroying the property of the 382; worship of the, 397

Dead, person supposed to have been, obliged to pretend to be born again, 218

Dead Sea, 283

Death, stories of the origin of, 20 sqq.

——, Water of, 50

Debata, a creator, 84

Deborah, Rebekah's nurse, buried under an oak, 334

Decalogue, the original, 360 sqq.; contrast between the ritual and the moral versions of the, 363; the moral, composed under prophetic influence, 363

Deer, the hamstrings of, cut out by some North American Indians, 257

Defoe, Daniel, on the angel of the plague, 308

Dejanira and Hercules, 253

Delaware Indians, their story of a great flood, 115

Delilah and Samson, 269 *sqq.*

Delphi, oracle at, 36, 218; the tripod at, 73; stone anointed at, 235

Delrio, Martin, on the consecration of church bells, 426

Demons repelled by armed men from women in childbed, 434 *sq.*

Déné tribes. *See* Tinnehs

Denmark, unlucky to count eggs, chickens, blossoms, and fruit in, 312

Deodand, English law of, 415 *sq.*

Derby, Borough English in, 176

Desauli, tutelary deity of Munda village, 341

Deucalion, his grave at Athens, 68; said to have founded the sanctuary and a commemorative service at Hierapolis on the Euphrates, 69 *sq.;* his flood associated with Thessaly, 76

—— and the flood, 67 *sqq.*

Deuteronomic Code, 353 *sqq.;* its prohibition of cuttings for the dead, 378

Deuteronomy, on the abolition of the "high places," 339, 354; date of, 356; ethical and religious character of, 356

Devon, Borough English in, 176

Dido, the mourning for, 380

Diegueño Indians of California, their story of the creation of man, 12

Dieri of Central Australia, silence of widows among the, 347

Diffusion of customs and beliefs, 47; geographical, of flood stories, 131 *sqq.*

Digest or *Pandects* of Justinian, 351

Dijon, trial and condemnation of a horse at, 413

Dillon, Captain P., on weeping as a salutation, 240

Diluvial traditions. *See* Flood

Dimas, son of Dardanus, 72

Diodorus Siculus on fiction of new birth at adoption, 216

Disguise against ghosts, 44

Divination, by a cup, 258 *sq.;* by water, 259; by ink, 260; by tea-leaves and coffee-grounds, 261; by molten lead or wax, 262

Diwata, a creator, 9

Dobu, homicides secluded in, 34 *sq.*

Dodona, sanctuary at, founded by Deucalion, 67

Dog, in stories of the creation of man, 9 *sq.;* brings message of mortality to man, 21; in story of the origin of death, 24; fortells a great flood, 114 *sq.;* sacrificial, in oaths of friendship, 155 *sq.,* 157, 161; sacrificial, used in rites of purification, 163; sacrificed in time of plague, 163. *See also* Dogs

Dogrib Indians, their story of a great flood, 121

Dogs, trial and punishment of, 400, 401, 414

Dolmens in Palestine, 346 *sq.*

Dooadlera, a creator, 6

Doorway of house, the dead buried at the, 320; the afterbirth buried at the. 320

Dorsetshire, divination by water in, 261

Douai, ultimogeniture in districts about, 177

Dove let out of ark, 52, 66, 70, 116, 130, 131

Dragon whose strength was in a pigeon, story of, 276 *sq.*

Dream, Jacob's, 223 *sqq.*

Dreams of the gods, 225 *sqq.*

Drinking, demons supposed to enter the body at, 437

—— out of a skull as a mode of inspiration, 302

Drium in Apulia, dream oracle of Calchas at, 228

Drowning, mode of avenging a death by, 256

Drowning man, fear to save a, 254

Druidical grove at Marseilles, 333

Drums beaten to drive away storm-spirits, 428; to keep demons from women in childbed. 436

Du Halde on ultimogeniture among the Tartars, 179, 180

Du Pratz, Le Page, on the Natchez story of the creation of man, 13; his account of the Natchez story of the flood, 112

Duck in story of a great flood, 123

Du-mu, the hero of the Lolo flood story, 83

Dunbar, Dr. William, on rules of inheritance among the Coles (Kols), 197

Dungi, king of Ur or Uru. 146

Duran, Diego, on a Mexican story like that of the Tower of Babel, 149

Durandus, G., on the virtue of church bells, 418, 419

Dusuns of British North Borneo their story of the origin of death, 26; their use of bells and other metal instruments to drive away evil spirits 432

Dyak stories of a great flood, 85 *sq.*

Dyaks of Borneo, their story of the creation of man, 7

—— of Dutch Borneo, beat gongs while a corpse is in the house, 431. *See also* Borneo, Sea Dyaks

Ea, Babylonian god of wisdom, 51, 53, 55, 56; a water deity, represented partly in fish form. 134

Eabani, the ghost of, called up by Gilgamesh, 296

Eagle foretells a great flood, 111

Eagles supposed to renew their youth, 18

Ear, of goat, rings made out of, 214

Earth, polluted by bloodshed, 36

Earth, chief of the, title of a priest, 37
——, Olympian, her precinct at Athens, 68
—— worshipped by tribes of Upper Senegal, 37
Earth-Initiate, a Californian creator, 11
——, the Maidu creator, 152
Earth-spirits, in rocks and stones, 233
Earthquake waves as causes of great floods, 139
Eating food on stones, magical effect of, 247
Ecclesiastical courts, their jurisdiction over wild animals, 403 sqq.
Echinadian Islands, Alcmaeon in the, 36
Ecuador, stories of a great flood in, 100, 104 sq.
Eden, the Garden of, 15 sq.
Egg, life of a wizard in an, 275 sq., 278
Egypt, absence of flood stories in, 129; modern, divination by water or ink in, 259 sq.; custom of bride stepping over blood on the threshold in, 322
Egyptian kings, ladders for the use of dead, 230
—— notion of the creation of man, 3
—— priests on deluges, 67
Eifel Mountains, the Benedictus bell in the, 420
Elgon, Mount, 38, 155
Elijah on Mount Horeb, God's revelation of himself to, 253; his sacrifice for rain on Mount Carmel, 340
Eliot, John, on ultimogeniture among the Garos, 194
Elisha and the child of the Shunammite, 3
Ellis, William, on Tahitian story of the creation, 5; on Polynesian flood stories, 94, 135
Elohim, the divine name in Hebrew, 60
Elohistic Document, 353
Elysius, his consultation of an oracle of the dead, 299
Encounter Bay tribe of South Australia, their story as to the origin of languages, 151 sq.
Endor, the witch of, 291 sqq.; the village of, 293
Engano, island, story of a great flood in, 84 sq.
Engedi, the springs of, 284
England, ultimogeniture in, 175; divination by tea-leaves and coffee-grounds in, 261; superstitious objection to count lambs in, 312
English law of deodand, 415 sq.
Enki, Sumerian god, 55, 56
Enlil, Babylonian god, 51, 53, 54, 55, 56
Enygrus, a kind of snake, thought to be immortal, 26
Ephraim, the lowlands of, 225
Ephraim and Manasseh, Jacob's blessing of, 174

Epidaurus, cures effected in dreams at the sanctuary of Aesculapius at, 226 sqq.
Epimetheus, 67
Erasinus, the river, sacrifice to, 253
Eriphyle and Alcmaeon, 36
Erythrina tomentosa, 213
E-sagil, or Esagila, temple at Babylon, 145
Esau defrauded by Jacob, 172 sq., 223
Eskimo of Alaska, their story of the creation of man, 11; their custom as to manslayers, 43; stories of a great flood among the, 128 sq.; divination by water among the, 260; their belief that human souls can be extracted by photography, 285; souls of sick children stowed away in medicine bag among the, 286; necromancy among the, 305; their objection to boil water during the salmon fishery, 368
—— of Labrador, necromancy among the, 305
Esthonians, their superstition as to boiling milk, 367
Ethiopian race of East Africa, 206
—— and Semitic usage, similarities of, 206 sq.
Euphrates, bull sacrificed to the, 253 sq.
Europe, ultimogeniture in, 175 sqq.; divination by molten lead or wax in, 262; belief in, that the power of witches and wizards resided in their hair, 272; superstition as to boiling milk in, 367; trial and punishment of animals in, 403 sqq.
Eurydice and Orpheus, 297
Eusebius on the dates of the floods of Ogyges and Deucalion, 71; on the terebinth at Hebron, 335; letter of Constantine to, 335; on the oak of Mamre, 336
Eusthathius on the terebinth of Mamre, 334
Eve, the Polynesian, 5
Evergreen oak in Palestine, 322 sq.
Evocation of the dead in ancient and modern times, 296 sqq.; by means of familiar spirits, 307
Ewe-speaking tribes of Togo-land, their story of the creation of man, 11; evocation of the dead among the, 302 sq.
Execution of animals, 397, 399, 400, 402, 412 sqq.
Exorcism of wild animals by the Catholic Church, 403 sqq.
——, bells used in, 418 sqq., 422 sqq., 427 sqq.
Expiation for homicide, 38 sqq.; for breach of treaty, 157; for breach of custom by fiction of new birth, 219 sq.
Expiations, use of skins of sacrificial victims at, 214
Exposure of famous persons in their infancy, legends of, 265 sqq.

Expulsion of ghosts of slain, 44
——, annual, of witches and wizards, 423; annual, of evil spirits, 432
Ezekiel, his denunciation of the women who hunted for souls, 288; on the worship of trees, 332; on the worship at "high places," 338 sq.; his proposed reforms, 359 sq.; on rites of mourning, 378
E-zida, ruined Babylonian temple at Borsippa, 145
Ezra, his promulgation of the Levitical law, 360

Fairies supposed to eat cakes that have been counted, 312
Fakaofor or Bowditch Island, story of the creation of man in, 5
Falaise, in Normandy, execution of a sow in, 413
Fall of man, 15 sqq.
Falls of the Nile, sacrifice of kids at the, 254
Familiar spirits, evocation of the dead by means of, 307
Fans of West Africa, their story of the creation of man, 11; bells worn by witch-doctors among the, 438
Faunus, oracle of, 228; caught by Numa, 253
Faust and Mephistopheles in the prison, 252
Fear of ghosts, 343, 347, 393 sq.
Fellaheen of Palestine, 167
Fernando Po, story of heavenly ladder in, 229
Festival, annual, at the Oak of Mamre, 336
—— of the Water-bearing at Athens, 68
Feuerbach, Renan on, 422
Fiction of new birth, in early law, 216 sq.; enacted by persons supposed to have died, 218; enacted by Brahman householder, 219; an expiation for breach of custom, 219; enacted by Maharajahs of Travancore, 220 sqq.
Field-mice, lawsuit against, 406
Fights of subjects at death of king, 387
Fig-tree in legend, 229
——, sacred, 38, 230
Fiji, treatment of manslayers in, 44; foundation sacrifices in, 169 sq.
Fijian chiefs, reverence for the thresholds of, 315
—— practice of catching souls of criminals in scarves, 288
Fijians, their story of the origin of death, 30; their expulsion of ghosts, 44; their story of a great flood, 90 sq.; kept canoes ready against a flood, 91, 139
Fillets used to catch souls, 288
Finow, king of Tonga, the mourning for, 388 sq.

Fire, how it was obtained after the flood, 85, 87 sq., 107; how fire was discovered by the friction of a creeper on a tree, 85
——, charcoal, custom of carrying bride into house over a, 317
Fire-boards held sacred, 200, 201
—— -wark among the Badagas, 433
Fish, in ancient Indian story of a great flood, 78; in Bhil story of a great flood, 79; miraculous, in flood stories, 134; unlucky to count, 311; not to be eaten, 374, 375
Fisher-folk in Scotland, their aversion to counting or being counted, 311
Fladda, one of the Hebrides, blue stone on which oaths were taken in, 248
Flathead Indians, their story of a great flood, 126; their bodily lacerations in mourning, 382
Flesh not to be brought into contact with milk, 370
Flies excommunicated by St. Bernard, 403
Flint knife used in sacrifice, 159
Flood, the Great, 46 sqq.
——, annual commemoration of the, 113
——, Babylonian story of, 48 sqq.;
Hebrew story of, 56 sqq.; discrepancy as to the duration of the, 61; ancient Greek stories of a great, 66 sqq.; shells and fossils as arguments in favour of a great, 71, 86, 128, 135; ancient Indian stories of a great, 78 sq.; modern Indian stories of a great, 79 sqq.
——, Song of the, 112
——, stories of a great, in Eastern Asia, 81 sqq.; in Australia, 88 sq.; in New Guinea and Melenesia, 89 sqq.; in Polynesia and Micronesia, 91 sqq.; in South America, 97 sqq.; in Central America and Mexico, 107 sqq.; in North America, 110 sqq.; in Africa, 129 sqq.; the geographical diffusion of, 131 sqq.; their relation to each other, 132 sqq.; their origin, 135 sqq.; partly legendary, partly mythical, 142
Floods caused by risings of the sea, 139; caused by heavy rains, 140 sq.
Folk-lore, in relation to the poets, 291; the emotional basis of, 422
Fontenay-aux-Roses, execution of a sow at, 413
Forbes, James, on fiction of new birth at Travancore, 221
Fords, water-spirits propitated at, 253 sq.
Fossil shells as evidence of the Noachian deluge, 71, 135 sq.
Fossils, marine, as evidence of great flood, 135, 136, 142
Foundation sacrifices among the Fijians, 169 sq.

Fracastoro, Girolamo, on evidence for a great flood drawn from sea-shells, 136

France, ultimogeniture in, 176 sq.; the shaving of witches in, 272; bride carried over the threshold in, 318; before the Revolution, local systems of law in, 351; trial and punishment of animals in, 403; church bells rung to drive away witches, 423

Friars Minor, in Brazil, their prosecution of ants, 410

Friesland, ultimogeniture in, 177

Frog in story of the origin of death, 24; great flood caused by a, 89

Froude, J. A., on the sound of church bells, 421

Fruits, mankind created afresh from, after the flood, 104

Fuegians, their story of a great flood, 107; their mourning customs, 384

Funerals, gladiatorial combats at, 387; metal instruments beaten at, 431

Furies, the sanctuary of the, 218; Nero haunted by the, 301

Gaboon, the Fans of the, 438

Gadarene swine, the case of the, 414

Gaidoz, M., on old people and their ages, 312

Gaikhos, their story like that of the Tower of Babel, 150

Galelareeze of Halmahera, their offering of hair to the dead, 385

Gall used to anoint manslayers, 41

Gallas of East Africa, their story of the origin of death, 31; their ethnical affinity, 206; their ceremony at adoption, 207; think it unlucky to count cattle, 309; their sacrifices to trees, 332; their objection to boil milk, 366; bells carried by priests and exorcists among the, 438

——, the Borâna, paint the faces of manslayers, 42

Gallinomeras, their mourning customs, 382

Game not eaten by pastoral people, 374 sq.; abundant in Masai country, 375

Gangamma, river god of the Badagas, 255

Garos of Assam, their Mongolian origin, 192; their husbandry, 192 sq.; their villages, 193; their mother-kin, 193; ultimogeniture among the, 194; their divination by water, 261

Gazelle Peninsula in New Britain, 32

Genesis, the account of the creation of man in, 1 sqq.; story of the Fall of Man in, 15 sqq.; the narrative of the flood in. 60

Geographical diffusion of flood stories, 131 sqq.

Geology and the stories of the great flood, 74 sq., 137

Georgia, Transcaucasian province, ultimogeniture in, 199

German belief about counting money, 312

—— superstition as to crossing the threshold, 319

Germany, ultimogeniture in, 177 sq.; church bells rung during thunderstorms in, 424 sq.

Gesture language employed by women after a death in Australia, 347

Gezer, in Palestine, human sacrifices at, 166 sqq.; sacred pillars at, 237

Ghost of murdered man or woman thought to haunt the murderer, 36, 38 sqq.; of husband, supposed to linger while flesh adheres to his bones, 348

Ghost-houses on bank of river, 255

Ghosts, disguises against, 44, 393; as causes of sickness, 213; troublesome, how disposed of, 213 sq.; given blood to drink, 297; fear of 343, 347, 393 sq.; certain mourning customs designed to propitiate the, 394 sq.; strengthened by drinking blood, 396

—— of slain animals supposed to avenge breaches of oaths, 161; of dead kings consulted as oracles in Africa, 301 sq.

—— of the slain, precautions taken by slayers against the, 41 sqq.; driven away, 44

Gibraltar, the Straits of, 75

Gideon, his interview with the angel, 333

Gilead, the wooded mountains of, 244, 251; rude stone monuments in, 246

Gilgamesh and the plant that renewed youth, 18 sq.; learns the story of the great flood from Ut-napishtim, 50 sq.

Gilgamesh epic, 18, 50; necromancy in the, 296

Gilgit, its situation and rulers, 267; an ogre king of, whose soul was made of butter, 279; annual festival of fire at, 281

Gillen, F. J. See Spencer, Sir Baldwin ..

Gipsies of Transylvania, their way of protecting women after childbirth, 163

Gladiatorial combats at Roman funerals, 387

Gloucester, Borough English in, 176

Goat brings message of immortality to men, 23, 24; cut in pieces at oath of fealty, 159 sq.; skin of sacrificial, used in ritual, 207 sq.; ceremony of being born from a, 7 sq., 223

Goat-skin in ritual, use of, 39, 41, 42

God's message of immortality to men, 23; revelation of himself to Elijah on Mount Horeb, 253

Gods, dreams of the, 225 sqq.

Goethe, on the original Ten Commandments, 360

Gold Coast, story of the origin of death told by the negroes of the, 23
Golden bells, the, 417
—— calves, worship of the, 231
—— cow in fiction of new birth, 220 sqq.
—— hair, a person's life of strength said to be in, 274
Golden Legend, The, on the virtue of church bells, 419
Gonds of India, 433, 434
Gongs, the use of, at exorcisms in China, 428 sq., 430; in Borneo, 431 sq.
—— beaten while corpse is in house, 431
Goniocephalus, 26
Goropius on the language of Paradise, 147
Grain, modes of counting, in Algeria and Palestine, 310
Grass or sticks offered at crossing rivers, 254
Grave, ceremony at, for disposing of troublesome ghost, 213; hair of mourners offered at, 379, 384, 393, 394
Graves, ladders placed in, 230; oracular dreams on 299 sq.
Gray, Archdeacon J. H., 306; on the evocation of the dead in China, 307
——, Thomas, on the curfew bells, 421
Great men, the need of them as leaders, 352 sq.
Greece, ancient, the fiction of a new birth in, 218; mourning customs in, 379 sq.
——, modern, bride not to touch the threshold in, 317
Greek flood stories not derived from Babylonian, 133
—— legend of the creation of man, 3
—— mode of ratifying oaths, 154
—— stories, ancient, of a great flood, 66 sqq.
—— superstition about counting warts, 312
—— tales of persons whose life or strength was in their hair, 274
Greeks, the ancient, their notion of the pollution of the earth by bloodshed, 36; their belief as to the ghosts of the slain, 38; their legend as to the origin and diversity of languages, 150 sq.; their worship of stones, 231 sq., 235; necromancy among the, 296 sqq.
—— and Trojans, their ceremonies at making a truce, 159
Greenlanders, their story of a great flood, 128 sq.
Grey, Lady Catherine, in the Tower, 420
——, Sir George, on the mourning customs of the Australian aborigines, 393
Griffon vulture, the great, 378
Grisons, ultimogeniture in the, 178
Grose, Captain Francis, on the Passing Bell, 418 sq.

Groves, sacred, the last relics of ancient forests, 339 sqq.
Growth of law, 350 sq.
Gruagach stones in the Highlands of Scotland, 235
Guancas, Peruvian Indians, their story of a great flood, 106
Guatemala, the Quiches of, 152
Guiana, British, story of the origin of death in, 27; stories of a great flood in, 101 sqq.
Guinea, tradition of a great deluge in, 129
Gyndes River punished by Cyrus, 256

Hadendoa, their objection to boil milk, 367
Haida Indians of Queen Charlotte Islands, their story of a great flood, 125
Hainault, ultimogeniture in, 177
Hair, the strength of people supposed to be in their, 272; cut in mourning for the dead, 377 sqq., 382, 383 sqq.; offered to the dead, 380, 381, 382, 383, 384, 385, 386, 393, 394, 397; of mourners offered at grave, or buried with the corpse, 379 sq., 381, 383, 384, 393, 394; of mourners thrown on the corpse, 384; of the dead worn by surviving relatives, 391; of mourners applied to corpse, 393, 394
Haka Chins, ultimogeniture among the, 189
Hakkas, their custom of handling a bride over the threshold, 316
Hale, Horatio, on Fijian story of a great flood, 139
Half skeletons of human victims at Gezer, 166, 167, 168, 169, 170, 171
Hall, C. F., on Eskimo story of a great flood, 129
Hamlet and the ghost, 252
Hammer, smith's thought to be endowed with magical virtue, 214
Hammurabi, king of Babylon, 54; the code of, 351
Hampshire, Borough English in, 175
Hamstrings of deer cut and thrown away by North American Indians, 257
Happy hunting grounds, 383
Hare brings message of mortality to men, 20, 22; origin of the, 21; and insect, story of, 22; and tortoise, story of, 22
Hareskin Indians, their story of a great flood, 121
Harlequins of history, 282
Hausas of North Africa, the, 25
Hawaii, stories of a great flood in, 94; lacerations of the body in mourning in, 387
Heap of Witness, 245, 246
Heaven and earth, stories of former connexions between, 228 sqq.

Heavenly ladder, 228 *sqq.*

Hebrew supposed to be the primitive language of mankind, 147

Hebrew distinction of clean and unclean animals, suggested explanation of, 376

—— mode of ratifying a covenant, 154

—— prophets denounce the worship of trees, 332 *sq.*, 338 *sq.*

—— story of the flood, 56 *sqq.*; its composite character, 60; compared with the Babylonian, 62 *sqq.*, 133; later Jewish additions to, 64 *sqq.*

—— usages in regard to milk and flesh diet, their origin in pastoral stage of society, 372, 376 *sq.*

—— words for oak, 331

Hebrews, the ancient, their lack of a sense of natural laws, 359

Hebron, 333, 334, 336, 337

Heidelberg, opinion of the doctors of, on a case of exorcism, 408

Heirship of Jacob, 172 *sqq.*

Helen, the suitors of, how they were sworn, 154

Helicon, Mount, 4

Hellanicus, on Deucalion's flood, 67

Hellas, ancient, 67

Hellespont punished by Xerxes, 256

Hen, sacrifice of, after childbirth, 163

Henry, A., 84

Hera, Greek name for Astarte at Hierapolis, 69; her adoption of Hercules, 216

Heraclea, in Bithynia, oracle of the dead at, 298

Hercules, carries off tripod from Delphi, 73; and the creation of the gorge of Tempe, 76; his oaths with the sons of Neleus, 155; ceremony of his adoption by Hera, 216; his wrestling with Achelous for Dejanira, 253

Herdsmen not allowed to eat vegetables, 373

Herero, disguise against ghosts among the, 44; refrain from cleansing their milk-vessels, 369

Hermes, 67; said to have introduced the diversity of languages, 151

Herodotus on the draining of Thessaly through Tempe, 76

Herrera, A. de, on the flood stories of the Peruvian Indians, 106

Herrick, on the bell-man, 423

Hervey Islands, mourning customs in the, 389

Herzegovina, custom in regard to bride crossing the threshold in, 317

Heshbon, 246

Hesiod on ceremony to be observed at crossing a river, 253

Hexateuch, the, 57

Hide of ox in oaths, 155

Hieraoplis, on the Euphrates, 68; the sanctuary at, said to have been founded by Deucalion, 69; the water of the flood said to have run away at, 69; ceremony commemorative of the flood at, 69; sacrifice of sheep at, 165

"High places" of Israel, 324 *sq.*; abolished, 338, 339, 354; denounced by Hebrew prophets, 338 *sq.*; Deuteronomy on, 339; still the seats of religious worship in Palestine, 339

Highlanders of Scotland, their Gruagach stones, 235

Highlands of Scotland, divination by tea-leaves in the, 261; unlucky to count people, cattle, or fish in the, 311

Hilprecht, H. V., 54

Hkamies. *See* Kamees

Hobley, C. W., 438; on Kikuyu rite of new birth, 208; on Kikuyu ceremony of adoption, 209 *sq.*

Holland, great floods in, 138 *sq.*

Hollis, A. C., on the Masai and Nandi, 206

Homer, on ceremony at truce, 159; the ghost of; evoked by Apion, 300; on the offering of hair to the dead, 380

Homicide purification for, 38, 41 *sq.*

Homicides shunned and secluded or banished, 34 *sq.*

Hooper, Lieutenant W. H., 116

Hopi or Moqui Indians of Arizona, their story of the creation of man, 13

Hor, Mount, the shrine of Aaron on, 250

Horace on the evocation of the dead by witches, 301

Horeb, Mount, God's revelation of himself to Elijah on, 253

Horse, its use in oaths, 154; tried and condemned, 413

Horses destroy first clay men, 9 *sq.*; white, sacrificed to river, 253; of dead man killed, 383; tails and manes of, cut off in mourning, 383

Hos or Larka Kols of Bengal, their language and racial affinity, 195 *sq.*; their country and mode of life, 196 their rules of descent, 197

Hos of Togoland, their priests wear little bells on their robes, 438

Hosea, on sacred pillars, 231; tomb of the prophet, 327; on the worship cf trees, 332

Hottentots, their stories of the origin of death, 20, 21; think it unlucky to count people, 309

House, inherited by youngest son, 176, 178, 179, 183, 198, 202; souls of family collected in a bag at moving into a new, 286

Houses, commercial, 186

"Houses of the soul," denounced by Isaiah, 290

Huarochiri, Indians of, their story of a great flood, 105

Hudson Bay erritory, the Montagnais of the, 116

Huichol Indians, their story of a great flood, 108 sq.

Human sacrifices as purification, 162; at Gezer, 166 sqq.; at laying foundations, 169 sq.; at making a covenant, 170

—— victims cut in two, 167 sqq.

Humboldt, A. de, on flood stories among the Indians of the Orinoco, 104, 135

Hungary, ultimogeniture in, 178

Huns, their mourning customs, 380

Hunter, Sir William, on the Khasis of Assam, 190

Hunting for souls, a practice denounced by Ezekiel, 288

Huxley, T. H., his essay on the flood, 46; on alleged flood caused by opening of the Bosphorus and Dardanelles, 74

Huxley lecture, 46

Hydromantia, 259

Ibos of Southern Nigeria, ultimogeniture among the, 202; their sacrifices to rivers, 255

Icelandic belief as to sitting on a threshold, 319

Ida, Mount, Dardanus said to have drifted to, 73

Identification of man with sacrificial victim, 215 sq.

Iguanas supposed to be immortal through casting their skins, 26

Images of dead ancestors used at the consultation of their spirits, 303

Imitative magic, 161

Immortality, man's loss of, 16 sqq.

Imprecations at peace-making, 159, 160

Inanimate objects punished for causing the death of persons, 398 sq.

Incas of Peru, their story of a great flood, 105 sq.

India, stories of the creation of man in, 9 sq.; stories of a great flood in, 79 sqq.; the fiction of a new birth in, 219; weeping as a salutation in, 241; form of divination for the detection of a thief in, 261

——, ancient, stories of a great flood in, 78 sq.; flood story in, not derived from the Babylonian, 133, 134; fiction of a new birth in, 218 sqq.; custom of bride stepping over the threshold in, 317

——, Northern, children buried under threshold to ensure their rebirth in, 320

Indian Archipelago, stories of a great flood in the, 84 sqq.

Indians, American. *See* American Indians

—— of British Columbia, their objection to a census, 310

Inger, a species of vermin, prosecuted by the authorities of Berne, 407

Initiation, blood of friends drunk by youths at, 396

Ink, divination by, 260

Ino or Pasaphea, sanctuary of, in Laconia, 228

Institutions of Israel, the ceremonial, their great antiquity, 352

Iolcus, sack of, 162

Iona, the black stones in, 248

Ireland, divination by coals in water in, 262; reptiles of, exorcized by St. Patrick, 403

Iron, the sound of, used to drive away spirits, 418

Iron bells worn by magicians and prophets, 438 sq.

Irragal, Babylonian god of pestilence, 52

Irrawaddy, its valley a line of migration, 194

Irrigation, sacrifices at, 212

Isaac, 172; how cheated by Jacob, 205; his evening meditation, 224

—— and Ishmael, 174

Isaiah, on worship of smooth stones, 231; his denunciation of "houses of the soul," 290; on the worship of oaks, 332; on rites of mourning, 377, 378

Ishmael and Isaac, 174

Ishar, Babylonian goddess, 52

Isidore of Saville, on the three great floods, 71

Isidorus, Neoplatonic philosopher, 258

Islay story of a giant whose soul was in an egg, 277 sq.

Ispahan, reverence for the threshold of the king's palace at, 315

Israel, ultimogeniture in, 172 sqq.; the "high places" of, 337 sqq.; great antiquity of the ceremonial institutions of, 352; its unquestioning faith in the supernatural, 359; cuttings for the dead in, 377 sqq.

Israelites, their ancestors nomadic herdsmen, 732, 377

Italy, ancient, dream oracles in, 228; oracle of the dead in, 299

Ituri River, ceremony at crossing the, 255

Ivory Coast, the Baoules of the, 289

Jabbok, Jacob at the ford of the, 251 sqq.

Jabesh, Saul buried under an oak or terebinth at, 334

Jackson, John, on foundation sacrifices in Fiji, 169 sq.

Jacob, the character of, 172; the frauds he practised on his brother and father, 172 sq.; the heirship of, 172 sqq.; his blessing of Ephraim and Manasseh, 174; and the kidskins, 204 sqq.; at Bethel, 223; his dream, 224; his ladder, 224; at the well, 237 sqq.; his departure from Haran, 243 sqq.; his dispute with Laban, 244; at the ford of the Jabbok, 251 sqq.; his sinew that shrank, 257; Mexican parallel to the story of his wrestling, 257 *sq.*; the daughters of, oak spirits in Palestine, 323, 328

Jacob and Esau, 204 *sqq.*

—— and Joseph, 174

Jacobs, Joseph, on ultimogeniture, 173

Jacobsen, Captain, 128

Jahwistic Document. *See* Jehovistic Document

Japanese have no tradition of a great flood, 131

Jaussen, Father Antonin, on the veneration for terebinths among the Arabs of Moab, 330

Java, cultivation of rice in, 185; mythical Rajah of, said to have acquired his strength from a stone, 247; bride carried by bridegroom into house in, 317

Jawbones of dead kings preserved by the Baganda, 301 *sq.*

Jebel Osh'a, 327

Jehovah, diversity in the use of the name in the Pentateuch, 60; in relation to sacred oaks and terebinths, 333

Jehovistic Document, 2 *sq.*, 55, 57, 59 *sqq.*, 353

—— version of the flood story, 60 *sqq.*

—— writer, 14, 15, 19

Jeremiah, on the worship of oaks, 332; on sacred poles (*asherim*), 338; on rites of mourning, 377, 378

Jeroboam, institutes worship of golden calves at Bethel, 231

Jerome, 290; as to the oak and terebinth, 331; on the, at Mamre, 335; on cuttings for the dead among the Jews, 379

Jerusalem, only legitimate altar at, 62; the fine ladies of, denounced by Isaiah, 290; Keepers of the Threshold in the temple at, 313, 314; concentration of the worship at, on suppression of local "high places," 338, 354; provision for the disestablished priests of the "high places" at, 356

Jeshimmon, the wilderness of Judea, 284

Jewish colony at Apamea Cibotos in Phrygia, 70

—— history, place of the Law in, 350 *sqq.*

Jews, their rule not to eat flesh and milk or cheese together, 371 *sq.*

Jhuming or jooming, a migratory system of cultivation, 180

Johor, in the Malay Peninsula, 82

Jonathan and David, their meeting, 239

Jordan, the region beyond, rude stone monuments in, 246; its springs, 328

Joseph, his meeting with his brethren, 238; his meeting with Jacob, 239; his cup, 258 *sqq.*

Joseph and Jacob, 174

Josephus, on the terebinth at Hebron, 334

Joshua, 249; the grave of, 325; and the stone of witness, 334

Josiah, king of Judah, his reformation, 62, 295, 338, 339, 354, 358, 359; and Deuteronomy, 356

Jubar, in the Altmark, the church bell rung during thunderstorms at, 424

Judea, the wilderness of, 283 *sq.*

Junior-right. *See* Ultimogeniture

Junius evokes the dead by incantations, 301

Juok, the Shilluk creator, 10

Jupiter, appealed to at making a treaty, 159

—— and Alcmena, 252

Jus Theelacticum, 177

Justinian, the *Digest* or *Pandects* of, 351

Jutland, North, mice, lice, fleas, and vermin not to be counted in, 312

Kabadi, in New Guinea, story of a great flood in, 89 *sq.*

Kabi, a tribe of Queensland, their mourning customs, 391

Kacharis, their womanly faces, 187

Kachcha Nagas of Assam, their story of the origin of the diversity of languages, 151

Kachins (Kakhyens, Chingpaws, Singphos), their Tartar origin, 184; ultimogeniture among the, 184 *sq.*; their agriculture, 186; their communal houses, 186; their Mongolian origin, 187; ultimogeniture among the Chinese, 187; their migration, 194 *sq.*; ward off demons from women at childbirth, 435. *See also* Singphos

Kafirs, mourning of widows among the, 381

Kai tribe of New Guinea, their story of the origin of death, 28

Kaitish tribe of Central Australia, their story of the origin of death, 30; customs observed by widows among the, 346, 347, 348; mourning of widows in the, 394

Kakadu tribe, their bodily lacerations in mourning, 391

Kakhyeen, their mode of avenging a death by drowning, 256

Kalmuks, their respect for the threshold, 316; demons kept off from women in childbed among the, 436

Kamars of Central India, their story of a great flood, 80

Kambinana, the Good Spirit, 32

Kamchadales, their story of a great flood, 84

Kamees or Hkamies, of Arakan, rule of inheritance among the, 189

Kamilaroi, their mourning customs, 390

Kansas, or Konzas, mourning customs of widows among the, 383

Kant on universal primeval ocean, 138

Karaite sect, the Jewish, reported magical rite of, 364

Karens of Burma, their story of the creation of man, 6; their story of a great flood, 81; their story like that of the Tower of Babel, 150; their ceremonies at peace-making, 161

Kariera tribe of Western Australia, their mourning customs, 391, 395

Karna, son of the Sun-god by the princess Kunti or Pritha, 266 sq.

Kataushys of Brazil, their story of a great flood, 100

Kathlamet-speaking Indians, their story of a great flood, 127

Kavirondo, Bantu tribes of, their precautions against the ghosts of the slain, 41; their mode of swearing friendship, 155; use of a cattle bell by widows among the, 431

——, the Nilotic. See Nilotic Kavirondo

Kawakipais or Diegueño Indians of California, their story of creation, 12

Kayans of Borneo, their evocation of the dead, 304; their custom of leaving trees for spirits, 342

Kedesh Naphtali, 323

Keepers of the Threshold, the, 313 sqq.

Kei Islands, story of the creation of man in the, 6; sacred stones in, 236; souls of infants stowed away for safety in coco-nuts in the, 286

Kennett, Professor R. H., on Jeremiah (ii. 34), 332 n.; on the original Ten Commandments, 362

Kent, Borough English in, 175

Kerak, in Moab, 330

Khasis of Assam, their story of the creation of man, 9; their language, 190; affinities, 190; agriculture, 190; their mother-kin, 190; ultimogeniture among the, 190 sq.

Khnoumou, Egyptian god, the creator of men, 3

Kid severed at peace-making, 156; in its mother's milk, not to see the, 360 sqq.

Kidskins, Jacob and the, 204

Kilimanjaro, Mount, 206

King, Norse custom at the election of a, 247. See also Kings

Kingfisher procures fire after the great flood, 87 sq.; in a story of a great flood, 117, 119

Kinglake, A. W., on divination by ink in Egypt, 260

"King's oak," 334

Kings, ghosts of dead, consulted as oracles in Africa, 301 sq.; in relation to oaks, 334

Kingsley, Mary H., on African stories of heavenly ladders, 228 sq.; on

witches hunting for souls in West Africa, 289

Kirantis, a tribe of the Central Himalayas beat copper vessels at funerals, 431

Kissi, souls of dead chiefs consulted as oracles among the, 303; their mourning customs, 381

Klemantans of Borneo, their form of adoption, 217

Knisteneaux. See Crees

Koiari of British New Guinea, their bodily lacerations in mourning, 835

Kolarian or Munda race, 195, 197

Kolosh, Russian name for the Tlinkits, 125

Kombengi, the Toradja maker of men, 6

Konkan, in Bombay Presidency, stones anointed in, 235, 236

Kookies of Northern Cachar, their use of a stone at marriage ceremony, 248. See also Kukis

Korkus, their story of the creation of man, 9; their fiction of a new birth, 219 sq.

Korwas, the, their respect for the threshold, 316

Koryaks, their method of averting plague, 163, 165; ultimogeniture among the, 201

Koshchei the Deathless, Russian story of, 274 sqq.

Kublai Khan, 314

Kukis of Manipur, their story of the origin of the diversity of language, 151; of Chittagong, their law of blood revenge 398

Kumaon, fiction of a new birth in, 218 sq.

Kumis, their story of the creation of man, 9

Kunti, or Pritha, mother of Karna by the Sun-god, 266

Kunyan, the hero of a flood story, 121 sq.

Kurmis, their respect for the threshold, 316

Kurnai of Victoria, their story of a great flood, 88; their bodily lacerations in mourning, 390

Kutus, on the Congo, silence of widows among the, 343

Kwakijutl Indians, silence of widows and widowers among the, 344

Kyganis, their bodily lacerations in mourning, 381

Laban, his dispute with Jacob, 244 sq.

Labrador, the Eskimo of, 305

Lacerations of the body in mourning, 377 sqq.

Laconia, sanctuary of Ino in, 228

Ladder, Jacob's, 224; the heavenly, 228 sqq.

Ladders to facilitate descent of goods or spirits, 230; in graves for the use of the ghosts, 230

Ladon, the river, 72

Lai, a Toradja god, 6

Lake Albert, the god of, and his prophetess, 438

—— Tyers in Victoria, aborigines about, their story of a great flood, 89

Lakshmi, goddess of wealth, 316

Lamarck on universal primeval ocean, 138

Lambs, unlucky to count, 311, 312

Land, private property in, 181, 186

Language, story of the origin of, 143; the diversities of, stories of their origin, 150 sqq.

—— spoken in Paradise, theories as to the, 147

Lapps unwilling to count themselves, 311

Larka Kols or Lurka Coles. See Hos

La Rochelle, bell at Protestant chapel at, punished for heresy, 415

Laubo Maros, a chief whose life was said to be in a hair of his head, 273

Lausanne, the Bishop of, his trial and condemnation of a species of vermin called inger, 407 sq.; leeches prosecuted at, 408

Law, legal fiction to mark a change of status in early, 216; a gradual growth, not a sudden creation, 350 sq.; of blood-revenge revealed to Noah, 398

——, the, of Israel, its place in Jewish history, 350; originally oral, not written, 354 sq.

Laws, new, rest on existing custom and public opinion, 351; local, in France, before the Revolution, their multiplicity and diversity, 351

Lead, divination by molten, 262

Leaping over the threshold, 318

Lebanon, the oaks of, 323

Leeches prosecuted at Lausanne, 408

Lees of palm-wine not allowed to be heated, 365

Legend and myth distinguished, 142

Legislation, primitive, reflects the tendency to personify external objects, 416 sq.

—— and codification distinguished, 350

Legitimacy of infants tested by water ordeal, 268 sq.

Leibnitz on universal primeval ocean, 137 sq.; on Hebrew as the supposed primitive language, 147

Leicester, Borough English in, 176

Lengua Indians of Paraguay, their story of the creation of man, 14; weeping as a salutation among the, 242

Lepchas of Sikkim, their womanly faces, 187

Lepers, special garb for, 38

Levitical code, its prohibition of cuttings for the dead, 379

—— law and the altar at Jerusalem, 61 sq.; promulgated by Ezra, 360

Lewin, Captain T. H., 9

Libanza, African god, 30

Libations to stones, 231, 235

—— of milk, honey, water, wine, and olive oil at a tomb, 300

Life, the bundle of, 283 sqq.

Lightning, custom in regard to person who has been killed by, 428

Lille, ultimogeniture in districts about, 177

Limentinus, Roman god of the threshold, 319

Lincolnshire, unlucky to count lambs in, 311

Lithuania, divination in, 262; superstitions as to the threshold in, 319

Little Book of the Covenant, 353

—— Wood Women, Bavarian belief as to, 312

Littleton on Borough English, 179

Livingstone, David, on a flood story in Africa, 130; on an African story like that of the Tower of Babel, 147

Livy, on Roman mode of making a treaty, 159; on the temple of Amphiaraus at Oropus, 225

Lizard in story of the creation of man, 11; brings message of mortality to men, 25; and chameleon, story of the, 25

Lizards, hated and killed by Zulus, 25; supposed to be immortal through casting their skins, 26, 31

Llama, speaking, in a flood story, 105

Locusts got rid of by payment of tithes, 405

Loftus, W. R., on flood at Baghdad, 141

Lolos, aboriginal race of Southern China, 83; their story of a great flood, 83; ultimogeniture among the, 189

Long Blo, a magical tree, 30

Longfellow on church bells in The Golden Legend, 419

Loon in story of a great flood, 115, 118, 120

Lorraine, bride carried over the threshold in, 318

Lotus-flower, golden, fiction of birth from a, 221

Louisiana, the Natchez Indians of, 13

Low, Sir Hugh, on use of bells in Borneo, 432 sq.

Lübeck, the Republic of, privilege of the youngest son in, 178

Lucan on the evocation of the dead by a Thessalian witch, 300 sq.; on Druidical sacrifices to trees, 333

Lucian on Deucalion's flood, 69; on the sanctuary at Hierapolis, 69; on the worship of stones, 225; on the sound of bronze and iron as a means of repelling spectres, 418

Lucullus sacrifices a bull to the Euphrates, 253

Lugal, Babylonian god, 32

Luiseño Indians of California, their story of a great flood, 111 *sq.*
Luo Zaho, supreme god in Nias, 7
Lurka Coles. *See* Hos
Lushais of Assam, their ceremonies to facilitate childbirth, 169; their migratory system of cultivation, 180 *sq.*; their villages, 181; ultimogeniture among the, 182
Lushei Kuki clans of Assam, their oath of friendship, 158
Lycorea on Parnassus, 68
Lyell, Sir Charles, on argument for universal deluge drawn from shells and fossils, 136
Lysippus, his image of Love, 232

Macalister, Professor Stewart, on human sacrifices at Gezer, 166, 169
Macaw as wife of two men, 105
MacDonald, King of the Isles, his oath on the black stones, 248
Macedonia, divination by coffee in, 261
Macedonian rite of purification, 162
Mackenzie, H. E., on Algonquin story of a great flood, 116
Macusis of British Guiana, their story of a great flood, 101
Madagascar, the Betsimisaraka of, 230; sacred stones in, 236; use of stone as a talisman in, 248; the Sihanaka of, 343
Magians sacrifice white horses to a river, 253
Magic, imitative, 161
——, sympathetic, 165, 171, 257; based on the association of ideas, 368
—— of strangers, dread of the, 168
Magic Mirror, a mode of divination, 259
Magical and religious aspects of oaths on stones, 249
Mahabharata, story of the exposure and preservation of Prince Karna in the, 267
Mahadeo creates man, 9 *sq.*
Mahadeva invoked at oaths, 249
Maidu Indians of California, their story of the creation of man, 11; their story of the origin of the diversity of languages, 152
Maimonides, on the prohibition of seething a kid on its mother's milk, 364
Mainere and *madelstad,* succession of the youngest, 177
Maitland, F. W., on Borough English, 176
Makanuaima, a creator, 101
Malacca, Malay code of, its provision as to cattle that have killed people, 399
Malachi, on the payment of tithes, 405
Malay Peninsula, the Mentras of the, 29; story of a great flood in the, 82 *sq.*
Malay region, traces of ultimogeniture in the, 198 *sq.*
—— wizards catch souls in turbans, 289

Malcolm III., Canmore, King of Scotland, 179
Malekula, one of the New Hebrides, story of the creation of man in, 6; bodily lacerations in mourning in, 385
Malwa, Western, the Bhils of, 198
Mamberano River, in Dutch New Guinea, natives of, their story of a great flood, 90
Mamre, the oaks or terebinths at, 333, 334, 336, 337
Man, creation of, 1 *sqq.*; the Fall of, 15 *sqq. See also* Men
Manasseh, King, his revival of necromancy, 295; Deuteronomy perhaps written in his reign, 356
Mandan Indians, their story of a great flood, 112 *sqq.*; their oracular stone, 234
Mangaia, mourning customs in, 389
Mangars of Nepaul, their ladders for the dead, 230
Manipur, ultimogeniture in, 183
Mankie, chief, 196, 197
"Mantle children," adopted children, 216
Mantras. *See* Mentras
Manu, the hero of the ancient Indian story of a great flood, 78 *sq.*, 134
Maoris, their story of the creation of man, 5; their story of a great flood, 94 *sqq.*; weeping as a salutation among the, 239; evocation of the dead among the, 303; bodily lacerations in mourning among the, 389 *sq.*
Marco Polo, 84; on keepers of the threshold at Peking, 314
Mare, child at birth placed inside a, 165; executed by the Parliament of Aix, 414
Marindineeze of New Guinea, their evocation of the dead, 304
Mariner, William, on bodily lacerations of the Tongans in mourning, 388
Mark of Cain, 33 *sqq.*
Marquesas Islands, bodily lacerations of women in mourning in the, 389
Marriage, use of sacrificial skins at, 211
—— by capture, supposed relic of, 318
Mars, the father of Romulus and Remus, 265
Marseilles, Druidical grove at, 333
Masai, the bodies of manslayers painted by the, 42; reported tradition of a great flood among the, 130; their ethnical affinity, 206; their use of victim's skin at sacrifices, 212 *sq.*; their ceremony at crossing a stream, 254; will not count men or beasts, 308 *sq.*; their sacrifices to trees, 332; their objection to boil milk, 366; their custom as to cleaning their milk-vessels, 369; their rule to keep milk and flesh apart, 370; their warriors not allowed to eat vegetables, 373;

formerly ate no game or fish, 375; country abundance of game in the, 375

Masarwas of Bechuanaland, their story of the origin of death, 22

Masseboth, sacred stones in Canaanite sanctuaries and "high places" of Israel, 237

Mati'-ilu, prince, his oath of fealty, 159 *sq.*

Mecca, the Black Stone at, 231

Medicine-men or witch doctors employed to detect witchcraft, 438

Medium, human, of rock-spirit, 234

Mediums, human, representing dead kings and chiefs, 302; their faces whitened in order to attract the attention of the spirits, 302; who communicate with the dead, 304

Meitheis of Manipur, ultimogeniture among the, 183 *sq.*

Melanesia, story of a great flood in, 91; worship of stones in, 232

Melanesian stories of the creation of man, 6; of the origin of death, 27 *sq.,* 32

Melissa, her ghost consulted by Periander, 297

Melu, a creator, 8

Men supposed to have been formerly immortal through casting their skins, 27 *sq. See also* Man

Menelaus and Proteus, 252

Menkieras of the French Sudan, their sacrifices to rocks and stones, 234

Mentras or Mantras of the Malay Peninsula, their story of the origin of death, 29

Mephistopheles and Faust in the prison, 252

Mercheta, or *marcheta,* due paid to a feudal lord on the marriage of a tenant's daughter, 179

Message, story of the Perverted, 20 *sq.,* 31 *sq.*

Messenia, the Boar's Grave at, 155

Messou, hero of a flood story, 115

Meteoric stones, oaths on, 249

Mexican parallel to the story of Jacob's wrestling, 257 *sq.*

Mexico, story of the creation of man in, 13; stories of a great flood in, 107 *sqq.*

Micah, on rites of mourning, 377 *sq.*

Mice, lawsuits brought against, 406, 411

Michael, the Archangel, his contention with Satan for the body of Moses 404

Michemis, a Tibetan tribe, use of bells at exorcism among the, 431

Michoacans, their story of the creation of man, 13; their story of a great flood, 107 *sq.*

Micronesia, story of a great flood in, 96 *sq.*

Midas and his ass's ears, 55; how he caught Silenus, 253

Midsummer Eve, divination on, 261; a witching time, 423

Migration to Mongoloid tribes from China into Burma and Assam, 194 *sq.*

Migratory system of agriculture, 180, 185

Mikirs of Assam, their story like that of the Tower of Babel, 150

Milk, offered to stones, 235; poured on sacred stones, 236; poured at tombs, 300; offered to trees, 332; not to seethe a kid in its mother's, 360 *sqq.*; not to be boiled for fear of injuring the cows, 364 *sq.*; the first, of a cow after calving, special rules as to the disposal of, 366, 367; not to be brought into contact with flesh, 370; not to be eaten with beef, 370 *sq.*; not to be brought into contact with vegetables, 370, 371, 372 *sqq.*

Milk-vessels not to be washed, 369; their materials supposed to affect the cow, 369

Millaeus on the shaving of witches, 272

Milton, on the Ladon, 72; on the bell-man, 423

Milya-uppa tribe, cut themselves in mourning, 392

Minahassa, in Celebes, souls of a family collected in a bag at a housewarming in, 286

Mindanao, one of the Philippines, stories of the creation of man in, 8, 9

Mingrelians of the Caucasus, their mourning customs, 381

Minos and Scylla, the daughter of Nisus, 274

Mirzapur, the Korwas of, 316

Mizpah, the Watch-tower, 246

Mkulwe, in East Africa, story like that of the Tower of Babel in, 148

Moab, the Arabs of, 162, 330, 379. *See also* Arabs

——, terebinths in, 329 *sq.*; rites of mourning in, 378

Moffatt, Robert, on absence of flood stories in Africa, 129 *sq.*

Mohammedan law as to division of property among sons, 204

—— saints in Syria, the tombs of, 324

Mohammedans of Sierra Leone and Morocco, their superstitions as to boiling milk, 364, 365, 367 *sq.*

Moisy, mad bull tried and hanged at, 413 *sq.*

Mole sacrificed in purification, 215

Moloch, sacrifice of children to, 332

Molossians, 67; their mode of swearing an oath, 155

Money, German belief about counting, 312

Mongolian type, 187

Mongoloid peoples, their migration from China into Burma and Assam, 194 *sq.*

—— tribes, ultimogeniture among, 180

Mongols, their tradition of a great flood, 84; ultimogeniture among the, 180

Montagnais Indians of Canada, their story of a great flood, 115 *sq.*

Montenegro, laceration of the face in mourning in, 380

Montezuma, hero of a flood story, 110

Moon, the creation of the, 8, 12; savage theory of the phases of the, 20; sends messages of immortality to men, 20 *sqq.*; associated with idea of resurrection, 29 *sqq.*; the ark interpreted as the, 137; temple of the, 162

Moors of Morocco, their notion of pollution caused by homicide, 35; their superstition as to boiling milk, 365, 367

Mopsus, the soothsayer, his oracle in Cilicia, 298

Moquis of Arizona, their story of the creation of man, 13; their use of bells to exorcize witches, 429

Moral standard, changes in the, 173

Mordvins, their custom of carrying a bride into the house, 317

Morning-Star Woman, the first woman, 12

Morocco, notions as to pollution of homicide in, 35; superstitious respect for the threshold in, 316, 319, 321; bride carried across the threshold of her husband's house in, 316; superstitions as to boiling milk in, 365, 367 *sq.*

Mortality of man, account of its origin, 16

Mosaic legislation, the so-called, its late date, 352

Moses, said to be a contemporary of Ogyges, 71; the historical character of, 263, 352 *sq.*; in the ark of bulrushes, 263; the infant, found and brought up by Pharaoh's daughter, 264; offspring of a marriage afterwards deemed incestuous, 268 *sq.*

Mota, the story of the creation of man in, 6

Mother assimilated to sheep, 208 *sq.*

Mother-kin among the Khasis, 190 *sq.*; among the Garos, 193

"Motherhoods" among the Garos, 193

Mountain, story of a moving, 101

Mourners disguise themselves from the ghost, 93 *sq.*

Mourning of murderer for his victim, 39 *sq.*; costume perhaps a disguise against ghosts, 44; for the dead, the custom of cutting the body and the hair in, 377 *sqq.*; customs of Australian aborigines designed to propitiate the ghosts, 393 *sq.*

Mrus, ultimogeniture among the, 195

Mud, head of manslayer plastered with, 43; plastered on bodies of mourners, 381

Mudarra, his adoption by his stepmother, 217 *sq.*

Mudburra tribe of Northern Australia, silence of widows in the, 344 *sq.*, 348

Mujati, Babylonian god, 52

Mukâms, shrines or tombs of reputed Mohammedan saints in Syria, 325 *sqq.*

Mukjarawaint, their bodily lacerations in mourning, 390

Munda or Kolarian race, 195, 197

Mundas, or Mundaris, their story of the creation of man, 10; their sacred groves, 340

Mungeli, Tahsil, India, weeping as a salutation among the people of, 241

Muratos of Ecuador, their story of a great flood, 100 *sq.*

Murray River, mourning customs of the aborigines on the, 390

Musk-rat brings up part of drowned earth after the flood, 115, 120, 121, compare 122, 123, 127

Mutilations, certain corporeal, to please the ghosts, 394 *sq.*

Myths of observation, 78, 142

Nabal and David, 284

Naga tribes of Assam, peace-making ceremonies among the, 157 *sqq.*

Nakawe, goddess of earth, 108

Namaquas, their story of the origin of death, 20

Nandi, their story of the origin of death, 21; their treatment of manslayers, 42 *sq.*; their modes of making peace, 155, 158; their ethnical affinity, 206; their use of sacrificial skins at marriage, 211; their periodical transference of power from older to younger generation, 215; their age-grades, 215; their respect for the threshold, 315, 316; silence of widows among the, 344; their objection to boil milk, 367; their milk-vessels, 369; do not eat meat and milk together, 371; do not eat certain wild animals, 374; use of bells at circumcision among the, 437

Naogeorgus, Thomas, on the use of church bells to drive away thunderstorms, 424

Napoleon, his code, 351

Narrinyeri of South Australia, their mourning customs, 391

Nasamones, of Libya, their oracular dreams on graves, 299

Natchez Indians of Louisiana, their story of the creation of man, 13; of the Lower Mississippi, their story of a great flood, 112

Natural laws hardly recognized by the ancient Hebrews, 359

Ndara, a Toradja goddess, 6

Ndengei, great Fijian god, 90

Nebo, Mount, 327

Nebuchadnezzar, king of Babylon, his capture of Jerusalem, 57

Necromancy among the ancient Hebrews, 295 sq.; among the ancient Greeks and Romans, 296 sqq.; in Africa, 301 sqq.; in Polynesia, 303; in the Indian Archipelago, 303 sqq.; among the Eskimo, 305; in China, 305 sqq.

Nenebojo, hero of an Ojibway flood story, 119 sq.

Neoptolemus, his grave at Delphi, 235

Nepaul, the Mangars of, 230

Nergal, Babylonian god of the dead, 296

Nero, his evocation of the ghost of Agrippina, 301

Nestorian Christianity in China, 84

Nets to keep off demons from women in childbed, 436

Neufville, J. B., on ultimogeniture among the Kachins, 185

Neusohl, in Hungary, the Passing Bell at, 420

New birth, ceremony of the, among the Akikuyu, 207 sqq., 215, 216; the rite of the, 216; fiction of, at adoption, 216 sq.; fiction of, enacted by Brahman householder, 219; fiction of, as expiation for breach of custom, 219; enacted by Maharajahs of Travancore, 220 sqq.

New Britain, story of the origin of death in, 32

—— England, execution of dogs in, 414

—— Guinea, story of the origin of death in, 28; custom in regard to the blood-wit in, 40; stories of a great flood in, 89 sqq.; divination by water in, 260; mode of recovering strayed souls of children in, 286

—— Guinea, British, mourning customs in, 385

—— Guinea, Dutch, story of a great flood in, 90; the Arafoos of, 257; the Marindineeze of, 304

—— Hebrides, the creation of man in the, 6; story of the former immortality of men in the, 28; story of a great flood in the, 91; worship of stones in the, 232; mourning customs in the, 385

—— South Wales, mourning customs of the Kamilaroi in, 390

—— Zealand, weeping as a salutation among the Maoris of, 239 sqq. See Maoris

Nez Perces, their story of a great flood, 126

Ngai, God, sacrifices for rain to, 340

Ngoni (Angoni) of British Central Africa, the, 25; their custom of painting the bodies of manslayers, 42. See also Angoni

Nias, story of the creation of man in, 7;

story of the origin of death in, 27; way of ratifying an oath in, 160; story told in, of a chief whose life was in a hair of his head, 273

Nicaragua, story of a great flood in, 107

Nicobar Islands, mourning customs in the, 393

Nicolaus of Damascus on the flood, 49

Niger, the Upper, the Bambaras of, 322

Nigeria, Southern, the Ibos of, 202, 255

Nile, the Karuma Falls of the, sacrifice at crossing, 254; King Pheron said to have thrown a dart into the, 256

Nilotic Kavirondo, seclusion and purification of murderers among the, 39; their precautions against the ghosts of the slain, 41

Nineveh, excavations at, 49

Ninib, Babylonian messenger of the gods, 51, 52, 53

Nippur, excavations at, 54

Nishinam tribe of California, silence of widows in the, 344

Nisir, mountain, 52

Nisus, king of Megara, and his purple or golden hair, 274

Njamus of British East Africa, their use of victim's skin at sacrifices, 212

Noachian deluge not the source of all flood stories, 132; argument in favour of, from marine shells and fossils, 135 sq.

Noah and the flood, 61 sqq.; on coins of Apamea Cibotos, 70; the law of blood revenge revealed to, 398

Nogais, a Tartar tribe, demons kept from women in childbed among the, 436

Norse custom at the election of a king, 247

North America, stories of a great flood in, 110 sqq.

—— American Indians, expel ghosts of the slain, 44; cut out and throw away the hamstrings of deer, 257; their laceration of the body in mourning, 381 sq. See America, American Indians

—— Berwick, Satan in the pulpit at, 272

Norway, sacred stones in, 235

Norwich, flood at, 140

Noses cut in mourning for the dead, 380

Nottingham, Borough English at, 175, 176

Nounoumas of Senegal, their customs in regard to bloodshed and homicide, 37; their sacrifices to trees, 333

Nuers of the White Nile, ultimogeniture among the, 202

Nukahiva, evocation of the dead in, 303 sq.

Numa, how he caught Picus and Faunus, 253; his divination by water, 259; his law concerning boundary stones, 403

Numitor, grandfather of Romulus and Remus, 265
Nyambe, an African sun-god, 247

Oak, Hebrew word for, 331; the worship of the, denounced Hebrew prophets, 333 *sq.*; in relation to kings, 334; spirit in triple form, 335
—— of Weeping, the, 334
Oaks in Palestine, 322 *sqq.*; three different kinds, 322 *sq.*; distribution in Palestine, 323; regarded with superstitious veneration by the peasantry, 323 *sqq.*
Oaths sworn on the pieces of animals, 154 *sq.*; Greek modes of ratifying, 154; of friendship ceremonies at taking, 155 *sqq.*
—— taken on stones, 248 *sq.*; religious and magical aspects of, 249
Oblivion, the Castle of, 250
Observation, myths of, 78, 142
Ocean, theory of a universal primeval, 138
Odenwald, ultimogeniture in, 178
Odoric, Friar, as to the Keepers of the Threshold at Peking, 314
Odyssey, evocation of the dead by Ulysses in the, 297
Offerings to stones, 231, 232, 233, 234
Og, king of Bashan, and Noah's ark, 65, 66
Ogyges, or Ogygus, the great flood in his time, 70 *sq.*
Ogygian, epithet applied to Boeotia and Thebes, 71
Oil poured on sacred stones, 225, 235
Ojhyâls, devil priests among the Gonds, 433
Ojibways of Ontario, their story of a great flood, 119 *sq.*
O-kee-pa, annual festival of the Mandan Indians, 114
Old Testament, traces of ultimogeniture in the, 174
Olympia, Zeus the God of Oaths at, 155; punishment of homicidal statute at, 402
Omahas, seclusion of homicides among the, 40; unwilling to number the years of their lives, 310; their mourning customs, 384
Onas, of Tierra del Fuego, their custom of lacerating the face in mourning, 384
Ontario, story of a great flood among the Ojibways of, 119 *sq.*
Ophrah, the oak or terebinth at, 333
Opus, the first city founded after the flood, 67
Oracles imparted in dreams, 225 *sqq.*; of the dead in ancient Greece, 297 *sqq.*; in Africa, 302
Oracular dreams on graves, 299
—— stones, 234
Oral law older than written law in Israel, 355
Oran, mode of counting grain at, 310

Orang Sakai of Sumatra, their bodily laceration in mourning, 385
Oraons of Chota Nagpur, tradition of their immigration, 195 *sq.*
Ordeal by water to test the legitimacy of infants, 268 *sq.*
Oregon or Columbia River, 382
Orestes, his offering of hair to the dead Agamemnon, 380
Origin of death, stories of the, 19 *sqq.*; of stories of a great flood, 135 *sqq.*; of language, 143; of ultimogeniture, 179, 202 *sqq.*
Orinoco, flood stories among the Indians of the, 104
Ornaments as amulets, 290
Oropus, sanctuary of Amphiaraus at, 225 *sq.*
Orpheus and Eurydice, 297
Ossetes of the Caucasus, their bodily lacerations in mourning, 381
Otaheite, mourning customs in, 386 *sq.* See Tahiti
Othrys, Mount, Deucalion said to have drifted to, 67
Otter in story of great flood, 116, 118, 120, 121, 123
Ownership of land, communal and individual, among the Kachins, 185
Ox, sacrificial, in oaths, 155, 157; that gored, the, 397 *sqq.*
Oxen outlawed at Rome for ploughing up boundary stones, 403

Pacific, earthquake waves in the, 139 *sq.*
Pacurius, king of Persia, how he detected the treason of a vassal, 250
Painting the bodies of manslayers, 41, 42, 43 *sq.*
Palestine, its reddish soil, 14; the races of, 167, 168; mode of counting grain in, 310; bride carried over the threshold in, 316; oaks in, 316 *sqq.*; the "high places" still the seats of religious worship in modern, 339
Palsy, a Samoan god, 27
Pamarys of Brazil, their story of a great flood, 100
Pampa del Sacramento, tradition of a great flood in the, 114
Panama, story of a great flood in, 107
Pandarus at the sanctuary of Aesculapius at Epidaurus, 227
Pandects of Justinian, 351
Pandora, the first woman, 67
Panopeus, scene of the creation of man, 3
Papagos of Arizona, their story of a great flood, 110
Paraguay, the Lengua Indians of, 14
Parian chronicler on the date of Deucalion's flood, 68
Paris, flood at, 140
Parnassus, 4; Deucalion said to have landed on, after the flood, 67

Pasiphae, or Ino, sanctuary of, in Laconia, 228

Passage between severed pieces of sacrificial victim, 154 *sqq.*; interpretation of the rule, 163 *sq.*, 170 *sqq.*

Passing Bell, the, 418, 420 *sqq.*

Pastoral peoples, ultimogeniture among, 179 *sq.*, 203; their rules based on a supposed sympathetic bond between a cow and its milk, 369; their rule not to let milk come into contact with flesh or vegetables, 369 *sqq.*; discourage agriculture, 373 *sq.*; abstain from eating wild animals, 374

—— tribes of Africa object to boil milk for fear of injuring their cattle, 364 *sqq.*

Patagonian Indians, birth ceremonies among the, 165; their mourning customs, 384

Pathian, the creator, 81

Patriarchal age, the, 153 *sqq.*; the end of the, 263

Patriarchs, long-lived of the Lolos, 83

Patroclus, the offering of hair to the dead, 380

Pausanias, on the Ladon, 72; on the valley of Pheneus, 73; on the sanctuary of Ino, 228

——, king of Sparta, his evocation of a ghost, 298

Peace-making ceremonies at, 155 *sqq.*

Peking, Keepers of the Threshold in the palace at, 314

Peleus and Astydamia, 162, 168; and Thetis, 252; his vow, 380

Pelew Islanders, their story of the creation of man, 6

Pelew Islands, story of a great flood in the, 96 *sq.*

Pelicans, why they are black and white, 88 *sq.*

Peneus, the river, 76

Peniel, 252

Pennant on St. Wenefride's bell, 425 *sq.*

Pentateuch, late date of the legal part of the, 350, 352; three bodies of law comprised in the, 353; position of the Priestly Code in the, 360

——, law of clean and unclean animals in the, 376

Perez and Zerah, 174

Periander, tyrant of Corinth, consults his dead wife, Melissa, 297

Permanent system of agriculture, 183, 184, 185 *sq.*

Perrot, Nicolas, on weeping as a salutation among the Sioux, 242 *sq.*

Persian kings, reverence for the threshold of their palace, 315

Persians adept in water-divination, 259

Persians, The, tragedy of Aeschylus, 300

Personification of water, 257; of external objects reflected in primitive legislation, 416 *sq.*

Peru, stories of a great flood in, 105 *sq.*

Perugino, the Virgins of, 422

Peruvian Indians, their story of the creation of man after the flood, 14; their offerings to river-gods, 254

Perverted Message, story of the, 20 *sq.*, 31 *sq.*

Pharae, in Achaia, sacred stones at, 231

Pheneus, the Lake of, 72 *sq.*

Phron, king of Egypt, said to have thrown a dart into the Nile, 256

Phiala, the Lake of, 323, 327

Philippine Islands, story of the creation of man in, 8; the Talalogs of the, 435

Philistine mourning rites, 378

Philistines, Samson and the, 269 *sqq.*

Philostratus on the ghost of Achilles, 300

Phoroneus, king of Argos, 151

Photography, belief that human souls can be extracted by, 285

Phrygian legend of a great flood, 70

Picardy, ultimogeniture in, 177

Picus caught by Numa, 253

Piedade no Maranhao, a province of Brazil, 410

Pig, sacrificial, in ratifying an oath, 160

Pillars, sacred, at Canaanite sanctuaries, 231

Pima Indians of Arizona, their story of the creation of man, 13; seclusion of manslayers among the, 43; their story of a great flood, 111

Pindar on Deucalion's flood, 67

Pirman, the Malay deity, 82

Pistacia terebinthus, 329

Plague, the Great, of London, 308

Plant that renew youth, 18 *sq.*

Plato, in the *Symposium,* on the primitive state of man, 14; on the ghosts of the murdered, 38; on Deucalion's flood, 67; on the trial and punishment of animals and inanimate objects, 401; his *Laws* compared with *The Republic,* 401 *sq.*

Playfair, Major A., on the Garos, 194

Pleiades, two stars removed from the, 65

Pleistocene period, man in the, 74

Plighting Stone, the, at Lairg in Sutherlandshire, 248

Pliny, on the Lake of Pheneus, 72; on the evocation of the ghost of Homer, 300

Plover in story of a great flood, 122

Plutarch, 4; on Deucalion's flood, 70; on oracles of the dead, 298, 299; on custom of carrying bride into house, 318, 319

Poets in relation to folk-lore, 291

Point Barrow, 11

Pollution, ceremonial, expiation for, 214

—— caused by homicide, 34 *sqq.*

Polynesia, story of the creation of man in, 5; stories of a great flood in, 91 *sqq.*

Polynesians, lacerations of the body and shearing of the hair in mourning among the, 386

Pomo Indians of California, mourning customs of the, 382

Ponto-Aralian Mediterranean, 74 sq.

Port Moresby in New Guinea, noises made by the natives to drive away storm-spirits and ghosts at, 428 sq.

Poseidon said to have opened the gorge of Tempe, 76; how he made Pterelaus immortal, 274

Praxiteles, his image of Love, 232

Precautions taken by slayers against the ghosts of the slain, 41 sqq.

Priest, the Jewish, his violet robe and golden bells, 417

Priestly Code, the, 350, 353, 360, 397, 417
—— Document, 2, 55, 57 sqq.
—— version of the flood story, 60 sqq.

Priests wear bells in Africa, 438

Primogeniture replacing ultimogeniture, 182, 189, 204, 205; regulating descent of chieftainship, 197

Proca, king of Alba Longa, 265

Procopius on the detection of the traitor Arsaces, 250

Prometheus, the creator of man, 3; father of Deucalion, 67

Property, private, in land, 181, 186; in moveables, 199

Prophet, the, ousted by the scribe, 355
—— of Wamala, the Banyoro god of plenty, 438

Prophetess of the god of Lake Albert, 438

Prophetic reformation of Israelitish religion, 338

Prophets, Hebrew, denounce the worship of trees, 332, 338 sq.; their freedom of thought and speech, 355

Propitiation of water-spirits at fords, 253 sqq.

Prosecution of animals in ancient Greece, 400 sq.; in modern Europe, 403 sqq.

Prostitution, religious, denounced by Hebrew prophets, 332

Proteus and Menelaus, 252

Prussians, the heathen, their worship of the oak at Romove, 333, 335

Prytanaeum, or town hall, court of the, at Athens, 400 sq.

Psophis, Alcmaeon in the valley of, 36

Pterelaus, king of Taphos, and his golden hair, 274

Pueblo Indians of Arizona, their use of bells to exorcize witches, 429

Puluga, a creator, 87

Pund-jel, an Australian creator, 4

Punishment of animals that have killed people, 397 sqq.; of inanimate objects which have caused the death of persons, 398 sqq.

Punjab, settlement of the Aryans in the, 78; dead infants buried at threshold to ensure their rebirth, in the, 320

Purification for homicide, 38 sqq., 41 sqq.
—— of mother of twins, 214 sq.
——, public, by passing between pieces of a victim, 162

Purificatory, sacramental, or protective theory of sacrificing victims of covenants, 158, 163, 164, 169, 171 sq.

Purus River, in Brazil, story of a great flood told by the Indians of the, 100

Pyramid Texts, the, 230

Pyrrha, wife of Deucalion, 67

Qat, Melanesian hero and creator, 6, 28, 91

Queen Charlotte Islands, the Haida Indians of, 125

Queensland, mourning customs in the tribes of, 391

Quercus pseudo-coccifera, 332, 337; aegilops, 323; infectoria, 323

Quiches of Guatemala, their story of the origin of the diversity of languages, 152

Rachel, her theft of her father's household gods, 244

Racine, his comedy Les Plaideurs, 401

Ragoba and his ambassadors to England, 220

Rags hung on trees by Syrian peasants, 328, 329; by the sick of Afghanistan, 341, 342

Raiatea, story of a great flood in, 93

Ram, its use in oaths, 154; black, as sacrificial victim, 212, 213; sacrificial, sleeping on skin of, 225, 228

Rama and the great flood, 79 sq.

Ramman, Babylonian storm-god, 50, 52

Rape of Lewes, Borough English in, 175

Rape of the Sabine women, 318

Raphael's picture of Jacob at the well, 59, 238

Raratonga, teeth knocked out in mourning in, 389

Rat in story of a great flood, 119. See also Rats

Ratification of covenant by cutting sacrificial victim in two, 154 sqq.

Rats, lawsuits brought against, 405 sq., 411 sq.

Rattan, the Rolled-up, connecting earth and heaven, 229

Raven makes first woman, 11; let out of ark, 52, 66, 116; in the religion and mythology of the Tlingits, 123 sqq.; how the raven restored mankind after the great flood, 125; in Haida mythology, 125
—— and dove in North American Indian story of a great flood, 123

Rawan, a demon king, 9

Rawlinson, Sir Henry, on the Gilgamesh epic, 50

Raziel, the angel, 65

Rebekah, 173, 205

Rebirth, infants buried under the threshold to insure their, 320

Receptacles for the souls of infants, 286

Red clay or earth, men fashioned out of, 5, 6, 9, 14

Redemption of people, 162

Reformation of King Josiah, 62, 338, 354, 359; prophetic, of Israelitish religion, 338

Reid, Thomas, on the law of deodand, 416

Religious and magical aspects of oaths on stones, 249

Rembau, a Malay state, ultimogeniture in, 198 *sq.*

Remigius, Mount, bell rung in thunderstorms on, 425

Renan, E., on Feuerbach, 422

Reptiles exorcized by St. Patrick, 403

Republic, Plato's, 401 *sq.*

Resurrection after three days, 29 *sq.*

—— associated with the new moon, 29

Retributive theory of sacrificing victims at covenants, 158 *sqq.*, 163, 164, 171

Rhea, Sylvia, mother of Romulus and Remus, 265

Rhine, ordeal of legitimacy by the, 269

Rhodesia, Bantu tribes of, spirits of dead chiefs consulted as oracles among the, 302

Rib, woman created out of a man's , 1, 2, 5, 6

Rice, the dry and wet systems of cultivation, 185 *sq.*

Right foot foremost at crossing the threshold, 317

"Right hand, son of the," title of the heir, 174

Rings made of skins of sacrificial animals, 207, 215

Ritual, sacrificial skins in, 206 *sqq.*; the use of bells in primitive, 439

River, the spirit or jinnee of the, 252

River-spirits, propitiation of, 254 *sqq.*

Rivers, ceremonies observed at the passage of, 253 *sqq.*; sacrifices to, 253, 254, 255; regarded as gods or the abodes of gods, 255

Rivers, Dr. W. H. R., on ultimogeniture among the Badagas, 198

Rock-spirits, malevolent, 234

Rocks, worship of, 234

Rockoro, Fijian god of carpenters, 90

Roman emperors, their evocation of the dead, 301

—— Pontifical, on the virtue of church bells, 418

Romans, their mode of making a treaty, 159; their way of protecting women at childbirth from Silvanus, 436 *sq.*

Rome, ancient, bride carried into her new home in, 317; laws of the Ten

Tables at, 380; gladiatorial combats at, 387; punishment of animals at, 403; the annual expulsion of ghosts at, 418

Romove, the sacred oak at, 333, 335

Romulus and Remus, story of their exposure and upbringing, 265

Rope severed at peace-making, 156

Roro-speaking tribes of New Guinea, their bodily lacerations in mourning, 385

Roscoe, Rev. John, on absence of flood stories in Africa, 130

Rottenburg in Swabia, church bells rung to drive away witches at, 423

Rotti, island, story of a great flood in, 86 *sq.*

Routledge, W. Scoresby, and Katherine, on the Kikuyu rite of new birth, 208

Ruahatu, Polynesian sea-god, 93, 94

Rubruquis, De, as to the warders of the threshold at the court of Mangu-Khan, 314

Rude stone monuments in the region beyond Jordan, 246

Rumeileh, ruins of a Roman fortress called, in Moab, 330

Russia, the Cheremiss of, 10, 342; ultimogeniture in, 178; heathen, the threshold the seat of house spirits in, 319; still-born children buried under the threshold in, 320

Russian story of Koschei the Deathless, 274 *sq.*

Saato, Samoan rain-god, 233

Sabbath of the Lolos, 83

Sabbaths, the witches', 423

Sabine women, rape of the, 318

Sacramental or purificatory theory of sacrificing victims at covenants, 158, 163, 164, 169, 171

Sacred groves the last relics of ancient forests, 339

—— oaks and terebinths, 322 *sqq.*

—— stones, 231 *sqq.*

Sacrifice of animals at the threshold, 321 *sq.*

Sacrifices to stones, 232, 234; to rivers, 253, 254 *sq.*; to the dead on the threshold, 322; to trees, 332 *sq.*; for rain, 340

Sacrificial skins in ritual, 206 *sqq.*

—— victim, identification of man with, 215 *sq.*

Sahara, oracular dreams on tombs in the, 299

St. Adelm's bell at Malmesbury Abbey, rung to drive away thunder, 426

St. Agatha, church bells rung on the night of, to drive away witches and wizards, 423

St. Bernard, his excommunication of flies, 403

St. Germains, the Abbey of, at Paris, its great bell rung to drive away thunder, 426

St. Juan Capristano, in California, 11

St. Julien, the commune of, its lawsuit against coleopterous insects, 405

St. Mark's, at Venice, the bells of, 422

St. Omer, ultimogeniture in neighbourhood of, 177

St. Patrick, his exorcism of reptiles, 403

St. Paul's Cathedral, the bell of old, rung in thunderstorms, 426

St. Wenefride's Well in Flintshire, holy bell at, 425 sq.

Saints, Mohammedan, their tombs in Syria, 324 sqq.

Sakarran, the Dyaks of, their story of the creation of man, 7

Salampandai, a Dyak god, maker of men, 7

Salsette, bride and bridegroom carried over the threshold in, 318

Salt, manslayers not allowed to eat, 43

Salteaux, or Chippeway Indians, their story of a great flood, 116 sqq.

Salutation, weeping as a, 238 sqq.

Samoa, worship of stones in, 233; bodily lacerations in mourning, 389

Samoan oath on a stone, 249

—— story of the origin of death, 27

Samothrace, Dardanus at, 72, 73; great flood at, 73 sq.

Samson, his character, 269 sq.; his home country, 270; his strength in his hair, 271

—— and Delilah, 269 sqq.

Samuel in relation to Saul, 291 sq.; his ghost evoked by the witch of Endor, 294

Sanchuniathon on the serpent, 18

Sanctuaries for men, animals and plants in Central Australia, 287

Sanctuary, the law of the one, 62, 354, 357

Sarcees, their story of a great flood, 123

Sargon, king of Babylonia, the story of his exposure and preservation, 266

Sarnas, sacred groves of the Mundas, 341

Satan, his sermon at North Berwick, 272

Satapatha Brahmana, story of a great flood in the, 78, 134

Sauks and Foxes, Indian tribe, their mourning customs, 383

Saul, his character and his relation to Samuel, 291 sqq.; his interview with the witch of Endor, 294; his interview with three men before his coronation, 334; buried under an oak or terebinth at Jabesh, 334; on one of the "high places," 339

Savigny, a sow tried and executed at, 412 sq.

Savoy, legal proceedings against caterpillars in, 409 sq.; animals as witnesses in, 415

Saxo Grammaticus, on Norse custom at election of a king, 247

Scandinavia, divination by water in, 260

Scapegoats, 352

Scarves, souls of criminals caught in, 288

Scent-bottles as receptacles of souls, 290

Scotland, Gruagach stones in, 235; divination in, 262; objection to count or be counted in, 311; the north-east of, cakes not to be counted in, 312; bride lifted over the threshold in, 318. See also Highlands, Highlanders.

Scott, Sir J. George, on ultimogeniture among the Kachins, 185; on systems of ownerships among the Kachins, 185

Scratching the face in mourning, 379, 380, 385

Scylla, how she betrayed her father Nisus, 274

Scythans, their mode of swearing oath of fealty, 155, 165; their bodily mutilations in mourning for a king, 380

Sea, risings of the, as causes of great floods, 139; attacked with weapons, 257

Sea Dyaks of Borneo, their story of the creation of man, 7; their story of a great flood, 85. See also Dyaks

Sebongoh Hill Dyaks, use of little bells among the, 433

Seclusion of homicides, 34 sqq.; of warriors who have slain enemies, 41 sqq.

Seilûn, the ancient Shiloh, 328

Selli, the, in ancient Hellas, 67

Semites, preceded by Sumerians in Babylonia, 54 sq.; swarmed from Arabian desert, 56

Semitic and Ethiopian usage, their similarities, 206 sq.

—— peoples, resemblance of their customs to those of certain tribes of Eastern Africa, 206

Senegal, Upper, worship of Earth in, 37

Serbian story of a warlock whose strength was in a bird, 276; of a dragon whose strength was in a pigeon, 276 sq.

Serpent and the Fall of Man, 15, 16, 17, 18 sq.; supposed to renew its youth by casting its skin, 18

Serpents supposed to be immortal because they cast their skins, 18, 26 sqq., 31 sq.

Serving for a wife, 195

Seven, the number, its prominence in Hebrew and Babylonian stories of the flood, 63

Severus, his ghost evoked by Caracalla, 301

Sexes created by Zeus, 14

Sextus Pompeius, his consultation of a Thessalian witch, 300 sq.

Shamash, Babylonian sun-god, 51

Shamsher, a prince in a folk-tale of Gilgit, 279 sqq.

Shans of China, ultimogeniture among the, 188; or Tai, their distribution and affinities, 188; their agriculture, 188

Shape-shifting of spirits, 252 sq.

Shechem, sacred oaks or terebinths at, 333 sq.; the vale of, 333

Sheep in the story of the origin of death, 23; brings message of immortality to men, 24; women assimilated to, 208, 209

—— and goat, stories of, 23 sq.

—— sacrificed in peace-making ceremonies, 159; in ceremony of redemption, 162; for the crops, 212; at threshold when bride enters her new home, 321 sq.

"Sheep of God," bird charged with message of immortality to men, 31

Shellfish supposed to be immortal through casting their skin, 27

Shells, fossil, as evidence of the Noachian deluge, 71, 135 sq.; marine, as evidence of a great flood, 86, 128; souls of enemies caught in, 289

Shetland Islands, dwelling-house inherited by youngest son in the, 176; objection to counting animals or things in the, 311

Shilluks, their story of the creation of man, 10

Shiloh, 328

Shortlands Islands, story of the origin of death in the, 28; leaves for roof of chief's house not to be counted in the, 310

Shri Badat, an ogre king of Gilgit, whose soul was made of butter, 279 sqq.

Shurippak, a Babylonian city, destroyed by flood, 51, 142

Siberia, North-eastern, the Yukaghirs of, 199 sq.

Siberian tradition of the creation of man, 6

Sick persons fed with the blood of their friends, 396

Sickness caused by ghosts, 213

Sienna, 422

Sierra Leone, bride carried into the house in, 317; objection to boil milk in, 364

Sigu, hero of a flood story, 101 sqq.

Sihai, the first man in Nias, 8

Sihanaka of Madagascar, silence of widows among the, 343 sq.

Silence imposed on widows for some time after the death of their husbands, 343 sqq.

Silent widow, the, 343 sqq.

Silenus caught by Midas, 253

Silesia, ultimogeniture in, 177; bride carried over threshold in, 317

Silvanus, women in childbed protected against, 436

Simpang-impang, a half-man, 85

Sin, Babylonian moon-god, 146

Sin of a census, 307 sqq.

Sindiân, the evergreen oak in Palestine, 322

Sinew that shrank, 257

Singbhum, 195

Singbonga, the Munda sun-god, 10

Singhalese, children at birth protected against forest spirits among the, 436

Singhpos or Chingpaws of Burma, their story of a great flood, 81

Sinyaxau, the first woman, 12

Sioux or Dacota Indians, weeping as a salutation among the, 242; their bodily lacerations in mourning, 383

Sippar, Babylonian city, 48, 49, 54

Siva, or Mahadeo, 9

Skin, story of the cast, 26 sqq., 31 sqq.; of sacrificial sheep in ritual, 165 sq.

Skins of sacrificial victims, persons wrapt in, 165; sacrificial, in ritual, 206 sq.

Skull, drinking out of, as a mode of inspiration, 302

Skye, sacred stones in, 235

Slave Coast, the Yoruba-speaking people of the, 433

—— Indians, their story of a great flood, 121

Slavonia, bride carried into husband's house in, 317

Slavonic countries, laceration of the face in mourning in, 280

—— parallels to the story of Samson and Delilah, 274 sqq.

Slavs, the South, form of adoption among, 217

Sleeping in sanctuaries in order to receive revelations in dreams, 225

Smith, Adam, on the punishment of inanimate objects, 416

——, George, his discovery of the Gilgamesh epic, 50

——, W. Robertson on the mark of Cain, 33; on sacramental or purificatory interpretation of covenant, 161, 164, 165, 166, 171; on hunting for souls, 288 n.; on the prohibition of seething a kid in its mother's milk, 364; on the offering of blood to the dead, 395

Smith regarded with superstitious awe by African tribes, 214

Smith River Indians of California, their story of a great flood, 112

Smoking to oracular stone, 234

—— as a means of inducing prophetic trance, 302

Snake, in story of the creation of man, 9; supposed to be immortal through casting its skin, 26

Snakes, water-spirits in the shape of, 256

Snake Indians, their bodily lacerations in mourning, 382 sq.

Snares to catch soul, 288 *sq.*

Sneezing as a symptom of life, 3, 5

Socrates, church historian, on the oak of Mamre, 335

Solomon, King, a younger son, 175

Solon, his legislation as to mourning customs, 380

Somali, their objection to heat camel's milk, 367

Somerset, Borough English in, 175

"Son of the right hand," title of the heir, 174

Song of the Flood, 112

Sorcha, the king of, and the herdsman of Cruachan, an Argyleshire story, 278

Soul, belief that a man's soul can be extracted from his body in his lifetime, 285

Souls of the dead, ladders for the use of the, 230; tied up for safety in a bundle, 286; human, extracted and stowed away for safety, 285 *sqq.*; caught in traps by witches and wizards, 288

South America, stories of a great flood in, 97 *sqq. See also* America *and* American Indians

Sowing, sacrifices before, 212

Sows tried and executed, 412 *sq.*

Sozomenus, church historian, on the oak of Mamre, 335; his account of the festival at the oak, 336

Spain, form of adoption in, 216 *sq.;* church bells rung to drive away witches in, 423

Spanish flies prosecuted by the inhabitants of Coire, 408

Spartan kings, kettles beaten at funerals of, 431

Speke, Captain, J. H., on water ordeal in Central Africa, 269; on scruples of Bahima in regard to milk, 372

——, Captain J. H., and J. A. Grant, on the objection to boil milk in Africa, 366

Spencer, Sir Baldwin, and F. J. Gillen, on the *churinga* of the Central Australian aborigines, 287; on the release of widows from the rule of silence Among the Arunta, 346

Sperchius, hair of Achilles vowed to the river, 380

Spider in story of creation of man, 10

Spirits, stones sacred to, 232 *sq.;* rivers supposed to be inhabited by malignant, 254; evil, supposed to be driven away by the sound of bells, 417, 418 *sq. See also* Demons

Spitting before crossing water after dark, 254

Spokanas, their story of a great flood, 126

Sprenger, inquisitor, his practice of shaving the heads of witches, 272

Stafford, Borough English in, 176

Stake driven into grave of troublesome ghost, 213

Stamford, Borough English in, 176

Statues and Statuettes representing the dead, employed at the consultation of their ghosts, 303

Status in early law, legal fiction of change of, 216

Stelvio, the commune of, its lawsuit against moles or field mice, 406

Stepping over sacrificed animals, 255

Stone, the Black, at Mecca, 231

——, the Plighting, at Lairg, 248

Stone monuments, rude, in the region beyond Jordan, 246 *sq.;* circles in Palestine, 247

Stones, men created afresh out of, after the flood, 67, 103, 104; oaths taken on, 161; oracular, 234; their magical effect in ratifying covenants, 247; employed in marriage ceremonies, 247

——, sacred, 231 *sqq.*; oil poured on, 225, 235 *sqq.*

Strambino, in Piedmont, the inhabitants of, prosecute caterpillars, 408 *sq.*

Strangers, dread of the magic of. 168

Strato, on the opening of the Bosphorus and the Straits of Gibraltar, 75

Strength of men, especially of witches and warlocks, supposed to be in their hair, 272 *sqq.*

Strymon, the river, white horses sacrificed to, 253

Stubbes, in *Anatomie of Abuses,* on the Passing Bell, 420

Sudan, the Anglo-Egyptian, objection to boil milk in, 367

——, the French, the Menkieras of, 234; the Nounoumas of, 333

Suffolk, burial of abortive calves in a gateway in, 321

Suk, of British East Africa, their rule of succession to property, 202; the pastoral, do not eat meat and milk milk together, 371; do not eat millet and milk together, 373; do not eat a kind of wild pig, 374

Sumatra, stories of a great flood in, 84 *sq.;* the Bataks of, 160, 199, 304; the Orang Sakai of, 385

Sumerian version of the flood story, 54 *sqq.*

Sumerians, the, 48, 54 *sqq.*, 352

Sun, the creation of the, 8, 12; the ark interpreted as the, 137; marries a woman, 229; supposed to descend annually into a fig-tree, 230

Sun-god creates man, 10; an African, 247; father of Karna by the princess Kunti or Pritha, 266

Sunars, bells worn by children and girls among the, 437

Supernatural birth in legend, 268

Surrey, Borough English in, 175

Sussex, Borough English in, 175

Swabia, ultimogeniture in, 178; church

bells rung to drive away thunder-storms in, 425

Sweden, divination in, 262

Switzerland, French custom of bride leaping over the threshold in, 318

Sympathetic magic, 165, 171, 257, 365, 369; based on the association of ideas, 368

Symposium of Plato, 14

Syria, cairns as witnesses in, 250; the Arabs of, averse to counting certain things, 313; bide stepping over blood in, 323; tombs of Mohammedan saints in, 324

Syrian belief that it is unlucky to tread on a threshold, 313

—— goddess, at Hierapolis, sacrifice of sheep to, 165

Szeukha, hero of a flood story, 111

Taanach, rock-hewn altar at, 167

Taaroa, chief god of Tahiti, 5; Polynesian creator, 92

Tabernacle in the widerness, 58

Tabor, Mount, 293, 323

Tagalogs of the Philippine Islands, ward off demons from women at childbirth, 435

Tahiti, story of the creation of man in, 5; stories of a great flood in, 92 *sqq.*; mode of divination by water in, 260; lacerations of the body in mourning in, 386 *sq.*, 395

Tai. *See* Shans of China

Tamanchiers, their story of the origin of death, 27

Tamanaques of the Orinoco, their story of a great flood, 104

Tamar and her twins, 174

Tamendonare, hero of a Brazilian flood story, 97 *sq.*

Tane, the Maori creator, 5, 94

Tangiers, custom observed at, on return from pilgrimage, 316

Tangkhuls of Assam, their oath on stones, 248

Tartar prince, his threshold not to be touched on pain of death, 314

Tartars, the Bedel, their story of the creation of man, 6

——, ultimogeniture among the, 179

Tasmania, mourning customs of the aborigines of, 393, 394

Tati Bushmen or Masarwas, their story of the origin of death, 22

Tatooed, manslayers, 41, 43

Taygetus, Mount, 228

Tcaipakomat, a creator of man, 12

Tchapewi, hero of a flood story, 121

Tchiglit Eskimo, their story of a great flood, 128

Tchuds, the Northern, ultimogeniture among, 178 *sq.*

Tea-leaves, divination by, 261

Tears of mourners offered to the dead, 386

Teeth of mourners knocked out, 387 *sq.*, 389

Tempe, the gorge of, 76 *sq.*

Ten Commandments, the original, 360 *sqq. See also* Decalogue

—— Tables, laws of the, on mourning rites, 380

Terebinths in Palestine, 322, 325, 327, 328, 329; venerated by the peasants, 329 *sq.*

Tertullian on sea-shells as evidence of a great flood, 135

Tezcatlipoca, Mexican god, his nocturnal rambles, 258

Tezpi, hero of a flood story, 108

Thaku, ceremonial pollution among the Akikuyu, 35, 38

Thasos, the trial and punishment of inanimate objects in, 402

Theagenes, a boxer, punishment of his statue, 402

Thebes in Boeotia, great antiquity of, 70, 71

Theophrastus on worship of stones, 235

Thespiae, in Boeotia, Love worshipped at, 232

Thessalian, witch, her evocation of the dead, 300 *sq.*

Thessaly, mountains of, parted in Deucalion's flood, 67, 76; said to have been originally a lake, 76

Thetis, caught by Peleus, 252

Thevet, André, on a flood story of the Indians of Brazil, 97

Thief, divination to detect a, 260, 261

Thlinkeet. *See* Tlingit

Thompson Indians of British Columbia, blacken the faces of manslayers, 43; their story of a great flood, 125 *sq.*

Thomson, W. M., on the oaks of Palestine, 323

Thonga of South-eastern Africa, their precautions against the ghosts of the slain, 41; their objection to boil milk, 366 *sq.*

Three angels worshipped at Hebron, 335

—— days, resurrection after, 29

—— men, interview of Abraham with, at the oaks of Mamre, 333, 334 *sq.*; interview of Saul with, before his coronation, 334

Threshold, the Keepers of the, 313 *sqq.*; sinful or unlucky to tread on a, 313 *sqq.*; bride at marriage carried over, 316 *sqq.*; supposed to be haunted by spirits, 319; sacrifice of animals at the, 321 *sq.*

Thresholds, ceremony performed at, to keep out Silvanus, 437

Thucydides on wanderings of Alcmaeon, 36

"Thunder-sheaves," dues paid to sexton for ringing the church bell in thunderstorms, 424

Thunderstorms, church bells rung to drive away, 424

Tiahuanaco, mankind created at, 14

Tibetan form of oath, 155

Tibullus on the evocation of the dead, 301

Tibur, oracle at, 228

Tickell, Lieut., on ultimogeniture among the Kols, 197

Tierra del Fuego, story of a great flood in, 107. *See also* Fuegians

Tigris in flood, 141

Tiki, the Maori creator, 5

Timor, disguise against ghosts in, 44; war of ratifying an oath in, 160; worship of stone in, 233 *sq.*

Tinneh Indians, their observances after manslaying, 43; their stories of a great flood, 121 *sqq.*

Tinnehs on Dénés, Indian nation of North-west America, 120; their mourning customs, 381

Tithes, the payment of, the best way of banishing locusts, 405

Tiu, hero of Maori story of a great flood, 95

Tlingit, or Thlinkeet Indians, their stories of a great flood, 123 *sqq.*; their mourning customs, 381 *sq.*

—— of Alaska, their explanation of the origin of the diversity of languages, 125, 152

Toaripi tribe of New Guinea, their bodily lacerations in mourning, 385

Tobacco offered to stones, 234

Tobias, his meeting with Raguel, 239

Todas of the Neligherry Hills, their worship of stones, 236; ceremonies performed by them at crossing rivers, 255

Todjo-Toradjas of Central Celebes, their story of the origin of death, 26

Togoland, the Ewe-speaking tribes of, 11; story of the origin of death in, 24; the Hos of, 438

To Kambinana, the Good Spirit, 32

To Koolawi of Celebes, their story of the origin of death, 29

To Korvuvu, charged with message of immortality to men, 32

Tombs, oracular dreams on, 299; of Mohammedan saints in Syria, 324 *sq.*

Tongans, their bodily lacerations in mourning, 388

Toradjas of Celebes, their legend of the creation of man, 6; their story of a great flood, 86; their stories of a creeper or rattan connecting earth and heaven, 229; their ladders for gods, 230; their way of deceiving water-spirits, 256; said to have attacked the tide with weapons, 257; their mode of catching the souls of enemies in shells, 289; their oracular dreams on graves, 300; their evocation of dead chiefs, 304; their objection to heating the lees of palm wine, 365; kill buffaloes that have killed men, 399; their personification of animals, 399 *sq.*

Torah, originally the oral decisions of the priests, 355

Torday, E., on the execution of a thieving dog, 400

Tortoise, brings message of immortality to men, 22

Toulouse, trial for witchcraft at, 272

Tower of Babel, 143 *sqq.*

Trakhan, king of Gilgit, story of his exposure and preservation, 267

Tralles, in Caira, water divination at, 259

Transference, periodical, of power from older to younger generation, 215

Transmission of independent origin of beliefs and customs, question of, 47

Transylvania, gipsies of, custom observed by women after childbed among the, 163

Travancore, the Maharajahs of, their fiction of a new birth, 220 *sqq.*

Treaty of peace, modes of concluding, 155 *sqq.*

Tree of the knowledge of good and evil, 15 *sqq.*; of life, 16 *sqq.*

Tree-god in triple form, 335

—— -spirit jabbed with spears, 213

Trees, sacred, bloody sacrifices to, 332; bones of dead deposited in, 344; cut down which have caused the death of persons, 398

Trial and punishment of animals in ancient Greece, 400 *sqq.*; in modern Europe, 403 *sqq.*

Tristram, Canon H. B., on rude stone monuments in Palestine, 246; on the oaks of Palestine, 323; on the terebinth, 329

Trojans and Greeks, their ceremony at making a truce, 159

Trow, the hero of a Dyak flood story, 86

Troy, or Dardania, founded by Dardanus, 73

True Steel, Serbian story of a warlock called, 276

Trumpeter-bird, why it has spindle shanks, 102

Tse-gu-dzih, Lolo god, 83

Tu, the Maori creator, 5

Tuaregs of the Sahara, their oracular dreams on graves, 299

Tucapacha, the Michoacan creator, 13

Tumbainot, hero of Masai flood story, 130 *sq.*

Tupi Indians of Brazil, weeping as a salutation among the, 241 *sq.*

Turbans, souls caught in, 289

Turia, a Samoan god, 233

Turkanas, rule of inheritance among the, 202

Turks, ultimogeniture among the, 180; their form of adoption, 217; their bodily lacerations in mourning, 385

Turtle in story of a great flood, 115

Twanas, their story of a great flood, 126

Twelfth Night, witches' Sabbath on, 423

Twins, purification of mother of, 214 *sq.*; parents of, wear bells at their ankles among the Baganda, 434

Tylor, Sir E. B., on myths of observation, 78, 142; on the legend of Cholula, 149; on the law of deodand, 416

Tyndareus, his mode of swearing the suitors of Helen, 154

Tzetzes, John, on the clash of bronze as a means of banning apparitions, 418, 429

Uassu, hero of a flood story, 100

Uganda Protectorate, spirits of rivers conceived in animal form in the, 254. *See* Baganda

Ukuni, objection to boil milk in, 366

Ultimogeniture, or junior-right, 172 *sqq.*; in Europe, 175 *sqq.*; F. W. Maitland on, 176; question of its origin, 179 *sqq.*, 200, 202 *sq.*; in Southern Asia, 180 *sqq.*; being replaced by primogeniture, 182, 189. 204, 205; in North-eastern Asia, 199 *sqq.*; in Africa, 201 *sq.*

—— and primogeniture, compromise between, 189

Ulysses, his evocation of the ghosts, 297; his offering of blood to the dead, 396

Uncleanness of women, the ceremonial, 352

Universal primeval ocean, theory of a, 137 *sq.*

Unkulunkulu, the Old Old One, sends message of immortality to men, 25

Unlucky to count or be counted, 308 *sqq.*; to tread on a threshold, 313 *sq.*

Unmatjera of Central Australia, 30; customs observed by widows among the, 346, 347, 348; mourning of widows among the, 394

Upotos of the Congo, their story of the origin of death, 30

Uproar made to drive away ghosts, 44

Uru, or Ur of the Chaldees, city of Babylon, 145 *sq.*

Ur-ak, king of Ur, 146

Ururi, in Central Africa, water ordeal in, 269

Ut-napishtim and the plant which renewed youth, 18; tells the story of the flood, 50 *sq.*; the hero of Babylonian flood story, 51 *sqq.*, 134

Utopias, political, 351

Vaca, Cabeça de, on weeping as a salutation among the North American Indians, 242

Valle, Pietro della, on the reverence for the threshold in the Persian king's palace, 315

Valmans of New Guinea, their story of a great flood, 89

Valonia oak in Palestine, 323

Varanus indicus, 26

Varro, on the antiquity of Thebes in Boeotia, 70, 71; on the date of the great flood, 71; on Pheneus as birthplace of Dardanus, 72; on the custom of lifting a bride over the threshold, 319; on scratching the face in mourning, 380

Vasconcellos, Simon de, on a flood story of the Brazilian Indians, 98

Vasse River, Western Australia, mourning custom on the, 393

Vate or Efate, mourning customs in, 385

Vedic hymns, no story of the great flood in the, 78

Vegetables, not to be brought into contact with milk, 370, 371, 372; not to be eaten by herdsmen, 373; not to be eaten by Masai warriors, 373

Venezuela, tradition of a great flood in, 114

Ventriloquism in necromancy, 295 *sq.*

Verona, petrifactions at, 135

Vesper bell, 421

Vesta, threshold sacred to, 319

Victims, sacrificial, in ratification of covenants and oaths, 154 *sqq.*

Victoria, mourning customs among the tribes of, 390

——, Western, the aborigines of, burn weapons which have killed their friends, 399

Villenose, the inhabitants of, prosecute caterpillars, 408

Violet robe of Jewish priest, 417

Virgil, on Anna's mourning for Dido, 380

Virginia, the Indians of, their offerings of hair in mourning, 384

Vuatom, story of the origin of death in, 26

Vulture, why it is black and white, 110; in flood story, 130 *sq.*

Wabende of East Africa, their story of the origin of death, 26

Wachaga of East Africa, their way of making peace by severing a kid and a rope, 156 *sq.*, 158, 171; war-baptism of lads among the, 166; their custom of cutting a boy and girl in two at making a covenant, 170 *sq.*; circumcision among the, 210; their use of sacrificial skins at covenants, 211; their use of victim's skins at sacrifices, 214; look upon a smith with superstitious awe, 214

Waduman tribe of Northern Australia, silence of widows in the, 344 *sq.*, 348

Wafipa of East Africa, their story of the origin of death, 26

Wa-giriama of British East Africa, their use of sacrificial skins at marriage, 211

Wagogo paint the faces of manslayers, 43; their objection to boil milk, 367

Wahumba, their objection to boil milk, 367

Wakka tribe, their mourning customs, 391

Wales, Borough English in, 176; bride lifted over the threshold in, 318. *See also* Welsh

Walpurgis Night, witches' Sabbath on, 423

Wamala, the god of plenty, and his prophet among the Banyoro, 438 *sq.*

Wamegi, their objection to boil milk, 367

Wanika, their mourning customs. 381

War-baptism of Wachaga lads, 166

Waralis of India, their worship of a stone, 235 *sq.*

Warramunga, silence of widows and other women after a death among the, 346 *sq.*; their mourning customs, 391 *sq.*

Warriors guarded against the ghosts of their victims by marks on their bodies, etc., 39, 41 *sqq.*

Warts, superstition about counting, 312

Warwickshire, unlucky to count lambs in, 312

Wa-Sania of British East Africa, 25; their story of the origin of the diversity of languages, 151; their dislike of being counted, 309

Washamba, circumcision among the, 210; do not eat meat with milk, 371

Washington State, stories of a great flood in, 126 *sq.*; the Flat-head Indians of, 126, 382

Wataturu, their rule as to eating a certain antelope, 375

Wataveta, their burial customs, 320

Water of Death, 50

Water personified, 257; ordeal to test the legitimacy of infants, 268 *sq.*

Water-bearing, the Festival of the, at Athens, 68

—— -divination, 259 *sqq.*

—— -lynxes, mythical animals in a flood story, 117 *sqq.*

—— -spirits shift their shapes, 252; propitiated at fords, 253; in the shape of snakes, 256; mode of deceiving, 256

Wawanga, of British East Africa, their use of sacrificial skins at marriage, 211; their use of victim's skin at sacrifices, 212, 213, 214 *sq.*

Wax, divination by molten, 262

Weapons that have killed persons destroyed or blunted, 399

Weeping as a salutation, 238 *sqq.*; among the Maoris, 239 *sq.*; among the Andaman Islanders, 241; in India, 241; among the American Indians, 241 *sqq.*

Weeping at meeting of friends in the Old Testament, 238 *sq.*

Weingarten, the "holy Blood-bell" in the monastry of, 425

Well, Jacob at the, 237 *sqq.*

Wellhausen, J., on the original Ten Commandments, 362

Welsh custom at crossing water after dark, 254

Wely, reputed Mohammedan saint, or his tomb, in Syria, 325, 327, 329, 330, 342

Wesphalia, ultimogeniture in, 177

Whale, ceremonies observed for the killing of a, 43

Wheat thrown over bride at threshold, 318

White clay smeared on body in sign of mourning, 345. 347

—— horses sacrificed to river, 253

Whitening bodies of mourners with pipe-clay, 394. *See also* Clay

—— the faces of mediums in order to attract the attention of the spirits, 302

Widow, the silent, 343 *sqq.*; married by her deceased husband's brother, 383, 384; haunted by her husband's ghost, 394

Widows, obliged to observe silence for some time after the death of their husbands, 343 *sq.*; in special relation to the younger brothers of their deceased husbands, 345 *sq.*, 348; haunted by their late husband's ghosts, 347, 348, 393 *sq.*

Wild animals, pastoral tribes abstain from eating, 374

Wilderness of Judea, 283 *sq.*

Wis-kay-tchach, a medicine man, hero of an Algonquin flood story, 116 *sqq.*

Wissaketchak, hero of a flood story, 121

Witch of Endor, 291 *sqq.*

Witches, ancient, their evocation of the dead, 301

—— and wizards, their power supposed to reside in their hair, 272; catch human souls in traps, 288 *sq.*; church bells rung to drive away, 422 *sq.*

Witness, the Heap of, 245, 246; the stone of, 334

Witnesses, cairns as, in Syria, 250

Wolf, Romulus and Remus suckled by a, 265

Wolves in Algonquin story of a great flood, 116 *sqq.*, 119

Woman, created out of a man's rib, 1, 2, 5, 6

Women as mediums or interpreters of ghosts, 302; as necromancers, 306; the ceremonial uncleanness of, 252

Woodpecker said to have assisted in feeding and guarding the infants Romulus and Remus, 265

Worship of stones, 231 *sq.*; of the dead, 397; of ancestors the most widely diffused and influential form of primitive religion, 397

—— of rivers, 253 *sq.*; among the Baganda, 254

Wotjobaluk of Australia, their story of the origin of death, 29 *sq.*

Wren in story of the creation of man, 13

Written code substituted for oral tradition at Josiah's reformation, 354 *sqq.*

Wurmlingen, church bell rung during thunderstorms at, 425

Würtemburg, ultimogeniture in, 177 *sq.*

Xenophon on scratching the face in mourning, 380

Xerxes, his sacrifice of white horses to the river Strymon, 253; his punishment of the Hellespont, 256

Xisuthrus, king of Babylon, hero of flood story, 48 *sq.*, 53, 56

Yabim of New Guinea, their custom in regard to the blood-wit, 40

Yehl or the Raven in the flood stories of the Tlinkits, 123 *sqq.*

Yezidis, bells worn by priest among the, 433

Yoruba-speaking peoples of the Slave Coast, bells worn by children among the, 433 *sq.*

Younger brothers of dead man in special relation to his widow, 345 *sq.*, 348

Youngest daughter the heir among the Khasis, 190 *sq.*, and among the Garos, 194; reason of the custom, 202 *sq.*

Youngest son as heir, 174. *See* Ultimogeniture

Youth supposed to be renewed by eating a plant, 18; by casting the skin, 18, 26 *sqq.*

Yukaghirs, their custom in regard to property, 199; ultimogeniture among the, 199 *sq.*

Zambesi, natives of the, their story like that of the Tower of Babel, 147

Zend-Avesta, its punishment of a worrying dog, 400

Zephaniah on those who leap on the threshold, 313

Zeus divides the sexes, 14; causes the flood, 67; the God of Escape, 67; his sanctuary at Dodona, 67; Olympian, his sanctuary at Athens, 68; Rainy, 68; his primitive rule over mankind, 151; the God of Oaths, 155; persuades Hera to adopt Hercules, 216; the infant, protected by the Curetes, 434, 437

Ziugiddu or Ziudsudda, hero of Sumerian flood story, 55 *sq.*

Zizyphus jujuba, 341

—— *-spina-Christi,* 325

Zulus, their story of the origin of death, 25

Zuyder Zee, origin of the, 138

Zyarats, mountain shrines in Afghanistan, 341 *sq.*